America's
TEST KITCHEN

THE BEST OF
America's
TEST KITCHEN

THE YEAR'S BEST RECIPES, EQUIPMENT REVIEWS, AND TASTINGS

2011

BY THE EDITORS AT
AMERICA'S TEST KITCHEN

PHOTOGRAPHY BY
CARL TREMBLAY, KELLER + KELLER, AND DANIEL J. VAN ACKERE

AMERICA'S TEST KITCHEN
17 Station Street, Brookline, MA 02445

Library of Congress Cataloging-in-Publication Data
The Editors at America's Test Kitchen

THE BEST OF AMERICA'S TEST KITCHEN 2011
The Year's Best Recipes, Equipment Reviews, and Tastings

1st Edition

Hardcover: $35 US
ISBN-13: 978-1-933615-64-6 ISBN-10: 1-933615-64-8
1. Cooking. 1. Title
2010

Manufactured in the United States of America

10 9 8 7 6 5 4 3 2 1

Distributed by America's Test Kitchen
17 Station Street, Brookline, MA 02445

EDITORIAL DIRECTOR: Jack Bishop
EXECUTIVE EDITOR: Elizabeth Carduff
ASSOCIATE EDITOR: Louise Emerick
DESIGN DIRECTOR: Amy Klee
ART DIRECTOR: Greg Galvan
ASSOCIATE ART DIRECTOR: Matthew Warnick
DESIGNER: Beverly Hsu
FRONT COVER PHOTOGRAPH: Carl Tremblay
STAFF PHOTOGRAPHER: Daniel J. van Ackere
ADDITIONAL PHOTOGRAPHY: Keller + Keller, Peter Tannenbaum, and Carl Tremblay
FOOD STYLING: Marie Piraino and Mary Jane Sawyer
ILLUSTRATOR: John Burgoyne
PRODUCTION DIRECTOR: Guy Rochford
SENIOR PRODUCTION MANAGER: Jessica Quirk
SENIOR PROJECT MANAGER: Alice Carpenter
PRODUCTION AND TRAFFIC COORDINATOR: Laura Collins and Kate Hux
ASSET AND WORKFLOW MANAGER: Andrew Mannone
PRODUCTION AND IMAGING SPECIALISTS: Judy Blomquist, Heather Dube, and Lauren Pettapiece
COPYEDITOR: Cheryl Redmond
PROOFREADER: Christine Corcoran Cox
INDEXER: Elizabeth Parson

PICTURED ON THE FRONT COVER: Ultimate Chocolate Cupcakes with Ganache Filling (page 251)

CONTENTS

STARTERS & SALADS

MAKE-AHEAD SWEET AND SOUR MEATBALLS

IN THE 1960s, SWEET AND SOUR MEATBALLS, SERVED as an appetizer, were as popular as the avocado green Crock-Pots or Salton hot trays used to serve them. The sweetness usually came from grape or cranberry jelly (as in Welch's "Tangy Grape BBQ Meatballs," circa 1968), while the tang came from vinegar and chili sauce or ketchup (think Heinz's "Ultimate Party Meatballs"). Sweet and sour cocktail meatballs are easy to serve for a crowd, and the sugary sauce is a guilty pleasure. That's what I remembered from my childhood, anyway.

After a few tests, I realized youth had clouded my judgment. Browning dozens of meatballs was a headache. The sauce was sickly sweet. I froze the meatballs in order to avoid much last-minute work, but, made with all-beef and filler, they turned hard and dry. Still, I was determined to bring sweet and sour meatballs into the 21st century with a fast, easy, tangy, delicious version that I could freeze without compromise.

Meatballs intended for the freezer need fat to keep them moist. I tested various meats and fat percentages before landing on 85 percent lean ground beef combined with ground pork, for tenderness. I also elected to use two egg yolks in place of a whole egg. Several common binders—bread crumbs, cracker crumbs, and cornflake crumbs—made the meatballs dry, so I turned to a panade. This French term refers to a paste made from bread softened in liquid (in this case, milk). These reformulated meatballs didn't dehydrate in the freezer.

Some of the recipes I'd tested seasoned the meatballs heavily, but the herbs and spices either disappeared into the sweet and sour sauce or clashed with it. In the end, salt and lots of pepper, garlic, and parsley proved that less was more. To form the meatballs quickly, I shaped them with a small melon baller. To brown them easily, I set them on a rimmed baking sheet in a 450-degree oven—the meatballs were done in 15 minutes. After they cooled, I froze them in zipper-lock bags.

Next I went to work on the sauce. Thus far I'd been testing with a very basic mix of chili sauce and jellied cranberry sauce. I began by pitting jams and jellies against one another. Tasters liked tangy apricot preserves best. Nobody liked the "shrimp cocktail" flavor the chili sauce evoked; they preferred ordinary tomato sauce. The basic components were now in place. Tasters demanded complexity, so I sautéed an onion, then stirred in the tomato sauce and apricot preserves. Still flat. The (unsweetened) tomato sauce gave me some leeway with the sugar, and ¼ cup of dark brown sugar contributed a pleasing molasses undertone. Dijon mustard and red pepper flakes helped balance the flavors, and Worcestershire sauce added much-needed depth.

I emptied the frozen meatballs into the bubbling sauce and waited just 10 minutes for them to warm before serving. Finally, I'd hit the mark.

—DIANE UNGER, *Cook's Country*

Make-Ahead Sweet and Sour Cocktail Meatballs
SERVES 20; MAKES ABOUT 80 MEATBALLS

Use a 1¼-inch melon baller or a 1-tablespoon measuring spoon to form the meatballs.

MEATBALLS
- 4 slices high-quality white sandwich bread, torn into pieces
- ½ cup whole milk
- 2 large egg yolks
- ½ pound ground pork
- ½ cup finely chopped fresh parsley
- 2 garlic cloves, minced
- 2 teaspoons pepper
- 1 teaspoon salt
- 2½ pounds 85 percent lean ground beef

SAUCE
- 1 tablespoon vegetable oil
- 1 onion, minced (about 1 cup)
- 1 (28-ounce) can tomato sauce
- 2½ cups apricot preserves
- ¼ cup packed dark brown sugar
- 3 tablespoons Worcestershire sauce
- 2 tablespoons Dijon mustard
- ¼ teaspoon red pepper flakes

1. FOR THE MEATBALLS: Adjust the oven racks to the upper-middle and lower-middle positions and heat the oven to 450 degrees. Using a fork, mash the bread, milk, and egg yolks in a large bowl until smooth. Add the pork, parsley, garlic, pepper, and salt and mix until incorporated. Add the beef and knead gently until combined.

2. Form the mixture into 1¼-inch meatballs (you should have about 80). Bake the meatballs on 2 rimmed baking sheets until cooked through and beginning to brown, 12 to 15 minutes, switching and rotating the sheets halfway through. Let the meatballs cool to room temperature, then refrigerate until firm, about 30 minutes. Transfer the meatballs to a large zipper-lock freezer bag and freeze for up to 1 month.

3. FOR THE SAUCE: Heat the oil in a Dutch oven over medium-high heat until shimmering. Cook the onion until softened, about 5 minutes. Whisk in the tomato sauce, preserves, sugar, Worcestershire, mustard, and red pepper flakes and bring to a boil. Reduce the heat to medium-low and simmer until the sauce is thickened, about 15 minutes. Let cool to room temperature. Transfer the sauce to an airtight container and freeze for up to 1 month.

4. Reheat the sauce, covered, in a Dutch oven over medium-low heat, stirring occasionally. Once the sauce reaches a simmer, stir in the frozen meatballs and cook until heated through, 10 to 15 minutes. Serve.

NOTES FROM THE TEST KITCHEN

MAKING THE MEATBALLS
To reheat, the baked-then-frozen meatballs can go straight from the freezer into the simmering sauce, which can also be made ahead and frozen separately.

1. Bake the meatballs, cool them on the counter on the baking sheet, then refrigerate them until firm.

2. Place the chilled meatballs in zipper-lock bags and freeze.

3. To reheat, dump the frozen meatballs directly into the simmering sauce.

SLOW-COOKER STICKY WINGS

PERFECT STICKY WINGS ARE MOIST AND LACQUERED with a slightly thick, sweet yet tangy sauce—the stickier and messier, the better. The sauce contains a range of sweet and savory ingredients, from honey, soy sauce, and chili sauce to jam and ketchup. Ordinary recipes variously bake the wings in a very hot oven, broil, or deep-fry them. Except when deep-fried, the wings tend toward flabbiness—they simply don't cook long enough to render the fat.

I wanted to make sticky wings in the slow cooker, and I knew I'd face some additional challenges: The appliance doesn't allow for evaporation, so food cooked in it risks tasting watered down and flavorless. Also, if the sauce couldn't reduce, how would it ever get sticky? The basic method in the slow-cooker recipes I tested went like this: Put wings and sauce in slow cooker, turn on, and wait. The basic results (no surprise) were flabby, greasy, not-at-all-sticky wings floating in a sea of chicken juices. On top of everything, they had so little flavor I barely knew I was eating chicken.

To begin my testing, I put together a basic sauce of soy sauce, brown sugar, and tomato paste (I'd fine-tune it later) and got to work. In test after test I decreased the sauce from the 3 cups I'd started with, hoping to be left with less liquid by the end of cooking. But the more I cut—all the way down to a single tablespoon—the more my sauce was diluted by the nearly 2 cups of chicken juices and grease released by the wings as they cooked. Stymied, I turned to something radical. I'd get rid of the sauce altogether, for now, anyway, and cook the wings bare. After three hours, I removed the wings from the cooker, discarded the troublesome fat and juices, and found myself with—wonder of wonders!— nicely rendered, juicy wings. Here I'd been worrying about the problems the slow cooker causes, and instead it had solved one: The low, slow heat melted the fat and extra juices off the wings.

For the sauce, I tested many possible combinations of the quasi-Asian ingredients that define sticky wings. In the end, tasters liked the basic soy sauce/tomato paste/ brown sugar mixture I'd been using, punched up by fresh garlic, fresh ginger, and cayenne. The combined ingredients were conveniently thick, so I could skip the step of cooking them down on the stovetop.

To get sticky wings that were sticky, I gradually came to accept that whatever other slow-cooker recipes did

SLOW-COOKER STICKY WINGS

or didn't do, mine would require the broiler. I'd need to take the rendered wings out of the slow cooker, paint them with sauce, and broil them. I did so, but I can't tell you how they tasted since they stuck to the baking sheet, as though super-glued. The next time, I lightly sprayed a rack with cooking spray and placed the rack on a baking sheet. I tossed the wings with half the sauce, broiled them on the rack, flipped, drizzled with the remaining sauce, and broiled again. The stickiness factor was spot-on, but the flavor, tasters complained, was merely skin deep.

Barbecue pit masters use rubs to flavor slowly cooking meat. Maybe I could adapt the technique for the slow cooker. I started again, this time coating the raw wings with ingredients pulled from my sauce: a paste-like puree of brown sugar, ginger, soy sauce, and cayenne. (I adjusted the sauce to account for the rub.) I hoped the rub would season the wings without adding moisture. Indeed, they emerged from the slow cooker rendered and seasoned, and after I broiled them with the sauce, they were sublimely sticky and seasoned inside and out.
—MEGHAN ERWIN, *Cook's Country*

Slow-Cooker Sticky Wings
SERVES 12

We prefer to use dark brown sugar in this recipe rather than light to achieve the right molasses-y flavor.

- ¾ **cup packed dark brown sugar**
- ¼ **cup soy sauce**
- 1 **(3-inch) piece fresh ginger, peeled and chopped**
- 4 **garlic cloves, peeled**
- ½ **teaspoon cayenne pepper**
- 4 **pounds chicken wings, halved at joint and wing tips removed**
- ¼ **cup water**
- ¼ **cup tomato paste**

1. Pulse ¼ cup of the sugar, 1 tablespoon of the soy sauce, the ginger, garlic, and ¼ teaspoon of the cayenne in a food processor until finely ground. Transfer the mixture to a slow cooker. Add the chicken wings and toss until combined.

2. Cover and cook on low until the fat renders and the chicken is tender, 3 to 4 hours. Using a slotted spoon, remove the wings from the slow cooker and transfer to a large bowl (discard the liquid in the slow cooker). Let the wings cool for 20 minutes (or cool briefly and refrigerate for up to 24 hours).

3. Adjust an oven rack to be 10 to 12 inches from the broiler element and heat the broiler. Set a wire rack inside a rimmed baking sheet lined with aluminum foil and spray the rack with vegetable oil spray. Whisk the water, tomato paste, remaining ½ cup sugar, remaining 3 tablespoons soy sauce, and remaining ¼ teaspoon cayenne in a bowl. Add half of the sauce to the bowl with the cooled wings and toss gently to coat. Arrange the wings, skin side up, on the prepared rack. Broil until the wings are lightly charred and crisp around the edges, 10 to 15 minutes. Flip the wings, brush with the remaining sauce, and continue to broil until well caramelized, about 3 minutes. Serve.

NOTES FROM THE TEST KITCHEN

KEYS TO PERFECT SLOW-COOKER STICKY WINGS
Most slow-cooker recipes for sticky wings cook the sauce and wings together, which results in a bland, greasy, watery mess. We cook the wings with a small amount of a potent paste so they can soak up flavor as they render fat, then we coat them with the sauce in two stages when broiling to finish.

THROW IT OUT
Four pounds of chicken wings render about 2 cups of fat. Most recipes incorporate this fat into the sauce. We throw it out.

SAUCE AND BROIL
A quick dump-and-stir sauce coats the wings just before they go under the broiler, with a second coating for reinforcement halfway through. The sauce caramelizes in under 20 minutes.

SPICED NUTS

NUTS ARE EXPENSIVE, SO IT'S DISAPPOINTING WHEN you make a batch of spiced nuts for the holidays that fall short. The best recipes produce nuts that are crisp and evenly coated with spices, and they don't turn soggy after a few days. In the test kitchen, we've had plenty of chances to perfect our technique. I decided to review our easy method and rummage through our spice rack to come up with some habit-forming variations.

Previous testing revealed that if I was going to flavor the nuts and bake them for close to an hour, it made no sense to use toasted, salted, or dry-roasted nuts. I started with a blank canvas—raw, unsalted nuts—knowing I could mix and match whichever types of nuts struck my fancy.

Different recipes use different tricks to get the spices to adhere. Some rely on oil or melted butter, but in my experience spiced nuts made this way have spotty coatings and leave fingers slick and greasy. Other recipes use simple syrup, which essentially makes for chewy nut candy, not a savory snack, and certainly not what I was looking for. Meanwhile mixing the nuts with corn syrup or maple syrup turns the nuts soft and gooey within a couple of days—I wanted something that would hold through the holiday season.

I eventually settled on a fourth approach, using egg whites to help the spices adhere. The whites proved too thick to coat the nuts evenly, so I added a splash of water to dilute them and salt, which helps keep the egg proteins apart and thus prevents them from coagulating. As an extra precaution against the whites leaving rubbery clots on the nuts as they bake, I drained the nuts thoroughly in a colander, letting any excess whites drip away. Only then did I toss the nuts with sugar and spices, for an even, delicate "shell" around each baked nut.

I baked the nuts low and slow in a 300-degree oven for about 45 minutes, long enough for both nut and coating to crisp. Higher temperatures scorched the coating before the nuts were toasted; lower temperatures and Christmas was over before the nuts were ready. To prevent them from sticking, I lined a baking sheet with parchment paper and sprayed it with cooking spray.

I learned quickly not to go crazy with the spices. Too heavy a hand and it was like eating potpourri. My master recipe uses a cinnamon, ginger, and coriander blend. I also developed variations: a hot-and-tart chili powder–lime (great with cashews, almonds, and peanuts); floral cardamom and orange zest (try almonds and pistachios); caramel-y Coca-Cola and five-spice powder (tropical macadamia nuts and cashews go nicely); and an Italian-themed rosemary and lemon (use hazelnuts, almonds, and walnuts, all of which grow there).

—MARÍA DEL MAR SACASA, *Cook's Country*

Crunchy Spiced Nuts

MAKES ABOUT 5 CUPS

You can use any variety of unsalted raw nuts. To double the recipe, adjust the oven racks to the upper-middle and lower-middle positions and bake the nuts on 2 baking sheets, switching and rotating sheets halfway through.

1	large egg white
1	tablespoon water
1	teaspoon salt
1	pound unsalted raw nuts
½	cup sugar
2	teaspoons ground cinnamon
1	teaspoon ground ginger
1	teaspoon ground coriander

1. Adjust an oven rack to the upper-middle position and heat the oven to 300 degrees. Line a baking sheet with parchment paper and coat with vegetable oil spray. Whisk the egg white, water, and salt in a large bowl. Add the nuts and toss to coat. Let the nuts drain thoroughly in a colander, 4 to 5 minutes.

2. Mix the sugar, cinnamon, ginger, and coriander in a large bowl. Add the drained nuts and toss to coat. Spread the nuts evenly onto the prepared baking sheet and bake until they are dry and crisp, 40 to 45 minutes, rotating the sheet halfway through. Cool the nuts completely, then break them apart and serve. (The nuts can be stored in an airtight container for up to 3 weeks.)

VARIATIONS
Chili-Lime Spiced Nuts

Use a combination of cashews, peanuts, and almonds in this spicy-sweet variation.

Follow the recipe for Crunchy Spiced Nuts, substituting 1 tablespoon lime juice for the water and adding 1 tablespoon grated lime zest to the egg white mixture. Substitute 2½ teaspoons chili powder, 1 teaspoon ground cumin, and ½ teaspoon cayenne pepper for the cinnamon, ginger, and coriander.

CRUNCHY SPICED NUTS

Orange-Cardamom Spiced Nuts

Almonds and pistachios are a good combination here.

Follow the recipe for Crunchy Spiced Nuts, substituting 1 tablespoon orange juice for the water and adding 1 tablespoon grated orange zest and ¼ teaspoon vanilla extract to the egg white mixture. Substitute 1 teaspoon ground cardamom and ½ teaspoon pepper for the cinnamon, ginger, and coriander.

Asian Spiced Nuts

We like macadamia nuts and cashews in this variation. The cola lends sweetness and depth of flavor.

Follow the recipe for Crunchy Spiced Nuts, substituting 1 tablespoon Coca-Cola for the water. Decrease the ginger to ½ teaspoon and substitute 1½ teaspoons five-spice powder for the cinnamon and coriander.

Rosemary-Lemon Spiced Nuts

Try a combination of almonds, walnuts, and hazelnuts for this Italian-inspired variation.

Follow the recipe for Crunchy Spiced Nuts, substituting 1 tablespoon lemon juice for the water and adding 1 tablespoon grated lemon zest to the egg white mixture. Substitute ½ cup packed light brown sugar, 1 tablespoon minced fresh rosemary, and ¼ teaspoon red pepper flakes for the granulated sugar, cinnamon, ginger, and coriander.

NOTES FROM THE TEST KITCHEN

THE BEST MINI PREP BOWLS
To speed the cooking process, we almost always measure out ingredients like ground spices, chopped herbs, and minced garlic and place them at the ready in "mini prep" bowls. These should be stable, easy to scrape out, and clean up free of stains and odors. We tested six sets in 6-ounce and 2-ounce sizes in a variety of materials (silicone, melamine, bamboo, and glass). The results? Old-fashioned dishwasher- and microwave-safe Pyrex bowls, the **Pyrex 4-piece 6-ounce Dessert Dish Set**, $5.99, won the day. The thick, heavy glass kept these spacious bowls from tipping, while fluted sides added extra grip.

HOT CRAB DIP

ALL ALONG THE MID-ATLANTIC AND SOUTHERN seaboards, where blue crab rules, its sweet meat finds its way into all kinds of dishes. One of the best is hot crab dip, a creamy, subtly spiced baked dip loaded with fresh crabmeat. Slathered onto crackers or toast points, it might just be the perfect hors d'oeuvre. Might, however, is the operative word. I have had some pretty bad batches. Often, the crab's flavor is buried by seasonings, while other recipes result in a dip with a texture as thin as bisque. Given crabmeat's considerable price, I wanted to develop the perfect rendition of this classic appetizer.

Unless you want to buy a bushel of crabs and pick your own meat, there are three options: fresh-picked, pasteurized, and canned. Fresh-picked meat comes in several forms (lump, backfin, claw) at varying prices. Pasteurized usually costs a bit less and canned is less yet. So what's best for dip? After making batches with each, I thought fresh and pasteurized worked well; canned did not. Its tinny, less-than-fresh flavor and watery texture were deemed unacceptable by all my tasters; this is one instance where quality is worth every penny.

Many hot dips rely on a combination of mayonnaise and sour cream, but I found that mayo was too gloppy and sour cream too runny. With the goal of sweet crab in a creamy, slightly tangy base in mind, I tried various dairy products, from yogurt, buttermilk, and sour cream to cream cheese, Monterey Jack, and heavy cream. In the end, cream cheese had the best flavor and texture if it was loosened a bit with milk. The cream cheese also contributed some appealing tanginess, but not enough. Lemon juice made the most sense, adding an acidic tang as well as a fresh brightness. I tested varying amounts and found that the more I added, the better the results. I settled on 3 tablespoons for 1 pound of crab.

The dip's flavorings should frame the crab, not obscure it. Many older recipes use onion powder and garlic salt, but these only add stale, artificial flavor. I started with Dijon mustard, which helped cut through the richness of the cream cheese, and I boosted it with a bit of minced onion and a full teaspoon of hot sauce. Next I tried adding Worcestershire sauce, a suggestion common in recipes I'd come across, and I found its sweet-tart, earthy flavor made for a good addition. I looked for a spice to accent the crab and settled on Old Bay seasoning, the quintessential spice blend for pairing with crabs and other seafood in the Mid-Atlantic region.

Many hot dips, including several of the crab dip recipes I found, are topped with buttery bread crumbs. I found that they added a richness that took away from the crab, so I decided to nix any sort of topping.

The method was simple enough. I mixed together everything except the crabmeat until well blended, then I used a rubber spatula to fold in the crab gently to ensure it maintained its large appealing chunks. About 20 minutes in a piping hot oven set at 475 degrees turned out a golden brown savory dip. Once prepared, the dip stores and travels well. All it needs is a few minutes in a hot oven to bring out its best.

—MATTHEW CARD, *America's Test Kitchen Books*

Hot Crab Dip

SERVES 12

This dip is best eaten warm, so bake it just before serving. Both fresh and pasteurized crabmeat work well in this recipe; don't use canned crabmeat. Serve with toast points or your favorite crackers.

2	(8-ounce) packages cream cheese, softened, cut into 1-inch chunks
¼	cup milk
3	tablespoons fresh lemon juice
2	tablespoons minced onion
2	teaspoons Worcestershire sauce
2	teaspoons Dijon mustard
1½	teaspoons Old Bay seasoning
1	teaspoon hot sauce
1	pound crabmeat, picked over for shells
2	tablespoons minced fresh parsley

1. Adjust an oven rack to the middle position and heat the oven to 475 degrees. Grease a shallow 2-quart baking dish.

2. Whisk the cream cheese, milk, lemon juice, onion, Worcestershire sauce, mustard, Old Bay, and hot sauce together in a large bowl until smooth. Gently fold in the crabmeat with a rubber spatula.

3. Transfer the mixture to the prepared baking dish and smooth the top. (The unbaked dip can be wrapped tightly with plastic wrap and refrigerated for up to 1 day; microwave on high until bubbling around the edges, 1 to 2 minutes, and stir before baking uncovered.) Bake until browned and bubbling, 20 to 25 minutes. Sprinkle with the parsley and serve.

NOTES FROM THE TEST KITCHEN

OUR FAVORITE HOT SAUCE
Though usually used in small doses, hot sauce can add just the vinegary heat a dish might need. Over the years, we've found that while most hot sauces share the same core ingredients—chile peppers, vinegar, and salt—their heat levels can vary drastically. To avoid a searingly hot sauce, we recommend using the test kitchen's favorite brand, **Frank's RedHot**, which has mellow heat and deep flavor. Some brands of hot sauce, such as Tabasco and La Preferida, are nearly twice as hot as Frank's; if using a brand other than Frank's in our recipes, start with half the amount and add more to taste.

PIMENTO CHEESE

A SOUTHERN STAPLE FOR AT LEAST A CENTURY, pimento cheese is a tangy, spreadable mixture made of cheddar cheese, jarred pimento peppers, and mayonnaise. It is typically slathered on crackers, toast, or crudités, or used as a sandwich filling, but if you ask any true Southerner, you'll be told pimento cheese tastes good on just about anything. While you can buy it premade at the grocery store, these are usually gloppy, bland mixtures. Homemade spreads are infinitely better and take less time to make than driving to the supermarket.

Wondering if the perfect recipe already existed, I whipped up several batches following the recipes I came across in my initial research, and I was surprised by the variations in ingredients, texture, and flavor. In the end, I decided that the best pimento cheese should exhibit a tangy flavor spiked by a bit of spice that was balanced, not overwhelming, and a creamy, but not smooth, texture. For a spread that had all of these traits, I realized the existing recipes weren't the answer. I would have to create my own.

Most recipes use extra-sharp cheddar cheese either by itself or in conjunction with a milder cheddar or Monterey Jack. I found batches made with all extra-sharp cheese tasted more complex and satisfying. Both white and orange varieties of extra-sharp cheddar worked fine, though I did find that cheddar aged more than one year produced a spread that had a crumbly, greasy texture.

As for the namesake ingredient, all the recipes I found called for the widely available 4-ounce jars of diced pimento peppers. These worked well so I saw no reason to change. (Regular roasted red peppers worked fine too, as long as they were well drained, patted dry, and chopped before being blended with the cheese.)

Mayonnaise acts as a binder for pimento cheese and adds a slight richness. I quickly realized that too much of the stuff made the spread greasy and bland, so I pared it back to the absolute minimum necessary to hold the mix together (just 6 tablespoons for 1 pound of cheese).

While some pimento cheese recipes are as simple as cheese, peppers, and mayonnaise, I preferred those with a bit more flavor. I quickly nixed the common additions of grated onions and chopped pickles in favor of minced garlic and a spoonful or two of hot sauce. In a few recipes the spread was spiked with sweet-tart Worcestershire sauce, and once I tried it, I knew it was a must.

As for mixing the spread, the recipes I found used one of two methods: hand blended or machine processed. I tasted batches of each and preferred the more homogenous texture of the spreads made in the food processor. While some recipes just instruct you to process all of the ingredients until smooth, I liked the cheese to have a bit of texture, so I pulsed it into the blended mayonnaise, peppers, and flavorings. Finally, after making over a dozen batches of pimento cheese, I understood why Southerners love the stuff so much.

—MATTHEW CARD, *America's Test Kitchen Books*

Pimento Cheese

SERVES 8

Both white and orange extra-sharp cheddar work well here; avoid long-aged cheddars. Don't substitute store-bought, preshredded cheese; it doesn't blend well and produces a dry spread. An equal amount of roasted red peppers may be substituted for the pimentos.

- 1 (4-ounce) jar pimento peppers, drained and patted dry (½ cup)
- 6 tablespoons mayonnaise
- 2 garlic cloves, minced
- 1½ teaspoons Worcestershire sauce
- 1 teaspoon hot sauce, plus more to taste
- 1 pound extra-sharp cheddar cheese, shredded (about 4 cups) (see note)
- Salt and pepper

Process the pimentos, mayonnaise, garlic, Worcestershire, and hot sauce together in a food processor until smooth, about 20 seconds. Add the cheese and pulse until uniformly blended, with fine bits of cheese throughout, about 20 pulses. Season with salt, pepper, and more hot sauce to taste. Serve or refrigerate until needed. (The pimento cheese can be refrigerated in an airtight container for up to 2 weeks; let sit at room temperature for 15 minutes before serving.)

MOROCCAN CARROT DIP

WHILE A VEGETABLE-BASED DIP SEEMS LIKE THE ideal alternative to the typical creamy, cheesy dips, most recipes are nothing more than pureed overcooked vegetables, with a minimum of seasoning, offering up an unappetizing muddy appearance. Could I create a fresh, complexly seasoned vegetable-based dip that was healthy but also appealing?

I began by looking at various international cuisines for inspiration, and the Moroccan combination of sweet, earthy carrots and warm spices struck me in particular. Further research revealed dozens of carrot dip recipes, combining mashed or pureed cooked carrots with various warm spices. A local Mediterranean restaurant serves a particularly outstanding carrot puree appetizer, with a fresh, clean flavor that is distinctly carrot-y but also deeply earthy and spicy, with a bright, appealing color. I settled on the goal of creating a dip with similarly undiluted carrot flavor, an aromatic and balanced depth from Moroccan spices, and a brilliant, fresh orange color.

My first step was to determine how to cook the carrots. Most recipes boil, steam, or microwave them, so I tried all three methods. I cut the carrots into ¼-inch-thick rounds and cooked each batch until just tender enough to mash with a potato masher. Tasters unanimously agreed that the boiled carrots looked and tasted washed out, and the steamed and microwaved carrots didn't fare much better.

Several tasters suggested oven-roasting the carrots, as this would concentrate the carrots' flavor and bring out their natural sweetness. These carrots definitely had a deep, sweet flavor, but the dip had an unappealing brown hue from the carrots' caramelization. I tried sautéing the carrots, in the hope I would get a similarly

MOROCCAN CARROT DIP

CALIFORNIA OLIVE OILS

California growers have spent the last two decades developing extra-virgin olive oils that might rival the best of Europe. Because the quality of olive oil degrades over time, the benefit of buying domestically is built in. Wondering if California could offer olive oils as good as our favorite import, Columela (a Spanish product), we purchased 10 olive oils from the state's largest and most established producers and tasted them blind (plain, with green apples to cleanse the palate, and on a crusty baguette with sea salt), and we included Columela in the tasting for comparison. In the end, our favorite Spanish oil came in first by a mere half point on a scale of 0 to 10. The domestic **California Olive Ranch Arbequina** won raves for its fresh, sweet, fruity flavor and pleasing hint of bitterness. For now, we believe Europe still maintains a stronghold in this intercontinental oil battle, but the California growers have clearly struck something promising. (See page 289 for more information about our testing results.)

concentrated flavor without so much browning, but by the time the carrots were cooked through they had also browned too much.

A hybrid cooking method seemed like the logical answer. However, oven-roasting just some of the carrots seemed fussy, as did oven-roasting the whole bunch for only a brief time, so I took oven-roasting off the table. I settled on first sautéing the carrots to concentrate their flavor, then simmering them in a small amount of liquid, effectively poaching or braising them. I needed enough liquid to finish cooking them through and avoid further browning, but not so much that I ended up boiling them. I started testing with the obvious choice of water. After trying varying amounts, ⅓ cup water for 2 pounds of carrots proved just right. Any less and the carrots started to brown before cooking through; any more and the flavor was too washed out.

To see if another liquid could enrich the flavor, I experimented with chicken broth and half-and-half in lieu of water. Both muted the carrot flavor rather than enhancing it. Vegetable broth seemed like a logical match, but the dip was too sweet and had an ambiguous vegetable flavor. Water, after all, was the best choice.

My attention then turned to the world of Moroccan spices. I wanted to keep things simple, so I limited myself to common pantry spices. I started with coriander, cumin, ginger, chili powder, cinnamon, turmeric, and paprika and stirred the spices into the carrots after their initial sauté. I let them cook a few seconds in the skillet before adding the water (this technique, called blooming, is used often in the test kitchen to eliminate spices' raw flavor).

I quickly learned that adding even a smidge too much spice gave the dip an unappealing ruddy tinge, and the dip lost its distinct carrot flavor. After testing varying amounts of each spice, I found that paprika and turmeric, even in small amounts, had ill effects on the color and didn't offer much flavor, so I eliminated them. After some tweaking, I achieved a balance of both warmth and heat using the remaining five spices, and less than 1 tablespoon total of spices ensured the carrot flavor and color stayed front and center. For depth I also stirred in two cloves of minced garlic.

Texture was the last issue. Up to this point I had been making a rough mixture using a potato masher, but some recipes use a fork, while still others puree the mixture in a food processor or blender. After one test I crossed off the fork method—it took far too long. Meanwhile, a few seconds in either the blender or food processor turned the carrot mixture into a very smooth puree, but tasters agreed it was too reminiscent of baby food. I decided to stick to the potato masher; I could quickly achieve a mostly smooth puree while leaving a few coarse bits throughout for textural appeal.

To finish, I added a couple of tablespoons of olive oil for smoothness and richness and a splash of white wine vinegar for brightness and for a balancing acid. A short time in the refrigerator allowed the flavors to meld, and a sprinkling of cilantro added freshness and contrasting color. This dip had everything I'd hoped for: appealing texture, bright color, and clean flavors, not to mention it was quick to make. It could definitely hold its own against its creamy, cheesy counterparts.

—JENNIFER LALIME, *America's Test Kitchen Books*

Moroccan Carrot Dip

MAKES ABOUT 2½ CUPS

For the dip to have a brilliant orange color and clean flavor, it is important to avoid browning the carrots when cooking them in step 1. Serve with pita chips.

- **3 tablespoons extra-virgin olive oil**
- **2 pounds carrots, peeled and sliced ¼ inch thick**
  Salt

2 garlic cloves, minced

¾ teaspoon ground coriander

¾ teaspoon ground cumin

¾ teaspoon ground ginger

⅛ teaspoon chili powder

⅛ teaspoon ground cinnamon

⅓ cup water

1 tablespoon white wine vinegar

　 Pepper

1 tablespoon minced fresh cilantro

1. Heat 1 tablespoon of the oil in a large saucepan over medium-high heat until shimmering. Add the carrots and ½ teaspoon salt and cook until they begin to soften, 5 to 7 minutes. Stir in the garlic, coriander, cumin, ginger, chili powder, and cinnamon and cook until fragrant, about 30 seconds. Add the water and bring to a simmer. Cover, reduce the heat to low, and cook, stirring occasionally, until the carrots are tender, 15 to 20 minutes.

2. Off the heat, mash the carrots with a potato masher, leaving a few coarse pieces for texture. Stir in the remaining 2 tablespoons oil and vinegar. Transfer to a bowl, cover, and refrigerate until the dip is chilled, about 30 minutes. Season with salt and pepper to taste and sprinkle with the cilantro before serving. (The dip can be refrigerated in an airtight container for up to 2 days. Season with additional vinegar, salt, and pepper to taste and sprinkle with the cilantro before serving.)

BRUSCHETTA

CENTURIES AGO, TUSCAN BRUSCHETTA MEANT nothing more than a slice of toasted country bread rubbed with garlic and oil. It's fair to say that in this country, at this time, the original concept has been all but lost. In its place, a toasted slab piled high with chopped tomatoes and basil has become standard. While this modern recipe sounds appealing, in reality it is tired and untidy. The tomatoes are rarely flavorful enough (save for a few weeks in August) to make much impact, and they invariably shed a lot of liquid. (And with nothing to hold the topping in place, much of it can wind up on your shirt.) The result is soggy and flavorless bruschetta.

My modern-day bruschetta recipes would feature smartly chosen, flavorful ingredients atop crisp, olive oil–brushed toasts for a substantial yet easy-to-eat appetizer or light entrée. Olives, marinated peppers, and artichoke hearts—all conveniently pantry-ready—fit the bill for punchy, concentrated flavors, as did sharp cheeses like feta and Parmesan. But judiciously selecting and carefully layering the ingredients wasn't enough to make the toasts easy to pick up, especially once the toppings were dressed with vinaigrette (the usual modern treatment). To make the whole package structurally sound from crust to crown, I needed something to act as a "glue" and anchor the toppings to the bread.

I spent a few days smearing bread with mayonnaise and viscous emulsified vinaigrettes before I realized that the solution might revolve around a technique and not a condiment jar. By pulsing one of the topping ingredients (like the artichokes or the feta cheese) in the food processor until it formed a rough paste, I was able to create a base onto which I could layer my other ingredients; this way, everything stayed firmly in place and no juices soaked through to the bread. Even better, tasters enjoyed the contrasting textures and flavors of the base spread and the chunkier elements. The only other concern was timing; to ensure optimum crunch, I made sure not to toast or top the bread until it was time to eat.

—ANDREA GEARY, *Cook's Illustrated*

Toasted Bread for Bruschetta

SERVES 4 AS A LIGHT MAIN COURSE OR 8 TO 10 AS AN APPETIZER

Toast the bread as close as possible to the time that you plan to serve the bruschetta. If you prefer, the bread can be grilled. After the ends are trimmed, the loaf of bread should yield 10 or 11 slices. To avoid an overpowering garlic flavor, use a light touch when rubbing the bread with the raw garlic.

1 loaf crusty country bread, about 10 by 5 inches, ends discarded, cut crosswise into ¾-inch-thick pieces

½ garlic clove, peeled

¼ cup extra-virgin olive oil

　 Salt

Adjust an oven rack to be 4 inches from the broiler element and heat the broiler. Broil the bread until deep golden on both sides, 1 to 2 minutes per side. Rub one side of each slice lightly with the garlic clove and brush this side with the olive oil. Season with salt to taste.

Bruschetta with Whipped Feta and Marinated Roasted Red Peppers

SERVES 4 AS A LIGHT MAIN COURSE OR 8 TO 10 AS AN APPETIZER

- 1 (24-ounce) jar roasted red peppers, rinsed, patted dry, and cut into ½-inch dice
- 1 garlic clove, minced
- 2 tablespoons red wine vinegar
- 2 tablespoons sugar
- ¼ teaspoon red pepper flakes
- ¼ teaspoon salt
- 8 ounces feta cheese, crumbled (about 2 cups)
- 2 tablespoons extra-virgin olive oil, plus extra for serving
- 2 teaspoons fresh lemon juice
- ¼ teaspoon pepper
- 1 recipe Toasted Bread for Bruschetta (see page 15)

Combine the roasted red peppers, garlic, vinegar, sugar, red pepper flakes, and salt in a medium bowl and set aside. Process the feta, olive oil, lemon juice, and black pepper in a food processor until smooth, about 10 seconds, scraping down the bowl once during processing. Divide the feta mixture among the toasts and spread to the edges. Using a fork, lift the peppers from the marinade and place on the toasts. Drizzle with olive oil and serve.

Bruschetta with Artichokes and Parmesan

SERVES 4 AS A LIGHT MAIN COURSE OR 8 TO 10 AS AN APPETIZER

Though we typically prefer frozen artichokes, canned work well here because they puree more uniformly.

- 1 (14-ounce) can artichoke hearts, rinsed and patted dry with paper towels
- 2 tablespoons finely shredded fresh basil
- 2 tablespoons extra-virgin olive oil, plus extra for serving
- 2 teaspoons fresh lemon juice
- 1 garlic clove, minced
- ¼ teaspoon salt
  Pepper
- 1 ounce finely grated Parmesan cheese (about ½ cup), plus 1 ounce Parmesan cheese, shaved into strips with a vegetable peeler
- 1 recipe Toasted Bread for Bruschetta (see page 15)

Pulse the artichoke hearts, basil, olive oil, lemon juice, garlic, salt, and ¼ teaspoon pepper in a food processor until a coarse puree forms, about 6 pulses, scraping down the bowl once during processing. Add the grated Parmesan and pulse to combine, about 2 pulses. Divide the artichoke mixture among the toasts and spread to the edges. Top with the shaved Parmesan, sprinkle with pepper to taste, drizzle with olive oil, and serve.

Bruschetta with Black Olive Pesto, Ricotta, and Basil

SERVES 4 AS A LIGHT MAIN COURSE OR 8 TO 10 AS AN APPETIZER

Because olives can be quite salty, be sure to use a light hand when seasoning the ricotta. Use only a high-quality whole-milk ricotta for this recipe; our recommended brand is Calabro.

- ½ cup pitted kalamata olives
- 2 tablespoons extra-virgin olive oil, plus extra for serving
- 1 small shallot, minced (about 2 tablespoons)
- 1½ teaspoons fresh lemon juice
- 1 garlic clove, minced
- 1½ cups ricotta cheese
  Salt and pepper
- 1 recipe Toasted Bread for Bruschetta (see page 15)
- 2 tablespoons finely shredded fresh basil

Process the olives, olive oil, shallot, lemon juice, and garlic in a food processor until a uniform paste forms, about 10 seconds, scraping down the bowl once during processing. Combine the ricotta with salt and pepper to taste in a small bowl. Divide the olive mixture among the toasts and spread to the edges. Carefully spread the ricotta over the olive mixture. Drizzle with olive oil, sprinkle with the basil, and serve.

NOTES FROM THE TEST KITCHEN

SHREDDING BASIL

To shred basil, simply stack several leaves on top of one another, roll them up, and slice. We have found that rolling the leaves lengthwise from tip to tail minimizes bruising and browning.

GRILLED VEGETABLE AND BREAD SALAD

WHAT'S NOT TO LOVE ABOUT FRESH VEGGIES combined with the heat and smoke of the grill? I could think of two things. First, there is the challenge of grilling them to just the right point—gently charred on the outside and tender within—while avoiding blackened and mushy vegetables. Then there's the issue of flavor: Usually there's just not enough of it. They may be appealing from a health standpoint, but plain grilled vegetables are sure to get boring fast. That's when the idea for an Italian-style vegetable and bread salad came to mind. Pair grilled vegetable chunks with cubes of rustic bread, fresh herbs, and a bright vinaigrette, and very little else is needed. With a little testing, I figured I'd have a surefire winner.

I began by determining the vegetables to use, focusing on Mediterranean flavors. Mindful of complementary cooking times, I matched zucchini with sweet red onion and red bell peppers. Cutting the zucchini lengthwise and the bell peppers into quarters gave me large pieces that were easy to handle on the grill. Once they cooked, they would be easy enough to cut up into bite-size chunks. For the grilling itself, most recipes I found for these vegetables suggested a total of 10 minutes for both sides over high heat. But when I tried this method, my vegetables were incinerated on the outside when the time was up. Trying again, I built a more moderate, medium-heat fire. Ten minutes later, my vegetables were perfectly browned and tender and full of smoky flavor. During this testing I also found that no matter how hard I tried to keep the onion rings intact, they always came apart and fell through the grate. Threading the onion slices onto metal skewers was an easy solution to ensure that not an onion was lost.

The bread cubes were up next. I knew the bread's quality would be key to a successful recipe, so I tried several varieties. Sliced white and supermarket bread was out; the overly smooth texture caused it to turn to mush when tossed with the dressing (at this point a simple combination of lemon juice and olive oil), and its surprisingly sweet flavor conflicted with the salad's savory flavors. I thought breads containing dried fruits or nuts might add a nice touch to the salad, but their garnishes seemed random and out of place. A high-quality rustic loaf or baguette worked the best. The sturdy texture and strong wheaty flavor paired well with the bolder grilled flavor of the vegetables, and it held up reasonably well once dressed. To make it a little sturdier and add appealing crunch, I decided to toast the bread in the oven before tossing it with the vegetables and dressing. This was exactly the texture the salad needed.

I thought I was on my last run-through when I noticed I had a fair amount of room left on the grill while the vegetables were cooking. I realized there was no need to toast the bread in the oven because it could be done quickly and easily right on the grill. Lightly coated with vegetable oil spray and seasoned with some salt and pepper, the bread toasted up to a beautiful golden brown. And as I had done with the vegetables, I grilled the bread in larger pieces for easier handling, then cubed it once cooked.

Now all I needed to do was put the finishing touches on my vinaigrette. Keeping with the Mediterranean theme, I started with a basic lemon juice and extra-virgin olive oil combination and added some mustard and garlic for tanginess and chopped basil and lemon zest for freshness. All I had to do was toss everything together. It seemed like it was almost there, but I wanted to add a little variety to the texture. Scattering a few ounces of crumbled goat cheese on top of the salad made the perfect finishing touch.

—DAN ZUCCARELLO, *America's Test Kitchen Books*

Grilled Vegetable and Bread Salad
SERVES 4

A rustic round loaf, or a baguette sliced on the extreme bias, works best for this recipe. Be sure to use high-quality bread.

- 3 tablespoons extra-virgin olive oil
- 2 tablespoons chopped fresh basil
- 4 teaspoons fresh lemon juice plus 1 teaspoon grated lemon zest
- 1 teaspoon Dijon mustard
- 1 garlic clove, minced
  Salt and pepper
- 1 red onion, sliced into ½-inch-thick rounds
- 2 red bell peppers, stemmed, seeded, and quartered
- 2 zucchini, halved lengthwise
  Vegetable oil spray
- 6 ounces French or Italian bread, cut into 1-inch-thick slices
- 2 ounces goat cheese, crumbled (about ½ cup)

GRILLED VEGETABLE AND BREAD SALAD

1. Whisk the oil, basil, lemon juice, lemon zest, mustard, garlic, ⅛ teaspoon salt, and ⅛ teaspoon pepper together in a large bowl and set aside.

2. Thread the onion rounds, from side to side, onto 2 metal skewers. Lightly coat the onion, bell peppers, and zucchini with vegetable oil spray and season with ⅛ teaspoon salt and ⅛ teaspoon pepper.

NOTES FROM THE TEST KITCHEN

HOW HOT IS YOUR FIRE?

To determine the heat level of the cooking grate itself, heat up the grill and hold your hand 5 inches above the cooking grate, counting how many seconds you can comfortably keep it there. Note that this works with both charcoal and gas grills.

Hot fire	2 seconds
Medium-hot fire	3 to 4 seconds
Medium fire	5 to 6 seconds
Medium-low fire	7 seconds
Low fire	10 seconds

GRILL COOKWARE: GREATER THAN GRATES?

Grill cookware promises to make it easier to grill small chunks of food so they don't fall into the fire. But can it give you the same results as grilling directly on the grates? Grill cookware comes in three starkly different designs (woks, skillets with handles, and rectangular sheet pans) and in materials from wire mesh, aluminum, and stainless steel to enameled cast iron and porcelain- or nonstick-coated steel. We rounded up models priced from $5.97 to $49.99 in all three styles and a range of materials. We also threw in an adjustable pan that allows the user to manipulate the size from large to small and a disposable aluminum model. The worst performers were the grill woks, which caused food to steam, and those pans with nonstick coating, which gave food a chemical smell and taste. But if you choose a good design and the right material, grill pans can be a definite improvement over futzing around to prevent food from falling through the grates. Our favorites were the **Weber Professional-Grade Grill Pan** (left), $19.99, and the **Williams-Sonoma Mesh Grill-Top Fry Pan** (right), $29.95. (See page 306 for more information about our testing results.)

3A. FOR A CHARCOAL GRILL: Open the bottom grill vents completely. Light a large chimney starter half full with charcoal briquettes (50 briquettes; 3 quarts). When the coals are hot, spread them in an even layer over the grill. Set the cooking grate in place, cover, and open the lid vents completely. Heat the grill until hot, about 5 minutes.

3B. FOR A GAS GRILL: Turn all the burners to high, cover, and heat the grill until hot, about 15 minutes. Turn all the burners to medium. (Adjust the burners as needed to maintain a medium fire; see at left.)

4. Clean and oil the cooking grate. Place the vegetables on one half of the grill and cook (covered if using gas) until spottily charred on both sides, 10 to 15 minutes, flipping them halfway through. Transfer the vegetables to a cutting board and remove the onion from the skewers.

5. While the vegetables cook, lightly coat the bread slices with vegetable oil spray and season with ⅛ teaspoon salt and ⅛ teaspoon pepper. Place the bread slices on the grill, opposite the vegetables, and cook (covered if using gas) until golden brown on both sides, about 4 minutes, flipping the slices halfway through. Transfer the bread to the cutting board with the vegetables.

6. Cut the vegetables into 1-inch pieces and the bread slices into 1-inch cubes. Add the vegetables and bread to the bowl with the vinaigrette and toss to coat. Divide the salad evenly among individual plates, sprinkle the cheese evenly over the salads, and serve.

CHOPPED SALADS, REFINED

CHOPPED SALADS HAD THEIR HEYDAY IN THE 1950s as a popular menu item for ladies who lunched. If you have encountered a good version, it's easy to see the appeal. The best are lively, thoughtfully chosen compositions of lettuce, vegetables, and sometimes fruit cut into bite-size pieces, with supporting players like nuts and cheese contributing hearty flavors and textures. Unfortunately, I've had more experience with the mediocre kind. These are little better than a random collection of cut-up produce from the crisper drawer, exuding moisture that turns the salad watery and bland. I wanted to come up with several recipes for chopped salads, each one offering complementary flavors and textures in every bite—not a random collection with little flavor or appeal.

Salting some of the vegetables to remove excess moisture was an obvious first step. I singled out two of the worst offenders for my starting point: cucumbers and

tomatoes. I halved a cucumber and scooped out its watery seeds before dicing it, tossing it with salt, and allowing it to drain in a colander set over a bowl. After 15 minutes, the cuke pieces had shed a full tablespoon of water. As for the tomatoes, I liked the idea of grape tomatoes because their good tomato flavor and small size make them appealing for a salad such as this one. Seeding them was out of the question; much of the tomato flavor is concentrated in the seeds and surrounding jelly. But I did cut them into quarters to expose more surface area to the salt, and in the end found this technique released a full 2 tablespoons of liquid from a pint of tomatoes after just 15 minutes.

As I tried more recipes, it became clear that the dressings weren't doing anything for the chopped salads. Most recipes called for a ratio of 3 parts oil to 1 part vinegar—the same proportions as for a leafy green salad. However, the ratio didn't translate all that well. I found that a more assertive blend of equal parts oil and vinegar was far better at delivering the bright, acidic kick needed in a chopped salad boasting hearty flavors and chunky textures.

But could I use the dressing to greater advantage? Tossing a green salad just before serving prevents the tender leaves from absorbing too much dressing and turning soggy. But I wanted just the opposite here. A little flavor absorption by some of the sturdier components of a chopped salad would actually be a good thing. Marinating ingredients such as bell peppers, onions, and fruit in the dressing for just five minutes before adding cheese and other tender components brought a welcome flavor boost.

I was now ready to focus on the composition of the salads. I determined that mild, crisp romaine and firm-tender cucumber were musts in every salad, as was the bite of red onion. I also liked the crunch of nuts along with the softer texture of cheese. For a Mediterranean combo, I added chickpeas, feta, and parsley to the standard mix. Another variation boasted red pepper with pear, cranberry, blue cheese, and pistachios; a third featured fennel and apple with tarragon, goat cheese, and walnuts. My tasters agreed; these vibrant, full-flavored salads were so good, they could revive the classic for a second life.

—BRYAN ROOF, *Cook's Illustrated*

Mediterranean Chopped Salad

SERVES 4 AS A LIGHT MAIN COURSE OR 6 AS A SIDE DISH

1   cucumber, peeled, halved lengthwise, seeded, and cut into ½-inch dice (about 1¼ cups) (see page 20)

1   pint grape tomatoes, quartered (about 1½ cups)

    Salt

3   tablespoons extra-virgin olive oil

3   tablespoons red wine vinegar

1   garlic clove, minced

1   (15-ounce) can chickpeas, drained and rinsed

½   cup pitted kalamata olives, chopped

½   small red onion, minced (about ¼ cup)

½   cup chopped fresh parsley

1   romaine heart, cut into ½-inch pieces (about 3 cups)

4   ounces feta cheese, crumbled (about 1 cup)

    Pepper

1. Combine the cucumber, tomatoes, and 1 teaspoon salt in a colander set over a bowl and drain for 15 minutes.

2. Whisk the oil, vinegar, and garlic together in a large bowl. Add the drained cucumber and tomatoes, chickpeas, olives, onion, and parsley. Toss and let stand at room temperature to blend the flavors, 5 minutes.

3. Add the romaine and feta and toss to combine. Season with salt and pepper to taste and serve.

Pear and Cranberry Chopped Salad

SERVES 4 AS A LIGHT MAIN COURSE OR 6 AS A SIDE DISH

1   cucumber, peeled, halved lengthwise, seeded, and cut into ½-inch dice (about 1¼ cups) (see page 20)

    Salt

3   tablespoons extra-virgin olive oil

3   tablespoons sherry vinegar

1   red bell pepper, stemmed, seeded, and cut into ¼-inch pieces (about 1 cup)

1   ripe but firm pear, cut into ¼-inch pieces (about 1 cup)

½   small red onion, minced (about ¼ cup)

½   cup dried cranberries

1   romaine heart, cut into ½-inch pieces (about 3 cups)

4   ounces blue cheese, crumbled (about 1 cup)

½   cup pistachios, toasted and chopped coarse

    Pepper

1. Combine the cucumber and ½ teaspoon salt in a colander set over a bowl and drain for 15 minutes.

2. Whisk the oil and vinegar together in a large bowl. Add the drained cucumber, bell pepper, pear, onion, and cranberries. Toss and let stand at room temperature to blend flavors, 5 minutes.

3. Add the romaine, blue cheese, and pistachios and toss to combine. Season with salt and pepper to taste and serve.

Fennel and Apple Chopped Salad

SERVES 4 AS A LIGHT MAIN COURSE OR 6 AS A SIDE DISH

Braeburn, Jonagold or Red Delicious apples would all work well here.

1   cucumber, peeled, halved lengthwise, seeded, and cut into ½-inch dice (about 1¼ cups) (see page 20)

    Salt

3   tablespoons extra-virgin olive oil

3   tablespoons white wine vinegar

1   fennel bulb, halved lengthwise, cored, and cut into ¼-inch dice (about 1½ cups) (see page 224)

2   apples, cored and cut into ¼-inch dice (about 2 cups)

½   small red onion, minced (about ¼ cup)

¼   cup chopped fresh tarragon

1   romaine heart, cut into ½-inch pieces (about 3 cups)

½   cup chopped walnuts, toasted

    Pepper

4   ounces crumbled goat cheese (about 1 cup)

1. Combine the cucumber and ½ teaspoon salt in a colander set over a bowl and drain for 15 minutes.

2. Whisk the oil and vinegar together in a large bowl. Add the drained cucumber, fennel, apples, onion, and tarragon. Toss and let stand at room temperature to blend flavors, 5 minutes.

3. Add the romaine and walnuts and toss to combine. Season with salt and pepper to taste. Divide salad among plates; top each with some goat cheese and serve.

WHEAT BERRY AND ARUGULA SALAD

IN SEARCH OF A NEW GRAIN SALAD TO ADD TO OUR repertoire that would also be on the healthful side, we landed on wheat berries. While wheat berries have the reputation of being a boring and bland side dish, they have a great nutty flavor and appealing texture that I felt had enormous potential if just dressed up a bit. Could I find a way to showcase wheat berries in a brightly flavored salad with appealing colors and textures?

First I needed to settle the best way to cook the wheat berries. Some recipes swore by simmering the kernels with exact proportions of water to wheat berries, though more relied on cooking the kernels like pasta, simply simmering the wheat berries in a large amount of water (both techniques required a long cooking time). I decided to go with the easier, more common method. After an hour of simmering, the grains had good texture, but I was disappointed to find the flavor had been somewhat diluted.

Taking another cue from pasta-cooking techniques, I added salt to the boiling water. Working with the test kitchen's standard ratio of 1 tablespoon of salt to 4 quarts of water, I cooked up another batch. This time I had an unexpected result; after an hour of cooking, the wheat berries were still incredibly hard. It turns out the salinity of the water was preventing the wheat from absorbing it. I decided to test separate batches, each with a different amount of salt. Right off the bat, tasters complained that the wheat berries cooked with 1 and 2 teaspoons of salt were still too hard. Those cooked with ¼ teaspoon and ½ teaspoon both produced grains with a pleasing texture and good flavor. In the end, I settled on just ½ teaspoon of salt, which allowed the wheat berries to achieve the proper tenderness while at the same time lending a good flavor boost. After draining and cooling the grains under running water to stop the cooking, I was ready to move on.

Next, I considered the additional components for my salad. A bed of arugula worked best in this setting, lending a slightly peppery flavor that complemented the mild grain. As for the dressing, I didn't want to simply douse it in olive oil; I was after something lighter and fresher. In the test kitchen we have sometimes turned to a spa technique of utilizing a fruit juice reduction to add bold flavor and rich texture to dressing. Cooking fruit juice down to a syrupy consistency allows it to take the place of most of the oil. I started by reducing orange juice, then added lime juice, honey, and cilantro for brightness and some cumin, paprika, and cayenne for a little Southwestern spice. Tasters appreciated the sweet flavor and touch of color from roasted red peppers. The salad needed some textural contrast, and chickpeas did this job well with the added benefit of providing protein and substance to help make it a meal. At this point my tasters loved the salad, but one suggested adding feta. Just 2 ounces crumbled into the salad continued the Mediterranean theme and created a cool, creamy counterpoint that made the perfect finishing touch.

—DAN ZUCCARELLO, *America's Test Kitchen Books*

Wheat Berry and Arugula Salad

SERVES 4

Wheat berries can be found in the health food section of most grocery stores. Once fully cooked, the wheat berries will still retain a chewy texture.

DRESSING

- 1 cup fresh orange juice (about 2 oranges)
- ¼ cup chopped fresh cilantro
- 2 tablespoons fresh lime juice
- 2 tablespoons water
- 1 tablespoon extra-virgin olive oil
- 2 teaspoons honey
- 2 garlic cloves, minced
- ½ teaspoon ground cumin
- ¼ teaspoon salt
- ¼ teaspoon paprika
- ⅛ teaspoon cayenne pepper

WHEAT BERRY AND ARUGULA SALAD

SALAD

- 1 **cup wheat berries**
- **Salt**
- 1 **(15-ounce) can chickpeas, drained and rinsed**
- ½ **cup jarred roasted red peppers, drained, patted dry, and chopped**
- 2 **ounces feta cheese, crumbled (about ½ cup)**
- **Black pepper**
- 8 **ounces baby arugula (about 8 cups)**

1. FOR THE DRESSING: Bring the orange juice to a simmer in a small saucepan over medium-high heat. Reduce the heat to medium and cook until the juice is syrupy and reduced to ⅓ cup, 12 to 15 minutes.

2. Transfer the orange juice syrup to a small bowl and refrigerate until cool, about 10 minutes. Whisk in the cilantro, lime juice, water, oil, honey, garlic, cumin, salt, paprika, and cayenne and set aside.

3. FOR THE SALAD: Bring 4 quarts water to a boil in a large pot. Add the wheat berries and ½ teaspoon salt, partially cover, and cook, stirring often, until tender but still chewy, about 1 hour. Drain the wheat berries and rinse them under cold running water until cool. Transfer the wheat berries to a large bowl and set aside.

4. TO ASSEMBLE THE SALAD: Stir the chickpeas, roasted red peppers, feta, and half of the dressing into the bowl with the wheat berries. Season with salt and black pepper to taste. In a separate bowl, toss the arugula with the remaining dressing and divide among 4 plates. Arrange 1 cup of the wheat berry mixture on top of each salad and serve.

NOTES FROM THE TEST KITCHEN

GETTING TO KNOW WHEAT BERRIES

Wheat berries, often erroneously referred to as "whole wheat," are whole, unprocessed kernels of wheat. Since none of the grain has been removed, wheat berries are an excellent source of fiber, protein, and iron and other minerals. Compared to more refined forms of wheat (cracked wheat, bulgur, and flour), wheat berries require a relatively long cooking time. In the test kitchen, we like to simmer them with a small amount of salt for about an hour until they are tender but still retain a good bite.

AMISH POTATO SALAD

THE SELF-SUFFICIENT AMISH LIVING IN COLONIAL America turned to pickling to preserve food for hard Pennsylvania winters. Vinegar was so readily used in Amish cooking that it was said that the table was incomplete without "seven sweet and sours." A prime example of their affinity for this combo is their simple potato salad studded with hard-boiled eggs and celery.

Before the advent of bottled dressing, boiled salad dressing was used as a creamy base for pasta or potato salads, including for the Amish version. Recipes began by gently cooking vinegar, sugar, water, a little oil or butter, flour for thickening, egg for emulsification and richness, and dry mustard over a double boiler (to prevent curdling) until the dressing turned thick and glossy. The dressing was refrigerated until needed, then thinned with milk or heavy cream and tossed with peeled and cubed boiled potatoes, chopped celery, and several mashed hard-boiled eggs. When I made an old-fashioned recipe in the test kitchen, the creamy, custardy egg-enriched dressing brought deviled eggs to mind, with a delicate balance of tart vinegar and mustard and sweetened dressing. The flavor was certainly worth preserving, but pulling out a double boiler for potato salad was beyond my commitment level. Surely there was an easier way.

Some modern recipes avoid cooking a dressing by mixing sugar, vinegar, and mustard into jarred mayonnaise. Though I liked the no-cook ease, this convenience version lacked the egg-enriched dressing's complexity. Looking over traditional recipes from Amish cookbooks, I selected the most balanced version, with ⅓ cup cider vinegar (which I preferred over brash white), ¼ cup sugar, 2 tablespoons vegetable oil, 2 tablespoons yellow mustard, 1 tablespoon flour, and one egg for 3 pounds of Yukon Gold potatoes (a good choice because of their sturdiness when boiled). I cooked the mixture in a saucepan, whisking constantly over low heat. The dressing thickened nicely the first time, but a second test went from silky to scrambled in seconds. Without the buffer of the double boiler, the dressing could too easily overcook. Could there be a way to avoid cooking the dressing and get the same rich, eggy flavor?

Since I had hard-cooked eggs on hand for mashing into the salad, I wondered if I could incorporate them into my dressing to avoid the bother of cooking it. True, hard-cooked egg might not thicken the dressing like cooking raw egg, but it would mimic the authentic flavor. To emulsify the ingredients, I filled the food processor with a hard-cooked yolk (the white lent a grainy texture), vinegar, sugar, oil, and mustard (I omitted the flour since it was only there to help thicken the dressing when cooking) and set the blade spinning. This dressing took me back to the rich, eggy flavor of the original, but now the dressing was too thin to coat the potatoes.

The original cooked dressings were quite thick; they were only thinned to the right coating consistency with fresh dairy right before use. Looking back to the no-cook, eggless recipe made with mayo I had found early on, I realized a thick, creamy dairy product might be the answer. Yogurt proved too watery, Miracle Whip too sweet, and mayo too greasy. Sour cream provided the best balance to my sweet and sour dressing and got me almost there, but the dressing was still a hair too loose. Could I omit the scant amount of oil now that the dressing included rich sour cream? As I'd suspected, not only did losing the oil tighten the texture, but it also brought the sweet and sour flavors to the forefront.

Now I only needed to fine-tune the salad. Employing a proven test kitchen technique for potato salads, I seasoned the hot, drained potatoes with a couple of tablespoons of the potent vinegary dressing (before it was mixed with the sour cream) to infuse them with flavor. A final addition of nutty celery seed sealed the deal. This Amish Potato Salad had the unique flavor of the old-world recipes, but with a foolproof modern method.

—CALI RICH, *Cook's Country*

Amish Potato Salad

SERVES 8

Spreading the hot potatoes in an even layer on a baking sheet and placing in the refrigerator promotes a quick chill and less chance of overcooked potatoes.

3	pounds Yukon Gold potatoes (about 6 to 8 medium), peeled and cut into ¾-inch chunks
	Salt
⅓	cup cider vinegar
¼	cup sugar
2	tablespoons yellow mustard
4	large hard-cooked eggs, peeled
½	teaspoon celery seed
¾	cup sour cream
1	celery rib, chopped fine
	Pepper

1. Bring the potatoes, 1 tablespoon salt, and enough water to cover the potatoes by 1 inch to boil in a large pot over high heat. Reduce the heat to medium and simmer until the potatoes are just tender, about 10 minutes.

2. While the potatoes simmer, microwave the vinegar and sugar in a small bowl until the sugar dissolves, about 30 seconds. Process the vinegar mixture, mustard, 1 hard-cooked egg yolk (reserve the white), the celery seed, and ½ teaspoon salt in a food processor until smooth. Transfer to a large bowl.

3. Drain the potatoes, then spread them in an even layer on a rimmed baking sheet. Drizzle 2 tablespoons of the dressing over the hot potatoes and toss until evenly coated. Refrigerate until cooled, about 30 minutes.

4. Whisk the sour cream into the remaining dressing. Add the remaining hard-cooked eggs and egg white and, using a potato masher, mash until only small pieces remain. Add the celery and cooled potatoes and stir until combined. Cover and refrigerate until well chilled, about 30 minutes. Season with salt and pepper. Serve. (The salad can be refrigerated in an airtight container for up to 2 days.)

NOTES FROM THE TEST KITCHEN

MAKING NO-COOK EGG DRESSING
We loved the flavor of Amish Potato Salad's traditional cooked-egg dressing, but we hated the process. Stepping away from the stove, we capture the same rich flavor by pureeing a hard-cooked egg yolk into the dressing base and then whisking in thick and creamy sour cream.

1. Processing a hard-cooked egg yolk into the dressing yields authentic flavor without any stovetop cooking.

2. Incorporating sour cream adds body and tang to the sweet and sour dressing.

SOUPS & STEWS

SLOW-COOKER FRENCH ONION SOUP

WHO DOESN'T LOVE FRENCH ONION SOUP? BUT IT'S hard to love making it, given the two hours of stovetop browning and stirring that it takes to caramelize a heap of onions. A slow cooker seemed like the perfect way to soften them without the bother of stirring or the fear they'd burn—assuming I could get them to brown and caramelize.

I tried several recipes, all promising classic French onion soup made in a slow cooker. Some dumped sliced onions and butter into the slow cooker and cooked them on low for one to two hours. After pouring in store-bought broth and cooking the mixture another four hours, I had crunchy onions adrift in thin, flavorless soup. Other recipes caramelized the onions in batches on the stovetop before transferring them to the slow cooker with commercial broth and herbs. This soup tasted somewhat better, but saved little work.

A recipe for slow-cooker caramelized onions suggested tossing the onions with butter, salt to draw out moisture, and sugar to aid browning and cooking them twice as long as for the soup recipe on the high setting. After four hours, these onions swam in their own sour, watery juice and had remained white as office paper. Frustrated, I left the slow cooker on. By the time the workday was over, the onions were finally beginning to brown. I lugged the appliance home, plugged it back in, and waited another four hours. At hour 12, the liquid was nearly gone and the onions were soft and brown around the edges. I warmed 2 cups each of beef and chicken broth (the combination gave the soup complexity), sherry, and thyme in the microwave and poured the mixture into the slow cooker. The house smelled like a French bistro, but the onions tasted waterlogged and the broth was thin and insipid.

For my next test, I turned to soy sauce, which the test kitchen has used before to add depth to slow-cooker stews. I mixed it with flour, which would help the soup thicken, as well as sherry and thyme, adding them to the slow cooker at the start in hope of aiding flavor development before stirring the mixture into the onions. This soup was a definite improvement, but because the slow cooker allows no evaporation, hence no concentration of flavors, it still lacked the deep, rich meatiness and silky texture of the classic.

The classic, of course, relies on homemade beef broth,

and homemade broth, in turn, starts with roasted beef bones for flavor and body. I didn't see any reason I couldn't add bones. I microwaved them first to simulate roasting, and then tucked them in around the perimeter of the slow cooker (where most of the heat is) with the onions. I proceeded with the recipe as before. Many hours later, the flavor passed muster, but tasters still weren't satisfied with the thin texture.

I tried adding tapioca, and after that, gelatin, without success. Then I got an admittedly insane idea from a test kitchen recipe I love for pork chops with apples: The silky sauce gets its texture from apple butter. For my next test, I added ¾ cup of apple butter to the onions. Many hours later, the onions were deep brown, the soup silky and deeply flavored. No one guessed my oddball secret ingredient.

To serve French onion soup, you ladle it into crocks, top it with French bread and Gruyère cheese, and broil to a bubbly, oozing, golden brown. Knowing most home cooks don't have soup crocks dedicated to this task, I decided it was more practical to lay slices of bread on a baking sheet, sprinkle them with grated cheese, and broil. I ladled the slow-cooker soup into bowls and topped each with cheese croutons. Ooh la la!

—DIANE UNGER, *Cook's Country*

Slow-Cooker French Onion Soup
SERVES 6 TO 8

You can slice the onions the night before and toast the croutons up to 1 day ahead. You can find beef bones in the freezer or meat section of most supermarkets, and apple butter near the jams and jellies.

SOUP
- 2 **pounds beef bones**
- 4 **tablespoons (½ stick) unsalted butter**
- 6 **large yellow onions (about 4 pounds), quartered and cut into ¼-inch-thick slices (see page 29)**
  Salt and pepper
- 1 **tablespoon brown sugar**
- 1 **teaspoon minced fresh thyme**
- ¾ **cup apple butter**
- ¾ **cup dry sherry**
- 5 **tablespoons unbleached all-purpose flour**
- ¼ **cup soy sauce**
- 2 **cups low-sodium chicken broth**
- 2 **cups low-sodium beef broth**

CROUTONS

1   loaf French bread, cut into ½-inch slices
10   ounces shredded Gruyère cheese (about 2½ cups)

1. FOR THE SOUP: Arrange the beef bones on a paper towel–lined plate. Microwave until well browned, 8 to 10 minutes. Meanwhile, set the slow cooker to high. Add the butter to the slow cooker, cover, and cook until melted. Add the onions, 2 teaspoons salt, 1 teaspoon pepper, brown sugar, and thyme. Stir the apple butter, sherry, flour, and soy sauce together in a small bowl until smooth. Pour over the onions and toss to coat. Tuck the bones under the onions around the edge of the slow cooker. Cover and cook on high until the onions are softened and deep golden brown, 10 to 12 hours (start checking onions after 8 hours).

2. Remove the bones from the slow cooker. Heat the beef and chicken broth in the microwave until beginning to boil. Stir the broth into the slow cooker. Season with salt and pepper to taste.

3. FOR THE CROUTONS: Adjust an oven rack to be about 6 inches from the broiler element and heat the oven to 400 degrees. Arrange the bread slices in a single layer on a baking sheet and bake until the bread is golden at the edges, about 10 minutes. Heat the broiler. Divide the cheese evenly among the croutons and broil until the cheese is melted and bubbly around the edges, 3 to 5 minutes.

4. Ladle the soup into bowls and top each serving with 2 croutons. Serve. (The onions can be cooked through step 1 up to 1 day ahead, transferred to a container, and refrigerated).

NOTES FROM THE TEST KITCHEN

SECRETS TO SLOW-COOKER FRENCH ONION SOUP

We found three ingredients were key to a deeply flavorful, silky soup with a rich brown color.

BEEF BONES
Beef bones, first microwaved to simulate roasting, contribute meaty flavor.

APPLE BUTTER
This unusual addition lends just the right subtle sweetness.

SOY SAUCE
Soy sauce, a test kitchen favorite in soups and stews, adds depth and color.

SLICING ONIONS FOR SLOW-COOKER FRENCH ONION SOUP

Most soup recipes start by chopping or mincing onions. But for our Slow-Cooker French Onion Soup, we wanted slices of onion that would retain their shape through 10 to 12 hours of gentle simmering. We found that cutting onions with the grain (rather than across it) yielded slices durable enough for the slow cooker.

1. Trim off both ends of the onion.

2. Turn the onion onto a cut end and slice it in half, pole to pole.

3. Peel each half, place the onion flat side down, and cut the onion into slices with the grain (pole to pole).

LIGHT CAULIFLOWER SOUP

WHEN IT COMES TO CREAMY PUREED VEGETABLE soups, cauliflower has never been at the top of the test kitchen's list. While we love its mild, earthy flavor, when married with broth and cream its delicate yet distinct flavor can all too easily be overshadowed. Many recipes for cauliflower soup boil the mild vegetable then puree it with heavy cream, but this results in over-cooked cauliflower so bland and a dairy component so, well, heavy, that you can't even taste the cauliflower in the cauliflower soup. Cauliflower soup should have a nutty, slightly sweet flavor that makes it an appeal-ing meal or side dish year-round. I wanted a healthy, flavorful recipe that would do this underestimated vegetable justice.

First I set out to find the best way to cook the cau-liflower. In the test kitchen, when we want to boost the flavor of vegetables we often roast them. The dry heat caramelizes their natural sugars, creating a deep, smoky-sweet flavor. It seemed like a good choice here. I found three basic techniques for roasting cauliflower: roasting cauliflower that has been blanched, roasting cauliflower that has been steamed, and roasting raw cauliflower. In each preparation the cauliflower florets are coated with oil, salt, and pepper at some point. I gave each one a try; the winner was clear. The cauli-flower that had been roasted raw had a nicely browned exterior and well-developed flavor that the other two couldn't match.

Now that the star of our soup had big flavor, I could turn to the other ingredients. Browned onions were an obvious choice for adding depth. Since I was already roasting the cauliflower in the oven, I decided to keep things easy and toss the onion with the cauliflower and roast the two together. But because cauliflower is so mild, I wondered if I could boost its flavor even more. After the vegetables had roasted for about 30 minutes, I moved them to the stovetop and sweated them briefly with a little garlic.

It was time to add the liquid. I tried vegetable broth, but tasters agreed it was overly sweet. Chicken broth created the right balance, and tasters liked the hint of acidity from a splash of white wine. At this point, because the cauliflower was already cooked, I only needed to simmer the florets with the liquid just long enough for the flavors to meld. After five minutes, I pureed the mixture in batches in the blender. It was time to determine the dairy component.

Like most cream of vegetable soup recipes, the cau-liflower soups I found relied on heavy cream for the dairy. But with all its fat, it was not an option for my soup. I tested all types of milk, half-and-half, and evaporated milk. Every variety of milk was too thin and flat for pairing with the deeper flavors of the roasted vegetables. Evaporated milk imparted its own sweetness that interfered. The half-and-half proved best, producing a soup with a smooth, velvety consistency and balanced roasted cauliflower flavor. I started testing with ¼ cup, but tasters thought this soup could take a larger dose of dairy, so I tested larger amounts and eventually settled on ½ cup. This soup was velvety and deeply flavorful, good enough to live up to its promise; you'd never guess each serving had a mere 140 calories and 9 grams of fat.

—ADELAIDE PARKER, *America's Test Kitchen Books*

Light Cauliflower Soup

SERVES 4

If the soup is too thick after the half-and-half has been added, stir in water, ¼ cup at a time, to achieve the desired consistency.

- 1 head cauliflower (about 2 pounds), trimmed, cored, and cut into ½-inch florets (about 6 cups)
- 1 onion, halved and sliced ½ inch thick
- 4 teaspoons canola oil
-    Salt and pepper
- 3 garlic cloves, minced
- ¼ cup dry white wine
- 1 bay leaf
- 3½ cups low-sodium chicken broth
- ½ cup half-and-half
- 1 tablespoon minced fresh chives

1. Adjust an oven rack to the middle position and heat the oven to 450 degrees.

2. Toss the cauliflower, onion, 1 tablespoon of the oil, ½ teaspoon salt, and ¼ teaspoon pepper together in a large bowl, then spread the mixture in an even layer on a rimmed baking sheet. Roast until the cauliflower is softened and lightly browned, 30 to 40 minutes, stirring halfway though.

3. Combine the roasted vegetables and remaining 1 teaspoon oil in a large Dutch oven. Cover and cook over medium-low heat, stirring occasionally, until the cauliflower is very soft, 3 to 5 minutes. Uncover, stir in the garlic, and cook until fragrant, about 30 seconds.

4. Stir in the wine and bay leaf and cook until the wine has reduced by half, about 1 minute. Stir in the broth and bring to a simmer over medium-high heat. Cover, reduce the heat to medium-low, and simmer for 5 minutes. Remove and discard the bay leaf.

5. Working in two batches, process the cauliflower mixture in a blender until smooth, about 1 minute. Transfer the cauliflower mixture to a clean Dutch oven, stir in the half-and-half, and cook over low heat until hot.

6. Season with salt and pepper to taste, ladle into bowls, and sprinkle each portion with some of the chives before serving. (The soup can be cooled and refrigerated in an airtight container for up to 3 days or frozen for up to 1 month. Thaw if frozen and reheat over low heat; do not boil.)

VARIATION

Light Curried Cauliflower Soup
Follow the recipe for Light Cauliflower Soup, adding 1½ teaspoons curry powder to the pot with the roasted vegetables in step 3. Substitute 2 tablespoons minced fresh cilantro for the chives.

NOTES FROM THE TEST KITCHEN

IMMERSION BLENDERS
Immersion blenders are a handy addition to any kitchen, saving on time, effort, and cleanup. Instead of awkwardly transferring hot soup in batches into a blender to puree, you simply stick the immersion blender into the cooking pot, push a button, and presto-chango, silken soup. It's also perfect for small mixing jobs like blending salad dressings, whipping small amounts of cream, or making smoothies. When we tested them in 2006, the KitchenAid Hand Blender earned top marks. Since then, new models have entered the market, and professional, restaurant-quality brands have dropped in price. We tested our old favorite against seven new models, priced from $25 to $100. Our winner was the **Kalorik Sunny Morning Stick Mixer**, $25. It won nearly every test we ran on it, it is comfortable to use, and its wide blade cage and detachable plastic shaft make for easy cleanup. (See page 304 for more information about our testing results.)

HEARTY TEN-VEGETABLE STEW

MOST GREAT STEW RECIPES ARE CHOCK-FULL OF meat because, honestly, in the dead of winter nothing sounds as satisfying. When looking for a meal to feed the belly and soul on a bone-chilling day, most home cooks think of a big pot of hearty, meaty stew bubbling away on the stove. But with so many heavy, meaty wintertime recipes out there, I felt the need for a reprieve from the beef, the chicken, and the pork. I wanted a vegetarian vegetable stew packed with a variety of vegetables that could satisfy just as well, but the vegetable stews I've come across simply throw vegetables into a pot and simmer away. They are either watery and bland or muddy and overloaded. There had to be a way to bring the vegetables to the forefront yet maintain balance, and at the same time win over even the most adamant carnivores. I headed into the test kitchen to see what I could do.

Based on previous test kitchen experience cooking all forms of stews, I knew onion, carrot, celery, and red bell pepper were in for their essential aromatic flavor, so I started by sautéing them until brown to coax out their natural sweetness. The addition of garlic, thyme, and tomato paste added further depth, and a little flour helped thicken the stew. At this point a bit of flavorful fond had built up, so I opted to deglaze my pot with wine, which would pick up the browned bits and at the same time add depth. I tried red wine first, but it overpowered the vegetables. White proved to be a much better choice, adding brightness, slight acidity, and depth all at once. After the wine reduced, I was ready to add the other liquid components, which would make the base for the soup. I began my testing with various amounts of vegetable broth and canned tomatoes, but the tomatoes brought too much acidity. This stew was better off with the vegetable broth alone.

Now for the real hurdle: What vegetables should be featured in my stew? In many stew recipes, root vegetables are a major component, not just for their earthy flavor but also because their starch acts as a thickener and gives stew that rich consistency it's known for. They seemed like a logical starting point, so I hit the grocery store and grabbed every kind of root vegetable available. Back in the test kitchen, I worked through the group. Turnips proved to be slightly bitter, not what I was looking for, while russet potatoes and sweet potatoes fell apart over the cooking time. In the end parsnips, celery root, and red potatoes won out for their unique flavors and appealing textures. I added them to the pot right after I poured in the broth, then I simmered the stew until the vegetables were tender. The size I cut these vegetables proved key. Too small and they disappeared into the stew, too large and they didn't cook through. In the end, I found 1-inch pieces were just right. They cooked through properly and gave the stew just the right hearty appearance. However, at this point I noticed a new problem. My stew was developing an overly sweet quality.

It shouldn't have been surprising, since nearly every ingredient I had added had a natural sweetness of its own. While the potatoes lent some balance, it wasn't enough. In most stews, meat helps provide balance, but clearly that wasn't an option here. Mushrooms are a typical vegetarian alternative to meat. First I tried portobellos, always a top choice for a meaty mushroom (consider the portobello burger), but they only muddled my stew's flavor, and they stayed spongy no matter how I cooked them. Working my way through the other supermarket mushroom options (remember, I wanted to keep this simple), I was surprised that everyday white button mushrooms won out. But how I incorporated them was crucial. Adding them straight to the broth resulted in chewy, spongy mushrooms. Sautéing the mushrooms until they were well browned before I added them to the liquid helped to deepen the mushrooms' flavor and kept them from being spongy. Browning the mushrooms also had the added bonus of creating even more flavorful fond in my pot.

The flavor was definitely less sweet, and more balanced, at this point, but I felt like it could still use more earthiness. Hearty greens seemed like a good idea, so once again I worked my way through all the options I could find. Mustard greens and escarole were both too bitter. Tasters liked both kale and curly leaf spinach, but the real winner was Swiss chard. It was hearty but not too tough, and I liked that there was no waste since both stems and leaves are edible. I added the stems with the aromatics and the leaves toward the end of the cooking to ensure they didn't disintegrate. This definitely helped to tip the scales further from the sweet side, but still not enough.

I didn't want to change the vegetables I had worked so hard to choose at this point, so the logical adjustment was the cooking liquid. Right now I was working with all vegetable broth, which also has a natural sweetness of its own. Using a mixture of vegetable broth and water went a long way to make this stew balanced. I settled on a ratio of nearly equal parts water and vegetable broth.

This stew was almost there, but it needed a touch of freshness and acidity. Summery zucchini struck me as a good addition, but it turned to mush when I added it with the root vegetables. Waiting to add it until the end of cooking with the chard leaves was an easy fix. A splash of lemon juice and a sprinkle of fresh parsley were the perfect finishing touches of freshness and acidity that my stew needed. This vegetable stew was hearty (I had managed to squeeze in a whopping ten vegetables) and satisfying, yet balanced and healthy. I was confident that it could hold its own any day of the week against even the best of the beef stews.

—CHRIS O'CONNOR, *America's Test Kitchen Books*

NOTES FROM THE TEST KITCHEN

THE NEW CHEF'S KNIFE: EAST MEETS WEST

In the European-American culinary tradition, a good chef's knife is the single most essential piece of kitchen equipment. This all-purpose knife has a thick, wedge-shaped blade that can push through tough foods and a curved edge that allows the blade to rhythmically rock when chopping. It won't chip or break easily and it's simple to resharpen. By contrast, in Japan there isn't one all-purpose knife, but instead various specialized knives; all are extremely thin, with a razor-sharp cutting edge honed on just one side that allows for incredibly precise cutting. These Japanese knives have a straighter edge than the chef knife (they are pulled along a cutting board rather than used in a rocking style), and are typically made of very hard steel to support the thinness of the blade. Only recently have knife makers merged the two styles. Called the *gyutou* (ghee-YOU-toe) in Japan, this hybrid knife fuses Japanese knife making with Western knife design. The result is a feather-light, lethally sharp, and wonderfully precise knife. We tested eight hybrid knives priced under $200 and our winning traditional chef's knife. We fell in love with two knives: the **Masamoto VG-10** (top), $136.50, and the **Misono UX-10** (bottom), $156. Both weigh 6 ounces and had among the slimmest spines in our lineup, giving them the narrowest profile for precision slicing. Cooks with a range of hand sizes and knife skills found each equally comfortable. (See page 301 for more information about our testing results.)

Hearty Ten-Vegetable Stew

SERVES 8

Kale greens or curly leaf spinach can be substituted for the chard; the kale will require about 5 additional minutes of simmering time to become tender. We prefer to use medium red potatoes, measuring 2 to 3 inches in diameter, in this recipe.

  2 tablespoons canola oil
  1 pound white mushrooms, sliced thin
     Salt
  8 ounces Swiss chard, stems and leaves separated, stems
     chopped fine and leaves cut into ½-inch pieces
  2 onions, minced (about 2 cups)
  1 celery rib, cut into ½-inch pieces
  1 carrot, peeled, halved lengthwise, and sliced
     1 inch thick
  1 red bell pepper, stemmed, seeded, and cut into
     ½-inch pieces
  6 garlic cloves, minced
  2 teaspoons minced fresh thyme, or ½ teaspoon dried
  2 tablespoons unbleached all-purpose flour
  1 tablespoon tomato paste
  ½ cup dry white wine
  3 cups low-sodium vegetable broth
  2½ cups water
  8 ounces red potatoes (about 2 medium), cut into
     1-inch pieces
  2 parsnips, peeled and cut into 1-inch pieces
  8 ounces celery root, peeled and cut into 1-inch pieces
  2 bay leaves
  1 zucchini, seeded and cut into ½-inch pieces
  ¼ cup minced fresh parsley
  1 tablespoon fresh lemon juice
     Pepper

1. Heat 1 tablespoon of the oil in a large Dutch oven over medium heat until shimmering. Add the mushrooms and ¼ teaspoon salt, cover, and cook until the mushrooms are very wet, about 5 minutes. Uncover and continue to cook until the mushrooms are dry and browned, 5 to 10 minutes.

2. Add the remaining 1 tablespoon oil, chard stems, onions, celery, carrot, bell pepper, and ½ teaspoon salt and cook until the vegetables are well browned, 7 to 10 minutes.

3. Stir in the garlic and thyme and cook until fragrant, about 30 seconds. Stir in the flour and tomato paste and

cook until lightly browned, about 1 minute. Stir in the wine, scraping up the browned bits, and simmer until nearly evaporated, about 2 minutes. Stir in the broth, water, potatoes, parsnips, celery root, and bay leaves and bring to a simmer.

4. Reduce the heat to medium-low, partially cover, and cook until the stew is thickened and the vegetables are tender, about 1 hour. Stir in the zucchini and chard leaves and continue to simmer until tender, 5 to 10 minutes.

5. Discard the bay leaves and stir in the parsley and lemon juice. Season with salt and pepper to taste and serve. (The stew can be cooled, transferred to an airtight container, and refrigerated for up to 3 days or frozen for up to 1 month. Thaw if frozen, then reheat over low heat.)

CHICKEN BOUILLABAISSE

I LOVE THE INTENSE GARLICKY FENNEL, ORANGE, and saffron flavors of bouillabaisse, the traditional Provençal stew packed with an assortment of fish and shellfish, onions and tomatoes, and served with crusty bread and a hefty dollop of rouille (a spicy, garlicky, bread-thickened mayonnaise). But buying and boning a half-dozen varieties of fresh seafood, making a stock, and then cooking each type of seafood is a task best left to restaurant chefs. Enter chicken bouillabaisse. A classic Provençal stew in its own right, it offers home cooks the promise of potent bouillabaisse flavor in a 45-minute chicken dinner. I had to try it.

Most of the recipes I found followed a similar process: Cook onions, leeks, fennel, and lots of garlic over a gentle flame until soft and sweet. Add chicken pieces along with saffron, cayenne pepper, tomatoes, and chicken stock and cook until the chicken is tender. Stir in a shot of pastis (an anise-flavored liqueur) and orange zest and simmer briefly. The dish is served with boiled potatoes along with rouille-slathered bread.

With such all-star ingredients in the pot, none of the recipes I tried was awful, but even the best needed tweaking. Most of the rouilles were heavy and dull. And while the fond created from searing the chicken flavored the broth, it seemed a shame to then submerge the crisped chicken. I wanted to find a way to get the chicken infused with the flavor of the broth but still keep some crisp skin.

CHICKEN BOUILLABAISSE

My stew base started with a fennel bulb, a leek, an onion, and a whole head of garlic sweated in olive oil. But since all of these aromatics turn sweet as they sweat, my tasters found the end result cloying. I knew I couldn't touch the fennel: It provides the anise backbone. Garlic was a better candidate. By cutting the amount down to a mere four cloves, I was able to retain garlicky flavor while dialing back on sweetness. I also experimented with eliminating the onion and found that tasters preferred the broth made with a leek alone.

A traditional bouillabaisse is only as good as its fish stock. Happily, with all the other flavorings contributing complexity to my stew, I found that store-bought chicken broth worked almost as well as homemade stock. To give the broth more body and a long-simmered flavor, I added a tablespoon each of flour and tomato paste with the saffron and cayenne. And instead of stirring in the orange zest late in the cooking, as most recipes instructed, I found it worked best when added with the broth. Tasters also preferred the pastis added at the start of the simmer, which burned off more of its alcoholic taste, leaving only the essence of licorice. As for the other ingredients, ½ cup of white wine brought the right brightness, while diced canned tomatoes were the best way to ensure consistently good tomato flavor year-round.

I moved on to the rouille. With a cup of oil and an egg yolk, it needed brightening, despite the presence of saffron and cayenne. Lemon juice helped, but Dijon mustard (a nontraditional ingredient) brought more tangy depth. To maximize the saffron flavor, I steeped the threads in hot water before adding them.

The only problem remaining was the chicken: The meat was tender and well flavored, but the skin was flabby. Many recipes brown the chicken with the skin on, then remove it before returning the chicken to the pot. This solves the flabby skin problem, but I couldn't get comfortable throwing out that nice crisped skin.

Then I realized a potential solution: the potatoes I was planning to boil separately. If I cooked them in the broth, they'd stick up above the liquid, creating a "raft" on which I could rest the chicken. These results looked good, but to my frustration, the skin was still flabby.

I realized the steam rising from the simmering liquid was soaking the skin. Maybe the fix was a switch from the stovetop to the oven, where the heat from above could keep moisture from condensing on the chicken. This was a giant step forward, but I still wasn't there. What if I placed the pot under the broiler just before

serving? That did it: The intense blast of heat re-crisped the skin in no time. With croutons and tangy rouille complementing the appealing chicken meat and skin, my stew made the most of its Provençal roots, and it didn't give tasters a chance to even think about fish.

—J. KENJI LOPEZ-ALT, *Cook's Illustrated*

Chicken Bouillabaisse

SERVES 4 TO 6

Leftover rouille can be used in sandwiches or as a sauce for vegetables and fish.

BOUILLABAISSE

- 3 **pounds bone-in, skin-on chicken pieces (split breasts cut in half, drumsticks, and/or thighs), trimmed**
  Salt and pepper
- 2 **tablespoons olive oil**
- 1 **large leek, white and light green parts only, halved lengthwise, sliced thin, and rinsed thoroughly**
- 1 **small fennel bulb, halved lengthwise, cored, and sliced thin (about 2 cups) (see page 224)**
- 4 **garlic cloves, minced**
- 1 **tablespoon unbleached all-purpose flour**
- 1 **tablespoon tomato paste**
- ¼ **teaspoon saffron threads**
- ¼ **teaspoon cayenne pepper**
- 3 **cups low-sodium chicken broth**
- 1 **(14.5-ounce) can diced tomatoes, drained**
- ½ **cup dry white wine**
- ¼ **cup pastis or Pernod**
- ¾ **pound Yukon Gold potatoes (1 large or 2 small), cut into ¾-inch cubes**
- 1 **(3-inch) strip orange zest**
- 1 **tablespoon chopped fresh tarragon or parsley**

ROUILLE AND CROUTONS

- 3 **tablespoons water**
- ¼ **teaspoon saffron threads**
- 1 **baguette**
- 4 **teaspoons fresh lemon juice**
- 2 **teaspoons Dijon mustard**
- 1 **large egg yolk**
- ¼ **teaspoon cayenne pepper**
- 2 **small garlic cloves, minced**
- ½ **cup vegetable oil**
- ½ **cup plus 2 tablespoons extra-virgin olive oil**
  Salt and pepper

1. FOR THE BOUILLABAISSE: Adjust the oven racks to middle and lower positions and heat the oven to 375 degrees. Pat the chicken dry with paper towels and season with salt and pepper. Heat the oil in a large Dutch oven over medium-high heat until just smoking. Add the chicken pieces, skin side down, and cook without moving until well browned, 5 to 8 minutes. Using tongs, flip the chicken and brown the other side, about 3 minutes. Transfer the chicken to a plate.

2. Add the leek and fennel. Cook, stirring often, until the vegetables begin to soften and turn translucent, about 4 minutes. Add the garlic, flour, tomato paste, saffron, and cayenne and cook until fragrant, about 30 seconds. Add the broth, tomatoes, wine, pastis, potatoes, and orange zest and bring to a simmer. Reduce the heat to medium-low and simmer for 10 minutes.

3. Nestle the chicken thighs and drumsticks into the simmering liquid with the skin above the surface of the liquid. Cook, uncovered, for 5 minutes. Nestle the breast pieces into the simmering liquid, adjusting the pieces as necessary to ensure the skin stays above the surface of the liquid. Bake on the middle rack, uncovered, until the breasts register 145 degrees and the thighs/drumsticks register 160 degrees on an instant-read thermometer, 10 to 20 minutes.

4. FOR THE ROUILLE: While the chicken cooks, microwave the water and saffron in a microwave-safe bowl until the water is steaming, 10 to 20 seconds. Allow to sit for 5 minutes. Cut a 3-inch piece off of the baguette and remove and discard the crust. Tear the piece of bread into 1-inch chunks (you should have about 1 cup). Stir the bread pieces and lemon juice into the saffron-infused water and soak for 5 minutes. Using a whisk, mash the soaked bread mixture until a uniform paste forms, 1 to 2 minutes. Whisk in the mustard, egg yolk, cayenne, and garlic until smooth, about 15 seconds. Whisking constantly, slowly drizzle in the vegetable oil in a steady stream until a smooth mayonnaise-like consistency is reached, scraping down the bowl as necessary. Slowly whisk in ½ cup of the olive oil in a steady stream until smooth. Season with salt and pepper to taste.

5. FOR THE CROUTONS: Cut the remaining baguette into ¾-inch-thick slices. Arrange the slices in a single layer on a rimmed baking sheet. Drizzle with the remaining 2 tablespoons olive oil and season with salt and pepper. Bake on the lower rack until light golden

brown (the croutons can be toasted while the bouillabaisse is in the oven), 10 to 15 minutes. (The rouille and croutons can be prepared either as the chicken cooks or up to 2 days in advance. Leftover rouille will keep refrigerated for up to 1 week.)

6. Remove the bouillabaisse and croutons from the oven and heat the broiler. Return the bouillabaisse to the oven and cook until the chicken skin is crisp and the breasts register 160 to 165 degrees and the thighs/drumsticks register 175 degrees on an instant-read thermometer, 5 to 10 minutes (smaller pieces may cook faster than larger pieces; remove individual pieces as they reach temperature).

7. Transfer the chicken pieces to a large plate. Skim the excess fat from the broth. Stir the tarragon into the broth and season with salt and pepper. Transfer the broth and potatoes to large shallow serving bowls and top with the chicken pieces. Drizzle 1 tablespoon of the rouille over each portion and spread 1 teaspoon rouille on each crouton. Serve, floating 2 croutons in each bowl and passing remaining croutons and rouille at the table.

NOTES FROM THE TEST KITCHEN

ENSURING CRISP BRAISED SKIN

Crisp skin on stewed chicken sounds like an oxymoron. But by resting the chicken on the potatoes as the bouillabaisse cooks, the skin stays out of the liquid and crisps. A final blast of broiler heat further enhances crispness.

SAFFRON: DOES BRAND MAKE A DIFFERENCE?
Saffron threads are the world's most expensive spice. So how important is brand? The answer: not very, if your recipe has other strong flavors. When we tasted four brands (two mail order, two supermarket, all high-grade red Spanish threads) in spicy, garlicky mayonnaise, we couldn't distinguish one from another. Only when we sampled the spices in plain chicken broth, with no other competing flavors, did the grassy, hay-like taste of our winner, **Morton & Bassett Saffron Threads**, $10.99 for 0.01 ounce, stand out. Despite being sold in the supermarket, this brand was the most expensive in the lineup. Unless saffron is the main flavoring in your recipe, you'll likely be fine with any brand of red threads.

UPDATED CHICKEN AND DUMPLINGS

DATING BACK TO THE EARLY 17TH CENTURY, chicken and dumplings is as classic as American food gets. Although the dish has taken on distinct regional differences—Northerners typically like their broth thick and their dumplings fluffy, while down South the broth is usually more soup-like, with flat, square dumplings—a general rule applies to the chicken. The more mature the bird, the better the flavor. Generations ago, an egg hen or rooster several years old would be simmered for four or even six hours until falling off the bone, producing a rich broth. The simple addition of dumplings made it a flavorful, thrifty meal.

Chickens sold in supermarkets today are usually no more than seven weeks old, and a few tests proved conventional wisdom right: No matter how long you cook them, whole young chickens yield unimpressive broth. To coax old-fashioned, full flavor from supermarket birds—and create dumplings that would please both Northern and Southern palates—it was time for some modern adjustments.

Great chicken broth needs two things: flavor and body. Would a particular part of a younger bird produce a flavorful broth? I made a series of broths with thighs, drumsticks, and breasts, both skin-on and skin-off. With or without skin, the stock made with just white meat was thin and flavorless, the meat dry and bland. Drumsticks performed better, but the skin-on thighs were a clear winner, with the most deeply flavored broth of the lot and meat that stayed tender.

To further boost flavor, I used a few proven test kitchen tricks. First, I replaced water with broth. Though store-bought broth can taste thin on its own, when cooked with real chicken parts, it turns decidedly richer. Second, I browned the meat before adding the liquid. Finally, I browned aromatics in the fond from the chicken and added alcohol. Carrots, celery, and onions introduced sweetness, while ¼ cup of dry sherry— preferred by tasters over white wine and vermouth— added acidity and depth.

Now I had to resolve the North-South debate about body. Northerners thicken with flour, while Southerners tend to leave well enough alone. I prepared two versions: The first batch I left plain, the other I

thickened with ½ cup of flour (the amount typical in many Yankee versions) just before deglazing with the sherry. My colleagues deemed the straight broth too thin, and they rejected the sludgy consistency of the thickened broth. Knocking the flour down to ¼ cup produced broth with just the right amount of body, but all agreed it muted the chicken flavor. Cutting the flour to 2 tablespoons still masked chicken essence. Switching to cornstarch had the same effect.

Looking for an alternative, I recalled that several hours of boiling converts the connective tissue in a chicken carcass to gelatin and thickens the broth. I didn't want my broth cooking for hours, but then I realized I'd left something out of my initial broth testing: wings. Because of their multiple joints, wings contain far more connective tissue than legs or breasts. If I added plenty of wings (a half dozen seemed right) with the thighs, could I extract enough gelatin to thicken the broth? This turned out to be just what was needed. Time to move on to the dumplings.

In the South, dumplings are made of dough rolled out to about ¼ inch thick and cut into squares that are then added to the pot. It's a tedious and messy process that yields dense, doughy dumplings. The Yankee approach is far simpler, resulting in fluffier dumplings made just

---

NOTES FROM THE TEST KITCHEN

BEST PARTS FOR BROTH
We found two parts of the chicken were key to our modernized chicken and dumplings.

NATURAL THICKENER
The multiple joints in chicken wings contain lots of collagen that converts into gelatin during cooking—a better broth thickener than flour, which masks the chicken flavor.

FULL O' FLAVOR
Pound for pound, chicken thighs impart richer flavor to broth than any other part of the bird. Plus, they require far less cooking time than a whole bird or carcass.

UPDATED CHICKEN AND DUMPLINGS

like drop biscuits. You simply mix flour and leavener in one bowl and fat and a liquid in another, combine the two mixtures rapidly, and drop biscuit-sized balls into the broth.

Given the differences in technique, I wasn't disappointed when (except for two holdouts, from Kentucky and Alabama) my colleagues preferred the lighter Yankee dumplings. The problem was, they weren't all that light.

Since the Yankee dumplings are so closely related to oven-baked drop biscuits, I tried using our standard drop biscuit recipe (flour, salt, sugar, baking powder and soda, butter, and buttermilk). These dumplings had great tangy buttermilk flavor, and because they had more leavener and butter, they were far from leaden. In fact, they were so fragile they disintegrated into the broth.

The ideal dumpling should have all the lightness of our drop biscuits, but enough structure to hold together in the broth. Knowing that fat coats flour and weakens its structure, I tried gradually cutting down on the recipe's 8 tablespoons of butter. At 4 tablespoons, their structure improved somewhat; removing any more compromised flavor. Since they were cooking in a moist environment, my next thought was cutting back the liquid. Reducing the amount of buttermilk from a full cup to ¾ cup was another improvement—but the dumplings were still far too delicate.

Perhaps the problem was too much leavener, which can lead to over-rising and poor structure. Completely eliminating the baking powder (only baking soda remained) gave them just the right density in the center, but they were still mushy around the edges. While eggs are not traditional biscuit ingredients, I tried adding one, hoping that the extra protein would help the dumpling hold together. A whole egg created too much eggy flavor. A single egg white added just the right amount of structure without affecting flavor. I also waited to add the dumplings until the broth was simmering, reducing their time in the broth.

One last problem remained: Steam was condensing on the inside of the pot's lid and dripping onto the dumplings, turning their tops soggy. Wrapping a kitchen towel around the lid of the Dutch oven worked like a charm, trapping the moisture before it had a chance to drip down and saturate my light-as-air dumplings and flavor-packed broth.

—FRANCISCO J. ROBERT, *Cook's Illustrated*

Updated Chicken and Dumplings

SERVES 6

We strongly recommend buttermilk for the dumplings, but you can substitute ½ cup plain yogurt thinned with ¼ cup milk. If you want to include white meat (and don't mind losing a bit of flavor in the process), replace 2 chicken thighs with 2 boneless, skinless chicken breast halves (about 8 ounces each). Brown the chicken breasts along with the thighs and remove them from the stew once they reach an internal temperature of 160 degrees, 20 to 30 minutes. The collagen in the wings helps thicken the stew; do not omit or substitute. Since the wings yield only about 1 cup of meat, using their meat is optional.

STEW

2½   pounds bone-in, skin-on chicken thighs, trimmed
     Salt and pepper
2   teaspoons vegetable oil
2   small onions, minced (about 1½ cups)
2   carrots, peeled and cut into ¾-inch pieces
1   celery rib, chopped fine
¼   cup dry sherry
6   cups low-sodium chicken broth
1   teaspoon minced fresh thyme
1   pound chicken wings
¼   cup chopped fresh parsley

DUMPLINGS

2   cups (10 ounces) unbleached all-purpose flour
1   teaspoon sugar
1   teaspoon salt
½   teaspoon baking soda
¾   cup cold buttermilk (see note)
4   tablespoons (½ stick) unsalted butter, melted and cooled
1   large egg white

1. FOR THE STEW: Pat the chicken thighs dry with paper towels and season with 1 teaspoon salt and ¼ teaspoon pepper. Heat the oil in a large Dutch oven over medium-high heat until shimmering. Add the chicken thighs, skin side down, and cook until the skin is crisp and well browned, 5 to 7 minutes. Using tongs, turn the chicken pieces and brown the second side, 5 to 7 minutes longer; transfer to a large plate.

Discard all but 1 teaspoon fat from the pot.

2. Add the onions, carrots, and celery to the pot. Cook, stirring occasionally, until caramelized, 7 to 9 minutes. Stir in the sherry, scraping up any browned bits. Stir in the broth and thyme. Return the chicken thighs, along with any accumulated juices, to the pot and add the chicken wings. Bring to a simmer, cover, and cook until the thigh meat offers no resistance when poked with the tip of a paring knife but still clings to the bones, 45 to 55 minutes.

3. Remove the pot from the heat and transfer the chicken to a cutting board. Allow the broth to settle for 5 minutes, then skim the fat from the surface using a wide spoon or ladle. When cool enough to handle, remove and discard the skin from the chicken. Using your fingers or a fork, pull the meat from the chicken thighs (and wings, if desired) and cut into 1-inch pieces. Return the meat to the pot.

4. FOR THE DUMPLINGS: Whisk the flour, sugar, salt, and baking soda in a large bowl. Combine the buttermilk and melted butter in a medium bowl, stirring until the butter forms small clumps. Whisk in the egg white. Add the buttermilk mixture to the dry ingredients and stir with a rubber spatula until just incorporated and the batter pulls away from the sides of the bowl.

5. Return the stew to a simmer, stir in the parsley, and season with salt and pepper to taste. Using a greased tablespoon measure (or #60 portion scoop), scoop level amounts of batter and drop them into the stew, spacing the dumplings about ¼ inch apart (you should have about 24 dumplings). Wrap the lid of the Dutch oven with a clean kitchen towel (keeping the towel away from the heat source) and cover the pot. Simmer gently until the dumplings have doubled in size and a toothpick inserted into the center comes out clean, 13 to 16 minutes. Serve immediately. (The stew can be prepared through step 3 up to 2 days in advance; bring the stew back to a simmer before proceeding with the recipe.)

SLOW-COOKER WHITE CHICKEN CHILI

BY DEFINITION, CHILI EQUALS HEAT AND LIVELINESS, and white chili should be no less interesting than the classic bowl of red. It should be a simple yet flavorful stew of shredded chicken and white beans. It's spiked with vibrant, spicy green chiles and earthy spices like cumin and coriander, then finished with a shower of fresh cilantro. I figured it would make a good candidate for the slow cooker: The chicken would cook gradually and flavor the broth, the beans would turn creamy, and the chiles would lace the dish with heat.

Many slow-cooker recipes dump chicken, beans, canned green chiles, onions, garlic, spices, and chicken broth into the slow cooker and let it go for hours. This hands-off approach had ease in its favor, but not much else. I found the results to be more like soup than stew, and by the end of cooking, the dish had no chile flavor—or any flavor at all, no matter how potent the spices were at the start. I resigned myself to doing a little work up front, with the hope that the results would justify the effort.

I identified the best features of the recipes I'd tested and set out to combine them. First, I sautéed the onions, garlic, chiles, and spices before putting them in the slow cooker, a classic cooking technique that builds a foundation of flavor and did indeed give the chili some backbone. Canned green chiles were squishy, rubbery, and had zero heat—and that was before they had cooked for hours. Fresh jalapeños improved the stew considerably. To build another layer of flavor, I reserved some of the sauté to stir in at the end of cooking.

I'd been adding boneless, skinless chicken breasts directly to the slow cooker but suspected that bone-in, skin-on thighs would add deeper flavor, especially if I browned them first. I browned the chicken, then removed and discarded its skin and used the rendered fat to sauté the onion mixture. The chili was notably better—the dark-meat thighs held up better to the long cooking time and weren't in as much danger of drying out.

The flavor was much improved, but the texture remained problematic. In the test kitchen, we know from experience that slow cookers don't allow for evaporation, and so I cut back the chicken broth. I also upped the amount of beans, from the two cans used in many recipes to three cans. The chili was now

SLOW-COOKER WHITE CHICKEN CHILI

significantly less soupy and became even better when I pureed one can of beans with some of the broth. The texture was good, but the flavor needed reinforcing.

The idea of corn crossed my mind, and after that there was no turning back. If you didn't grow up in the South or Southwest, you might not know about hominy, dried white or yellow corn that has had the hull and germ removed. I had a hunch it would puree nicely and add flavor, too. I emptied a can into the food processor with the beans. It made for a velvety-smooth chili base with a hearty note of toasted corn. Perfect.

To finish, I stirred in the usual cilantro and was about to add a squeeze of lime when I spied a jar of pickled jalapeños. I chopped a few tablespoons and stirred them in instead. They gave the chili just the right kick and sweetness.

—MARÍA DEL MAR SACASA, *Cook's Country*

NOTES FROM THE TEST KITCHEN

BUILDING FLAVOR FOR WHITE CHICKEN CHILI
The slow cooker has a reputation for washing out flavors. Here's how we fight that.

1. Puree hominy (with the beans and chicken broth) to give the broth heft, velvety texture, and subtle corn flavor.

2. Brown the chicken parts, then sauté onions, jalapeños, garlic, and spices in the rendered fat to add layers of flavor.

3. To brighten the flavors, stir in minced pickled jalapeños and half the sautéed aromatics just before serving.

Slow-Cooker White Chicken Chili
SERVES 6 TO 8

You will need about 6 chicken thighs for this recipe; 4 bone-in, skin-on split chicken breasts may be substituted, though the flavor will not be as deep.

 3 (15-ounce) cans cannellini beans, drained and rinsed
 1 (16-ounce) can white hominy, drained and rinsed
 3 cups low-sodium chicken broth
   Salt
 3 pounds bone-in, skin-on chicken thighs, trimmed
   Pepper
 1 tablespoon vegetable oil
 2 onions, minced
 4 jalapeño chiles, seeded and chopped fine
 6 garlic cloves, minced
 4½ teaspoons ground cumin
 2 teaspoons ground coriander
 ¼ cup finely chopped fresh cilantro
 2 tablespoons drained jarred pickled jalapeños, minced

1. Puree 1 can of the beans, the hominy, broth, and ¾ teaspoon salt in a blender until completely smooth. Pour the pureed mixture into a slow cooker.

2. Pat the chicken dry with paper towels and season with salt and pepper. Heat the oil in a large skillet over medium-high heat until just smoking. Cook the thighs, skin side down, until the skin is well browned and the fat has rendered, about 5 minutes. Remove and discard the skin, then add the skinned thighs to the slow cooker.

3. Pour off all but 2 tablespoons of the fat from the skillet. Add the onions, jalapeños, and ½ teaspoon salt and cook until golden brown, stirring occasionally, about 8 minutes. Add the garlic, cumin, and coriander and cook until fragrant, about 30 seconds. Transfer half of the onion mixture to the slow cooker; reserve the remaining mixture in the refrigerator.

4. Add the remaining 2 cans beans to the slow cooker. Cover and cook on low until the chicken is tender, about 4 hours. Transfer the chicken to a bowl. When cool enough to handle, discard the bones and shred the chicken into bite-size pieces. Stir the cilantro, pickled jalapeños, shredded chicken, and reserved onion mixture into the slow cooker and let warm. Serve. (The chili can be refrigerated in an airtight container for up to 2 days.)

JOE BOOKER STEW

EVERYBODY'S HEARD OF CHICKEN AND DUMPLINGS, but did you know the dish has company? Soup dumplings, fruit dumplings, cheese dumplings … Dumplings were once as common a starch as potatoes. One beef and dumpling recipe rarely found in modern cookbooks is Joe Booker stew. It can be traced to Maine, where ice fishermen and loggers ate it to warm themselves during bone-chilling New England winters. Joe Booker stew is a thrifty, long-simmered dish made from what was on hand: salt pork, root vegetables, veal or beef, and water. The homely dumplings (flour, water, leavener) made it a one-pot dinner. The identity of Mr. Booker remains a mystery to historians, and it was equally mysterious to me why this delicious stew ever disappeared.

The first printed recipe I could find, from Imogene Walcott's 1939 *The New England Yankee Cookbook,* calls for rendering half a pound of chopped salt pork, discarding the cracklings, then browning the onions and beef (I used chuck, the test kitchen's choice for stews) in the rendered fat. Water is added and, an hour later, rutabaga, carrots, and potato. The stew simmers until the vegetables are tender. The recipe says to "serve with dumplings," assuming every cook worth her salt had a dumpling recipe. I used a recipe from a Boston cookbook of the same vintage: Roll dough, cut into rounds, and set them atop simmering stew for 10 minutes.

Joe Booker has a lighter, cleaner taste than modern beef stews because of the plentiful vegetables and the water (no broth or wine). Yet it shouldn't be watery and thin, as my first test was. The dumplings were lean, flavorless, undercooked—and too much trouble.

Before tackling the dumplings, I needed to work on the stew itself. Discarding the rendered salt pork seemed the antithesis of Yankee thrift; perhaps I could use it to boost the stew's flavor. I let it render in a Dutch oven for 15 minutes, then left it in the pot as I made a stew. It was inedibly salty and greasy. For my next test, I started by microwaving the salt pork to speed the rendering. Seven minutes later, it was brown and crisp, and I noticed salt crystals on its surface. I rinsed them off, browned the stew meat in some of the rendered fat and browned some onion in a few teaspoons of oil, and added the partly desalinized pork cubes. I removed the pieces of pork after an hour of simmering. This stew had good pork flavor and was not too salty. To further boost the meatiness, I tested substituting beef broth for the water

NOTES FROM THE TEST KITCHEN

SORTING OUT SALT PORK
Many stew and baked bean recipes call for salt pork, which is made from the same cuts as bacon: the sides and belly of the pig. Salt pork is salt cured, but it's not smoked (bacon is) and it's fattier than bacon. We liked salt pork in Joe Booker Stew and used its rendered fat to brown and flavor the meat and vegetables. If you can't find salt pork, use bacon, but it will add a smoky undertone. Don't confuse salt pork with fatback, which is unsalted and uncured and comes from the layer of fat running along the pig's back.

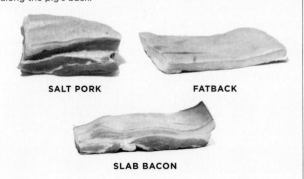

SALT PORK   FATBACK

SLAB BACON

MAKING SCOOP-AND-DROP DUMPLINGS
No need to roll, cut, or knead the dumplings for Joe Booker Stew. These dumplings come together in minutes.

1. After combining the flour, baking powder, and seasonings, simply stir in the mixture of milk and melted butter.

2. Use a small ice cream scoop (or 2 large spoons) to gently drop the dumplings onto the simmering stew, about ¼ inch apart.

but this was a mistake, as the broth's flavor took over. A combination of 4 cups each of water and beef broth was better, giving heft without masking the stew's delicacy.

I returned to the dumplings. They are typically made of flour, salt, leavener, and seasonings mixed with water, milk, or cream. Butter, lard, or oil can be added. Dumplings may be rolled and cut, or spooned and dropped. For ease, after my first test using the roll-and-cut style I switched to drop dumplings, adding extra water to turn the dough into a batter and replacing the cream of tartar and baking soda with a generous amount of baking powder for more lift. Using an ice cream scoop, I dropped spoonfuls of the batter onto the simmering stew, covered the pot, and waited 20 minutes (twice as long as my first test, to guard against doughy dumplings).

These dumplings were better, if still lean and bland. Stirring in leftover rendered salt pork fat overwhelmed them, but milk instead of water helped, and 3 tablespoons of melted butter turned them rich and tender. I'd previously stumbled upon a beef stew recipe with parsley dumplings. With ½ cup parsley, my dumplings—and my stew—perked right up. Move over chicken and dumplings, it's time to make room for Joe Booker.

—DIANE UNGER, *Cook's Country*

Joe Booker Stew

SERVES 6 TO 8

You can substitute peeled, chopped turnip or parsnip for the rutabaga. Use a Dutch oven with at least a 6-quart capacity. You can substitute bacon for the salt pork, but note that you will also add a smoky flavor if using bacon.

STEW

- **8 ounces salt pork, quartered**
  Vegetable oil, as needed
- **1 (3-pound) boneless beef chuck-eye roast, trimmed and cut into 1-inch pieces (see page 46)**
  Pepper
- **2 onions, chopped**
- **2 tablespoons unbleached all-purpose flour**
- **4 cups low-sodium beef broth**
- **4 cups water**
- **2 teaspoons minced fresh thyme**
- **1½ pounds red potatoes, scrubbed and cut into ¾-inch chunks**
- **1½ pounds rutabaga, peeled and cut into ¾-inch chunks**
- **1 pound carrots, peeled and cut into ¾-inch chunks**

DUMPLINGS

- **2 cups unbleached all-purpose flour**
- **½ cup finely chopped fresh parsley**
- **5 teaspoons baking powder**
  Salt and pepper
- **1 cup milk**
- **3 tablespoons unsalted butter, cut into ½-inch pieces**

1. FOR THE STEW: Place the salt pork in a bowl and microwave until the fat renders and the pork is golden, 5 to 8 minutes. Pour off the fat, reserving 2 tablespoons (if you have less, supplement with vegetable oil). When the pork is cool enough to handle, rinse it under running water to remove excess salt and set aside.

2. Pat the beef dry with paper towels and season with pepper. Heat 2 teaspoons of the reserved pork fat in a large Dutch oven over medium-high heat until just smoking. Cook half of the beef until well browned all over, about 8 minutes. Transfer to a bowl and repeat with 2 teaspoons more pork fat and the remaining beef. Add the remaining 2 teaspoons pork fat and the onions to the pot and cook until golden brown, about 5 minutes. Stir in the flour and cook until lightly browned, about 1 minute.

3. Return the beef and any accumulated juices to the pot. Stir in the broth, water, thyme, and rinsed salt pork and bring to a boil. Reduce the heat to low and simmer, covered, until the meat is nearly tender, about 1 hour. Remove and discard the salt pork. Add the potatoes, rutabaga, and carrots to the pot and continue to simmer, covered, until the vegetables are just tender, 20 to 30 minutes.

4. FOR THE DUMPLINGS: When the vegetables are nearly tender, combine the flour, parsley, baking powder, 1 teaspoon salt, and 1 teaspoon pepper in a large bowl. Combine the milk and butter in a liquid measuring cup and microwave, stirring once or twice, until the butter melts, about 1 minute. Stir the warm milk mixture into the flour mixture until incorporated.

5. Once the vegetables are tender, use a small ice cream scoop or 2 large spoons to drop golf ball–size dumplings (about 2 tablespoons) into the stew (you should have about 15 dumplings). Simmer gently, covered, until the dumplings have doubled in size and a toothpick inserted into the center comes out clean, 18 to 22 minutes. Serve. (The stew can be prepared through step 3, covered, and refrigerated for up to 3 days. To serve, bring the stew to a simmer and proceed with step 4.)

JOE BOOKER STEW

BEST BEEF STEW

EVERY WINTER, I LOCK MYSELF IN THE KITCHEN with a piece of beef chuck, vegetables, and my Dutch oven and set about the alchemic task of turning a tough cut of beef tender. And every winter, I emerge a few hours later, disappointed. It's the smell that keeps me going at it: As the stew simmers, it fills the house with a rich aroma, but the taste is never as complex as the scent. It's not that my beef stew is bad, but it's nowhere near good enough to merit the several hours of waiting.

Of the dozen or so recipes I have tried, from quick-and-easy versions with canned beef broth, heavy thickeners, and tiny pieces of beef to better (but still disappointing) four-hour versions, the only one that delivered truly satisfying flavor came from the famed Michelin-starred chef Thomas Keller. The problem? It required four days, a dozen dirty pots and pans, and nearly 50 ingredients. The results were fit for royalty, but it was hardly the approachable, home-cooked meal I was aiming for. There had to be a compromise.

The basic process for beef stew is straightforward: Brown chunks of beef in a Dutch oven, add aromatics and thickener, cover with liquid, and simmer until everything is tender and the flavors meld. The key to developing complexity is to maximize flavor in every step. American beef stew is first and foremost about the beef, so picking the right cut is essential. Supermarket "stew meat" was a nonstarter; the jumble of bits and chunks was impossible to cook evenly. Cuts like tenderloin, strip, and rib-eye, while great for searing or grilling, turned mealy with prolonged cooking. Cuts like hanger or skirt steak offered great flavor, but their texture was stringy. While well-marbled blade steaks and short ribs (favored by Keller) worked well, in the end they were no better than chuck-eye roast. It's one of the cheapest, beefiest cuts in the supermarket, and it turns meltingly tender when properly cooked.

The first key to rich, meaty flavor is proper browning, which meant searing the meat in two batches for a big pot of stew. Then I caramelized the usual choices of onions and carrots (rather than just adding them raw to the broth, as many recipes suggest). Though at first I planned to remove the meat while sautéing the vegetables, I found that by leaving it in the pot, its residual heat helped the onions and carrots cook faster and more evenly. I quickly sautéed crushed garlic before

---

NOTES FROM THE TEST KITCHEN

TRIMMING A CHUCK ROAST
To ensure consistent texture and flavor, avoid packaged stew meat (which can include odd-size pieces from all over the cow) and instead start with a chuck roast that you trim and cut into chunks yourself.

1. Pull apart the roast at its major seams (marked by lines of fat and silver skin). Use a knife as necessary.

2. With a sharp chef's knife or boning knife, trim off any thick layers of fat and silver skin. Cut the meat into chunks as directed.

THE SECRET TO MEATY FLAVOR
To boost meaty flavor in food, we often add ingredients high in glutamate. This common amino acid is the building block for MSG and occurs naturally in various foods, including mushrooms, cheese, tomatoes, and fish. The addition of two such glutamate-rich ingredients—tomato paste and salt pork—to our beef stew intensified its savory taste. But when we added a third glutamate-packed ingredient, anchovies, the beefy flavor seemed to increase exponentially. Evidence published recently in *Proceedings of the National Academy of Sciences* explains why: Besides glutamate, anchovies contain the compound inosinate. Scientists have found inosinate has a synergistic effect on glutamate, heightening its meaty taste by up to fifteenfold.

SMALL FRY, BIG TASTE
Salty little anchovies boost the meaty flavor significantly in our beef stew.

adding ¼ cup of flour to lightly thicken the stew. Next I deglazed the pan with 2 cups of red wine and simmered the liquid to reduce it and to let its raw flavor dissipate. I then added 2 cups of chicken broth (favored over tinny canned beef broth) and let the stew simmer for 2½ hours in the oven (which provides a more even heat than the stovetop).

The stew was bare bones, but I'd worry about additions later. For now, I needed to focus on the flavor of the broth, which was not developing very well. My stew still lacked real meatiness. I decided to attack the problem in a more scientific manner.

We've long known that ingredients rich in glutamates—compounds that give meat its savory taste—can enhance the flavor of a dish. Tomatoes are one such ingredient. I experimented with various canned tomato products, finally landing on tomato paste, which lent the right background note.

Thinking of other glutamate-rich ingredients, I wondered about cured meats that have a super-concentrated flavor. Bacon was too smoky, but salt pork worked well, adding a subtle depth to both broth and beef. Then I remembered another salted product that's packed with glutamates: anchovies. I mashed one up and incorporated it with the garlic and tomato paste. It was a smashing success. I found I could add up to four fillets with increasingly better results before the fishiness revealed itself. Finally, my stew was packed with meaty depth. But one problem remained: texture.

Keller's stew starts with homemade veal stock. As it cooks, collagen in the veal bones is transformed into gelatin, which gives the final stew a luxurious, mouth-coating texture—something that my flour-thickened broth lacked. Theoretically, powdered gelatin should work as well, but once I removed the flour, I needed to add nearly ½ cup of gelatin powder to thicken the stew sufficiently. What about a combination of flour and gelatin? I made the stew with ¼ cup of flour just as before but added a single packet of bloomed gelatin after removing the stew from the oven. After just three minutes of simmering on the stovetop, the liquid developed a rich, glossy sheen that looked (and tasted) every bit as rich as the veal stock–based version.

The rest of the recipe was simple: I added a handful of frozen pearl onions toward the end of cooking along with frozen peas. Starchy russets broke down too easily, but medium-starch Yukon Golds added halfway through

cooking were a success. As I ladled myself a bowl of the supremely meaty and satisfying stew, I couldn't help but appreciate that, sometimes, the little things really do matter.

—J. KENJI LOPEZ-ALT, *Cook's Illustrated*

Best Beef Stew

SERVES 6 TO 8

Use a good-quality medium-bodied wine, such as Côtes du Rhône or Pinot Noir, for this stew. Try to find beef that is well marbled with white veins of fat. Meat that is too lean will come out slightly dry. Four pounds of blade steaks, trimmed of gristle and silver skin, can be substituted for the chuck-eye roast. While the blade steak will yield slightly thinner pieces after trimming, it should still be cut into 1½-inch pieces. Look for salt pork that is roughly 75 percent lean.

2 garlic cloves, minced

4 anchovy fillets, minced fine (about 2 teaspoons)

1 tablespoon tomato paste

1 (4-pound) boneless beef chuck-eye roast, trimmed and cut into 1½-inch pieces (see page 46)

2 tablespoons vegetable oil

1 large onion, halved and sliced ⅛ inch thick

4 carrots, peeled and cut into 1-inch pieces

¼ cup unbleached all-purpose flour

2 cups red wine (see note)

2 cups low-sodium chicken broth

4 ounces salt pork, rinsed of excess salt

2 bay leaves

4 sprigs fresh thyme

1 pound Yukon Gold potatoes, scrubbed and cut into 1-inch pieces

1½ cups frozen pearl onions, thawed

2 teaspoons (about 1 packet) unflavored powdered gelatin

½ cup water

1 cup frozen peas, thawed

Salt and pepper

1. Adjust an oven rack to the lower-middle position and heat the oven to 300 degrees. Combine the garlic and anchovies in a small bowl and press the mixture with the back of a fork to form a paste. Stir in the tomato paste and set the mixture aside.

2. Pat the meat dry with paper towels (do not season the meat). Heat 1 tablespoon of the vegetable oil in a large Dutch oven over high heat until just starting to smoke. Add half of the beef and cook until well browned on all sides, about 8 minutes total, reducing the heat if the oil begins to smoke or the fond begins to burn. Transfer the beef to a large plate. Repeat with the remaining beef and 1 tablespoon vegetable oil, leaving the second batch of meat in the pot after browning.

3. Reduce the heat to medium and return the first batch of beef to the pot. Add the onion and carrots to the pot and stir to combine with the beef. Cook, scraping the bottom of the pan to loosen any browned bits, until the onion is softened, 1 to 2 minutes. Add the garlic mixture and cook, stirring constantly, until fragrant, about 30 seconds. Add the flour and cook, stirring constantly, until no dry flour remains, about 30 seconds.

4. Slowly add the wine, scraping the bottom of the pan to loosen any browned bits. Increase the heat to high and allow the wine to simmer until thickened and slightly reduced, about 2 minutes. Stir in the broth, salt pork, bay leaves, and thyme. Bring to a simmer, cover, transfer to the oven, and cook for 1½ hours.

5. Remove the pot from the oven. Remove and discard the bay leaves and salt pork. Stir in the potatoes, cover, return the pot to the oven, and cook until the potatoes are almost tender, about 45 minutes.

6. Using a large spoon, skim any excess fat from the surface of the stew. Stir in the pearl onions. Cook over medium heat until the potatoes and onions are cooked through and the meat offers little resistance when poked with a fork (the meat should not be falling apart), about 15 minutes. Meanwhile, sprinkle the gelatin over the water in a small bowl and allow to soften for 5 minutes.

7. Increase the heat to high, stir in the softened gelatin mixture and the peas. Simmer until the gelatin is fully dissolved and the stew is thickened, about 3 minutes. Season with salt and pepper to taste. Serve. (The stew can be cooled, covered tightly, and refrigerated for up to 2 days. Reheat it gently before serving.)

HOLLYWOOD CHILI

IN THE DAYS WHEN MOVIE STARS WERE REALLY stars, they met at Chasen's, a glamorous red-boothed restaurant on the border of Hollywood. Ronald proposed to Nancy, the Brat Pack tossed back martinis, Alfred Hitchcock rubbed shoulders with Humphrey Bogart there. The stargazing was good, and so too was the rich, gently spiced chili, so popular it spawned its own legends—Elizabeth Taylor had 10 quarts shipped to her in Rome where she was filming *Cleopatra,* for one. What made it distinctive and delicious? A glut of green peppers, a mix of hand-ground beef chuck and pork butt, and heart-stopping amounts of butter to brown the meat. In 1995, after 60 years, Chasen's was shuttered, inspiring a book, a documentary, and obituaries mourning a "bygone era." The chili, however, is timeless.

Curious, I cooked a batch based on a recipe in *Chasen's: Where Hollywood Dined—Recipes and Memories.* Lacking the special large-holed grinder that Chasen used, I (tediously) hand-diced beef chuck roast and pork butt, then browned the meat in a stick of butter with chopped green peppers, onion, and garlic. I simmered dried pinto beans that I'd soaked overnight, reserving the cooking water for the chili pot. At the end, I stirred in canned diced tomatoes, cumin, and chili powder.

After an hour, the chili was meaty, rich, and tomato-heavy—but a little dull. Chasen's served it tableside from a copper chafing dish with shredded cheese and sour cream. I reached for hot sauce instead, hoping some heat would bring the recipe into the new millennium.

But that wasn't the only tweak this recipe needed. I wanted to minimize the kitchen work. I turned to the food processor. However, trimming fat and gristle from the meat and cutting it into manageable chunks before processing was more work than I'd anticipated. Worse, instead of grinding the meat, the processor shredded it, making the chili stringy and chewy. I switched to ground beef and ground pork. But while the ground beef was pleasantly tender in the chili, the pork was sandy and dry, and adding it late in the game didn't help.

For my next test, I stuck with the ground beef but returned to the hand-chopped pork butt. Although this chili was excellent, the chopping and trimming remained a deal-breaker. Seeking a substitute for the pork butt, I first tried country-style pork ribs. I seared the ribs in butter and tossed them into the chili pot with the tomatoes. After an hour, I fished them out, pulled the meat from the bone, chopped it coarse, and stirred it into the chili. The bones had reinforced the chili's meaty flavor, but the chili was greasy. My next contender, blade chops, which are less fatty, had similar virtues, without the drawback of grease. They were a winner.

Using canned beans streamlined the recipe further. To add body, I replaced the diced tomato in the original with canned tomato sauce and crushed tomatoes. Chipotle chiles in adobo sauce brought depth and heat. At this point, I thought I was done, but tasters still complained that the chili was bland. Was all that butter muting its edge? I cut it back by half, to 4 tablespoons: Bingo. Chasen's regulars Jimmy Stewart and Frank Sinatra will never show up at my house for dinner. No matter; I can console myself with a great bowl of chili.

—DIANE UNGER, *Cook's Country*

Hollywood Chili

SERVES 6 TO 8

Chipotle chiles are smoked and dried jalapeños: wear rubber gloves when handling them.

- 3 pounds bone-in pork blade chops, about 1½ inches thick
  Salt and pepper
- 4 tablespoons (½ stick) unsalted butter
- 2 pounds 85 percent lean ground beef
- 3 green bell peppers, chopped fine
- 2 onions, minced (about 2 cups)
- ¼ cup chili powder
- 2 teaspoons ground cumin
- 4 garlic cloves, minced
- 1 teaspoon minced canned chipotle chile in adobo sauce, plus 2 teaspoons adobo sauce
- 2 (28-ounce) cans crushed tomatoes
- 1 (29-ounce) can tomato sauce
- 1 cup water
- 3 (15-ounce) cans pinto beans, drained and rinsed

1. Pat the pork dry with paper towels and season with salt and pepper. Melt 1 tablespoon of the butter in a large Dutch oven over medium-high heat. Add the pork and cook until well browned, about 5 minutes per side. Transfer the pork to a plate. Add the beef to the pot and cook over medium-high heat, stirring occasionally, until no longer pink, about 5 minutes. Drain the beef and set aside.

2. Return the Dutch oven to medium heat and melt the remaining 3 tablespoons butter. Add the peppers and onions and cook until softened, about 5 minutes. Stir in the chili powder, cumin, and garlic and cook until fragrant, about 30 seconds.

3. Stir in the chipotle, adobo sauce, crushed tomatoes, tomato sauce, and water and bring to a boil. Return the pork and beef to the pot, along with any accumulated juices. Reduce the heat to low and simmer, covered, stirring occasionally, until the pork is tender, about 1 hour.

4. Transfer the pork to a cutting board. When cool enough to handle, remove the meat from the bones, discarding the fat, and chop coarsely. Use a wide spoon to skim any fat from the surface of the chili. Stir the chopped pork and pinto beans into the pot, return to a simmer, and cook, uncovered, stirring occasionally, for 30 minutes. Season with salt and pepper to taste. Serve. (The chili can be refrigerated for up to 3 days).

NOTES FROM THE TEST KITCHEN

MAKING HOLLYWOOD CHILI
The original Hollywood chili relied on a custom grinder for its mix of beef chuck and pork butt. We pair supermarket ground beef with pork blade chops for the same meaty impact.

1. Start by browning bone-in pork chops in butter, then remove them from the pan and use the rendered fat to brown the ground beef.

2. After building the base of the chili with peppers, onions, spices, chipotle, adobo sauce, tomato sauce, and crushed tomatoes, stir in the ground beef and reserved chops.

3. One hour later, remove the cooked chops, separate the meat from the bones, coarsely chop the meat, and stir it back into the chili with the pinto beans. Simmer for 30 minutes.

GRILLED ASPARAGUS

ASPARAGUS IS MY GO-TO VEGETABLE WHEN I WANT to grill something simple: Just snap off the woody ends, toss the spears with oil, and cook them over a hot fire. Minutes later, the spears come off the grill sweet and juicy with crisp, charred tips. The method doesn't get any easier—but (as it does with all vegetables grilled in this straightforward way) the one-note result does get monotonous. By exploring other techniques, I wondered if I could smarten the flavor of this vegetable, all the while keeping the method and the ingredients uncomplicated.

First, I needed to home in on the essential elements: ideal spear size and grilling method. Pencil-thin asparagus, while great for steaming, burned before it had a chance to cook through; plus, grilling is all about the crust and these spears didn't offer much of it. Thicker (about ½ inch in diameter near the base) spears offered plenty of surface area for maximum char, not to mention a meaty, crisp-tender texture. As for the grilling method, a simple medium-hot fire worked best (see "How Hot Is Your Fire?" page 19). The trimmed, olive oil–brushed spears were on and off the fire in roughly eight minutes, perfectly cooked through and with a nice char yet not burned.

When it came to kicking up the flavor, a punchy marinade—applied either before or after grilling—seemed like an obvious place to start. But simply soaking the raw spears in vinaigrette got me nowhere. The inherent toughness of the outer skin on the spears meant little of the dressing's flavor could penetrate; when I pulled the asparagus from the dressing, the bulk of the flavor slid right back into the bowl. But the alternative didn't fare much better. Dressing the asparagus spears after they came off the grill turned their crisp texture soggy.

The answer to tastier spears turned out to be as simple as brushing the asparagus with melted butter, rather than oil, before placing them on the grill. When I swapped fats, tasters remarked that the spears tasted nuttier and more flavorful, and were even crisper and browner than spears brushed with oil. The reason was twofold: Because butter contains small amounts of protein and lactose (milk sugar), it enhances the browning of anything it touches, creating hundreds of rich, nutty new flavor compounds in a process known as the Maillard reaction. Furthermore, butter is about 20 percent water, and this moisture subjects the asparagus to a brief period of steaming before it burns off from the intense heat of the grill—just long enough to break down the cell structure of the spears' outer skin and allow more of the sugars inside to be coaxed out and caramelized.

The use of melted butter was so simple and effective that I couldn't resist building on the idea with a few flavored butters. Garlic was an obvious choice, as were the fresh, tangy flavors of lemon, lime, and orange zests—especially when combined with a shake or two of heady spices including chili powder, cayenne, and cumin. Now all I needed was a good grilled steak to share the plate.

—YVONNE RUPERTI, *Cook's Illustrated*

Grilled Asparagus with Garlic Butter
SERVES 4 TO 6

This recipe works equally well on a gas or charcoal grill; just make sure the fire is medium-hot (see "How Hot Is Your Fire?" page 19). Use asparagus that is at least ½ inch thick near the base. Do not use pencil-thin asparagus; it cannot withstand the heat and will overcook. Age affects the flavor of asparagus enormously. For the sweetest taste, look for spears that are bright green and firm, with tightly closed tips.

3   tablespoons unsalted butter, melted
3   small garlic cloves, minced
1½   pounds thick asparagus spears, tough ends trimmed (see note)
     Salt and pepper

1. Combine the butter and garlic in a small bowl. Brush the asparagus with the butter mixture and season with ¼ teaspoon salt and pepper to taste.

2A. FOR A CHARCOAL GRILL: Open the bottom grill vents completely. Light a large chimney starter filled with charcoal briquettes (100 briquettes; 6 quarts). When the coals are hot, pour them in an even layer over the grill. Set the cooking grate in place, cover, and heat the grill until medium-hot, about 5 minutes.

2B. FOR A GAS GRILL: Turn all the burners to high, cover, and heat the grill until hot, about 15 minutes. (Adjust the burners as needed to maintain a medium-hot fire; see page 19).

GRILLED ASPARAGUS WITH GARLIC BUTTER

3. Clean and oil the cooking grate. Grill the asparagus, uncovered, turning once, until just tender and caramelized, 2 to 5 minutes per side, moving the asparagus as needed to ensure even cooking. Transfer the asparagus to a platter and serve.

VARIATIONS

Grilled Asparagus with Chili-Lime Butter
Follow the recipe for Grilled Asparagus with Garlic Butter, substituting 1 teaspoon grated lime zest, ½ teaspoon chili powder, ¼ teaspoon cayenne, and ⅛ teaspoon red pepper flakes for the garlic.

Grilled Asparagus with Orange-Thyme Butter
Follow the recipe for Grilled Asparagus with Garlic Butter, substituting 1 teaspoon grated orange zest and 1 teaspoon minced fresh thyme for the garlic.

Grilled Asparagus with Cumin Butter
Follow the recipe for Grilled Asparagus with Garlic Butter, reducing the garlic to 2 cloves and adding 1 teaspoon grated lemon zest, ½ teaspoon ground cumin, and ½ teaspoon ground coriander to the butter in step 1.

NOTES FROM THE TEST KITCHEN

THE BEST GRILL TONGS
To the uninitiated, all grill tongs look the same. But small design nuances have a huge impact on how well tongs handle asparagus or corn, flip a whole chicken, or turn an awkward, floppy rack of ribs on the grill. We bought eight pairs and headed to the backyard to see how they compared. More than half the tongs we bought failed us because they were bulky or oddly shaped, had teeth that were too flat or too sharp, or required Hulk-like strength to use. The **OXO Good Grips 16-inch Locking Tongs**, $14.99, won out. Comfortable, lightweight, and sturdy, they passed every test with top marks. (See page 307 for more information about our testing results.)

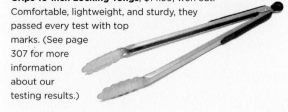

ROASTED CABBAGE

POTATOES AND CARROTS MAY BE THE USUAL candidates for roasting, but the test kitchen has found that time spent in a very hot oven can draw out the best in other veggies too, including broccoli and cauliflower. The sweet, deep flavors they develop could charm even an avowed vegetable loather. I wondered if wedges of cabbage, a vegetable generally reserved for coleslaw or soup and not known for winning fans, would fare as well. After all, it is in the same crucifer family as broccoli and cauliflower. Though cabbage turns mushy and smells bad when overcooked, I had a hunch that a little time in a hot oven could help turn its sad image around.

I started with a straightforward approach, cutting a head of cabbage into 1-inch wedges, cutting out the core, then brushing the wedges with oil and seasoning them with salt and pepper. I arranged the wedges on a baking sheet and, with the fear that too high a temperature might obliterate the leaves, I roasted them at a cautious 400 degrees (the test kitchen roasts broccoli at 500 degrees). These wedges seemed almost steamed; I was well aware that their soggy state wasn't going to win any converts. My cabbage needed to cook more quickly. Next time I set the oven dial to 450 degrees and I also preheated the baking sheet (a trick I borrowed from the test kitchen's roasted broccoli recipe), hoping to give the oiled, seasoned wedges an initial blast of heat. This was a big improvement, but I still had a big issue with browning.

Most vegetables need only the occasional shake of the pan to brown and roast evenly, but to brown both sides of these cabbage wedges, I'd have to flip them, one by one. Inevitably, some (or most) of the delicate wedges flopped apart during the flip (if not before), and I ended up with cabbage shreds. These shreds could never brown evenly—not before they burned, anyway. To fix this, I cut the cabbage very carefully, making sure to leave the core intact. Now each wedge had something to hold on to.

As I was flipping the wedges, I had an epiphany. I remembered that cabbage, like broccoli, is low in natural sugars. When the test kitchen roasts broccoli, we add a smidge of sugar to the salt and pepper seasoning.

Maybe if I did the same here, it would help caramelize the tops of the wedges and let me skip the flip altogether. I sugared, preheated, roasted, and neither flipped nor flopped: The cabbage wedges had a wonderful nutty flavor and were tawny brown on both the top and bottom. A final drizzle of balsamic vinegar ensured that everyone went back for seconds—quite a coup for cabbage.

—MEGHAN ERWIN, *Cook's Country*

Roasted Cabbage Wedges
SERVES 4 TO 6

1 teaspoon sugar
1 teaspoon salt
¼ teaspoon pepper
1 head green cabbage
3 tablespoons vegetable oil
2 teaspoons balsamic vinegar

1. Adjust an oven rack to the upper-middle position. Place a rimmed baking sheet on the rack and heat the oven to 450 degrees. Combine the sugar, salt, and pepper in a small bowl. Quarter the cabbage through the core and cut each quarter into 1-inch wedges, leaving the core intact (you will have about 16 wedges). Brush the cabbage wedges all over with the oil and sprinkle with the salt mixture.

2. Arrange the cabbage on the hot baking sheet and roast until the cabbage is tender and lightly browned around the edges, about 25 minutes. Drizzle the cabbage with the vinegar. Serve.

NOTES FROM THE TEST KITCHEN

PREPPING CABBAGE FOR ROASTING

To keep cabbage wedges together so they brown evenly, quarter the cabbage, taking care to cut directly through the core. Cut each quarter through the core into 1-inch-thick wedges.

CRISPY ROASTED POTATOES

MOST OF THE TIME, ROASTED POTATOES ARE MADE using the generic treatment: chop medium, drizzle with oil, toss into the oven at some high-ish temperature, pull out when they've got color. This one-size-fits-all approach is seldom disastrous; the problem is consistency. For every batch of golden-crisped wedges with perfectly velvety interiors, there's a surfeit of duds sporting mealy innards, leathery crusts, and uneven browning.

A survey of roasted-potato recipes revealed that foolproof techniques are few and far between. Most employed very hot ovens and long roasting times to get a well-browned exterior at the expense of a velvety interior, and often that beautifully browned crust was tough and chewy. The recipes that produced a creamy interior ended up pale-golden and not the least bit crisp. I set out to achieve the perfect balance: crisp outside, silky-smooth inside.

The initial group of recipes wasn't devoid of lessons. An unmistakable pattern had emerged: The best exterior texture came from recipes that parcooked the spuds by either boiling or simmering before moving them to the oven. As these recipes also called for shorter roasting times, the results seemed counterintuitive.

Puzzled, I dusted off some of the food-science tomes in our library. No surprise that no actual crisping was occurring during parcooking, but an important step in the process was getting a serious jump-start. For a potato to brown and crisp, two things need to happen, both of which depend on moisture. First, starch granules in the potatoes must absorb water and swell, releasing some of their amylose, a water-soluble type of starch. Second, some of the amylose must break down into glucose. Once the moisture evaporates on the surface of the potato, the amylose hardens into a shell, yielding crispness, and the glucose darkens, yielding an appealing brown color. In the oven, this is a lengthy process because the starch granules swell slowly, releasing little amylose. In contrast, parboiled potatoes are swimming in moist heat, releasing lots of amylose on the potato's surface. By the time parcooked spuds go in the oven, they are ready to begin browning and crisping almost immediately.

Would all this science stand up to kitchen tests? I cut up two batches of standard russet potatoes into

CRISPY ROASTED POTATOES

1½-inch chunks. I parboiled the first batch until tender, spread the chunks on a baking sheet drizzled with ¼ cup olive oil, and roasted them at 450 degrees, flipping them partway through cooking. The second batch went straight into the oven. After about 45 minutes, the parcooked spuds were nicely browned and fairly crisp, with relatively creamy interiors. The oven-only batch took an hour to reach the same level of browning and crispness—at which point the interiors were far more dried out.

So parcooking was key. But was boiling best? Surely, some of that great exterior starch was getting washed off. I prepped another batch, this time using a gentler form of moist heat: steaming. When I pulled this batch out of the oven, yes, the color was a deep brown but the texture was tacky and chewy, almost like taffy. Too much starch and sugar had led to a gluey residue. The magic formula, then, was to draw out the starch and sugar quickly, but to wash away the excess. I found that 10 minutes of slightly gentler simmering (bringing to a boil, then immediately reducing the heat so the vigorous action of boiling wouldn't wash away too much starch) produced the best texture yet.

Although I was achieving a modicum of crispness and browning, the browning was uneven. Also, tasters wanted creamier interiors and—by the way—could the exteriors be crisper still, please? The uneven browning wasn't hard to solve. I identified two culprits: First, the chunky potato cubes demanded several turns to give every surface time against the baking sheet. Two, the partially cooked potatoes were so delicate that it was hard to transfer them to the oven without a few breaking apart into pieces that cooked at a different rate.

I found that reducing the parcooking time to just 5 minutes was long enough to get the starch breakdown going but short enough that the potatoes could be handled without breaking. As for the shape, I sliced the potatoes into rounds—since they had only two cut surfaces, I only had to flip them once. A few tests later, I arrived at ½-inch-thick rounds as optimal for providing the right ratio of crisp exterior to creamy interior.

Now for the tricky part: upping crispness and creaminess. Creaminess depended on interior moisture, which escapes as the potatoes cook, yet crispness depended on adequate roasting time. One was the enemy of the other. Although jump-starting the starch-breakdown process

had cut down the roasting time, I still needed to allow time for the surface moisture to evaporate. (Until that happens, the temperature at the potato's surface can't rise beyond 212 degrees—the boiling point of water—far below the temperature needed for crisping.)

The big breakthrough came courtesy of our science editor, who observed that the parcooking was doing more than jump-starting the surface starch. It was also speeding up the evaporation process by creating a rough surface. A rougher surface offers more escape routes for moisture than the flat surface of a raw potato, and the damaged exterior cells surrender their moisture more readily than intact cells. So why not try roughing up the surface even more?

Using a fork to gently scrape the surfaces of the parcooked potatoes, I roasted another batch. Sure enough, I achieved the best results yet, but scraping individual potato slices seemed absurd. For my next experiment, I tried tossing the potatoes—vigorously—with olive oil and salt, hoping the salt would mimic the friction of the fork. In the process, a thick layer resembling mashed potatoes formed on the exterior. Success! Once roasted, the spuds were crisper than ever—and nicely seasoned.

I'd reduced the roasting time to less than an hour and preheating the baking sheet shaved off a few more minutes. The abbreviated session in the dry heat had a noticeable effect on the interior, allowing more retention of moisture and thus a creamier texture. The only way to up the creaminess would be to reduce the roasting time further, but I wasn't willing to sacrifice the incredible exterior texture I had worked so hard to achieve.

That's when it dawned on me to revisit potato choice. I had been using russets, which have a high starch content and low moisture. With the parcooking and surface-roughing steps, I had starch in spades. But moisture I could use. Substituting Red Bliss potatoes (high moisture, low starch) gave me creamy interiors, but at the expense of too much crispness. When I substituted Yukon Golds (medium starch, medium moisture), I reached the finish line. They crisped up just as perfectly as the russets, yet the extra moisture kept the interiors far creamier. The results were crisp as a chip and creamy as a bowl of mashed potatoes—the best of both worlds.

—FRANCISCO J. ROBERT, *Cook's Illustrated*

KEYS TO MAKING CRISP, EVENLY BROWNED SPUDS

1. Cut the potatoes into ½-inch rounds, which require only one flip, making it far easier to ensure each side gets equal time facedown on the pan.

2. Simmer the potatoes to bring the starch to the surface, jump-starting the crisping process.

3. Preheat the rimmed baking sheet to give cooking a head start, leading to crisper results.

4. Toss the parboiled potatoes vigorously with salt and oil to damage the surface cells, which speeds up evaporation.

JUST SCRATCHING THE SURFACE

Parcooked potato slices brown faster in the oven than raw slices, and "roughing them up" by tossing them vigorously with salt and oil led them to brown faster still. Why? Surface area. Browning can't start until surface moisture evaporates. The roughed-up slices have more exposed surface area than smooth slices and thus more escape routes for moisture.

ROUGHED-UP SURFACE = FAST EVAPORATION   **SMOOTH SURFACE = SLOW EVAPORATION**

Crispy Roasted Potatoes
SERVES 4 TO 6

The steps of parcooking the potatoes before roasting and tossing the potatoes with salt and oil until they are coated with starch are the keys to developing a crisp exterior and creamy interior. The potatoes should be just undercooked when they are removed from the simmering water in step 1.

2½ pounds Yukon Gold potatoes (about 5 medium), rinsed and cut into ½-inch-thick slices
    Salt
5 tablespoons olive oil
    Pepper

1. Adjust an oven rack to the lowest position, place a rimmed baking sheet on the rack, and heat the oven to 450 degrees. Place the potatoes and 1 tablespoon salt in a Dutch oven and add cold water to cover by 1 inch. Bring to a boil over high heat, then reduce the heat and gently simmer until the exteriors of the potatoes have softened but the centers offer resistance when pierced with a paring knife, about 5 minutes. Drain the potatoes well and transfer to a large bowl. Drizzle the potatoes with 2 tablespoons of the oil and sprinkle with ½ teaspoon salt. Using a rubber spatula, toss to combine. Drizzle the potatoes with 2 tablespoons more oil and ½ teaspoon salt and continue to toss until the exteriors of the potato slices are coated with a starchy paste, 1 to 2 minutes.

2. Working quickly, remove the baking sheet from the oven and drizzle the remaining 1 tablespoon oil over the surface. Carefully transfer the potatoes to the baking sheet and spread into an even layer (skin side up if an end piece). Bake until the bottoms of the potatoes are golden brown and crisp, 15 to 25 minutes, rotating the baking sheet after 10 minutes.

3. Remove the baking sheet from the oven and, using a metal spatula and tongs, loosen the potatoes from the pan and carefully flip each slice. Continue to roast until the second side is golden and crisp, 10 to 20 minutes longer, rotating the baking sheet as needed to ensure the potatoes brown evenly. Season with salt and pepper to taste and serve immediately.

DUCHESS POTATOES

DUCHESS POTATOES ARE AN ELEGANT FRENCH-pedigreed classic in which mashed potatoes are enriched with egg, piped into decorative rosettes, and baked until golden brown. The egg lightens the potato, creating a dainty, almost weightless fluff that contrasts with the crispy, craggy exterior. In 1867, an article in *Galaxy* magazine lamenting the state of American cooking noted duchess potatoes on the menu of a rare good dinner. For the next century, the dish made regular appearances on the menus of country clubs, ocean liners, and fancy-pants restaurants, but by the 1970s it seemed stuffy and out of step with the times, and thus it fell into culinary disrepute. Which is a shame, because duchess potatoes really are something very special.

I tested recipes dating back almost a century as well as modern versions, and they all had similar ingredients and technique. Recipes combined boiled, mashed russet potatoes (fluffy russets contribute to fluffy duchess) with butter, eggs, cream or milk, and a pinch of nutmeg. The mix is placed in a pastry bag, piped, and baked. The potatoes looked suitably impressive, and tasters liked the airiness of the little peaks, but they found the texture cottony and dry and the mash too lean for elegant party fare.

Baking was drying the mounds out (broiling won't cook the egg to a safe temperature, so I ruled it out). As a group, recipes skimped on cream and butter, which wasn't helping. But when I added more, the mixture slumped into puddles. My challenge was to make a puree firm enough to pipe, yet rich and creamy enough to be worth the effort.

Most recipes called for boiling the potatoes. Even drained and dried (by cooking on the stovetop for a minute), they remained too waterlogged to pipe. Baking added an hour to an already time-consuming recipe. Microwaving, however, took just 20 minutes or so, and since it used no liquid, I could safely mash 1 cup of cream into 3 pounds of potatoes—more than twice the cream in most recipes I'd tested.

As for the butter, 6 tablespoons (the amount I found was needed to achieve a rich, buttery taste) mashed into the hot potatoes melted, making the mixture too loose to pipe. So I cooled the mash before adding the butter in small chunks. With this method I had no trouble piping, but the butter oozed out in the oven. I got the idea to add half of the butter while the potatoes were hot (the mash absorbed it) and the other half once they'd cooled (which, as I'd hoped, melted into buttery pockets in the oven but didn't leak out).

Unfortunately, weighed down with extra butter and cream, my duchess lacked the light, puffy texture that should distinguish her. That lift comes from the eggs. In my initial testing, recipes called for anywhere from one to four. More eggs made the potatoes taste (surprise!) eggy, so I settled on one whole egg and one yolk (for added richness), but that amount wasn't enough to lighten my creamy, buttery puree.

If lift was what I was after, might baking powder work? Admittedly, it was a weird idea, but in the test kitchen, we'll try anything once. I stirred ½ teaspoon into the potato puree, piped, baked, and hoped. About 20 minutes later, I had my answer: rich, buttery, yet practically weightless potatoes. Sure, piping duchess potatoes takes time. Good things do. Incidentally, the potatoes won't suffer any if you pipe them a day ahead, handy when company is coming.

—LYNN CLARK, *Cook's Country*

Duchess Potatoes

SERVES 8

For the smoothest, most uniform texture, use a food mill or ricer to mash the potatoes.

- 3 pounds russet potatoes (about 6 medium), scrubbed
- 1 cup heavy cream
- 6 tablespoons unsalted butter, cut into ¼-inch cubes and softened
- 1 large egg plus 1 large egg yolk, lightly beaten
- 1¼ teaspoons salt
- ½ teaspoon pepper
- ½ teaspoon baking powder
- Pinch nutmeg

1. Adjust an oven rack to the upper-middle position and heat the oven to 475 degrees. Prick the potatoes all over with a fork, place on a plate, and microwave until tender, 18 to 25 minutes, turning the potatoes over after 10 minutes.

2. Cut the potatoes in half. When cool enough to handle, scoop the flesh into a large bowl and mash until no lumps remain. Add the cream, 3 tablespoons of the butter, the eggs, salt, pepper, baking powder, and nutmeg and continue to mash until the potatoes are smooth. Let cool to room temperature, about 10 minutes. Gently fold in the remaining 3 tablespoons butter until the pieces are evenly distributed.

3. Following the photos, pipe eight 4-inch-wide mounds of potato onto a rimmed baking sheet. Spray lightly with vegetable oil spray and bake until golden brown, 15 to 20 minutes. Serve. (Once piped onto the baking sheet, the potatoes can be covered loosely with plastic wrap and refrigerated for 24 hours. Remove the plastic and spray lightly with vegetable oil spray before baking.)

NOTES FROM THE TEST KITCHEN

PIPING DUCHESS POTATOES
With a pastry bag fitted with a star tip, making beautiful duchess potatoes is child's play. But you can just as easily make them without a pastry bag.

A. WITH A PASTRY BAG: Start each portion by piping a 4-inch circle on the baking sheet. Continue to pipe upward in circles until you've made a 3-inch peak.

B. WITHOUT A PASTRY BAG: Scoop the potatoes into a zipper-lock bag, snip off a corner, and pipe as directed. Use the tines of a fork to created rippled edges.

SWEET POTATO CASSEROLE

EVERY YEAR BETWEEN OCTOBER AND DECEMBER, an estimated 35 million pounds of marshmallows are sold in America. Sweet potato casserole accounts for much of that tonnage. The casserole was popularized by a recipe booklet that the Campfire marshmallow company printed in 1930, "How Famous Chefs Use Campfire Marshmallows," in which solemn chefs in imposing toques touted marshmallows as a way to dress up dinner. The booklet includes some half-dozen recipes for mashed sweet potatoes with marshmallow crusts, not to mention a recipe for Campfire Marshmallow Mayonnaise. Mercifully, the latter has disappeared, but sweet potato casserole has earned an enduring place in our hearts, and on our Thanksgiving tables.

Sadly, over the years, sweet potato casserole has become something of an embarrassment. Have you ever noticed, though, the guests who make the most fun of it are the same ones discreetly getting seconds? After testing a handful of recipes, I could see both sides. The marshmallow topping was visually stunning and tasted irresistible, and the nostalgia factor was huge with my tasters. But many casseroles emerged from the oven watery, too sweet, and so dolled up with spices you might mistake them for dessert—and that was before they donned their marshmallow caps. Also, with so much going on, the flavor of the sweet potatoes got lost. My goal: Restore the reputation of a venerable—if often mistreated—casserole.

Sweet potato casserole is made by roasting or boiling sweet potatoes until tender (or, heaven forbid, reaching for the syrupy canned ones); mashing them with butter, cream, sugar, and spices; spooning them into a baking dish; topping them with mini marshmallows; and broiling until brown. Boiling the sweet potatoes washed out their flavor and made the casserole watery, while roasting took too long. I wondered if an unusual test kitchen method for mashed sweet potatoes might work. I simmered 5 pounds of peeled and cubed sweet potatoes, covered, in ½ cup of cream and 12 tablespoons of melted butter, then took them off the heat and mashed them. They weren't firm enough for a casserole. I decreased the butter and cream to 6 tablespoons each—any less and the potatoes burned. Still soggy. I tried leaving the heat on medium-low while I mashed. Poof! The excess moisture vanished.

SWEET POTATO CASSEROLE

Unfortunately, by cutting back on the cream and butter, I'd inadvertently dialed back on the richness that befits a holiday dish. To restore it, I tried adding eggs (they altered the texture and turned the casserole into a soufflé), then evaporated milk (it made the casserole taste too lean). Mentally ticking off other dairy products in my effort to add fat, I hit on cheese. Cheese with marshmallows? Yuck. I changed my mind when a colleague suggested tangy (but otherwise neutral) cream cheese. Just 2 ounces made the casserole richer without making it wetter. Even better, its tang tempered the sweetness of the casserole.

It sure needed tempering. Some recipes add as much as 3 cups of sugar. I eliminated all of it. But tasters missed the sugar, never mind previous complaints. I added back 2 teaspoons, just enough to reinforce the sweet potatoes' natural sweetness. In such a small amount, brown sugar added no discernible flavor, so I stuck with white. Next, I tested spices. Tasters rejected ginger, nutmeg, and cinnamon on the grounds they turned what should be a side dish into a pie. In the end, I stopped at salt and pepper. The marshmallows made enough of a statement on their own; I needn't go crazy with the spices.

I felt I'd restored dignity and deliciousness to the bottom half of the casserole, so I turned a critical eye on the topping. If you're thinking it was just a matter of sprinkling on a few handfuls of mini marshmallows, think again. Cranky tasters grumbled that the roasted marshmallows were chalky and dried out. I did some checking and found that mini marshmallows, unlike full-sized ones, are coated with cornstarch to keep them from sticking to each other in the bag. I ditched the minis and instead topped the casserole with large marshmallows that I cut in half through the equator (if left uncut, the large marshmallows were too thick and gooey). The golden brown topping was creamy, crispy, and starch-free. I'd put this sweet potato casserole up against that of any famous chef, however tall his hat.

—LYNN CLARK, *Cook's Country*

Sweet Potato Casserole

SERVES 8 TO 10

If you prefer silky-smooth potatoes, use a hand mixer to beat the potatoes in step 3. Use sharp, clean scissors sprayed with cooking spray (to prevent sticking and make cleanup easier) to snip the marshmallows in half through the equator.

- **5 pounds sweet potatoes (6 to 7 medium), peeled and cut into 1-inch chunks**
- **6 tablespoons heavy cream**
- **6 tablespoons unsalted butter, cut into 6 pieces**
- **2 teaspoons sugar**
- **1 teaspoon salt**
- **½ teaspoon pepper**
- **2 ounces cream cheese**
- **1 (10-ounce) bag marshmallows, halved crosswise**

1. Combine the potatoes, cream, butter, sugar, salt, and pepper in a Dutch oven. Cook covered, stirring occasionally, over medium heat until the potatoes begin to break down, 20 to 25 minutes.

2. Reduce the heat to medium-low and continue to cook, covered, until the liquid has been absorbed and the potatoes are completely tender, 15 to 20 minutes. Meanwhile, adjust an oven rack to the upper-middle position and heat the oven to 450 degrees.

3. Add the cream cheese to the pot. Using a potato masher, mash until the cream cheese is fully incorporated and the sweet potatoes are smooth. Continue to cook, stirring constantly, until the potatoes are thickened, about 5 minutes.

4. Transfer the potato mixture to a 2-quart baking dish and top with a single layer of marshmallows. Bake until the marshmallows are browned, about 5 minutes. Serve. (After transferring the sweet potato mixture to the baking dish, the mixture can be refrigerated, covered, for up to 2 days. Microwave until warm for 4 to 7 minutes before topping with the marshmallows and baking as directed.)

NOTES FROM THE TEST KITCHEN

STEAM, DON'T BOIL

We steam the sweet potatoes in a little butter and cream for a sturdier texture and more concentrated flavor in our Sweet Potato Casserole.

SCALLOPED CORN

I DECIDED TO MAKE SCALLOPED CORN—A CREAMY casserole of corn topped by a crisp cracker-crumb crust—after a friend described how she and her cousins used to fight over the last helping at her grandma's table. To my dismay, however, the family recipe contained not a single fresh ingredient: canned creamed corn, crumbled soda crackers, jarred this, and powdered that. I was ready to write scalloped corn off as a dumping ground for convenience products until I unearthed a bounty of recipes from the 1890s, the heyday of the dish. Some included tomatoes, indicating the seasonality of the casserole, and all alternated layers of what they called "green corn" (picked young) with cracker crumbs for thickening. A few recipes included milk or cream; others dotted the layers with butter before topping the casserole with more cracker crumbs and baking it in a "moderate" oven. These fresh versions were bound to be an improvement over the canned contenders, right?

Not so fast. Whether old or new, the casseroles were uniformly pasty from the bloated cracker crumbs within, while the canned creamed corn versions were slimy. Tasters much preferred fresh corn, but it took over an hour for the kernels to soften in the oven, after which corn no longer tastes fresh and summery. The crumb topping—there for crunchy contrast—was either sandy and bland or parched from the long, dehydrating spell in the oven. This recipe had a promising concept but needed an overhaul. My goals were to thicken the casserole without crackers or cans, to shorten the cooking time and retain a fresher corn flavor, and to improve the crumb topping.

Working off the skeleton of an old recipe, I tackled the base, baking a mixture of 5 cups corn kernels, about 1 cup cream, a few tablespoons butter—no crackers, no thickener, and (no surprise) no cohesion. I went through other recipes looking for the ingredient to bind the casserole together. Eggs (even just one) turned the dish into corn pudding while the amount of cornmeal needed to do the job turned it into porridge. Both cornstarch and flour smothered the corn flavor. Many recipes thicken creamy soups and chowders by pureeing a portion of the mixture, leaving the remainder whole for contrasting texture. So I blended 2 cups of corn with the cream and, per request (or should I say, demand) from tasters, at the same time nearly doubled the amount of whole kernels to 9 cups, or about 12 ears of corn. A switch

from heavy cream to half-and-half made the dish lighter and fresher; for the same reason, I ejected the butter.

To cut down the cooking time, I covered the baking dish with foil, which helped slightly. Then I got a better idea: Why not make the corn mixture on the stovetop, then top it with crumbs and finish it in the oven? I simmered the kernels with 1¼ cups half-and-half, and in about 20 minutes the corn was very tender. The blender still came in handy for giving the dish a luscious, creamy texture: I blended 2 cups of the corn mixture into a smooth puree, which I then stirred back into the saucepan before pouring everything into the baking dish.

For the topping, I began with the traditional combination of crushed soda crackers and butter. Now that the corn was already tender and warm, the casserole needed barely 10 minutes in a hot oven to brown the crumbs, so the dry, dusty texture problem solved itself. On a hunch, I mixed some fresh bread crumbs in with the crackers. They added a light crispiness tasters liked, but the flavor was humdrum. I experimented with different cracker types hoping one variety might provide the right flavor, eventually landing on Ritz. They were a perfect fit: a little salty, a little sweet, and not a bit boring. Just like the rest of my rejuvenated scalloped corn.

—KRIS WIDICAN, *Cook's Country*

Scalloped Corn

SERVES 4 TO 6

You'll need about half of a sleeve of Ritz crackers. Add up to 1 tablespoon sugar to the cooking mixture in step 2 if your corn is out of season.

- 14 Ritz crackers
- 1 slice high-quality white sandwich bread, torn into pieces
- 3 tablespoons unsalted butter, melted
- 12 ears corn, husks and silk removed
- 1¼ cups half-and-half
- 1½ teaspoons salt
- ¼ teaspoon pepper

1. Adjust an oven rack to the middle position and heat the oven to 450 degrees. Spray an 8-inch square baking dish with vegetable oil spray. Pulse the crackers, bread, and butter in a food processor until coarsely ground.

2. Following the photo, cut the kernels from the ears of corn. Bring the kernels, half-and-half, salt, and pepper to a boil in a large saucepan. Reduce the heat to medium-low and simmer, covered, until the corn is tender, 20 to 30 minutes.

3. Puree 2 cups of the corn mixture in a blender until thick and smooth. Return the puree to the pot with the cooked corn and stir to combine. Transfer the corn mixture to the prepared dish. Top with the crumb mixture and bake until golden brown, 7 to 10 minutes. Serve. (Once transferred to the baking dish in step 3, the filling can be refrigerated, covered, for up to 3 days. Refrigerate the crumb topping separately. Bring the filling to room temperature, cover with foil, and bake for 20 minutes at 400 degrees. Increase the temperature to 450 degrees, remove the foil, top with the crumb mixture, and bake until golden brown, 7 to 10 minutes.)

NOTES FROM THE TEST KITCHEN

CUTTING KERNELS FROM THE COB
Cutting the kernels off ears of corn can be tricky, as the cobs can roll around on the cutting board. Here's how we do it.

Use a chef's knife to cut the cobs in half. Stabilize the cob halves by standing them on their cut ends, then slice the kernels from the cob.

BLEND FOR BEST RESULTS
Other scalloped corn recipes muck up the works with added ingredients like layered crumbs, flour, or eggs. We get better flavor and texture by limiting ourselves to two main ingredients—half-and-half and corn—and pureeing a portion of them to thicken the casserole.

ALL ABOUT THE CORN
Blending some of the cooked corn with half-and-half gives the casserole a thick, creamy consistency and keeps the focus where it should be—on the corn.

HUSHPUPPIES

MOST OF US ARE AT LEAST FAMILIAR WITH hushpuppies—crispy-on-the-outside, fluffy-on-the-inside fried cornmeal dumplings served throughout the South with fried fish and barbecue. They were born out of thrift in a hardscrabble time, perhaps from leftover bits of cornmeal batter used to fry catfish. In the beginning, hushpuppies were made with no fat (or very little), no dairy, and no flour, and were seasoned with nothing but salt. They were fried in whatever was on hand, usually lard. Early recipes produced hard, dense hushpuppies—I know because I tested a few. As time went on, cooks added eggs, dairy (milk or buttermilk), and seasonings such as pepper and grated onion.

To lighten the hushpuppies, some cooks began replacing a portion of the cornmeal with flour, adding baking powder or soda, and folding in whipped egg whites. (If you ask me, those whipped whites go a step too far, turning a homespun fried bread into a fluffy, froufrou fritter, plus they require more work than a humble food should.) I didn't want to reinvent the hushpuppy, I just wanted a recipe I could count on. I wanted to cherry-pick from the recipes I'd researched to get the very best hushpuppy—flavorful, crisp on the outside, and tender within—for the least effort.

Working with a basic batter that whisked together cornmeal and flour, whole eggs, baking powder, water, and salt, I started by testing varying ratios of cornmeal and flour. Obviously, the more cornmeal in the batter, the deeper the corn flavor, but more cornmeal also made for dense, gritty hushpuppies. At the other end of the scale, some recipes skewed so heavily toward flour that the hushpuppies turned out more like cakey, fluffy doughnuts than genuine hushpuppies. After a handful of tests, with the help of my tasters, I determined that ¾ cup cornmeal and ½ cup flour produced a hushpuppy that nicely balanced the two extremes.

For the liquid component of the batter, I tested water, milk, and finally buttermilk, always combined with eggs. (One recipe I found called for beer, but the flavor was strong and seemed way off base.) My tasters preferred the buttermilk for its slight tang. Once I'd settled on buttermilk, it made sense to add baking soda. Not only would soda react with acidic buttermilk to produce lighter hushpuppies, but it would also help them brown and achieve the requisite crunchy crust. In my next test, ½ teaspoon soda performed admirably, yielding hot, crusty, golden-brown hushpuppies with a striking yellow interior.

Still, with nothing but salt to season them, the hushpuppies tasted, thus far, pretty plain. I added cayenne pepper and finely minced onion (grating, called for in some recipes, was a hassle), both fairly typical additions based on my research and both befitting a classic. (I'd seen other recipes that called for such oddball ingredients as oregano, lemon zest, garlic, even chopped pickles.) While the batter sat for a few minutes to thicken, I heated the oil—far more likely to be on hand these days than lard. Then I dropped tablespoonfuls of the batter into the bubbling oil and fried the hushpuppies. One recipe I'd come across said the hushpuppies would "roll over on their backs" when they were done. Right on call, a number of my fritters did just that, flipping over all on their own in the hot fat just like a good dog should.

—DIANE UNGER, *Cook's Country*

Hushpuppies

MAKES ABOUT 25 HUSHPUPPIES

Avoid using instant grits for this recipe. Coarse- and stone-ground cornmeal will work, but they will make the hushpuppies gritty. If you don't have buttermilk, whisk 1½ teaspoons lemon juice into ¾ cup milk and let it stand for 10 minutes.

- ¾ cup (3 ¾ ounces) yellow cornmeal (see note)
- ½ cup (2½ ounces) unbleached all-purpose flour
- 1½ teaspoons baking powder
- ¾ teaspoon salt
- ½ teaspoon baking soda
- ¼ teaspoon cayenne pepper
- ¾ cup buttermilk
- 2 large eggs
- ¼ cup minced onion
- 2 quarts peanut or vegetable oil

1. Combine the cornmeal, flour, baking powder, salt, baking soda, and cayenne in a large bowl. Whisk in the buttermilk, eggs, and onion until combined. Let the batter sit at room temperature for 10 minutes or up to 1 hour.

2. Heat the oil in a large Dutch oven over medium-high heat to 350 degrees. Drop half of the batter into the oil in heaping tablespoons and fry until deep golden brown, 2 to 3 minutes, turning the hushpuppies halfway through (some should turn over on their own). Transfer to a wire rack set over a rimmed baking sheet and repeat with the remaining batter. Serve. (The hushpuppies can be refrigerated in an airtight container for up to 2 days. Reheat in a 450-degree oven for about 10 minutes.)

VARIATIONS

Corn and Red Pepper Hushpuppies

Follow the recipe for Hushpuppies, adding 1 cup corn kernels (fresh or frozen, thawed), ½ red bell pepper, seeded and chopped fine, and 2 thinly sliced scallions to the batter in step 1.

Crab and Chive Hushpuppies

Follow the recipe for Hushpuppies, adding ½ pound crabmeat (picked over for shells), 2 tablespoons Dijon mustard, and 2 tablespoons minced fresh chives to the batter in step 1.

Ham and Cheddar Hushpuppies

Follow the recipe for Hushpuppies, adding 4 ounces finely chopped deli ham, 4 ounces shredded sharp cheddar cheese, 2 tablespoons Dijon mustard, and 2 thinly sliced scallions to the batter in step 1.

NOTES FROM THE TEST KITCHEN

BAD DOG, GOOD DOG

OLD YELLER
All-cornmeal hushpuppies are dense and dry as a bone.

A TENDER PUP
A combination of flour and cornmeal produces hushpuppies that are crisp on the outside and tender within.

NO-FUSS POLENTA WITH BROCCOLI RABE, SUN-DRIED TOMATOES, AND PINE NUTS

NO-FUSS POLENTA

THIS SIMPLE, HEARTY DISH OF LONG-COOKED cornmeal dates back to sixteenth-century Rome, where *polenta sulla tavola* was poured onto the table to soak up flavors from previous meals. These days, polenta passes for haute restaurant cuisine. Its nutty corn flavor is equally satisfying, whether embellished with simple butter and cheese or served as a base for braised veal shanks or an exotic mushroom ragout. Today it is prepared either as a warm, porridge-like spoon food or as firmer squares that are grilled or fried. Both have their merits, but when the cold weather sets in, a bowl of the soothing, silky-textured stuff can't be beat.

The recipe sounds easy: Boil water, whisk in cornmeal, and stir until softened. But the devil is in the details: Polenta can take up to an hour to cook, and if you don't stir almost constantly, it forms intractable clumps. I wanted to find a better way.

Here's what's going on in a pot of polenta: When the starchy part of the corn kernels (the endosperm) comes in contact with hot water, it eventually absorbs liquid, swells, and bursts, releasing starch in a process known as gelatinization. At the same time, the grains soften, losing their gritty texture. But the tough pieces of endosperm require plenty of time and heat for the water to break through. And the pot must be stirred constantly; if polenta heats unevenly, some of its starch gelatinizes much faster than the rest, forming little pockets of fully cooked polenta, which are nearly impossible to fully break up once formed.

I tried a shortcut with parboiled "instant" brands that are ready in minutes, but tasters complained that these cooked up gluey, with lackluster flavor. It was time for a tour of cornmeal options. The typical supermarket offers a bewildering assortment of products, and their labels confuse matters further. The same dried ground corn can be called anything from yellow grits to polenta to corn semolina. Labels also advertise "fine," "medium," and "coarse" grinds, but I discovered no standards exist—one manufacturer's medium grind might be another's heartiest coarse option. Then there's the choice between whole-grain and degerminated corn (which is treated before grinding to remove both hull and germ but leaving endosperm intact).

My best bet was to try everything. I eventually settled on the couscous-size grains of coarse-ground degerminated cornmeal (often labeled "yellow grits"). They delivered the hearty yet soft texture I was looking for, plus plenty of nutty corn flavor. The only downside: The large, coarse grains took a full hour to cook through, during which time the mixture grew overly thick and my arm ached from stirring. I had been sticking to the typical 4–1 ratio of water to cornmeal. After experimenting, I found a 5–1 ratio (7½ cups water to 1½ cups cornmeal) produced the right loose consistency.

Now the hard part: whittling down the one-hour cooking time and decreasing the stirring. The rate at which water penetrates the corn is proportional to temperature, so raising the heat seemed logical, but even a heavy-bottomed pot couldn't protect the polenta from burning badly.

Maybe the key was in the cornmeal itself. There had to be a way to give that water a head start on penetrating the grains. Would soaking the cornmeal overnight help, the way it does with dried beans? I combined the cornmeal and water the night before, then cooked them together the next day. The results were uninspiring. While the grains did seem to absorb some of the liquid, this small improvement didn't alter the cooking time enough to make the extra step worth it.

Casting about for ideas, I came back to beans. The goal in cooking dried beans and dried corn is essentially identical. In a bean, water has to penetrate the hard outer skin to gelatinize the starch within. In a corn kernel, the water has to penetrate the endosperm. To soften bean skins and speed up cooking, some cooks advocate adding baking soda during cooking. Would this work for cornmeal?

I started up another batch, adding ¼ teaspoon baking soda to the cooking water as soon as it came to a boil. To my delight, the polenta cooked up in 20 minutes. But it was overkill. The baking soda acted so effectively that the cooked porridge turned gluey. It also added a strange flavor. I found that even ⅛ teaspoon soda was excessive. Just a pinch turned out to be plenty, producing polenta that cooked in a mere 30 minutes without any gluey texture or objectionable flavors.

As for stirring time, the solution came quite by accident. I'd just whisked the cornmeal into the boiling water when I got called away from the kitchen. Without thinking, I threw a lid on the pot (traditionally you cook polenta uncovered), turned the heat to its lowest level, and left the polenta to sputter untouched for nearly the entire 30 minutes. Rushing back to the stove, I expected to find a clumpy, burned-on-the-bottom mess, but instead I found perfectly creamy polenta. The baking soda must have helped the granules break down and release their starch in a uniform way so that the bottom layer didn't cook any faster than the top. And the combination of covering the pot and adjusting the heat to low cooked the polenta so gently and evenly that the result was lump-free, even without vigorous stirring.

I eventually found that after one relatively brief whisk as soon as the ingredients went in and another, shorter one five minutes later, I didn't even have to lift the lid until it was time to add the cheese. Two cups of grated Parmesan plus a pair of butter pats gave this humble mush enough nutty tang and richness to make it a satisfying dish, with or without a topping—and with the barest amount of effort.

—YVONNE RUPERTI, *Cook's Illustrated*

No-Fuss Parmesan Polenta

SERVES 6 TO 8 AS A SIDE DISH, OR 4 AS A MAIN COURSE WITH A TOPPING

Coarse-ground degerminated cornmeal such as yellow grits (with grains the size of couscous) works best in this recipe. Avoid instant and quick-cooking products, as well as whole-grain, stone-ground, and regular cornmeal. Do not omit the baking soda—it reduces the cooking time and makes for a creamier polenta.

NOTES FROM THE TEST KITCHEN

THE BEST CORNMEAL GRIND FOR POLENTA

We found coarser grains brought the most desirable and pillowy texture to our creamy polenta. However, grind coarseness can vary dramatically from brand to brand since there are no standards to ensure consistency: One manufacturer's "coarse" may be another's "fine." Here's how to identify the optimal coarsely ground texture.

TOO FINE
The super-fine grains of quick-cooking cornmeal speed the cooking process but lack corn flavor.

STILL TOO FINE
Regular cornmeal (such as Quaker) has a similarly sand-like texture that also cooks up gluey.

JUST RIGHT
A coarser cut, about the size of couscous, retains a soft but hearty texture after cooking.

BAKING SODA'S SOFT AND SPEEDY TOUCH

For polenta to lose its hard, gritty texture and turn creamy, enough water must penetrate the corn's cell walls so that the starch granules within swell and burst (or "gelatinize"). Baking soda added to the cooking liquid can reduce the time it takes for gelatinization to occur, thus shortening cooking time. Here's why: Corn cell walls are held together by pectin. When alkaline sodium bicarbonate (a.k.a. baking soda) is present, the pectin breaks down, weakening the corn's structure and allowing water to enter and gelatinize the starch in less than half the time.

MAKING A FLAME TAMER

Our recipe for No-Fuss Parmesan Polenta relies on heat so low it barely disturbs the pot's contents. A flame tamer (or heat diffuser), a metal disk that can be fitted over an electric or gas burner to reduce the heat, can help to ensure the heat is as gentle as possible. If you don't have a flame tamer (it costs less than $10 at most kitchen supply stores), you can easily make one.

Squeeze a 3-foot length of aluminum foil into a ½-inch rope. Twist the rope into a ring the size of the burner.

The polenta should do little more than release wisps of steam. If it bubbles or sputters even slightly after the first 10 minutes, the heat is too high and you may need a flame tamer (see page 68). For a main course, serve the polenta with a topping (recipes follow) or with a wedge of rich cheese or a meat sauce. Served plain, the polenta makes a great accompaniment to stews and braises.

7½ cups water
1½ teaspoons salt
   Pinch baking soda
1½ cups coarse-ground cornmeal (see note)
4 ounces Parmesan cheese, grated (about 2 cups), plus extra for serving
2 tablespoons unsalted butter
   Pepper

1. Bring the water to a boil in a heavy-bottomed 4-quart saucepan over medium-high heat. Stir in the salt and baking soda. Slowly pour the cornmeal into the water in a steady stream, while stirring back and forth with a wooden spoon or rubber spatula. Bring the mixture to a boil, stirring constantly, about 1 minute. Reduce the heat to the lowest possible setting and cover.

2. After 5 minutes, whisk the polenta to smooth out any lumps that may have formed, about 15 seconds. (Make sure to scrape the sides and bottom of the pan.) Cover and continue to cook, without stirring, until the grains of polenta are tender but slightly al dente, about 25 minutes longer. (The polenta should be loose and barely hold its shape; it will continue to thicken as it cools.)

3. Remove from the heat, stir in the Parmesan and butter, and season with pepper to taste. Let stand, covered, for 5 minutes. Serve, passing extra Parmesan separately.

No-Fuss Polenta with Sautéed Cherry Tomatoes and Fresh Mozzarella

SERVES 4

Don't stir the cheese into the sautéed tomatoes or it will melt prematurely and turn rubbery.

3 tablespoons extra-virgin olive oil
2 garlic cloves, sliced thin
   Pinch red pepper flakes
   Pinch sugar
2 pints cherry tomatoes, halved
   Salt and pepper
1 recipe No-Fuss Parmesan Polenta
6 ounces fresh mozzarella, cut into ½-inch cubes (about 1 cup)
2 tablespoons thinly sliced fresh basil

Heat the oil, garlic, red pepper flakes, and sugar in a 12-inch nonstick skillet over medium-high heat until fragrant and sizzling, about 1 minute. Stir in the tomatoes and cook until they just begin to soften, about 1 minute. Season with salt and pepper to taste and remove from the heat. Spoon the tomato mixture, along with any accumulated juice, over the polenta, top with the mozzarella, and sprinkle with the basil. Serve.

No-Fuss Polenta with Broccoli Rabe, Sun-Dried Tomatoes, and Pine Nuts

SERVES 4

½ cup sun-dried tomatoes packed in oil, rinsed, patted dry, and chopped coarse
3 tablespoons extra-virgin olive oil
6 garlic cloves, minced
½ teaspoon red pepper flakes
   Salt
1 bunch broccoli rabe (about 1 pound), trimmed and cut into 1½-inch pieces
¼ cup low-sodium chicken broth
1 recipe No-Fuss Parmesan Polenta
3 tablespoons pine nuts, toasted

Heat the sun-dried tomatoes, oil, garlic, red pepper flakes, and ½ teaspoon salt in a 12-inch nonstick skillet over medium-high heat, stirring frequently, until the garlic is fragrant and slightly toasted, about 1½ minutes. Add the broccoli rabe and broth, cover, and cook until the broccoli rabe turns bright green, about 2 minutes. Uncover and cook, stirring frequently, until most of the broth has evaporated and the broccoli rabe is just tender, 2 to 3 minutes. Season with salt to taste. Serve over the polenta, sprinkling individual portions with pine nuts.

FARRO RISOTTO

I'M A FAN OF A CREAMY, VELVETY PLATE OF RISOTTO as much as the next guy, but sometimes I find myself wanting a grain that has a similarly rich, indulgent appeal but is a little more rustic and hearty. At the same time, I don't want to settle for the somewhat everydayness of brown rice. In my search for a grain that falls somewhere between the two, I came across farro. A whole-grain relative of wheat, farro emigrated from central Italy to the United States about a decade ago, though only in the past few years has it gained widespread popularity, appearing on more and more restaurant menus as well as in supermarkets. Italians, who have enjoyed farro for centuries, prepare the grain much like how they cook Arborio rice for risotto, by cooking the farro slowly into a creamy dish called farrotto. The apparent difference between the two, and thus farro's appeal to me, lay in the heartier, nutty flavor and more satisfying chew of the farro. I was sold. I set out to come up with an easy-to-make, accessible farrotto recipe of my own, one that took half an hour or less yet still produced a dish that was creamy and rich, while highlighting farro's unique flavor and texture.

It made sense to begin testing with the test kitchen's brand new risotto cooking method (see recipe page 74). It was definitely simple; there were only two additions of warmed liquid and a few stirs during cooking, in comparison to the fussier traditional risotto cooking method of incremental additions of liquid and constant stirring. But the 5 cups of warmed liquid added at the beginning was far too much; it was all liquid and no creamy sauce, and the fact that this recipe used the lid (relying on residual heat to finish the cooking) only worsened the issue because the excess liquid couldn't evaporate. If I cut back on the liquid, the grains cooked unevenly. This method wasn't going to work, but I did learn a few valuable lessons. First the farro clearly required less liquid than Arborio rice, and second, because of this lesser amount of liquid, stirring was a must to ensure even cooking.

For my next test, I tried the test kitchen's older risotto method, which called for less liquid than the new method, no lid, and more (though not nonstop) stirring. I started by sautéing onions until soft, then I added the farro, toasted the grains briefly, then poured in a splash of wine for depth. I ladled about half the warmed broth (3 cups) into the pot and let it simmer for a full 12 minutes and gave it just a few stirs. Then I finished the last few minutes with incremental broth additions and constant stirring. This method was the best yet, producing tender, evenly cooked grains with a subtle chew, and they were swimming in a creamy, but not gummy, sauce. After a few rounds of tests, I found that a roughly 2–1 ratio of liquid to grain was just right, and because the acidic wine conflicted with the farro's flavor, I dropped it and stuck with just water and broth. My tasters were impressed that the transformation took just 25 minutes. But I had to wonder, could I make the process any easier?

I reviewed my progress and what I'd learned. Stirring was a must for even cooking; a 2–1 ratio of liquid and cooking without a lid allowed for the right consistency (not to mention no lid made sense because I had to stir fairly often). Could I simplify adding the liquid? I wondered if I could pour it in all at once, and furthermore, did it even need to be warmed liquid? For this next run-through I added all the liquid (unheated) all at once to the grains in the pot, I stirred the mixture often, and I cooked it without a lid. This batch took exactly the same amount of time as the previous successful test, the results looked identical, and tasters couldn't tell the difference. And given how much easier it was to add the broth at once, and that I didn't have to heat it up separately first, I had a clear winner.

With my simplified method in place, I turned my attention to flavorings. While onions were certainly a good start, I felt that a few more aromatics might give the dish more depth. Tasters liked garlic and thyme, and carrots provided a pleasant earthy sweetness. Up to this point I had been finishing my farro side dish in the classic risotto style with butter and Parmesan, and while tasters liked the richness, some felt it masked the subtle nuttiness of the farro. I decided to try going in the opposite direction and use a fresher finish, substituting fresh chopped parsley and lemon juice for the butter and Parmesan. To my surprise, tasters unanimously preferred this lighter, brighter version. Still rich and creamy from the farro's natural starch, the dish now seemed to be in perfect balance. I had finally arrived at a satisfying, accessible side dish that paid proper homage to this ancient grain.

—DAN SOUZA, *America's Test Kitchen Books*

FARRO RISOTTO WITH FENNEL, RADICCHIO, AND BALSAMIC VINEGAR

Farro Risotto

SERVES 4 TO 6

To make this dish vegetarian, substitute low-sodium vegetable broth for the chicken broth.

1 onion, minced
1 carrot, peeled and chopped fine
1 tablespoon olive oil
  Salt and pepper
3 garlic cloves, minced
1 teaspoon minced fresh thyme
1½ cups farro
2 cups low-sodium chicken broth
1½ cups water
2 tablespoons chopped fresh parsley
1 teaspoon fresh lemon juice

1. Combine the onion, carrot, oil, and ¼ teaspoon salt in a large saucepan. Cover and cook over medium-low heat, stirring occasionally, until the vegetables are softened, 8 to 10 minutes. Stir in the garlic and thyme and cook until fragrant, about 30 seconds.

2. Stir in the farro and cook until lightly toasted, about 2 minutes. Stir in the broth and water and bring to a simmer. Reduce the heat to low and continue to simmer, stirring often, until the farro is tender, 20 to 25 minutes.

3. Stir in the parsley and lemon juice. Season with salt and pepper to taste and serve.

VARIATIONS

Farro Risotto with Arugula, Lemon, and Parmesan
Follow the recipe for Farro Risotto, omitting the carrot and stirring in 2 ounces baby arugula, ½ cup grated Parmesan cheese, and ½ teaspoon grated lemon zest with the parsley in step 3 before serving.

Farro Risotto with Fennel, Radicchio, and Balsamic Vinegar
Follow the recipe for Farro Risotto, substituting 1 fennel bulb, chopped fine, for the carrot and 2 teaspoons balsamic vinegar for the lemon juice. Stir in ½ small head radicchio, sliced thin, with the parsley in step 3 before serving.

NOTES FROM THE TEST KITCHEN

THE BEST LARGE SAUCEPAN
A few years ago we gave the All-Clad Stainless 4-Quart Saucepan top honors among large saucepans. At the time, this pot had a unique "fully clad" design that gave it a corner on the market. The others, without this design, were more likely to burn food. But now other manufacturers are producing multi-ply, fully clad pans, some at a price cheaper than our old favorite. We rounded up eight models priced from $49.97 to $384.95 to see how much we needed to spend to get a great fully clad saucepan. The real differences came down to design and maneuverability. We found a good-quality, fully clad, easy-to-maneuver pan in the Cuisinart MultiClad Unlimited 4-Quart Saucepan for just $69.99, but it did rate behind one other pan: the **All-Clad Stainless 4-Quart Saucepan with Lid and Loop**, $194.99, which gained top marks once again. (See page 300 for more information about our testing results.)

FARRO
Farro is a whole-grain form of wheat that has been enjoyed for centuries in Tuscany and central Italy. Italians traditionally cook farro in the same manner as Arborio rice to create a creamy dish called farrotto. Thanks to praise for farro from scores of culinary magazines and top chefs, it is gaining favor with home cooks and is more widely available in natural and gourmet food stores. We love it for its slightly sweet, big, nutty flavor and chewy texture, not to mention its health benefits (it is high in fiber and protein). We found the best way to cook farro is to leave it uncovered and stir it often. Uncovered, the liquid was able to evaporate slowly as the farro cooked. Frequent stirring helped release the starches in the farro (much like a traditional risotto recipe) creating a rich and creamy consistency—without any butter or cream!

ALMOST HANDS-FREE RISOTTO

ACCEPTED WISDOM FOR COOKING RISOTTO dictates near-constant stirring to achieve the perfect texture: tender grains with a slight bite, bound together in a light, creamy sauce. As the rice cooks, it releases a starch called amylopectin. This starch absorbs liquid and expands, thickening the broth. Constantly stirring jostles the rice grains, agitating them and promoting the release of amylopectin from their exterior.

But most of us have neither the time nor the patience for 30 minutes of stirring. That's why a few years ago our test kitchen came up with an easier method. It starts like a traditional recipe: Sweat aromatics, add 2 cups of Arborio rice (a short-grained rice ideal for risotto because of its high amylopectin and starch content), toast the grains in hot fat, and pour in dry white wine, stirring until the liquid is just absorbed. Then, rather than adding the broth in traditional half-cup intervals, we add roughly half the liquid—3 cups of broth and water—at once and simmer for a full 12 minutes with only a few stirs during the process. For the last nine minutes, the traditional, incremental method is resumed as we slowly add the remaining hot broth while stirring constantly. The resulting risotto turns out every bit as creamy and al dente as those stirred for 30 minutes. Why? Once it starts bubbling, all that liquid jostles the rice grains in much the same way as constant stirring, accelerating the release of starch. But, I wondered, could I take things even further? Could I eliminate the final nine-minute stir and still deliver a perfect pot of risotto?

I had only so many variables to consider, so I started with the liquid. What if I added more from the start? If I started by pouring in 5 cups of liquid, the contents of the pot would be very fluid for the first 15 to 20 minutes of cooking, allowing the rice to bob around and cook more evenly, with minimal stirring. Only when the rice released enough starch and the sauce started to thicken, impeding fluidity, would I need to resume stirring. I gave this theory a shot, anxiously dipping my spoon into the pot as soon as the rice and sauce started to take on that familiar glossy sheen. I was pleasantly surprised. More water up front helped,

though quite a few crunchy bits of uncooked rice from the cooler top of the pan lingered. But I was getting somewhere.

Simply adding more liquid at the start wasn't enough; I needed to keep that moist heat evenly distributed, top to bottom, throughout cooking. That had never been a problem when I was stirring in portions of liquid every few minutes in the final stretch, but now I needed my cooking vessel to do more of the legwork—and my saucepan wasn't cutting it.

A Dutch oven has a thick, heavy bottom, deep sides, and a tight-fitting lid—all of which are meant to trap and distribute heat as evenly as possible, which seemed ideal here. I cooked up a new batch, starting it in a Dutch oven and covering it as soon as I added my liquid. Traditionally, the lid is left off, but with this no-stir method I was free to use it to my advantage, hopefully ensuring that the top of the rice would stay as hot as the bottom. The first 19 minutes of cooking were easy—I had to lift the lid only twice for a quick stir—but after that, the liquid once again turned too viscous for the rice (which was still undercooked) to move around the pot without assistance. Even over low heat, the rice still needed at least five minutes of constant stirring to turn uniformly al dente.

That's where the second half of the Dutch oven success story comes in. Conceptually, this uneven heat problem was not unlike a challenge we faced when developing our recipe for Slow-Roasted Beef. Aiming to cook the roast as gently and evenly as possible, we turn the heat way down—and then shut the oven off completely, leaving the beef to rest in the still-warm environment until it crawled up to temperature. Here, the heavy metal pot would function in much the same way, retaining heat long after it comes off the burner. If the risotto required its final stirring because the bottom was still cooking faster than the top, what if I removed the Dutch oven from the burner during the final minutes of cooking? Without sitting over a direct flame, the rice should turn perfectly al dente just from the residual heat.

For my next batch, after the initial 19-minute covered cooking period I gave the risotto a quick three-minute stir to get the sauce to the right consistency, followed by a five-minute covered, off-heat rest. As I removed the lid, a big plume of steam escaped, indicating that my rice was indeed still hot. As I stirred in some butter, a handful of Parmesan, a few herbs, and a squeeze of lemon juice, I could tell I was on the right track; the risotto looked perfectly creamy, thickened (but not sticky), and velvety. A single taste confirmed it: Using the same ingredients, the proper pot, and an up-to-speed technique, I'd made risotto with just as much love as any Italian nonna—without going stir-crazy.

To turn my risotto into a simple one-dish meal, I developed a recipe incorporating chicken. Using

bone-in, skin-on pieces ensured the meat wouldn't dry out, and by searing the chicken in the Dutch oven used for the risotto, I deepened its flavor and added rich fond to the pot. I then transferred the chicken pieces to the simmering broth to gently poach as the aromatics and rice cooked. Cut in half, they were cooked through right on time. I just had to pick the chicken off the bones, discard the skin, and incorporate it just before serving.

—ANDREA GEARY, *Cook's Illustrated*

NOTES FROM THE TEST KITCHEN

SECRETS TO MAKING ALMOST HANDS-FREE RISOTTO

In the traditional approach to risotto, near-constant stirring for 25 minutes accomplishes two things: It maximizes the release of starch from the rice, for a creamier sauce, and it ensures that the whole pot cooks evenly. Here's how we achieved the same goals, with only 3 minutes of stirring after the broth is added.

1. Add a full 5 cups of liquid at the start, which, once brought to a boil, jostles the rice grains much like stirring, accelerating the release of creamy starch.

2. Cover the pot with a lid. Coupled with the heavy-bottomed Dutch oven and low heat, it helps distribute the heat as evenly as stirring, so every grain is as tender as the next.

3. Rest the risotto in the pot off the heat on the counter at the end of cooking to provide additional insurance that the rice turns perfectly al dente, from the top of the pot to the bottom.

Almost Hands-Free Risotto with Parmesan and Herbs

SERVES 6

This more hands-off method does require precise timing, so we strongly recommend using a timer. The consistency of risotto is largely a matter of personal taste; if you prefer a brothy risotto, add extra broth in step 4. This makes a great side dish for braised meats.

- 5 **cups low-sodium chicken broth**
- 1½ **cups water**
- 4 **tablespoons (½ stick) unsalted butter**
- 1 **large onion, minced (about 1½ cups)**
  Salt
- 1 **large garlic clove, minced**
- 2 **cups Arborio rice**
- 1 **cup dry white wine**
- 2 **ounces Parmesan cheese, grated (about 1 cup)**
- 2 **tablespoons chopped fresh parsley**
- 2 **tablespoons chopped fresh chives**
- 1 **teaspoon fresh lemon juice**
  Pepper

1. Bring the broth and water to a boil in a large saucepan over high heat. Reduce the heat to medium-low to maintain a gentle simmer.

2. Heat 2 tablespoons of the butter in a large Dutch oven over medium heat. When the butter has melted, add the onion and ¾ teaspoon salt. Cook, stirring frequently, until the onion is softened but not browned, 4 to 7 minutes. Add the garlic and stir until fragrant, about 30 seconds. Add the rice and cook, stirring frequently, until the grains are translucent around the edges, about 3 minutes.

3. Add the wine and cook, stirring constantly, until fully absorbed, 2 to 3 minutes. Stir 5 cups of the hot broth mixture into the rice, reduce the heat to medium-low, cover, and simmer until almost all the liquid has been absorbed and the rice is just al dente, 16 to 19 minutes, stirring twice during cooking.

4. Add ¾ cup more hot broth mixture, and stir gently and constantly until the risotto becomes creamy, about 3 minutes. Stir in the Parmesan. Remove the pot from the heat, cover, and let stand for 5 minutes. Stir in the remaining 2 tablespoons butter, parsley, chives, and lemon juice. Season with salt and pepper to taste. If desired, add up to ½ cup remaining broth mixture to loosen the texture of the risotto. Serve.

Almost Hands-Free Risotto with Chicken and Herbs

SERVES 6

Adding chicken breasts to the risotto turns a side dish into a main course. Check the chicken periodically in step 2; the thinner ends of the chicken breasts will likely cook through more quickly than the thicker ends. If you prefer a brothy risotto, add the extra broth in step 6.

- 5   **cups low-sodium chicken broth**
- 2   **cups water**
- 1   **tablespoon olive oil**
- 2   **(12-ounce) bone-in, skin-on chicken breasts, cut in half crosswise**
- 4   **tablespoons (½ stick) unsalted butter**
- 1   **large onion, minced (about 1½ cups)**
      Salt
- 1   **large garlic clove, minced**
- 2   **cups Arborio rice**
- 1   **cup dry white wine**
- 2   **ounces Parmesan cheese, grated (about 1 cup)**
- 2   **tablespoons chopped fresh parsley**
- 2   **tablespoons chopped fresh chives**
- 1   **teaspoon fresh lemon juice**
      Pepper

1. Bring the broth and water to a boil in a large saucepan over high heat. Reduce the heat to medium-low to maintain a gentle simmer.

2. Heat the olive oil in a large Dutch oven over medium heat until just starting to smoke. Add the chicken, skin side down, and cook without moving until golden brown, 4 to 6 minutes. Flip the chicken and cook the second side until lightly browned, about 2 minutes. Transfer the chicken to the saucepan of simmering broth and water and cook until the chicken registers 160 to 165 degrees on an instant-read thermometer, 10 to 15 minutes. Transfer to a large plate.

3. Add 2 tablespoons of the butter to the Dutch oven and cook over medium heat. When the butter has melted, add the onion and ¾ teaspoon salt. Cook, stirring frequently, until the onion is softened but not browned, 4 to 7 minutes. Add the garlic and stir until fragrant, about 30 seconds. Add the rice and cook, stirring frequently, until the grains are translucent around the edges, about 3 minutes.

4. Add the wine and cook, stirring constantly, until fully absorbed, 2 to 3 minutes. Stir 5 cups of the hot broth mixture into the rice. Reduce the heat to medium-low, cover, and simmer until almost all the liquid has been absorbed and the rice is just al dente, 16 to 19 minutes, stirring twice during cooking.

5. Add ¾ cup more hot broth mixture, and stir gently and constantly until the risotto becomes creamy, about 3 minutes. Stir in the Parmesan. Remove the pot from the heat, cover, and let stand for 5 minutes.

6. Meanwhile, remove and discard the skin and bones from the chicken and shred the meat into bite-size pieces. Gently stir the shredded chicken, the remaining 2 tablespoons butter, and the parsley, chives, and lemon juice into the risotto. Season with salt and pepper to taste. If desired, add up to ½ cup remaining broth mixture to loosen the texture of the risotto. Serve.

VARIATION

Almost Hands-Free Saffron Risotto with Chicken and Peas

Follow the recipe for Almost Hands-Free Risotto with Chicken and Herbs, adding ¼ teaspoon saffron threads to the rice with the broth mixture in step 4. Stir ¾ cup frozen peas into the risotto with the Parmesan in step 5.

MAKE-AHEAD BREAKFAST CASSEROLE

ON BUSY MORNINGS WHEN YOU HAVE TO FEED A crowd, few things are easier than popping a breakfast casserole into the oven. The beauty of it is, of course, that you make it the day before—combining dried cubes of bread with browned sausage in a casserole dish, scattering that with cheese, pouring on eggs mixed with milk or cream, and letting it soak overnight. The next morning, you slip the casserole into the oven and it bakes into puffy, golden, savory goodness. Right?

Not so fast. The recipes I tried had a host of problems: Some were the texture of baby food, others were so overloaded with sausage that they tasted of nothing but, and too many versions slanted toward heavy and greasy. I was looking for a flavorful, balanced breakfast casserole with a crisp top and a soft, custardy inside.

I decided to tackle the texture first. Many recipes call for cubed white sandwich bread, but even when I gently "staled" the cubes in the oven first, the bread drank up too much custard and turned to mush after an overnight stay in the refrigerator. Sturdier Italian bread, which I sliced rather than cubed, held up better. I then experimented with leaving the slices in the oven until they were toasted, not merely dry. The texture and flavor of the casserole improved even more.

Most recipes using a 13 by 9-inch dish call for a dozen eggs, which is about the right amount to meld with one loaf of sliced Italian bread. The 6 cups of milk or cream, however, was too much by far. Even the toasted bread practically dissolved in so much liquid. A few tests proved that 4 cups was ideal. In further side-by-side tests, tasters preferred whole milk to either cream or half-and-half; the latter two options were too heavy and too rich. To give this casserole a little extra character, I added a splash of hot sauce for a touch of vinegary heat.

Recipes vary widely on the amounts of sausage and cheese they call for. To determine the right ratios for heft without heaviness, I subjected tasters to more breakfast casseroles than most people eat in a lifetime. When I used a lot of sausage, its seasoning took over and the casserole was greasy; too little sausage and it seemed like an afterthought. One pound of breakfast sausage, crumbled and browned with onion, struck the right balance. The casserole got another boost in flavor when I used extra-sharp cheddar in place of the typical sharp cheddar.

Shingling the bread in two layers and layering the sausage-onion mixture and the cheese ensured flavor in every bite. I was close, but the casserole was dry in spots; the custard wasn't soaking in evenly. I wrapped the casserole with plastic wrap, then placed a spare baking dish loaded with cans on top to compress it. Problem solved.

—KRIS WIDICAN, *Cook's Country*

Make-Ahead Breakfast Casserole
SERVES 8 TO 10

You can find unsliced loaves of Italian bread in the bakery section of your supermarket. Frank's RedHot is the test kitchen's top-rated hot sauce. If using a spicier sauce such as Tabasco, reduce the amount to 1½ teaspoons.

- 1 (14-inch) loaf Italian bread, ends trimmed
- 1 pound bulk pork sausage
- 1 small onion, minced (about ½ cup)
- 12 ounces extra-sharp cheddar cheese, shredded (about 3 cups)
- 12 large eggs, lightly beaten
- 4 cups whole milk
- 1 tablespoon hot sauce (see note)
- 1½ teaspoons salt
- 1 teaspoon pepper

1. Adjust the oven racks to the upper-middle and lower-middle positions and heat the oven to 400 degrees. Slice the bread in half lengthwise, then slice each half crosswise into ½-inch-thick pieces. Spread the bread in single layers on 2 rimmed baking sheets and bake until golden, 15 to 20 minutes, flipping the bread and switching and rotating the sheets halfway through. Cool for 15 minutes.

2. Cook the sausage in a large skillet over medium heat until no longer pink, about 5 minutes. Add the onion and cook until golden, about 5 minutes.

3. Grease a 13 by 9-inch baking dish. Shingle half of the bread in the prepared pan so the edges overlap slightly. Top with half of the sausage mixture and 1 cup of the cheese. Repeat with the remaining bread, remaining sausage mixture, and remaining 2 cups cheese.

4. Whisk the eggs, milk, hot sauce, salt, and pepper in a large bowl and pour evenly over the casserole. Following the photos on page 79, wrap the casserole with plastic wrap and weight it. Refrigerate for at least 1 hour or up to 24 hours.

5. Adjust an oven rack to the middle position and heat the oven to 350 degrees. Let the casserole stand at room temperature while the oven is heating. Remove the weights, unwrap the casserole, and bake until the edges and center have puffed and the top is golden brown, about 1 hour. Cool for 10 minutes and serve.

VARIATIONS

Make-Ahead Breakfast Casserole with Chorizo and Pepper Jack

Follow the recipe for Make-Ahead Breakfast Casserole, replacing the bulk pork sausage with 1 pound chorizo sausage, halved lengthwise and sliced thin, and the cheddar with 3 cups shredded pepper Jack cheese. In step 2, add ¼ cup chopped fresh cilantro to the chorizo mixture after it has been removed from the heat.

Make-Ahead Breakfast Casserole with Italian Sausage and Fontina

Follow the recipe for Make-Ahead Breakfast Casserole, replacing the bulk pork sausage with 1 pound hot or sweet Italian sausage, casings removed, and the cheddar with 3 cups shredded fontina cheese. In step 2, add ¼ cup chopped fresh basil to the sausage mixture after it has been removed from the heat.

NOTES FROM THE TEST KITCHEN

WEIGHTING WHILE YOU WAIT

To make sure the toasted bread fully absorbs the custard, we weight our casserole, first covering the assembled casserole with plastic wrap. Both of the following methods ensure a uniform casserole.

A. USING CANNED GOODS: Place a spare 13 by 9-inch dish on top of the wrapped casserole and set canned goods on top for extra weight.

B. USING BOXES OF BROTH: Carefully place boxes of broth (or boxes of sugar) evenly on top of the wrapped casserole. (You do not need a spare dish for this method.)

EASY CHEESY QUICHE FOR TWO

WITH ITS ALLURING COMBINATION OF CREAMY custard and flaky crust, quiche is easy to love. But most recipes make enough to serve a crowd, whether it's a 9-inch quiche or dozens of cocktail-hour minis. That's fine for a party, but when you are just serving a couple at home on Sunday morning, the idea of eating quiche leftovers for days is less than ideal. I wanted a quiche that showcased the custard's silky texture and the crispiness of the buttery crust but would serve just two people.

My first challenge was deciding what size pie plate to use. I eventually settled on a 6-inch pie plate, which I thought would provide just the right amount of quiche for two. For the pie dough, I followed the standard formula of flour, fat, and water, ultimately settling on 4 tablespoons of butter and 2 tablespoons of shortening to 1 cup of flour, which provided the most buttery flavor and tender texture without compromising the structure of the dough. After rolling out the dough and fitting it into the pie plate, I allowed the crust to chill for 20 minutes (to prevent the crust from shrinking while it baked), then parbaked it in a 375-degree oven until light golden brown in color to ensure a crisp crust.

It was time to tackle the filling. It would, like most standard quiches, be a combination of eggs, dairy, cheese, and herbs. Eggs contribute structure, moisture, and flavor to quiche so I started there. Most recipes for a 9-inch quiche serving six to eight people include somewhere between three and six eggs. Early on, I found that recipes with too many eggs resulted in a rubbery texture; too few eggs and the quiche was too soft to cut neatly and the flavor was too mild. After a number of tests, I settled on two eggs and ⅔ cup of dairy for my downsized recipe. This produced a quiche that was firm-textured yet not rubbery, rich but not overly eggy.

As for the type of dairy, I tried milk and cream alone, as well as half-and-half. By itself, milk tasted too lean and cream was far too rich; half-and-half was best by far, rich-tasting and with a substantial but not dense texture.

When it came to the cheese, I didn't want to get carried away—some recipes I tested seemed more like a cheese tart than a custardy quiche. For my easy quiche for two, I found that ½ cup of cheddar brought just enough rich cheese flavor without overwhelming the custard. For an herb, I wanted something mild but bright; a bit of minced chives worked perfectly.

After mixing the cheese and chives into the custard, I poured the mixture into the parbaked crust and moved it to a moderate 350-degree oven. After about 30 minutes, I had just the quiche I had been hoping for: a tender, flaky crust and a custard that was creamy but not overly rich.

Of course, taking the quiche out of the oven at just the right time was also essential to obtaining a perfectly creamy custard. I found that watching the quiche, not the clock, was the trick here. Once the surface of the quiche was puffed and had a light golden brown color, I opened the oven door and did a quick test for doneness by inserting a knife blade into the custard, about 1 inch from the edge. When the quiche was done, the knife blade came out clean; at this point the center still appeared slightly soft, but I found that the residual heat finished the baking while the quiche cooled on the rack.

My easy cheese quiche was good, but I thought the addition of ham or bacon might take it up a notch, so I created two just-as-easy variations—a ham and Swiss quiche and a classic quiche Lorraine (made with bacon and Gruyère). Served slightly warm or at room temperature, all three quiches were a piece of cake—or custard.

—DAN ZUCCARELLO, *America's Test Kitchen Books*

Easy Cheesy Quiche for Two

SERVES 2

You will need a 6-inch pie plate for this recipe. If desired, you can substitute 1 round of store-bought pie dough, such as Pillsbury Just Unroll!, for the homemade pie dough. If the pie dough becomes too soft to work with, simply refrigerate it until firm. It is important to add the custard to the pie shell while it is still warm; if the crust has cooled, rewarm it in the oven for 5 minutes before adding the custard. To avoid spills, we place the crust on the oven rack then pour in the filling in step 7; work quickly here to avoid letting too much heat escape from the open oven.

CRUST

- 1 cup (5 ounces) unbleached all-purpose flour
- ½ teaspoon salt
- 2 tablespoons vegetable shortening, cut into ½-inch pieces and chilled
- 4 tablespoons (½ stick) unsalted butter, cut into ¼-inch pieces and chilled
- 3–5 tablespoons ice water

FILLING

- ⅔ cup half-and-half
- 2 large eggs, lightly beaten
- 2 teaspoons minced fresh chives or parsley
- ⅛ teaspoon salt
- ⅛ teaspoon pepper
- 2 ounces cheddar cheese, shredded (about ½ cup)

1. FOR THE CRUST: Process the flour and salt together in a food processor until combined. Scatter the shortening over the top and process until the mixture resembles coarse cornmeal, about 10 seconds. Scatter the butter pieces over the top and pulse until the mixture resembles coarse crumbs, about 10 pulses. Transfer the mixture to a medium bowl.

2. Sprinkle 3 tablespoons of the ice water over the mixture. Using a stiff rubber spatula, stir and press the dough until it sticks together. If the dough does not come together, stir in the remaining water, 1 tablespoon at a time, until it does.

3. Turn the dough out onto a clean counter. Shape into a ball and flatten into a 5-inch disk. Wrap with plastic wrap and refrigerate for 1 hour. Before rolling out the dough, let it sit on the counter to soften slightly, about 10 minutes.

4. Roll out the dough into a 10-inch round, about ⅛ inch thick, on a lightly floured counter. Following the photos on page 82, fit the dough into a 6-inch pie plate and trim, fold, and crimp the edge. Cover loosely with plastic wrap and freeze for 20 minutes.

5. Adjust an oven rack to the lower-middle position and heat the oven to 375 degrees. Line the chilled crust with a sheet of lightly greased foil and fill with pie weights. Bake until the pie dough looks dry and is light in color, 25 to 30 minutes.

6. FOR THE FILLING: Whisk the half-and-half, eggs, chives, salt, and pepper together in a large measuring cup. Stir in the cheese until well combined.

7. Remove the pie shell from the oven and reduce the oven temperature to 350 degrees. Remove the pie weights and foil and transfer the pie shell to a foil-lined rimmed baking sheet. Return the pie shell to the oven. Carefully pour the egg mixture into the warm shell until it reaches about ½ inch from the top edge of the crust (you may have extra egg mixture).

8. Bake the quiche until the top is lightly browned, the very center still jiggles and looks slightly underdone,

EASY QUICHE LORRAINE FOR TWO

FITTING PIE DOUGH FOR QUICHE FOR TWO

1. Loosely roll the dough around a rolling pin, then gently unroll it over the pie plate.

2. Lift the dough and gently press it into the pie plate, letting the excess hang over the plate.

3. Trim the pie dough so that it hangs over the pie plate by ½ inch, then tuck the dough underneath itself to form a tidy, even edge that sits on the lip of the pie plate.

4. Use the index finger of one hand and the thumb and index finger of the other to create fluted ridges perpendicular to the edge of the pie plate.

MAKING PIE DOUGH BY HAND

If you don't have a food processor, you can mix the dough by hand. Freeze the butter in its stick form until very firm. Whisk together the flour and salt in a medium bowl. Add the chilled shortening and press it into the flour using a fork. Grate the frozen butter on the large holes of a box grater into the flour mixture, then cut the mixture together, using two butter or dinner knives, until the mixture resembles coarse crumbs. Add the water as directed.

and a knife inserted about 1 inch from the edge comes out clean, 30 to 40 minutes.

9. Let the quiche cool for at least 30 minutes or up to 1 hour. Serve slightly warm or at room temperature. (The wrapped dough can be refrigerated for up to 2 days or frozen for up to 1 month. If frozen, let the dough thaw completely on the counter before rolling it out.)

VARIATIONS

Easy Quiche Lorraine for Two

Cook 2 slices bacon, cut into ¼-inch pieces, in an 8-inch skillet over medium-low heat until crisp, about 10 minutes. Using a slotted spoon, transfer the bacon to a paper towel–lined plate and pour off all but 1 tablespoon of the bacon fat. Add ¼ cup minced onion to the skillet and cook over medium heat until softened and lightly browned, 5 to 7 minutes. Follow the recipe for Easy Cheesy Quiche for Two, substituting Gruyère cheese for the cheddar and adding the cooked bacon and onion to the filling in step 6.

Easy Ham and Swiss Quiche for Two

Follow the recipe for Easy Cheesy Quiche for Two, substituting Swiss cheese for the cheddar and adding 2 thin slices deli ham (about 2 ounces), cut into ¼-inch pieces, to the filling in step 6.

DUTCH BABY

A CROSS BETWEEN A POPOVER AND A GIANT, EGGY pancake, a Dutch baby bakes in a skillet in a "brisk oven" (as an old recipe we found puts it). It puffs up spectacularly and then, moments out of the oven, deflates to form a bowl with crisp sides and a thin, custardy bottom. It's finished with a squeeze of lemon juice and a generous dusting of confectioners' sugar. This pancake is thought to come from Germany, not Holland— the name is a corruption of "Deutsch." The "baby" is usually traced to Manca's Café in Seattle, famous for more than 50 years for the small (hence, baby) oven-baked pancakes it dubbed Dutch babies. Over the years, the baby has grown up: Today it's inevitably large.

That suited me. A big, puffy pancake was just what I had in mind. Most recipes have you whisk together a 1–1 ratio of flour to milk with several eggs, pour the mixture into a heavily buttered skillet, and bake for 20 minutes. Where ordinary pancakes call for baking soda and powder, a Dutch baby relies on the conversion of water to steam for lift—the milk, eggs, and butter in the batter all contain substantial amounts of water. Perhaps because the oven temperature, amount of batter per skillet, and skillet type and size varied widely in the recipes I found, so did the results of my first set of tests. Some Dutch babies had soft sides, others had thick and soggy bottoms, and then there were those that never rose above the skillet rim. I wanted a puffy, well-risen pancake (large enough to serve four people) with crisp sides and a tender bottom.

To feed four, I'd need enough batter for a 12-inch skillet. Most recipes call for ½ cup flour, ½ cup milk, and 3 eggs, but many (especially older ones) are maddeningly vague about skillet size. I poured a batter made with these ingredient amounts into a 12-inch skillet but came up short. Keeping the flour-to-milk ratio constant, I tested increasing amounts, and eventually concluded that 1¼ cups of each gave me the right volume for the pan. Since I'd more than doubled the milk and flour, logic dictated I double the eggs as well. But when I did so, the bottom thickened, and the final result tasted like a fluffy omelet instead of a proper pancake. I scaled back the eggs one by one and, despite the extra flour and milk, found that three still sufficed.

I wanted my baby to be big, and I figured separating the eggs and beating the whites to stiff peaks would ensure height. But instead of a baby with height I got a soufflé-like concoction with a lumpy, foamy middle. Worse, the edges were no taller than before. Next, I experimented up and down with baking temperature: Finally, at 450 degrees I got the highest rise without any burning. To ensure that the batter rose evenly, I tested various skillets. A traditional cast-iron skillet worked well, but I had even better luck with an ordinary skillet, as its gently sloping sides promoted an even rise.

Now if only I could get the sides to crisp. Knowing that fat makes baked goods tender, I wondered: If I replaced the whole milk in my Dutch baby with skim milk, might less fat translate to more crispness? Indeed

it did. Next, I replaced ¼ cup of the flour with an equivalent amount of cornstarch, an ingredient known for its crisping powers. But I wasn't quite done. Past experience had taught me that a hot skillet would give the batter a head start on crisping. Some recipes preheat the skillet on the stovetop just long enough to melt the 3 tablespoons of butter that grease the pan, but I got better results preheating the pan in the oven. Because the knob of butter scorched in the blazing-hot skillet, I tried substituting vegetable oil, which has a higher smoke point. This solved one problem but caused another: Everybody missed the taste of butter. The next time, I greased the pan with 2 tablespoons oil (making sure to brush the sides, too) and stirred 1 tablespoon melted butter into the batter.

For a final flavor tune-up, I whisked a teaspoon of vanilla extract and 2 teaspoons of lemon zest into the batter. Whoa, baby!

—MARÍA DEL MAR SACASA, *Cook's Country*

Dutch Baby

SERVES 4

You can use whole or low-fat milk instead of skim, but the Dutch Baby won't be as crisp. For a treat, serve with an assortment of berries and lightly sweetened whipped cream.

2	tablespoons vegetable oil
1	cup (5 ounces) unbleached all-purpose flour
¼	cup cornstarch
2	teaspoons grated lemon zest plus
	2 tablespoons fresh lemon juice
1	teaspoon salt
3	large eggs
1¼	cups skim milk
1	tablespoon unsalted butter, melted and cooled
1	teaspoon vanilla extract
3	tablespoons confectioners' sugar

1. Adjust an oven rack to the middle position and heat the oven to 450 degrees. Brush the surface and sides of a 12-inch skillet with the oil. Place the skillet on the oven rack and heat until the oil is shimmering, about 10 minutes.

2. Meanwhile, combine the flour, cornstarch, lemon zest, and salt in a large bowl. Whisk the eggs in another bowl until frothy and light, about 1 minute. Whisk the milk, butter, and vanilla into the eggs until incorporated. Whisk one-third of the milk mixture into the flour mixture until no lumps remain, then slowly whisk in the remaining two-thirds milk mixture until smooth.

3. Carefully pour the batter into the heated skillet and bake until the edges of the Dutch Baby are deep golden brown and crisp, about 20 minutes. Transfer the skillet to a wire rack and sprinkle the Dutch Baby with the lemon juice and confectioners' sugar. Cut into wedges and serve.

NOTES FROM THE TEST KITCHEN

MAKING A DUTCH BABY

1. Brush the entire interior surface of the pan, including the sides, with vegetable oil.

2. Heat the greased pan in the oven before pouring in the batter to initiate a big rise.

3. Remove the Dutch Baby when its edges are deep golden brown and crisp and it resembles a giant popover, about 20 minutes.

4. Transfer the skillet to a wire rack and sprinkle the Dutch Baby with lemon juice and confectioners' sugar. Expect it to deflate after it sits a few minutes.

BUTTERMILK WAFFLES

UNLIKE SOME OF THE THINGS I'LL MAKE FOR A special breakfast—a quiche or an omelet, say—a waffle is hard to get disastrously wrong. Sure, it may come out a little dense or a tad cottony. It may wilt too quickly. But topped with the usual gobs of butter and maple syrup, even a flawed waffle is never terrible.

The compensating effects of butter and syrup may be why so many waffle recipes settle for not-bad rather than chasing the defining balance of contrasts: a crisp, golden-brown dimpled crust surrounding a moist, fluffy interior. Or "waffle" recipes, I should say, as a survey revealed that most are merely repurposed pancake recipes. Not surprisingly, a batter meant to cook on the flat, open surface of a griddle doesn't turn out the same in the enclosed, rigid environment of a waffle iron.

But even recipes designed specifically for a waffle iron had their downsides: To help ensure the proper lift, the best either involved an overnight rise or the patience to whip up egg whites just so. I wanted a recipe that didn't require day-ahead forethought—or even much more than measuring out some flour and cracking an egg.

Waffles and pancakes have obvious structural differences, but the flavor profiles of buttermilk versions are the same. As such, it made sense to start with the test kitchen's recently developed Buttermilk Pancakes recipe and fine-tune that recipe for waffle duty. I made a batter with slightly less sugar and a tad more salt than our pancakes, but otherwise the same: 2 cups flour, 1 tablespoon sugar, ¾ teaspoon salt, 1 teaspoon baking powder, ½ teaspoon baking soda, 2 cups buttermilk, ¼ cup sour cream (which we found provides far tangier flavor than buttermilk alone), two eggs, and 3 tablespoons melted butter and poured it into the preheated waffle iron. The result: the terrific flavor I expected but a gummy, wet interior and not much in the way of a crust.

What was causing the texture to suffer? Comparing the griddle with the waffle iron, it wasn't hard to guess. To get crisp, the exterior of a waffle must first become dry. Although a waffle iron is hardly airtight—steam escapes easily via the open sides—all that moist steam racing past the crisping waffle was slowing down the process. The waffle iron's weight bearing down while the waffle was trying to rise doesn't help. I needed a drier batter with much more leavening oomph.

I first tried decreasing the amount of liquid in the batter, losing almost half of the buttermilk and adding

BUTTERMILK WAFFLES

SECRETS TO CRISPY, FLUFFY WAFFLES

We found two ingredients were key to creating perfect, easy-to-make waffles.

VEGETABLE OIL

For crispier results, we swapped out the typical melted butter for oil. Unlike butter, oil contributes no moisture to the waffle. Oil also helps keep the waffle crisp after it comes off the heat: As a pure fat, it is better able to repel water.

SELTZER

The carbon dioxide bubbles in seltzer act the same way as whipped egg whites to provide lift to the waffle—without all the work.

THE BEST WAFFLE IRON

Few kitchen appliances have a more specific job description than your waffle iron, yet the marketplace is still rife with machines turning out pallid, soggy results. Our now-retired favorite model, the VillaWare Uno Series Classic Waffler 4-Square, reliably made crisp, toasty waffles, and we were anxious to find one just as good. We rounded up six traditional (not Belgian) irons, among them our previous Best Buy from Black and Decker, as well as round and clover- (or heart-) shaped newcomers. Each featured adjustable temperature settings, nonstick surfaces, and indicator lights. The best irons consistently produced uniformly crisped, evenly cooked waffles—and in the specific shade selected. For the highest marks, an audible alert was a must, as it frees you from the tedium of hovering over the iron. Heat-resistant handles and casings were also important. Our new winner, the clover-shaped **Chef's Choice WafflePro Express**, $69.95, stood out for speedily cooking a perfect waffle in the promised shade—and emitting a loud beep to let you know breakfast is ready.

extra sour cream (to compensate for the loss of some of the fat and tangy flavor), which yielded a net ½ cup less liquid. The resulting waffles were somewhat less wet inside, but they were still quite dense.

Shifting my focus to leaveners, I tried the technique I had hoped to outlaw: whipping the egg whites into a foam and then folding it in at the last stages of mixing. These waffles had a vastly superior texture thanks to the millions of tiny air bubbles produced in the process. (When the batter heats up in the waffle iron, these air bubbles expand, giving the waffle volume.) But getting the whites to this stage was definitely a pain—subjecting myself to the rigors of meringue-work before breakfast wasn't exactly the low-effort method I had in mind. There had to be an easier way. More baking soda and baking powder seemed like a good idea, but tasters complained of a metallic aftertaste when I increased them.

Then I had an idea that seemed like kind of a long shot: In Japanese tempura batters, seltzer or club soda is often used in place of still water. The idea is that the tiny bubbles of carbon dioxide released from the water will inflate the batter the same way as a chemical leavener—minus the metallic aftertaste. On a whim, I replaced the buttermilk in my recipe with a mixture of seltzer and powdered buttermilk. The resulting waffles were incredibly light. In fact, they were so light that tasters claimed them to be "insubstantial," and "all surface crunch with no interior."

I wondered if the bubbly seltzer now made the baking powder and soda superfluous. When tested, waffles made without chemical leaveners had excellent texture but lacked a uniform brown exterior. That's because browning occurs best in an alkaline environment, and without the help of mildly alkaline baking soda, the buttermilk and seltzer in the recipe made the batter too acidic for browning to happen. Adding back ½ teaspoon of baking soda produced waffles that were perfect—at least when they first emerged. But after mere moments on the plate, they would begin to soften.

The problem is that as soon as the waffle comes away from the heat source, its interior moisture starts to migrate outward, softening the crisp crust. I needed to find a way to prevent this. A little research informed me that the key is fat. Fat and water naturally repel each other. So I thought if I could get more fat into the mix, the surface portion of the batter would be better able to stop water from softening the exterior.

After some experimentation, I found that the solution was not merely adding more fat, but also the type of fat I was using. I had been working with butter, which is about 20 percent water. Meanwhile, oil contributes no water at all, so there is less moisture available to move to the surface of the waffle in the first place. Another test proved waffles made with oil (I ended up using ¼ cup) stayed significantly crispier than those I had made with melted butter. Additionally, when oil is swapped in, the difference in the amount of water is made up with fat. The fattier the batter, the more it repels whatever interior moisture manages to rise to the surface of the waffle. The result: The surface stays crisp, and the moisture stays inside the waffle, where it belongs. I was afraid that tasters would miss the butter flavor, but in fact they didn't even notice, commenting only on how excellent the texture was. Besides, I could always add more butter at the table if I wanted to.

These waffles were so good, so easy, and so foolproof that, since they practically cook themselves, I may never make any other kind of hotcakes again.

—ANDREA GEARY, *Cook's Illustrated*

Buttermilk Waffles

MAKES ABOUT EIGHT 7-INCH ROUND WAFFLES

While the waffles can be eaten directly from the waffle iron, they will have a crisper exterior if rested in a warm oven for 10 minutes. Buttermilk powder is available in most supermarkets and is generally located near the dried milk products or in the baking aisle (leftover powder can be kept in the refrigerator for up to a year). Seltzer or club soda gives these waffles their light texture; use a freshly opened container for maximum lift. Avoid sparkling water such as Perrier, which is not bubbly enough. Serve with butter and maple syrup.

  2   **cups (10 ounces) unbleached all-purpose flour**
  ½   **cup dried buttermilk powder**
  1   **tablespoon sugar**
  ¾   **teaspoon salt**
  ½   **teaspoon baking soda**
  ½   **cup sour cream**
  2   **large eggs**
  ¼   **cup vegetable oil**
  ¼   **teaspoon vanilla extract**
  1¼ **cups unflavored seltzer water (see note)**

1. Adjust an oven rack to the middle position and heat the oven to 250 degrees. Set a wire rack in a rimmed baking sheet and place the baking sheet in the oven. Whisk the flour, buttermilk powder, sugar, salt, and baking soda in a large bowl to combine. Whisk the sour cream, eggs, oil, and vanilla in a medium bowl to combine. Gently stir the seltzer into the wet ingredients. Make a well in the center of the dry ingredients and pour in the wet ingredients. Gently stir until just combined. The batter should remain slightly lumpy with streaks of flour.

2. Heat a waffle iron and bake the waffles according to the manufacturer's instructions (use about ⅓ cup for a 7-inch round iron). Transfer the waffles to the rack in the warm oven and hold for up to 10 minutes before serving.

CHRISTMAS KRINGLE

MOST OF WISCONSIN HAS A REPUTATION FOR DAIRY, brats, and beer, but in Racine, kringle is king. Recipes for this oval-shaped, supremely buttery Danish arrived with the many Danish immigrants who settled in Racine in the 1800s. Kringle, often eaten at Christmas, combines the richness of sweet yeast dough with some of the flakiness of puff pastry. It's variously filled with jammy fruit, sweetened cream cheese, or sugared and spiced nuts, and is drizzled with glaze. Aside from stunning amounts of butter, kringle requires one thing above all: patience. Traditional kringle takes three days and calls for bakers to fold the dough dozens of times, stopping repeatedly to let it chill and relax. I wondered how I would ever chill and relax with so much work ahead.

After I returned from visiting five bakeries in Racine, I uncovered recipes that purported to cut down the time and labor. I settled on a pecan-butter filling, the most popular Racine variation, then mixed, rolled, and shaped nine kringles. I baked them after their overnight rest. They looked impressive but how they tasted was a different matter. Some were heavy and cakey, others lean and bready. Many were greasy rather than buttery, and several were encased in stiff, achingly sweet frostings. I wanted a kringle that rivaled the real McCoy in every respect, except for the hours required to make it.

I stepped back to get a handle on the difference between authentic and quick (comparatively speaking)

PECAN KRINGLE

kringle. Authentic kringle is made with Danish dough, a cousin of croissant and puff pastry dough that adds eggs to the mix of milk, flour, yeast, and sugar for an especially rich, tender texture. The dough is chilled, rolled out, wrapped around a slab of butter, rolled again, folded into thirds, and chilled again. This process forms layers of butter that melt and steam in the oven, making the dough separate into thin, light pastry sheets. In quick kringle recipes, cubes of cold butter are cut into flour, sugar, and yeast, after which water, milk, cream, or sour cream and sometimes eggs are stirred in. The dough is simply rolled, filled, shaped into an oval, and rested.

One dough from my initial tests stood out. It used 2 cups sour cream as its sole wet ingredient (with 2 cups butter, 4 cups flour, 2 tablespoons sugar, and one envelope yeast). The recipe yielded two kringles with a tender, flaky crumb. Our science editor explained the acidic sour cream weakened the dough's gluten structure, mimicking the flaky texture of an authentic kringle. Unfortunately, this version was greasy. I reduced the butter bit by bit to 1¼ cups—the greasiness disappeared. So did the tenderness. I experimented with using cornstarch (which has no gluten) for some of the flour, but it had little effect. Next, I replaced some of the butter with shortening, a known tenderizer. Restraint was key, as butter is the mark of any self-respecting Danish. I hit the sweet spot at ¼ cup shortening and 1 cup butter.

During my visit to Racine, Eric Olesen, baker and co-owner of O&H Bakery, had told me, "The key to a light and tender kringle is letting the dough relax, and that takes time." But how much time? To speed my kringle along, I whittled down the overnight rest, ultimately reducing it to four hours with no ill effect.

I turned my attention to the filling and glaze. Bakeries in Racine layer on the brown sugar, butter, and cinnamon mix, which they top with ground pecans. To streamline the process, I pulsed everything in a food processor (toasting the pecans first to bring out their flavor) and spread the mixture over the dough in a single layer. My working recipe used an excessively thick glaze made from confectioners' sugar and milk. I thinned it, added vanilla extract, and applied it with a light hand.

Tender, buttery, flaky, and easier and quicker to make, my kringle was ready for a showdown. I ordered a kringle from O&H, king of kringle bakeries in the town billing itself Kringle Capital of the U.S. I called tasters for a side-by-side tasting. Mine more than held its own.

—CALI RICH, *Cook's Country*

Pecan Kringle

MAKES 2 KRINGLES, EACH SERVING 8

To bake only one kringle, adjust the oven rack to the middle position. If the dough appears shaggy and dry after adding the sour cream in step 2, add up to 2 tablespoons ice water until the dough is smooth. If the capacity of your food processor is less than 11 cups, pulse the butter and shortening into the dry mixture in two batches at the beginning of step 2.

FILLING

- 1 cup pecans, toasted
- ¾ cup packed light brown sugar
- ¼ teaspoon ground cinnamon
- ⅛ teaspoon salt
- 4 tablespoons (½ stick) unsalted butter, cut into ½-inch pieces and chilled

DOUGH

- 4 cups (20 ounces) unbleached all-purpose flour
- 16 tablespoons (2 sticks) unsalted butter, cut into ½-inch pieces and chilled
- 4 tablespoons vegetable shortening, cut into ½-inch pieces and chilled
- 2 tablespoons confectioners' sugar
- 2¼ teaspoons (about 1 envelope) instant or rapid-rise yeast
- ¾ teaspoon salt
- 2 cups sour cream
- 1 large egg, lightly beaten

GLAZE

- 1 cup confectioners' sugar
- 2 tablespoons whole or low-fat milk
- ½ teaspoon vanilla extract

1. FOR THE FILLING: Process the pecans, brown sugar, cinnamon, and salt in a food processor until the pecans are coarsely ground. Add the butter and pulse until the mixture resembles coarse meal. Transfer to a bowl.

2. FOR THE DOUGH: Add the flour, butter, shortening, confectioners' sugar, yeast, and salt to the empty food processor and pulse until the mixture resembles coarse meal. Transfer to a bowl and stir in the sour cream until a dough forms. Turn the dough out onto a lightly floured counter and divide in half. Pat each half into a 7 by 3-inch rectangle and wrap in plastic wrap. Refrigerate the dough for 30 minutes, then freeze until firm, about 15 minutes.

MAKING KRINGLE

1. Working on a lightly floured counter, roll the dough into a 28 by 5-inch rectangle, with one long side closest to you. The dough should be about ¼ inch thick.

2. Leaving a ½-inch border around the sides and edges, spread half of the filling over the bottom half of the dough.

3. Brush the edge of the uncovered dough with water and fold the dough over the filling, pinching to close the long seam.

4. Fit one end of the folded dough inside the other to make an oval and press to seal.

RATING DECAFFEINATED COFFEES

A great piece of kringle pairs perfectly with a great cup of coffee, and lately we've been wondering whether grocery store decaf coffee has improved as much as the high-octane stuff. We tasted seven nationally distributed supermarket brands, all sold preground, to find out. Tasters sampled each coffee first black, and then with milk. Our top-ranked brands contained only Arabica beans, a lower-caffeine varietal known for good flavor. Surprisingly, one of the cheaper ordinary brands, **Maxwell House Decaf Original Roast**, actually edged out the premium brands to prevail. Tasters praised it as "mellow and smooth" with "detectable complexity," and "a slight nutty aftertaste."

3. Following the photos, roll one dough half into a 28 by 5-inch rectangle, cover the bottom half of the dough strip with half of the filling, leaving a ½ inch border around the sides and edges. Brush the edges with water, fold the dough over the filling, and pinch the seams closed. Shape the dough into an oval, tuck one end inside of the other, and pinch to seal. Transfer the kringle to a parchment-lined rimmed baking sheet, cover with plastic wrap, and refrigerate for at least 4 or up to 12 hours. Repeat with the remaining dough and filling.

4. Adjust the oven racks to the upper-middle and lower-middle positions and heat the oven to 350 degrees. Discard the plastic wrap, brush the kringles with the beaten egg, and bake until golden brown, 40 to 50 minutes, switching and rotating the sheets halfway through. Transfer the kringles to a wire rack and let cool for 30 minutes.

5. FOR THE GLAZE: Whisk the confectioners' sugar, milk, and vanilla in a bowl until smooth. Drizzle the glaze over the kringles. Let the glaze set for 10 minutes. Serve warm or at room temperature. (The kringles can be stored in an airtight container at room temperature for up to 2 days.)

VARIATIONS

Cream Cheese Kringle

Follow the recipe for Pecan Kringle, omitting the pecan filling. In step 1, combine 8 ounces softened cream cheese, ¼ cup granulated sugar, and ½ teaspoon grated lemon zest in a bowl. In step 3, spread half of the cream cheese mixture over the bottom of the dough and continue with the recipe as directed. Repeat with the remaining dough and cream cheese mixture.

Double Berry Kringle

Do not substitute raspberry jam for the preserves; it will leach out of the kringle.

Follow the recipe for Pecan Kringle, omitting the pecan filling. In step 1, combine ½ cup raspberry preserves and ¼ cup finely chopped dried cranberries in a bowl. In step 3, spread half of the preserves mixture over the bottom half of the dough and continue with the recipe as directed. Repeat with the remaining dough and preserves mixture.

OVERNIGHT COFFEE CAKE FOR TWO

A MOIST, BUTTERY SLICE OF COFFEE CAKE IS A breakfast that's pretty hard to beat. But I have two big issues with standard coffee cake recipes, "big" being the operative word. A standard recipe yields enough to serve a crowd, so if you aren't expecting company you're stuck with a lot of extra, and leftover coffee cake doesn't hold up that well after a day or two. They're also a big pain to make. If I don't get up a few hours early (and who wants to on Sunday morning?), by the time the coffee cake is out of the oven it's almost lunchtime. I wanted a scaled-down recipe for moist, richly flavored coffee cake that would provide enough for breakfast, with maybe a snack-size piece leftover, and I wanted to be able to mix the batter the night before and refrigerate it so that all I'd have to do was roll out of bed the next morning and bake it off.

The test kitchen had already developed an overnight sour cream coffee cake (made with all-purpose flour, white and light brown sugar, eggs, butter, sour cream, baking powder, and baking soda) that boasts a moist crumb and sweet, buttery streusel, so all I'd have to do is downsize the recipe and I'd be finished, right? Wrong. Scaling the ingredients back proportionally to accommodate a 6-inch round cake pan instead of a 9-inch was a failure. Tasters were quick to point out the flaws: The streusel sank into the cake and the crumb was dry, not moist. Because of baking's chemical nature, simply cutting a recipe proportionally doesn't always go smoothly, as I had just seen firsthand. I was going to need to let go of the cake's original ratios and rethink the ingredient proportions through good old-fashioned trial and error.

I had been making my coffee cake with one egg, and I wondered if upping the eggs from one to two might add the moisture that was lacking and contribute additional protein for a heartier batter to hold up my currently sinking streusel. No dice. Rather than adding richness and structure, it made the batter too eggy. What if I lessened the flour? I was surprised that a small adjustment was all it needed. Cutting back from ¾ cup to ⅔ cup worked perfectly; the batter was just dense enough to hold up the topping while the cake baked, and the cake came out of the oven moister than before. But tasters agreed it needed more moisture still.

I decided to look at the fat, thinking that increasing the amount of sour cream might be the answer. I increased the sour cream from ¼ cup to ⅓ cup, but my tasters complained the resulting cake was too tangy. I wondered how the cake would turn out if I tinkered with the butter instead. I had been using 1 tablespoon of melted butter, so I tested cakes made with 2 and 3 tablespoons of butter. The batter made with 3 tablespoons of butter baked up into a cake that was too greasy and rich; however, the batter made with 2 tablespoons had just enough fat to bake up to a perfectly tender, moist cake after an overnight stay in the fridge.

My cake was nearly finished—it just needed the streusel topping. A simple combination of light brown sugar, granulated sugar, flour, and butter spiced with cinnamon and enriched with crunchy walnuts did the trick. Fresh out of the oven—with no dirty dishes left to do—this tender coffee cake is the perfect start to any day.

—DAN ZUCCARELLO, *America's Test Kitchen Books*

Overnight Coffee Cake for Two

MAKES ONE 6-INCH COFFEE CAKE

You will need one 6-inch round cake pan for this recipe.

STREUSEL

- 1 tablespoon light brown sugar
- 1 tablespoon granulated sugar
- 1 tablespoon unbleached all-purpose flour
- 1 tablespoon unsalted butter, cut into ½-inch pieces and chilled
- ¼ teaspoon ground cinnamon
- 2 tablespoons chopped walnuts, pecans, or almonds

CAKE

- ⅔ cup (3⅓ ounces) unbleached all-purpose flour
- ½ teaspoon baking powder
- ¼ teaspoon baking soda
- ⅛ teaspoon ground cinnamon
- ⅛ teaspoon salt
- ¼ cup sour cream
- 1 large egg, at room temperature
- 3 tablespoons light brown sugar
- 2 tablespoons unsalted butter, melted and cooled
- 1 tablespoon granulated sugar

1. FOR THE STREUSEL: Using your fingers, combine the brown sugar, granulated sugar, flour, butter, and cinnamon in a small bowl until the mixture resembles coarse meal. Stir in the nuts and set aside.

2. FOR THE CAKE: Grease a 6-inch round cake pan, then line the bottom with parchment paper. Whisk the flour, baking powder, baking soda, cinnamon, and salt together in a medium bowl. Whisk the sour cream, egg, brown sugar, melted butter, and granulated sugar together in another bowl until smooth. Gently fold the sour cream mixture into the flour mixture with a rubber spatula until just combined. (The batter will be lumpy with a few spots of dry flour; do not overmix.)

3. Scrape the batter into the prepared pan and smooth the top. Sprinkle the streusel evenly over the top of the cake. Wrap the pan tightly with plastic wrap and refrigerate for up to 24 hours or freeze for up to 1 month (do not thaw the frozen cake before baking). (To bake the cake right away, do not wrap the pan with plastic wrap. Bake the cake as directed in step 4, reducing the baking time to 25 to 30 minutes.)

4. When ready to bake, adjust an oven rack to the lower-middle position and heat the oven to 350 degrees. Unwrap the cake and bake until the top is golden and a toothpick inserted into the center comes out with a few crumbs attached, 30 to 35 minutes if refrigerated, or 40 to 45 minutes if frozen, rotating the pan halfway through.

5. Let the cake cool in the pan for 10 minutes. Run a small knife around the edge of the cake, then flip it out onto a wire rack. Peel off the parchment paper, flip the cake right-side up, and let cool completely before serving.

VARIATIONS

Overnight Lemon-Blueberry Coffee Cake for Two
You can substitute frozen blueberries for the fresh ones; they must be thawed, rinsed, and dried, but they do not need to be tossed with flour.

Toss ¼ cup fresh blueberries with ½ teaspoon unbleached all-purpose flour. Follow the recipe for Overnight Coffee Cake for Two, adding ¼ teaspoon grated lemon zest to the dry ingredients and the floured berries to the finished batter in step 2.

Overnight Cranberry-Orange Coffee Cake for Two
Follow the recipe for Overnight Coffee Cake for Two, adding ¼ teaspoon grated orange zest to the dry ingredients and 3 tablespoons dried cranberries to the finished batter in step 2.

LIGHT CHEESE BREAD

THE ULTIMATE CHEESE BREAD IS ADDICTIVE. MOIST and hearty, a perfect slice is studded throughout with pockets of cheese and topped with a crunchy, cheesy crust. It's a multi-purpose baked good, perfect toasted for breakfast topped with an egg, as a snack, or for serving alongside a bowl of soup. But we all know addictive, crave-worthy foods are rarely diet food. (After all, most of us can stop after one apple, but cookies? That's another story.) Most cheese bread recipes require so much cheese and butter that the amount of fat in a serving goes beyond the acceptable for a snack or side item. I set out to make a cheese bread that had a moist crumb and boasted a good cheesy tang, but I wanted it to be light enough that I could enjoy it without the guilt.

I began by reviewing the test kitchen's full-fat recipe for cheese bread. First I tried cutting back the cheese and using low-fat dairy ingredients. The original recipe called for 4 ounces each of shredded Parmesan and cheddar, 1¼ cups whole milk, 3 tablespoons butter, and to top it all off, ¾ cup sour cream. That makes for one rich loaf. I reduced the Parmesan by half, changed to low-fat milk and low-fat sour cream, and swapped out the full-fat cheddar in favor of the 50 percent reduced-fat variety. I wasn't surprised when this bread turned out to be a flavorless doorstop. After all, I had cut out most of the richness and cheesiness. I needed to look deeper into my bag of bread baking tricks.

Looking over other quick-bread recipes, I noticed that buttermilk was turning up in a lot of ingredient lists. Why? It lends both tangy flavor and nice richness—and conveniently for me, it's also low in fat. I decided to see how far I could go on cutting back the fat in the dairy products, so I nixed the milk, butter, and sour cream for my next test and I used just buttermilk (I left the one egg as is). I also went back to regular extra-sharp cheddar—tasters all agreed that even if I had to use less of the full-fat version, the reduced-fat cheddar wasn't working here. The full-fat cheese returned the great cheesy flavor to my loaf (3 ounces did the trick), and it was nicely complemented by the tang of the buttermilk. But without the butter, my cheese bread had a crumb that was on the spongy side. Clearly, some fat had to be added back into the mix. Oil pops up in a lot of quick breads, and since I wanted to avoid the saturated fat in the butter if I could, I tried supplementing some of the buttermilk with canola oil. A few tests proved it took just 1 tablespoon of canola oil to reclaim some of the richness and moisture of full-fat cheese bread. This moist, cheesy loaf with a nice crumb was definitely on the right track. However, the flavor of my loaf still needed some finessing.

To enhance the flavor of the cheese, I added ¼ teaspoon of dry mustard and a pinch of cayenne pepper. For a rich flavor and good color in the crust, I revisited the Parmesan cheese. At first, I just sprinkled some on top of the batter before putting my loaf pan into the oven. This was fine, but not outstanding. Then I hit on the idea of coating the pan's bottom with cheese as well, guaranteeing a cheesy, crispy exterior all the way around. But how little cheese could I get away with? After some trial and error, I decided that a few tablespoons for the pan, a few tablespoons for the top, and about ¼ cup mixed into the batter provided a good nuttiness and saltiness throughout my loaf and great exterior texture without adding too much fat.

After 45 minutes in the oven, my cheese bread had a moist crumb and full, cheesy flavor—and with just 6 grams of fat (about half the amount of the original) and only 170 calories per slice, this was one indulgence I wasn't worried about getting addicted to.

—ERIKA BRUCE, *America's Test Kitchen Books*

Light Cheese Bread

MAKES ONE 8-INCH LOAF

Shredding the Parmesan on the large holes of a box grater and sprinkling it over the top of this bread adds a nice texture and helps prevent the cheese from burning; do not grate it fine or use pre-grated Parmesan. The texture of this bread improves as it cools, so resist the urge to slice the loaf while it is piping hot.

2 ounces Parmesan cheese, shredded on
   the large holes of a box grater (about ⅔ cup)
2½ cups (12½ ounces) unbleached all-purpose flour
1 tablespoon baking powder
1 teaspoon salt
¼ teaspoon dry mustard
⅛ teaspoon cayenne pepper
⅛ teaspoon black pepper
3 ounces extra-sharp cheddar cheese,
   cut into ¼-inch cubes (about ¾ cup)

1¼ cups low-fat buttermilk
1 tablespoon canola oil
1 large egg

1. Adjust an oven rack to the middle position and heat the oven to 350 degrees. Lightly coat an 8½ by 4½-inch loaf pan with vegetable oil spray, sprinkle 3 tablespoons of the Parmesan evenly over the bottom of the pan, and set aside.

2. Whisk the flour, baking powder, salt, mustard, cayenne, and black pepper together in a large bowl. Stir in 3 tablespoons more Parmesan and the cheddar, breaking up any clumps. In a medium bowl, whisk the buttermilk, oil, and egg together until smooth. Gently fold the buttermilk mixture into the flour mixture with a rubber spatula. (Do not overmix.) The batter will be heavy and thick.

3. Scrape the batter into the prepared pan and smooth the top. Sprinkle the remaining Parmesan evenly over the top. Bake until golden brown and a toothpick inserted into the center comes out clean, 45 to 50 minutes, rotating the pan halfway through.

4. Let the loaf cool in the pan for 5 minutes, then turn it out onto a wire rack and let cool for 1 hour before serving. (The bread can be wrapped tightly in plastic wrap and stored at room temperature for up to 3 days.)

VARIATIONS

Light Cheese Bread with Roasted Red Peppers and Scallions

Be sure to pat the roasted red peppers dry before adding them to the buttermilk.

Follow the recipe for Light Cheese Bread, adding ½ cup jarred roasted red peppers, drained, patted dry, and chopped, and 2 scallions, minced, to the buttermilk mixture.

Light Cheese Bread with Chipotle Chiles

Follow the recipe for Light Cheese Bread, omitting the cayenne pepper and adding 2 teaspoons minced chipotle chiles in adobo sauce to the buttermilk mixture.

Light Cheese Bread with Sun-Dried Tomatoes and Garlic

Follow the recipe for Light Cheese Bread, adding ¼ cup chopped sun-dried tomatoes and 2 garlic cloves, minced, to the buttermilk mixture.

SPROUTED GRAIN BREAD

WHILE BREAD MADE FROM SPROUTED GRAINS ISN'T new—a few commercial bakers have been making it for over 40 years, some of them noting it's been around since Biblical times—its popularity has really jumped in the past decade as people try to eat more healthfully. Word has gotten out that sprouted grain bread goes beyond your typical whole-grain loaf. How? Sprouting grains (which is done by hydrating whole grains or seeds to allow them to start germinating; think of seedlings) releases enzymes that boost vitamin content and make the vitamins more accessible to your body. Sprouted grain bread also has a unique earthy, complex flavor and nutty texture that makes it a great change of pace. So what's the downside? First, it comes with a hefty price tag—often more than $4 a loaf—and second, supermarket loaves are often sold frozen. As much as I like the idea of eating sprouted grain bread, I am rarely willing to purchase an expensive, frozen loaf of bread, no matter how good it is for me. However, I had to wonder, could I come up with my own easy-to-follow recipe so I could enjoy fresh-baked sprouted grain bread more regularly?

Despite its rising popularity, sprouted grain bread still isn't widely consumed, so I was a little concerned about finding existing recipes to give me a jumping-off point. However, with a little digging I was able to find a few, both by notable bakers and adventurous home cooks. These recipes gave me hope, but they also caused considerable doubt about how easy this recipe could be. While some vaguely called for "assorted grains" (which produced wildly different results depending upon which grains were chosen), others demanded specific, hard-to-find specialty grains (making them just as expensive as a store-bought loaf). Given that this kind of bread takes almost a week to make (sprouting the grains or seeds can take up to four days), these recipes just didn't seem worth the effort. My goal was a tall order: I wanted an affordable, easy-to-make sprouted grain bread recipe with an appealingly fresh, nutty flavor and texture.

According to most of the recipes I found, the process for making the bread should go something like this: A mix of whole grains and possibly beans (such as wheat berries, rye berries, barley, spelt, millet, amaranth, lentils, chickpeas) is soaked overnight to hydrate and activate the dormant germ. Then the grains are drained and

left at room temperature anywhere from six hours to four days until small "tails" sprout. Next, these sprouted grains are ground to a paste, mixed with yeast, salt, and sometimes honey, and kneaded into a dough. Following standard bread baking procedure the dough is then allowed to rise until doubled in size, shaped, allowed to rise a second time, and baked. With the basics set out, I started by focusing on the grains.

A number of recipes called for seven or more grains, but I doubted that many grains was an absolute necessity for making a complexly flavored loaf. So I limited myself to using up to four grains. Each one would have to make a noticeable contribution to the bread, whether in terms of taste or texture, to make the cut. After scouring my local market for whole grains, I rounded up lentils, popping corn (an often-overlooked whole grain), wheat berries, quinoa, and dried chickpeas. After letting them all sprout, which took a few days, I made a loaf using 100 percent of each sprouted grain. The wheat berries, lentils, and quinoa all produced great-tasting loaves, each with a distinct, satisfying flavor. The corn and chickpeas, meanwhile, turned out sour-tasting bread that won little favor with tasters. With the three approved grains nailed down, I mixed and matched various ratios until I hit upon a winning combination. With 50 percent wheat berries, and 25 percent each lentils and quinoa, I had a balanced loaf that was sweet,

NOTES FROM THE TEST KITCHEN

PREPARING SPROUTED GRAINS
After combining the grains and water, store the rehydrated grains, covered, at room temperature, rinsing and draining them daily until small sprouts appear on each type of grain, about 3 days (left). (Note that not every individual grain needs to sprout, just a few examples of each type of grain. We have found that the lentils are usually the slowest to sprout.) Before making the bread, process the sprouted grains in a food processor to a smooth, sticky paste (right), 2 to 3 minutes, scraping down the bowl often.

SPROUTED GRAINS

PROCESSED GRAINS

SPROUTED GRAIN BREAD

nutty, earthy and satisfying. Unfortunately, it was also absolutely leaden.

While certainly disappointing, the results weren't altogether surprising. Since a dough's ability to trap gas and rise is directly related to its gluten content (a bread dough with more gluten can trap more gas and thus bakes into a taller, lighter loaf), my almost-gluten-free dough (with just a small amount contributed by the wheat berries) was destined to fall short. Some recipes suggested using vital wheat gluten, a powder of pure gluten derived from wheat flour, to fix this shortcoming. I located the hard-to-find ingredient and made a loaf. While the result was certainly taller than before, the vital wheat gluten gave the bread a rubbery crumb and strange bitter flavor. It definitely wasn't worth the effort it took to track down.

I turned my attention to using a more conventional form of gluten in my recipe: flour. But I had to be careful; I wanted my loaf to have the nutritional benefits and taste of sprouted grains, not flour, so I needed to pick a flour with a high percentage of gluten so I could minimize the amount I had to add. Bread flour was the answer. After a few more tests, I found the winning combination was about 3 parts sprouted grains to 2 parts flour. This gave me a tall, classic-looking loaf of bread that had complex sprouted grain flavor, and a surprisingly tender crumb.

The hard part was over, so I worked on finessing the texture. A few store-bought brands get added crunch by mixing a portion of unprocessed grains into the dough. I tried leaving one-quarter of my sprouted grains unprocessed, but I found when any of these landed on the exterior of the bread, they dried out during baking and became hard enough to crack a tooth. Next I tried swapping in a mix of sunflower, pumpkin, and sesame seeds for the unprocessed grains. Tasters agreed this was the best loaf yet. I mixed a portion of the seeds into the dough and sprinkled the rest on top to give the crust added crunch and flavor. A little egg white wash ensured the seeds would stay put and a few quick scores across the top before baking ensured a finished, professional looking loaf of bread.

After sprouting my way through pounds and pounds of grains, I could finally sit down and enjoy a slice of my fresh, never-frozen sprouted grain bread.

—DAN SOUZA, *America's Test Kitchen Books*

Sprouted Grain Bread
MAKES ONE 9-INCH LOAF

Note that this bread can take up to 4 days to make, although most of the time is hands off. Do not substitute all-purpose flour for the bread flour.

SPROUTED GRAINS

- ¾ cup wheat berries
- ¼ cup quinoa
- ¼ cup brown lentils
- 2 cups cool water

DOUGH

- ½ cup warm water (110 degrees)
- 3 tablespoons honey
- ¼ cup unsalted sunflower seeds, toasted
- 2 tablespoons pumpkin seeds, toasted
- 2 tablespoons sesame seeds, toasted
- 1¾–2¼ cups (9⅔–12⅔ ounces) bread flour
- 2¼ teaspoons (about 1 envelope) instant or rapid-rise yeast
- 1½ teaspoons salt
  Vegetable oil spray
- 1 large egg white, whisked together with 1 teaspoon water, for brushing

1. FOR THE SPROUTED GRAINS: Combine the wheat berries, quinoa, lentils, and water in a large container, cover, and let soak at room temperature until the grains are fully hydrated and softened, at least 12 hours or up to 24 hours.

2. Drain the grains through a fine-mesh strainer then return to the container. Cover and let sit at room temperature, rinsing and draining the grains daily, until small sprouts appear on each type of grain, 1 to 3 days.

3. Process the sprouted grains in a food processor to a smooth, sticky paste, 2 to 3 minutes, scraping down the bowl often.

4. FOR THE DOUGH: Whisk the water and honey together in a liquid measuring cup. Combine the sunflower, pumpkin, and sesame seeds in a small bowl. Combine the processed sprouted grains, 1¾ cups of the bread flour, yeast, and salt together in a standing mixer fitted with the dough hook.

5. With the mixer on low speed, add the water mixture and mix until the dough comes together, about

2 minutes. Stop the mixer, cover the bowl with plastic wrap (no need to remove it from the mixer), and let sit at room temperature for 20 minutes.

6. Remove the plastic wrap and knead the dough on medium-low speed until it is smooth and elastic, about 8 minutes. If after 4 minutes more flour is needed, add the remaining ½ cup bread flour, 2 tablespoons at a time, until the dough clears the sides of the bowl but sticks to the bottom. Add 6 tablespoons of the seeds and continue to knead until incorporated, 1 to 2 minutes.

7. Turn the dough out onto a lightly floured counter and knead by hand to form a smooth, round ball. Place the dough in a large, lightly greased bowl and cover with greased plastic wrap. Let rise in a warm place until nearly doubled in size, 1½ to 2 hours.

8. Spray a 9 by 5-inch loaf pan with vegetable oil spray. Turn the dough out onto a lightly floured counter. gently press the dough into a 9-inch square, roll into a tight cylinder, and pinch the seam closed.

9. Place the loaf, seam side down, in the prepared pan. Spray the loaf lightly with vegetable oil spray, cover loosely with greased plastic wrap, and let rise in a warm place until the loaf has nearly doubled in size, 45 to 75 minutes. Meanwhile, adjust an oven rack to the lower-middle position and heat the oven to 350 degrees.

10. Brush the loaf with the egg white–water mixture and sprinkle with the remaining 2 tablespoons seeds. Cut three ¼-inch-deep diagonal slashes across the top of the loaf with a razor blade or sharp knife, then spray lightly with water.

11. Bake until the crust is golden and the center of the bread registers 210 degrees on an instant-read thermometer, 40 to 50 minutes, rotating the loaf halfway through baking.

12. Cool the loaf in the pan for 15 minutes, then flip out onto a wire rack and let cool to room temperature, about 2 hours, before serving. (Once all of the grains have sprouted in step 2, they can be thoroughly patted dry with paper towels, transferred to a clean airtight container, and refrigerated for up to 1 week before being processed into a paste. Alternatively, do not let the dough rise in step 7, but refrigerate it overnight or for up to 16 hours; let the dough sit at room temperature for 30 minutes, then continue with step 8.)

CHEWY GRANOLA BARS

WHETHER GRABBED ON THE WAY OUT THE DOOR as an on-the-go breakfast, packed into a lunch, or eaten as an after-school snack, a chewy granola bar is a convenient and healthy food choice for kids and adults alike. I remember eating my fair share growing up, but when I recently bought a box from the supermarket, I was pretty disappointed with what I found. Not only were the flavor and texture one-dimensional, but I realized after reading the label that these "healthy" bars were packed with processed ingredients and preservatives. Another visit to the supermarket aisles wasn't any more encouraging: I was hard-pressed to find a chewy granola bar that didn't contain a laundry list of unpronounceable (and unappealing) ingredients. Instead of wasting any more time in the supermarket reading ingredient labels, I decided I would be better off in the test kitchen, developing my own chewy granola bar recipe. My parameters were simple: I wanted a chewy, nut- and oat-packed granola bar that would appeal to both adults and kids, require minimal effort, and use readily available pantry ingredients.

A little outside research turned up a long list of chewy granola bar recipes, but they all required ingredients like brown rice syrup and agave nectar. The test kitchen already had a couple of great crunchy granola bar recipes, so that seemed like my best place to start. These recipes follow a pretty straightforward method. Nuts and oats are toasted in a skillet with oil or butter until fragrant and lightly browned and then transferred to a bowl. Next, a mix of honey and brown sugar is cooked in the skillet until fully dissolved. The two mixtures are then quickly combined, patted into a foil-lined 13 by 9-inch baking pan, and baked in a 300-degree oven for about 25 minutes. Once slightly cooled, the mixture is cut into neat bars, which are then cooled to the perfect brittle, crunchy texture. Given the short list of ingredients, it seemed that the binder (in this case honey and brown sugar) had to be largely responsible for the texture of these bars. Hoping to come up with just the right chewy granola bar binder, I grabbed an assortment of sweeteners and headed into the test kitchen.

My initial thought was that the crunchy texture was a result of the brown sugar recrystallizing as it cooled. By this logic, I figured if I dropped the brown sugar in favor of all honey (naturally a liquid) my bars would maintain a chewy texture once cooled. For my next test I heated honey alone, just enough to make it loose and easy to combine with the oats. But one bite of the resulting bars and my excitement faded. These all-honey bars were all crunch and no chew. I tried substituting maple syrup and molasses for the honey, but got equally disappointing results.

Taking a step back, I wondered if those 25 minutes in the oven weren't a larger cause of crunchiness, since baking would drive out moisture. Could I keep the chew by avoiding the oven? For my next batch, I followed the same method, but instead of popping the pan into the oven, I let it sit at room temperature until the honey cooled. These bars fell apart in a sticky mess; the honey was too loose. For the next test, I stirred the oats with honey that I had reduced in the skillet by about half; maybe double-strength honey would do the trick. When freshly mixed, these bars looked and tasted promising. But after 20 minutes of cooling, these bars were as crunchy as my early batches. To add insult to injury, they were also cloyingly sweet. I headed back to the drawing board.

While hanging around the test kitchen, I noticed a fellow test cook preparing a batch of turtle brownies. As she pressed a pecan half into a gooey, sticky layer of caramel, the light bulb went off. Caramel, a mixture of white sugar cooked to roughly 350 degrees and a liquid (either half-and-half or cream) can be made to almost any consistency, from hard candy to a silky sauce. And caramel maintains that consistency once cooled to room temperature so it would be much easier to predict the final texture of a caramel-bound bar. Since I had a pretty good idea of how chewy I wanted the bars to be, I tested ratios of sugar to half-and-half until I had a caramel of the proper consistency (something that fell right between caramel ice cream sauce and toffee). I eagerly stirred this caramel into my working oat-nut mixture, pressed it into the pan, and let the caramel cool. Voilà! Thirty minutes later I had bars that, while not perfect, were miles ahead of anything I had made before. They had just the right amount of chew and a slightly smoky sweetness that played well with the oats and nuts. Now I just needed to refine the oat mixture.

The test kitchen's original crunchy granola bar recipe

I had been working with contained 3 cups of rolled oats and a handful of chopped almonds. With the help of the oven, all these oats toasted up nicely to create perfectly crunchy bars. But in my no-bake bar, all these oats were overwhelming, and they tasted slightly raw and leaden. I needed another component that could replace some of the oats with a contrasting texture and add a toasty flavor. I figured my answer would be on the cereal aisle. After much testing, I landed on a winner: Multigrain Cheerios. These crunchy rings added a nice toasty flavor and helped reinforce the hearty feel of my bars, and at the same time their airiness lightened the bars' texture. To keep things interesting, I added a mix of nuts (tasters liked almonds, cashews, and pumpkin seeds the best), and came up with a few appealing variations with additions like peanut butter, dried fruits, and ginger. With dozens and dozens of failed pans of granola behind me, I had finally created a chewy, easy-to-make, pantry granola bar I could call my own.

—DAN SOUZA, *America's Test Kitchen Books*

Chewy Granola Bars

MAKES 16 BARS

Do not substitute quick-cooking or instant rolled oats in this recipe, or the granola will taste sandy rather than chewy. You can substitute 1½ cups Rice Krispies cereal for the Cheerios if desired.

- ⅓ cup slivered almonds
- ⅓ cup unsalted cashews, chopped coarse
- ¼ cup unsalted pumpkin seeds
- 3 tablespoons unsalted butter
- 2 cups old-fashioned rolled oats (see note)
- 1½ cups Multigrain Cheerios
- ¼ teaspoon salt
- ⅓ cup water
- 1 cup (7 ounces) sugar
- ¼ cup half-and-half
- 1 teaspoon vanilla extract

1. Following the photos on page 256, line a 13 by 9-inch baking pan with a foil sling and coat lightly with vegetable oil spray. Toast the almonds, cashews, and pumpkin seeds in a 12-inch skillet over medium

CHEWY GRANOLA BARS

heat, stirring often, until fragrant and golden brown, 5 to 7 minutes. Transfer the toasted nuts and seeds to a large bowl.

2. Add the butter to the skillet and melt over medium heat. Stir in the oats and cook, stirring often, until golden and fragrant, 4 to 6 minutes. Transfer the toasted oats to the bowl with the toasted nuts and seeds and stir in the Cheerios and salt.

3. Pour the water into a clean heavy-bottomed medium saucepan. Following the photos, pour the

NOTES FROM THE TEST KITCHEN

MAKING CARAMEL

1. Pour the water into a clean heavy-bottomed medium saucepan, then pour the sugar into the center of the pan (don't let it hit the pan sides). Gently stir the sugar with a clean heatproof spatula to wet it thoroughly.

2. Bring the mixture to a boil over medium-high heat and cook, without stirring, until the sugar has dissolved and the caramel has a faint golden color (about 300 degrees on a candy thermometer), 4 to 8 minutes.

3. Reduce the heat to medium-low and continue to cook, stirring only as needed, until the caramel has a dark amber color (about 350 degrees on a candy thermometer), 1 to 3 minutes.

4. Off the heat, whisk in the half-and-half (the mixture will steam and bubble vigorously) until the caramel is smooth and just barely bubbling, 30 to 60 seconds.

sugar into the center of the pan (don't let it hit the pan sides), and gently stir with a clean heatproof spatula to wet the sugar thoroughly. Bring to a boil over medium-high heat and cook, without stirring, until the sugar has dissolved completely and the caramel has a faint golden color (about 300 degrees on a candy thermometer), 4 to 8 minutes.

4. Reduce the heat to medium-low and continue to cook the sugar-water mixture, stirring only as needed, until the caramel has a dark amber color (about 350 degrees on a candy thermometer), 1 to 3 minutes. Off the heat, whisk in the half-and-half (the caramel will steam and bubble vigorously) until smooth and just barely bubbling, 30 to 60 seconds. Whisk in the vanilla.

5. Working quickly, stir the hot caramel into the nut-oat mixture until thoroughly combined. Transfer the mixture to the prepared baking pan and pack very firmly into an even layer. Let the granola cool completely, about 30 minutes. Remove the granola from the dish using the foil, cut into 16 bars, and serve. (The bars can be stored in an airtight container, between layers of parchment paper to prevent sticking, for up to 5 days.)

VARIATIONS

Chewy Peanut Butter Granola Bars
Follow the recipe for Chewy Granola Bars, substituting ⅔ cup unsalted dry-roasted peanuts, chopped coarse, for the almonds and cashews. Add 2 tablespoons chunky peanut butter to the caramel with the vanilla in step 4.

Chewy Ginger-Cardamom Granola Bars
Follow the recipe for Chewy Granola Bars, stirring 2 tablespoons coarsely chopped crystallized ginger, ¾ teaspoon ground ginger, and ¼ teaspoon ground cardamom into the toasted nut-oat mixture with the Cheerios in step 2.

Chewy Harvest Fruit Granola Bars
We like the combination of cherries, cranberries, and apricots, but any dried fruit can be used here.

Follow the recipe for Chewy Granola Bars, stirring ½ cup dried fruit, chopped coarse, into the toasted nut-oat mixture with the Cheerios in step 2.

CAT HEAD BISCUITS

NOT LONG AGO, I DID A DOUBLE TAKE WHEN I SPIED "cat head biscuits" on a billboard advertising a cafe near Greensboro, North Carolina. Say what?! "They're a big ol' biscuit," the waiter told me when I reached the place. "Big as a cat's head." A few minutes later, biscuits arrived warm from the oven—huge and as soft and fluffy as a dinner roll. The pull-apart sides were like pillows, the tops golden brown and craggy, the insides tender and moist. The problem? I'd have to travel nearly 1,000 miles to eat them. Unless I came up with a recipe of my own.

Cat head biscuits were born out of Appalachian frugality in a place and era (early 20th century) where butter—and time—were extravagances. The cook rubbed lard into flour and leaveners and then stirred in sour milk to make a wet dough. She (or he) pinched off large blobs, nestled them in a cast-iron skillet, and baked.

I made a recipe based on those I'd found: 3 cups all-purpose flour, 1 tablespoon baking powder, ½ teaspoon baking soda, ¾ cup shortening, and 1¼ cups buttermilk. Yield: six large, soft biscuits, their downy texture thanks in part to the acidic, tenderizing buttermilk. But tasters rejected the shortening's "strong artificial flavor." My next batch, made with butter, corrected flavor but screwed up the texture: These were flaky, not fluffy. I compromised with 8 tablespoons of butter plus 4 of shortening. Putting the shortening back in tenderized the biscuits—but not enough.

Could the flour even things up? One recipe specified "Southern flour." I tracked down White Lily, a famous Southern brand. White Lily has several traits all-purpose doesn't: One, lower protein content, which yields a more delicate baked good. Two, bleach (while some all-purpose flours are bleached, the test kitchen's favorite is Pillsbury Unbleached), which inhibits gluten formation, increasing tenderness. Three, fine milling (delicacy again). Finally, phosphate, which contributes to rise and lightness when mixed with an acid (here, buttermilk). So it was no surprise that the next batch, made with White Lily, produced biscuits that were light as air.

But unless you live in the South, White Lily is hard to find. Might cake flour (also bleached, fine-milled, and with an even lower protein content) approximate it? Unfortunately, cake flour produced a cottony biscuit that barely held together. An equal mix of cake and all-purpose flours got me back to a soft, fluffy biscuit.

Much more than the ingredients, the techniques used to make these biscuits were strange. Most biscuits specify cold fat, which is "cut" into the dry ingredients. Not these. Here I was rubbing in softened butter with my (warm) hands. Why did this work? In traditional biscuits, the chilled fat promotes flaky texture by melting in the oven, forming pockets of steam. For cat head biscuits, I was after fluffy, not flaky. I also puzzled over why cat head biscuits weren't quickly kneaded until the dough coalesced. Let's see: Kneading develops gluten, which develops structure, which was what I didn't want. Nor was kneading practical given the sticky, wet dough. Rather than stamp out biscuits or pinch off hunks of dough, I scooped out six hefty lumps. I also experimented with pans and found a basic cake tin worked fine. Because the biscuits were snuggled together, the sides stayed soft as the biscuits baked. These biscuits were light, fluffy, and true to name, big as a cat's head.

—CALI RICH, *Cook's Country*

Cat Head Biscuits

MAKES 6

This recipe will also work with 3 cups White Lily flour in place of both the all-purpose and cake flours.

- 1½ cups (7½ ounces) unbleached all-purpose flour
- 1½ cups (6 ounces) cake flour
- 1 tablespoon baking powder
- 1 teaspoon salt
- ½ teaspoon baking soda
- 8 tablespoons (1 stick) unsalted butter, cut into ½-inch pieces and softened
- 4 tablespoons vegetable shortening, cut into ½-inch pieces
- 1¼ cups buttermilk (see page 103)

1. Adjust an oven rack to the upper-middle position and heat the oven to 425 degrees. Grease a 9-inch cake pan. Combine the flours, baking powder, salt, and baking soda in a large bowl. Rub the butter and shortening into the flour mixture until the mixture resembles coarse meal. Stir in the buttermilk until combined.

2. Following the photo, use a greased ½-cup measure or large spring-loaded ice cream scoop to transfer 6 heaping portions of dough into the prepared pan, placing 5 scoops around the pan's perimeter and 1 scoop in the center.

3. Bake until the biscuits are puffed and golden brown, 20 to 25 minutes. Cool in the pan for 10 minutes, then transfer to a wire rack. Serve. (The biscuits can be stored in an airtight container at room temperature for up to 2 days.)

NOTES FROM THE TEST KITCHEN

FORMING CAT HEAD BISCUITS

Many biscuits are kneaded, rolled, stamped out, and then baked. For Cat Head Biscuits, we scoop the sticky dough and nestle the biscuits in a cake pan. (A spring-loaded ice cream scoop does the job well.)

THE SECRET TO FLUFFY CAT HEAD BISCUITS

Southern bakers swear by White Lily all-purpose flour, which they say makes biscuits soft and downy, exactly the texture we sought for our Cat Head Biscuits. But what if you don't live in the South and can't easily get your hands on a bag? We found we could replicate it by combining equal amounts of ordinary all-purpose flour (made from a mix of high- and low-gluten wheats) and cake flour (a soft, fine-textured flour).

WHITE LILY
The soft and fluffy standard-bearer

ALL-PURPOSE FLOUR
Contributes structure

CAKE FLOUR
Contributes softness

CRACKLIN' CORNBREAD

SOUTHERNERS ARE PURISTS ABOUT CORNBREAD. Flour and sugar are an abomination, and if you don't bake the batter in a hot, greased cast-iron skillet (for the crispest crust possible), you might as well wear a "Yankee" sticker on your forehead. Among the most beloved variations is "cracklin' cornbread," which is speckled with crispy, salty bits of rendered pork skin. It's hard to argue that there's a version of cornbread much better. It's a perfect match with chili, barbecue, meatloaf, or just all by itself. If you've got the time to render the skin to make it from scratch, you're in for a treat. But if you don't, relying on commercial cracklings, or pork rinds, to save time is definitely *not* the answer—the two are about as similar as plastic roses are to a fragrant blossom. Could I duplicate this cornbread to make it a weeknight possibility without making the cracklings?

As a jumping-off point, I used the test kitchen recipe for Southern skillet cornbread. For that recipe, the test kitchen made a few key discoveries. Although stone-ground cornmeal has a great pure corn flavor, it made a cornbread that was too gritty; regular, finely ground cornmeal was the way to go. Buttermilk was preferable to milk (it added a sharp tang that worked well with the corn), and a combination of butter (for flavor) and vegetable oil (which can withstand high heat without burning) worked best for the fat. A couple of eggs and 1 teaspoon each of baking soda and baking powder produced a cornbread with just the right lift and texture.

From there, I started experimenting with ingredients that might add the same flavor as cracklings. Among my more bizarre (and least successful) mock cracklings were Fritos that I fried in bacon grease. A more reasonable, though also unsuccessful attempt, involved chopped salt pork—it was closer but, alas, it was too salty and tough. Fried bacon, however, added flecks of chewy, salty pork throughout. My cornbread really started to crackle when I replaced the ¼ cup of butter in our original recipe with the same amount of bacon fat I'd rendered. Now the smokiness was really in the forefront.

The ingredients were set, but I wasn't quite finished perfecting my recipe. During testing, the cornbread sometimes stuck. (Hey, we don't all have perfectly

seasoned skillets.) Then I discovered a neat trick: When the skillet and 1 tablespoon oil were good and hot, instead of pouring the batter, I dolloped it in. Adding the batter in spoonfuls helped the oil stay on the bottom of the pan (rather than being pushed to the sides), which ensured the cornbread's easy release. After about 15 minutes in a hot 450-degree oven, I had a perfect round of cracklin' cornbread. I turned out the dark golden bread five minutes after it was done, so it wouldn't steam and soften in the skillet. There was really only one way to serve it: crunchy crust side up.
—MEGHAN ERWIN, *Cook's Country*

Cracklin' Cornbread

SERVES 10

You will need a 10-inch ovensafe skillet for this recipe; for the crunchiest crust, bake the cornbread in a cast-iron pan. Avoid coarsely ground cornmeal, which will make the cornbread too gritty.

 6   slices bacon, chopped fine
2¼   cups (11¼ ounces) cornmeal (see note)
 1   teaspoon baking powder
 1   teaspoon baking soda
 ½   teaspoon salt
 2   cups buttermilk
 ¼   cup vegetable oil
 2   large eggs, lightly beaten

1. Adjust an oven rack to the middle position and heat the oven to 450 degrees. Cook the bacon in a 10-inch ovensafe skillet over medium heat until crisp, about 8 minutes. Transfer the bacon to a paper towel–lined plate. Pour off the fat from the skillet, reserving ¼ cup.

2. Combine the cornmeal, baking powder, baking soda, and salt in a large bowl. Whisk in the buttermilk, 3 tablespoons of the oil, the reserved bacon fat, eggs, and crisp bacon.

3. Heat the remaining 1 tablespoon oil in the empty skillet over medium-high heat until just smoking. Spoon the cornmeal mixture, ½ cup at a time, into the skillet. Transfer the skillet to the oven and bake until the top begins to crack and the sides are golden brown, 12 to 16 minutes. Cool the cornbread in the pan for 5 minutes, then turn it out onto wire rack. Serve.

PASTA WITH PECORINO AND BLACK PEPPER

MY GO-TO PANTRY MEAL IS AS SIMPLE AS IT GETS: Boil some pasta, toss it with a quick drizzle of olive oil and some good, sharp cheese, and voilà—a light dinner that, while no one would mistake it for haute cuisine, is satisfying nonetheless. Recently at Lupa, Mario Batali and Joe Bastianich's New York trattoria, I tried *pasta alla cacio e pepe* (pasta with cheese and pepper), a dish that took the same concept to new heights. Described by the waiter as a popular Roman "spaghetti party" dish often thrown together to cap off a night on the town, it combined long, thin pasta with Pecorino Romano and fresh-cracked black pepper. The strands came napped in a barely creamy sauce boasting intense cheese flavor and speckled with the pepper. If results like these were possible with a real recipe (or even a few guidelines), I was done noodling around on my own.

An Internet search turned up dozens of approaches, including one from Batali: Toss a pound of cooked pasta with ¼ cup of olive oil and 2 tablespoons of butter, add plenty of grated cheese and black pepper along with pasta water to keep it moist, toss, and serve. Maybe the chefs at his restaurant have superior skills (or Batali is withholding something); when I tried his recipe, I couldn't get it to work. Instead of emulsifying into a creamy sauce after being tossed into the hot pasta, the Pecorino merely solidified into clumps and ended up stuck to the tongs. Ditto with the other recipes I found.

Perhaps I was grating the Pecorino too coarse and it wasn't melting properly? I tried again with cheese shredded on the grater's smallest holes. Still no luck: Although the cheese melted more quickly, it formed clumps just as fast. I tinkered around with the amount of cheese and pasta water, but no matter what I did, the cheese still clumped.

A talk with our science editor revealed the likely problem. Cheese consists mainly of three basic substances: fat, protein, and water. In a hard lump of Pecorino, the three are locked into position by the solid structure of the cheese. But when the cheese is heated, its fat begins to melt and its proteins soften. The fat acts as a sort of glue, fusing the proteins together. Cornstarch, he suggested, might be useful for coating the cheese and preventing the proteins from sticking together, so

I added some as I tossed the pasta. It worked, but there was a catch: By the time I used enough cornstarch to prevent clumping, it dulled the flavor of the cheese, and I wasn't about to trade flavor for texture.

Was there another way to get starch into the mix? Pasta releases starch into the cooking water as it boils, so maybe I could use this to my advantage. I reduced my cooking water from 4 quarts down to 2 quarts per pound of pasta. After cooking the spaghetti, I whisked some grated cheese into a cup of the semolina-infused water that remained. My results were the best yet, but some of the cheese was still clumping.

Hitting the books again, I discovered another factor that affects how proteins and fat interact: emulsifiers.

NOTES FROM THE TEST KITCHEN

AUTHENTIC PECORINO ROMANO
Imported Pecorino Romano is a hard aged sheep's milk cheese with a distinctively pungent, salty flavor that bears almost no resemblance to domestic cheeses simply labeled "Romano." These wan stand-ins are made with cow's milk and lack the punch of the real deal. Most authentic Pecorino Romano will have the name stamped into the rind of the cheese, but this isn't always the case so your best bet is to read the label. Using authentic Italian Pecorino Romano is important in any recipe calling for Pecorino Romano, but it is especially key in our recipe for Spaghetti with Pecorino Romano and Black Pepper, where it's the star.

THE BEST BLACK PEPPER
In recipes calling for ground pepper, we greatly prefer grinding our own to the preground variety, which has a faded aroma and flavor. When a recipe calls for a small dose, any freshly ground pepper will be fine. But if you're cooking a peppery specialty, like our Spaghetti with Pecorino Romano and Black Pepper, or if you like to grind fresh pepper over your food before eating, choosing a superior peppercorn can make a difference. We tested several varieties, and tasters gave top marks to highly aromatic peppercorns with complex flavor, and they preferred moderate heat rather than an overpowering strong heat. Our favorite was **Kalustyan's Indian Tellicherry Black Peppercorns** (left), which is sold by a Manhattan emporium online, but a close second was supermarket brand **Morton & Bassett Organic Whole Black Peppercorns** (right).

Milk, cream, and fresh cheeses have special molecules called lipoproteins that can associate with both fat and protein, acting as a sort of liaison between the two and keeping them from separating. But as cheese ages, the lipoproteins break down, losing their emulsifying power. No wonder my Pecorino Romano, which is aged for at least eight months, was clumping. How could I get an infusion of totally intact lipoproteins? The answer was simple: add milk or cream.

Since I was already using butter, why not replace it with the same amount of cream? (At the same time, I also took the olive oil down to 2 teaspoons to satisfy a few tasters who found the dish greasy.) This time, the cheese easily formed a light, perfectly smooth sauce when I tossed it with the spaghetti. Now for the real test: I placed a serving of pasta on the table and let it cool for a full five minutes. Even as it cooled, there wasn't a clump in sight.

I may never learn what really goes on in Lupa's kitchen, but my innovative version is worthy of any late-night Roman spaghetti party.

—YVONNE RUPERTI, *Cook's Illustrated*

Spaghetti with Pecorino Romano and Black Pepper

SERVES 4 TO 6

High-quality ingredients are essential in this dish, most importantly, imported Pecorino Romano. For a slightly less rich dish, substitute half-and-half for the heavy cream. Do not adjust the amount of water for cooking the pasta; the amount used is critical to the success of the recipe. Make sure to stir the pasta frequently while cooking so that it doesn't stick to the pot. Draining the pasta water into the serving bowl warms the bowl and helps keeps the pasta hot until it is served. Letting the dish rest briefly before serving allows the flavors to develop and the sauce to thicken.

- 4 **ounces Pecorino Romano, grated fine (about 2 cups), plus 2 ounces grated coarse (about 1 cup), for serving**
- 1 **pound spaghetti**
   Salt
- 2 **tablespoons heavy cream**
- 2 **teaspoons extra-virgin olive oil**
- 1½ **teaspoons pepper**

1. Place the finely grated Pecorino in a medium bowl. Set a colander in a large bowl.

2. Bring 2 quarts water to a boil in a large Dutch oven. Add the pasta and 1½ teaspoons salt and cook, stirring frequently, until the pasta is al dente. Drain the pasta into the colander set in the bowl, reserving the cooking water. Pour 1½ cups of the cooking water into a liquid measuring cup and discard the remainder and then place the pasta in the empty bowl.

3. Slowly whisk 1 cup of the reserved pasta water into the finely grated Pecorino until smooth. Whisk in the cream, oil, and pepper. Gradually pour the cheese mixture over the pasta, tossing to coat. Let the pasta rest for 1 to 2 minutes, tossing frequently, adjusting the consistency with the remaining ½ cup reserved pasta cooking water as needed. Serve, passing the coarsely grated Pecorino separately.

PASTA WITH TOMATO AND ALMOND PESTO

THIS SIDE OF THE ATLANTIC, "PESTO" IS SYNONYmous with a rich concoction made with lots of basil, Parmesan cheese, garlic, pine nuts, and good olive oil. This particular type of sauce originated in Genoa, a city in northern Italy's Liguria region; in Italy, you can find countless variations on this theme, with ingredients ranging from parsley and arugula to almonds, walnuts, pecans, sun-dried tomatoes, even fennel. I've always been intrigued by a "red" variation that hails from Trapani, a village on the western tip of Sicily. Here almonds replace pine nuts, but the big difference is the inclusion of fresh tomatoes—not as the main ingredient, but just enough to tint the sauce and lend fruity, vibrant sweetness.

The Trapanese pesto recipes I'd found in Italian cookbooks used similar techniques and stuck to a core list of ingredients. But when I mixed up a few, the results were distinctly different. One resembled chunky tomato salsa, another was thin and watery, and another was buried in cheese. Only a creamy, reddish-ocher pesto created by Lidia Bastianich, the renowned Italian-American chef and host of the PBS cooking series *Lidia's Italy* (from her book of the same name), came close to the clean, bright sauce I was after. If I could fine-tune her recipe

PASTA WITH TOMATO AND ALMOND PESTO

to work with supermarket tomatoes, I'd have a new quick pasta sauce to add to my repertoire.

Like most pesto recipes, Bastianich's came together in just minutes: Pulse tomatoes, basil leaves, toasted almonds, garlic, coarse salt, and red pepper flakes (more on that later) together in a food processor; add olive oil in a slow, steady stream to emulsify; adjust the seasonings; toss with pasta and cheese and serve. The tomatoes contribute bright flavor, while the ground almonds thicken the sauce and offer their own delicate taste and richness.

In fact, once the oil and cheese came into play, tasters wondered if the sauce was a tad too rich, even when used sparingly on pasta. I needed a better sense of the pesto's origins, so we called Bastianich herself. She explained that in Trapani, fishermen bring smaller, unsold fish home to their families, and everyone eats the leftover catch fried over a bed of pesto-tossed pasta. "It's a way to make a little bit of fish go a long way," she said.

In that scenario—stretching a meal—the richness made sense. But I wanted something a bit lighter and brighter. The tomatoes seemed like a good place to start. Farmers market tomatoes would surely be best, but I wanted a year-round pesto, which meant relying on year-round tomatoes. I plucked UglyRipes, grape tomatoes, and cherry tomatoes from the produce aisle and gave each a try. The UglyRipes were out—their quality was inconsistent. The cherry and grape tomatoes proved equal contenders, sharing a similar brightness and juiciness that was far more reliable. I settled on a generous 2½ cups.

Almonds, just like pine nuts in the Genovese version, are integral to this pesto because they contribute body while retaining just enough crunch to offset the tomatoes' pulpiness. Toasting was a must to release oils and flavor prior to processing. I found that blanched, slivered almonds browned more evenly than whole nuts and avoided the muddy flavor often contributed by papery skins. One-quarter cup, plus a relatively modest ⅓ cup extra-virgin olive oil, added a combination of pleasant grittiness and creamy texture without too much richness.

Basil is the star of Genovese pesto, but its role in the Trapanese version is a supporting one. A half-cup added just enough flavor to work in tandem with the tomatoes. For a variation, I swapped out the almonds for pine nuts and the basil for a slightly heavier dose of peppery arugula.

Save for boiling the pasta, my pesto was all but on the table. But something was missing—something small. Bastianich's recipe offered the option of increasing the pepperoncini, by which she meant the dried red peppers native to Tuscany. But I had another association: hot vinegar peppers. On a whim, I added a scant ½ teaspoon. Presto! This was just the kind of zingy touch the sauce needed.

—YVONNE RUPERTI, *Cook's Illustrated*

Pasta with Tomato and Almond Pesto
SERVES 4 TO 6

A half-teaspoon of red wine vinegar and ¼ teaspoon of red pepper flakes can be substituted for the pepperoncini. If you don't have a food processor, you may use a blender. In step 2, pulse the ingredients until roughly chopped, then proceed with the recipe, reducing the processing times by half.

¼	cup slivered almonds
12	ounces cherry or grape tomatoes (about 2½ cups)
½	cup fresh basil leaves
1	garlic clove, minced
1	small pepperoncini, stemmed, seeded, and minced (about ½ teaspoon)
	Salt
	Pinch red pepper flakes (optional)
⅓	cup extra-virgin olive oil
1	pound pasta, preferably linguine or spaghetti
1	ounce Parmesan cheese, grated (about ½ cup), plus extra for serving

1. Toast the almonds in a small skillet over medium heat, stirring frequently, until pale golden and fragrant, 2 to 4 minutes. Let cool.

2. Process the cooled almonds, tomatoes, basil, garlic, pepperoncini, 1 teaspoon salt, and red pepper flakes (if using) in a food processor until smooth, about 1 minute. Scrape down the sides of the bowl. With the machine running, slowly drizzle in the oil, about 30 seconds.

3. Meanwhile, bring 4 quarts water to a boil in a large pot. Add the pasta and 1 tablespoon salt and cook until al dente. Reserve ½ cup of the cooking water, then drain the pasta and return it to the pot.

4. Stir the pesto and ½ cup of the Parmesan into the pasta, adjusting the consistency with the reserved pasta cooking water as needed so that the pesto coats the pasta. Serve with extra Parmesan.

VARIATION

Pasta with Tomato, Pine Nut, and Arugula Pesto

Follow the recipe for Pasta with Tomato and Almond Pesto, substituting pine nuts for the almonds and replacing the basil with ¾ cup lightly packed arugula. Add 1¼ teaspoons grated lemon zest and 1 teaspoon fresh lemon juice to the food processor with the other ingredients in step 2.

NOTES FROM THE TEST KITCHEN

WHOLE WHEAT PASTA STEPS UP

Given the push these days toward whole grains, it's no surprise that supermarket shelves now carry whole wheat or multigrain noodles from just about every major pasta manufacturer. To separate the wheat from the chaff, we recently bought 18 nationally distributed brands of whole wheat and multigrain spaghetti and sampled them plain with olive oil, rating them on flavor and texture. We narrowed the field to 10 finalists and tested these with homemade marinara and pesto. Some were puzzlingly similar to white pasta while others were heavy, dense, and rough. So what did our tasting panel find? First, most of the 100 percent whole wheat and 100 percent whole grain pastas fell quickly to the bottom of the rankings, garnering descriptions like "mushy," "doughy," "sour," and "fishy." But there was one dark horse in the bunch, Italian-made **Bionaturae Organic 100% Whole Wheat Spaghetti** (7 grams protein and 6 grams fiber per serving), made entirely of whole wheat but with an appealingly chewy and firm texture like the pastas with little or no whole grains. Some tasters even deemed it "more flavorful than white pasta." The manufacturer's secret? Custom milling (which ensures good flavor), extrusion through a bronze not Teflon die (which helps build gluten in the dough), and a slower drying process at low temperatures (which yields sturdier pasta). (See page 290 for more information about our testing results.)

PASTA ALLA NORMA

PASTA ALLA NORMA IS A LIVELY COMBINATION OF tender eggplant and robust tomato sauce that is seasoned with herbs, mixed with al dente pasta, and finished with shreds of salty, milky ricotta salata (salted and pressed sheep's milk ricotta cheese). The textures and flavors have much more nuance than the typical pasta with tomato sauce, and the eggplant lends pasta alla Norma a heartiness that makes it superbly satisfying. This pasta is a classic in Sicily, where it was named for a nineteenth-century opera in which a druid priestess, Norma, perishes alongside her Roman lover. As the story goes, the opera was such a sensation that it inspired a Sicilian chef to create this dish in tribute to the opera and its composer, Vincenzo Bellini, a native son.

But even a classic faces pitfalls. Preparing the eggplant is a big production, usually requiring salting before frying, and it often ends up soggy and oil-slicked. The flavors in the dish can easily drown out the subtle essence of the eggplant. Meanwhile, the tomatoes either coagulate into a heavy, overwhelming sauce or there are so few they can't form an adequate foundation. I went into the kitchen to develop a bold, complex pasta, a weeknight meal with rich tomato and eggplant flavors and a smooth, silky texture.

Most pasta alla Norma recipes salt cubed eggplant for about an hour to draw out its excess moisture. To find out if I could skip or at least shorten salting, I prepared batches with eggplant I had salted for an hour, a half-hour, 15 minutes, and not at all. After tasting the results side by side, I was forced to conclude that salting for an hour was best: It drew out the most moisture, which helped the eggplant brown better and cook faster.

Next I considered how to cook the eggplant. One of the first recipes I tried called for frying two eggplants cut into strips in 3 inches of oil. The eggplant soaked up about half its weight in oil, turning silky and rich, but it made for a heavy, greasy sauce and required almost 40 minutes of watchful batch-cooking. Frying was out. I briefly considered roasting, but this also seemed slow for a weeknight meal. My best bet was sautéing in a lesser amount of oil. Unfortunately, when I tried it, the eggplant was almost always underdone, and it still required cooking in batches. Hoping to cook the eggplant more deeply, I peeled the skin before cubing and sautéing—but the difference was barely discernible.

PASTA ALLA NORMA

Looking for new ideas, I recalled a method for removing moisture from eggplant developed by a colleague working on a caponata recipe. Instead of salting the eggplant and leaving it to drain, he zapped salted cubes in the microwave for 10 minutes. The salt draws out moisture that microwaving turns into steam, all the while causing the eggplant to collapse and compress its air pockets. And because the pockets have collapsed, the eggplant also soaks up less oil. He also found that placing the eggplant on coffee filters for microwaving did an even better job of absorbing moisture than regular old paper towels. Using this method with my pasta alla Norma was a resounding success. Not only was it much faster than traditional salting, but the results were actually better: The eggplant pieces came out of the microwave surprisingly dry, a great start for browning. Furthermore, microwaving shrank the cubes to a size that could handily be cooked in one batch in a 12-inch skillet. Browning the eggplant for a full 10 minutes deeply caramelized the eggplant, giving it a round, full flavor with toasty notes that accented the vegetable's elusive sweetness.

Finally, I tried different types of eggplants: portly globe; smaller, more svelte Italian; and slender, lavender-colored Chinese. All worked, but I preferred globe eggplant, which has a tender yet resilient texture and far fewer seeds than the others. Cut into cubes, the globe eggplant retained its shape even after sautéing.

The base for pasta alla Norma is a simple tomato sauce, to which the eggplant is added. I was sure that fresh tomatoes would be best, but after a few rounds of testing, I concluded the trouble of peeling and salting them (a must to avoid a stringy, watery sauce) required more effort than I wanted here. I set out to come up with a simpler, year-round option. Diced canned tomatoes yielded a bright-tasting sauce, but since the eggplant was cut into cubes, this sauce was too chunky. My tasters preferred a sauce made with canned crushed tomatoes—a full 28 ounces—for their thick consistency, which lent cohesion.

To season the sauce, I used four cloves of minced garlic. A dash of red pepper flakes added a suggestion of heat, a generous dose of basil brought fresh flavor, and a tablespoon of olive oil stirred in at the end gave the sauce rich, round, fruity notes.

The sauce tasted fine tossed with the pasta, especially when sprinkled with a generous dose of ricotta salata

cheese, yet something was missing. It lacked backbone. I was considering a break with tradition by adding pancetta or prosciutto when a colleague suggested anchovies. Of course! Cooked in oil with the garlic and pepper flakes, one minced fillet was good, but two were even better, giving the sauce a deep, savory flavor without any trace of fishiness.

To determine how best to bring the elements together, I made a couple more batches. For the first, I browned the eggplant, set it aside, made the sauce in the same

NOTES FROM THE TEST KITCHEN

RICOTTA SALATA'S UNDERSTUDIES
Ricotta salata, a firm, tangy Italian sheep's milk cheese that bears little resemblance to the moist ricotta sold in tubs, is an essential component of traditional pasta alla Norma. If you can't find it, consider these options instead.

FRENCH FETA
Milder but tangy, this is a close cousin to ricotta salata in flavor and texture.

PECORINO ROMANO
Hard and dry, with a slightly more assertive aroma and flavor than ricotta salata.

COTIJA
Made with cow's milk, this Mexican cheese has a firm yet crumbly texture, but is less complex than ricotta salata.

THE RIGHT EGGPLANT FOR THE JOB
Bulbous globe eggplants not only contain far fewer seeds than smaller sister varieties like Italian and Chinese, but their firm flesh retains its shape even after cooking, making them an ideal choice in virtually any cooking application.

skillet, and then added the eggplant to the sauce and simmered them together long enough to heat through. For the second, I built the tomato sauce right on top of the browned eggplant so that they simmered together for about 10 minutes. The latter wound up a bit mushy and somewhat muddled, but the former had crisp, clear qualities—the eggplant's caramelization could still be tasted, and its tender texture had integrity.

Even with only a few minutes of simmering, the eggplant had a tendency to soak up tomato juices, causing the sauce to become rather thick, so the final adjustment was adding a little reserved pasta cooking water when tossing the sauce with the pasta. With that, all the components were perfectly in tune. My pasta alla Norma was on the table in well under an hour, without theatrics and with bold, balanced flavors.

—DAWN YANAGIHARA, *Cook's Illustrated*

Pasta alla Norma

SERVES 4

This recipe calls for both regular and extra-virgin olive oil. The higher smoke point of regular olive oil makes it best for browning the eggplant; extra-virgin olive oil stirred into the sauce before serving lends fruity flavor. If you don't have regular olive oil, use vegetable oil. We prefer kosher salt in step 1 because it clings best to the eggplant. If using table salt, reduce the amount to ½ teaspoon. Do not stir the eggplant more often than called for in step 2, as doing so may cause the eggplant cubes to break apart. Ricotta salata is traditional, but French feta, Pecorino Romano, and cotija (a firm, crumbly Mexican cheese) are acceptable substitutes. Our preferred brands of crushed tomatoes are Tuttorosso and Muir Glen.

- 1 **large eggplant (1¼ to 1½ pounds), cut into ½-inch cubes**
  Kosher salt (see note)
- 3 **tablespoons olive oil**
- 4 **garlic cloves, minced**
- 2 **anchovy fillets, minced**
- ¼–½ **teaspoon red pepper flakes**
- 1 **(28-ounce) can crushed tomatoes**
- 1 **pound ziti, rigatoni, or penne**
- 6 **tablespoons chopped fresh basil**
- 1 **tablespoon extra-virgin olive oil**
- 3 **ounces ricotta salata, shredded (about 1 cup)**

1. Toss the eggplant with 1 teaspoon salt in a medium bowl. Line the surface of a large microwave-safe plate with a double layer of coffee filters and lightly coat with vegetable oil spray. Spread the eggplant in an even layer over the coffee filters. Microwave the eggplant, uncovered, until dry to the touch and slightly shriveled, about 10 minutes, tossing once halfway through. Cool slightly.

2. Transfer the eggplant to a medium bowl, drizzle with 1 tablespoon of the olive oil, and toss gently to coat. Discard the coffee filters. Heat 1 tablespoon more olive oil in a 12-inch nonstick skillet over medium-high heat until shimmering. Add the eggplant and distribute in an even layer. Cook, stirring every 1½ to 2 minutes, until well browned and fully tender, about 10 minutes. Remove the skillet from the heat, transfer the eggplant to a plate, and set aside.

3. Add the remaining 1 tablespoon olive oil, garlic, anchovies, and red pepper flakes to the empty but still-hot skillet and cook using the residual heat so the garlic doesn't burn, stirring constantly, until fragrant and the garlic becomes pale golden, about 1 minute (if the skillet is too cool to cook the mixture, set it over medium heat). Add the tomatoes, return the skillet to medium-high heat, and bring to a boil. Reduce the heat to medium and simmer, stirring occasionally, until the sauce has slightly thickened, 8 to 10 minutes.

4. Meanwhile, bring 4 quarts water to a boil. Add the pasta and 2 tablespoons salt and cook until al dente. Reserve ½ cup of the cooking water, then drain the pasta and return it to the pot.

5. While the pasta is cooking, return the eggplant to the skillet with the tomatoes and gently stir to incorporate. Bring to a simmer over medium heat and cook, stirring occasionally, until the eggplant is heated through and the flavors are blended, 3 to 5 minutes. Stir the basil and extra-virgin olive oil into the sauce and season with salt to taste. Add the sauce to the cooked pasta, adjusting the consistency with the reserved pasta cooking water so that the sauce coats the pasta. Sprinkle with the ricotta salata and serve immediately.

VARIATION

Pasta alla Norma with Olives and Capers

Follow the recipe for Pasta alla Norma, substituting chopped fresh parsley for the basil and adding ½ cup slivered kalamata olives and 2 tablespoons drained, rinsed capers along with the parsley and extra-virgin olive oil to the sauce in step 5.

HEARTY ITALIAN MEAT SAUCE

THE ITALIAN-AMERICAN CLASSIC KNOWN AS SUNDAY gravy is not a dish, it's a feast. Bowls of lightly sauced pasta and slow-cooked tomato "gravy" are served alongside platters of meat that have been braised for hours in this gravy. These can include ribs, meatballs, pork shoulder, hot and sweet sausages, and the dish's typical crowning glory: braciole, stuffed, rolled Italian beef that's a meal on its own. Why such extravagance? Italians who immigrated to the United States in the late nineteenth and early twentieth centuries found meat far more abundant and affordable here than in their home country, and Sunday gravy became a weekly celebration of this good fortune.

After trying a handful of recipes, which were all-day productions, I couldn't help but be impressed by the sheer plenitude and the richness of the sauce. But was so much time and effort—and meat—necessary? My goal: a full-flavored meal on the table in less than four hours, with no more than an hour of hands-on cooking.

In the classic recipes, you first mix and shape meatballs and make braciole, then brown these and the sausages, ribs, and pork shoulder in batches. Next, you sauté flavorings like onions, oregano, and garlic, scraping up the fond left in the pan to flavor the sauce. Tomatoes go in, and the meats return to simmer until tender—for a few hours or, often, much longer. The meats get transferred to a platter and a little sauce is stirred into pasta, with the remaining sauce passed separately.

The browning alone took 40 minutes, so as a start on making the dish more manageable, I limited myself to one kind of sausage and one cut of pork. For the sausage, tasters preferred the mild kick that hot Italian links gave the sauce over the fennel taste of sweet sausage. As for pork, I tried neck bones, butt, pork chops, and all manner of ribs. Baby back ribs were our favorite; they weren't too fatty and turned moist and tender in just a few hours, and the bones added richness to the sauce.

Next up, the braciole. After making several versions, all following the same laborious approach (pound lean steaks; fill with a stuffing of cheese, prosciutto, and herbs; roll and tie with twine; brown and simmer), the same issue kept cropping up. Tasters loved the beefy flavor it lent the sauce and the salty taste of the filling, but the lean cut always turned out a little dry. I could fix the problem, but did I really need to?

If I could nail down truly standout meatballs, maybe they could serve as the meal's centerpiece, instead of braciole. I had a head start with a proven test kitchen technique: Instead of all ground beef, we often use a mixture of ground beef and pork. Meatloaf mix, a combination of ground beef, pork, and veal, produced even juicier results. I then incorporated a panade made of bread and buttermilk to ensure tenderness and add subtle tanginess. Garlic, parsley, and red pepper flakes, plus an egg yolk for richness, boosted the flavor even further. But these meatballs became lopsided from sticking to the bottom of the Dutch oven and were so tender that they broke apart at the end of the long simmer. I solved this by browning them separately in a nonstick skillet, then adding them to the sauce in the last 15 minutes of cooking.

With such moist, richly flavored meatballs, tasters weren't missing the braciole, but what they did miss were the distinctive flavors of its filling. Why not simply incorporate some of those same ingredients into my meatballs? When I added a couple of ounces of finely chopped prosciutto and a half-cup of Pecorino Romano to the ground meat along with the other flavorings, it led to a sauce that tasted surprisingly close to the gravy made with bona fide stuffed beef—with far less work.

With my meats settled, I could move on to perfecting the sauce. As a benchmark, I compared a sauce simmered for four hours with the full spectrum of Sunday gravy meats to my pared-down working recipe (simmered for just 2½ hours—the time it took for the ribs to become tender). While the difference wasn't huge, tasters found that the classic sauce did have deeper, meatier flavor.

Before finessing flavor, I had some streamlining to do. Up to this point, I had been using whole canned tomatoes, pureeing them in a blender, and adding them to the pan with tomato paste, as the better recipes I found suggested. Substituting tomato puree wasn't an option; it added an unwelcome cooked flavor to the sauce. Crushed tomatoes, however, were a winner, producing a sauce with nice thickness and body.

As an easy first step toward building complexity, I sautéed the onions until they were just beginning to brown. I also experimented with intensifying the flavor of tomato paste: Instead of merely browning the tomato paste, I cooked it until it nearly blackened, concentrating its sweetness. Though in Italy meat sauces aren't known for assertive garlic flavor, tasters appreciated the added intensity from four cloves.

Now, what could I do to inject more meaty flavor? Without braciole—and with the meatballs added at the end—my sauce was benefiting only from the juices of the sausages and ribs. I experimented with some of the usual suspects, including soy sauce and Marmite, a flavor enhancer made from yeast extract. The best booster turned out to be an ingredient rarely found in tomato sauce: beef broth. Just ⅔ cup added the right rich depth.

One last tweak: Instead of simmering the meat and the sauce together on the stovetop, which requires constant monitoring, I covered the Dutch oven and transferred it to the even heat of the oven, where I could leave it unattended for most of the time.

Three and a half hours after first setting foot in the kitchen, I had a sauce to rival any Italian grandmother's Sunday gravy, and a feast I'd be proud to invite family and friends to share.

—BRYAN ROOF, *Cook's Illustrated*

Hearty Italian Meat Sauce

SERVES 8 TO 10

We prefer meatloaf mix (a combination of ground beef, pork, and veal) for the meatballs in this recipe. Ground beef may be substituted, but the meatballs won't be as flavorful. Six tablespoons of plain yogurt thinned with 2 tablespoons milk can be substituted for the buttermilk. This recipe makes enough to sauce 1½ pounds of pasta. The sauce can be prepared through step 4 and then cooled and refrigerated in the Dutch oven for up to 2 days. To reheat, drizzle ½ cup water over the sauce (do not stir in) and warm on the lower-middle rack of a preheated 325-degree oven for 1 hour before proceeding with the recipe.

SAUCE

- 2 tablespoons olive oil
- 1 (2¼-pound) rack baby back ribs, cut into 2-rib sections
  Salt and pepper
- 1 pound hot Italian sausage
- 2 onions, minced (about 2 cups)
- 1¼ teaspoons dried oregano
- 3 tablespoons tomato paste
- 4 garlic cloves, minced
- 2 (28-ounce) cans crushed tomatoes
- ⅔ cup beef broth
- ¼ cup chopped fresh basil

MEATBALLS

- 2 slices high-quality white sandwich bread, crusts removed, torn into ½-inch pieces
- ½ cup buttermilk (see note)
- ¼ cup chopped fresh parsley
- 2 garlic cloves, minced
- 1 large egg yolk
- ½ teaspoon salt
- ¼ teaspoon red pepper flakes
- 1 pound meatloaf mix (see note)
- 2 ounces thinly sliced prosciutto, chopped fine
- 1 ounce Pecorino Romano cheese, grated (about ½ cup)
- ½ cup olive oil
- 1½ pounds spaghetti or linguine
- 2 tablespoons salt
  Grated Parmesan cheese, for serving

1. FOR THE SAUCE: Adjust an oven rack to the lower-middle position and heat the oven to 325 degrees. Heat the oil in a large Dutch oven over medium-high heat until just smoking. Pat the ribs dry with paper towels and season with salt and pepper. Add half of the ribs to the pot and brown on both sides, 5 to 7 minutes total. Transfer the ribs to a large plate and brown the remaining ribs. After transferring the second batch of ribs to a plate, brown the sausages all over, 5 to 7 minutes. Transfer the sausages to a plate with the ribs.

2. Reduce the heat to medium, add the onions and oregano and cook, stirring occasionally, until beginning to brown, about 5 minutes. Add the tomato paste and cook, stirring constantly, until very dark, about 3 minutes. Stir in the garlic and cook until fragrant, about 30 seconds. Add the crushed tomatoes and broth, scraping up any browned bits. Return the ribs and sausage to the pot, bring to a simmer, cover, and transfer to the oven. Cook until the ribs are tender, about 2½ hours.

3. FOR THE MEATBALLS: Meanwhile, combine the bread, buttermilk, parsley, garlic, egg yolk, salt, and red pepper flakes in a medium bowl and mash with a fork until no bread chunks remain. Add the meatloaf mix, prosciutto, and Pecorino Romano to the bread mixture. Mix with your hands until thoroughly combined. Divide the mixture into 12 portions. Roll the portions into balls, transfer the meatballs to a plate, cover with plastic wrap, and refrigerate until ready to use.

4. When the sauce is 30 minutes from being done, heat the oil in a large nonstick skillet over medium-high heat until shimmering. Add the meatballs and cook until well browned all over, 5 to 7 minutes. Transfer the meatballs to a paper towel–lined plate. Remove the sauce from the oven and skim the fat from the top with a large spoon. Transfer the browned meatballs to the sauce and gently submerge. Cover, return the pot to the oven, and continue cooking until the meatballs are just cooked through, about 15 minutes.

5. Meanwhile, bring 6 quarts water to a boil in a large pot. Add the pasta and salt and cook until al dente. Reserve ½ cup of the cooking water, then drain the pasta and return it to the pot.

NOTES FROM THE TEST KITCHEN

NOT YOUR NONNA'S GRAVY
By choosing our ingredients carefully, we created a sauce with almost the same flavor as the more time-consuming traditional approach.

RIGHT RIB
These baby back pork ribs turn tender after just 2½ hours of cooking; the bones enrich the sauce.

MISSING LINK
Who needs sweet Italian sausage when you've already got the mild kick of the spicy links?

MORE THAN A MEATBALL
Prosciutto and Pecorino Romano give our meatballs authentic flavor.

BEEFY BOOSTER
Though unconventional, a touch of beef broth reinforces the meatiness of the sauce.

COOKING TOMATO PASTE FOR SUNDAY GRAVY

Cooking the tomato paste until nearly blackened concentrates its sweetness and adds complexity to the sauce.

---

6. TO SERVE: Using tongs, transfer the meatballs, ribs, and sausages to a serving platter and cut the sausages in half. Stir the basil into the sauce and season with salt and pepper to taste. Toss the pasta with 1 cup of the sauce until lightly coated, adding the reserved pasta cooking water as needed. Serve the pasta, passing the remaining sauce and the meat platter separately.

MANICOTTI WITH MEAT SAUCE

IT MIGHT FEEL LIKE AN AGE-OLD CLASSIC, BUT stuffing pasta (or Italian crepes called *crespelle*) to make the dish known as manicotti is a relatively modern addition to the Italian culinary scene. But in spite of its late start, when manicotti got big, it got really big. Today, you can easily find manicotti in the supermarket freezer case, but it can barely touch the flavor and texture of homemade. Of course, most people buy it frozen because making stuffed manicotti with meat sauce is truly a labor of love. It takes time and effort to brown ground beef, build a tomato sauce, cook and cool pasta tubes, pipe in the ricotta filling, sauce the stuffed pasta, and bake the ensemble. The reward is a hearty, homey, knockout dish—or at least it should be. I painstakingly prepared a number of recipes, only to discover the harsh realities of bland fillings, sauce and meat that never melded, and shredded pasta tubes. Where was the love?

Manicotti was originally made by rolling sheets of fresh pasta around a filling. This sounded easier than grappling with dried manicotti tubes, but making fresh pasta was out of the question for a weekday supper. What about no-boil lasagna noodles? Could giving them a quick soak to make them pliable save me trouble? After soaking 16 noodles (enough to fill a 13 by 9-inch dish) in hot water, I patted them dry, portioned out the filling, and started rolling. I filled these noodles much more quickly than dried tubes, and with no ripping. In a finished casserole, they were indistinguishable.

One pound of ground beef and two 28-ounce cans of crushed tomatoes made enough sauce to cover the filled tubes. But the beef flavor was faint. If I had all day, I'd let the sauce simmer and develop flavor. I remembered that a colleague had used the food processor to jump-start his Bolognese sauce: Once the ground beef was

BAKED MANICOTTI WITH MEAT SAUCE

broken down, its flavor permeated the tomatoes. This technique worked just as well for my manicotti sauce. For rounder flavor, I tested using meatloaf mix and ground pork in combination with the ground beef, but they didn't contribute much. Hot Italian sausages were a modest improvement, and pepperoni—though it may sound odd—was better still. When I ground pepperoni slices with the beef, tasters couldn't identify the new addition but loved the spicy, meaty taste it imparted.

Tasters agreed that the standard filling of equal parts ricotta and mozzarella (plus an egg for binding) tasted flat. So I exchanged 1 cup of the mozzarella for more assertive Parmesan. While the taste improved, the texture took a nosedive. Provolone fixed both. A taster suggested adding meat to the filling. I reserved 1 cup of the sautéed meat mixture and stirred it into the ricotta mixture; now it tasted meaty to the core. My manicotti isn't effortless, but it is definitely easy, and the robust, flavorful payoff is worth a little exertion.

—CALI RICH, *Cook's Country*

NOTES FROM THE TEST KITCHEN

MAKING MEATY MANICOTTI

Manicotti shells are hard to fill without tearing. For easy-to-fill manicotti, we reinvented the noodle.

1. After soaking the no-boil lasagna noodles briefly in hot water, place them on a kitchen towel to dry. With the short side of the noodles facing you, spread the filling across the bottom of each noodle and roll it into a tube.

2. Arrange the rolled manicotti, seam side down, on top of the meat sauce in the baking dish.

FOOD STORAGE CONTAINERS

Packing up leftovers ought to be easy, but food storage containers are one of life's persistent little annoyances. Once you dig through a slippery stack of containers to match tops and bottoms that aren't too stained or warped, you have to fuss over them for a tight seal. Then come the other quandaries: Does it fit in the fridge or freezer? Will it leak if it tips over? Can you microwave in it? Do you have to remember to wash it only on the top rack of the dishwasher? Should you worry about possible health risks with plastics containing bisphenol-A (BPA)? We don't think food storage containers should take this much thought. We selected eight BPA-free plastic food storage containers, choosing square or rectangular as close as possible to 8-cup capacity, and worked them over, testing for leaking, durability, odor-retention, and design. We put them in the microwave, the freezer, and the refrigerator. We ran them through dozens of dishwasher cycles, submerged them in water, and even dropped them to see how they held up. The flat **Snapware MODS Large 8-Cup Rectangle**, $6.99, survived all our tests and met our goals for a food storage container. (See page 310 for more information about our testing results.)

Baked Manicotti with Meat Sauce

SERVES 6 TO 8

You will need 16 no-boil lasagna noodles for this recipe (note that the test kitchen's preferred brand, Barilla, comes 16 to a box, but other brands contain only 12). It is important to let the dish cool for 15 minutes after baking.

SAUCE

- 1 onion, chopped (about 1 cup)
- 6 ounces sliced deli pepperoni
- 1 pound 85 percent lean ground beef
- 1 tablespoon tomato paste
- 5 garlic cloves, minced
- ¼ teaspoon red pepper flakes
- 2 (28-ounce) cans crushed tomatoes
  Salt and pepper

MANICOTTI

- 24 ounces ricotta cheese (about 3 cups)
- 10 ounces mozzarella cheese, shredded (about 2½ cups)
- 6 ounces provolone cheese, shredded (about 1½ cups)
- 1 large egg, lightly beaten
- ½ teaspoon salt
- ½ teaspoon pepper
- ¼ cup finely chopped fresh basil
- 16 no-boil lasagna noodles

1. FOR THE SAUCE: Pulse the onion and pepperoni in a food processor until coarsely ground. Add the beef and pulse until thoroughly combined.

2. Transfer the beef mixture to a large saucepan and cook over medium heat, breaking up the mixture with a wooden spoon, until no longer pink, about 5 minutes. Using a slotted spoon, transfer 1 cup of the beef mixture to a paper towel–lined plate. Add the tomato paste, garlic, and red pepper flakes to the pot with the remaining meat mixture and cook until fragrant, about 1 minute. Stir in the tomatoes and simmer until the sauce is slightly thickened, about 20 minutes. Season with salt and pepper to taste.

3. FOR THE MANICOTTI: Adjust an oven rack to the upper-middle position and heat the oven to 375 degrees. Combine the ricotta, 2 cups of the mozzarella, 1 cup of the provolone, the egg, salt, pepper, basil, and reserved meat mixture in a large bowl. Bring 2 quarts water to a boil and pour into a 13 by 9-inch baking dish. Soak the noodles until pliable, about 5 minutes. Drain the noodles on a kitchen towel and dry the baking dish.

4. Spread half of the meat sauce over the bottom of the baking dish. Following the photos on page 118, top each noodle with ¼ cup of the cheese filling, roll, and arrange, seam side down, on top of the sauce in the baking dish. Spread the remaining sauce over the manicotti. Cover the baking dish with foil and bake until the manicotti is bubbling around the edges, about 40 minutes. Remove the foil and sprinkle with the remaining ½ cup mozzarella and ½ cup provolone. Bake until the cheese is melted, about 5 minutes. Cool for 15 minutes. Serve. (The sauce can be made ahead and stored in an airtight container for up to 3 days.)

LIGHT SPINACH LASAGNA

THE AMERICANIZED VERSIONS OF THIS ITALIAN classic are thankfully simpler than the original (no homemade noodles, for one), but (perhaps not surprisingly) they also cut out the bulk of the flavor and appeal. These stateside versions are typically heavy and bland, with army-green spinach and béchamel that tastes mostly like glue. Then there's the fact that between all the sauce and cheese, one serving of spinach lasagna can tally nearly 500 calories and 27 grams of fat. That's far from the "healthier" alternative to meat lasagna you would hope for. I wanted a recipe I could put together on a weeknight that offered vibrant spinach, a flavorful sauce, and a healthy balance of cheese.

To begin, I tackled the spinach. I already knew that in most simplified recipes, the spinach's drab color and bland flavor are actually caused by the type of noodles used. Traditional Italian recipes use homemade fresh pasta, and because fresh pasta cooks in an instant, these lasagnas require only a brief stay in the oven, just enough time for the layers to bind but not so much as to overcook the spinach. Meanwhile, most Americanized recipes call for convenient no-boil noodles, which certainly save you labor, but they require at least 50 minutes of baking to become tender. This long stint in the oven robs the spinach of its vibrancy.

Obviously, I could rescue the spinach by shortening the oven time. So I swapped out the no-boil noodles for conventional dried lasagna noodles, cooked al dente, which would ensure my lasagna would need just 20 minutes to bake. With this method, I made one lasagna with fresh spinach and one with frozen. In a side-by-side tasting, I was surprised to find my fellow test cooks were just as happy with the flavor and color of the frozen spinach as the fresh, so I settled on the more convenient frozen. I did find it was key to wrap the defrosted spinach in a kitchen towel and wring out the excess liquid before proceeding in order to guard against a waterlogged lasagna.

Next I moved on to the béchamel. A classic milk sauce thickened with a roux made from flour and butter, béchamel was obviously problematic to my healthier recipe goals. I quickly cut out some fat by using low-fat milk instead of whole, but there was still the issue of thickening, since the roux, with its 5 tablespoons of butter, was out of the question. Cornstarch has pulled through for the test kitchen in myriad similar situations, so I felt it was worth a try here. I whisked 2 tablespoons cornstarch into cold milk to make a slurry before stirring it into the sauce. Surprised for the second time in my lasagna makeover testing, I noticed that the cornstarch worked like a charm. It thickened the sauce perfectly without being gummy, and it didn't taste at all starchy.

To boost the flavor of my revamped béchamel sauce, I sautéed 1 cup of onions with plenty of garlic before pouring in the milk. Adding two bay leaves and freshly grated nutmeg (typical béchamel seasonings) lent depth, and sprinklings of salt and pepper were the only other refinements needed. I could have stuck to the traditional layering process of noodles, sauce, spinach and multiple types of cheese, but I wanted to keep this recipe simple.

I decided this was a good place for combining a few steps, so I stirred grated Parmesan cheese into the sauce along with the spinach and set the mixture aside.

Most recipes for spinach lasagna call for both ricotta and mozzarella cheeses, but tasters noted that the ricotta layer in my recipe was cooking up too dry. For my next test, instead of ricotta I covertly added scoops of cottage cheese to my lasagna, which I pureed with an egg to help smooth out some of its curds. Tasters approved of this moist, creamy layer, and no one caught on to my ingredient swap. To see if I could cut out any fat, I tried low-fat and fat-free cottage cheese instead of regular, but everyone agreed these both tasted too lean. This was one place the extra fat was definitely worth keeping. To give my lasagna a flavor boost, I tried replacing mild shredded mozzarella with fontina, a semi-firm cheese with buttery, nutty tones that melts beautifully. Its complexity was a welcome addition, and though fontina contains more fat and calories than mozzarella, I found I could reduce the amount of shredded cheese from 2 cups to 1½ cups and still end up with bolder flavor than what the lasagna was getting with mozzarella.

After several dozen tests, I was getting pretty weary of dealing with parboiling conventional noodles. There had to be a way to make no-boil noodles work here. The solution was to soak the no-boil noodles in boiling water for just 5 minutes. After only 20 minutes in a 425-degree oven, the softened no-boil noodles in my lasagna were perfectly cooked and the spinach had kept all its healthy green vitality. The only cooking left to do involved a quick trip to the broiler to brown the cheese.

With its bright spinach, balanced layers of cheese and sauce, easy method, and healthier profile (just 14 grams of fat and 350 calories per serving), this was one lasagna that beat out any other version I could find, Old World or New.

—ADELAIDE PARKER, *America's Test Kitchen Books*

Light Spinach Lasagna

SERVES 8

We prefer Barilla no-boil lasagna noodles for their delicate texture resembling that of fresh pasta. Be sure to use Italian fontina rather than bland and rubbery Danish or American fontina. To make the cheese easier to shred, freeze it for 30 minutes to firm it up. You will need a broiler-safe baking dish for this recipe.

SAUCE

- 1 onion, minced (about 1 cup)
- 1 teaspoon canola oil
  Salt
- 4 garlic cloves, minced
- 3 cups 1 percent low-fat milk
- 2 bay leaves
- ½ teaspoon freshly grated nutmeg
- 2 tablespoons cornstarch
- 2 (10-ounce) packages frozen chopped spinach, thawed, squeezed dry, and chopped fine
- 1 ounce Parmesan cheese, grated (about ½ cup)
  Pepper

LAYERS

- 8 ounces whole-milk cottage cheese (about 1 cup)
- 1 large egg
- ¼ teaspoon salt
- 12 no-boil lasagna noodles
- 2 ounces Parmesan cheese, grated (about 1 cup)
- 6 ounces Italian fontina cheese, shredded (about 1½ cups)

1. FOR THE SAUCE: Combine the onion, oil, and ⅛ teaspoon salt in a large saucepan. Cover and cook over medium-low heat, stirring occasionally, until softened, 8 to 10 minutes. Stir in the garlic and cook until fragrant, about 30 seconds. Stir in 2¾ cups of the milk, bay leaves, and nutmeg. Bring to a simmer over medium-low heat.

2. Whisk the cornstarch and remaining ¼ cup milk together, then whisk into the pot. Continue to simmer, whisking constantly, until thickened, about 6 minutes. Off the heat, remove and discard the bay leaves. Stir in the spinach and Parmesan until incorporated and no clumps of spinach remain. (You should have about 3½ cups sauce.) Season with salt and pepper to taste. Cover to keep warm, and set aside.

3. FOR THE LAYERS: Adjust an oven rack to be 6 inches from the broiler element, adjust a second oven rack to the middle position, and heat the oven to 425 degrees.

4. Process the cottage cheese, egg, and salt in a food processor (or blender) until very smooth, about 30 seconds. Transfer to a bowl and set aside.

5. Pour 1 inch of boiling water into a 13 by 9-inch broiler-safe baking dish, then add the noodles one at a time. Let the noodles soak until pliable, about 5 minutes, separating them with the tip of a sharp knife to prevent sticking. Remove the noodles from the water and place in a single layer on clean kitchen towels. Discard the water, dry the baking dish, and coat the interior with vegetable oil spray.

6. TO ASSEMBLE AND BAKE: Spread ½ cup of the sauce evenly over the bottom of the baking dish. Position 3 of the noodles on top of the sauce. Spread ¾ cup more sauce evenly over the noodles, sprinkle evenly with the Parmesan, and top with 3 more of the noodles. Spread ¾ cup more sauce evenly over the noodles, sprinkle evenly with ¾ cup of the fontina, and top with 3 more of the noodles. Spread ¾ cup more sauce evenly over the noodles, followed by the cottage cheese mixture. Finish with the remaining 3 noodles, remaining ¾ cup sauce, and remaining ¾ cup fontina.

7. Cover the baking dish with foil and bake the lasagna on the middle oven rack until bubbling, about 20 minutes. Remove the baking dish from the oven and remove the foil. Heat the broiler. Transfer the baking dish to the upper oven rack and broil the lasagna until the cheese is spotty brown, 4 to 6 minutes. Let the lasagna cool for 15 minutes before serving.

NOTES FROM THE TEST KITCHEN

INSULATED CARRIERS
Insulated carriers used to be for pizza delivery workers or caterers only, but we found four models designed to keep your famous lasagna piping hot all the way to the potluck or picnic. After all, no one wants to eat a lukewarm casserole—or worse, food that's unsafe. We prefer carriers with sturdy handles and zippers that fit snugly around a standard 13 by 9-inch baking dish. Overall, the best performer was the **Pyrex Portables 3-Quart Oblong with Black Carrier**, $29.99, which kept hot food hot and safe to eat (over 140 degrees) for nearly 3 hours. What's more, its sleek carrier fit like a glove around the baking dish it came with. Have carrier, will travel.

ST. LOUIS PIZZA

IT'S TRUE, YOU CAN MAKE TERRIFIC PIZZA ON A yeastless crust. It may sound crazy, but folks in St. Louis have been doing it for years. With its wafer-thin crust, thick, sweet tomato sauce, gooey Provel cheese (another local secret), and signature square slices, St. Louis pizza is unmistakable. Imo's, a popular local chain, is credited with creating it, and it's said that founder Ed Imo, a former tile-layer, subconsciously cut the circular pizza into tile-shaped squares (the "square beyond compare," as the jingle goes). The chain, and its pizza, have since crossed into Illinois and Kansas, and as a proud St. Louis native I hoped to introduce it to the remaining 47 states.

Although you can find St. Louis pizza at many pizzerias in the region, home recipes for it are as sparse as the prairie. In the test kitchen, we usually start recipe development with existing recipes, but in this case the pizzeria recipe was top secret—Imo's wasn't talking. Since the crust resembles crackers, I started by looking over cracker recipes for ideas, but soon enough I lucked onto an Internet recipe claiming to be the real thing, St. Louis pizza, so I began my testing there. And fortunately, I also had years of eating the real Imo's pizza to go by.

According to the recipe I found, St. Louis pizza crust mixes flour (2 cups) with corn syrup (2 tablespoons), olive oil (2 tablespoons), water (½ cup), baking powder, and salt into a dough that is rolled paper-thin. (Ordinary pizza dough, by comparison, has yeast, more olive oil, and neither baking powder nor corn syrup.) This easy crust required no mixer, no yeast, barely any kneading, and no rising time. It was topped with a dump-and-stir tomato paste–heavy sauce and sprinkled with Provel, which resembles American cheese. The pizza baked for 12 minutes in a hot oven. When I tasted it, my challenges were clear. The crust, which should be crisp at the edges, tender in the center, and light brown was instead pale, tough, and bland. The sauce needed some serious perking up. And since you can't buy Provel outside of St. Louis (I used some I'd carried back after a recent visit home), I'd have to find a substitute.

The crust should be both tender and crisp, seemingly opposing goals: Think flour tortilla meets saltine cracker. For tenderness, in place of the water I tried seltzer and beer, both of which facilitate tenderness by making the dough a little acidic. But neither made much difference

ST. LOUIS PIZZA

here. Milk, my next experiment, worked all too well, making the pizza crust wholly soft. In the end, after weeks of tinkering with the liquid ingredients, I decided I was getting nowhere and would stick with the tap water. I'd have to find room for improvement elsewhere in the ingredient list.

To get a crisp crust, St. Louis pizzerias fire a pizza oven to upward of 800 degrees. The fact that my oven wasn't getting anywhere close to that mark had to be a large part of the problem. The first thing I did was replace the corn syrup with drier granulated sugar, which led to a modest textural improvement. Next, I tried brushing the bottom of the dough with olive oil before topping it; this failed to make any difference. Prebaking it without the topping did give me a crisp crust, but I refused to add an extra step to what should be an easy recipe.

Finally, I considered the flour. It was more than a lucky guess that led me from there to cornstarch. The test kitchen has used it successfully in the past to crisp food (it works by absorbing moisture) and at the same time, because it has no gluten, cornstarch helps make cakes and cookies tender. I tested various amounts and found that a mere 2 tablespoons gave me the light brown crust with a tender middle and audibly crunchy edges that I was after. And for flavor, simply increasing the salt in the dough by ½ teaspoon did wonders.

The tomato sauce in my working recipe was easy—no sautéing onions, mincing garlic, or long simmers. But on the downside, it was pasty and flat. To loosen it and freshen the flavor, I replaced some of the paste with tomato sauce. I added a tablespoon of sugar for the slight sweetness that distinguishes St. Louis pizza, and stirred in dried oregano and fresh basil. The fresh herb isn't typical, but it gave the pizza such a flavor lift that once I'd tried it, there was no going back.

Provel cheese is said to have been created for St. Louis pizza (though St. Louisans also like it in sandwiches) and was designed to melt nicely without any stringiness. I tested Provel side by side with an assortment of other cheeses. A mix of mild American cheese and creamy Monterey Jack came closest to the real thing, but in test after test, something—I couldn't pinpoint what—seemed to be missing. Then I noticed an item on the Provel's ingredient list I'd overlooked: smoke flavoring. A few drops of liquid smoke later, I had approximated the flavor and texture of Provel, and St. Louis pizza, in our New England test kitchen.

—MEGHAN ERWIN, *Cook's Country*

St. Louis Pizza

MAKES TWO 12-INCH PIZZAS

We like to use a baking stone (also called a pizza stone), which heats evenly and helps crisp crusts, but if you don't have one, bake the pizzas on a preheated inverted rimmed baking sheet.

SAUCE

- 1 (8-ounce) can tomato sauce
- 3 tablespoons tomato paste
- 2 tablespoons chopped fresh basil
- 1 tablespoon sugar
- 2 teaspoons dried oregano

CHEESE

- 8 ounces shredded white American cheese (about 2 cups)
- 2 ounces shredded Monterey Jack cheese (about ½ cup)
- 3 drops liquid smoke

DOUGH

- 2 cups (10 ounces) unbleached all-purpose flour
- 2 tablespoons cornstarch
- 2 teaspoons sugar
- 1 teaspoon baking powder
- 1 teaspoon salt
- ½ cup plus 2 tablespoons water
- 2 tablespoons olive oil

1. FOR THE SAUCE AND CHEESE: Whisk together the tomato sauce, tomato paste, basil, sugar, and oregano in a small bowl and set aside. Toss the cheeses with the liquid smoke in a medium bowl and set aside.

2. FOR THE DOUGH: Combine the flour, cornstarch, sugar, baking powder, and salt in a large bowl. Combine the water and olive oil in a liquid measuring cup. Stir the water mixture into the flour mixture until the dough starts to come together. Turn the dough onto a lightly floured counter and knead 3 or 4 times, until it is cohesive.

3. Adjust an oven rack to the lower-middle position, place a pizza stone (or an inverted baking sheet) on the rack, and heat the oven to 475 degrees. Divide the dough into 2 equal pieces. Working with 1 piece of dough at a time, press the dough into a small circle and transfer it to a piece of parchment paper dusted lightly with flour. Following the photos on page 124, use a rolling pin to roll and stretch the dough to form a 12-inch circle, rotating the parchment as needed. Lift the parchment and pizza dough off the counter onto an inverted baking sheet.

4. Top 1 dough round with half of the sauce and half of the cheese. Carefully pull the parchment paper and pizza off the baking sheet and onto the hot baking stone. Bake until the underside is golden brown and the cheese is completely melted, 9 to 12 minutes. Remove the pizza and the parchment from the oven and transfer the pizza to a cooling rack. Cool for 2 minutes. Repeat with the second dough round and the remaining sauce and cheese. Cut the pizzas into 2-inch squares and serve. (The dough can be made in advance. At the end of step 2, tightly wrap the ball of dough in plastic wrap and refrigerate for up to 2 days.)

VARIATIONS

St. Louis Pizza with Pepperoni

Follow the recipe for St. Louis Pizza through step 3. Arrange 7 ounces thinly sliced pepperoni on a paper towel–lined plate, cover with 2 more paper towels, and microwave for 2 minutes. Let cool. Proceed with the recipe, arranging the pepperoni on the pizza before sprinkling with cheese.

St. Louis Pizza with Peppers, Mushrooms, and Onions

Follow the recipe for St. Louis Pizza through step 3. Heat 2 tablespoons vegetable oil in a large skillet over medium-high heat until shimmering. Cook 2 onions, sliced thin, and 2 red bell peppers, sliced thin, until browned, about 10 minutes. Transfer to a bowl and

---

NOTES FROM THE TEST KITCHEN

MAKING ST. LOUIS PIZZA

St. Louis Pizza has a paper-thin crust. Here's how we transfer the dough from countertop to oven without tearing.

1. Roll out the dough on parchment paper so it doesn't stick and you can move it easily.

2. Place the parchment and dough on an inverted baking sheet, then top it with sauce and cheese.

3. To get the pizza into the oven, slide both parchment and pizza onto the hot baking stone.

WHERE THERE'S (LIQUID) SMOKE, THERE'S NO FIRE

Anyone who is passionate about barbecue knows nothing beats the real smoke flavor that comes from slowly smoldering chunks of hickory or mesquite. To mimic that flavor indoors, we used liquid smoke for our St. Louis Pizza. Many people assume that the process of making liquid smoke involves distasteful chemical shenanigans, but that's not the case. Liquid smoke is made by collecting smoke from smoldering wood chips in a condenser that quickly cools the vapors, causing them to liquefy. The droplets are captured and filtered twice before being bottled. (Once, we were crazy enough to try making liquid smoke in the test kitchen: The process took an entire day, and all we got was 3 tablespoons. Never again.) Our top-rated brand, **Wright's All-Natural Hickory Seasoning Liquid Smoke**, contains nothing but smoke and water. Be forewarned, this stuff is extremely concentrated—a few drops go a long way.

A CUT ABOVE

A shoddy pizza cutter drags melted cheese out of place and fails to cut through crisp crust cleanly. A good pizza cutter gets the job done quickly, neatly, and safely. The basic wheel cutter is the most common variety and we tested eight of them to find the best one. While all of them cut through thin-crust pizza without a problem, only a few could cleanly slice through deep-dish pies loaded with cheese and toppings. Our favorite pizza wheel is the extremely sharp **Mario Batali The Italian Kitchen Pizza Wheel**, $15.95.

set aside. Heat 1 tablespoon more vegetable oil in the skillet over medium-high heat until shimmering. Cook 1 pound white mushrooms, sliced thin, until browned, about 10 minutes. Transfer to the bowl with the onions and peppers and toss to combine. Proceed with the recipe, distributing the sautéed vegetables over the pizza before sprinkling with cheese.

HEALTHY PIZZA WITH MULTIGRAIN CRUST

WHILE MOST OF US EQUATE PIZZA WITH JUNK FOOD, that's not always the case. Great pizza should be a cooperative effort of three main components: crust, sauce, and toppings. When these components are in harmony, pizza can easily be a balanced meal: You've got vegetables, dairy, and grains, and perhaps a little meat. Picture a crisp crust, fresh vegetables and sauce, and a sprinkling of cheese. The problems pop up when this balance is thrown off—think gobs of cheese, dense and doughy crust, and greasy toppings. It's then that a slice of pizza can become an unhealthy mess. Could I come up with an easy, from-scratch pizza recipe that was also healthy? I wanted a crisp-tender crust and flavorful, fresh sauce and toppings. And above all, I set my sights on starting my recipe with a multigrain crust, which would give my pizza a one-of-a-kind flavor and texture as well as a nutritional punch. Pie in the sky? Hopefully not.

As it is, the crust is probably the trickiest part of pizza making at home. While traditional pizza dough is nothing more than bread dough with oil added, we've found in the test kitchen that minor changes can yield dramatically different results. I wanted a dough that was easy to shape and stretch thin, and it needed to bake up crisp and chewy, full of multigrain flavor. We had already developed a good whole wheat crust recipe, so it seemed like a good starting place.

This existing whole wheat pizza dough recipe is pretty straightforward, blending bread flour, whole wheat flour, yeast, water, salt, and oil in a food processor. It produces a crust that is fairly thin, crispy on the bottom, and has a good amount of chew. It also holds up well under the weight of different toppings. So my first step was introducing more grains. I quickly learned it wasn't going to be as simple as adding more grains to the dough. When I incorporated a mix of flaxseed

and rye, bran, and barley flours, all I got was a crust that was tough and dense. Substituting the grains for some of the bread flour was better, but the grains were too hard when the pizza was done. I needed a way to soften the grains before adding them to the dough. For my next test, I started by bringing the water in our dough recipe to a simmer and letting the grains soak in it. After they'd soaked for 30 minutes I incorporated them into the dough mixture and proceeded with the recipe. This was a big step in the right direction; these grains incorporated into the dough much better. But because the grains had absorbed a fair amount of the liquid, my crust was too dense. Going up from 1½ cups of water to 1¾ cups did the trick.

Tasters agreed that my multigrain crust had the nutty flavor and appealing texture I was after, but after making it a few times I was a little tired of collecting and measuring all the different grains. That is when a fellow test cook, who had recently developed a multigrain bread recipe, suggested using a multigrain hot cereal mix instead. Usually located in the supermarket health-food aisle, hot cereal mix is a blend of whole grains already mixed and ready to go (our favorite brand, Bob's Red Mill, includes wheat, rye, oats, oat bran, barley, rice, and flaxseed). I gave it a test and, once steeped in the warm water, the mix became soft like a porridge that easily blended into the dough. And better yet, when it was baked, it tasted just as good as the custom mix I had put together.

Next, I moved on to the sauce. I was after something fresh, simple, and light, so I wasn't surprised that in a side-by-side tasting of several cooked versus no-cook sauces, tasters agreed a no-cook sauce nailed my goals. I settled on a blend of canned whole tomatoes, olive oil, garlic, and salt for its fresh taste and simplicity. All I had to do was combine the ingredients in a food processor.

Up next was the cheese. I tested several varieties of mozzarella, including whole-milk, part-skim, reduced-fat, and nonfat, just to see how much fat I could cut out before it turned my pizza into diet food. While whole-milk mozzarella tasted great and melted exceptionally well, its high fat content meant I could only use a small amount, which made the pizza look obviously healthy and obviously skimpy. Tasters agreed, they'd rather have more of a lower fat cheese. Nonfat and reduced-fat mozzarellas tasted bland and their textures were rubbery, but part-skim mozzarella had a rich full flavor and good melting ability that made it the winner. I also added a sprinkling of freshly grated Parmesan, which gave the pizza an extra flavor boost and nice saltiness.

As for the toppings, sticking with vegetables was the obvious choice for adding flavor with minimal calories and fat. For color, texture, and nutrients, I liked the idea of broccoli, but adding it to the pizza raw didn't work: It was still far from done by the time the pizza was ready. Precooking was a must, so I quickly sautéed the broccoli until it was lightly browned to intensify its flavor, then I added some water to the pan and steamed it until tender. Garlic is always a good match for broccoli and a natural for pizza, so I added a few cloves to the pan with the

broccoli. And finally I tossed in some sun-dried tomatoes for a hint of sweetness. This topping combination was a hit, and keeping the amount of each ingredient in check ensured the pizza's components stayed in balance. All I had to do was prepare the dough and the sauce, precook the vegetables, then assemble and bake.

Thanks to a few tricks, my three key pizza components worked well together to create a healthy multigrain pizza that was fresh, satisfying, and tallied only 260 calories and 10 grams of fat for two slices. That beats takeout any day.

—CHRIS O'CONNOR, *America's Test Kitchen Books*

NOTES FROM THE TEST KITCHEN

MAKING GARLICKY BROCCOLI AND SUN-DRIED TOMATO PIZZA WITH MULTIGRAIN CRUST

1. Before making the dough, soften the dry cereal mix. Stir the boiling water and cereal mix together, cover, and let stand, stirring occasionally, until the mixture resembles a thick porridge and is just warm, about 30 minutes.

2. While the dough rests, make a quick no-cook tomato sauce and prepare the broccoli topping by sautéing broccoli with garlic and sun-dried tomatoes.

3. After preparing the dough and rolling out one of the rounds, transfer the round to a rimless (or inverted) baking sheet lined with parchment paper and reshape as needed, then brush the outer edge of the dough with oil.

4. Top the dough round with the tomato sauce, mozzarella, Parmesan, and half the broccoli mixture, leaving a half-inch border around the edge. Slide the paper and pizza onto a hot baking stone and bake for 8 to 13 minutes.

BAKING STONES TAKE THE HEAT

Clay or ceramic baking stones enable you to make ultra-crisp, chewy pizzas at home and improve the crust and crumb of any hearth-baked bread. Baking stones absorb both heat and moisture, which keeps the oven hot and dries out the pizza or bread's crust, guaranteeing crispness. We tested seven stones in different shapes, sizes, and materials to find out if all baking stones can take the heat. We judged the stones on two main criteria: design (including ease of use, installation, and storage) and performance (including heat conductivity, evenness of browning, and crispness of baked goods). For the most part, there was little issue with performance. With little variation, all seven stones produced evenly colored and crisp crusts in pizzas. Design, however, was another story. The **Baker's Catalogue Pizza Baking Stone**, $52.95, came out on top. It is a good-size baking stone (about 14 by 16 inches) that is not too heavy, with smooth, rimless edges that make it easy to slide loaves onto the surface.

A PACKAGE DEAL: SEVEN-GRAIN CEREAL

Scavenging for different grains is challenging and takes up precious time. When making our multigrain pizza dough, we prefer the ease of one-stop shopping: one bag of hot cereal mix, which already has seven grains. Be sure to buy hot cereal mix rather than boxed cold breakfast cereals that may also be labeled "seven-grain." Our favorite brand of seven-grain mix is **Bob's Red Mill**, which includes a mix of wheat, rye, oats, oat bran, barley, rice, and flaxseeds.

Garlicky Broccoli and Sun-Dried Tomato Pizza with Multigrain Crust

MAKES TWO 14-INCH PIZZAS

For an accurate measurement of boiling water, bring a full kettle of water to a boil, then measure out the desired amount. You can substitute unbleached all-purpose flour for the bread flour; however, the resulting crust will be a little less chewy. We prefer the softer texture of canned whole peeled tomatoes here; however, diced canned tomatoes can be substituted in a pinch. Garnish the pizza with a sprinkling of fresh chopped basil after cooking.

DOUGH

- 1¾ cups boiling water (see note)
- 1 cup (5 ounces) seven-grain hot cereal mix (see page 126)
- 2–2¼ cups (11 to 12⅓ ounces) bread flour
- 1 cup (5½ ounces) whole wheat flour
- 2¼ teaspoons (about 1 envelope) instant or rapid-rise yeast
- 1½ teaspoons salt
- 3 tablespoons olive oil

SAUCE AND TOPPINGS

- 1 (28-ounce) can whole peeled tomatoes, drained and juice reserved
- 1 tablespoon extra-virgin olive oil
- 5 garlic cloves, minced
- ½ teaspoon salt
- 4 teaspoons olive oil
- 8 ounces broccoli florets, cut into 1-inch pieces (about 3 cups)
- ¼ cup water
- ½ cup oil-packed sun-dried tomatoes, rinsed, patted dry, and sliced thin
- Pepper
- 3 cups shredded part-skim mozzarella cheese (about 12 ounces)
- ¼ cup grated Parmesan cheese

1. FOR THE DOUGH: Following the photos on page 126, stir the boiling water and cereal mix together in a medium bowl, cover, and let stand, stirring occasionally, until the mixture resembles a thick porridge and is just warm (about 110 degrees), about 30 minutes.

2. Pulse 2 cups of the bread flour, whole wheat flour, yeast, and salt together in a food processor to combine. Dollop the porridge mixture evenly over the top and drizzle in the oil. Process the mixture until a rough ball forms, 30 to 40 seconds. Let the dough rest for 2 minutes, then process for 30 seconds longer. If the dough is sticky and clings to the blade, add the remaining ¼ cup bread flour, 1 tablespoon at a time, and pulse to incorporate.

3. Turn the dough out onto a lightly floured counter and knead it into a smooth, round ball. Place the dough in a large, lightly oiled bowl and cover tightly with greased plastic wrap. Let rise in a warm place until nearly doubled in size, 1 to 1½ hours, before using. (If desired, you can slow the dough's rising time by letting it rise in the refrigerator for up to 16 hours; let the refrigerated dough soften at room temperature for 30 minutes before using. Once risen, the dough can be sealed in a zipper-lock bag and frozen for up to 1 month; let thaw on the counter for 2 to 3 hours, or overnight in the refrigerator, before using.)

4. FOR THE SAUCE AND TOPPINGS: Meanwhile, pulse the drained tomatoes, extra-virgin olive oil, 2 of the garlic cloves, and salt together in a food processor until coarsely ground and no large pieces remain, about 12 pulses. Transfer the mixture to a liquid measuring cup and add the reserved canned tomato juice until the sauce measures 2 cups.

5. Adjust an oven rack to the lower-middle position, place a baking stone on the rack, and heat the oven to 500 degrees. Let the baking stone heat for at least 30 minutes (but no longer than 1 hour).

6. Meanwhile, heat 2 teaspoons of the olive oil in a 12-inch nonstick skillet over medium heat until shimmering. Add the broccoli and cook until lightly browned, about 5 minutes. Stir in the remaining 3 garlic cloves and cook until fragrant, about 30 seconds. Add the water, cover, and cook for 3 minutes. Uncover, add the sun-dried tomatoes, and cook until the broccoli is tender and the water is evaporated, about 2 minutes. Season with salt and pepper to taste and transfer to a bowl.

7. Turn the dough out onto a lightly floured counter, divide it into 2 equal pieces, and cover with greased plastic wrap. Working with 1 piece of dough at a time (keep the other piece covered), press and roll the dough into a 14-inch round on a lightly floured counter. Transfer the dough to a rimless (or inverted) baking sheet lined with parchment paper and reshape as needed.

8. Lightly brush the outer ½-inch edge of the dough with a teaspoon more oil. Spread 1 cup of the pizza

CHICAGO DEEP-DISH PIZZA

sauce over the dough, leaving a ½-inch border at the edge. Sprinkle with 1½ cups of the mozzarella, 2 tablespoons of the Parmesan, and half the broccoli mixture.

9. Slide the parchment paper and pizza onto the hot baking stone. Bake the pizza until the edges are brown and the cheese is golden in spots, 8 to 13 minutes. (Assemble the second pizza while the first bakes.)

10. Remove the pizza from the oven by sliding the parchment paper back onto the baking sheet. Discard the parchment paper and slide the pizza onto a cutting board. Slice the pizza into 8 slices and serve hot. Let the stone reheat for 5 minutes before baking the second pizza.

CHICAGO DEEP-DISH PIZZA

UNLESS YOU'VE BEEN TO CHICAGO, YOU MAY DISMISS deep-dish pizza with the same scorn as bad-boy chef and author Anthony Bourdain, who views it as a doughy, tasteless "crime against food" that's nothing more than a platform for loading on cheese and toppings. But as I discovered on a trip to Chicago, the real deal has little to do with the overwrought impostors served up in franchise pizzerias. Sure, a Chicago crust is thick, but instead of being bland and bread-like, it offers the textural contrast of a good biscuit—airy inside, lightly crisp outside, and flaky throughout, with a rich taste that can hold its own.

I began my research at Chicago's original Pizzeria Uno, the 1943 birthplace of deep-dish pizza (not to be confused with the chain Uno Chicago Grill), and continued to such legendary spots as Gino's East and Lou Malnati's. Most of the pies I sampled shared the same high sides, rich and flaky crust, and toppings that reversed the usual order—first a blanket of mozzarella, maybe some sausage, and finally tomato sauce. None of these pizzerias would give me their recipes, but taste alone told me the key rested with two unorthodox ingredients: cornmeal and butter.

Back in Boston, a little research unearthed dozens of recipes claiming to replicate authentic Chicago deep-dish pizza that proved at least part of my hunch right: Cornmeal was definitely part of the deal. But while all the recipes I found listed far more fat than what you find in classic pizza dough (which relies on just a few tablespoons of olive oil), only a handful actually called for

butter. And those that did simply melted it and worked it into a recipe that, but for ½ cup cornmeal and a tiny bit of sugar, sounded an awful lot like classic pizza dough: Combine flour, cornmeal, salt, sugar, and yeast in a bowl, add melted butter and water, transfer ingredients to a stand mixer, and knead into a dough. Allow the dough to rise, divide it in half, and let it rise again until doubled in size. Then, instead of stretching each dough ball into a circle to be baked directly on a pizza stone, press the dough into a 9-inch round pan, add some toppings, and bake it on a stone in a 500-degree oven.

First impression? Not bad. The crust was more chewy than flaky, but the buttery flavor came through, and the cornmeal added nice earthiness and crunch.

But how to transform the crust from bread-like to biscuit-like? Maybe the answer had to do with biscuit techniques. First, I swapped melted butter for cold butter: cold butter melts in the oven and then steam fills the thin spaces left behind, resulting in flaky, buttery layers. Second, I traded my stand mixer for a food processor; for biscuits, we use it to cut butter into the dry ingredients instead of kneading the dough. Third, following biscuit protocol, I waited to add my liquid—water—until after the butter and dry ingredients were combined. I was cautiously optimistic, but my hopes soon crumbled—literally. This crust was so brittle it fell apart like a cracker.

I returned to the standing mixer and melted butter. While pondering other flaky baked goods, it occurred to me: Why not try laminating? This baking term refers to the layering of butter and dough used to create baked goods like ultra-flaky croissants, Danishes, and puff pastry through a sequence of rolling and folding. After melting part of the butter, I mixed it with the dough, allowed the dough to rise, and rolled it into a 15 by 12-inch rectangle. I spread the remaining 4 tablespoons of slightly softened butter over the surface and rolled the dough into a cylinder to create layers of buttery dough. To amplify this effect, I then flattened the cylinder into a rectangle, divided it in half, and folded each half into thirds, like a business letter.

So far, so good—except all that handling caused the temperature of the dough to rise. By the time I patted each half into a ball and tried to roll the balls flat, the dough had warmed so much that the butter had practically melted, leading to a crust that was more tender and breadlike than flaky—I was right back where I started. The solution? Moving the dough into the refrigerator

MAKING THE CRUST FOR CHICAGO DEEP-DISH PIZZA

1. After rolling out the dough into a 15 by 12-inch rectangle, spread the softened butter over the dough, leaving a ½-inch border along the edges.

2. Roll the dough into a tight cylinder, starting at the short end closest to you.

3. Flatten the dough cylinder into an 18 by 4-inch rectangle, then halve the cylinder crosswise.

4. Fold each dough half into thirds to form a ball and pinch the seams shut.

5. After letting the dough balls rise in the refrigerator for 40 to 50 minutes, roll out each ball into a 13-inch disk about ¼ inch thick.

6. Transfer the dough disks to the oiled pans and lightly press the dough into the pans, pressing it into the corners and up the sides.

for its second rise so that any butter that had melted or gotten overly soft could harden right back up again. This gave me a pizza with just the flaky texture I wanted.

My only additional tweak was adding 2 tablespoons of oil to each pan to crisp the edges. This worked so well that I wondered if the pizza stone was still necessary. One more test and I had my answer: It wasn't.

With my crust all set, I considered the cheese and the sauce—in that order. Sliced mozzarella, common to most recipes, had been my starting point, but when I pitted it against freshly shredded mozzarella, the latter won out for its smoother texture and the way it formed a consistent barrier between dough and sauce.

As for the sauce, I decided to try our Quick Tomato Sauce, which creates surprisingly complex flavor in a mere 15 minutes from canned crushed tomatoes. For a slightly thicker rendition that was more compatible with my Chicago pizza, I simmered it for an extra 15 minutes. This bright-tasting sauce won raves.

More than 100 pizzas later, I was satisfied with my own rich and tasty homage to this distinctive Midwestern pie.

—FRANCISCO J. ROBERT, *Cook's Illustrated*

Chicago Deep-Dish Pizza

MAKES TWO 9-INCH PIZZAS

You will need a standing mixer with a dough hook for this recipe. Place a damp kitchen towel under the mixer and watch it at all times during kneading to prevent it from wobbling off the counter. Handle the dough with slightly oiled hands to prevent sticking. The test kitchen prefers Dragone Whole Milk Mozzarella; part-skim mozzarella can also be used, but avoid preshredded cheese here. Our preferred brands of crushed tomatoes are Tuttorosso and Muir Glen. Grate the onion on the large holes of a box grater.

DOUGH

3¼ cups (16¼ ounces) unbleached all-purpose flour

½ cup (2¾ ounces) yellow cornmeal

2¼ teaspoons (about 1 envelope) instant or rapid-rise yeast

2 teaspoons sugar

1½ teaspoons salt

1¼ cups water, at room temperature

3 tablespoons unsalted butter, melted, plus 4 tablespoons, softened

1 teaspoon plus 4 tablespoons olive oil

SAUCE

- **2** tablespoons unsalted butter
- **¼** cup grated onion (see note)
- **¼** teaspoon dried oregano
  Salt
- **2** garlic cloves, minced
- **1** (28-ounce) can crushed tomatoes
- **¼** teaspoon sugar
- **2** tablespoons chopped fresh basil
- **1** tablespoon extra-virgin olive oil
  Pepper

TOPPINGS

- **1** pound mozzarella, shredded (about 4 cups)
- **¼** cup grated Parmesan cheese

1. FOR THE DOUGH: Mix the flour, cornmeal, yeast, sugar, and salt in the bowl of a standing mixer fitted with a dough hook on low speed until incorporated, about 1 minute. Add the water and melted butter and mix on low speed until fully combined, 1 to 2 minutes, scraping the sides and bottom of the bowl as needed. Increase the speed to medium and knead until the dough is glossy and smooth and pulls away from sides of the bowl, 4 to 5 minutes. (The dough will only pull away from the sides while the mixer is on. When the mixer is off, the dough will fall back to the sides.)

2. Using your fingers, coat a large bowl with 1 teaspoon of the olive oil, rubbing excess oil from your fingers onto the blade of a rubber spatula. Using the oiled spatula, transfer the dough to the oiled bowl, turning once to oil the top. Cover the bowl tightly with plastic wrap. Let the dough rise at room temperature until nearly doubled in volume, 45 to 60 minutes.

3. FOR THE SAUCE: While the dough rises, heat the butter in a medium saucepan over medium heat until melted. Add the onion, oregano, and ½ teaspoon salt and cook, stirring occasionally, until the liquid has evaporated and the onion is golden brown, about 5 minutes. Add the garlic and cook until fragrant,

about 30 seconds. Stir in the tomatoes and sugar, increase the heat to high, and bring to a simmer. Lower the heat to medium-low and simmer until the sauce has reduced to 2½ cups, 25 to 30 minutes. Off the heat, stir in the basil and oil, then season with salt and pepper to taste.

4. TO LAMINATE THE DOUGH: Adjust an oven rack to the lowest position and heat the oven to 425 degrees. Using a rubber spatula, turn the dough out onto a dry counter and roll into a 15 by 12-inch rectangle. Following the photos on page 130, use an offset spatula to spread the softened butter over the surface of the dough, leaving a ½-inch border along the edges. Starting at the short end, roll the dough into a tight cylinder. With the seam side down, flatten the cylinder into an 18 by 4-inch rectangle. Cut the rectangle in half crosswise. Working with 1 half, fold the dough into thirds like a business letter, then pinch the seams together to form a ball. Repeat with the remaining half of dough. Return the dough balls to the oiled bowl, cover tightly with plastic wrap, and let rise in the refrigerator until nearly doubled in volume, 40 to 50 minutes.

5. Coat two 9-inch round cake pans with 2 tablespoons olive oil each. Transfer 1 dough ball to a dry counter and roll out into a 13-inch disk about ¼ inch thick. Transfer the dough round to a cake pan by rolling the dough loosely around the rolling pin, then unrolling the dough into the pan. Lightly press the dough into the pan, working it into the corners and 1 inch up the sides. If the dough resists stretching, let it relax for 5 minutes before trying again. Repeat with the remaining dough ball.

6. For each pizza, sprinkle 2 cups of the mozzarella evenly over the surface of the dough. Spread 1¼ cups of the tomato sauce over the cheese and sprinkle 2 tablespoons of the Parmesan over the sauce for each pizza. Bake until the crust is golden brown, 20 to 30 minutes. Remove the pizza from the oven and let rest for 10 minutes before slicing and serving.

SLOW-COOKER BRAISED SHORT RIBS

SHORT RIBS ARE A TOUGH CUT OF MEAT THAT requires a long, slow braise to achieve melting, fork-tender perfection. Recipes for wine-braised ribs have you brown the meat to render some of the fat, and then sauté onions, carrots, and celery in the pot. Next, you stir in tomato paste, red wine, and broth (scraping up the flavorful browned bits known as fond) before returning the ribs to the pot to simmer. Given the usual three-hour cooking time, it's no surprise that most slow-cooker cookbooks include a recipe.

What did surprise me was that the recipes I tested weren't any good: In general, the ribs tasted boiled and drab, and the sauce was watery and dotted with fat. The closed, moist environment of a slow cooker allows no evaporation, so the flavors couldn't become concentrated and deepened. Clearly, I'd have to work on developing flavor before the ingredients entered slow-cooker lockdown. I put together a basic sauce (figuring I'd refine it later), then turned to the meat.

In the test kitchen, we use English-style ribs for braises. Their single bone and thick layer of meat make for hefty, uniform portions. I knew browning the ribs in a skillet first was key. But the ribs' curved bones prevented the meat from lying flat in the pan, in turn preventing the full development of fond, and thus flavor. Since I'd be removing the meat from the bone before serving anyway, I sliced it off the bone upfront, trimming fat at the same time. This allowed for more browning, and more fond development.

I tossed the raw bones into the slow cooker with the browned meat, but they added surprisingly little flavor. I cooked them in the skillet first to enhance their taste, but that pesky curve inhibited proper browning, so they made a lackluster statement. Roasting the bones (as restaurant chefs do when making stock) took too much time. Wondering if I could "roast" the bones in the microwave, I laid them in a baking dish and hit "start." After about 15 minutes, the bones looked like they'd spent hours in an oven, and indeed, they added unequivocal depth to the sauce.

Now the sauce was flavorful, but it lacked enough acid to balance the rich, fatty beef. I doubled the red wine from 1 cup to 2 cups—with scant effect. Next, I reduced the 2 cups back to 1 cup on the stovetop to concentrate the flavors—this gave the sauce real muscle. Two tablespoons of balsamic vinegar added a subtle sweetness that pulled the dish together.

For a glossy, velvety consistency, I rejected cornstarch (gluey) and flour (starchy) in favor of instant tapioca, which I added with the broth. One problem remained: Short ribs ooze fat as they cook. To fix this, many recipes chill them overnight so that the gelled fat can be scraped from the cooking liquid and discarded. I didn't want to add a day to my cooking, so I simply fished out the ribs and set them aside, discarded the bones, strained the sauce, and then reached for the fat separator—an easy fix. At last I had short ribs that were perfectly cooked and a sauce with sheen, body, and layers of flavor.

—MARÍA DEL MAR SACASA, *Cook's Country*

Slow-Cooker Red Wine–Braised Short Ribs
SERVES 4

We prefer English-style ribs here, each of which contains a single, large rib bone and a thick piece of meat, rather than thinner, flanken-style ribs. You will need 6 to 8 English-style ribs. If a 13 by 9-inch dish won't fit in your microwave, use the largest dish that will in step 1.

- 5 **pounds bone-in beef short ribs, trimmed**
- **Salt and pepper**
- 2 **tablespoons vegetable oil**
- 2 **onions, chopped (about 2 cups)**
- 1 **carrot, peeled and chopped**
- 1 **celery rib, chopped**
- 2 **tablespoons tomato paste**
- 1 **teaspoon dried thyme**
- 2 **cups dry red wine**
- 2 **tablespoons balsamic vinegar**
- 2 **cups low-sodium chicken broth**
- 2 **tablespoons Minute tapioca**
- 2 **bay leaves**
- 2 **tablespoons chopped fresh parsley**

1. Following the photos, cut the meat from the bones and set aside. Arrange the bones in a 13 by 9-inch baking dish and microwave until well browned, 10 to 15 minutes, rearranging the bones halfway through. Transfer to the slow cooker.

2. Pat the meat dry with paper towels and season with salt and pepper. Heat the oil in a 12-inch skillet over medium-high heat until just smoking. Cook the meat until well browned, about 5 minutes per side. Transfer to the slow cooker.

3. Cook the onions, carrot, and celery in the empty skillet over medium heat until browned, about 8 minutes. Stir in the tomato paste and thyme and cook until beginning to brown, about 1 minute. Stir in the wine and vinegar and simmer, scraping up any browned bits, until reduced to 1 cup, about 5 minutes. Stir in the broth, tapioca, and bay leaves and bring to a boil. Transfer the sauce to the slow cooker with the meat.

4. Cover the slow cooker and cook on low until the meat is fork-tender, about 8 hours (or cook on high for 4 to 5 hours). Transfer the meat to a serving platter. Strain and defat the cooking liquid and discard the solids. Stir the parsley into the sauce and season with salt and pepper to taste. Pour 1 cup of the sauce over the meat. Serve, passing the remaining sauce at the table.

NOTES FROM THE TEST KITCHEN

UNLOCKING BEEFY FLAVOR

1. For English-style short ribs (our preference here to flanken-style), insert a knife between the rib and meat and, staying as close to the bone as possible, saw the meat off the bone.

2. Microwave the bones for 10 to 15 minutes and add them to the slow cooker to add rich, roasted flavor.

SWISS STEAK

IN 1930, A GOOD HOUSEKEEPING COOKBOOK, *Meals, Tested, Tasted, and Approved,* featured a dish sometimes known as Swiss steak (the cookbook called it Tomato Steak). Round steaks were pounded, floured, browned, and then smothered in carrots, tomatoes, and turnips, which cooked down during a long oven braise to a savory, satisfying gravy. The steaks, meanwhile, became almost tender enough to eat with a spoon. The recipe enabled frugal housewives to transform a tough, cheap cut of meat and ordinary vegetables into a delicious and filling meal. Sadly, over the years, Swiss steak became the province of school cafeterias and the victim of mid-century convenience trends (onion soup mixes, etc.). But made right, it's an easy, inexpensive supper. I set out to restore and, better yet, perfect it.

I began by making that original recipe along with a handful of others, which variously added celery and bell peppers and used different cuts of meat, like cube steak and blade steak. The promise of the dish—its ease, economy, and tangy, beefy flavors—was evident. But none of the recipes lived up to it. Gravies were bland, pasty, or watery. The meat by turn was dry, mangled, gristly, or too thin to qualify as a meaty steak.

Starting with a basic gravy of onions, canned tomato sauce, and water, I began by testing different cuts of meat. It had to be economical, as would befit Swiss steak. Tasters rejected the round steak as lean, dry, and livery, and cube steaks as mangled, shaggy, and too thin for Swiss steak. I moved on to blade steaks. In their favor: a thick shape and good beefy flavor. Against them: a line of gristle running down the middle. A deal breaker, tasters said.

The butcher suggested chuck roast, a well-marbled cut popular in stews. I carved the roast into steak-size pieces—or tried to. But the same pockets of fat that made this cut juicy also prevented me from cutting it into neat steaks. This Swiss steak was moist, tender, and appropriately beefy—it just wasn't steak. Since I was going to the trouble of butchering, maybe I ought to butcher a blade roast into steaks. With a little ingenuity, could I trim the gristle? I cut a whole blade roast into four chunks, turned the chunks on their sides, cut again, then sliced off the gristle. I was headed in the right direction.

By the way, Swiss steak doesn't come from Switzerland. Rather, the recipe's name comes from the technique of pounding raw meat to tenderize it, which resembles swissing, a method of smoothing out cloth between two rollers. (A 1930s recipe instructed pounding flour into the steak "until it could take no more.") But the problem is, pounding doesn't actually tenderize meat. The only way to tenderize a tough piece of meat is to physically shorten the muscle fibers. Consider cube steak. Cut from the round, cube steak is naturally tough. That's why the individual round steaks are fed through a machine that "cubes" the meat at multiple angles with needle-like blades. The blades sever the muscle fibers, rendering tough meat tender. Pounding meat only compresses the muscle fibers, ensuring a consistent thickness. So call me a heretic, but I skipped the swissing step; the slow braise (about two hours in a 300-degree oven) made the meat plenty tender. As for the flour,

stirring a tablespoon into the gravy to thicken it was simpler than dredging the meat and had the same effect.

Thus far, my gravy mix of tomato sauce, water, and raw onions tasted uninspired. I added, in turn, turnips, carrots, bell peppers, and celery. The tomato sweetened the sauce without carrots, and tasters insisted I eliminate the other vegetables. So I simply sautéed the onions in the fat from the browned steaks, then bolstered them with tomato paste, garlic, and thyme. Next, I replaced the water with chicken broth. After that, I discovered that diced tomatoes supplied more body than sauce. Swiss steak's original name, tomato steak, gave me the idea to stir in minced sun-dried tomatoes, which really pulled the dish together.

—LYNN CLARK, *Cook's Country*

NOTES FROM THE TEST KITCHEN

BUTCHERING BLADE ROAST FOR SWISS STEAK

Top blade roast, a shoulder cut with great flavor, has a pesky line of gristle that runs horizontally through its center. Follow these simple steps to remove it and cut perfect Swiss steaks.

1. Place the roast on a carving board and cut it crosswise into 4 even pieces.

2. Turn one steak on its side to expose the line of gristle that runs through its center.

3. Remove the gristle by cutting through the meat on either side of gristle to yield 2 "steaks." Repeat with the remaining pieces of blade roast to yield a total of 8 steaks.

Swiss Steak with Tomato Gravy

SERVES 6 TO 8

Top blade roast may also be labeled chuck roast first cut, top chuck roast, flat iron roast, or simply blade roast. Use low-sodium chicken broth or the gravy will be too salty.

- 1 (3½ to 4-pound) boneless top blade roast
  Salt and pepper
- 2 tablespoons vegetable oil
- 1 onion, halved and sliced thin
- 2 tablespoons tomato paste
- 1 tablespoon unbleached all-purpose flour
- 3 garlic cloves, minced
- ½ teaspoon dried thyme
- 1 (14.5-ounce) can diced tomatoes
- 1½ cups low-sodium chicken broth
- 1 tablespoon sun-dried tomatoes packed in oil, rinsed, patted dry, and minced
- 1 tablespoon finely chopped fresh parsley

1. Adjust an oven rack to the middle position and heat the oven to 300 degrees. Following the photos, cut the roast crosswise into quarters and remove the line of gristle to yield 8 steaks.

2. Pat the steaks dry with paper towels and season with salt and pepper. Heat 1 tablespoon of the oil in a large Dutch oven over medium-high heat until just smoking. Brown 4 of the steaks, about 3 minutes per side. Transfer the steaks to a plate and repeat with the remaining 1 tablespoon oil and 4 steaks.

3. Add the onion to the empty pot and cook until softened, about 5 minutes. Add the tomato paste, flour, garlic, and thyme and cook until fragrant, about 1 minute. Stir in the diced tomatoes and broth and bring to a boil.

4. Return the steaks and any accumulated juice to the pot. Transfer the pot to the oven and braise, covered, until the steaks are fork-tender, about 2 hours. Transfer the steaks to a platter, tent with foil, and let rest for 5 minutes. Skim the fat from the sauce. Stir in the sun-dried tomatoes and parsley. Season with salt and pepper to taste, pour the sauce over the steaks, and serve.

SUPER-CRUSTY GRILLED STEAKS

THE BEST STEAKS ARE SALTY, SIZZLING, AND ALMOST singed on the outside and juicy, red, and almost buttery within. It's this contrast between the exterior and interior that makes for perfect steak. Steakhouses achieve a formidable crust with industrial-strength grills and broilers (some pushing temperatures into quadruple digits) that instantly evaporate surface moisture on the meat, leaving a dry surface upon which to build a substantial caramelized crust. Home rigs can't get that hot (500 degrees is all you can ask for), so you can kiss good crust goodbye.

I wanted to use any old backyard grill to get that same delicious charred crust on our favorite tender (and expensive) cuts: strip, filet mignon (a.k.a. tenderloin), and rib-eye. Most of us buy prepackaged supermarket steaks, which sit in a pool of juice on a Styrofoam tray. The obvious first step was to dry them. I blotted them with paper towels, heated the grill, seasoned the steaks with salt and pepper, and cooked them to medium-rare over a hot fire. They were pretty good eating, but the exteriors stayed pale and moist.

Many steakhouses dry-age beef for weeks to tenderize the meat (enzymes in the meat slowly break down) and concentrate the flavor by way of dehydration. I wondered if a byproduct of that dehydration—less moisture to be exuded during cooking, thus a drier surface—could help me develop a steakhouse-worthy crust. So I tried quickly "aging" my steak overnight in the refrigerator (uncovered on a wire rack). It worked, but in the end I decided it was too much advance work for a simple grilled steak. But I was on the right track.

Aware that salt draws moisture out of foods, I salted the steaks and let them sit on paper towels for an hour before cooking. The paper towels became soggy, but the grilled steaks still failed to form a respectable crust. Moving on, I sprinkled the steaks with sugar with the idea it might caramelize into a crusty coating. The sugar burned, the steaks tasted sweet—a complete failure.

In the test kitchen, we often talk about how the freezer robs food of moisture. Its intensely dry environment causes rapid evaporation. Nine times out of 10, it's an effect we're trying to counteract, but could it work in my favor here? I froze unwrapped steaks for an hour, then placed them on a hot grill. It did the trick! Since the steaks had been frozen for just an hour, the interiors remained tender and juicy, but the exteriors were sufficiently dehydrated to develop a first-class crust. (Starting out with cold meat also bought me almost a minute of extra grill time to develop char.)

Next, I tried salting the steaks before partially freezing them, which not only assured a well-seasoned steak but also drew moisture to the surface, where it evaporated. For one final test, I mixed the salt with a teaspoon of cornstarch—a champ at absorbing moisture. That allowed me to cut the freezing time in half—to just 30 minutes—and still achieve a bone-dry exterior.

My own house might not have the swagger and mahogany of a steakhouse, but I had what I wanted most: a perfect grilled steak.

—LYNN CLARK, *Cook's Country*

Super-Crusty Grilled Steaks
SERVES 4

To minimize flare-ups, trim excess fat and gristle from the steaks before grilling. Serve with Classic Steak Sauce (recipe follows), if desired. We prefer these steaks cooked to medium-rare, but if you prefer them more or less done, see "Testing Meat for Doneness" on page 139.

1 teaspoon salt
1 teaspoon cornstarch
4 strip, rib-eye, or tenderloin steaks, about 1½ inches thick
Pepper

1. Combine the salt and cornstarch in a small bowl. Pat the steaks dry with paper towels and rub with the

SUPER-CRUSTY GRILLED STEAKS

salt mixture. Arrange the steaks on a wire rack set inside a rimmed baking sheet and freeze until the steaks are firm and dry to the touch, at least 30 minutes or up to 1 hour.

2A. FOR A CHARCOAL GRILL: Open the bottom grill vents completely. Light a large chimney starter filled with charcoal briquettes (100 briquettes; 6 quarts). When the coals are hot, pour them in an even layer over the grill. Set the cooking grate in place, cover, and heat the grill until hot, about 5 minutes.

2B. FOR A GAS GRILL: Turn all the burners to high, cover, and heat the grill until hot, about 15 minutes. (Adjust the burners as needed to maintain a hot fire; see page 19).

3. Season the steaks with pepper. Clean and oil the cooking grate. Grill the steaks (covered if using gas) until the meat registers 120 to 125 degrees on an instant-read thermometer, about 5 minutes per side. Transfer to a plate, tent with foil, and let rest for 5 minutes. Serve.

NOTES FROM THE TEST KITCHEN

KEYS TO A GOOD CRUST

We discovered two important tricks to achieving a steakhouse crust on our grilled steaks.

1. Rubbing each steak with salt and cornstarch accelerates drying.

2. Freezing the steaks for 30 minutes causes rapid evaporation of moisture.

A BRIGHT IDEA: GRILL LIGHTS

After sundown, grilling enthusiasts can literally be left out in the dark. Enter the grill light. Attached to a side table or cabinet handle, it should illuminate the grate so you can read a thermometer and cook food properly. We waited until dark to grill with four models, as well as a cap with lights built into the brim. The latter was a bust; its twin beams barely illuminated the food. Among the lights, we disliked clip attachments that only gripped flat surfaces and plastic components that ended up too close to the fire. Our favorite, the **Camp Chef Chef's Grill Light**, $25, attaches anywhere, and its 24-inch flexible neck can bend or stretch to shine light on any part of the grill. Five LED lights on this winner illuminated food clearly, and the sturdy C-clamp held tight even when knocked.

TESTING MEAT FOR DONENESS

An instant-read thermometer is the most reliable method for checking the doneness of chicken, beef, and pork. To use an instant-read thermometer, simply insert it through the side of a chicken breast, steak, or pork chop. The chart below lists temperatures at which the meat should be removed from the heat (the temperature of the meat will continue to climb another 5 to 10 degrees as it rests before serving).

WHEN IS IT DONE?

MEAT	COOK UNTIL IT REGISTERS	SERVING TEMPERATURE
Chicken and Turkey Breasts	160 to 165 degrees	160 to 165 degrees
Chicken Thighs	175 degrees	175 degrees
Duck Breasts		
Medium-rare	120 to 125 degrees	130 degrees
Medium	130 to 135 degrees	140 degrees
Medium-well	140 to 145 degrees	150 degrees
Well-done	150 to 155 degrees	160 degrees
Pork	140 to 145 degrees	150 degrees
Beef and Lamb		
Rare	115 to 120 degrees	125 degrees
Medium-rare	120 to 125 degrees	130 degrees
Medium	130 to 135 degrees	140 degrees
Medium-well	140 to 145 degrees	150 degrees
Well-done	150 to 155 degrees	160 degrees

Classic Steak Sauce

MAKES 1¼ CUPS

Raisins may seem unusual here, but they add depth and sweetness. For accurate measurement of boiling water, bring a full kettle of water to a boil, then measure out the desired amount.

  ½ **cup boiling water (see note)**
  ⅓ **cup raisins**
  ¼ **cup ketchup**
  3 **tablespoons Worcestershire sauce**
  2 **tablespoons Dijon mustard**
  2 **tablespoons white vinegar**
     Salt and pepper

Combine the water and raisins in a bowl and let sit, covered, until the raisins are plump, about 5 minutes. Puree the raisin mixture, ketchup, Worcestershire, mustard, and vinegar in a blender until smooth. Season with salt and pepper to taste. (The sauce can be refrigerated in an airtight container for up to 1 week.)

STEAK TIPS WITH MUSHROOM-ONION GRAVY

STEAK TIPS SMOTHERED IN MUSHROOM AND ONION gravy is a classic combination, and it always beckons with its promise of juicy meat and hearty, satisfying flavors. But often it's nothing more than chewy, overcooked beef swimming in either a thin, generic brown sauce or a thick sludge of bland gravy. When I researched recipes, I quickly realized why this meal is often disappointing. It usually calls for small, easily overcooked strips of beef and flavor-sacrificing shortcuts like canned cream of mushroom soup, dried onion soup mix, or ketchup. It wasn't hard to envision a much better rendition, one that featured tender, meaty pieces of steak covered in a sauce enriched by the essence of fresh mushrooms and onions. If I could figure out an efficient way to coax full flavor from these simple ingredients—ideally using one pan—I'd have a great addition to my weeknight repertoire.

First, I needed a basic framework. After some initial tests, I found it was possible to cook the entire dish in one skillet, first searing the beef and setting it aside, then building the gravy, and finally adding the meat back to the gravy to cook through. Beyond convenience, this method offered two key advantages: the initial sear left my skillet full of the crusty browned bits known as fond, which provided a flavorful base for the sauce, and adding the partially cooked beef to the gravy and simmering until it cooked through allowed the flavors to mingle and build depth.

The next task was finding the right beef for the job. Though you occasionally find the dish made with expensive cuts like strip steak, rib-eye steak, and tenderloin, I didn't want to pay top dollar for a midweek meal. I turned to cheaper cuts: flank steak, round steak, and, of course, the most common choice, sirloin steak tips (also known as flap meat). This beefy cut has a wealth of internal marbling that melted into the coarse muscle fibers of the steak, adding tenderness when the meat was cooked to medium-rare. Flank steak made a suitable substitute if steak tips were unavailable but wasn't nearly as meaty-tasting, while round steak lacked intramuscular fat, easily turning bland, dry, and chalky after simmering in the gravy. Steak tips were ideal after all.

I wanted to develop a flavorful, well-seared crust yet leave the interior slightly underdone, so it wouldn't turn chewy and tough when I returned it to the pan to simmer with the gravy. I experimented with cutting the meat into various sizes and eventually settled on 1½-inch chunks. These gave me plenty of surface area to brown in a reasonable amount of time and were large enough that they didn't overcook in the sauce. To promote browning and a flavorful crust on the meat, I sprinkled the pieces with a little sugar before searing. These steak tips tasted pretty darn good, but could I get them even juicier?

One of the test kitchen's proven methods for beefing up steak flavor and juiciness is a quick soak in soy sauce. The salty soy draws juices out of the steak, and then the reverse happens as the soy, along with the moisture, flows back in, bringing deep flavor into the meat. Adding the sugar to the soy sauce instead of sprinkling it on separately bolstered flavor even more. After its 30-minute soak in the sugar-soy mixture and a quick sear, I produced the beefiest steak yet, with a substantial crust and plenty of fond left behind. I figured the rest would be gravy.

Up to this point, I had been adding a little vegetable oil to the pan and starting my sauce with half a pound of sliced white mushrooms. The flavor proved more mild than meaty, so I tried increasing the amount of mushrooms. But even with a pound of mushrooms, the flavor was still lacking. Costlier creminis were only slightly earthier and while portobellos had better flavor tasters found them leathery. Plus, unless I scooped out their black gills (a tedious process), the portobellos left the gravy unappealingly murky. Next I tried adding ¼ ounce of dried porcinis (hydrated in some beef broth) to the pan along with the white mushrooms. While their texture was only subtly perceptible, the porcinis contributed the intense mushroom flavor I was looking for.

My next consideration was the sauce's liquid component. Homemade stock was out of the question for this weeknight meal. I would make do with canned beef broth—a beefy but mild alternative—and then try adding some of the usual suspects to boost flavor: Worcestershire sauce, tomato paste, red wine, and more soy sauce. Tasters felt lukewarm about each addition, telling me that these ingredients actually overpowered the meatiness.

Then I stumbled upon a better way to boost the gravy's flavor. To cook the mushrooms in the same pan that I used to cook the beef, I needed to make sure they released moisture quickly enough to dissolve the fond before it burned. Lightly salting the mushrooms immediately after placing them in the pan helped break down their cell walls and set their juices flowing more quickly. Once the mushrooms had "deglazed" the pan and started to brown, I added a thinly sliced onion and more salt to the skillet (to expedite the onion's release of moisture) and waited until the vegetables were deeply browned, their liquid had cooked off, and even more browned bits clung to the pan. I now had a triple-header for flavor: a classic meat fond compounded by two layers of vegetable fond.

To thicken the broth into gravy, I tried adding cornstarch, but it created a gelatinous sauce that reminded tasters of a bad beef stir-fry. Sprinkling flour over the mushrooms as they sautéed was much more effective in creating a rich, lump-free gravy. As a finishing touch, I added a minced garlic clove and ½ teaspoon of chopped thyme, which accented the woodsy flavor of the mushrooms.

After making a final batch and gently simmering the meat and gravy together for five minutes to meld their flavors, tasters told me I was done. I took a few bites and agreed: My homemade steak tips were far better than anything I'd ever been served in a pub.

—KEITH DRESSER, *Cook's Illustrated*

Steak Tips with Mushroom-Onion Gravy
SERVES 4 TO 6

Steak tips, also known as flap meat, are sold as whole steak, cubes, and strips; we prefer to purchase whole steak tips and cut them ourselves. If you can only find cubes or strips, reduce the cooking time slightly to avoid overcooking any smaller or thinner pieces. Cremini mushrooms can be used in place of the white mushrooms. Serve over rice or egg noodles.

1   tablespoon soy sauce
1   teaspoon sugar
1½   pounds sirloin steak tips, trimmed and
     cut into 1½-inch chunks
¼   ounce dried porcini mushrooms, rinsed
1¾   cups low-sodium beef broth
     Salt and pepper
2   tablespoons vegetable oil
1   pound white mushrooms, sliced ¼ inch thick
1   large onion, halved and sliced thin
4   teaspoons unbleached all-purpose flour
1   garlic clove, minced
½   teaspoon minced fresh thyme
1   tablespoon chopped fresh parsley

1. Combine the soy sauce and sugar in a medium bowl. Add the beef, toss well, and marinate for at least 30 minutes or up to 1 hour, tossing once.

2. Meanwhile, cover the porcini mushrooms with ¼ cup of the broth in a small microwave-safe bowl. Cover with plastic wrap, cut several vents in the plastic, and microwave for 30 seconds. Let stand until the mushrooms soften, about 5 minutes. Lift the mushrooms from the liquid with a fork and mince (you should have about 1½ tablespoons). Strain the liquid through a fine-mesh strainer lined with a paper towel into a medium bowl. Set the mushrooms and liquid aside.

3. Sprinkle the meat with ½ teaspoon pepper. Heat 1 tablespoon of the oil in a 12-inch skillet over medium-high heat until smoking. Add the meat and cook until well browned on all sides, 6 to 8 minutes. Transfer to a large plate and set aside.

4. Return the skillet to medium-high heat and add the remaining 1 tablespoon oil, the white mushrooms, porcinis, and ¼ teaspoon salt. Cook, stirring frequently, until all the liquid has evaporated and the mushrooms start to brown, 7 to 9 minutes. Scrape the pan to loosen the fond. Add the onion and ¼ teaspoon salt and

BUYING THE RIGHT STEAK TIPS

Steak tips (also called "flap meat" or "sirloin tips") have a big beefy flavor and tender texture (when sliced properly against the grain) that make this cut one of our favorite inexpensive steaks. But since "steak tips" is a catch-all phrase for almost any type of beef cut into strips, it can be tricky to identify. The easiest way is to look at the grain: Flap meat has a large-grained texture that is distinct from other beef cuts, which tend to have a finer, tighter grain. And be sure to buy a whole steak (right), not strips (center) or cubes (left).

GET IT COARSE-GRAINED
Look for a whole "steak tip" steak (right) with a large-grained texture.

KEYS TO RICH, HEARTY STEAK TIPS AND GRAVY

1. Soak the steak tips in soy sauce and sugar to boost the meaty flavor and browning.

2. Sear the steak tips to create flavorful browned bits (fond) that serve as the base for a rich gravy.

3. Cook mushrooms, then onions, in the pan with the fond left by the meat until they are deeply caramelized to form an extra layer of flavorful fond.

continue to cook, stirring frequently, until the onion begins to brown and dark bits form on the bottom of the pan, 6 to 8 minutes longer. Add the flour, garlic, and thyme and cook, stirring constantly, until the vegetables are coated with flour, about 1 minute. Stir in the remaining 1½ cups beef broth and the porcini soaking liquid, scraping the bottom of the pan to loosen the browned bits, and bring to a boil.

5. Nestle the steak pieces into the mushroom and onion mixture and add any accumulated juice to the skillet. Reduce the heat to medium-low and simmer until the steak registers 130 degrees on an instant-read thermometer, 3 to 5 minutes, turning the beef several times. Season with salt and pepper to taste, sprinkle with parsley, and serve.

OLD-FASHIONED ENCHILADAS

WHEN I THINK OF HOMEMADE ENCHILADAS, I THINK of ground beef mixed with an overload of chili powder, cooked almost bone dry, rolled in a tortilla, and slathered with a flavorless red sauce (perhaps from a can) and gobs of cheese. What comes out of the oven, albeit speedy and easy, doesn't go far in terms of satisfying your belly, much less your soul. But American-style enchiladas weren't always so uninspired. When Mexican immigrants first adapted enchiladas to the local tastes and ingredients, sure, they toned down the spices and added extra cheese, but the flavor was still plenty big, a reflection of a long cooking time and well-chosen ingredients. These "Americanized" enchiladas were filled with tender shredded meat that had been braised for hours, and they were topped with a slow-simmered, deeply flavored sauce that had a bold, yet well-balanced, kick. Today it's surprisingly hard to find a legit old-fashioned American enchilada recipe, as everyone has seemingly traded in the full-flavored, soul-satisfying original for the sake of speed and convenience.

So when I spotted a recipe called Grandma's Enchiladas, sent in for our Lost Suppers recipe contest, it really caught my attention. Josie Landon, the entrant, was from Idaho, so I admit I was a little skeptical at first (shouldn't the best enchiladas come from New Mexico or South Texas?), but after I read her entry, I knew these enchiladas were the real deal. Josie's recipe came from the grandmother of one of her good childhood friends, and it called for building a sauce that included five spices (not just the usual chili powder), and then cooking a chuck roast right in the sauce, low and slow. When the meat was done, it was shredded and the enchiladas were assembled, topped with sauce and cheese, then put into the oven to heat through. This sounded just like the kind of old-fashioned, slow-cooked recipe I'd been dreaming of. I couldn't wait to give it a test run.

Starting with the sauce, Josie called for sautéing onions and garlic, then adding spices (cumin, cayenne, chili powder, coriander, and black pepper), chopped fresh tomatoes, water, tomato paste, and a splash of red wine. She simmered this mixture for 30 minutes or longer (she noted several hours is best), then pureed it in the blender. It had all the markings of a great, full-bodied sauce and I was well rewarded after one test. I didn't want to change much; however, I did end up with 13 cups of the stuff—great if you want fill the freezer but I wanted to make just enough to serve a small group. So I scaled it down to make just 3 cups. I also swapped out the fresh tomatoes for canned sauce, which meant I didn't have to cook the tomatoes down, dramatically shortening the cooking time. (Also, using canned sauce meant I didn't have to drag out our blender.) I wasn't too worried about shortchanging the flavor when I made this change to Josie's recipe because I knew the sauce would have plenty of time to concentrate in the next step, when it was cooking with the meat.

Josie cooked a 4-pound chuck roast with 2 to 3 cups of the sauce in a slow cooker for 8 to 10 hours, then shredded it. This meat was full-flavored and ultra-tender, but I wasn't keen on it taking 10 hours. There was also some extra meat, so I scaled down to 3 pounds, and I found I could get the same results in less time by cubing the roast prior to cooking instead of leaving it whole. I cooked it in the sauce just as Josie had, but instead of using a slow cooker I placed the sauce and meat in a pot and put it in a 300-degree oven, covered, for a few hours. I found that browning the meat before it went in the oven further deepened its flavor. Once the meat was tender, I shredded the meat and strained the sauce. Both had exactly the deep, rich flavor I was after.

Assembling the enchiladas was simple. I spread a little of the sauce over the bottom of a casserole dish just as Josie instructed, then I spooned the meat into the tortillas and rolled them up before placing them in the

pan. Josie topped the enchiladas with sauce and then cheddar cheese, two steps that I agreed were a given, but I also added some the sauce and cheese to the inside of the enchiladas to get saucy, cheesy appeal throughout. An old test kitchen trick of spraying the tortillas with vegetable oil before rolling ensured the tortillas didn't dry out during baking.

Less than 30 minutes later, out of the oven came hearty, meaty enchiladas in a smoky-spicy sauce that had all the flavor and comfort-food appeal I could have possibly hoped for. Clearly, good old-fashioned cooking was anything but lost.

—JENNIFER LALIME, *America's Test Kitchen Books*

ASSEMBLING ENCHILADAS

1. Grease a 13 by 9-inch baking dish, then spread ¾ cup of the sauce over the bottom of the dish.

2. Place ⅓ cup of the beef mixture evenly down the center of each warmed tortilla. Tightly roll the tortillas and place them seam side down in the baking dish.

3. Pour the remaining 1 cup sauce over the enchiladas to coat evenly.

4. Sprinkle the enchiladas with the remaining 1 cup cheese and cover the baking dish tightly with foil before baking.

OLD-FASHIONED ENCHILADAS

Old-Fashioned Enchiladas

SERVES 6

This recipe calls for dry red wine; we prefer to use Côtes du Rhône or generically labeled "table" wines that use a combination of grapes. Avoid oaky wines like Cabernet Sauvignon.

- 1 (3-pound) boneless beef chuck-eye roast, trimmed and cut into 1½-inch pieces (see page 46)
  Salt and black pepper
- 2 tablespoons vegetable oil
- 2 onions, minced (about 2 cups)
- 3 tablespoons chili powder
- 2 teaspoons ground cumin
- 2 teaspoons ground coriander
- ¼ teaspoon cayenne pepper
- 4 garlic cloves, minced
- 2 (15-ounce) cans tomato sauce
- ¼ cup dry red wine
- 8 ounces cheddar cheese, shredded (about 2 cups)
- 12 (6-inch) corn tortillas
  Vegetable oil spray
- ¼ cup chopped fresh cilantro, for serving
  Lime wedges, for serving

1. Adjust an oven rack to the lower-middle position and heat the oven to 300 degrees. Pat the beef dry with paper towels and season with salt and black pepper. Heat 1 tablespoon of the oil in a large Dutch oven over medium-high heat until just smoking. Add half of the beef and cook until well browned on all sides, about 8 minutes, turning as needed. Transfer the beef to a bowl. Repeat with the remaining 1 tablespoon oil and the remaining beef.

2. Pour off all but 1 tablespoon fat from the pot. Add the onions and ½ teaspoon salt and cook, stirring occasionally, until softened, 5 to 7 minutes. Stir in the chili powder, cumin, coriander, cayenne, and ¼ teaspoon black pepper and cook until the spices darken slightly and are fragrant, about 2 minutes. Stir in the garlic and cook until fragrant, about 30 seconds. Stir in the tomato sauce and wine and bring to a simmer, scraping up any browned bits.

3. Return the beef, along with any accumulated juice, to the sauce. Bring to a simmer, then cover the pot and place it in the oven. Cook until the meat is tender, 2 to 2½ hours. Transfer the beef to a plate. Pour the sauce

through a fine-mesh strainer, discarding the solids, and set aside. (You should have about 2 cups sauce.)

4. Adjust an oven rack to the middle position and increase the temperature to 375 degrees. Grease a 13 by 9-inch baking dish. Following the photos on page 143, spread ¾ cup of the sauce over the bottom of the dish and set aside.

5. When the meat is cool enough to handle, shred it into bite-size pieces and place it in a bowl. Add ¼ cup of the sauce and 1 cup of the cheese and toss to combine.

6. Spray the tortillas on both sides with vegetable oil spray and arrange on a rimmed baking sheet. Bake until the tortillas are warm and pliable, about 1 minute. Spread the tortillas out over a clean counter. Place ⅓ cup of the beef mixture evenly down the center of each tortilla. Tightly roll the tortillas around the filling, then lay them seam side down in the baking dish.

7. Pour the remaining 1 cup sauce over the enchiladas to coat evenly. Sprinkle with the remaining 1 cup cheese and cover tightly with foil. Bake until the enchiladas are heated through and the cheese is melted, 20 to 25 minutes. Serve with the cilantro and lime wedges.

EMPANADAS

AS ALL-IN-ONE MEALS GO, EMPANADAS—THE SOUTH American equivalent of Britain's pasties, or meat turnovers—are a difficult act to beat: a moist, savory filling encased in a tender yet sturdy crust. Though by no means tough, the crust is resilient enough to hold up to travel, making empanadas a favorite working-man's lunch in Latin America (and an ideal make-ahead candidate for us). With so much going for them, what's not to love?

For starters, all the work. Although there are endless crust and filling variations, most recipes demand more time and fuss (not to mention the deep-frying mess involved with many recipes) than the average home cook has to spare. I decided early on to make things easier for myself: That meant forgoing deep-frying or esoteric ingredients. Even a braised shredded beef stuffing, as many recipes suggest, would prolong my kitchen work unnecessarily. Instead, I narrowed my focus to ground beef–filled pies encased in a simple, flaky crust that would be hearty enough to stand as a main course on my dinner table.

Finding a popular flavor profile for the filling was as easy as opening a Chilean cookbook. *Empanadas de pino* combine savory-sweet spiced beef with raisins, briny olives, and hard-cooked eggs. The best pino recipes sautéed onions and garlic with a few spices, then added tiny, hand-chopped chunks of beef before the eggs, raisins, and olives were stirred in. Starting with packaged ground beef seemed like an easy streamlining step, but even with moist, 85 percent lean ground chuck, the finished pino had a rubbery, pebbly texture. For help, I turned to an Italian meatball-softening trick: blending the ground beef with a milk-and-bread mixture known as a panade. As the mixture cooks, starches in the bread absorb moisture from the milk and form a gel around the protein molecules, which lubricates the meat in much the same way as fat. Adding a slice of bread mashed with 2 tablespoons of milk to my ground chuck markedly improved the texture, but the filling really took shape when I replaced the milk with an equal amount of chicken broth, intensifying the meaty flavor.

To round out the flavor of the filling, tasters liked a hefty dose of aromatics: two onions and four cloves of garlic. The winning spice mix was a combination of cumin, cayenne, and cloves, which I sautéed in oil, or "bloomed," in the pan before adding the beef. Finally, a handful of cilantro leaves and a few teaspoons of vinegar, along with the chopped eggs, raisins, and green olives, brought freshness, sweetness, and acidity to the mix.

Until now, I'd been wrapping the filling in the test kitchen's Foolproof Pie Dough. The pastry combines butter (for flavor) and shortening (for tenderness) with water and the unusual addition of vodka. Since gluten (the protein matrix that makes pie crusts tough) doesn't form in alcohol, using the high-proof alcohol (tequila works just as well) allows you to add more liquid to the mix; the result is dough that's both more workable and more tender. (Any trace of alcohol flavor burns off during baking.)

That said, my tasters found the buttery, flaky crusts too similar to British pasties. Hoping to introduce more Latin-inspired flavors, I traded some of the flour for masa harina, the ground, dehydrated cornmeal used to make Mexican tortillas and tamales. Though unusual, the cornmeal provided welcome nutty richness and rough-hewn texture. Even better, less flour meant less protein in the dough; less protein meant I didn't need shortening (to tenderize the dough) and could switch to all butter for better flavor. Dividing the dough into a dozen smaller rounds before rolling them out into individual shells hastened the process.

Most pastry shells (and empanada crusts) receive an egg wash before baking for a lustrous finish, but I'm not one for cosmetics if they don't also improve flavor and texture. For a crisp crust, I brushed the shells with a little oil. Now the tops boasted shine and crunch, but the undersides dulled in comparison. No problem; preheating the baking sheet (as you would a pizza stone) and drizzling the surface with oil helped crisp up the bottoms. The result was a crust so shatteringly crisp that it almost passed for fried, giving way to a filling as flavorful as those of the best hand-chopped pinos.

I'd more than succeeded in bringing this recipe home; in fact, I would put my unconventional crust up against a more authentic version any day. And next time I get a craving for empanadas, I won't have to call my travel agent.

—BRYAN ROOF, *Cook's Illustrated*

Beef Empanadas

SERVES 4 TO 6

The alcohol in the dough is essential to the texture of the crust and imparts no flavor—do not omit it or substitute water. Masa harina can be found in the international aisle with other Latin foods or in the baking aisle with the flour. If you cannot find masa harina, replace it with additional all-purpose flour (for a total of 4 cups).

FILLING

- 1 slice high-quality white sandwich bread, torn into quarters
- 2 tablespoons plus ½ cup low-sodium chicken broth
- 1 pound 85 percent lean ground beef
  Salt and black pepper
- 1 tablespoon olive oil
- 2 onions, minced (about 2 cups)
- 4 garlic cloves, minced
- 1 teaspoon ground cumin
- ¼ teaspoon cayenne pepper
- ⅛ teaspoon ground cloves

½ cup fresh cilantro, chopped coarse

2 hard-cooked eggs, chopped coarse

⅓ cup raisins, chopped coarse

¼ cup pitted green olives, chopped coarse

4 teaspoons cider vinegar

DOUGH

3 cups (15 ounces) unbleached all-purpose flour

1 cup (5 ounces) masa harina (see note)

1 tablespoon sugar

2 teaspoons salt

12 tablespoons (1½ sticks) unsalted butter, cut into ½-inch pieces and chilled

½ cup cold vodka or tequila

½ cup cold water

5 tablespoons olive oil

1. FOR THE FILLING: Process the bread and 2 tablespoons of the chicken broth in a food processor until a paste forms, about 5 seconds, scraping down the sides of the bowl as necessary. Add the beef, ¾ teaspoon salt, and ½ teaspoon black pepper and pulse until the mixture is well combined, 6 to 8 pulses.

2. Heat the oil in a 12-inch nonstick skillet over medium-high heat until shimmering. Add the onions and cook, stirring frequently, until beginning to brown, about 5 minutes. Stir in the garlic, cumin, cayenne, and cloves and cook until fragrant, about 1 minute. Add the beef mixture and cook, breaking the meat into 1-inch pieces with a wooden spoon, until browned, about 7 minutes. Add the remaining ½ cup chicken broth and simmer until the mixture is moist but not wet, 3 to 5 minutes. Transfer the mixture to a bowl and cool for 10 minutes. Stir in the cilantro, eggs, raisins, olives, and vinegar. Season with salt and black pepper to taste and refrigerate until cool, about 1 hour.

3. FOR THE DOUGH: Pulse 1 cup of the flour, the masa harina, sugar, and salt in a food processor until combined, about 2 pulses. Add the butter and process until the mixture is homogeneous and the dough resembles wet sand, about 10 seconds. Add the remaining 2 cups flour and pulse until the mixture is evenly distributed around the bowl, 4 to 6 quick pulses. Empty the mixture into a medium bowl.

4. Sprinkle the vodka and water over the mixture. Using your hands, mix the dough until it forms a tacky

MAKING EMPANADAS

1. Divide the dough in half, then divide each half into 6 equal pieces.

2. Roll each piece of dough into a 6-inch round about ⅛ inch thick.

3. Place about ⅓ cup of filling on each round, then brush the edges with water.

4. Fold the dough over the filling, then crimp the edges using a fork to seal.

mass that sticks together. Following the photos, divide the dough in half, then divide each half into 6 equal pieces. Transfer the dough pieces to a plate, cover with plastic wrap, and refrigerate until firm, about 45 minutes.

5. TO ASSEMBLE: Adjust the oven racks to the upper-middle and lower-middle positions, place 1 baking sheet on each rack, and heat the oven to 425 degrees. While the baking sheets are preheating, remove the dough from the refrigerator. Roll each dough piece out on a lightly floured counter into a 6-inch circle

KEYS TO A CRISP EMPANADA CRUST

1. Drizzle oil onto the preheated baking sheets, which simulates a shallow fry, crisping up the bottom of the pies.

2. Brush the empanadas with oil rather than an egg wash before baking. This helps transfer heat more quickly and evenly, improving browning.

about ⅛ inch thick, covering each rolled-out dough round with plastic wrap while rolling out the remaining dough. Place about ⅓ cup of the filling in the center of each dough round. Brush the edges of each round with water and fold the dough over the filling. Trim any ragged edges, then crimp the edges of the empanadas shut using a fork.

6. Drizzle 2 tablespoons of the oil over the surface of each hot baking sheet, then return the sheets to the oven for 2 minutes. Brush the empanadas with the remaining 1 tablespoon oil. Carefully place 6 empanadas on each baking sheet and cook until well browned and crisp, 25 to 30 minutes, switching and rotating the baking sheets halfway through. Cool the empanadas on a wire rack for 10 minutes before serving. (After step 5, the empanadas can be covered tightly with plastic wrap and refrigerated for up to 2 days.)

VARIATION

Beef Empanadas with Corn and Black Bean Filling
Follow the recipe for Beef Empanadas, omitting the raisins and cooking ½ cup frozen corn kernels and ½ cup rinsed canned black beans along with the onions in step 2.

LIGHT PHILLY CHEESESTEAKS

WITH ALL THE LOCAL PRIDE THAT YOU FIND BEHIND the one-of-a-kind Philadelphia cheesesteak, it's a little intimidating to set out to re-create the famed sandwich at home. But, as incredible as this meaty, cheesy, comfort-food classic is, I didn't want to have to hop a plane or train (or drive) for an afternoon every time I craved one. On top of that, what if I wanted a lighter version? The typical cheesesteak, after all, is a fairly greasy mix of beef and onions topped with gobs of provolone or the local favorite, Cheez Whiz. I wanted a beefy, cheesy sandwich that really satisfied but didn't make me feel like I had just consumed a week's worth of calories and fat. It sounded a bit like mission impossible, but I decided it was worth a shot.

The key to a good cheesesteak lies in the texture of the meat (some would call it "frizzled"), so I started by taking note of the cooking method used by most Philly-area cheesesteak stands. A good-size rib-eye roast is cut into credit card–thin slices on the deli slicer, then the meat is cooked on a well-greased griddle over a heap of browned onions. With two heavy-duty spatulas, the adept cooks chop the meat and onions together then, as the meat finishes cooking, they drape slices of cheese over the top and let it melt. After a few final spatula swipes, the whole mixture is placed in a toasted sub (or hoagie) roll. It is this thinly sliced, spatula-chopped meat that makes the sandwich.

I began by looking for the best cut of beef for my recipe. Rib-eye, traditional though it is, was too fatty for my lighter version. I considered blade, top sirloin, and top round, and I chose steaks over roasts to better control the quantity. These steaks all worked well, tasting beefy and tender, but in the end, my tasters preferred the leaner quality of the top round.

Next I needed to find a way to get those ⅛-inch-thick slices, without a professional-grade deli slicer. When partially frozen, the meat was easier to slice, but I still found it challenging to cut paper-thin slices. Looking around the test kitchen, my eyes settled on the food processor. Could it work like a deli slicer?

I cut the steaks into 1-inch-wide fingers for easier handling before running them through the food processor's feed tube. This first attempt met with little success; the solid blocks of frozen steak were too hard, and it was too difficult for the blade of the slicing disk to cut the meat neatly. Still, I felt I was on to something, so next I tried freezing the steaks only partially (roughly 30 minutes, depending on the freezer's settings) in the hope it would allow the blade to better do its job. This turned out to be the solution, and I was able to make quick work of slicing the steaks.

I was ready to bring the remaining ingredients in line. Working with a nonstick skillet, which would require less oil than a traditional one, I started by quickly browning some chopped onion, then added the bite-size pieces of steak. Once the meat was just cooked through, I was ready to add the cheese. I knew I'd need to keep the cheese to a minimum if I wanted to make my cheesesteak lighter, but the sandwich still needed enough to earn its name and have that gooey appeal. Tasters quickly voted in favor of provolone over artificial Cheez Whiz. I was able to cut back the typical number of cheese slices, down to five slices rather than eight, and use reduced-fat provolone without getting a single raised eyebrow from tasters. I layered the provolone cheese over the meat and onions, let it melt slightly, and then stirred the melted cheese into the meat and onions to ensure a uniformly cheesy mixture. Even with less cheese, these sandwiches looked plenty appealing—and everyone appreciated that an overload of grease wasn't visible. I'd cut the calories in half and the fat down from 35 grams to 13 grams—even the native Philadelphians in our test kitchen were amazed at the great authentic flavor in my homemade lighter Philly cheesesteak.

—DAN ZUCCARELLO, *America's Test Kitchen Books*

Light Philly Cheesesteaks

SERVES 4

Don't overfreeze the beef, as it will be difficult for the slicing disk of the food processor to shave the meat. Top with pickled hot peppers, sautéed bell peppers, sweet relish, or hot sauce, if desired.

- 1 **(1-pound) top round steak, trimmed of all visible fat, cut into 1-inch-wide strips, and partially frozen**
- 1 **onion, chopped (about 1 cup)**
- 2 **teaspoons canola oil**
  Salt and pepper
- 5 **slices reduced-fat deli-style provolone cheese**
- 4 **(6-inch) sub rolls, slit partially open and lightly toasted**

NOTES FROM THE TEST KITCHEN

PREPARING MEAT FOR PHILLY CHEESESTEAKS

1. Trim the fat from the steak and cut the meat into 1-inch-wide strips. Place the strips of meat on a large plate and freeze until the exterior hardens but the interior remains soft, 25 to 50 minutes.

2. Using a food processor fitted with the slicing disk, shave the partially frozen meat as thin as possible.

REDUCED-FAT POTATO CHIPS

A serving of regular potato chips has 10 grams of fat, but with reduced-fat chips crowding the snack aisle, we wondered if we could find an acceptable light chip for pairing with our light cheesesteak. We purchased eight national brands and held a blind taste test. Surprise, we liked best the ones that reduced the fat the least. Manufacturers reduce the fat in one of three ways: One method bakes, oils, and salts potato slices, resulting in 3 grams of fat per serving; another quickly fries sliced potatoes, then removes some of the oil picked up during frying by steaming and baking (these are 6 to 7 grams of fat per serving); and finally, some are made by combining sugar, binders, and leaveners with dehydrated potatoes to form a dough, which is cut into "chips" and baked (1 ½ to 3 grams fat per serving). The chips made using the hybrid fry-then-bake method were the big winners. **Ruffles Reduced Fat** and **Lay's Kettle Cooked Reduced Fat Extra Crunchy Potato Chips** fooled us into thinking we were munching on "regular" chips (Cape Cod 40% Reduced Fat Potato Chips weren't far behind). For a modest fat reduction, these three make fine choices. As for the processed chips? Run screaming. (See page 291 for more information about our testing results.)

1. Following the photos on page 149, shave the partially frozen meat using a food processor fitted with the slicing disk. Set the shaved meat aside.

2. Combine the onion, 1 teaspoon of the oil, and ¼ teaspoon salt in a 12-inch nonstick skillet. Cover and cook over medium-low heat, stirring occasionally, until softened, 8 to 10 minutes. Uncover, increase the heat to medium-high, add the remaining 1 teaspoon oil, meat, ¼ teaspoon salt, and ⅛ teaspoon pepper, and cook until the meat is no longer pink, 2 to 3 minutes.

3. Reduce the heat to low, place the slices of cheese over the meat, and continue to cook until the cheese has melted, about 1 minute. Stir the melted cheese and meat together to combine. Spoon ½ cup of the meat mixture into each toasted bun and serve.

BEEF BARBECUE SANDWICHES

IT'S TRUE, I TEND TO THINK OF MYSELF AS A PRETTY experienced barbecue eater. Texas Barbecued Beef Ribs, Alabama Chicken, Chicago Sticky Ribs, Baltimore Pit Beef; I've pretty much covered the barbecue map here in our test kitchen. So when I saw that we'd received a recipe called Grandma Wooly's Beef Barbecue for our Lost Suppers contest, I wrote Grandma off before I'd even read the first line. I figured there couldn't possibly be any sort of barbecue I wasn't already familiar with. I couldn't have been more wrong.

A read-through of Dorothy Woolever's, a.k.a. Grandma Wooly's, recipe (as submitted by her grandson Charles from Rochester, New York) revealed a sort of shredded beef barbecue you won't find in backyards in Chicago, or Texas, or St. Louis. About the only places you would find it are the homes of the Woolevers themselves— this was a personal, not a regional, specialty. With its combination of pickling spice, dry mustard, and cider vinegar, I wasn't sure what exactly this barbecue was going to taste like, but I felt pretty confident it wouldn't be anything familiar.

The recipe started by covering 2 pounds of stew meat with water and simmering it on the stovetop until tender, at least three to four hours as noted by Charles. I opted for a boneless chuck-eye roast that I cut into

cubes myself, rather than buying pre-cut cubed stew meat since these pieces are often cut into varying sizes that won't cook evenly. I also decided to brown the meat first to deepen its flavor. I covered it with water and set it to simmer for several hours.

Once the meat was tender, I added cider vinegar, sugar, dry mustard, and ketchup to the cooking liquid as the recipe directed, followed by a couple of tablespoons of pickling spices that had been bundled together in cheesecloth (so that the spices could be removed easily at the end of cooking). The simmering continued for four or five more hours, until the meat was fall-apart tender, by which point the liquid in the pot had also cooked down into a sauce with just the right consistency for coating the pieces of meat. I shredded what large chunks of meat remained into bite-size pieces and piled the saucy shredded barbecue onto buns. It was time to give it a try.

What resulted was in a league of its own. The meat was definitely ultra-tender, infused with flavor from cooking in the sauce, but the real key was the sauce itself: tangy, sweet, and spicy all at once. This barbecue immediately earned a high spot on my list of all-time favorites. I didn't need to change much about Grandma's recipe, but I did decide to move the cooking from the stovetop to the oven, which would provide more even heat and require less babysitting. This adjustment also cut the cooking time in half. My tasters agreed that the sauce was a smidge sweet, and since plenty of sweetness was coming from the 1½ cups of ketchup, I dropped altogether the tablespoon of sugar that the original recipe had called for. Tasters also noted that the pickling spices came on a little strong, so I cut them in half, down to 1 tablespoon. This ensured the spices' flavor was still present (after all, they are the secret ingredient in the recipe) but now they were complementary, not overwhelming. This barbecue was tender, flavorful, and most certainly one-of-a-kind.

Charles had it exactly right when he wrote in his entry, "It's remarkable in that the deep flavors of the finished dish belie the simplicity of the ingredients. This recipe is, indeed, way more than the mere sum of its parts!" I couldn't agree more, and I hope he won't mind that this Woolever family tradition is going to become a tradition in my own house as well.

—DAN ZUCCARELLO, *America's Test Kitchen Books*

BEEF BARBECUE SANDWICHES

Beef Barbecue Sandwiches

Pickling spice can be found in the spice aisle of your local supermarket.

- 1 tablespoon pickling spice
- 2 pounds boneless beef chuck-eye roast, trimmed and cut into 1½-inch pieces (see page 46)
  Salt and pepper
- 2 tablespoons vegetable oil
- 2½ cups water
- 1½ cups ketchup
- 1 tablespoon cider vinegar
- 1 teaspoon dry mustard
- 8 hamburger buns, toasted

1. Adjust an oven rack to the lower-middle position and heat the oven to 300 degrees. Tie the pickling spice in cheesecloth to make a sachet.

2. Pat the beef dry with paper towels and season with salt and pepper. Heat 1 tablespoon of the oil in a Dutch oven over medium-high heat until just smoking. Add half of the beef and cook until well browned on all sides, about 8 minutes, turning as needed. Transfer the beef to a bowl. Return the pot to medium-high heat and repeat with the remaining 1 tablespoon oil and the remaining beef.

3. Stir the water into the pot, scraping up any browned bits. Return the beef, along with any accumulated juice, to the pot. Bring to a simmer, cover, and transfer the pot to the oven. Cook, stirring occasionally, until the beef is almost tender, about 1 hour.

4. Stir in the ketchup, vinegar, mustard, and spice sachet. Continue to cook until the meat is tender, about 1 hour longer.

5. Discard the spice sachet and transfer the meat to a plate. When cool enough to handle, pull the meat into thin shreds, discarding the excess fat and gristle. Stir the beef back into the sauce and season with salt and pepper to taste. Serve on the buns.

PIMENTO CHEESEBURGERS

MOST AMERICANS ARE VAGUELY AWARE OF PIMENTO cheese as the orange stuff Southerners smear on crackers or celery sticks and wash down with sweet tea. The neon spread—made with orange cheddar, chopped pimentos, mayonnaise, and, depending on whom you ask, onion, Worcestershire, olives, or hot sauce—tastes as bright as it looks. It is so beloved as a burger topping in and around Columbia, South Carolina, that Southern food authority John T. Edge calls pimento cheeseburgers the city's "national food." I called the Rockaway Athletic Club restaurant to ask about its famous version. Owner David Nelson revealed that the cheese recipe comes from "my mama," but he had a good long laugh when I asked what was in it. I might as well have asked the Coca-Cola Company for its secret formula or the U.S. government how to build a nuclear bomb.

Calls to other Columbia restaurants famous for their burgers (the Palmetto Sandwich Shop, the Mousetrap, and the Kingsman, among them) made two things perfectly clear. First, these aren't ordinary cheeseburgers, where a ho-hum slice of cheese plays second fiddle to the burger. Nope, with "pimento cheese burgers," the emphasis is firmly on the cheese. And second, no matter how polite and charming the reply, no one was going to give me the secret recipe for pimento cheese. I'd have to concoct my own.

I began with finely grated extra-sharp cheddar (sharp and mild varieties lacked zip), chopped pimentos (which are jarred sweet red peppers), and mayonnaise. Then I tested the most common add-ins. My tasters—including a genuine Carolina native—went minimalist. They gave the nod to cayenne pepper and dry mustard, both of which added bite, and they deemed everything else superfluous.

Pimento cheese at the ready, I seasoned four burger patties with salt, pepper, and Worcestershire (the sauce suited the burger better than it did the cheese), added a panade of bread soaked in milk to guard against overcooking, and started grilling. When the burgers were almost done, I slathered on the spread. Unfortunately the same mayonnaise that made the pimento cheese easy to spread also caused it to slide off the sizzling burgers and scorch. Minus the moistening power of the mayonnaise, however, the cheddar hardened into a greasy, orange scab. I went back to some recipes I'd collected when I began my testing and came across a few pimento cheese recipes that contained cream cheese as well as mayonnaise; I tried the combo in my cheese blend. This mixture was spreadable, melted gently, and stayed put atop the patty.

These burgers were on their way, but my tasters had become so fond of the pimento cheese, they demanded more. Could I not only top the burgers with pimento cheese, but also stuff some of it inside the burgers? I carefully formed patties around a central blob of the soft cheese spread, but the cheese oozed out of several and burned during cooking. I tried chilling the spread for several hours before using it in the burgers, figuring I'd buy myself more time before it melted on the grill. Maybe I earned an extra minute or two, but again cheese dripped out of some of the grilling burgers. All right then, I'd freeze the cheese, not merely chill it. I did so in measures of 2 tablespoons. The cheese stayed solid while I shaped the patties, which allowed me to take more care. After several construction experiments, I found that the cheese stayed put during grilling if I divided the meat for each patty in half, allowing me to wrap the cheese securely inside two layers of ground meat. That way, I could be sure the cheese was firmly centered in, and contained by, the meat.

The burgers looked great as they rested on a platter, but the first bite triggered a burst of orange lava that burned the chin of more than one taster. The fix was twofold: Omit the mayonnaise from the portion of pimento cheese destined for inside the burgers, and wait for the burgers to rest for five minutes before taking a bite. That way, the cheese wouldn't spurt. Proud of my formula, not to mention my novel construction technique, I could finally see for myself why other pimento cheeseburger creators wanted to keep their recipes a secret!

—MARÍA DEL MAR SACASA, *Cook's Country*

Grilled Pimento Cheeseburgers
SERVES 4

Pimento cheese gets its signature color from orange cheddar cheese—don't use white in this recipe. Allow the burgers to rest a full five minutes before eating them or the hot, cheesy center will spurt out.

6	ounces extra-sharp cheddar cheese, grated fine (about 1½ cups)
⅓	cup drained jarred pimentos, chopped fine
2	ounces cream cheese, softened
½	teaspoon dry mustard
⅛	teaspoon cayenne pepper
1	tablespoon mayonnaise
2	slices high-quality white sandwich bread, torn into pieces
¼	cup whole milk
1½	pounds 85 percent lean ground beef
1	tablespoon Worcestershire sauce
½	teaspoon salt
½	teaspoon black pepper

1. Mix the cheddar cheese, pimentos, cream cheese, mustard, and cayenne in a bowl until well combined. Following the photos on page 154, drop four 2-tablespoon portions of the pimento cheese mixture onto a plate, pat lightly to flatten, and cover tightly with plastic wrap. Freeze until firm, at least 2 hours. Combine the remaining pimento cheese mixture with the mayonnaise, cover with plastic wrap, and refrigerate.

2. Using a potato masher, mash the bread and milk in a large bowl. Add the beef, Worcestershire, salt, and black pepper and gently knead until well combined. Divide the meat into 4 equal portions. Mold half of 1 portion of meat around 1 piece of the frozen cheese, then surround this mini-patty with the remaining half portion of meat. Repeat with the remaining frozen cheese and 3 portions meat to form 4 hamburgers.

3A. FOR A CHARCOAL GRILL: Open the bottom grill vents completely. Light a large chimney starter filled half full with charcoal briquettes (50 briquettes; 3 quarts). When the coals are hot, pour them in an even

BUILDING A BETTER PIMENTO CHEESEBURGER

1. Drop four 2-tablespoon portions of pimento cheese onto a plate and pat lightly to flatten. Cover with plastic wrap and freeze until firm, at least 2 hours.

2. After dividing the meat into 4 portions, use half of 1 portion of meat to enclose 1 portion of frozen cheese.

3. Mold the remaining half portion of meat around the mini-patty and seal the edges. Flatten the meat with the palm of your hand to form a 1-inch-thick patty. Repeat with remaining cheese and meat to form 4 hamburgers.

THE BEST KOSHER DILL PICKLES

When we set out to find the best kosher dill pickle, we were surprised to learn that "kosher" in this case merely indicates the presence of garlic and the pickle's sour, salty profile. We gathered five nationally distributed brands of whole kosher dills, both "processed" and "fresh" to find the best. Processed dills are made by brining whole cucumbers in large tanks, where they ferment for weeks or months. During the last stage of fermentation, dill weed is added. The pickles are rinsed and sealed in shelf-stable jars with vinegar and seasoning. Fresh pickles are produced by placing cucumbers directly into jars, filling the jars with seasoned brine, and immediately refrigerating them. Once the pickles have absorbed the seasonings, they are ready. These pickles, sold refrigerated, have a shorter shelf life than processed pickles. Our tasting's results were definitive: The two fresh pickle brands we tried had the best flavor and texture, with the right crunch and authentic garlicky dill-pickle flavor. **Boar's Head Kosher Dill Whole Pickles**, our winner, were the only pickles in our lineup with fresh garlic, and their "firm, crisp" texture ensured they nabbed the top spot.

layer over the grill. Set the cooking grate in place, cover, and heat the grill until hot, about 5 minutes.

3B. FOR A GAS GRILL: Turn all the burners to high, cover, and heat the grill until hot, about 15 minutes. Turn all the burners to medium. (Adjust the burners as needed to maintain a medium fire; see page 19).

4. Clean and oil the cooking grate. Grill the burgers until well browned and cooked through, about 6 minutes per side.

5. Spread the cheese-mayonnaise mixture evenly on top of the burgers and cook (covered if using gas) until the cheese mixture is slightly melted, about 1 minute. Transfer the burgers to a plate, tent with foil, and let rest for 5 minutes before serving. (The pimento cheese balls can be frozen for up to 1 week and the spread can be refrigerated for up to 1 week. When ready to grill, continue with the recipe from step 2.)

VARIATION

Stovetop Pimento Cheeseburgers

Follow the recipe for Grilled Pimento Cheeseburgers through step 2. Heat 2 teaspoons vegetable oil in a 12-inch nonstick skillet over medium heat until just smoking. Add the patties and cook until well browned, about 6 minutes. Flip the burgers, cover the skillet, and cook until the burgers are well done, about 6 minutes. Continue with the recipe from step 5.

RED BEANS AND RICE

EATING RED BEANS AND RICE ON MONDAYS IS A tradition in New Orleans, where for decades custom held that the first day of the workweek be devoted to laundry. Doing laundry took all day, and having a pot of beans simmering on the back burner was a way to accomplish dinner at the same time. Even as speedy machines replaced the low-tech washboard, red beans and rice has remained a Louisiana staple.

Though beans and rice are hardly unique to New Orleans, the Cajun spin is revelatory: modest ingredients transformed into a creamy stew replete with smoke and spice and unctuous texture, served atop white rice—a neutral foil to all that heady flavor. With only basics, however, mistakes aren't easily hidden. One false move and the magic fades, marred by blown-out beans, bland or pasty sauces, and flavors that never quite come together. What's more, given that many authentic recipes call for ingredients hard to come by north of the Big Easy, this deceptively simple recipe can flummox even a seasoned home cook. As a Boston native who grew up eating baked beans, I was all too familiar with the challenges associated with bean cookery. Perhaps, with a little Beantown-bred ingenuity, I could whip up a version to make any Cajun cook proud.

Surveying the recipes out there, I cooked up several to get my bearings. I learned one thing in short order: If you're on the prowl for ways to ruin a pot of beans, there's no need to look far. Even recipes from Cajun-cuisine luminaries—Paul Prudhomme, Emeril Lagasse, and others—had issues, including dried-spice overkill and one ill-fated porkfest (six ham hocks for a single pot!). Plus, the beans ran the gamut of textural problems. I decided to start with a stripped-down recipe and then build it up again.

First, the legumes. Canned beans were a nonstarter so I looked at the dried options. New Orleans cooks prefer local Camellia Brand red kidney beans, citing their tender skins and ultra-creamy interiors. I ordered a few bags from Louisiana and cooked them up, comparing them to nationally available Goya red kidney beans. Sure enough, the Camellia beans were smoother, softer, and overwhelmingly preferred by tasters. But how many of us would mail-order ingredients for a casual meal?

A few experts suggested using "small red beans" (also called Mexican red beans), which are common in Caribbean and Latin American cooking. Happily, these beans were readily available at the neighborhood supermarket. I prepared two batches of beans, one kidney and one small red, rehydrating them in water overnight, then simmering them for a few hours with sautéed chopped onion, celery, and green bell pepper. Hands down, tasters preferred the small red beans, praising the smooth interior texture and the yielding yet still-intact skins, versus the "mealy" texture and chewy skins of the kidney beans.

Now that the beans' innards were staying inside the skins where they belonged, they weren't getting quite as well seasoned. Easy enough to fix: We recently discovered that brining beans overnight in salt water not only improves texture but seasons them throughout.

As for the meat component, legit Louisiana recipes in my collection included as many as three different pork products, among them sausage, ham, and pork shoulder. As fussy as it seemed, I was determined to get a similar depth of meaty flavor into my beans.

The sausage part was easy. Andouille is the usual choice, and just 8 ounces provided depth and complexity. Many recipes also call for tasso: pork coated with spices, onion powder, and granulated garlic, then hot-smoked until it resembles jerky. It lends a peppery kick to the dish. Since it's also difficult to find outside Louisiana, I searched for a substitute and eventually determined the flavor could be approximated with a few slices of bacon punched up with paprika, black pepper, and cayenne. (I would also add minced garlic and extra fresh onion to the sautéed veggies later.)

Some New Orleans cooks consider pickled pork shoulder mandatory. I had no hope of finding any outside Louisiana, so I made some myself, adding diced pork shoulder to vinegar, then pickling it for three days. Added to my working recipe, it contributed a welcome brightness, but a three-day pickling process was as absurd as mail-ordering beans. On a whim, I replaced the pickled pork with plain vinegar. This simple trick worked: Just 1 teaspoon of red wine vinegar added to the pot about an hour into cooking and a few splashes added right before serving provided all the right brightness, and most of my tasters were none the wiser.

All I had left was to sharpen the flavors. Many Cajun recipes, including beans and rice, start out with sautéed green pepper, onions, and celery—a slight variation on the French mirepoix (which swaps peppers for carrots). I found that when all three were used in equal quantities, the green pepper and celery stood out too much. (Plus, I needed to make up for the extra onion flavor the real tasso would have contributed.) Further testing revealed that a ratio of 2 parts onion to 1 part each green pepper and celery yielded the best balance. A few cloves of garlic and the flavor really started to pop.

The cooking liquid also needed tweaking. While the oldest recipes I found called for plain water, many modern recipes call for chicken broth. Canned broth did add complexity, but it also lent too much chicken flavor. I eventually settled on a ratio of 1 part broth to 2 parts water. As final improvements, I added bay leaves and fresh thyme for herbal notes.

This modern version of red beans and rice is neither the daylong epic of yesteryear nor an exercise in instant gratification. The dish takes about two hours of cooking, but most of that time is unattended simmering, interrupted by an occasional stir of the pot—just enough time to get the laundry done.

—ANDREA GEARY, *Cook's Illustrated*

RED BEANS AND RICE

Red Beans and Rice

SERVES 6 TO 8

If you are pressed for time you can "quick-brine" the beans. In step 1, combine the salt, water, and beans in a large Dutch oven and bring to a boil over high heat. Remove the pot from the heat, cover, and let stand for 1 hour. Drain and rinse the beans and proceed with the recipe. If you can't find andouille sausage, substitute kielbasa. Tasso can be difficult to find, but if you use it, omit the bacon and paprika in step 2 and cook 4 ounces finely chopped tasso in 2 teaspoons vegetable oil until lightly browned, 4 to 6 minutes, then proceed with the recipe. In order for the starch from the beans to thicken the cooking liquid, it is important to maintain a vigorous simmer in step 2.

Salt

1 **pound (about 2 cups) small red beans, rinsed and picked over**

4 **slices bacon, chopped fine**

1 **onion, minced (about 1 cup)**

1 **small green bell pepper, seeded and chopped fine**

1 **celery rib, chopped fine**

3 **garlic cloves, minced**

1 **teaspoon chopped fresh thyme**

1 **teaspoon sweet paprika**

2 **bay leaves**

¼ **teaspoon cayenne pepper**

Black pepper

6 **cups water**

3 **cups low-sodium chicken broth**

8 **ounces andouille sausage, halved lengthwise and sliced ¼ inch thick**

1 **teaspoon red wine vinegar, plus extra for seasoning**

1 **recipe Basic White Rice (recipe follows)**

3 **scallions, white and green parts, sliced thin**

Hot sauce, for serving (optional)

1. Dissolve 3 tablespoons salt in 4 quarts cold water in a large bowl or container. Add the beans and soak at room temperature for at least 8 hours or up to 24 hours. Drain and rinse well.

2. Heat the bacon in a large Dutch oven over medium heat, stirring occasionally, until browned and almost fully rendered, 5 to 8 minutes. Add the onion, bell pepper, and celery; cook, stirring frequently, until the vegetables are softened, 6 to 7 minutes. Stir in the garlic, thyme, paprika, bay leaves, cayenne, and ¼ teaspoon black pepper and cook until fragrant, about 30 seconds. Stir in the beans, water, and broth and bring to a boil over high heat. Reduce the heat and vigorously simmer, stirring occasionally, until the beans are just soft and the liquid begins to thicken, 45 to 60 minutes.

3. Stir in the sausage and 1 teaspoon red wine vinegar and cook until the liquid is thick and the beans are fully tender and creamy, about 30 minutes. Season with salt, black pepper, and additional vinegar to taste. Serve over the rice, sprinkling with the scallions and passing hot sauce separately, if desired. (The beans can be cooled, covered tightly, and refrigerated for up to 2 days. To reheat, add enough water to the beans to thin them slightly.)

NOTES FROM THE TEST KITCHEN

KEYS TO BETTER RED BEANS
We found three tricks were key to getting authentic flavor and texture for our modern version of Red Beans and Rice.

THE RIGHT BEANS
Small red beans cooked up creamier than kidney beans and were easier to find than the authentic Camellia beans.

OVERNIGHT BRINE
Salting the dried beans during their overnight rehydration session keeps them well seasoned and smooth textured.

ACID REDUX
Adding red wine vinegar at two different points, once during cooking and again (to taste) before serving, provided all the bright acidity of traditional "pickle meat."

Basic White Rice

MAKES ABOUT 6 CUPS

- **2 cups long-grain white rice**
- **1 tablespoon unsalted butter or vegetable oil**
- **3 cups water**
- **1 teaspoon salt**

1. Place the rice in a colander or fine-mesh strainer and rinse under cold running water until the water runs clear. Place the colander over a bowl and set aside.

2. Heat the butter in a large saucepan over medium heat. Add the rice and cook, stirring constantly, until the grains become chalky and opaque, 1 to 3 minutes. Add the water and salt, increase the heat to high and bring to a boil, swirling the pot to blend the ingredients. Reduce the heat to low, cover, and simmer until all the liquid is absorbed, 18 to 20 minutes. Off the heat, remove the lid and place a kitchen towel, folded in half, over the saucepan. Replace the lid and let stand for 10 to 15 minutes. Fluff the rice with a fork and serve.

NOTES FROM THE TEST KITCHEN

THE BEST ANDOUILLE SAUSAGE

Traditional andouille (pronounced an-DOO-ee) sausage from Louisiana is made from ground pork, salt, garlic, and seasoned with plenty of black pepper, then slowly smoked over pecan wood and sugarcane for up to 14 hours. Used in a wide range of Louisiana dishes, such as gumbo, jambalaya, and red beans and rice, it bolsters any dish with intense smoky, spicy, earthy flavor. We tasted four brands, looking for the right combination of smokiness and heat with a traditionally chewy but dry texture. Not surprisingly, a sausage straight from Louisiana won the day: **Jacob's World Famous Andouille**. Tasters voted these mail-order Louisianan links with a burgundy tint the smokiest and spiciest in the lineup. Coming in second, Wellshire Andouille Sausage from Whole Foods held its own in the heat department.

THE BEST LONG-GRAIN WHITE RICE

Higher-quality white rice offers a pleasing "al dente" texture and a natural, slightly buttery flavor. While most of this subtle variation comes from the varietal of rice, processing also affects flavor. All white rice has been milled, a process that removes the husk, bran, and germ. The longer the rice is milled, the whiter it becomes. Many brands (except organic) are enriched to replace lost nutrients. Cooked long-grain white rice grains should be fluffy and separate. We tasted six national brands of long-grain white rice, plain (steamed in our favorite rice cooker) and in pilaf. **Lundberg Organic Long-Grain White Rice** stood out for its nutty, buttery flavor and its distinct, smooth grains.

INDOOR PULLED PORK

NOT TO MINIMIZE ANYONE'S ACCOMPLISHMENTS, but when it comes to barbecue, professional pit masters have it made: A commercial smoker goes a long way toward getting great results. Even home cooks who live in temperate climates have a leg up, since (with proper technique) a kettle grill works almost as well as a pit. But here in New England, if you get a hankering for pulled pork in winter, you're in a bind. You either have to wait until spring, when the snow melts and the winds die down, or bring the operation indoors.

The phrase "indoor barbecue" is usually code for "braised in a Dutch oven with bottled barbecue sauce." This results in mushy, waterlogged meat and candy-sweet sauce—a far cry from what I was after. I wanted moist, tender, shreddable meat with deep smoke flavor all the way through, plus a dark, richly seasoned crust.

With any kind of barbecue, a good amount of fat is necessary for moisture and flavor. Well-marbled Boston butt (from the upper portion of the front leg of the pig) is a favorite for pulled pork because of its high level of marbling. Since I was shredding the meat anyway, I opted for the boneless version. I'd fine-tune my dry rub later, but for now, I applied a mixture of salt, pepper, and sugar to a 5-pound roast.

I considered my next key decision: oven temperature. On the grill, barbecue temperatures hover between 250 and 300 degrees. For the oven, I opted for the 300-degree end of the scale, hoping to have my meat on the table as soon as possible.

I wanted supremely moist meat, so I brined the pork in salt water before placing it in the oven. Six hours later, the meat had developed a substantial black crust (or "bark"), but one taste revealed that this bark, while flavorful, was dry as a bone, and the meat underneath was tough and almost impossible to shred. Why should the standard five or six hours on a grill produce tender meat with a crisp yet moist crust, while the same time in an oven only delivered barely edible leather?

I knew for meat to become tender, its connective tissue must break down. This requires both heat and time. Meat needs to hold an internal temperature of around 200 degrees for at least an hour in order for collagen (a key protein component of connective tissue) to dissolve. Apparently, my meat was heating too slowly in the oven—though I wondered why, since 300 degrees was at the top end of the temperature scale for barbecue.

It soon dawned on me that there's a crucial difference between real barbecue and oven barbecue. On a grill, as moisture escapes from damp wood chips and steaming meat, it's trapped underneath the dome of the lid, creating a moist cooking environment. To create extra steam, some cooks even place a pan of water beside the coals. An oven, by contrast, is ventilated to remove any moisture that builds up inside. Since moist air transfers heat more effectively than dry air, an oven is less efficient than either a grill or a smoker.

Confident of my reasoning, I boosted the oven temperature to 325 degrees to jump-start collagen breakdown, then set a pan of water on the lowest oven rack, directly underneath the pork. No luck; my oven was still too dry. What if I trapped the moisture right up against the meat? But an aluminum foil shield did this too well. The meat came out moist and tender in only 4½ hours, but there was no bark.

I'd need to use a dual method: covering the pork for part of the time to speed up cooking and keep it moist, then uncovering it for the remainder to allow the meat to develop a crust. I experimented until I found the perfect balance: Three hours of covered cooking rendered the meat meltingly tender, while an hour and a half uncovered helped a nice crust to form. This bark was so good that my tasters pleaded for more, a request I accommodated by splitting the pork butt in half horizontally before cooking, greatly increasing its surface area. (Surprisingly, I found I still needed the same amount of cooking time to ensure tender meat.)

I'd achieved the right texture, now I needed to master the defining feature of barbecue: smoky flavor. I ignited wood chips in a foil packet on the stovetop and put them in the oven with the pork, but they extinguished quickly. I tried grinding the chips in a spice grinder, hoping they would stay lit longer. One ruined spice mill later, I was no better off. We used smoky Lapsang Souchong tea to impart smoky flavor to our recipe for Oven-Barbecued Spareribs, but those ribs are exposed to smoke for a mere 30 minutes. After 4½ hours of tea smoke, my pork butt tasted too strongly of, well, tea.

There was another option: When developing our Skillet-Barbecued Pork Chops, we learned that liquid smoke is a natural product derived from condensing the moist smoke of smoldering wood chips. Starting modestly because of its strength, I tried adding a teaspoon of liquid smoke to my gallon of brine. To my delight, the smoky flavor made its way into the meat without overwhelming it and tasted completely natural. Seeking deeper flavor, I ended up using a full 3 tablespoons in the brine; more than that made no further impact. But I thought my pork could still be a little smokier.

I was reminded that pulled pork can be cooked with a dry rub or a wet rub. What if I used both methods, thereby incorporating smoke flavor two ways? First, I fortified my dry rub with smoked paprika, then supplemented the dry rub with a wet rub of mustard mixed

NOTES FROM THE TEST KITCHEN

GETTING SMOKE FLAVOR WITHOUT A FIRE

1. Add liquid smoke to the brine to draw smoky flavor deep into the meat.

2. Rub the pork with more liquid smoke to give the crust, or bark, a pronounced smoky flavor.

3. Add smoked paprika to the dry rub to bring in additional smokiness and help the bark develop its color.

with a little more liquid smoke. Success! My pork finally had a deep, well-developed smokiness.

All I needed now was a sauce. Not wanting to limit myself to just one barbecue region or style, I developed a classic sweet and tangy sauce, a vinegar sauce (Lexington, North Carolina, style), and a mustard sauce (South Carolina style). Since my pork emerged from the oven complete with flavorful drippings, I enriched each sauce with ½ cup of the defatted liquid. My indoor barbecue may involve some degree of illusion—but I'd challenge any barbecue lover not to be taken in by the (liquid) smoke and mirrors.

—BRYAN ROOF, *Cook's Illustrated*

Indoor Pulled Pork with Sweet and Tangy Barbecue Sauce

SERVES 6 TO 8

Sweet paprika may be substituted for smoked paprika. Covering the pork with parchment and then foil prevents the acidic mustard from eating holes in the foil. Serve the pork on hamburger rolls with pickle chips and thinly sliced onion. Lexington Vinegar Barbecue Sauce or South Carolina Mustard Barbecue Sauce (recipes follow) can be substituted for the Sweet and Tangy Barbecue Sauce. Alternatively, use 2 cups of your favorite barbecue sauce thinned with ½ cup of the defatted pork cooking liquid in step 5.

PORK

- 1 cup plus 2 teaspoons salt
- ½ cup plus 2 tablespoons sugar
- 3 tablespoons plus 2 teaspoons liquid smoke
- 1 boneless pork butt (about 5 pounds), cut in half horizontally (see photos)
- ¼ cup yellow mustard
- 2 tablespoons black pepper
- 2 tablespoons smoked paprika (see note)
- 1 teaspoon cayenne pepper

SAUCE

- 1½ cups ketchup
- ¼ cup light or mild molasses
- 2 tablespoons Worcestershire sauce
- 1 tablespoon hot sauce
- ½ teaspoon salt
- ½ teaspoon black pepper

1. FOR THE PORK: Dissolve 1 cup of the salt, ½ cup of the sugar, and 3 tablespoons of the liquid smoke in 4 quarts cold water in a large container. Submerge the pork in the brine, cover with plastic wrap, and refrigerate for 2 hours.

2. While the pork brines, combine the mustard and remaining 2 teaspoons liquid smoke in a small bowl and set aside. Combine the black pepper, paprika, remaining 2 tablespoons sugar, remaining 2 teaspoons salt, and cayenne in another small bowl; set aside. Adjust an oven rack to the lower-middle position and heat the oven to 325 degrees.

3. Remove the pork from the brine and dry thoroughly with paper towels. Rub the mustard mixture over the entire surface of each piece of pork, then sprinkle the entire surface of each piece with the spice mixture. Place the pork on a wire rack set inside a foil-lined rimmed baking sheet. Place a piece of parchment paper over the pork, then cover with aluminum foil, sealing the edges to prevent moisture from escaping. Roast the pork for 3 hours.

4. Remove the pork from the oven and remove and discard the foil and parchment. Carefully pour off the liquid in the bottom of the baking sheet into a fat separator and reserve for the sauce. Return the pork to the oven and cook, uncovered, until well browned and tender, and the roast registers 200 degrees on an instant-read thermometer, about 1½ hours. Transfer the pork to a serving dish, tent loosely with foil, and let rest for 20 minutes.

5. FOR THE SAUCE: While the pork rests, pour ½ cup of the defatted cooking liquid from the fat separator

---

NOTES FROM THE TEST KITCHEN

CUTTING PORK BUTT IN HALF
Halving the pork increases its surface area, which creates more flavorful bark.

Holding your knife parallel to the cutting board, press one hand flat against the top of the pork butt while cutting horizontally.

into a medium bowl. Whisk in the ketchup, molasses, Worcestershire, hot sauce, salt, and pepper.

6. Using 2 forks, shred the pork into bite-size pieces. Toss the meat with 1 cup of the sauce and season with salt and pepper to taste. Serve, passing the remaining sauce separately. (The shredded and sauced pork can be cooled, tightly covered, and refrigerated for up to 2 days. Reheat it gently before serving.)

Lexington Vinegar Barbecue Sauce
MAKES ABOUT 2½ CUPS

This sauce can be substituted for the Sweet and Tangy Barbecue Sauce in our recipe for Indoor Pulled Pork on page 160 if desired.

- 1 cup cider vinegar
- ½ cup ketchup
- ½ cup water
- 1 tablespoon sugar
- ¾ teaspoon salt
- ¾ teaspoon red pepper flakes
- ½ teaspoon pepper

Combine all the ingredients in a medium bowl with ½ cup of the defatted cooking liquid (in step 5) and whisk to combine.

South Carolina Mustard Barbecue Sauce
MAKES ABOUT 2½ CUPS

This sauce can be substituted for the Sweet and Tangy Barbecue Sauce in our recipe for Indoor Pulled Pork on page 160 if desired.

- 1 cup yellow mustard
- ½ cup white vinegar
- ¼ cup packed light brown sugar
- ¼ cup Worcestershire sauce
- 2 tablespoons hot sauce
- 1 teaspoon salt
- 1 teaspoon pepper

Combine all the ingredients in a medium bowl with ½ cup of the defatted cooking liquid (in step 5) and whisk to combine.

SAUTÉED PORK CUTLETS

ON PAPER, A PACKAGE OF SUPERMARKET PORK cutlets offers everything the time-pressed cook could want in a weeknight meal: thrift, minimal preparation, and dinner in minutes. But on your plate, these advantages don't mean a thing. Prepackaged center-cut pork loin is usually poorly butchered into ragged and uneven scaloppini, for predictably dry, stringy results. I didn't need to work through more than one batch of cutlets to confirm my fears: By the time the cutlets took on any color, not a drop of moisture was left in them, and all semblance of tenderness had evaporated.

If the bulk of my problems revolved around dry meat, brining or salting (a.k.a. dry-brining) was a must. Both methods alter the shape of the muscle proteins, making the meat less prone to squeezing out water as it cooks. Of the two, I opted for the speedier brining. A 30-minute soak was enough to give ¼-inch-thick cutlets the moisture boost they needed, as well as seasoning them throughout.

But brining worked too effectively. The retained moisture kept the meat so wet it steamed, and the cutlets were cooked through before they could brown. I needed to trigger browning while the exterior was still wet. In a recipe we had recently developed for Skillet-Roasted Fish Fillets, the solution to this very problem was to sprinkle sugar over the moist surface of the fish before putting it in the pan, since sugar caramelizes at a lower temperature than protein. But instead of sprinkling the sugar on the cutlets, could I simply mix it into the brine? Just 1½ teaspoons added to the brining liquid did the trick, helping the cutlets develop a more golden brown crust without turning them into candy.

But could I get the meat to go darker still? The only other element to play with was cooking fat. I'd been using olive oil, but if I included some butter, its sugars and milk proteins would allow for better browning and boost flavor at the same time. (Butter alone wouldn't be feasible. With its low smoke point, it would burn too easily.) Half a tablespoon of butter heated with a tablespoon of oil not only deepened the browning, but left me enough flavorful fond for a pan sauce.

Still, perfectly cooked though they were, my cutlets lacked one critical thing: deep meaty taste. Maybe I was asking too much of the ultra-lean loin. I soon found myself back at the supermarket, scanning the butcher's case for something that would give me richer pork flavor.

Determined as I was, my options for pork scaloppini were limited. I needed another relatively large cut that would slice neatly, cook quickly, and maintain tenderness. Tenderloin—the thin, tapered muscle that runs along the opposite side of the spine from the larger loin muscle—was one option. But while its texture is more supple than the loin's, this cut has even less flavor.

After further research, I stumbled across a scaloppini recipe calling for an unusual cut: pork leg. Little known in the United States but common in Canadian butcher shops, this cut comes from the larger muscles in the upper hind leg of the pig—the same joint cured and smoked to produce ham. These muscles are packed with flavor. Could scaloppini fashioned from this cut be the solution? To my disappointment, at the supermarket I discovered fresh ham is packed with more

than just flavor: It's also full of connective tissue, awkwardly shaped bones, and fat deposits that needed to be removed before I could create cutlets. Sure, they were flavorful, but there was no way my "quick" weeknight dinner was going to start with 30 minutes of butchering.

Observing the deep red meat of the ham gave me another idea. When buying pork chops, if you ask the butcher for a blade-end cut (the end closest to the front of the pig), you get a chop with a small eye of pale meat from the lean pork loin and plenty of flavorful darker red meat from the hog's fattier shoulder. This was the meat I was after. Cutting scaloppini from a whole blade-end roast was one option, but an easier (albeit unusual) option occurred to me: boneless country-style spare ribs. A common choice for braising, smoking, or grilling, these meaty ribs combine a large portion of the flavorful shoulder meat with minimal connective tissue and only a bit of bland loin (and occasionally none at all).

Even better, because the ribs are sold portioned into relatively small pieces, they required little work to be fashioned into cutlets. It was a matter of trimming each rib of external fat, slicing it lengthwise into two or three pieces, and pounding each of them into ¼-inch-thick cutlets. Even though these ribs were fattier than meat from the loin, pork these days is still bred to be lean, and I found 30 minutes in a sweetened brine was still necessary for the best flavor and browning. (Ditto on the oil-butter combo for the cooking fat.) After just four minutes total in a hot skillet, these cutlets cooked up exactly as I'd hoped: tender, juicy, and flavorful on the inside, with a deep brown crust.

All that was left was to whip up a couple of pan sauces. I first homed in on a mustard-cider variation (both great complements to pork). As the pork brined, I reduced a flour-thickened mixture of cider and stock flavored with dry mustard, shallots, and sage. After removing the cooked cutlets from the pan, I deglazed the fond-crusted skillet with my reduction, then swirled in coarse mustard and butter for a rich, glossy sauce that coated my tender, browned cutlets beautifully. A similarly prepared sauce featuring lemon juice and capers did the same.

No longer was this dish just a pedestrian effort for a weeknight repertoire. Meaty pork cutlets dressed up this nicely might just make it into my Saturday night rotation.

—ANDREW JANJIGIAN, *Cook's Illustrated*

NOTES FROM THE TEST KITCHEN

COMMON (AND UNCOMMON) CUTS FOR CUTLETS
We rejected two of the most popular cuts for pork cutlets that come from the whole loin—the center-cut loin and tenderloin—in favor of an unusual but far more flavorful choice.

OUR CHOICE:
COUNTRY-STYLE RIBS
Individual ribs cut from the blade (front) end of the loin, these ribs contain mostly dark meat from the fatty, flavorful shoulder.

RUNNER-UP:
CENTER-CUT LOIN
Cut from the large muscle that runs through the loin section, this option is relatively tender, but extremely lean and thus prone to drying out.

RUNNER-UP:
TENDERLOIN
This small, tapering muscle located inside the rib cage about halfway down spine, is the most tender part of the pig. It can be easily fashioned into uniform cutlets but is lean, with moderate flavor.

SAUTÉED PORK CUTLETS WITH MUSTARD-CIDER SAUCE

Sautéed Pork Cutlets with Mustard-Cider Sauce

SERVES 4

We prefer natural to enhanced pork (which has been injected with a salt solution to increase moisture and flavor). If the pork is enhanced, do not brine. Look for ribs that are about 3 to 5 inches long. Cut ribs over 5 inches in half crosswise before slicing them lengthwise to make pounding more manageable.

    Salt
1½ teaspoons sugar
1½ pounds boneless country-style pork spareribs,
    trimmed (see note)
4½ teaspoons unsalted butter, cut into 6 equal pieces
 1 small shallot, minced
 1 teaspoon unbleached all-purpose flour
 1 teaspoon dry mustard
 ½ cup low-sodium beef or chicken broth
 ¼ cup apple cider
 ½ teaspoon minced fresh sage
    Pepper
 1 tablespoon olive oil
 2 teaspoons whole-grain mustard

1. Dissolve 1 tablespoon salt and the sugar in 2 cups water in a medium bowl. Cut each pork rib lengthwise into 2 or 3 cutlets about ⅜ inch wide. Gently pound the cutlets to ¼-inch thickness between 2 layers of plastic wrap. Submerge the cutlets in the brine, cover with plastic wrap, and refrigerate for 30 minutes. (Do not overbrine.)

2. Meanwhile, melt 2 pieces of the butter in a small saucepan over medium heat. Add the shallot and cook until softened, about 1½ minutes. Stir in the flour and dry mustard and cook for 30 seconds. Gradually whisk in the broth, smoothing out any lumps. Stir in the cider and sage, bring to a boil, then reduce to a gentle simmer and cook for 5 minutes. Remove the pan from the heat, cover, and set aside.

3. Adjust an oven rack to the middle position and heat the oven to 200 degrees. Remove the cutlets from the brine, dry thoroughly with paper towels, and season with pepper. Heat the oil in a 12-inch skillet over medium-high heat until just smoking. Add 1 more piece butter, let it melt, then quickly lay half of the

cutlets into the skillet. Cook until browned on the first side, 1 to 2 minutes.

4. Using tongs, flip the cutlets and continue to cook until browned on the second side, 1 to 2 minutes. Transfer the cutlets to a large plate and keep warm in the oven. Repeat with the remaining cutlets and 1 more piece butter.

5. Return the empty skillet to medium heat, add the reserved broth mixture, and bring to a simmer. Cook, scraping up the browned bits, until the sauce

is slightly thickened and has reduced to about ½ cup, about 2 minutes. Stir in any accumulated pork juice and simmer for 30 seconds longer.

6. Off the heat, whisk in the whole-grain mustard and remaining 2 pieces butter. Season the sauce with salt and pepper to taste, spoon it over the cutlets, and serve immediately.

VARIATION

Sautéed Pork Cutlets with Lemon-Caper Sauce
Follow the recipe for Sautéed Pork Cutlets with Mustard-Cider Sauce, substituting ¼ cup white wine for the cider, 2 teaspoons lemon juice for the sage, and 2 tablespoons rinsed capers, 1 teaspoon minced fresh parsley, and 1 teaspoon finely grated lemon zest for the whole-grain mustard.

SUNDAY PORK ROAST WITH MUSHROOM GRAVY

FOR MOST PEOPLE, ROAST PORK WITH MUSHROOM gravy starts with a relatively lean pork loin, which cooks in about an hour. Then, when the meat is done, many cooks make the gravy by sautéing sliced mushrooms in the drippings, thickening the mixture with flour, and finally whisking in chicken broth. This method is fast, but the results are not so flavorful. Pork loin is mild, and quick gravy, which can't help but lack depth, doesn't give it much of a boost.

The most flavorful roasts start with one of the most flavorful cuts on the hog: the shoulder, also called Boston butt. This cut is usually associated with pulled pork, which is cooked low and slow to melt out the fat and tough connective tissue. The test kitchen also loves this cut as a roast, as long as it gets the time it needs—about six hours in a 300-degree oven (which explains why we think of it as a Sunday roast). With the details of the roast already determined, my challenge would be to produce rich, mushroom-y gravy befitting this succulent roast.

Chicken broth is a workhorse ingredient in the test kitchen that we add to poultry, beef, and vegetable dishes, but adding it to the gravy for my roast at the end of cooking wouldn't give it a chance to develop any pork flavor. To do that, it would have to go into the roasting pan with the meat for a stint. The pork needed some time on its own to brown and render first, so I didn't want to add the broth at the outset of the cooking time. Waiting to add it at the three-hour mark, I discovered, gave it enough time to drink up flavor. But tasters agreed that the flavor wasn't exactly right; it was too close to chicken soup. So I replaced half the broth with water, hoping this adjustment would allow the pork flavor to come to the forefront. This worked perfectly. A cup each of water and broth, combined with the pork drippings, yielded enough liquid for a gravy base. I was essentially making a meaty pork broth—complete with an onion and bay leaf—and its richness greatly enhanced the gravy.

The flavor was meaty and rich, but since this was going to be a mushroom gravy, I wondered if I could imbue my pork broth with mushroom flavor by tossing the mushrooms into the roasting pan. Three hours, conveniently, gave them time to become tender and start to caramelize, especially as some of the liquid in the roasting pan gradually evaporated. For the deepest possible mushroom flavor, I tried, in turn, meaty portobellos and dense, rich shiitakes. When I tested them side by side with ordinary white mushrooms, however, there wasn't a heck of a lot of difference. After three hours in a roasting pan, a mushroom is a mushroom is a mushroom. So I went with the best buys, white or cremini mushrooms; I quartered two 10-ounce packages and scattered them around the roast. When the pork was done, I strained the flavorful liquid, setting the mushrooms aside. I put some of the pork fat into a saucepan, stirred in flour to make a roux, then whisked in the pan juices. One taste confirmed that I was very close.

All that was left was to fine-tune the flavors. Dried thyme and sage suited the roast nicely. I got double the flavor by using them twice: first rubbing them on the roast (with salt and pepper) before cooking, and later adding them to the roasting pan with the broth mix and mushrooms. This was a Sunday supper worth waiting for.

—CALI RICH, *Cook's Country*

Sunday Pork Roast with Mushroom Gravy

SERVES 6 TO 8

Boneless pork shoulder, often labeled Boston butt, is usually sold wrapped in netting, which should be removed. Don't use a nonstick roasting pan, as the dark surface may overbrown the outside of the roast.

  1 **(4 to 5-pound) boneless pork shoulder roast, fat trimmed to ⅛ inch thick (see note)**
1½ **teaspoons dried thyme**
1½ **teaspoons dried sage**
  2 **teaspoons salt**
  1 **teaspoon pepper**
  1 **onion, halved**
20 **ounces white or cremini mushrooms, quartered**
  1 **cup low-sodium chicken broth**
  1 **cup water, plus extra as needed**
  1 **bay leaf**
  2 **tablespoons unbleached all-purpose flour**

1. Adjust an oven rack to the lower-middle position and heat the oven to 300 degrees. Pat the pork roast dry with paper towels and rub all over with 1 teaspoon of the thyme, 1 teaspoon of the sage, the salt, and pepper. Tie the roast at 1-inch intervals with kitchen twine.

2. Arrange the roast, fat side up, in a roasting pan and cook until beginning to brown, about 3 hours. Add the onion, mushrooms, broth, 1 cup water, bay leaf, remaining ½ teaspoon thyme, and remaining

½ teaspoon sage to the pan and continue to roast until the meat is well browned and a skewer inserted in the center meets no resistance, about 3 hours. Transfer the roast to a carving board, tent with foil, and let rest for 30 minutes.

3. Discard the onion and bay leaf. Strain the contents of the roasting pan through a fine-mesh strainer into a fat separator, reserving the mushrooms. Let the liquid settle, then pour the defatted pan juices (you should have about 1 cup) into a measuring cup and add enough water to yield 1½ cups.

4. Transfer 2 tablespoons of the fat from the separator to a large saucepan and heat over medium-high heat until shimmering. Stir in the flour and cook until golden, stirring constantly, 1 to 2 minutes. Slowly whisk in the pan juices and bring to a boil. Add the reserved mushrooms and simmer over medium-low heat until the gravy is slightly thickened, about 5 minutes. Remove the twine from the roast. Cut the roast into 1-inch-thick slices and serve with the gravy. (The rubbed roast may be wrapped in plastic wrap and refrigerated overnight at the end of step 1.)

HEALTHY STUFFED PORK LOIN

THE APPEALINGLY MILD, MEATY FLAVOR AND affordable price tag of pork loin make it one of my favorite choices when entertaining a small group, and because it's a lean cut it is also a perfect option when I am trying to keep the menu healthy. Many home cooks, myself included, have at some point turned to stuffing a pork loin in the hope of boosting its mild flavor and keeping it from drying out since there's not much fat to help in that department. While the concept is sound, the problems I've encountered with stuffed pork loin recipes abound. There are recipes in which the meat turns dry and tough and overcooks by the time the stuffing is done, and then there are the roasts where a stuffing does more harm than good, adding only dull flavor or poor texture. And then there are the countless recipes that rely on a flawed stuffing technique, whether it is overcomplicated or ineffective (with stuffing that

---

NOTES FROM THE TEST KITCHEN

THE SECRET TO BIG MUSHROOM FLAVOR
Most recipes for pork roast and mushroom gravy don't start the gravy until the meat is done. Our gravy gets underway earlier in the process, ensuring deep flavor.

By adding the mushrooms (along with water and broth) to the pan midway through the pork roast's cooking time, we create a mushroom-and-pork broth that is deeply flavored and makes an unbeatable base for the gravy.

oozes out into the pan or ends up looking messy and unappealing). I wanted to solve all of these issues with a single recipe. My stuffed pork loin needed to be easy to prepare, full of flavor without requiring much added fat, and perfectly cooked.

Simplifying the stuffing process was going to be my first—and most important—hurdle. Looking through existing recipes, I found quite a few methods. One required boring a hole through the center of the roast with a knife and sharpening steel. No thanks. A second method seemed more promising, creating a stuffed pork loin that looked similar to a jellyroll. The roast was slit crosswise six or seven times but not cut entirely through, so that it could be opened up like a book into one long, thin piece of meat. The meat was then coated with stuffing, rolled into a log, and tied. This method produced elegant results and allowed for a notable amount of stuffing, but it required excellent knife skills to cut such thin layers and was a lot more work than I wanted to do. A third technique I often found involved creating a pocket for the stuffing by making a cut lengthwise into the top of the roast, then stuffing the meat and sealing it off with wooden skewers. While this method required a minimum of effort, the appearance was sloppy.

I decided my best bet was to land somewhere between the jellyroll method and the top-loading pocket method. I started by making a deep cut lengthwise down the center of the roast (similar to the pocket but cutting through at both ends), careful not to cut all the way through to the cutting board. Then I made two more cuts, horizontally through each half, but again not cutting all the way through. This allowed me to open the pork loin up like a letter into a single, flat piece (much like the jellyroll method but far simpler). From here I packed a stuffing (a test recipe for now) down the center of the roast and closed it back up by wrapping the sides of the pork loin up and around the filling. To hold it together I simply tied the roast at 1-inch intervals. I was careful not to tie the roast too tightly; when I did, the stuffing squeezed out through the openings on each end. My new method took about five minutes to do and it allowed for enough stuffing so that each bite of the meat was ensured a good amount of stuffing to go with it.

I needed to decide on what was going to go into my stuffing. The recipes I'd found used everything from bread crumbs to fresh fruit and dried fruit to nuts, meats, and cornbread (along with herbs and spices, of course). One test ruled out a bread crumb–based stuffing. The bread soaked up an excess of moisture and juice from the pork, resulting in a mushy stuffing. Fresh fruit seemed like my best bet for a healthy, flavorful stuffing; as a bonus, it released its own moisture and thus helped keep the pork juicy. But choosing the right fruit was key: peaches turned to mush and pears were too subtle. Apples, a classic fruit to match with pork, held the most promise. I considered Red Delicious, Golden Delicious, and Granny Smith, and in the end settled on the firm, slightly tart Granny Smiths (Golden Delicious were too sweet, and Red Delicious did not hold up well during the long cooking time). A stuffing made with raw apples got me close—the apples released a good amount of moisture and kept the meat properly juicy—but they were still too crunchy by the time the pork was finished. Precooking the stuffing was the answer. Not only did it soften the apples just enough to ensure they were the perfect just-cooked-through texture by the end, but it gave me a chance to build more flavor into my stuffing. I added shallots for bite and a touch of honey to balance the tartness of the Granny Smiths. Dried cranberries added color and appealing fruitiness, and fresh thyme and some red pepper flakes rounded things out. This stuffing was sweet, tart, and savory all at once, and it was just moist enough to help keep the pork loin from drying out without washing out its flavor. Rubbing a combination of chopped rosemary and thyme with a little coriander over the roast before I put it in the oven infused the meat with yet another layer of flavor.

All that was left was cooking it through. Many stuffed pork loin recipes brown the stuffed roast on the stovetop before roasting. While this might add appealing color and flavor, dealing with a large rolled-and-stuffed roast on the stovetop was a pain. Simply sliding the pork loin in the oven to roast was my easiest and best route, giving me a roast with plenty of color and flavor. I found that about an hour in a 375-degree oven was all it took.

Slicing into my stuffed pork roast, I knew I had a winner. The meat was juicy and the filling had stayed put, and one bite proved the flavor was right on track. And as impressive as it looked, my dinner guests would never realize how easy it was to make.

—CHRIS O'CONNOR, *America's Test Kitchen Books*

HEALTHY STUFFED PORK LOIN

Healthy Stuffed Pork Loin

SERVES 8

We found that leaving a ⅛-inch-thick layer of fat on top of the roast is ideal; if your roast has a thicker fat cap, trim it to be about ⅛ inch thick.

- 1 tablespoon unsalted butter
- 1 pound (about 2 medium) Granny Smith apples, peeled, cored, and cut into ¼-inch pieces
- 2 shallots, halved and sliced thin
- 2 teaspoons honey
- ½ cup low-sodium chicken broth
- ¼ cup dried cranberries
- 1 tablespoon minced fresh thyme or 1 teaspoon dried
- Pinch red pepper flakes
- Salt and pepper
- 1 (3-pound) boneless pork loin roast (see note)
- 1 teaspoon minced fresh rosemary or ¼ teaspoon dried
- 1 teaspoon ground coriander

1. Adjust an oven rack to the lower-middle position and heat the oven to 375 degrees. Melt the butter in a 12-inch skillet over medium heat. Add the apples, shallots, and honey, cover, and cook until the apples release their liquid, 3 to 5 minutes. Uncover and continue to cook, stirring often, until the shallots and apples are well browned, 10 to 12 minutes.

2. Stir in the chicken broth, cranberries, 1 teaspoon of the thyme, and the red pepper flakes and cook until the apples are soft and the pan is almost dry, 1 to 2 minutes. Transfer the filling to a bowl and season with salt and pepper to taste.

3. Following the photos, slice the pork loin open lengthwise down the middle, then make a long cut into each side without cutting all the way through, and press the roast open flat. Season the inside with salt and pepper, mound the stuffing evenly down the center, then tie the pork around the filling into a tidy roast using butcher's twine.

4. Pat the outside of the roast dry with paper towels. Mix the remaining 2 teaspoons thyme, rosemary, coriander, ¼ teaspoon salt, and ⅛ teaspoon pepper together, then rub the herb mixture evenly over the outside of the roast.

5. Place the roast in a 13 by 9-inch baking dish. Roast until the pork registers 140 to 145 degrees on an instant-read thermometer, 50 to 70 minutes.

6. Transfer the roast to a carving board, tent loosely with foil, and let rest for 20 minutes. Remove the twine, slice the pork, and serve. (The pork loin can be filled and tied through step 3, then wrapped tightly in plastic wrap and refrigerated for up to 1 day.)

VARIATION

Healthy Stuffed Pork Loin with Figs and Balsamic
Follow the recipe for Healthy Stuffed Pork Loin, substituting ⅓ cup dried figs, chopped coarse, for the cranberries and adding 1 tablespoon balsamic vinegar to the skillet with the broth.

NOTES FROM THE TEST KITCHEN

PREPARING STUFFED PORK LOIN

1. Slice the pork open down the middle, from end to end, about two-thirds through the meat.

2. Gently press the pork loin open. Carefully slice into the sides of the roast, being careful not to cut through, and press the pork flat.

3. Season the inside of the pork with salt and pepper, then mound the filling evenly down the center of the roast.

4. Wrap the sides of the pork around the filling, then tie the roast closed with butcher's twine at 1-inch intervals. Don't tie the roast too tight or you may squeeze out the filling.

POULTRY

HONEY ROAST CHICKEN

OVER THE YEARS, WE'VE MADE ROAST CHICKEN every which way in the test kitchen. This time, I hoped to introduce honey, remembering a moist chicken with a lovely, lingering honey flavor I'd enjoyed once from a takeout shop. I imagined a chicken that was crisp and beautifully flavored, but when I attempted to replicate it by liberally coating a whole chicken with warm (thinned) honey before roasting, the chicken skin ended up burned yet flabby and the meat bloody. (If I cooked the chicken long enough to get the meat done, the honey, and my roasting pan, turned to cinders.) Moreover, my bird was underseasoned and barely tasted of honey.

For that first test I had used a favorite test kitchen roasting technique: I heated the oven to 375 degrees and cooked two chickens (to serve six to eight) on a roasting rack, breast side down, for 35 minutes. I flipped the birds over, increased the heat to 450 degrees, and roasted them for another 30 to 40 minutes. The method protects the more delicate breast meat while giving the longer-cooking dark meat time to cook through. After the chicken is turned, the breast browns and crisps without drying out. Ordinarily, anyway. When I brushed on the honey, the skin got soggy.

I dug out a recipe I'd seen for a soy-honey brine, figuring the brined chicken would be nicely seasoned and honey-flavored to the bone—with no burning. Instead, I found that the soy masked the honey. In all honesty, I didn't want to take the time (or refrigerator space) to brine two chickens anyway, so I turned to honey butter, which I rubbed under their skin before roasting as before. Yet again, the honey burned and its flavor was faint. To prevent burning, I protected the chickens with foil—which worked fine, if my goal was steamed, soggy chicken skin.

Having exhausted ways to add honey flavor before the birds went into the oven, I was finally convinced I'd be better off incorporating the honey late in the game. So for my next test, I first rubbed a simple mixture of salt and pepper on the birds. It was better yet when I used some of the rub under the skin and some on the outside of the chickens. For a burnished look, I added paprika. Then I returned to the question of honey.

For balance, I mixed some honey with lemon juice and zest, and I brushed this glaze on the chickens 10 minutes before they were done. I found that glazing at the end had an unexpected benefit: The chicken skin, coated with nothing but spices for almost an hour, had rendered and crisped up nicely. However, when it came to the flavor of my new glaze, tasters compared the glaze to Luden's cough drops, so I switched to cider vinegar for tang. As for how it actually glazed the chicken, well, not so much. The glaze kept running off, so I tried adding cornstarch to thicken it. This helped, but even so, it was inevitable that a little dripped onto the roasting pan, where it sizzled and burned. To prevent that, I added water and chicken broth to the roasting pan when I flipped the chickens, which, conveniently, gave me the makings of a tasty sauce. After the chickens finished cooking, I brushed them again with the glaze. Meanwhile, I reduced the sauce and the juice in a pan, whisked in a few tablespoons of butter for richness and gloss, and added an extra tablespoon of vinegar for brightness. Now this was like the honey-glazed chicken I remembered, only better.

—DIANE UNGER, *Cook's Country*

Honey Roast Chicken
SERVES 6 TO 8

The test kitchen's favorite brand of chicken broth is Swanson Certified Organic Free Range Chicken Broth.

   Salt and pepper
1 teaspoon sweet paprika
2 (3½ to 4-pound) whole chickens, giblets discarded
1 teaspoon cornstarch
1 cup plus 1 tablespoon water
1 cup plus 1 tablespoon cider vinegar
½ cup honey
1 cup low-sodium chicken broth
1 teaspoon minced fresh thyme
2 tablespoons unsalted butter, cut into pieces and chilled

1. Adjust an oven rack to the middle position and heat the oven to 375 degrees. Combine 1 tablespoon salt, 2 teaspoons pepper, and the paprika in a small bowl. Pat the chickens dry with paper towels. Following the photos on page 174, rub the mixture under the skin and over the outside of each chicken. Tuck the wings behind the back and tie the legs together with butcher's twine for each bird.

HONEY ROAST CHICKEN

2. Stir the cornstarch and 1 tablespoon of the water together in a bowl until no lumps remain and set aside. Bring 1 cup of the vinegar and the honey to a simmer in a small saucepan over medium-high heat. Cook, stirring occasionally, until reduced to ½ cup, 3 to 5 minutes. Slowly whisk the cornstarch mixture into the glaze. Return to a simmer and cook for 1 minute.

3. Arrange the chickens, breast side down, on a V-rack set inside a roasting pan. Roast the chickens until just golden, about 35 minutes. Remove the chickens from the oven and, using a wad of paper towels, flip the breast side up. Raise the oven temperature to 450 degrees. Pour the remaining 1 cup water and the broth into the roasting pan. Return the chickens to the oven and roast until the thighs register 165 to 170 degrees on an instant-read thermometer, 30 to 40 minutes. Brush the chickens evenly with a thick layer of glaze and continue to roast until the glaze is golden brown, about 10 minutes. Transfer the chickens to a carving board, brush with the remaining glaze, and let rest for 15 minutes.

4. Meanwhile, pour the pan juice and any accumulated chicken juice into a saucepan and skim the fat. Stir in the thyme, bring to a simmer, and cook until the sauce is slightly thickened and reduced to 1 cup, about 10 minutes. Off the heat, whisk in the butter and remaining 1 tablespoon vinegar. Season with salt and pepper to taste. Carve the chickens and serve, passing the sauce at the table.

CIDER-BRAISED CHICKEN

BRAISING PORK CHOPS IN APPLE CIDER INFUSES them with apple flavor. I wanted to adapt the method for chicken, so a natural starting point for my recipe was to simply braise chicken in apple cider. I browned chicken pieces until they were golden, set them aside, and then sautéed onions and garlic in the same pan. I returned the chicken to the pan, poured in cider until the meat was nearly submerged, and placed it in a low oven (the consistently gentle heat of the oven works better than the stovetop for braising). I left the cover off, knowing that a moist environment wouldn't allow the chicken skin to render and become crisp. Well, the skin was still soggy and flabby, and the dish tasted nothing like apples; the chicken juice had diluted the cider, which clearly needed lots of support to deliver deep apple flavor.

First, I trained my attention on the chicken. Braised chicken skin is often rubbery because the fat hasn't been rendered correctly. Most recipes call for browning the chicken until "golden brown," usually about five minutes per side. I took the time to thoroughly render the skin—a full 10 minutes over medium-high heat until it had turned deep chestnut brown. (It took just five minutes to brown the skinless flip side.)

For even crisper skin, I ignored the "low and slow" rule of braising and tried cranking the heat up to 450 degrees. In just 10 minutes, the chicken was done and the skin was better, but still not perfect. Things really turned the corner when I re-thought the technique I'd been using of flipping the chicken pieces halfway through their oven time. As long as I didn't overcook the chicken, I found I could leave it

---

NOTES FROM THE TEST KITCHEN

SECRETS TO HONEY ROAST CHICKEN

1. To ensure deeply seasoned chicken, gently loosen the skin and rub the chicken with a salt-pepper-paprika spice mix inside and out.

2. Wait until the chicken is almost done before glazing it with a honey-vinegar mix. By this point, the skin is crispy and the honey won't burn.

3. To accentuate the honey flavor, make a sauce from the pan drippings, which are faintly sweet from the glaze runoff.

skin side up. At the same time, I reduced the amount of liquid in the pan so that it reached just halfway up the chicken pieces, leaving the skin exposed to the drier heat. With that adjustment, the finish line was really in sight.

I was ready to focus on the sauce. The extra browning of the chicken left plenty of fond in the pan, and the high-heat roasting sans lid let the liquid evaporate in the oven, which helped concentrate the apple flavor. To give the braise more interest, I chopped up one apple and stirred it in after the onions. A McIntosh turned to mush, a Granny Smith was too tart and firm, but buttery Golden Delicious, Cortland, and Jonagold each retained their integrity when cooked.

The addition of the apple worked so well that I decided to look for additional apple products to fortify the braising liquid. Applesauce gave the dish a grainy feel; apple butter was so intense it overwhelmed the delicate chicken, and both apple jelly and apple juice concentrate made the sauce too sweet. I thought that drier hard apple cider could replace some (or all) of the fresh cider, but tasters missed the fruitiness of the fresh cider. The addition of apple brandy, however, echoed the earthiness of the apples and gave the sauce depth.

To thicken the braising liquid and turn it into a sauce, I browned 2 teaspoons of flour with the garlic at the start. Fresh thyme provided warmth and herbal softness. To further underline the dish's apple character, I added splashes of cider vinegar and additional apple brandy before serving.

—ADAM RIED, *Cook's Country*

Cider-Braised Chicken

SERVES 4

Either white or dark meat (or a combination) will work. Plain brandy, cognac, or Calvados (a French apple brandy) can be used in place of the apple brandy.

3	pounds bone-in, skin-on chicken pieces (split breasts cut in half, drumsticks, and/or thighs)
	Salt and pepper
2	teaspoons vegetable oil
1	onion, minced (about 1 cup)
2	garlic cloves, minced
2	teaspoons minced fresh thyme
2	teaspoons unbleached all-purpose flour
1	large Golden Delicious, Cortland, or Jonagold apple, peeled, cored, and cut into ¾-inch chunks
1	cup apple cider
¼	cup apple brandy
1	teaspoon cider vinegar

1. Adjust an oven rack to the middle position and heat the oven to 450 degrees. Pat the chicken dry with paper towels and season with salt and pepper. Heat the oil in a 12-inch oven-safe skillet over medium-high heat until just smoking. Cook the chicken, skin side down, until well browned, about 10 minutes. Flip the chicken and brown the second side, about 5 minutes. Transfer to a plate.

2. Pour off all but 1 tablespoon of the fat from the skillet. Add the onion to the skillet and cook until softened, about 5 minutes. Stir in the garlic, thyme, and flour and cook, stirring frequently, until fragrant and the flour is absorbed, about 1 minute. Add the apple, cider, and 3 tablespoons of the brandy and bring to a boil.

3. Nestle the chicken, skin side up, into the sauce and roast until the breasts register 160 to 165 degrees and the thighs/drumsticks register 175 degrees on an instant-read thermometer, about 10 minutes. Transfer the chicken to a platter. Stir the vinegar and remaining 1 tablespoon brandy into the sauce. Season with salt and pepper to taste. Serve, passing the sauce separately.

NOTES FROM THE TEST KITCHEN

KEYS TO CRISP-SKINNED CIDER-BRAISED CHICKEN
We avoid flabby skin with a hybrid technique that combines braising and pan roasting.

1. Brown the chicken, skin side down, in a skillet on the stovetop for 10 minutes until it is deep brown. Brown the second side for 5 more minutes.

2. After building the sauce in the skillet and returning the chicken to the pan, finish cooking the chicken skin side up and uncovered in a hot oven.

BATTER-FRIED CHICKEN

THERE ARE DOZENS OF WAYS TO PREPARE FRIED chicken, from brines to flour dredges, from honey-dipped to double-dunked. But one appealing method has practically disappeared: batter-frying. In the 19th century, recipes for it were common. Chicken parts were dipped in a batter not unlike pancake batter and shallow-fried in lard. On occasion, the chicken was cooked first, then battered and deep-fried, apparently to keep the batter from burning before the chicken was cooked through. The recipes I found promised a delicate, fantastically crunchy coating encasing moist, nicely seasoned chicken. Whatever the specifics, merely reading about batter-fried chicken made me hungry.

I was pleased when I found a few modern recipes to get me started. The batters sounded simple enough: flour, salt, eggs, and milk or buttermilk. Depressingly, the coatings these recipes produced were a disappointment. They were soft, doughy, and doughnut-like, and just as in some of the old recipes I'd been reading about, the batter burned before the chicken was cooked through.

Before I solved any of those problems, I needed to settle on a technique. Recipes were divided between deep- and shallow-frying. I tried both methods, and there was no contest: With shallow-frying, the batter consistently burned on the bottom.

Deep-frying method determined, I turned to textural issues. I had a hunch the egg in the batter was contributing to the soft texture, which was just flat-out wrong for fried chicken. After all, these were basically pancake batters, so naturally they'd be soft and fluffy. Taking out the egg did make the coating less soft, but it still darkened too quickly. I tried batters made with whole milk, skim milk, and buttermilk, all to no avail. Were the milk sugars in the dairy causing the batter to burn, I wondered? I put in a call to our science editor, who confirmed my suspicions. It turns out that when wet batter hits hot frying oil, the moisture in the batter vaporizes, leaving behind the solids, which adhere to the chicken. In this case, the sugars in the milk solids were browning too fast.

Obviously, I needed liquid of some sort to turn my flour mixture into batter. I tried beer, club soda (which is sometimes used in tempura batter), and, finally, plain old water. Wouldn't you know it? Ordinary water worked best, bringing to mind some of the Civil War–era batter-fried chicken recipes I'd researched. They'd called for water, too; presumably, times were hard and water was free.

Based on plenty of test kitchen experience, I made an executive decision to soak the chicken parts in a salt-sugar-water brine to keep them moist and flavorful as they fried. Then I stirred together a very simple batter of flour, water, salt, and plenty of black pepper. I really wasn't sure how thick the batter was supposed to be, so I opted for the consistency of pancake batter to be sure it would stick. I dunked the pieces in batter and slipped them gently into the hot oil so that it wouldn't spatter. The results were promising. After 10 minutes, the batter hadn't burned (always a good sign), and by the time the chicken was cooked through, the exterior was a pretty golden brown. But the texture was more like a thick carapace than the thin, crispy coating I'd set my heart on.

I thinned the batter down with more water than I had used before. For crispiness, I turned to cornstarch, an ingredient the test kitchen has had luck using in the past. After testing varying amounts, I replaced half of the flour in the batter with an equal amount of cornstarch. At this point, it occurred to me that baking powder might add lift and lightness without doughiness. Along with this leavener, I stirred in black pepper, paprika, and cayenne for simple but unambiguous flavor, then dried off the brined chicken parts and put them into the batter to coat them thoroughly. I lifted out the pieces with tongs, let the excess batter drip off (now the coating was so thin you could see through it), and lowered them carefully into the deep, hot fat.

Some 15 minutes later, I marveled at my own handiwork. The chicken looked amazing, and a single bite confirmed I'd hit the mark. The meat was juicy yet cooked through. The picture-perfect, golden-brown crust snapped and crackled, and tasters loved its pleasant peppery bite. Just as I'd hoped, batter-fried chicken was incredibly easy, crispy as all get-out, and indisputably delicious.

But that's not the end of the story. Hard as it was to stop my colleagues from gobbling up all the chicken, I set aside a few pieces in the refrigerator. Two days later, I placed them on a wire rack set inside a baking sheet and warmed them in a 450-degree oven for about 10 minutes. Guess what? They were as good as the day I'd fried them.

—DIANE UNGER, *Cook's Country*

BATTER-FRIED CHICKEN

Batter-Fried Chicken

SERVES 4 TO 6

We prefer eating this chicken the day it is made, but it reheats and recrisps surprisingly well.

> **Salt**
> ¼ **cup sugar**
> 4 **pounds bone-in, skin-on chicken pieces (split breasts cut in half, drumsticks, and/or thighs)**
> 1 **cup unbleached all-purpose flour**
> 1 **cup cornstarch**
> 5 **teaspoons black pepper**
> 2 **teaspoons baking powder**
> 1 **teaspoon sweet paprika**
> ½ **teaspoon cayenne pepper**
> 1¾ **cups cold water**
> 3 **quarts peanut or vegetable oil**

1. Dissolve ¼ cup salt and the sugar in 1 quart cold water in a large bowl. Submerge the chicken in the brine, cover with plastic wrap, and refrigerate for 30 minutes or up to 1 hour.

2. Whisk the flour, cornstarch, black pepper, baking powder, 1 teaspoon salt, paprika, and cayenne together in a large bowl, then add the water and whisk until smooth. Refrigerate the batter while the chicken is brining.

3. Heat the oil in a large Dutch oven over medium-high heat to 350 degrees. Remove the chicken from the brine and pat it dry with paper towels. Whisk the batter to recombine, then transfer half of the chicken to the batter. One piece at a time, remove the chicken from the batter, allow excess batter to drip back into the bowl, and transfer the chicken to the oil. Fry the chicken, adjusting the burner as necessary to maintain an oil temperature between 300 and 325 degrees, until deep golden brown and the breasts register 160 to 165 degrees and the thighs/drumsticks register 175 degrees on an instant-read thermometer, 12 to 15 minutes. Drain the chicken on a wire rack set inside a rimmed baking sheet. Bring the oil back to 350 degrees and repeat with the remaining chicken. Serve. (The chicken can be stored, refrigerated, in an airtight container for up to 2 days. To reheat, adjust an oven rack to the middle position and heat the oven to 450 degrees. Place the chicken on a wire rack set inside a rimmed baking sheet and bake for 10 minutes.)

NOTES FROM THE TEST KITCHEN

MAKING BATTER-FRIED CHICKEN

1. Whisk together a thin batter made from water, flour, baking powder, spices, and cornstarch.

2. To avoid a doughy coating, let the excess batter drip off the chicken back into the bowl before transferring the chicken to the oil.

3. To prevent the chicken pieces from sticking together in the oil, don't crowd the pot. Fry the chicken in two batches.

NASHVILLE HOT FRIED CHICKEN

LATE ONE AFTERNOON AT PRINCE'S HOT CHICKEN Shack in Nashville, Tennessee, the regulars are lined up to place their orders at the tiny takeout window. A woman asks, "Do you have any lip balm?" I shake my head no, wondering if she really planned to borrow some from a stranger. "I was going to suggest you put some on before you eat," she says, "'cause this fried chicken is so hot it's gonna chap your lips!" The chicken arrives, craggy and crusted with red-brown spices. It's perched atop a slice of white bread and speared by a toothpick threaded with pickles, both meant to counteract the heat. I taste the medium-hot chicken. A slow burn builds. I gingerly try the hot. My eyes water, my nose runs, and I begin to sweat.

Over two days in Nashville, I sweated through many hot fried chicken quarters and grew to understand the addicting endorphin rush that hot fried chicken devotees describe. Before I left town, I would need to get someone to divulge the recipe. No luck. At every restaurant, the tiny order windows kept my prying eyes from taking in much. I'd have to figure out Nashville hot fried chicken on my own.

Back home, I found only three recipes for it, either online or in cookbooks. All started with chicken quarters and spice mixtures of garlic powder, sugar, salt, and eye-popping amounts of cayenne pepper. One recipe suggested dredging the chicken in flour and spices; one called for sprinkling on the spice mixture after frying; and the third called for brushing the fried chicken with a lard-based spice paste. The first batch was a burning disaster. Twenty-five minutes in the hot oil (quarters take longer to fry than smaller pieces) incinerated the cayenne pepper. Sprinkling the spices on after frying produced chicken smothered in powdery seasoning. The post-fry paste had promise, but it spread unevenly, leaving pockets of fiery, dusty spices. As for the meat, it was dry and bland—far from the moist, deeply seasoned chicken I'd eaten in Nashville.

We've fried plenty of chickens in the test kitchen and have developed some proven techniques. We brine the raw chicken in a saltwater solution to keep the meat juicy. For an extra-crispy coating, we dredge the chicken in flour twice before frying. We usually fry small pieces for even cooking, but for authenticity's sake, and for a more balanced meat-to-spice ratio, Nashville hot fried chicken requires quarters. As long as I fried two equal-sized quarters at a time, the pieces should cook evenly.

The post-fry spice paste was a good start. But I needed to make it loose enough to coat the chicken, yet not so wet as to make the chicken soggy. Melting the lard worked nicely, but I hated the taste. Nashville residents may have terrific (all-natural) lard at their disposal, but most of us can only find the sour, plasticky-tasting hydrogenated stuff. I turned to oil. I mixed a couple of tablespoons of the frying oil with 2 tablespoons of cayenne and ½ teaspoon each of salt, garlic powder, and sugar. This paste was too thick to brush evenly, so I increased the oil to ¼ cup. Now more of a spicy oil than a paste, it coated the chicken evenly without soaking it. But even at 2 tablespoons of cayenne, the heat wasn't up to Nashville level, nor did it penetrate the chicken meat. I added a teaspoon of bracing dry mustard and

upped the cayenne to a blistering 3½ tablespoons, but it remained superficial, and now the spices burned so hot, they sent tasters scrambling for a cold drink.

I'd already noticed that when the spicy paste hit the hot chicken, the spices softened slightly. What if I heated them by design? Blooming spices—cooking them for 30 seconds in oil—softens and deepens their flavor. I heated them in ¼ cup oil in a small saucepan until fragrant, fried the chicken, and brushed it with the toasted spice oil. The taste was more complex yet still lip-burningly hot.

Thanks to the brine, the meat was salty and moist, but it lacked heat. To turn it up, I added a couple of tablespoons of hot sauce to the brine. It was virtually undetectable. I kept upping the quantity until I was adding ½ cup hot sauce. Finally, the heat was more than skin deep.

As I wrapped up my last few tests, I noticed that tasters were dividing themselves into two groups: the smaller group circled the stove and pounced on the insanely spicy chicken pieces as soon as I plucked them from the fryer. Most people, however, kept a cool distance. "You've made an authentic version, but so what?" they said. "It's too hot to eat." So I dialed back some of the spices for the less-hot version that follows—it's still pretty darn spicy. If you dare, cook up a batch of the original, Nashville Extra-Hot Fried Chicken.

—LYNN CLARK, *Cook's Country*

Nashville Hot Fried Chicken

SERVES 4 TO 6

Chicken quarters take longer to cook than smaller pieces. To ensure that the exterior doesn't burn before the inside cooks through, keep the oil temperature below 325 degrees while the chicken is frying.

½ **cup hot sauce**

½ **cup plus ½ teaspoon sugar**

   Salt

1 **(3½ to 4-pound) whole chicken, quartered (see page 180)**

3 **quarts plus 3 tablespoons peanut or vegetable oil**

1 **tablespoon cayenne pepper**

½ **teaspoon sweet paprika**

¼ **teaspoon garlic powder**

2 **cups unbleached all-purpose flour**

½ **teaspoon black pepper**

1. Whisk the hot sauce, ½ cup of the sugar, and ½ cup salt into 2 quarts cold water in a large bowl until the salt and sugar dissolve. Submerge the chicken in the brine, cover with plastic wrap, and refrigerate for 30 minutes or up to 1 hour.

2. Heat 3 tablespoons of the oil in a small saucepan over medium heat until shimmering. Add the cayenne, paprika, ½ teaspoon salt, the remaining ½ teaspoon sugar, and the garlic powder and cook until fragrant, about 30 seconds. Transfer to a small bowl.

3. Remove the chicken from the brine. Combine the flour, ½ teaspoon salt, and the black pepper in a large bowl. Dredge the chicken pieces 2 at a time in the flour mixture. Shake the excess flour from the chicken and transfer to a wire rack set inside a rimmed baking sheet. (Do not discard the flour mixture.)

4. Adjust an oven rack to the middle position and heat the oven to 200 degrees. Heat the remaining 3 quarts oil in a large Dutch oven over medium-high heat to 350 degrees. Return the chicken pieces to the flour mixture and turn to coat. Fry half of the chicken pieces, adjusting the burner as necessary to maintain an oil temperature between 300 and 325 degrees, until deep golden brown and the breasts register 160 to 165 degrees and the thighs/drumsticks register 175 degrees on an instant-read thermometer,

---

NOTES FROM THE TEST KITCHEN

QUARTERING CHICKEN

1. Slice between the drumstick and the breast. Hold the chicken with one hand and use the other to bend back the leg and pop out the joint.

2. Cut through the leg joint. Do not separate the thigh from the drumstick. Repeat steps 1 and 2 to detach the other leg quarter.

3. To separate the whole breast from the backbone, cut through the ribs with kitchen shears on either side of the backbone.

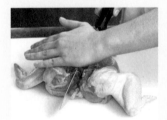

4. With the whole breast skin side down, cut through the breastbone to separate the breast and wing section into halves.

KEYS TO FIERY FLAVOR

To make a version of Nashville Hot Fried Chicken that's worthy of the name, you have to season chicken down to the bone.

1. Add hot sauce to a standard salt and sugar brine. As the chicken soaks, it picks up heat and flavor.

2. Heat the spices in oil to soften their dry, harsh edge and amplify their flavor.

3. After the chicken has been fried, brush it with the spicy oil. Waiting until after it is cooked prevents the cayenne from burning.

20 to 25 minutes. Drain the chicken on a clean wire rack set inside a rimmed baking sheet and place in the oven. Bring the oil back to 350 degrees and repeat with the remaining chicken. Stir the spicy oil mixture to recombine and brush over both sides of the chicken. Serve.

VARIATION

Nashville Extra-Hot Fried Chicken

Our original recipe packs a punch but would never pass muster with aficionados of true Nashville hot fried chicken. This extra-hot version is the heat level you'd get if you ordered the "hot" at Prince's Hot Chicken Shack. Don't say we didn't warn you.

Follow the recipe for Nashville Hot Fried Chicken, increasing the oil to ¼ cup, cayenne to 3½ tablespoons, and sugar to ¾ teaspoon in step 2, and add 1 teaspoon dry mustard to the oil mixture.

PAN-SEARED CHICKEN BREASTS

WHAT COOK DESPERATE FOR A QUICK DINNER hasn't thrown a boneless, skinless chicken breast into a hot pan, keeping fingers crossed for edible results? The fact is, pan-searing is a surefire way to ruin this cut. Unlike a split chicken breast, which has the bone and skin to help keep the meat moist and juicy, a boneless, skinless breast is fully exposed to the intensity of the hot pan. Inevitably, it emerges moist in the middle and dry at the edges, with an exterior that's leathery and tough. But there's no denying the appeal of a cut that requires no butchering. What would it take to get a pan-seared boneless, skinless breast every bit as flavorful, moist, and tender as its skin-on counterpart?

The problem is that the center of a thick chicken breast takes a long time to reach 165 degrees. Meanwhile, the outer layers are busy overcooking, losing moisture, and turning stringy and tough. One unconventional recipe tried to solve the problem by parcooking the chicken in water before searing. In theory, the idea was sound: Poaching would cook the breasts gently and evenly, and the parcooked, warm chicken should take much less time to develop a flavorful brown crust than straight-from-the-fridge meat. Less time in a hot

skillet equals less moisture lost. The chicken was juicy and brown, all right—but also flavorless, since much of the chicken's juice seeped into the cooking liquid and subsequently got poured down the drain.

I tried ditching the water bath in favor of the oven, still keeping the same gently-parcook-then-sear order, a technique we've used successfully in the test kitchen with thick-cut steaks. I placed four chicken breasts in a baking pan, cooked them in a 275-degree oven until they hit 150 degrees, and then seared them. They browned quickly and beautifully, but while the meat was moist enough on the inside, the exterior had dehydrated so much that I practically needed a steak knife to cut it.

What about salting? Like brining, salting changes the structure of meat proteins, helping them to retain more moisture as they cook. Ideally, chicken should be salted for at least six hours to ensure full penetration and juiciness. But boneless, skinless breasts are supposed to be quick and easy, so I wasn't willing to commit more than 30 extra minutes. Poking holes into the meat with a fork created channels for the salt to reach the interior of the chicken, maximizing a short salting time. This made the interior even juicier, but the exterior was still too dried out.

If the issue was really the chicken's exterior, should it be somehow protected from the oven's dry heat? I tried the exact same method, this time wrapping the baking dish tightly in foil before cooking. Bingo! This cover-and-cook method proved so effective that I could combine the 30-minute salting step with the roasting step.

I now had breasts that were supremely moist and tender on the inside with a flavorful, browned exterior. With a little more effort, could I do better still? To protect thin cutlets from the heat of the pan and encourage faster browning, many recipes dredge them in flour. Raw breasts are malleable, which means they make good contact with the pan. The parcooked breasts, on the other hand, had already firmed up slightly, so only some of the flour was able to come in contact with the hot oil in the pan, leading to spotty browning.

Dredging was out, and I didn't want to go the full breading route. The only other thing I could think of was a technique from Chinese cooking called velveting. Here the meat is dipped in a mixture of oil and cornstarch, which provides a thin, protective layer that keeps the protein moist and tender even when exposed to the ultra-high heat of stir-frying. Though I'd never heard of using this method on large pieces of meat like breasts, I saw no reason it wouldn't work. I brushed my parcooked chicken with a mixture of 2 tablespoons melted butter (which would contribute more flavor than oil) and a heaping tablespoon of cornstarch before searing it.

As soon as I put the breasts in the pan, I noticed that the buttery slurry helped the chicken make better contact with the hot skillet, and as I flipped the pieces, I was happy to see an even, golden-brown crust. However, tasters reported that the cornstarch was leaving a slightly pasty residue. Replacing the cornstarch with flour didn't work; the protein in flour produced a crust that was tough and bready instead of light and crisp. Achieving exactly the right amount of protein and starch in the coating turned out to be the key. A mixture of 3 parts flour to 1 part cornstarch created a thin, browned, crisp coating that kept the breast's exterior as moist as the interior—some tasters thought it was even better than chicken skin itself.

Served on its own or with a simple pan sauce, this tender, crisp-coated chicken far surpassed any other pan-seared breasts I've ever made. Start to finish, they did take a little longer to cook than the fastest methods, but the hands-on time was almost the same as for breasts you just throw into the skillet. Now that I know how good boneless chicken breasts really can be, if I don't have time to cook them right, I'll just cook something else.

—KEITH DRESSER, *Cook's Illustrated*

Pan-Seared Chicken Breasts

SERVES 4

For the best results, buy similarly sized chicken breasts. If your breasts have the tenderloin attached, leave it in place and follow the upper range of baking time in step 1. For optimal texture, sear the chicken immediately after removing it from the oven.

- 4 **(6 to 8-ounce) boneless, skinless chicken breasts, trimmed (see note)**
- 2 **teaspoons kosher salt or 1 teaspoon table salt**
- 1 **tablespoon vegetable oil**
- 2 **tablespoons unsalted butter, melted**
- 1 **tablespoon unbleached all-purpose flour**
- 1 **teaspoon cornstarch**
- ½ **teaspoon pepper**
- 1 **recipe Lemon and Chive Pan Sauce (optional; recipe follows)**

1. Adjust an oven rack to the lower-middle position and heat the oven to 275 degrees. Following the photo on page 183, use a fork to poke the thickest half of each breast 5 to 6 times, then sprinkle each breast with ½ teaspoon kosher salt (or ¼ teaspoon table salt). Place the chicken, skinned side down, in a 13 by 9-inch baking dish and cover tightly with foil. Bake until the chicken registers 145 to 150 degrees on an instant-read thermometer, 30 to 40 minutes.

2. Remove the chicken from the oven and transfer, skinned side up, to a paper towel–lined plate and pat dry with paper towels. Heat the oil in a 12-inch skillet over medium-high heat until smoking. While the pan is heating, whisk the butter, flour, cornstarch, and pepper together in a small bowl. Lightly brush the tops of the chicken with half of the butter mixture. Place the chicken in the skillet, coated side down, and cook until browned, 3 to 4 minutes. While the chicken browns, brush the second side with the remaining butter mixture. Using tongs, flip the chicken, reduce the heat to medium, and cook until the second side is browned and the chicken registers 160 to 165 degrees, 3 to 4 minutes. Transfer the chicken to a platter and let rest while preparing the pan sauce (if not making a pan sauce, let the chicken rest for 5 minutes before serving).

Lemon and Chive Pan Sauce

MAKES ABOUT ¾ CUP

- 1 **shallot, minced (about 3 tablespoons)**
- 1 **teaspoon unbleached all-purpose flour**
- 1 **cup low-sodium chicken broth**
- 1 **tablespoon fresh lemon juice**
- 1 **tablespoon minced fresh chives**
- 1 **tablespoon unsalted butter, chilled**
  Salt and pepper

Add the shallot to the empty skillet and cook over medium heat until softened, about 2 minutes. Add the flour and cook, stirring constantly, 30 seconds. Add the broth, increase the heat to medium-high, and bring to a simmer, scraping the pan bottom to loosen the browned bits. Simmer rapidly until reduced to ¾ cup, 3 to 5 minutes. Stir in any accumulated chicken juice, return to a simmer, and cook for 30 seconds. Off the heat, whisk in the lemon juice, chives, and butter; season with salt and pepper to taste. Spoon over the chicken and serve.

SECRETS TO BETTER PAN-SEARED CHICKEN BREASTS

1. Poke the thicker part of the breasts with the tines of a fork before salting to allow the salt to penetrate the meat more quickly, which results in juicy interiors in a minimum of time.

2. Bake the chicken at a low temperature in a foil-covered dish to ensure even cooking and to keep the exterior from drying out.

3. Brush butter, flour, and cornstarch onto the breasts to create a "skin" to protect the meat during searing.

4. Briefly sear the parcooked coated breasts to keep them moist and create crisp exteriors.

PASTRY BRUSHES

Since manufacturers have released a number of new models since our last testing a few years ago (at which time we declared the OXO Good Grips Silicone Pastry Brush king), we chose eight new pastry brushes, both natural and silicone, and went back into the kitchen to see if any came close to our original favorite. We tested the brushes on a variety of tasks: painting runny egg wash on dumplings, basting grilled chicken with barbecue sauce, oiling a hot pan, and brushing crumbs from a cake before frosting it. Yet again, the light, maneuverable **OXO Good Grips Silicone Pastry Brush**, $6.99, came out in front. (See page 305 for more information about our testing results.)

OLD-FASHIONED TAMALE PIE

THE IDEA BEHIND TAMALE PIE—THAT YOU CAN GET the flavor of a tamale in one crowd-friendly, easy-to-prepare dish—makes perfect sense. But sadly, the tamale pies I've had aren't much like an actual tamale. They have always been casseroles made with ground (never shredded) meat, beans, and vegetables in a tomato-y sauce under a cornmeal topping that is covered with cheese. The flavor is usually flat and the spices stale. And then there's the textural issue. While tamales are traditionally steamed, a method that keeps the exterior fluffy and the meat inside moist, tamale pies are baked, so the texture of the cornmeal topping is often dried out from the oven's heat (what saves the meat filling is the decidedly un-tamale-like tomato sauce).

My low opinion of tamale pies changed when I tasted a recipe we received for our Lost Suppers contest called Granny's Tamale Pie from Betty Hesterberg of Bozeman, Montana. Of the several recipes we received for tamale pie, Betty's in particular caught my eye from the start. "My mother got this recipe from the elderly wife of a sheep rancher, who would make this dish and heat it up over the fire at herding camps," she stated. I've never seen or heard of a 1950s-style casserole getting heated up over a campfire; this one showed promise. Betty called for layering shredded meat between a cornmeal filling, baking the pie in a Dutch oven set in a water bath, and serving the results with a smoky-spicy sauce on the side rather than making a sauce part of the pie filling. Notably, she didn't call for a single shred of cheese. This promised to be a different kind of tamale pie—and that was a good thing.

Betty started her recipe by poaching meat for the filling. She called for dark meat chicken or game birds (she said she always made it with pheasant growing up), and while the game had a rustic appeal, I opted for bone-in chicken thighs to keep things simple. I browned the meat first for deeper flavor, and I decided to cook it in chicken broth rather than water as Betty had done, with the goal of getting a deeper flavor since the cooking liquid would come into play later for the sauce.

After the meat was cooked and shredded, I moved on to the cornmeal filling. Betty's recipe began by sautéing salt pork that she ground herself with some garlic and onion in a Dutch oven. The combination sounded like a good start, but salt pork can be hard to come by and

OLD-FASHIONED TAMALE PIE

grinding it was tedious, so I swapped it out for chopped bacon. After the bacon's fat had rendered, I removed the bacon from the pot and set it aside for the time being. Following Betty's instructions, I stirred a large can of tomatoes, creamed corn, and black olives into the pot (she noted a family tradition of using olives with the pits, but I saw no reason to do so and changed to pitted olives). Next, the cornmeal batter, a mixture of eggs, cornmeal, and milk, went in, and I cooked this mixture for a few minutes until it thickened. At this point I stirred the bacon back in (leaving it in the pot the whole time would have turned it chewy). So far, so good.

It was time for assembly. Following Betty's instructions, I measured out half the thickened cornmeal mixture, leaving a base layer of it in the pot. I scattered the shredded chicken on top and covered this chicken layer with the remaining cornmeal mixture. This was already feeling much more along the lines of a real tamale, but the next step is what really separated Betty's recipe from the pack. She didn't just slide the pot in the oven for a few hours and call it a day. She called for baking the pie, covered, in a water bath. This technique would allow the tamale pie to steam just like real tamales. I set the pot in a roasting pan filled partially with water, and moved it all to the oven to bake for a few hours.

While the pie baked I put together the sauce, a simple combination of tomato sauce, Mexican-style chili powder (hotter than your standard chili powder), flour for thickening, and some of the liquid from poaching the chicken. Betty toasted the flour first to deepen the flavor, a trick that was something like making a dry roux. This sauce tasted great, but I felt like it was a little too hot for my New England palate, so I swapped out the hot Mexican-style chili powder for regular chili powder, and I added cumin and coriander for a rounder flavor. After I whisked the sauce together, I set it aside until the pie was ready.

What came out of the oven definitely looked better than any tamale pie I'd ever seen. The cornmeal was golden, flecked with tomatoes, corn, and olives. A spoonful revealed this pie also tasted unlike any other. The gentle cooking of the water bath made this pie moist and fluffy, and the chicken had remained tender and juicy. Served with the sauce, it had a flavor and texture that was just like taking a bite out of a tamale.

—JENNIFER LALIME, *America's Test Kitchen Books*

Old-Fashioned Tamale Pie
SERVES 6 TO 8

You will need a large roasting pan, ideally one that is 16 by 13 inches, to accommodate the water bath in this recipe.

PIE
- 3 pounds bone-in, skin-on chicken thighs, trimmed
- Salt and pepper
- ½ cup vegetable oil
- 3 cups low-sodium chicken broth
- 8 slices bacon, chopped
- 1 onion, minced (about 1 cup)
- 2 garlic cloves, minced
- 2 (14.5-ounce) cans diced tomatoes, drained
- 1 (14.75-ounce) can creamed corn
- 1 (6-ounce) can pitted ripe black olives, drained and chopped
- 1 cup whole milk
- 3 large eggs
- 2 cups yellow cornmeal

SAUCE
- 3 tablespoons unbleached all-purpose flour
- 1 tablespoon chili powder
- 1 teaspoon ground cumin
- 1 teaspoon ground coriander
- 1½ cups enriched chicken broth (reserved from making the pie filling)
- 1 (8-ounce) can tomato sauce
- Salt and pepper
- ¼ cup chopped fresh cilantro, for serving

1. FOR THE PIE: Adjust an oven rack to the lower-middle position and heat the oven to 325 degrees.

2. Pat the chicken dry with paper towels and season with salt and pepper. Heat 1½ teaspoons of the oil in a large Dutch oven over medium-high heat until just smoking. Add half of the chicken and cook until golden brown on both sides, about 10 minutes, flipping halfway through. Transfer the chicken to a plate and remove the skin. Return the pot to medium-high heat and repeat with 1½ teaspoons more oil and the remaining chicken.

3. Stir the broth into the pot, scraping up any browned bits. Return the chicken, along with any accumulated juice, to the pot. Bring to a simmer, cover, and cook until the thickest part of the thighs registers 175 degrees on an instant-read thermometer, about 1 hour.

4. Transfer the chicken to a plate. Measure out and reserve 1½ cups of the broth for the sauce. Discard any remaining broth (or save for another use). When the chicken is cool enough to handle, shred the meat into bite-size pieces and set aside.

5. Bring a kettle of water to a boil. Meanwhile, cook the bacon in the Dutch oven over medium-low heat until crisp, about 10 minutes. Using a slotted spoon, transfer the bacon to a paper towel–lined plate.

6. Increase the heat to medium and heat the bacon fat until shimmering. Add the onion and ½ teaspoon salt and cook, stirring occasionally, until softened, 5 to 7 minutes. Stir in the garlic and cook until fragrant, about 30 seconds. Stir in the remaining 7 tablespoons oil, the tomatoes, corn, olives, and ½ teaspoon pepper and bring to a simmer.

7. Meanwhile, whisk the milk and eggs together in a bowl. Whisk in the cornmeal until incorporated and smooth. Slowly pour the cornmeal mixture into the pot while stirring constantly in a circular motion to prevent clumping, and cook until the mixture thickens slightly, about 1 minute. Off the heat, stir in the reserved bacon.

8. Measure out and reserve half (about 4 cups) of the cornmeal mixture. Smooth the cornmeal mixture left in the pot into an even layer, then top with the shredded chicken. Pour the reserved cornmeal mixture over the chicken and smooth into an even layer, covering the meat completely.

9. Cover the pot and place it inside a large roasting pan. Place the roasting pan in the oven and carefully pour enough boiling water into the pan to reach one-third of the way up the sides of the Dutch oven. Bake until the cornmeal mixture is dry to the touch and lightly browned, 1½ to 2 hours. Cool for 10 minutes.

10. FOR THE SAUCE: While the pie bakes, cook the flour in a medium dry skillet over medium heat, stirring frequently, until light golden brown, 3 to 5 minutes. Stir in the chili powder, cumin, and coriander and cook until fragrant, about 30 seconds. Stir in the reserved broth and tomato sauce, bring to a simmer, and cook until thickened, about 2 minutes. Season with salt and pepper to taste.

11. When the pie has cooled, sprinkle it with the cilantro and serve, passing the sauce separately.

HEALTHY SKILLET CHICKEN POT PIE

WITH ITS RICH SAUCE, TENDER CHUNKS OF CHICKEN, and perfectly cooked vegetables all nestled under flaky pie dough or biscuits, chicken pot pie might be the perfect comfort food. That is, of course, if you don't factor in how long it takes to make or all the fat and calories it has (an average serving tallies 720 calories and 39 grams of fat). My goal was twofold: develop an easier skillet chicken pot pie and make sure it delivered all of the comforting goodness of the original, with less than a third of the fat, calories, and cholesterol.

I focused first on the chicken. Recipes call for dark meat, white meat, or a mix. I opted to use boneless, skinless chicken breasts since they are a lower-fat option than dark meat and would cook more quickly than bone-in pieces. I tested three basic cooking methods: sautéing bite-size pieces of meat; sautéing whole breasts and shredding the meat afterward; and poaching whole breasts in broth and shredding the meat afterward. Incorporated into a basic working recipe, the sautéed chicken pieces were too dried out, and the sautéed breasts had formed a crusty outer layer tasters didn't like. However, they did like the deep flavor of the whole sautéed breasts. The poached and shredded chicken was moist and juicy and absorbed the sauce, but it lacked flavor compared to the sautéed breasts. As a compromise, I sautéed the breasts on one side, then flipped them and poached them in the sauce. This chicken had the flavor and texture I was after, and poaching the chicken right in the sauce further streamlined my recipe. With my chickens in a row, I moved on to the vegetables.

Since I was after a healthier chicken pot pie, I wanted to pack in a larger-than-average variety of vegetables. Restricted to my 12-inch skillet, I was after only those I could cook right in the sauce along with the chicken. After browning the chicken, I sautéed some of the usual suspects—carrots, celery, and onion—in the fat left in the pan, then added the sauce (a basic working recipe for now) and chicken, added a working topping, and cooked it through. Tasters liked this familiar mix, but craved some fresher, brighter flavors. The sweetness of red bell pepper was a big hit. I also wanted to incorporate some green vegetables, but broccoli, asparagus, and green beans all turned out army-green and unappealing. Instead, I opted for green vegetables that would cook quickly and could be added toward the end to preserve their color and texture. Frozen peas worked well, as did baby spinach. I could easily stir both into the sauce before adding the topping and moving the whole thing to the oven. With that, I was ready to tackle the sauce.

Chicken pot pie filling gets its gravy-like consistency from a roux, traditionally made by cooking equal parts flour and butter together (as much as 6 tablespoons). Because the flour in a roux is cooked, it has a nutty, appealing flavor, and mixing it with butter allows it to blend easily into the broth. Once stirred into the filling, the mixture thickens the broth into a rich, velvety gravy. But this much butter was out of the question here. Cornstarch, often a substitute for roux in healthy recipes, produced a gelatinous, unappealing sauce. Simply adding flour to the broth didn't work either: The flour's raw flavor stood out and the filling clumped. Toasting the flour in a dry skillet until fragrant and golden fixed the raw flavor issue. I knew from experience that making a slurry—a mixture of a starch and a cold liquid—before adding it to a hot pan would allow for thickening without clumping. So I let the flour cool to room temperature before stirring in the cool broth and adding this slurry to the pan with the vegetables. This trick worked like a charm.

For richness, most chicken pot pie fillings add a half-cup or more of heavy cream. Looking into lighter options, whole milk diluted the pie's rich chicken flavor, but a few tablespoons of half-and-half provided good richness with considerably less fat than heavy cream. Finally, I fortified the sauce with garlic, thyme, and bay leaves, as well as sherry and fresh parsley for some brightness. All that was left was topping it off.

There are basically two ways to top a chicken pot pie: with individual biscuits or a savory pie crust. While both provide great contrast to a saucy pot pie, I chose biscuits because they are generally quicker and less fussy to make. Biscuits rely on butter for both tenderness and flakiness, so I knew that while I wanted to cut back on the butter, I wouldn't eliminate it. Starting with one of our buttermilk drop-biscuit recipes (even easier than roll-out biscuits), I gradually cut the butter back from 5 tablespoons to just 3 tablespoons and still got tender, flaky biscuits. I tried baking the biscuits directly on top of the pie filling by dropping the raw dough onto the filling and finishing it in the oven. Unfortunately, this gave me soggy-bottomed biscuits. For my next test, I parbaked the biscuits for 10 minutes, during which

time I continued to prepare the filling. Then I placed my parbaked biscuits on top of my filling, moved the whole thing to the oven, and baked it until the biscuits were golden. Perfection!

—DAN SOUZA, *America's Test Kitchen Books*

Healthy Skillet Chicken Pot Pie

SERVES 6

Make sure to use a 12-inch oven-safe skillet for this recipe.

BISCUITS

- 1½ cups (7½ ounces) unbleached all-purpose flour
- 1½ teaspoons baking powder
- ½ teaspoon baking soda
- ¼ teaspoon salt
- ½ cup buttermilk (see page 103)
- 3 tablespoons unsalted butter, melted

FILLING

- 6 tablespoons unbleached all-purpose flour
- 1½ pounds boneless, skinless chicken breasts, trimmed
  Salt and pepper
- 1 tablespoon canola oil
- 1 pound carrots, peeled and cut into ¼-inch-thick rounds
- 2 red bell peppers, stemmed, seeded, and chopped coarse
- 1 onion, minced (about 1 cup)
- 1 celery rib, sliced ¼ inch thick
- 2 garlic cloves, minced
- 2 teaspoons minced fresh thyme
- 4 cups low-sodium chicken broth
- ⅓ cup dry sherry
- 2 bay leaves
- 4 ounces baby spinach (about 4 cups)
- ¾ cup frozen peas
- 3 tablespoons half-and-half
- 2 tablespoons minced fresh parsley

1. FOR THE BISCUITS: Adjust an oven rack to the lower-middle position and heat the oven to 425 degrees. Line a baking sheet with parchment paper. Whisk the flour, baking powder, baking soda, and salt together in a large bowl. In a separate bowl, whisk the buttermilk and melted butter together. Gently stir the buttermilk mixture into the flour mixture until just combined and no pockets of flour remain.

2. Divide the dough evenly into 6 pieces, shape into balls, and, following the photos, space them evenly on the prepared baking sheet. Bake until the biscuits have risen and set but are still pale, about 10 minutes. Transfer the biscuits to a wire rack.

3. FOR THE FILLING: Toast the flour in a 12-inch skillet over medium-high heat, stirring often, until fragrant and light golden, 5 to 7 minutes. Transfer the flour to a large bowl to cool. Wipe the skillet clean with paper towels.

4. Pat the chicken dry with paper towels and season with salt and pepper. Heat the oil in the skillet over medium-high heat until just smoking. Add the chicken and cook until browned on one side, 3 to 4 minutes. Transfer the chicken to a plate, leaving the fat behind in the skillet.

5. Add the carrots, bell peppers, onion, and celery to the fat left in the skillet and cook, stirring occasionally, until the vegetables are softened, 7 to 9 minutes. Stir in the garlic and thyme and cook until fragrant, about 30 seconds.

6. Whisk the broth, sherry, and bay leaves into the bowl of cooled, toasted flour until evenly combined, and then whisk the mixture into the skillet. Add the browned chicken, bring to a simmer, cover, and cook over medium-low heat until the chicken registers 160 to 165 degrees on an instant-read thermometer, 12 to 15 minutes.

7. Transfer the chicken to a plate and shred it into bite-size pieces when cool enough to handle. Meanwhile, continue to simmer the sauce over medium-high heat until the vegetables are tender and the sauce is thickened, 5 to 8 minutes.

8. Discard the bay leaves. Stir in the spinach, a handful at a time, until wilted, about 1 minute. Off the heat, stir in the shredded chicken, peas, half-and-half, and parsley. Season with salt and pepper to taste.

9. Arrange the biscuits on top of the filling in the skillet, about 1½ inches apart. Transfer the skillet to the oven and bake until the biscuits are golden and the filling is bubbling, about 10 minutes. Let cool for 5 minutes before serving. (The baked biscuits can be stored in an airtight container at room temperature for up to 1 day. The filling can be prepared through step 8 and refrigerated in an airtight container for up to 1 day. Before topping with the biscuits and baking as directed, gently reheat the filling in a covered 12-inch skillet over medium-low heat until hot, adding additional broth as needed to loosen the consistency.)

NOTES FROM THE TEST KITCHEN

MAKING SKILLET CHICKEN POT PIE

1. Parbake the biscuits before laying them on top of the filling to ensure their bottoms won't be gummy. Bake them until risen and set but not yet browned; they will continue to bake on top of the filling.

2. For a butter-free roux with a nice roasted flavor, toast the flour, then set it aside to cool.

3. Brown the chicken on just one side for deeper flavor, then remove it from the pan so that you can cook the vegetables and build the sauce in the pan, incorporating the flavorful fond left behind.

4. Make a slurry by whisking the sherry and broth with the cooled toasted flour before adding the mixture to the skillet to ensure this butter-free roux will thicken properly and without lumps.

5. After adding the browned chicken to the skillet and simmering gently to cook it through, remove the chicken and shred it into bite-size pieces.

6. Stir in the spinach, then the chicken, peas, parsley, and half-and-half. Arrange the biscuits evenly over the filling. Transfer the skillet to the oven and bake until the filling is bubbling and hot and the biscuits are golden.

EASY CHICKEN TACOS

CHICKEN SOFT TACOS ARE EVERYWHERE, FROM forgettable 99-cent offerings at mall food courts to deeply satisfying versions at Mexican restaurants. At the mall, bland, underseasoned white meat is seared, chopped, and stuffed into a factory-made taco. At the other end of the spectrum, a whole chicken is broken down and poached in seasoned liquid to moist, fall-off-the-bone, deeply flavored perfection. Unfortunately, the tastier taco takes hours to make and requires a mile-long list of hard-to-find, exotic ingredients. For a fast week-night dinner, I hoped to combine speed with quality.

I tested a variety of recipes, from Tex-Mex to Southwestern to regional Mexican, and quickly crossed those calling for 24-hour marinades and obscure ingredients off my list. Some of the quick-cooking recipes briefly marinated boneless chicken breasts in lime juice, cilantro, garlic, and spices like chili powder and cumin; cooked them over high heat; chopped the meat; and then stuffed it in a tortilla and piled on toppings. To begin my testing, I made such a marinade. The flavors needed work, but I wanted to pick the best cooking method first.

I knew the fast sear was out. In my initial testing, that method had yielded leathery, desiccated meat. In the test kitchen, we often brine chicken in salt water to keep it juicy, but this extra step (about an hour in brine) didn't fit into my time frame. I considered another test kitchen technique: reserving a few tablespoons of marinade to toss with the chicken after it was cooked and cut up, almost like a dressing. It's meant to add extra flavor, but I figured the dressing would moisten the seared chicken, too, disguising any textural flaws. Unfortunately, it didn't work out that way.

I reconsidered the elaborate Mexican recipes that slowly simmer whole chickens in flavored broths and wondered if I could borrow the technique (poaching) for chicken breasts. I simmered chicken broth in a skillet, added the breasts, and cooked them, covered, for 10 minutes. The chicken emerged tender and moist. Unfortunately, it was also insipid.

Might a more flavorful solution be as near as my marinade? I added the marinade ingredients (garlic, lime juice, fresh jalapeños, and lots of cilantro) to the poaching liquid, but on my first try, the flavors were out of balance. While bright, the chicken was aggressively

tart. I discarded the lime and reached for a carton of orange juice. While I was at it, I eliminated the chicken broth altogether and used ½ cup of the OJ instead. A touch of sweetness now tempered the vivid acidity. For smokier, more full-bodied flavor, I replaced the jalapeños with 2 teaspoons of chipotle chiles. Better, but not perfect.

But even with all these adjustments, I had to concede the white meat lacked robustness. It was time to call in the reinforcements. I was raised in Latin America, where—those from the United States may be surprised to learn—Worcestershire sauce and yellow mustard are pantry staples. In my home, these everyday items went into many basic chicken and beef marinades. I added some Worcestershire to the poaching liquid to mimic the more complex flavor of dark meat. A squirt of mustard pulled everything together, adding sharpness that balanced the sweet juice and smoky chipotle.

A pool of flavorful liquid remained in my skillet after the chicken was poached. It struck me that I could improve my taco by reducing it to make a sauce. As I was making the tacos again, this time sautéing the garlic and chipotle chiles in oil to build a base for the sauce, a colleague suggested I use butter instead of oil. "Tacos made with butter? Really?!" But she was on to something: A few pats of creamy butter added richness to the very lean breast meat.

I held back the mustard until the chicken was poached and the liquid reduced, about 15 minutes later. Whisking

---

NOTES FROM THE TEST KITCHEN

SECRETS TO MAKING EASY TACOS WITH BIG FLAVOR
We found that a handful of unexpected, yet ordinary, ingredients add just the right depth and dimension to our simple chicken tacos.

YELLOW MUSTARD, WORCESTERSHIRE, ORANGE JUICE, AND BUTTER

EASY CHICKEN TACOS

the mustard in at the end helped thicken and emulsify the sauce. Finally, I shredded the chicken (a side-by-side test showed shreds absorbed more sauce than cubed chicken) and tossed it with the sauce along with a final sprinkling of fresh cilantro. I reached for a steamy tortilla, piled it with chicken and toppings, and eagerly tucked into my easy, delicious chicken taco.

—MARÍA DEL MAR SACASA, *Cook's Country*

Easy Chicken Tacos

SERVES 6

To warm the tortillas, wrap them in foil and heat in a 350-degree oven for 15 minutes. Top the tacos with shredded lettuce, grated cheese, diced avocado, tomato, and sour cream.

- 3 **tablespoons unsalted butter**
- 4 **garlic cloves, minced**
- 2 **teaspoons minced canned chipotle chile in adobo sauce**
- ¾ **cup chopped fresh cilantro**
- ½ **cup orange juice**
- 1 **tablespoon Worcestershire sauce**
- 1½ **pounds boneless, skinless chicken breasts, trimmed**
- 1 **teaspoon yellow mustard**
  Salt and pepper
- 12 **(6-inch) flour tortillas, warmed**

1. Melt the butter in a 12-inch skillet over medium-high heat. Add the garlic and chipotles and cook until fragrant, about 30 seconds. Stir in ½ cup of the cilantro, the orange juice, and Worcestershire and bring to a boil. Add the chicken and simmer, covered, over medium-low heat until the chicken registers 160 to 165 degrees on an instant-read thermometer, 10 to 15 minutes, flipping the chicken halfway through. Transfer to a plate and tent with foil.

2. Increase the heat to medium-high and cook until the liquid is reduced to ¼ cup, about 5 minutes. Off the heat, whisk in the mustard. Shred the chicken into bite-size pieces and return it to the skillet. Add the remaining cilantro to the skillet and toss until well combined. Season with salt and pepper to taste. Serve with the tortillas.

THAI CHICKEN WITH BASIL

IN CHINA, THE SECRET TO A SUCCESSFUL STIR-FRY lies not in what goes into the wok, but what's under it: an intense coal fire or a massive high-output burner. The super-high heat rapidly cooks meats and vegetables, and imparts an intense smoky flavor. But on a recent trip to Thailand, I discovered there's more than one way to heat a wok. On nearly every street corner in Bangkok, vendors scoop hot meals out of woks set up on pushcarts. These boast only mild flames but manage to produce stir-fries every bit as complex and flavorful as those from the hottest Cantonese kitchen.

To learn how this was accomplished, I met with chef-instructor Sanusi Mareh of the Silom Thai Cooking School in Bangkok, who taught me a secret that turned the familiar stir-fries on their heads. Unlike a high-heat stir-fry, in which the aromatics are added toward the end to prevent scorching, the key to a low-temperature method is to sauté the aromatics over medium-low heat at the beginning. The flavor compounds in the aromatics infuse the oil they're cooked in, which in turn coats the protein, giving the dish deep, complex flavor. It's a method pervasive in Thai cooking.

Mareh taught me how to make one of my all-time favorite Thai street dishes: *gai pad krapow*, or chicken with hot basil. The process was simple: I finely chopped chicken with a pair of cleavers, cooked it with a big handful of hot basil in oil flavored with garlic, shallots, and Thai chiles, then finished it with fish sauce, Thai oyster sauce, and sugar. Served with steamed jasmine rice, it had a bright, clean flavor defined by the aromatic, grassy basil and a perfect balance of heat and sweetness. It was one of the best, simplest stir-fries I'd ever made.

Back in the test kitchen, making this recipe wasn't as easy. Unevenly cooked aromatics lent a bitter burnt flavor. Mincing a pound of chicken by hand is manageable with two cleavers, but a chore with a chef's knife. And the signature ingredient, hot basil, is nearly impossible to find in this country.

My first task was to develop a foolproof method for infusing the oil with aromatics. I'd already burned my first attempt: a dozen finely chopped Thai chiles, three cloves of garlic, and three finely sliced shallots cooked in 2 tablespoons of oil. Adding extra oil to the skillet (we prefer a skillet to a wok for American stoves) helped them cook more evenly, but I had to use a full ¼ cup of oil to make a difference, which made the dish greasy. Turning down the heat from medium to medium-low and starting in a completely cold skillet further increased my chances of success. I also dialed back the oil to 2 tablespoons. After six to eight minutes, my aromatics were a perfectly even shade of golden brown.

The dish I had in Thailand was almost unbearably spicy, so I decided to tone down the heat and reduced the chiles to six. Lowering the heat made the dish seem cloyingly sweet, so I also cut the amount of sugar in half, down from 2 tablespoons to 1.

Chopping chicken by hand was a nonstarter, so I tried store-bought ground chicken. Bad idea. It was ground too fine and cooked up into a mealy, mushy texture. Next I tried chopping meat in the food processor. Dark meat was more forgiving but contained fatty stringy bits, so I decided to stick with breast meat. Since I was pulling the processor out, I used it to chop the garlic and chiles, further streamlining this simple dish.

Getting a flavorful sear in a high-heat stir-fry requires cooking meat in batches, letting it sit undisturbed in a hot nonstick skillet. The difficulty is that lean white-meat chicken can go from tender to tough in the blink of an eye. A low-temperature stir-fry, thankfully, is much more foolproof. (Since the aromatic oil and sauce provide so much complexity, the lack of browning isn't an issue.) I added all of the meat to the skillet in a single batch, stirring it constantly to promote even cooking. To further guarantee moist meat, I added a tablespoon of fish sauce to the food processor as I chopped the chicken, then let the mixture rest for 15 minutes in the refrigerator. The fish sauce acted as a brine, seasoning the meat and helping it retain moisture.

I moved on to the sauce. With no access to Thai-style oyster-flavored sauce, I'd been substituting Chinese. However, its thicker consistency and heavier flavors were weighing down the dish. Simply decreasing the amount didn't work; the dish went from overloaded to lacking complexity. Then I thought about a Thai condiment that diners often add to their dish to brighten the flavor: white vinegar. Adding a mere teaspoon balanced the heaviness of the oyster-flavored sauce and brought brightness. While I was in the business of brightening flavors, I made an unconventional move, setting aside a tablespoon of my raw garlic-chile mixture to be added to the sauce at the end of cooking. The combination of fresh and cooked aromatics was an instant hit.

Only one problem remained: incorporating the flavor of basil. Unlike sweet Italian or even Thai basil, hot basil has a robust texture that can stand up to prolonged cooking, giving it plenty of time to release its distinctive aroma into the chicken. Simply substituting Italian basil didn't work: Added any time before the last minute and it became wilted and slimy. And when it only spent a short time in the skillet, it didn't offer enough flavor. I needed a way to keep the leaves bright and fresh tasting, while at the same time lending the dish a deep basil flavor.

Then it clicked: Since I was already using the oil-infusing technique to deliver garlic, chile, and shallot flavor, why not use the same method for my basil? I gave it a try, chopping a cup of basil leaves along with the chiles and garlic, then cooking them all together. The basil released its flavor into the dish, and the small pieces did not suffer from sliminess. To add fresh texture and bright green color, I stirred in an additional cup of whole basil leaves right before serving. I now had a dish infused with a deep basil flavor that could transport me back to Bangkok with about 20 minutes of work.

—J. KENJI LOPEZ-ALT, *Cook's Illustrated*

Thai Chicken with Basil
SERVES 4

Since tolerance for spiciness can vary, we've kept our recipe relatively mild. For a very mild version, remove the seeds and ribs from the chiles. If fresh Thai chiles are unavailable, substitute 2 serranos or 1 medium jalapeño. In Thailand, red pepper flakes and sugar are passed at the table, along with extra fish sauce and white vinegar. Serve with steamed rice and vegetables, if desired. You do not need to wash the food processor bowl after step 1.

- 2 **cups fresh basil leaves, tightly packed**
- 3 **garlic cloves, peeled**
- 6 **green or red Thai chiles, stemmed**
- 2 **tablespoons fish sauce, plus extra for serving**
- 1 **tablespoon oyster-flavored sauce**
- 1 **tablespoon sugar, plus extra for serving**
- 1 **teaspoon white vinegar, plus extra for serving**
- 1 **pound boneless, skinless chicken breasts, trimmed and cut into 2-inch pieces**
- 3 **shallots, peeled and thinly sliced (about ¾ cup)**
- 2 **tablespoons vegetable oil**
  Red pepper flakes, for serving

1. Pulse 1 cup of the basil leaves, the garlic, and chiles in a food processor until chopped fine, 6 to 10 pulses, scraping down the sides of the bowl once during processing. Transfer 1 tablespoon of the basil mixture to a small bowl, stir in 1 tablespoon of the fish sauce, the oyster-flavored sauce, sugar, and vinegar, and set aside. Transfer the remaining basil mixture to a 12-inch heavy-bottomed nonstick skillet.

2. Pulse the chicken and the remaining 1 tablespoon fish sauce in the food processor until the meat is chopped into ¼-inch pieces, 6 to 8 pulses. Transfer the chicken to a medium bowl and refrigerate for 15 minutes.

3. Stir the shallots and oil into the basil mixture in the skillet. Heat the mixture over medium-low heat (the mixture should start to sizzle after about 1½ minutes; if it doesn't, adjust the heat accordingly), stirring constantly, until the garlic and shallots are golden brown, 5 to 8 minutes.

4. Add the chicken, increase the heat to medium, and cook, stirring and breaking up the chicken with a potato masher or rubber spatula, until only traces of pink remain, 2 to 4 minutes. Add the reserved basil–fish sauce mixture and continue to cook, stirring constantly, until the chicken is no longer pink, about 1 minute. Stir in the remaining 1 cup basil leaves and cook, stirring constantly, until the basil is wilted, 30 to 60 seconds. Serve immediately, passing the extra fish sauce, sugar, vinegar, and red pepper flakes separately.

GRILL-ROASTED TURKEY BREAST

FOR THANKSGIVING, I NORMALLY GRILL-ROAST A whole bird, but in the summer months, grilling a mild-mannered turkey breast over a smoky fire can be just the ticket. The problem is that ultra-lean turkey breast easily dries out. Plus there's the matter of its irregular shape (thick on one end and tapered on the other) that can lead to uneven cooking. I was determined to get around these issues and deliver a grill-roasted breast with all the richness and juiciness I associate with the thighs and legs, along with crisp, well-rendered skin.

Grill-roasting involves cooking over indirect heat at a fairly constant temperature, mimicking the environment of an oven. Because the fiery heat can quickly turn low-fat meat such as turkey breast chalky and dry, the test kitchen often turns to either salting or brining to keep the meat moist throughout cooking. Since the latter could interfere with my goal of crisp skin, I opted for salting. When meat is salted, its juice is initially drawn out of the flesh and beads of liquid pool on its surface. Eventually, the salty liquid slowly migrates back into the meat, keeping it moist as it cooks. Salting a whole bone-in skin-on turkey breast took about an hour and was a good first step in improving flavor and texture.

Grill-roasting typically requires a grill setup that the test kitchen refers to as a modified two-level fire, in which all the coals are pushed to one side of the grill to create two temperature zones. I placed the salted breast on the hotter side of the grill first to crisp the skin, then moved it to the cooler side to cook through. My colleagues agreed that while I had made some progress, there were still spots dry as a bone.

Breast meat starts to dry out when it reaches temperatures above 165 degrees, so I'd have to keep as much meat as possible below this point. The test kitchen had recently demonstrated that low heat helps meat cook evenly. We roasted turkey breasts in 400- and 275-degree ovens and then recorded their temperature readings taken at ¼-inch intervals from the centers to the exteriors. In the turkey cooked in a 400-degree oven, over 50 percent of the breast registered higher than 165 degrees (with the very surface reaching over 200 degrees). In the turkey cooked in a 275-degree oven, 80 percent of the breast remained under 165 degrees, with the surface temperature only reaching 176 degrees.

These findings shaped my next test. I started a turkey breast slowly on the grill's cooler side until its internal temperature reached 150 degrees. The meat was moist, and though its skin was not yet crisp, most of its fat had rendered. A quick sear on the hotter side of the grill took care of the skin, and after resting, the breast had reached the ideal serving temperature of 165 degrees.

The skin was crackling crisp and most of the flesh was moist and juicy. I was about to call it a day until one taster pointed out that the tapered ends were overcooked and dry. Repositioning the tapered ends away from the hot side of the grill helped, but not enough.

Inspiration struck when I started thinking about the myriad ways I've prepared chicken breasts in restaurants. One of the fancier approaches is a roulade. The method involves stuffing a butterflied boneless breast with a filling, then rolling it into a tight cylinder. The roulade is first browned, then braised or baked. It makes an elegant presentation, and its uniform width leads to even cooking. Could I modify this technique for a turkey breast?

I bought a boneless, skinless turkey breast, butterflied it, salted it, rolled it into a cylinder, and grilled it with my low/high heat method. The meat was evenly cooked, but without its protective skin, the exterior developed a leathery crust. Returning to a whole bone-in, skin-on breast, I removed the breasts from the bone and sprinkled them with salt. Next, I arranged the breasts so the thick end of one was pressed against the tapered end of the other, creating even thickness throughout. I tied the meat and skin with butcher's twine and grill-roasted the meat with my dual-temperature method.

NOTES FROM THE TEST KITCHEN

BONING A TURKEY BREAST

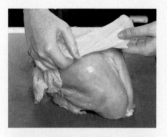

1. Starting at one side of the turkey breast and using your fingers to separate the skin from the meat, peel the skin off the meat and reserve.

2. Using the tip of a knife, cut along the rib cage to remove each breast half completely. Sprinkle each breast with 2 teaspoons kosher salt (or 1 teaspoon table salt).

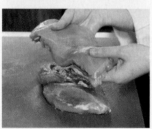

3. Arrange one breast, cut side up. Top it with the second breast, cut side down, placing its thick end over the other breast's tapered end. Drape the skin over the breasts and tuck the ends under.

4. Tie a 3-foot piece of butcher's twine lengthwise around the roast. Then, tie five to seven pieces of twine at 1-inch intervals crosswise along the roast, starting at its center, then at either end, and then filling in the rest.

THE BEST BONING KNIFE: NO BONES ABOUT IT

We love our sturdy chef's knife for tasks like chopping onions, hacking up chicken bones, or pushing through butternut squash. But when it comes to the intricate work of trimming silver skin from tenderloins or removing the breast from a whole bird, a boning knife is best. A good boning knife is at least 6 inches long, very sharp, and agile, letting you maneuver nimbly around joints and bones. Despite the appearance lately of newer models with innovative blades promising greater flexibility or smoother cutting, after testing we found our old winner, the **Victorinox (formerly Victorinox-Forschner) Fibrox 6-Inch Straight Boning Knife**, $15.95, still reigned supreme—and at a fraction of the cost of the other contenders. The nonslip grip and narrow, straight blade of this knife let testers remove the smallest bones with precision and comfort.

CHEAP DIGITAL THERMOMETERS

Everybody in the test kitchen fights over the ThermoWorks Splash-Proof Super-Fast Thermapen, but its near-three-digit price tag ($96) demands a cheaper alternative. However, our Best Buy by default, the Maverick Redi-Chek Professional Chef's Digital Thermometer ($13), isn't up to speed with its 47-second read time. (Higher-rated models were discontinued.) To find a replacement, we ran core tests on six new $35-and-under models—temping ice water, boiling water, and pan-seared chicken breasts—to assess their accuracy, response time, and design. When the last readout flashed on the screen, we had a tie between the **ThermoWorks Super-Fast Waterproof Pocket Thermometer** (left), $24, and the **CDN ProAccurate Quick-Read Thermometer** (right), $16.95. Neither winner bests the speed or wide temperature range of the Thermapen, but they are just as accurate—and far more wallet-friendly. (Plus, their response times leave the Redi-Chek in the dust.)

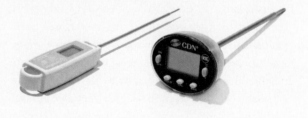

I was definitely on to something. The only setback was that the skin did not cover the meat well, creating a few desiccated patches where the flesh was exposed during grilling. To solve this, I pulled the skin off the breasts before removing the bone. After arranging the breasts thick end to thin end, I strategically draped the large piece of skin around the meat, leaving no areas uncovered save for a narrow seam on the underside. I secured the package with twine, coated the skin lightly with vegetable oil, and proceeded. The roast held its shape beautifully, and when I brought the turkey inside to my colleagues, they finally praised it as moist, evenly cooked, and crisp all around.

With my basic recipe established, I played around with flavorings. Sprinkling wood chips over the hot coals while the turkey roasted lent a touch of smokiness to the mild meat. I also came up with a fresh herb butter to slather onto the breasts before tying. While it may not be the most conventional-looking turkey that's ever come off my grill, it was certainly the best—and my satisfied tasters agreed.

—FRANCISCO J. ROBERT, *Cook's Illustrated*

Grill-Roasted Boneless Turkey Breast

SERVES 6 TO 8

We prefer either a natural (unbrined) or kosher turkey breast for this recipe. Using a kosher turkey breast (rubbed with salt and rinsed during processing) or self-basting turkey breast (injected with salt and water) eliminates the need for salting in step 2. If the breast has a pop-up timer, remove it before cooking.

 1 **whole bone-in, skin-on turkey breast (5 to 7 pounds) (see note)**
 4 **teaspoons kosher salt or 2 teaspoons table salt**
 ½ **cup wood chips, soaked in water for at least 30 minutes (optional)**
 1 **teaspoon vegetable oil**
    Pepper

1. Following the photos on page 194, remove the skin from the breast meat and then remove the breasts from the bone structure (discard the bones or save for stock).

2. Sprinkle the entire surface of each breast with 2 teaspoons kosher salt (or 1 teaspoon table salt). Assemble and tie the turkey breasts following the photos on page 194, then place the roast on a wire rack set inside a rimmed baking sheet and refrigerate, uncovered, for 1 hour.

3A. FOR A CHARCOAL GRILL: Open the bottom grill vents halfway. Light a large chimney starter filled with charcoal briquettes (100 briquettes; 6 quarts). When the coals are hot, pour all the coals over half of the grill, leaving the other half empty. Sprinkle the soaked wood chips (if using) over the coals. Set the cooking grate in place, cover, and open the lid vents halfway. Heat the grill until hot, about 5 minutes.

3B. FOR A GAS GRILL: Place the wood chips (if using) in a shallow aluminum pie plate and place the plate on the primary burner (the burner that will remain on during cooking) and reposition the cooking grate(s). Turn all the burners to high, cover, and heat the grill until hot, about 15 minutes. Leave the primary burner on high and turn off the other burner(s). (Adjust the burner(s) as needed to maintain a medium-hot fire; see page 19).

4. Rub the surface of the roast with the oil and season with pepper to taste. Clean and oil the cooking grate. Place the roast on the grate over the cooler side of the grill. Cover the grill and grill-roast until the meat registers 150 degrees on an instant-read thermometer, 40 to 60 minutes, turning the roast 180 degrees halfway through.

5. Slide the roast to the hot side of the grill and cook (covered if using gas) until the roast is browned and the skin is crisp on all sides, 2 to 2½ minutes per side (8 to 10 minutes total). Transfer the roast to a carving board and let rest for 20 minutes. Cut the roast into ½-inch-thick slices, removing the twine as you cut. Serve immediately.

VARIATION

Grill-Roasted Boneless Turkey Breast with Herb Butter

Place ¼ cup tarragon leaves, 1 tablespoon thyme leaves, 2 minced garlic cloves, and ¼ teaspoon pepper on a cutting board; mince to a fine paste. Combine the herb paste and 4 tablespoons softened unsalted butter in a medium bowl. Follow the recipe for Grill-Roasted Boneless Turkey Breast through step 1. After salting each breast, place cut side up on the counter. Lift the tenderloin away from each breast, leaving it partially attached, and spread the butter evenly over the cut side of each breast. Replace the tenderloin and proceed with the recipe as directed.

SEAFOOD

PAN-ROASTED FISH FILLETS

PAN-ROASTED FILLETS OF THICK-CUT HALIBUT, COD, and other white fish have become fixtures on restaurant menus nearly everywhere. When well executed, the cooking method yields moist, white slabs of tender, flavorful fish with a chestnut-brown crust—nothing like the stringy, overbaked fillets most of us serve at home.

Hoping to replicate the success of this method, home cooks—and those who write recipes for them—in the past have latched on to pan-roasting, but the results have been mixed. Here's the problem: To yield truly outstanding results, recipes for pan-roasted fish require keen attention and a practiced hand—that is, the skill of an experienced restaurant chef, not the busy home cook confronting an unfamiliar recipe. My goal was a foolproof, point-and-shoot recipe for succulent, well-browned, thick-cut fish fillets.

From an initial round of testing, I knew I needed fillets no less than 1 inch thick, and preferably thicker; skinnier fillets end up overcooked by the time they've achieved a serious sear. I wanted my recipe to work with popular white fish like halibut, cod, sea bass, and red snapper. Since skin-on fillets are not always available, I started my testing with skinless fillets. I carefully patted them dry to minimize sticking, then seasoned them with kosher salt (easier to distribute evenly than fine-grained table salt) and pepper. To cook four fillets at a time with ample room for flipping, a 12-inch skillet was a must, and a few quick tests confirmed a nonstick pan was also critical.

I started with a technique we've successfully used with skin-on salmon fillets: oven-searing. I placed the fish in a preheated skillet in a hot oven. The approach works great with a high-fat fish like salmon; if left on, the fatty skin forms a protective barrier between the meat and the hot pan. For delicate, skinless white fish fillets, however, this technique was a bust.

I moved on to a technique I'd witnessed in various restaurant kitchens: Sear the fish on one side in a blazing-hot skillet, flip it, then add a big pat of butter to the pan and repeatedly baste the fish as it cooks. A few burned fingers later, I realized that spooning hot butter in a sizzling skillet for any longer than a minute or two is impractical at home, so I switched to a safer method: Sear in a hot pan, flip, then transfer to a hot oven to cook the fish through.

How hot, exactly, should the pan be? I seared fish at every temperature beyond a cold start, documenting texture, appearance, and flavor. No matter what I did, the results were problematic. If I added the fish to the pan just as a sheen of oil started to smoke, I could produce an attractive and flavorful sear in about three minutes, but I also got a tough, dried-out interior. On the other hand, starting in a cooler pan or cooking for less time left the fish tender but failed to develop the crust. For now, a compromise would have to work. I scaled back the sear to a light golden brown—about 1½ minutes. It didn't look or taste nearly as good as the darker sear, but I could live with it.

As for the oven, 425 degrees was the way to go. Any hotter and the fish dried out before it cooked through, and lower temperatures did nothing for texture or flavor. In a 425-degree oven, it took 7 to 10 minutes for the fillets to be just opaque. I found it best to err on the side of undercooking (just a touch translucent at the center) to preserve as much moisture as possible.

Despite testing my way through twenty-odd pounds of various fillets, I felt as though I hadn't accomplished much. Sure, the fish was tender, tasted good, and proved technically easy to prepare, but it didn't have the flavor—much less the visual appeal—of a proper restaurant sear. Temporarily putting my working recipe on hold, I focused on another experimental method. In an old recipe for seared pork chops, rather than trying—and failing—to get a good sear on both sides of the chop without drying out the meat, we'd discovered that it was better to give just one side a perfect sear, producing enough flavorful compounds to compensate for the pale second side and ensuring juicy, tender meat. Unfortunately, fish and pork are not the same. Even with just one side seared to a beautiful, crusty brown, the delicate flesh of my fish still overcooked.

To get flavor, I needed plenty of browning, but for texture, I couldn't let the fish get too hot. Part of the solution might be to increase the rate of browning. But what if I also insulated the fish at the same time, to protect it against drying out? Many recipes call for dusting the fillets with flour before searing. It sounded promising, since the proteins and sugars in the flour would contribute to browning. At first it seemed to work. The coated fish developed a flavorful crust much faster than uncoated fish, and in fact, these were the best fillets yet, but the flour lent a pasty texture to the crust. I ran into the same problem no matter what starch I tried: flour (all-purpose, pastry, and Wondra), cornmeal, cornstarch, potato starch, potato flour, rice flour, semolina, and even Cream of Wheat.

Thinking back to that pork chop recipe in which we seared only one side, I remembered an odd ingredient choice: sugar sprinkled over the chop before searing. The idea is that the sugar commingles with exuded juices from the chop, accelerating browning and giving the meat a rich color and deep flavor that's anything but sweet. Could I use the same approach for my fish? I dusted a few fillets with a touch of granulated sugar (about ⅛ teaspoon) and placed them

NOTES FROM THE TEST KITCHEN

A SPOONFUL OF SUGAR

Fish begins to dry out when its internal temperature reaches 120 to 135 degrees, far below the 300 degrees it takes for a good sear. Here's how we got the fish to brown at a lower temperature: When sugar is added to the fish's surface and is exposed to the pan's heat, it quickly breaks down to glucose and fructose. Fructose rapidly caramelizes at around 200 degrees—a temperature the exterior of the fish easily reaches soon after hitting the pan. A little sugar sprinkled on a fillet will lead to faster browning, helping a good crust to form quickly.

WITH SUGAR   SUGAR-FREE

REMOVING SKIN FROM FISH FILLETS

If you happen to buy skin-on fillets, some quick knife work can remove it.

1. With a sharp knife, separate a corner of the skin from the fish.

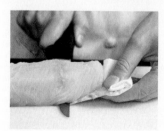

2. Using a paper towel to hold the skin, slide the knife between the fish and the skin to separate them.

SECRETS TO MOIST, WELL-BROWNED FISH

1. Buy fillets at least 1 inch thick that won't cook through too quickly.

2. Sprinkle one side of each seasoned fillet with sugar to expedite browning.

3. Sear just on the sugared side to add flavor and help ensure a moist interior.

4. Roast the seared fish briefly in a hot (425-degree) oven to cook it through without drying it out.

in a hot skillet. I knew I was on the right track when just a minute later, a well-browned crust had already formed. There's no way my fish had time to dry out in that period. Tasting it after it came out of the oven less than 10 minutes later confirmed my observation: well-browned, flavorful fish that was, most important, tender. Best of all, not one taster noticed any sweetness; they just remarked on how good the fish looked and tasted, especially with a squeeze of lemon or a piquant relish. Let restaurant chefs have their recipes—this method for pan-roasted fish is a trick you really can try at home.

—MATTHEW CARD, *Cook's Illustrated*

Pan-Roasted Thick-Cut Fish Fillets

SERVES 4

Thick white fish fillets with a meaty texture, like halibut, cod, sea bass, or red snapper, work best in this recipe. Because most fish fillets differ in thickness, some pieces may finish cooking before others—be sure to immediately remove any fillet that reaches 135 degrees. You will need an oven-safe nonstick skillet for this recipe.

- 4 (6 to 8-ounce) skinless white fish fillets, 1 to 1½ inches thick
  Kosher salt and pepper
- ½ teaspoon sugar
- 1 tablespoon vegetable oil
  Lemon wedges or relish (recipes follow), for serving

Adjust an oven rack to the middle position and heat the oven to 425 degrees. Dry the fish thoroughly with paper towels and season with salt and pepper. Sprinkle ⅛ teaspoon sugar evenly over 1 side of each fillet. Heat the oil in a 12-inch oven-safe nonstick skillet over high heat until smoking. Place the fillets in the skillet, sugared sides down, and press down lightly to ensure even contact with the pan. Cook until browned, 1 to 1½ minutes. Using 2 spatulas, flip the fillets and transfer the skillet to the oven. Roast the fillets until the centers are just opaque and the fish registers 135 degrees on an instant-read thermometer, 7 to 10 minutes. Immediately transfer the fish to individual plates and serve with lemon wedges or relish.

Green Olive, Almond, and Orange Relish

MAKES ABOUT 1½ CUPS

If your olives are marinated, rinse and drain them before chopping.

- ½ cup slivered almonds, toasted
- ½ cup green olives, chopped coarse
- 1 small garlic clove, minced
- 1 teaspoon grated orange zest plus ¼ cup fresh orange juice
- ¼ cup extra-virgin olive oil
- ¼ cup minced fresh mint
- 2 teaspoons white wine vinegar
  Salt
  Cayenne pepper

Pulse the almonds, olives, garlic, and orange zest in a food processor until the nuts and olives are finely chopped, 10 to 12 pulses. Transfer the relish to a bowl and stir in the orange juice, olive oil, mint, and vinegar. Season with salt and cayenne to taste. Spoon over the fish and serve immediately.

Roasted Red Pepper, Hazelnut, and Thyme Relish

MAKES ABOUT 1½ CUPS

- ½ cup hazelnuts, toasted and skinned
- ½ cup jarred roasted red peppers, drained, patted dry, and chopped coarse
- 1 small garlic clove, minced
- ½ teaspoon grated lemon zest plus 4 teaspoons fresh lemon juice
- ¼ cup extra-virgin olive oil
- 2 tablespoons chopped fresh parsley
- 1 teaspoon chopped fresh thyme
- ¼ teaspoon smoked paprika
  Salt and pepper

Pulse the hazelnuts, roasted peppers, garlic, and lemon zest in a food processor until finely chopped, 10 to 12 pulses. Transfer the relish to a bowl and stir in the lemon juice, olive oil, parsley, thyme, and paprika. Season with salt and pepper to taste. Spoon over the fish and serve immediately.

GRILLED TUNA STEAKS

GRILLED TUNA IS AN EXERCISE IN CONTRASTS: AN intense smoky char wrapped around a cool, delicately flavored, tender, and moist center that pairs with nearly any flavoring. Grilling tuna just right might be old hat for a seasoned chef, but as a once-a-year treat in the backyard, my tuna wasn't quite on a par with the pros'. A few days of testing turned out steak after steak with either a rare center and no char, or a great sear enveloping a dry, mealy interior. And in every case, a strong fishy odor dominated what I'd always regarded as a very mild fish.

Tuna is extremely lean, making it especially prone to drying out. An overcooked steak or salmon fillet, while not ideal, has enough interior fat to keep it relatively moist; overcook your tuna and the best you've got is a nice treat for the family cat. It simply must be served rare or medium-rare, which is where the grill method becomes tricky. How do you char the outside of a tuna steak while leaving the interior untouched?

I began by selecting fresh 1-inch-thick tuna steaks—any thinner, and I'd never be able to keep them on the grill long enough to achieve a decent crust without overcooking their insides. I followed our standard method to keep fish from sticking: I covered the grill with aluminum foil while it preheated over a modified two-level fire for dual-zone cooking, allowing me to easily brush away any built-up debris. I then applied several layers of oil with paper towels to build up a nonstick surface before adding the steaks. The fish gave a promising sizzle when it hit the superheated grate, but the finished product was far from ideal: The exteriors were dry and stringy with a fishy aroma, and though it bore distinct grill marks, most of the fish emerged unappetizingly gray with a pallid flavor to match.

Dried herbs and spices brown much faster than meat, so I reasoned that giving my tuna a good coating of them before cooking should yield more of the charred flavor I was after. It certainly worked, but the intense flavors of the coating overwhelmed the subtle tuna. I decided to step away from spices and herbs and move on to another ingredient that can enhance browning: oil.

Oil doesn't brown on its own, but it does perform two important functions: First, it helps to distribute heat evenly over the surface of the fish; ideally, this would

take some of the heat from the grill grate and transfer it to those areas of the fish not actually touching the grate. Second, it adds a little fat to the lean fish, which keeps the exterior from tasting too dry and stringy. But when I pulled my olive oil–rubbed steaks off the fire, the tuna (though slightly moister) still lacked grill flavor and had a surprisingly fishy odor.

With some research I discovered that in order to moisten the tuna's flesh, oil needs to be able to penetrate and coat the muscle fibers on a microscopic level. But tuna is full of water, and as we all know, oil and water don't mix. To get the oil to coat the muscle fibers, I needed it to be in a state where it wouldn't repel water. I immediately thought of a vinaigrette. In a thoroughly emulsified salad dressing, the oil is dispersed in tiny droplets in the vinegar (often with the aid of an emulsifying agent such as egg yolk, mustard, or mayonnaise), where it would be unaffected by water from the fish. As long as the flavor of the vinaigrette did not overpower the taste of the tuna itself, coating the fish in such an emulsion might be just the ticket.

For my next test, I prepared a simple dressing of olive oil, red wine vinegar, and Dijon mustard, which I brushed onto the fish before grilling it. The effect was immediate. The dressing (and its oil) clung to the fish, moistening its outer layer and solving the problem of dry, stringy flesh.

To my surprise, the vinaigrette had two other effects: It reduced fishy odor and boosted grill flavor. Our science editor explained the reason for less fishiness: The acid in the vinaigrette helps neutralize an odoriferous compound in fish called trimethylamine, created when the flesh is exposed to heat. As for the boost in smokiness, I did some more investigating and found that much of smoke flavor comes from small, oil-soluble particles coming off the burning coals. Normally, in lean foods like tuna, these compounds quickly dissipate before they can dissolve in the small amount of available fat, taking grill flavor with them. But by coating the tuna in an oily emulsion, it had more fat for the flavorful compounds to dissolve in than plain tuna, yielding smokier-tasting fish. Now only one hurdle remained: improving browning.

In the test kitchen we often add sugar to brines and marinades for pork chops or poultry to enhance browning—would the same work for fish on the hot grill? I whisked 2 teaspoons of sugar into a batch of vinaigrette and grilled up the fish. The sugar helped achieve the browning I wanted, but only after eight minutes on the hot grill, by which time the delicate fish was overdone. I knew that before table sugar—sucrose—can brown, it has to first break down into the simpler sugars fructose and glucose. Larger cuts of meat that take a while to cook can accommodate that timeline, but tuna is on the grill for less than five minutes. Since honey is made primarily of simple sugars, it is already primed for browning. Maybe it would be the answer for quick-cooking tuna, since it should deliver the same degree of browning faster.

Indeed, the honey's effect on browning was dramatic, and its sweetness was barely noticeable in the vinaigrette. The fish came off the grill with everything I'd hoped for: attractive grill marks, a nicely charred, pleasantly smoky crust, and a rosy, melt-in-your-mouth center. Another bonus: By making a little extra vinaigrette, I had a ready-to-go sauce built right into the recipe.

—ANDREW JANJIGIAN, *Cook's Illustrated*

Grilled Tuna Steaks with Red Wine Vinegar and Mustard Vinaigrette

SERVES 6

We prefer our tuna served rare or medium-rare. If you like your fish cooked medium, observe the timing for medium-rare, then tent the steaks loosely with foil for 5 minutes before serving. To achieve a nicely grilled exterior and a rare center, it is important to use fish steaks that are at least 1 inch thick.

- 3 tablespoons plus 1 teaspoon red wine vinegar
  Salt
- 2 tablespoons Dijon mustard
- 2 tablespoons chopped fresh thyme or rosemary
- 2 teaspoons honey
- ¾ cup olive oil
- 6 (8-ounce) tuna steaks, 1 inch thick
  Pepper

1. Whisk the vinegar, ½ teaspoon salt, mustard, thyme, and honey together in a large bowl. While whisking constantly, slowly drizzle the oil into the vinegar mixture until lightly thickened and emulsified. Measure out ¾ cup of the vinaigrette and set aside for cooking the fish. Reserve the remaining vinaigrette for serving.

GRILLED TUNA STEAKS WITH RED WINE VINEGAR AND MUSTARD VINAIGRETTE

2A. FOR A CHARCOAL GRILL: Open the bottom grill vents completely. Light a large chimney starter filled with charcoal briquettes (100 briquettes; 6 quarts). When the coals are hot, pour all the coals in an even layer over half of the grill, leaving the other half empty. Set the cooking grate in place and loosely cover the grate with a large piece of heavy-duty foil. Cover the grill and heat until hot, about 5 minutes.

2B. FOR A GAS GRILL: Turn all the burners to high and loosely cover the grate with a large piece of heavy-duty foil. Cover the grill and heat the grill until hot, about 15 minutes. Leave the primary burner on high and turn off the other burner(s). (Adjust the burner as needed to maintain a hot fire; see page 19.)

3. Remove the foil with tongs and discard. Clean and oil the cooking grate, oiling 5 to 10 times until the grate is black and glossy.

4. Brush both sides of the tuna steaks liberally with the vinaigrette reserved for cooking and season with salt and pepper to taste. Grill the fish (covered if using gas) without moving until grill marks form and the bottom surface of the fish is opaque, about 1½ minutes. Carefully flip and continue cooking until grill marks form on the second side, about 1½ minutes longer for rare (opaque at the perimeter and translucent red at the center when checked with the tip of a paring knife) or 3 minutes for medium-rare (opaque at the perimeter and reddish pink at the center). Transfer to a platter and serve immediately, passing the reserved vinaigrette.

VARIATIONS

Grilled Tuna Steaks with Provençal Vinaigrette
Follow the recipe for Grilled Tuna Steaks with Red Wine Vinegar and Mustard Vinaigrette, substituting 2 tablespoons minced fresh parsley for the thyme and adding ¼ cup chopped pitted oil-cured black olives, 1 tablespoon minced fresh oregano, 2 minced anchovies, and 1 minced garlic clove to the vinaigrette in step 1.

Grilled Tuna Steaks with Chermoula Vinaigrette
Follow the recipe for Grilled Tuna Steaks with Red Wine Vinegar and Mustard Vinaigrette, substituting 2 tablespoons minced fresh parsley for the thyme and adding ¼ cup minced fresh cilantro, 4 minced garlic cloves, 1 teaspoon sweet paprika, 1 teaspoon ground cumin, and ½ teaspoon ground coriander to the vinaigrette in step 1.

Grilled Tuna Steaks with Soy-Ginger Vinaigrette
Follow the recipe for Grilled Tuna Steaks with Red Wine Vinegar and Mustard Vinaigrette, substituting 3 tablespoons plus 1 teaspoon rice wine vinegar for the red wine vinegar and omitting the salt and thyme. Add 2 thinly sliced scallions, 3 tablespoons soy sauce, 1 tablespoon toasted sesame oil, 2 teaspoons minced fresh ginger, and ½ teaspoon red pepper flakes to the vinaigrette in step 1.

LAZY MAN'S LOBSTER FOR TWO

LOBSTER IS A CLASSIC CHOICE FOR AN ELEGANT dinner for two. Most people boil or steam their crustaceans and serve them whole with a side of drawn butter. While there's nothing wrong with this simple, traditional approach, fumbling around with a cooked lobster, hammering down on shells, and poking around for meat isn't exactly a tidy affair. I wanted a refined lobster dinner for a couple that delivered the sweet, rich flavor of lobster and didn't require a bib to eat. Searching for ideas, I came across a dish known as "lazy man's lobster," a New England favorite featuring lobster meat in a rich cream sauce baked under a bread-crumb topping. Basically, it's a lobster gratin similar to the classic lobster Newburg but without the egg-enriched sauce. It seemed like a winner on paper, streamlined and simple yet elegant and indulgent, but most recipes I tried were lacking in flavor (lobster or otherwise) and too rich from an overload of cream. I set out to create my own version of lazy man's lobster, one that was full of flavor and not too heavy—and perfect for just two.

I first considered ways to incorporate the lobster. A few recipes make lobster stock, which is then added to cream and reduced. While this method certainly promised deeper lobster flavor, making my own stock was a project beyond what I was willing to do, even for a special dinner. Some recipes removed the lobster meat from the shell and sautéed it. Removing the meat cooked is hard enough; doing it when raw makes it that much harder, so that method was out. In other recipes, precooked lobster meat was added to reduced cream that had been flavored with aromatics. I opted for this streamlined approach.

Early tests helped me determine that 12 ounces of cooked lobster meat was just right for two people. Any less and the lobster faded to the background, any more upset the balance between the lobster, the sauce, and the crumb topping. Steaming my own lobsters was my preferred route. However, I found that purchasing precooked lobster meat (which, depending on where you live can be found at a good fish market or even a local supermarket) worked as a good second choice.

With the lobster settled, I moved on to the details of the cream sauce. I began by cobbling together a straightforward but flavorful sauce using ½ cup heavy cream, a shallot, some thyme, and a bit of flour before stirring in the precooked lobster meat. For a stronger herbal presence, I added minced tarragon, a classic pairing with shellfish. Tasters complained the sauce was too heavy, so I stirred in ¼ cup sherry, another traditional match that helped to cut the richness of the cream and played off the sweetness of the lobster meat well. But it wasn't quite enough; tasters still thought the sauce was somewhat leaden. But cutting the heavy cream down to ¼ cup created a sauce that wasn't rich enough for an elegant dish such as this. In the end, I compromised, settling on ⅓ cup. Tasters also thought the sauce could use some zing; a pinch of cayenne added a little heat that contrasted nicely with the sauce's creaminess.

Using individual gratins seemed like the best route for this recipe, for both easy portioning and elegant oven-to-table presentation (though an 8-inch square baking dish also works). After preparing the cream sauce and stirring in the cooked lobster, I divided the mixture between two 2-cup gratin dishes. All I needed to do was finalize the topping. Bread crumbs made from high-quality sandwich bread offered the best texture and achieved nice browning after a short stint in the oven. I tried other test kitchen crumb topping favorites, but none worked as well: Saltines were too bland, Ritz too rich, and panko too crunchy. To boost the flavor of the bread crumbs, I added a touch of grated Parmesan cheese, a little oil, more minced tarragon, and paprika. With the filling already cooked on the stovetop, the gratins needed only 15 minutes in a 400-degree oven to just heat through and become bubbling hot with a golden crown. This is an elegant dinner that's sure to impress, and happily, no mallet, pliers, or bib are required.

—DAN ZUCCARELLO, *America's Test Kitchen Books*

NOTES FROM THE TEST KITCHEN

HOW TO COOK LOBSTER

We found the best way to cook a lobster is steaming. For our Lazy Man's Lobster for Two, you will need 12 ounces of cooked meat (see the chart below for meat yields). Fit a large Dutch oven with a steamer basket and add water to the pot until it just touches the basket's bottom. Bring the water to a boil over high heat, then add the lobsters to the steamer basket. Following the times in the chart, cover and steam the lobsters until they are bright red and fully cooked. Be sure to check the pot periodically to make sure the water has not boiled dry; add more water as needed. Remove the lobsters from the steamer basket and let them cool slightly before shelling. (Cooked lobster meat can be refrigerated in an airtight container for up to two days.)

LOBSTER	STEAMING TIME	MEAT YIELD
Soft-Shell		
1¼ lbs	11 to 12 minutes	3½ to 4 oz
1½ lbs	13 to 14 minutes	5½ to 6 oz
Hard-Shell		
1¼ lbs	13 to 14 minutes	5½ to 6 oz
1½ lbs	15 to 16 minutes	7½ to 8 oz

SHELLING A LOBSTER

1. After the lobster is cooked and slightly cooled, remove the tail and claw appendages by twisting them off the body over a large bowl to prevent a mess. Discard the lobster body.

2. Use scissors to cut the tail shell open and pull the meat out with a fork.

3. Twist the claw from the connecting joint. Use lobster crackers or a mallet to break open the connecting joint and claw, and remove the meat from both with a cocktail fork if necessary.

Lazy Man's Lobster for Two

SERVES 2

You can either buy cooked lobster meat or you can cook 2 (1¼ to 1½-pound) lobsters and shell the meat yourself (see page 205). You will need two shallow 2-cup gratin dishes (measuring approximately 9 by 6 inches), or you can substitute one 8-inch square baking dish.

FILLING

- 1 tablespoon vegetable oil
- 1 shallot, minced
- 1 teaspoon minced fresh thyme
- Pinch cayenne pepper
- 4 teaspoons unbleached all-purpose flour
- ¼ cup dry sherry
- 1 cup low-sodium chicken broth
- ⅓ cup heavy cream
- 12 ounces cooked lobster meat (see note), chopped coarse
- 1 tablespoon minced fresh tarragon
- Salt and pepper

TOPPING

- 1 slice high-quality white sandwich bread, torn into pieces
- 2 tablespoons grated Parmesan cheese
- 1 tablespoon minced fresh tarragon
- 1 teaspoon vegetable oil
- ⅛ teaspoon sweet paprika

1. FOR THE FILLING: Heat the oil in a 10-inch skillet over medium heat until shimmering. Add the shallot, thyme, and cayenne and cook until the shallot is softened, 2 to 3 minutes. Stir in the flour and cook for 30 seconds. Stir in the sherry and simmer until it has nearly evaporated, about 2 minutes. Whisk in the broth and cream and simmer until the liquid has thickened and reduced to ¾ cup, 10 to 12 minutes.

2. Off the heat, add the cooked lobster meat and tarragon; season with salt and pepper to taste. Divide the mixture evenly between 2 shallow 2-cup gratin dishes. (The gratins can be covered tightly with plastic wrap and refrigerated for up to 24 hours. Remove the plastic wrap and microwave briefly on medium until warm, 2 to 4 minutes, before topping and baking.)

3. FOR THE TOPPING: Adjust an oven rack to the middle position and heat the oven to 400 degrees. Pulse the bread in a food processor to coarse crumbs, about 10 pulses. Combine the bread crumbs, Parmesan, tarragon, oil, and paprika in a bowl. (The topping can be stored in an airtight container at room temperature for up to 24 hours.)

4. Sprinkle the topping evenly over the gratins. Bake until the sauce is bubbling and the topping is golden brown, about 15 minutes. Let cool for 10 minutes before serving.

PAN-SEARED SCALLOPS

LIKE A LOT OF SEAFOOD PREPARATIONS, PAN-SEARED scallops are as easy as it gets for a restaurant chef: Slick a super-hot pan with oil, add the shellfish, flip them once, and serve. The whole process takes no more than a couple of minutes and produces golden-crusted beauties with tender, just-cooked interiors. But try the same technique at home and you're likely to run into trouble. The problem is that most home stovetops don't get nearly as hot as professional ranges, so it's difficult to properly brown the scallops without overcooking them. Moreover, restaurant chefs pay top dollar for scallops without chemical additives, which are known in the industry as "dry." The type available in most supermarkets, called "wet" scallops, are treated with a solution of water and sodium tripolyphosphate (STP) to increase shelf life and retain moisture. Unfortunately, STP lends a soapy, off-flavor to the scallops, and the extra water only compounds the problem of poor browning. I wanted to achieve superior pan-seared scallops, whether using supermarket wet scallops or the pricier dry variety. I would have to find a solution to the browning-without-overcooking conundrum and a way to get rid of the chemical taste of STP.

My first stop was the supermarket fish counter. Scallops are available in a range of sizes: A pound of the hard-to-find large sea variety contains 8 to 10 scallops, while a pound of the petite bay variety may have as many as 100 pencil eraser–sized scallops. Since small scallops are more prone to overcooking than large, I opted for the biggest commonly available size: 10 to 20 per pound. I decided to work with wet scallops first. After all, if I could develop a good recipe for finicky wet scallops, it would surely work with premium dry scallops.

I started by seasoning 1½ pounds (the right amount for four people) with salt and pepper. I heated 1 tablespoon of vegetable oil in a 12-inch stainless-steel skillet, then added the scallops in a single layer and waited for them to brown. After three minutes, they were steaming away in a ¼-inch-deep pool of liquid. At the five-minute mark, the moisture in the skillet evaporated and the flesh began to turn golden. But at this point it was too late: The scallops were already overcooked and tough, and I hadn't even flipped them.

To dry out the scallops, I tried pressing them between kitchen towels. When 10 minutes didn't work, I tried a full hour—even leaving a third batch overnight in the refrigerator. The results were disheartening. While slightly drier than unblotted scallops, the pressed batches still exuded copious amounts of liquid in the skillet

(and they still tasted soapy; I'd focus on that later). My conclusion: Beyond a 10-minute blot, there's not much point in an extended drying time.

It was becoming clear that to dry out the waterlogged scallops for good browning, I'd have to get the pan as hot as possible. Without a high-output range, it was important to pay careful attention to technique. I started by waiting to add the scallops to the skillet until the oil was beginning to smoke, a clear indication of heat. I also cooked the scallops in two batches instead of one, since crowding would cool down the pan. Finally, switching to a nonstick skillet ensured that as the scallops cooked, the browned bits formed a crust on the meat instead of sticking to the skillet. These were steps in right direction, but the scallops were still overcooked and rubbery by the time they were fully browned.

Would switching from oil to butter help my cause? Butter contains milk proteins and sugars that brown rapidly when heated, so I hoped that it would help the scallops turn golden before they overcooked. But my

NOTES FROM THE TEST KITCHEN

GOING FOR A SOAK
Wet scallops have been treated with sodium tripolyphosphate (STP), which lends a disagreeable flavor. We tried to get rid of the STP by soaking the scallops in water. We tested soaking one batch of scallops in a quart of water for 30 minutes, a second batch for an hour, and left a third untreated. Compared to the untreated batch, the results from soaking weren't encouraging— tasters were still able to clearly identify an unpleasant chemical flavor in both soaked samples. It turns out that the phosphates in STP form a chemical bond with the proteins in scallops. The bonds are so strong that they prevent the STP from being washed away, no matter how long the scallops are soaked. (A lab test found that the one-hour soak removed a mere 11 percent of the STP.) We found our best solution was to mask the chemical flavor by soaking the scallops in a solution of lemon juice, cold water, and salt. (See the recipe headnote on page 208 for instructions.)

ARE YOUR SCALLOPS WET OR DRY?
If you are unsure whether your scallops are wet (treated with chemicals) or dry (untreated), conduct this quick test: Place 1 scallop on a paper towel–lined, microwave-safe plate and microwave on high power for 15 seconds. If the scallop is dry, it will exude very little water. If it is wet, there will be a sizable ring of moisture on the paper towel. (The microwaved scallop can be cooked as is.)

PREPPING SCALLOPS

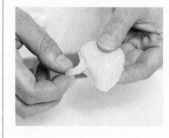

The small, crescent-shaped muscle that is sometimes attached to the scallop will be incredibly tough when cooked. Use your fingers to peel this muscle away from the side of each scallop before cooking.

BASTING SPOONS
In the test kitchen, we use a basting spoon for everything from skimming fat to scooping up pan sauce or basting a turkey. We tested five models in stainless steel, silicone, and fiberglass, preferring spoons with long, comfortable handles and thin shallow bowls that were easy to maneuver around every type of pan, from a low skillet to a deep Dutch oven. Our favorite was the **Rösle Basting Spoon with Hook Handle**, $28.95. The shallow bowl of this stainless-steel winner made tipping the pan unnecessary, and its long handle kept our hands away from the heat.

hopes were dashed when in my next batch, the butter that I'd swapped for oil actually made matters worse: It burned before the scallops were cooked through.

Then I recalled a method I'd used when cooking steaks and chops in restaurants: butter-basting. I gave it a try with my scallops, searing them in oil on one side and adding a tablespoon of butter to the skillet after flipping them. I tilted the skillet to allow the butter to pool, then used a large spoon to ladle the foaming butter over the scallops. Waiting to add the butter ensured that it had just enough time to work its browning magic on the shellfish, but not enough time to burn. The scallops now achieved a deep golden brown crust in record time, and their moist interiors were preserved. They weren't quite as tender and juicy as dry scallops, but they were darn close.

Only one problem remained, and it was a big one: the soapy flavor of STP. I already knew from earlier tests that blotting removes neither excess water nor STP, but what about the opposite approach: soaking in water to wash out the STP? It was a flop. No matter how long or carefully I rinsed the scallops, the STP still remained.

I thought things over and decided that if I couldn't remove the STP, I would try to mask it. I thought maybe a saltwater brine was the answer because it would penetrate the scallops deeply. The brine did provide even seasoning, but not enough to mask the chemical flavor. I noted that the phosphate in STP is alkaline. What if I covered it up by putting acidic lemon juice in the brine? Problem solved. Only the most sensitive tasters now picked up on a hint of chemical off-flavors; most tasted only the sweet shellfish complemented by the bright flavor of citrus.

With my wet-scallop approach established, it was finally time to test my recipe on dry scallops. I skipped the soaking step, which was unnecessary in the absence of STP, and proceeded with the recipe. The result? Scallops that rivaled those made on a powerful restaurant range, golden brown on the exterior and juicy and tender on the interior. I was happy to serve them with just a squeeze of lemon, but fancier occasions call for a sauce. For those instances, I developed a couple of recipes based on a classic accompaniment: browned butter.

—BRYAN ROOF, *Cook's Illustrated*

Pan-Seared Scallops

SERVES 4

We strongly recommend purchasing dry scallops (those without chemical additives; see page 206 for more about wet versus dry scallops). If you can only find wet scallops, soak them in a solution of 1 quart cold water, ¼ cup lemon juice, and 2 tablespoons table salt for 30 minutes before proceeding with step 1, and season the scallops with pepper only in step 2. Prepare the sauce (if serving) while the scallops dry (between steps 1 and 2) and keep it warm while cooking them.

> 1½ pounds dry sea scallops (about 16 scallops), tendons removed (see page 207)
>   Salt and pepper
> 2 tablespoons vegetable oil
> 2 tablespoons unsalted butter, cut into 2 pieces
>   Lemon wedges or sauce (recipes follow), for serving

1. Place the scallops on a rimmed baking sheet lined with a clean kitchen towel. Place a second clean kitchen towel on top of the scallops and press gently on the towel to blot liquid. Let the scallops sit at room temperature for 10 minutes while the towels absorb moisture.

2. Remove the second towel and sprinkle the scallops on both sides with salt and pepper. Heat 1 tablespoon of the oil in a 12-inch nonstick skillet over high heat until just smoking. Add half of the scallops in a single layer, flat side down, and cook, without moving, until well browned, 1½ to 2 minutes.

3. Add 1 tablespoon of the butter to the skillet. Using tongs, flip the scallops and continue to cook, using a large spoon to baste the scallops with the melted butter, tilting the skillet so the butter runs to one side, until the sides of the scallops are firm and the centers are opaque, 30 to 90 seconds longer (remove smaller scallops from the pan as they finish cooking). Transfer the scallops to a large plate and tent loosely with foil. Wipe out the skillet with a wad of paper towels and repeat with the remaining 1 tablespoon oil, remaining scallops, and remaining 1 tablespoon butter. Serve immediately with lemon wedges or sauce.

Lemon Brown Butter Sauce

MAKES ABOUT ¼ CUP

- 4 **tablespoons (½ stick) unsalted butter**
- 1 **small shallot, minced (about 4½ teaspoons)**
- 1 **tablespoon minced fresh parsley**
- 2 **teaspoons fresh lemon juice**
- ½ **teaspoon minced fresh thyme**
- **Salt and pepper**

Heat the butter in a small heavy-bottomed saucepan over medium heat and cook, swirling the pan constantly, until the butter turns dark golden brown and has a nutty aroma, 4 to 5 minutes. Add the shallot and cook until fragrant, about 30 seconds. Remove the pan from the heat and stir in the parsley, lemon juice, and thyme. Season with salt and pepper to taste. Cover to keep warm.

Tomato-Ginger Sauce

MAKES ABOUT ½ CUP

- 6 **tablespoons (¾ stick) unsalted butter**
- 1 **plum tomato, cored, seeded, and diced**
- 1 **tablespoon grated fresh ginger**
- 1 **tablespoon fresh lemon juice**
- ¼ **teaspoon red pepper flakes**
- **Salt**

Heat the butter in a small heavy-bottomed saucepan over medium heat and cook, swirling the pan constantly, until the butter turns dark golden brown and has a nutty aroma, 4 to 5 minutes. Add the tomato, ginger, lemon juice, and red pepper flakes and cook, stirring constantly, until fragrant, about 1 minute. Season with salt to taste. Cover to keep warm.

CRAB CAKES

CITIZENS OF MARYLAND HOLD THIS TRUTH TO BE self-evident: The best crab cakes are all about the crab. That's why Marylanders typically serve their famous crab cakes with nothing but a squeeze of lemon. Not to be crabby, but that's easy for them: Fresh and fabulous crabmeat at a reasonable price is as common in Maryland as ants at a picnic. Where does that leave the rest of us? Refusing to be discouraged, I took as my model one of Maryland's best-loved versions: the jumbo-size, award-winning crab cakes from J.W. Faidley Seafood, made from handpicked blue crabmeat bound with minimal mayonnaise and crushed saltines and seasoned with Dijon mustard. The bar was high, but my goal was to make something as meaty, succulent, and sweet.

Nine recipes and a day of picking, chopping, binding, shaping, and frying later, I found I had achieved little of note. I had pecked at greasy crab cakes (ugh! an entire stick of butter) and pasty ones (blame the glut of crumbs). I had despaired over one recipe of crab cakes overpowered by Old Bay seasoning, mustard, and raw onion, and another that tasted of nothing but lackluster crab and mayonnaise. Crab cakes that dialed back on binder had problems of their own. They were so soggy that they were hard to form, and even the ones I could get to hold together fell apart in the skillet.

It was time to head off on my own. I put together a working recipe using 1 pound lump crabmeat, one whole egg, ¾ cup crushed saltines, ¼ cup mayonnaise, and 1 tablespoon Dijon mustard. Picking over the crabmeat to make a batch, I happened to notice how much liquid was pooling in my mixing bowl. Not a single recipe had suggested I begin by pressing the crabmeat dry. Geez. Obviously, I'd need less binder if the crab was drier from the start. Step one of my recipe was settled: Dry crabmeat with paper towels.

Next I gradually cut back on the cracker crumbs. My tasters liked ¼ cup of crushed saltines, but with that amount the crab cakes weren't sturdy enough to withstand pan-frying in oil. I tried both fresh and toasted bread crumbs in place of the saltines. The saltines absorbed the most moisture (and we liked the taste best),

KEYS TO MEATY CRAB CAKES THAT HOLD TOGETHER

Here's how we got our Maryland Crab Cakes to coalesce without too much binder.

1. We dry the crabmeat with paper towels, which allows us to use fewer crushed crackers for binding.

2. We chill the crab cakes so they can set up and the cracker crumbs can absorb moisture before broiling.

3. We broil the crab cakes on a baking sheet so we don't have to flip them to brown the second side.

IN THE MARKET FOR CRAB

Our recipe for Maryland Crab Cakes calls for 1 pound of crabmeat. Fresh jumbo lump blue crabmeat from the Chesapeake Bay, in Maryland, prized for its tenderness, sweet flavor, and big meaty pieces, is best. But we don't all have access to it. So we tested our recipe with every other type of crab we could procure, from fresh to frozen, East Asian to Maine, pasteurized to imitation. Tasters compared some to cat food, others to bad tuna. But not all were terrible. On the positive side, the next best thing to fresh Maryland blue crab is, we concluded, pasteurized canned blue crab from Maryland. It's drier and firmer than fresh but still has good crab flavor. Unlike canned tuna, pasteurized canned crab must be refrigerated. It's produced by heating the crabmeat to 185 degrees to prevent bacteria growth; sometimes it's bleached, which also stops bacteria. Pasteurized canned crabmeat will last 6 to 12 months—that's before you open the can. Once the can is open, eat the meat within three days. Read the label carefully when you're shopping. We found one brand labeled "Maryland" that actually came from Indonesia and was merely canned in Maryland. Also, don't try to save money by buying imitation crabmeat. It was so dry and stringy in our crab cakes, we doubted any amount of mayonnaise could fix it.

so I stuck with them. Next, I lost the egg white—and gained slightly firmer crab cakes. In search of ideas to strengthen the cakes further, I reviewed my research and read that Marylanders often broil crab cakes. Hmm. I divided my mixture into generous ½-cup portions, mounded them on a greased baking sheet, and broiled just long enough for them to warm and brown (about 15 minutes). Since I no longer had to flip the crab cakes, they held together—and did so even better when I chilled them first.

With the basic components and cooking technique set, I turned my attention to the flavor. Most supermarket crabmeat has been pressure-steamed, canned in brine, and pasteurized. This process prolongs shelf life but diminishes flavor. To make up for this shortcoming, I gently mixed in hot sauce, minced scallions, and Old Bay (but not too much, just a teaspoon). Since I wasn't planning on serving these crab cakes with tartar sauce, I wondered if a richer cake was in order. I reconsidered an earlier recipe I'd rejected that used an entire stick of melted butter. Butter and shellfish are a time-tested pairing, after all. Ultimately, I replaced just 2 tablespoons of mayonnaise in my recipe with the same amount of melted butter. At the same time, I greased my sheet pan with butter instead of the nonstick spray I'd been using. Delicious.

One nagging concern remained: The undersides of the crab cakes were soggy. For my final test, I dunked one side of each crab cake in extra saltine crumbs before refrigerating. Later, as the crab cakes broiled, the bottoms lightly fried in the butter, crisping and browning. These crab cakes might not have been made in Maryland, but they sure tasted just as good.

—DIANE UNGER, *Cook's Country*

Maryland Crab Cakes

SERVES 4

Jumbo lump crabmeat is available at the fish counter of most supermarkets. If you can't find it, you can use refrigerated pasteurized lump crabmeat. To make the cracker crumbs, grind 14 saltines in a food processor.

- **1 pound lump crabmeat, picked over for shells**
- **½ cup saltine crumbs (see note)**
- **3 scallions, minced**
- **2 tablespoons unsalted butter, melted, plus 1 tablespoon unsalted butter, softened**

MARYLAND CRAB CAKES

2   tablespoons mayonnaise

1   large egg yolk

1   tablespoon Dijon mustard

2   teaspoons hot sauce

1   teaspoon Old Bay seasoning

     Lemon wedges, for serving

1. Dry the crabmeat well with paper towels. Using a rubber spatula, gently combine the crabmeat, ¼ cup of the cracker crumbs, the scallions, melted butter, mayonnaise, egg yolk, mustard, hot sauce, and Old Bay in a large bowl.

2. Divide the mixture into 4 equal portions and shape into tight, mounded cakes. Press the top of each cake in the remaining ¼ cup cracker crumbs. Transfer the cakes, crumb side down, to a large plate and refrigerate, covered, for at least 1 hour or up to 8 hours.

3. Adjust an oven rack to be 6 inches from the broiler element and heat the broiler. Grease an 8 by 8-inch square area in the center of a rimmed baking sheet with the softened butter. Transfer the crab cakes to the prepared baking sheet, crumb side down. Broil until the crab cakes are golden brown, 12 to 15 minutes. Serve with the lemon wedges.

SOUTH CAROLINA SHRIMP BOIL

NEW ENGLAND HAS ITS CLAMBAKES. NEW ORLEANS, its crawfish boils. In the coastal hamlet once known as Frogmore, South Carolina, and surroundings, they've got Frogmore stew—it has no frogs and it's not stew. It's a South Carolina shrimp boil by another (very charming) name. Frogmore stew is made by simmering local shell-on shrimp, smoked sausage, corn on the cob, and potatoes in a broth seasoned with Old Bay. When it's time to eat, the broth is discarded and the shrimp and vegetables are heaped, higgledy-piggledy, onto newspaper-covered picnic tables cluttered with paper towels and "waster" buckets for spent cobs and shells. The dish is equally popular at backyard picnics and casual seaside restaurants all along the Carolina coast.

Yet as a Carolina native, I can attest that the one-pot appeal of Frogmore stew is often its downfall. Home cooks are apt to add everything to the pot at the same time, or let everything boil away madly while they tend to other dishes. In those instances, the fresh, summery charm of Frogmore stew vanishes, replaced with a mishmash of blown-out potatoes, mealy corn, and rubbery shrimp. The recipes I tested added the potatoes first and the shrimp last, but didn't agree on the sausage and corn. The Old Bay dominated some versions; in others, it was just a rumor.

The best recipe I tested began by browning smoky, spicy andouille sausage to render its fat and boost flavor. The cook was then instructed to set the sausage aside and add 16 cups of water and 1 tablespoon of Old Bay to the now-empty pot. Halved red potatoes and quarters of corn on the cob went into the pot, simmering until the potatoes were barely tender. Next, the browned sausage and, five minutes later, the shrimp went into the pot. The staggered cooking ensured intact potatoes, plump corn, and nicely cooked sausage and shrimp (as long as you watched closely). Unfortunately, the flavors were washed out.

You don't eat the broth in Frogmore stew, but if it has no flavor, the stuff you do eat won't either. I tested adding garlic, onion, celery, and bell pepper to the broth, but they didn't add much given the short cooking time. Instead of emptying a canister of Old Bay into the water, I attempted to get the same effect by subtraction. I reduced the water to 5 cups, barely enough to cover the 1½ pounds of potatoes, four ears of corn, 1½ pounds of sausage, and 2 pounds of shrimp I was using. For yet more flavor, I tested replacing a cup of the water with an equal amount of clam juice, as well as chicken broth and beer. Tasters preferred the clam juice, since it reinforced the taste of the sea. Some recipes call for tomatoes. I tried it. We liked it. Tomatoes were in.

I had been adding the shrimp to the simmering liquid during the last few minutes of cooking, but that gave them scant time to soak up flavor. I tossed them with additional Old Bay before adding them to the pot, but the spice washed right off. To get it to adhere, I'd have to get the shrimp out of the broth. Might a metal steamer basket be the answer? I tossed the shrimp with 2 teaspoons Old Bay and placed them in the basket, which I set directly on the simmering vegetables and sausage. With the shrimp elevated above the liquid, the seasoning stayed put. Ten minutes later, they were juicy and much more flavorful. Plus, cooking them this way was more forgiving, so I could relax, right in line with the spirit of a casual seafood boil.

—CALI RICH, *Cook's Country*

South Carolina Shrimp Boil

SERVES 8

This dish is always made with shell-on shrimp, and we think peeling them is half the fun. If you prefer peeled shrimp, use only 1 teaspoon of Old Bay in step 3. See photo if you are using shell-on but prefer for them to be deveined. If you can't find andouille sausage, you can substitute kielbasa and add ¼ teaspoon cayenne pepper to the broth in step 2.

1½ pounds andouille sausage, cut into 2-inch lengths
2 teaspoons vegetable oil
4 cups water
1 (14.5-ounce) can diced tomatoes
1 (8-ounce) bottle clam juice
5 teaspoons Old Bay seasoning
1 bay leaf
1½ pounds small red potatoes (about 9), halved
4 ears corn, husks and silk removed, cut into 2-inch rounds
2 pounds extra-large (21 to 25 per pound) shrimp (see note)

1. Heat the sausage and oil in a large Dutch oven over medium-high heat until the fat renders and the sausage is browned, about 5 minutes. Using a slotted spoon, transfer the sausage to a plate.

2. Bring the water, tomatoes, clam juice, 3 teaspoons of the Old Bay, the bay leaf, potatoes, and corn to a boil in the empty pot. Reduce the heat to medium-low and simmer, covered, until the potatoes are just tender, about 10 minutes.

3. Return the browned sausage to the pot. Toss the shrimp with the remaining 2 teaspoons Old Bay and transfer to a collapsible steamer basket. Following the photos, nestle the steamer basket into the pot. Cook, covered, stirring the shrimp occasionally, until cooked through, about 10 minutes. Strain the stew and discard the bay leaf. Serve.

NOTES FROM THE TEST KITCHEN

LAYERED COOKING
Our staggered cooking method develops flavor and guarantees that each ingredient is perfectly cooked.

1. Brown the sausage to render its fat and give the stew a spicy base of flavor.

2. Simmer the potatoes and corn for 10 minutes with the seasoning and cooking liquid to give them enough time to soak up flavor and become tender.

3. For tender sausage, return the browned sausage to the pot for the last 10 minutes of cooking.

4. Steam the seasoned shrimp over the simmering stew to ensure they are tender and well flavored.

DEVEINING SHRIMP
You don't have to remove the flavorless, harmless "vein" that runs down the back of shrimp, but lots of eaters can't get past the fact it's the shrimp's intestinal tract.

To devein the shell-on shrimp for our South Carolina Shrimp Boil, use a small pair of scissors to cut through the shell to expose and free the underlying vein.

VEGETARIAN ENTRÉES

SPANISH TORTILLA

IN SPAIN, YOU WILL DISCOVER *TORTILLA ESPAÑOLA* in tapas bars, restaurants, and homes, usually served with a garlicky mayonnaise, as an evening snack or light supper. This egg-and-potato omelet (no relation to Mexican corn or flour tortillas) is made by slow-cooking sliced potatoes and onions in olive oil until meltingly tender, mixing them with beaten eggs, and frying it all into a golden-brown cake. Spanish tortilla has an intensely rich flavor and velvety texture that is immensely appealing—but only if someone else is doing the cooking. The typical Spanish tortilla recipe calls for simmering potatoes in 3 to 4 cups of extra-virgin olive oil. While Spaniards strain and reuse the oil to make several tortillas a week, from my point of view using so much oil for a single, somewhat humble meal seemed excessive. I wanted to keep the satisfying flavor and unctuous texture but lose the quart of oil.

I decided to stick with the traditional volume of olive oil until I could determine the proper type and ratio of ingredients. I started by cooking a generous amount of potatoes in 4 cups of oil. Waxy Red Bliss potatoes and new potatoes were out—no matter how long they were cooked, they remained too firm. Yukon Golds worked better, but starchy russets were best of all, turning soft and creamy. One and a half pounds of russets yielded a 1½-inch-thick tortilla that just fit inside a 10-inch skillet—perfect for four people as a light dinner. I found that ⅛-inch-thick slices of quartered potatoes yielded the best distribution of egg and potato. For the onion, tasters favored the mellow flavor of standard yellow onions over shallots, Spanish onions, and sweet Vidalias.

Recipes varied wildly in the ratio of eggs to potatoes. One egg per pound of potatoes was clearly too little; there wasn't enough egg for the tortilla to set. Ten eggs per pound made it overwhelmingly eggy. Five eggs per pound (or eight eggs per 1½ pounds) of potatoes was just enough to let the tortilla set firm but tender, with the eggs and potatoes melding into one another instead of competing.

Up to this point, I had been cooking the potatoes and onions in oil until soft, mixing them with eggs in a bowl, then pouring the mix back into the skillet, shaking it gently to keep the eggs from sticking. Traditional recipes call for flipping the tortilla with the help of a single plate when the bottom is set but the top is still liquid. This might be old hat for Spanish cooks, but the result when I tried was an egg-splattered floor. I tried skipping the flip and finishing the tortilla by browning the second side under the broiler, but this puffed up the eggs like a soufflé—not the authentic dense and creamy texture I wanted. What if I just trapped the heat inside the pan to set the top? I cooked another tortilla, this time placing a lid on the pan as soon as the bottom of the egg-and-potato mixture was set. Two minutes later, the top was cooked just enough to make flipping less risky—but not easy. Fed up, I fudged tradition and grabbed another plate. By sliding the tortilla out of the pan and onto one plate, then placing another upside-down over the tortilla, I could easily flip the whole thing and slide the tortilla back in the pan.

I could finally set my sights on scaling down the oil. Unfortunately, with a reasonable ½ cup oil the potatoes on the bottom of the pan browned and overcooked before the potatoes on the top began to soften. Perhaps, once again, cooking with the lid on would help? I tossed the potatoes and onions in ¼ cup of olive oil, heated another ¼ cup oil in a skillet, then added the potatoes and onions and covered it, stirring occasionally. Better, but still not great—even with the stirring, the potatoes on the bottom of the pan developed tough brown spots. Turning the heat down to medium-low and extending the cooking time to over 20 minutes prevented these spots, but now the potatoes were turning mushy.

The problem was that with a deep pan of oil, it's easy to cook a large volume of potatoes without disturbing them. The potatoes slowly soften, and as they cook, the starch on their exterior hardens, forming a sheath that keeps their shape intact. In less oil, however, the potatoes were half frying, half steaming—and without sheath formation, they were disintegrating at the slightest touch. I realized that I'd made my potato choice while I was still using the traditional cooking method. With less oil, did russets still make sense?

I started a new tortilla using slightly firmer, less starchy Yukon Golds, which I had initially rejected. With less oil, they were clearly a winner: starchy enough to become meltingly tender as they cooked, but sturdy enough to stir and flip halfway through cooking with fewer breaks. In fact, the new approach worked so well that I found I could reduce the oil to a mere 6 tablespoons. The rich flavor was still present as long as I relied on a high-quality extra-virgin olive oil, a much more appealing prospect since I was now using only a moderate amount.

My tortillas were nearing perfection, but my colleagues were curious about incorporating additional ingredients. This was a cinch, since Spanish tortillas are like American diner omelets in one important way: While perfectly good plain, they can take on an infinite variety of fillings. I prepared two tortillas with typical additions (roasted red peppers and peas, and Spanish chorizo) and served them with a batch of garlicky mayonnaise. Praising the exceptionally creamy potatoes and eggs studded with salty sausage or sweet vegetables, tasters quickly finished their slices and came back for seconds. My tortillas still delivered true Spanish flavor.

—J. KENJI LOPEZ-ALT, *Cook's Illustrated*

Spanish Tortilla with Roasted Red Peppers and Peas

SERVES 4 AS A LIGHT MAIN COURSE OR 6 AS AN APPETIZER

Spanish tortillas are often served warm or at room temperature with olives, pickles, and Garlic Mayonnaise (recipe follows) as an appetizer. They may also be served with a salad as a light entrée. For the most traditional tortilla, omit the roasted red peppers and peas. There's no need to wash the bowl in step 1. It is OK if some of the potato slices break into smaller pieces when poked with the paring knife in step 1. You will need a 10-inch nonstick skillet for this recipe.

- 6 **tablespoons plus 1 teaspoon extra-virgin olive oil**
- 1½ **pounds Yukon Gold potatoes (3 to 4 medium), peeled, quartered lengthwise, and cut crosswise into ⅛-inch-thick slices**
- 1 **small onion, halved and sliced thin**
- 1 **teaspoon salt**
- ¼ **teaspoon pepper**
- 8 **large eggs**
- ½ **cup jarred roasted red peppers, drained, patted dry, and cut into ½-inch pieces**
- ½ **cup frozen peas, thawed**
  Garlic Mayonnaise (optional; recipe follows)

HOW TO FLIP A TORTILLA

1. After browning the first side, loosen the tortilla with a rubber spatula and slide it onto a large plate.

2. Place the second plate face down over the tortilla. Invert the tortilla on the second plate so that it is browned side up.

3. Slide the tortilla back into the pan, browned side up, then tuck the edges into the pan with a rubber spatula.

BUYING EGGS

Eggs come in three grades (AA, A, and B), six sizes (peewee to jumbo), and a rainbow of colors. But the only grade we could find in the market was Grade A, the only colors were brown and white, and the only sizes were jumbo, extra-large, large, and medium. After extensive tasting, we couldn't discern any consistent flavor differences among these egg sizes. For consistency, our recipes call for large eggs. It's important to use the size called for in any recipe, especially when baking. As for color, the shell's hue depends on the breed of the chicken. Despite marketing hype that color makes a difference, we found that shell color has no effect on flavor.

1. Toss 4 tablespoons of the oil, the potatoes, onion, ½ teaspoon of the salt, and pepper in a large bowl until the potato slices are thoroughly separated and coated in oil. Heat 2 tablespoons more oil in a 10-inch nonstick skillet over medium-high heat until shimmering. Reduce the heat to medium-low, add the potato mixture to the skillet, and set the bowl aside. Cover and cook, stirring with a rubber spatula every 5 minutes, until the potatoes offer no resistance when poked with the tip of a paring knife, 22 to 28 minutes.

2. Meanwhile, whisk the eggs and remaining ½ teaspoon salt in the reserved bowl until just combined. Using a rubber spatula, fold the hot potato mixture, red peppers, and peas into the eggs until combined, making sure to scrape all of the potato mixture out of the skillet. Return the skillet to medium-high heat, add the remaining 1 teaspoon oil, and heat until just beginning to smoke. Add the egg-potato mixture and cook, shaking the pan and folding the mixture constantly for 15 seconds. Smooth the top of the mixture with a rubber spatula. Reduce the heat to medium, cover, and cook, gently shaking the pan every 30 seconds until the bottom is golden brown and the top is lightly set, about 2 minutes.

3. Using a rubber spatula, loosen the tortilla from the skillet, shaking back and forth until the tortilla slides around freely in the pan. Following the photos on page 217, slide the tortilla onto a large plate. Invert the tortilla onto a second large plate and slide it, browned side up, back into the skillet. Tuck the edges of the tortilla into the skillet with a rubber spatula. Return the pan to medium heat and continue to cook, gently shaking the pan every 30 seconds, until the second side is golden brown, about 2 minutes longer. Slide the tortilla onto a carving board or serving plate and allow to cool for at least 15 minutes. Cut the tortilla into cubes or wedges and serve with Garlic Mayonnaise, if desired.

VARIATION

Spanish Tortilla with Chorizo and Scallions
Use a cured, Spanish-style chorizo for this recipe. Portuguese linguiça is a suitable substitute.

Follow the recipe for Spanish Tortilla with Roasted Red Peppers and Peas, omitting the roasted red peppers and peas. In step 1, prepare the potato mixture as directed, then heat 4 ounces Spanish-style chorizo, diced medium, with 1 tablespoon oil in a 10-inch nonstick skillet over medium-high heat, stirring occasionally, until the chorizo is browned and its fat has rendered, about 5 minutes. Once the chorizo is browned, reduce the heat to medium-low and add the potato mixture to the skillet with the chorizo and rendered fat. Continue with the recipe as directed, folding 4 thinly sliced scallions (green and white parts) into the eggs in step 2.

Garlic Mayonnaise
MAKES ABOUT 1¼ CUPS

 2 large egg yolks
 2 teaspoons Dijon mustard
 2 teaspoons fresh lemon juice
 1 garlic clove, minced
 ¾ cup vegetable oil
 1 tablespoon water
 ¼ cup extra-virgin olive oil
 ½ teaspoon salt
 ¼ teaspoon pepper

Process the yolks, mustard, lemon juice, and garlic in a food processor until combined, about 10 seconds. With the machine running, slowly drizzle in the vegetable oil, about 1 minute. Transfer the mixture to a medium bowl and whisk in the water. Whisking constantly, slowly drizzle in the olive oil, about 30 seconds. Whisk in the salt and pepper and serve. (The mayonnaise can be refrigerated in an airtight container for up to 4 days.)

FRESH VEGETABLE TART

AMONG ALL THE SAVORY TARTS AND PIES, ONE OF my favorites is the vegetable tart, a simple dish with a tender crust filled with a layer of mild cheese, and a true emphasis on fresh vegetables. A colorful vegetable tart is perfect for a summertime lunch or light dinner, and it makes for a great presentation at a dinner party among the ho-hum dips and chips. However, while a vegetable tart may sound like the epitome of a healthy choice, after testing a number of existing recipes I knew this was usually not the case. Typically the cheese and crust turned this seemingly light meal into a rare indulgence, not to mention taking the emphasis away from the starring ingredient. I set out to come up with a fresh vegetable tart that delivered on its light and healthy promise.

I focused first on the crust. I liked the classic appearance of a traditional tart shell, and I needed one that was sturdy enough to support the toppings without being so dense it could break a tooth. Puff pastry was out since it's too flaky, and I wanted something with less butter and shortening than regular pie dough. After

FRESH VEGETABLE TART

MAKING A PRESS-IN CRUST

1. Transfer the processed dough to a 9-inch tart pan with a removable bottom.

2. Working outward from the center, press the dough into an even layer, sealing any cracks.

3. Working around the edge, press the dough firmly into the corners of the pan with your fingers.

4. Go around the edge once more, pressing the dough up the sides and into the fluted ridges.

5. Lay plastic wrap over the dough and smooth out any bumps using the palm of your hand.

some additional research, I found that olive oil crusts are traditional in many regions of Italy. This sounded like an idea worth exploring.

Cobbling together a recipe, I decided to avoid the more temperamental rolled-out crust in favor of a simpler press-in crust. My first attempt at an olive oil press-in crust fared well, though its texture was much too tender—more like a shortbread than a sturdy tart crust. Reducing the amount of oil made it sturdier, but I had to be careful. Too little oil led to a chewy crust. Six tablespoons (compared to the 8 tablespoons I had used for my first test) proved to be the happy medium. I also tried incorporating some whole wheat flour into the mix for additional strength. I found that a 3-1 ratio of all-purpose to whole wheat flour worked best, lending strength without making the crust tough. The whole wheat flour also gave the crust a rustic flavor that went over well with tasters. I knew from test kitchen experience that parbaking the crust before adding any filling would ensure the crust would bake through evenly. About half an hour in a 375-degree oven did the trick.

Next I turned to the filling, starting with the cheese. Since I wanted the vegetables to be the star, I didn't need much, just a thin, creamy layer to hold on to the vegetables and add appealing contrasting texture. I made two tarts with shredded mozzarella—one with part-skim and one with reduced-fat—a third tart with part-skim ricotta, and a fourth that was mixture of part-skim ricotta and reduced-fat mozzarella. The two mozzarella-only versions yielded unappealing, rubbery layers of cheese that congealed when cooled. All ricotta was better, but too watery. The ricotta-mozzarella combination was a hit. The ricotta provided just the right creamy texture, and the mozzarella helped hold the filling together and prevented it from oozing too much when the tart was sliced. At the recommendation of a fellow test cook, I also sprinkled a thin layer of Parmesan over the bottom of the shell. Not only did this add flavor and texture, but it created a layer of protection from the slightly moist ricotta (and eventually the vegetables), ensuring that my crust would stay crisp and sliceable.

Moving on to the vegetables, first I had to determine which ones to use. Since my parbaked crust required little additional cooking, I needed to pick vegetables that would cook quickly. After some experimentation, I decided to stick with a fairly typical Italian combination of sliced zucchini and plum tomatoes—both capable of turning perfectly tender in a relatively short time. As I suspected, once in the oven, the zucchini and plum tomatoes exuded moisture during cooking, and the resulting tart was a waterlogged mess. To fix the problem, I salted the vegetables after slicing them and allowed them to drain on paper towels for 30 minutes, then blotted them dry and layered them in the shell over the cheese. This tart came out of the oven with just a glossy sheen of moisture, still slightly juicy but far from waterlogged.

For a final flavor boost, I drizzled a touch of olive oil mixed with minced garlic and thyme over the tart before baking. When I pulled the tart out of the oven, I let it cool for a few minutes and sprinkled it with some chopped fresh basil. This vegetable tart was light but still full of bright vegetable flavor. It definitely delivered on its promise.

—DAN ZUCCARELLO, *America's Test Kitchen Books*

Fresh Vegetable Tart
SERVES 6

The filling in this tart is relatively thin, so be sure to press the dough only ¾ inch up the sides of the tart pan. We like the flavor and creaminess of part-skim ricotta here; do not use fat-free ricotta. Serve with a salad to make this a light, summery meal.

CRUST
- ¾ cup plus 3 tablespoons (about 4⅔ ounces) unbleached all-purpose flour
- ¼ cup plus 1 tablespoon (about 1¾ ounces) whole wheat flour
- 1 tablespoon sugar
- ½ teaspoon salt
- 6 tablespoons extra-virgin olive oil
- ¼ cup ice water
- 1 ounce Parmesan cheese, grated (about ½ cup)

FILLING
- 1 small zucchini (about 6 ounces), ends trimmed, sliced ¼ inch thick
- 2 plum tomatoes, cored and sliced ¼ inch thick
  Salt
- 2 teaspoons extra-virgin olive oil

- 1 garlic clove, minced
- ½ cup part-skim ricotta cheese (see note)
- 1 ounce part-skim mozzarella cheese, shredded (about ¼ cup)
  Pepper
- 2 tablespoons chopped fresh basil

1. FOR THE CRUST: Process the all-purpose flour, whole wheat flour, sugar, and salt together in a food processor until combined. Drizzle the oil over the flour mixture and pulse until the mixture resembles coarse sand, about 12 pulses. Add 3 tablespoons of the ice water and continue to process until large clumps of dough form and no powdery bits remain, about 5 seconds. If the dough doesn't clump, add the remaining 1 tablespoon water and pulse to incorporate, about 4 pulses. (The dough should feel quite sticky.)

2. Following the photos on page 220, transfer the dough to a 9-inch tart pan with a removable bottom and pat it into an even layer. Press the dough up the sides of the pan, then lay plastic wrap over the dough and smooth out any bumps using the palm of your hand. Leaving the plastic wrap on top of the dough, place the tart pan on a large plate and freeze the tart shell until firm, about 30 minutes.

3. Adjust an oven rack to the middle position and heat the oven to 375 degrees. Set the tart pan on a large baking sheet and remove the plastic wrap. Press a double layer of foil into the frozen tart shell and over the edges of the pan and fill with pie weights. Bake until the tart shell is golden brown and set, 30 to 40 minutes, rotating the baking sheet halfway through. Transfer the baking sheet to a wire rack and carefully remove the weights and foil.

4. Sprinkle the Parmesan evenly over the bottom of the tart shell, return the baking sheet to the oven, and continue to bake until the cheese is golden, 5 to 10 minutes longer. Let the tart shell cool on the baking sheet while making the filling. Increase the oven temperature to 425 degrees.

5. FOR THE FILLING: While the tart shell is cooling, spread the zucchini and tomatoes over several layers of paper towels. Sprinkle with ½ teaspoon salt and let drain for 30 minutes; gently blot the tops of the zucchini and tomatoes dry with more paper towels.

6. Combine 1 teaspoon of the oil and the garlic in a small bowl. In a separate bowl, mix the remaining

1 teaspoon oil, the ricotta, and mozzarella together and season with salt and pepper to taste.

7. Spread the ricotta mixture evenly over the bottom of the tart shell. Shingle the zucchini and tomatoes attractively on top of the ricotta in concentric circles. Drizzle the vegetables with the oil mixture. Bake the tart on the baking sheet until the cheese is bubbling and the vegetables are slightly wilted, 20 to 25 minutes, rotating the baking sheet halfway through.

8. Let the tart cool on the baking sheet for 10 minutes, then sprinkle with the basil. To serve, remove the outer metal ring of the tart pan, slide a thin metal spatula between the tart and the tart pan bottom, and carefully slide the tart onto a platter or carving board. Serve warm.

STUFFED ACORN SQUASH

THESE DAYS MOST RESTAURANTS ARE OFFERING vegetarian options, but typically the choices are limited at best, usually either a ho-hum pasta dish or perhaps some vegetables that seem more like a scaled-up side dish. And rarely do they come across as healthy, often dependent on an overabundance of starches or cheese. Recipes for home cooks don't do much better. I wanted a healthy vegetarian entrée that felt like a full, satisfying meal that even a carnivore would be happy about eating as the main dish. When I began considering the options, stuffed vegetables seemed like a good place to start. A quick search turned up countless recipes for the usual suspects: stuffed tomatoes, stuffed zucchini, and stuffed eggplant. These all felt like a side dish, so I kept looking for the right vegetable for the job. Then I came across a handful of recipes for stuffed winter squash. If I could come up with the right filling and the right cooking method to marry the squash and filling without a lot of fuss, hearty and rich-tasting winter squash sounded like the foundation for a winning vegetarian entrée.

After considering all the varieties of winter squash, I quickly settled on acorn squash. Not only does it boast plenty of visual appeal on the plate, but half of a squash, once stuffed, seemed like just the right amount for one person. I knew from test kitchen experience that the best way to develop flavor in winter squash is to roast it, but because roasting a squash can take up to an hour, it was clear I'd need to precook the squash before filling. My plan was simple: Precook the squash, prepare the filling, and then marry the two by cooking the combined dish briefly in the oven.

So with my strategy in place, the first question was at what temperature and for how long I should roast the squash. After a few tests, I confirmed that roasting the halved and seeded acorn squash in a 400-degree oven for about 45 minutes did the trick. Lower temperatures simply took too long, and higher temperatures burned the edges of the squash before it had a chance to cook through. I found that roasting the squash cut side down on a foil-lined baking sheet in the lower part of the oven helped to caramelize the flesh of the squash, concentrating its sweet, nutty flavor. Now that the squash was cooked, it was ready to be filled.

After testing several filling bases, I found that bread cubes were a quick and convenient option, but their mushy texture after being cooked in the hollowed out squash made them a poor choice. Cooked grains proved a much more reliable route. I tested couscous and brown rice, and in the search for something heartier, I grabbed some barley off the shelf. Couscous, while a good choice for vegetables like zucchini, was too delicate to stand up to the meaty squash. Brown rice was better, but barley was the clear winner. It made a rustic, hearty filling base that tasters gave a unanimous thumbs-up. There are a few varieties of barley sold, and for the best texture and a reasonable cooking time, I opted to use pearl barley rather than hulled or instant. (See page 224 for more information about barley.)

When preparing barley as a side dish, in the past the test kitchen has had success cooking barley like risotto, adding liquid incrementally to create a velvety sauce that envelops the grain during cooking. While this is appealing on its own, it seemed a little rich and out of place in this context. Furthermore, the risotto method is time consuming and I was already pre-roasting the squash as it was. I wanted to keep things simple, so I settled on boiling the barley in water like pasta and simply draining it. This took just 20 minutes or so, and I could get it cooking while the squash was in the oven.

STUFFED ACORN SQUASH WITH BARLEY

While the barley cooked, I began to explore flavorings for the filling. I started by sautéing some aromatics for depth, settling on fennel to complement the earthy barley, along with some minced onion and a generous amount of garlic. As for spices and herbs, ground coriander lent warmth while thyme added fresh floral flavor. Next I stirred the cooked and drained barley into the pan. For textural contrast, tasters approved toasted pine nuts. Then all I had to do was fill the precooked squash with my filling and pop it in the oven for 10 minutes to meld the two components.

My barley-stuffed squash was getting there, but the filling seemed like an afterthought, just some barley grains stuffed in a seeded squash half. The two didn't feel unified. Maybe making the filling more cohesive would help, I thought. Cheese seemed like a logical choice, and 1 cup of Parmesan cheese lent an appealing nutty richness and also helped bind the grains together without making the filling overly cheesy. But still, it wasn't enough. As I was scooping out a bite of the moist squash to pair with a spoonful of barley from my latest test batch, I had an idea. What better way to bind the barley and marry it with the squash than to mix the two together? For my next test, after roasting the squash I scooped out the cooked flesh, leaving a thin border, and stirred it into the barley until well combined. Then I mounded the squash-barley mixture into the squash shells. Eureka! This was the cohesive, hearty, and appealing meal I was after.

All my recipe needed was a few finishing touches. I took ¼ cup of the Parmesan cheese out of the filling and used it as a topping instead, which lent more visual appeal once browned in the oven. Finally, a splash of balsamic vinegar drizzled over the stuffed squash just before serving brightened the flavors and elevated the stuffed squash to where it belonged—center stage at dinnertime.

—SUZANNAH MCFERRAN, *America's Test Kitchen Books*

NOTES FROM THE TEST KITCHEN

TRIMMING AND CORING FENNEL

1. Cut off the stems and feathery fronds.

2. Trim a very thin slice from the base from the bulb and remove any tough or blemished outer layers.

3. After cutting the bulb in half through the base, use a small, sharp knife to remove the pyramid-shaped core. Slice or chop the fennel as directed.

BARLEY

Our recipe for Stuffed Acorn Squash gets a hearty, nutty-flavored filling that also happens to be nutritious with the help of barley. While barley might be most familiar as a key ingredient in beer, this cereal grain is a nutritious high-fiber, high-protein, and low-fat cereal grain with a nutty flavor that is similar to that of brown rice. It is great in soups and in salads, as risotto, and as a simple side dish. Barley is available in multiple forms. Hulled barley, which is sold with the hull removed and the fiber-rich bran intact, is considered a whole grain and is higher in a few nutrients (iron, magnesium, potassium, thiamine, riboflavin, and fiber) compared to pearl (or pearled) barley, which is hulled barley that has been polished to remove the bran. Then there is quick-cooking barley, which is available as kernels or flakes. Hulled barley, which is hard to find in most supermarkets, takes a long time to cook and should be soaked prior to cooking. Pearl barley cooks much more quickly, making it a more versatile choice when you are adding it to soups or making risotto or a simple pilaf. Use it as a stand-in for rice alongside recipes such as stir-fries or curries.

Stuffed Acorn Squash with Barley

SERVES 4

Make sure to use pearl barley, not hulled barley, in this recipe—hulled barley takes much longer to cook. For more information on barley, see page 224.

2 **small acorn squash (about 1½ pounds each), halved and seeded**

2 **teaspoons olive oil**

    Salt and pepper

¾ **cup pearl barley, rinsed and drained**

1 **onion, minced (about 1 cup)**

1 **fennel bulb, halved lengthwise, cored, and chopped fine (see page 224)**

6 **garlic cloves, minced**

1 **teaspoon minced fresh thyme or ¼ teaspoon dried**

1 **teaspoon ground coriander**

2 **ounces Parmesan cheese, grated (about 1 cup)**

2 **tablespoons minced fresh parsley**

2 **tablespoons pine nuts, toasted**

1 **tablespoon unsalted butter**

4 **teaspoons balsamic vinegar**

1. Adjust the oven racks to the upper-middle and lower-middle positions and heat the oven to 400 degrees. Line a rimmed baking sheet with foil and lightly spray with vegetable oil spray.

2. Brush the cut sides of the squash with 1 teaspoon of the oil, season with salt and pepper, and lay them cut side down on the prepared baking sheet. Roast on the lower-middle rack until tender (the tip of a paring knife can be slipped into the flesh with no resistance), 45 to 55 minutes. Remove the squash from the oven and increase the oven temperature to 450 degrees.

3. Meanwhile, bring 3 quarts water to a boil in a large saucepan. Stir in the barley and ¼ teaspoon salt. Return to a boil, then reduce to a simmer and cook until the barley is tender, 20 to 25 minutes. Drain and set aside.

4. Wipe the saucepan dry and add the remaining 1 teaspoon oil, the onion, and fennel. Cover and cook over medium-low heat, stirring occasionally, until the vegetables are softened, 8 to 10 minutes. Stir in the garlic, thyme, and coriander and cook until fragrant, about 30 seconds.

5. Off the heat, stir in the barley, ¾ cup of the Parmesan, the parsley, pine nuts, and butter. Season with salt and pepper to taste.

6. Flip the roasted squash over and scoop out the flesh, leaving a ⅛-inch thickness of flesh in each shell. Gently fold the squash flesh into the barley mixture, then mound the mixture into the squash shells (about 1 cup of filling per shell).

7. Sprinkle with the remaining ¼ cup Parmesan. Bake on the upper-middle rack until the cheese is melted, 5 to 10 minutes. Drizzle with the balsamic vinegar and serve. (The stuffed squash can be assembled through step 6, covered loosely with plastic wrap, and refrigerated for up to 4 hours. Finish and bake as directed, increasing the baking time to 25 to 30 minutes.)

BLACK BEAN BURGERS

THESE DAYS YOU CAN BUY A PRETTY GOOD VEGGIE burger from the freezer aisle at the supermarket, but like just about any dish, homemade is better—when you've got the right recipe. Most veggie burger recipes turn out bland, grain-based patties, call for a daunting amount of chopping and precooking before even forming the veggie burgers, require obscure ingredients, or simply don't hold together. I wanted to come up with a veggie burger that was satisfying, had appealing texture and flavor, and most of all was easy and inexpensive to make. Black beans appear in various vegetarian entrées as the main protein source, from tacos and chili to casseroles and hearty salads, and they are also seen as the starring ingredient in vegetarian burgers. The framework is simple: Black beans are mashed and combined with herbs, seasonings, and a binder, then formed into patties and pan-seared. With their meaty, satisfying flavor and general appeal, black beans struck me as a great foundation for my own veggie burger.

I started by testing a few existing recipes, and the problems were clear. Even black bean burgers proved to be a labor of love, requiring mashing, chopping, and measuring before mixing everything together— much more involved than their beefy brethren. And many of these recipes were just not worth this effort— countless patties came out of the pan dry, pasty, or falling apart, not to mention bland in flavor. Nevertheless, I saw the potential. I just needed to find a way to get moist patties with appealing texture, robust flavor, and the ability to go from pan to plate without falling into pieces.

I looked first at the beans. Most of the recipes for burgers I had tested called for two cans of beans. Canned beans were not only a time-saver compared to soaking and simmering dried beans, but two cans conveniently provided the right amount to make six burgers. Although canned beans have a slightly mushier texture than dried beans, I was confident I could overcome that drawback with good prep and some additional ingredients.

My test recipes had revealed two main preparation styles for the beans: mashing some and leaving some whole, or mashing all of them. Not surprisingly, burgers made with all mashed beans had an unappealingly pasty consistency. The burgers with a combination of half mashed and half whole beans fared much better, offering a good textural contrast. But these burgers had another problem; I could rarely make a patty that didn't fall apart before it was cooked through, even in spite of the egg most of these recipes used for binding.

I wondered if more eggs would help hold the burgers together. Opening up a few more cans of beans, I experimented with batches of burgers made with two and three eggs. The batch with three eggs was too moist, making a mixture more like a batter than a burger. The batch with two eggs, however, had the proper amount of moisture and held together perfectly.

It was time to look at additional ingredients. A few recipes I had come across included not just herbs and spices but also chopped vegetables. This idea seemed promising since it could result in more flavor and texture. I tested common choices for vegetables first: onion, garlic, shallot, celery, mushrooms, and bell pepper. Tasters felt that the onion and garlic were overpowering, but milder shallot provided a nice pungency. Celery and mushrooms both added a meaty texture and rich flavor, but they required precooking to avoid tasting raw—too much work for this recipe. Finely chopped raw bell pepper added the flavor and texture I was looking for. As for herbs and spices, tasters liked Southwestern flavors best—cilantro, cumin, and cayenne. As a final addition, a little olive oil brought my burgers' richness to just the right level.

Now my burgers had excellent flavor and texture, but with more ingredients in the mix, an old problem cropped up again: The burgers were falling apart. Egg

didn't seem like the answer this time, and recognizing that the mashed beans played a part in binding, I tried increasing the ratio of mashed beans to whole. I finally settled on a 3–1 ratio. These burgers held together well, and with the whole beans and bell pepper lending texture, they weren't too mushy. To further ensure stability, I also incorporated fresh bread crumbs to help absorb any excess moisture from the vegetables.

I put a patty in the skillet, and after 10 minutes my burger was ready for the bun and all the fixings. One bite proved it; this black bean burger was hearty, filling, and full of flavor. I'd definitely be making these again and again.

—DAN ZUCCARELLO, *America's Test Kitchen Books*

Black Bean Burgers

SERVES 6

Avoid overmixing the bean mixture in step 3 or the texture of the burgers will be mealy. Serve with your favorite toppings on whole wheat rolls or with a salad.

- 2 slices high-quality white sandwich bread, torn into pieces
- 2 large eggs
- 3 tablespoons olive oil
- 1 teaspoon ground cumin
- ½ teaspoon salt
- ⅛ teaspoon cayenne pepper
- 2 (15-ounce) cans black beans, drained and rinsed
- 1 red bell pepper, stemmed, seeded, and chopped fine
- ¼ cup minced fresh cilantro
- 1 shallot, minced (about 3 tablespoons)

1. Adjust an oven rack to the middle position and heat the oven to 350 degrees.

2. Pulse the bread in a food processor to coarse crumbs, about 10 pulses. Spread the crumbs on a rimmed baking sheet and bake, stirring occasionally, until golden brown and dry, 10 to 12 minutes. Set aside to cool to room temperature.

3. Whisk the eggs, 1 tablespoon of the oil, the cumin, salt, and cayenne together in a small bowl. Place 2½ cups of the beans in a large bowl and mash them with a potato masher until mostly smooth. Stir in the bread crumbs, egg mixture, remaining ½ cup beans, bell pepper, cilantro, and shallot until just combined. Divide the bean mixture into 6 equal portions, about ½ cup each, and lightly pack into 1-inch-thick patties.

4. Heat 1 tablespoon more oil in a 12-inch nonstick skillet over medium heat until shimmering. Carefully lay half of the patties in the skillet and cook until well browned on both sides, 8 to 10 minutes, flipping them halfway through.

5. Transfer the burgers to a plate and tent loosely with foil. Return the skillet to medium heat and repeat with the remaining 1 tablespoon oil and the remaining burgers. Serve.

VARIATION

Black Bean Burgers with Corn and Chipotle Chiles
Follow the recipe for Black Bean Burgers, substituting 1 tablespoon minced canned chipotle chile in adobo sauce for the cayenne pepper. Reduce the amount of red bell pepper to ¼ cup and add ¾ cup frozen corn, thawed and drained, to the bean mixture in step 3.

NOTES FROM THE TEST KITCHEN

CANNED BLACK BEANS

Most canned black beans have three main ingredients: beans, water, and salt. So how different could they taste? Plenty different, we found out when we sampled six national brands in a blind test. The three brands that scored the highest all have more than 400 milligrams of sodium per ½-cup serving; simply adding salt to the low-scoring brands that had far less salt didn't help. Tasters also disliked mushy beans. The difference between firm and mushy beans hinges on a balance between chemistry (in the form of salt and other additives) and how hot and how long the beans are cooked during canning. The beans need salt for good flavor, but too much can make them mushy. This is why two of our salty, highly ranked brands include calcium chloride, which counteracts the softening power of sodium. **Bush's Best Black Beans**, our winning brand, does not. How they achieve firm beans with lots of salt and no calcium chloride is proprietary manufacturing information, we're told, but odds are that to preserve more of their firm texture, Bush's quickly processes their beans with less heat than the other brands. (See page 296 for more information about our testing results.)

CHEESE FRENCHEES

I LOVE THE MIDWEST FOR A LOT OF REASONS: Kansas City Sticky Ribs, the slightly sweet yeast buns with meat filling known as runsas, and St. Louis Gooey Butter Cake, just for starters. So when I learned about the Cheese Frenchee through an entry for our recent Lost Suppers recipe contest, I had a feeling I was about to add one more thing to my Midwest-loving list.

The Cheese Frenchee was described by Pam Patterson, the contest entrant, as "a deep-fried grilled cheese sandwich," but I quickly learned there is more to it than that. It's a grilled cheese sandwich made with a touch of mayo, which is then cut into triangles, battered, and rolled in a crunchy coating before being deep-fried. A little research revealed that it was probably the most beloved menu item at the food chain known as King's Food Host USA. The chain began in Lincoln, Nebraska, in 1955 as King's Drive-In and grew to include roughly 160 restaurants in 17 states, mostly in the Midwest (today King's, sadly, no longer exists). King's itself had a retro charm that had me hooked almost as much as the sound of the Frenchee. Pam recalled that "the novelty of this restaurant was the telephone situated at each booth. You placed your order by picking up the phone and giving it to the hostess over the phone. In a time when many households had only one phone in the entire house, having a telephone tableside was very thrilling!" Needless to say, I was pretty thrilled to give the Frenchee a go.

I started with Pam's recipe. I made several sandwiches by placing a slice of American cheese between two slices of white sandwich bread that I had spread with mayonnaise (about 1 tablespoon per slice) just as Pam indicated, then I cut each sandwich on the diagonals into four triangles. Next, I set up the batter and coating stations. The batter was straightforward, just milk and a couple of large eggs, beaten. However, Pam's instructions for the coating were a little more vague: She simply called for "2 cups cracker crumbs." I wasn't sure if this meant soda crackers like saltines or something richer, like Ritz crackers. So after dipping the sandwich triangles in the egg mixture, I rolled half of them in crushed saltines and the other half in crushed Ritz. I then placed the coated triangles on a baking sheet as Pam instructed and refrigerated them for an hour so that they would "set." I agreed with Pam that this was an essential step, since

CHEESE FRENCHEES

otherwise the coating would just fall off during frying and the sandwich would turn to mush.

An hour later it was time to fry. I heated a good amount of vegetable oil to 375 degrees in a large Dutch oven and added a few breaded triangles to the pot, turning them when the first side turned light golden brown, as Pam noted, to brown the second side. Pam wasn't specific about cooking time, but I found the frying step didn't take long, no more than a minute or two per side. After they were fried Pam said to drain them, which I did by placing the sandwiches on a paper towel–lined plate.

Like grilled cheese, it was clear these sandwiches would be best when eaten shortly after cooking, while the cheese was still warm and gooey. And it only took one bite to confirm I had a winner on my hands; the outside of this sandwich was crunchy and golden, and the cheese inside was gooey and melted, just as I'd hoped. I only had to make a few tweaks to Pam's recipe to get it just right. My tasters liked the saltine coating just fine (and I later learned it would have been the more authentic choice), but everyone agreed the rich, buttery Ritz cracker coating really put the indulgent Frenchee over the top. I also decided to increase the amount of cheese. Pam had called for four to five slices and I settled on six, divvied up evenly among the sandwiches, which helped cover the bread for each sandwich

and maximize the amount of cheese without overdoing it. The coating on a few sandwiches fell off in spots, but all I had to do to remedy this problem was to press on the crumbs right after I'd coated the sandwiches to make sure the crumbs adhered.

These sandwiches pretty much epitomized perfect comfort food. And while Pam wrote that King's Food Host served their Frenchees with a side of french fries or onion rings, I was happy with just a little ketchup for dipping. Score one more win for the Midwest.

—SUZANNAH MCFERRAN, *America's Test Kitchen Books*

Cheese Frenchees

SERVES 4

Try dipping the sandwiches in ketchup—a Frenchee fanatic told us that's how she ate them growing up in Oklahoma.

1½	sleeves Ritz crackers (50 crackers), pulsed in a food processor to coarse crumbs
⅔	cup milk
2	large eggs
½	cup mayonnaise
8	slices high-quality white sandwich bread
6	(¾-ounce) slices American cheese
3–4	quarts vegetable oil

1. Line a large rimmed baking sheet with parchment paper. Spread the cracker crumbs in a shallow dish. Whisk the milk and eggs together in a medium bowl.

2. Spread 1 tablespoon of the mayonnaise on one side of each slice of bread. Arrange 1½ slices of the cheese on 4 of the slices of bread and top with the remaining 4 slices bread, with the mayonnaise side facing the cheese. Cut each sandwich diagonally into quarters.

3. One at a time, dip the sandwich quarters into the egg mixture, then coat with the cracker crumbs, pressing to adhere. Place on the prepared baking sheet and refrigerate until set, about 1 hour.

4. Pour the oil into a large Dutch oven until it measures 2 inches deep. Heat the oil to 375 degrees over medium-high heat. Lay half of the chilled sandwich quarters in the oil and fry until golden brown on both sides, 2 to 3 minutes, flipping halfway through. Transfer the sandwich quarters to a large paper towel–lined plate to drain briefly. Repeat with the remaining sandwich quarters. Serve.

POOR MAN'S MEATBALLS

WHETHER IT'S A FINANCIAL RECESSION, THE GREAT Depression, or there's just a large family to feed, when times get really tough, meat is often one of the first things to get cut from the shopping list. And in its place, home cooks get creative with the suppers they put on the table for their families. Some are perhaps not so noteworthy, but many others deserve a second look, turning simple, inexpensive ingredients into much more than the sum of their parts. Such was the case with a recipe, submitted by Donna Bardocz for our Lost Suppers contest, called "Aunt Nina's Breadballs and Sauce." Aunt Nina had learned this recipe from her own mother, Grandma Coppola, who made breadballs for her twelve children when her husband came home empty-handed from hunting. Made in much the same way as meatballs but with bread crumbs, eggs, cheese, and herbs and then served with a tomato sauce, these "meatless meatballs" piqued my interest.

A little research (and a few more conversations with Donna) turned up the fact that breadballs aren't quite the, well, oddballs I first thought. The concept comes from Italy, where similar recipes are made as appetizers, but they can work equally well for an affordable dinner. One Italian recipe compares such breadballs to a light gnocchi, which sounded like an ideal vegetarian comfort-food entrée to me. It was time to take Aunt Nina's recipe to the kitchen and find out what these breadballs were all about.

Donna's recipe was straightforward. She started by mixing a day-old loaf of Italian bread (I presumed we should tear it into pieces first) with an egg and ½ to 1 cup of water, just enough to wet the bread to form it into a ball. Then she mixed in minced onion, a couple of cloves of minced garlic, parsley, basil, and 1 cup of Parmesan. I gave this method a shot but had some trouble getting the latter ingredients to incorporate well and distribute evenly among the bread, so I decided to whisk together the water (I used a full cup), egg, seasonings, and cheese until combined, and only then did I mix in the bread to make the "dough."

Next it was time to form and fry the breadballs. Donna didn't indicate how big to make them, so I settled on balls that were 1½ inches in diameter, the same size as the test kitchen's meatballs. This gave me 30 breadballs, enough to serve six to eight people, which seemed about right for a family-friendly meal that could serve a few extra friends or provide some leftovers. Next I heated vegetable oil in a skillet as Donna's recipe directed and fried the breadballs until golden brown. I set them aside and moved on to the sauce.

Donna's sauce was essentially a dump-and-cook method, offering a simplicity that I found appealing and just right for a dish like this one. She combined a chopped onion, several cloves of minced garlic, a 12-ounce can of tomato paste, 4½ cups water, several tablespoons of sugar, a can of tomato sauce, and a large can of whole tomatoes. She seasoned the sauce with basil, oregano, and parsley, then cooked the mixture over low heat for one to two hours. I followed suit, combining all the ingredients and setting the sauce to simmer. I stirred it occasionally, but mostly I waited with anticipation to try the results.

When a few hours had passed, I ladled the sauce over the breadballs and gave them a taste. This was definitely a recipe worth adding to my repertoire. It was comforting, tasted flavorful yet familiar, and would appeal to just about anyone. I was sold.

I decided to make only a few tweaks to Donna's original recipe. To boost the flavor of the breadballs, I added another ½ cup cheese and another clove of garlic, and I omitted the onion since it created distracting crunchy bits in the breadballs. I also decided to cook the breadballs through in the sauce after I had browned them to boost their flavor even more. I started by browning the balls in the same pot where I would build the sauce, then once browned I set them aside, got the sauce going, and then added the balls back to the pot to cook through while the sauce reduced. Unfortunately, with this method the breadballs, which I had fried until golden brown, had a tendency to fall apart in the sauce. However, simply frying them a little longer, until they were well browned and a good crust had formed, ensured they held together throughout the long simmer in the sauce. Cooking the breadballs in the sauce not only boosted their flavor like I had hoped but it also helped tenderize them.

Donna's sauce was simple yet flavorful, though I realized I could get similar long cooked flavor and the perfect consistency in less time by reducing the amount of water and simmering it covered (with the breadballs) for one hour. I found it a little sweet so I cut back on the sugar, and I added a dash of red pepper flakes for kick. I also swapped out the whole tomatoes for diced, which held up a little better during the simmer and added a nice texture. To deepen the onion's flavor, I sautéed it before adding the other sauce components to the pot.

Donna might have called these "Poor Man's Meatballs," but they were so good I'd consider them anything but.

—DAN ZUCCARELLO, *America's Test Kitchen Books*

Poor Man's Meatballs and Tomato Sauce

SERVES 6 TO 8

Let the breadballs form a good crust during frying or they will fall apart when simmered. To keep them from sticking to the pan, make sure the oil is shimmering before you start cooking and don't move them for the first few minutes of browning.

BREADBALLS

- 1 cup water
- 1 large egg
- 3 garlic cloves, minced
- 1 tablespoon chopped fresh parsley or ¾ teaspoon dried
- 1 tablespoon chopped fresh basil or ¾ teaspoon dried
- ¼ teaspoon pepper
- 1 (16-ounce) loaf Italian bread, torn into small pieces
- 3 ounces Parmesan cheese, grated (about 1½ cups)
- 6 tablespoons olive oil

SAUCE

- 1 onion, minced (about 1 cup)
  Salt
- 2 (6-ounce) cans tomato paste
- 1 tablespoon sugar
- 3 garlic cloves, minced
- 2 teaspoons dried oregano
- ⅛ teaspoon red pepper flakes
  Pepper
- 2 cups water
- 1 (28-ounce) can diced tomatoes
- 1 (15-ounce) can tomato sauce
- 1 tablespoon chopped fresh parsley
- 1 ounce Parmesan cheese, grated (about ½ cup)
- 1 tablespoon chopped fresh basil

1. FOR THE BREADBALLS: Whisk the water, egg, garlic, parsley, basil, and pepper together in a large bowl. Add the bread and cheese and mix with your hands until well combined. With wet hands, form the mixture into 1½-inch breadballs (you should have about 30 breadballs).

2. Heat ¼ cup of the oil in a Dutch oven over medium-high heat until shimmering. Add half of the breadballs and cook until well browned on the first side, 2 to 4 minutes. (Do not move the breadballs until they are well browned on the first side.) Continue to cook until they are well browned on all sides, about 5 minutes longer, turning as needed. Transfer the breadballs to a bowl. Add the remaining 2 tablespoons oil to the pot and return it to medium heat until the oil is shimmering. Repeat with the remaining breadballs.

3. FOR THE SAUCE: Pour off all but 1 tablespoon of the oil from the pot and return to medium heat until shimmering. Add the onion and ½ teaspoon salt and cook, stirring occasionally, until softened, 5 to 7 minutes. Stir in the tomato paste, sugar, garlic, oregano, red pepper flakes, and ¼ teaspoon pepper and cook until the tomato paste begins to brown, 2 to 4 minutes. Add the water, tomatoes, and tomato sauce. Bring to a simmer, cover, and cook, stirring occasionally, for 1 hour.

4. Return the breadballs to the pot, cover, and continue to simmer until the sauce is thickened slightly and the breadballs are tender, about 30 minutes longer. Off the heat, stir in the parsley and season with salt and pepper to taste. Serve, sprinkling each portion with Parmesan and basil.

NOTES FROM THE TEST KITCHEN

DON'T THROW IN THE TOWEL

Many dish towels can't handle even the smallest kitchen mishap. Some towels have zero absorbency, while others wipe up spills easily but stain just as readily. Then there are towels that shrink to the size of a tissue in the dryer or break delicate stemware with their bulk. We tested eight towels, from $2.50 to $8.99, in our search for a dish towel that would soak up liquid, dry dishes without streaks or destruction, and look good as new after washing. We soon discovered that while innovative materials promised better absorption, they often failed to deliver, and when it came to microfiber, we couldn't get past its uncomfortably prickly texture. In the end, we preferred the feel and absorbency of cotton, but terry cloth was too bulky, and flimsy herringbone and flour sack towels couldn't stand up to demanding kitchen work. Only the **NOW Designs Ripple Towel**, $7.95, passed all our tests with near perfect scores. It's the towel we've been waiting for. Now, we have no excuse for not drying the dishes. (See page 311 for more information about our testing results.)

DESSERTS

OLD-FASHIONED PECAN PIE

LONG BEFORE KARO SYRUP WAS A GLEAM IN THE eye of its inventors, 19th-century homemakers were setting "transparent pies" to cool on windowsills. Made with sugar, butter, and eggs and sweetened with molasses or maple, cane, or sorghum syrup, these pies resembled pecan pie without the nuts. Then manufacturers came up with a flavorless, cheap liquid sugar made from highly processed cornstarch. In 1902, the Corn Products Refining Company of New York and Chicago aggressively marketed it as Karo corn syrup: "Great spread for daily bread, a table delight, appreciated morning, noon, or night." Three decades later, the wife of a Karo executive baked a transparent pie with the newfangled syrup and added pecans. The company printed her recipe in a promotional booklet, pie history was made, and Karo took off.

In truth, I've never entirely understood the popularity of pecan pie, or Karo pie, as it's sometimes called in the South. Flavorless Karo syrup brings nothing but undifferentiated, over-the-top sweetness. I wanted to return the pie to its roots—at least what I imagined them to be. And I wanted to actually taste the pecans rather than smothering them in tooth-aching sweetness. As I'd never tasted cane syrup or sorghum syrup (the latter is made from a cereal grass), I mail-ordered a few bottles from the mostly small, local Southern companies that still produce them.

When these old-fashioned syrups arrived in the test kitchen, I tried them on their own and then I tested them baked in pies. Tasters were delighted by their range of flavor, from full-bodied and molasses-y to light and buttery to honeyed—and everything in between. And while the darker syrups overwhelmed the pecan pies, the more delicate ones were sensational, with far more flavor than I'd ever managed to coax from either light or dark corn syrup. So now that I knew what I was missing, I set out to approximate it using ordinary pantry ingredients.

NOTES FROM THE TEST KITCHEN

MOVE OVER, KARO

Before Karo syrup monopolized the market, pies were made with many other types of syrup, including sorghum (made from a cereal grass) and cane (made from the boiled-down juice of the sugarcane plant). These syrups still exist, and you can mail-order them, but otherwise you'll probably need to travel to places like Louisiana or Kentucky to find them. We tasted a range of such syrups, including Steen's 100% Pure Cane Syrup and Townsend's Sweet Sorghum, then tried to duplicate their complex flavors from products we could buy at the supermarket. In the end, a combination of three ordinary sweeteners created an old-fashioned flavor that easily bested Karo.

MOLASSES
Brings a robust, slightly bitter quality

LIGHT BROWN SUGAR
Adds warmth and caramel tones

MAPLE SYRUP
Adds delicate complexity

THE BEST HAND-HELD MIXER

A good hand-held mixer is an essential appliance in any kitchen. It is compact, portable, and relatively inexpensive. And even if you own a standing mixer, there are some jobs, like whipping cream or beating eggs, where it's just easier to grab a hand-held mixer. Over the years, however, we've been disappointed by many models; they can be little more than glorified whisks. And who hasn't encountered the disconcerting smoky odor of a hand-held mixer's motor as the beaters slog their way through particularly stiff dough? We headed into the kitchen with eight leading models to see if we could separate the wimps from the workhorses. Many models had their shortcomings, including lack of power and excessive splattering. The overall winner was the **Cuisinart Power Advantage 7-Speed Hand Mixer**, $49.95, for its powerful, quiet motor, digital controls, and useful extra-low speed. The only thing this mixer can't do is knead bread dough. But the cookies, cakes, and frostings you make with it will be identical to those made in a standing mixer that costs almost three times as much. (See page 303 for more information about our testing results.)

As a reference point, I started with the original 1930s Karo recipe, which has changed little since that time: 3 eggs, 1 cup sugar, 1 cup light or dark Karo syrup, 2 tablespoons butter or margarine, and 1¼ cups pecans. The pie is baked at 350 degrees in an unbaked pie shell. I started my experimenting with granulated sugar, which, like cane syrup, is made from sugarcane. My idea was to make my own faux sugarcane syrup out of sugar and water. I found a recipe online that purported to do so and, following its instruction, I caramelized sugar in a skillet, added water, and boiled until the syrup thickened slightly. Along the way, I burned the caramel twice and lacquered the stove in bubbling syrup. Even when I got it right, the results didn't much resemble the cane syrups I'd tasted. As for the other sweeteners, even the mildest variety of honey tasted like, well, honey; no one thought it suited pecan pie. Maple syrup came the closest to the syrups I'd tasted, but the maple flavor was too pronounced. Many sugar tests later, I discovered I could mellow the maple and achieve the flavors I sought by combining it with light brown sugar and just a single tablespoon of molasses.

I heated the sugars briefly, which dissolved the brown sugar, thus eliminating graininess. I stirred in the butter. My working recipe called for 2 tablespoons. Other recipes I'd tested use as many as 8 tablespoons. I settled on 4 for appreciable buttery flavor without greasiness. Now, the filling tasted as good as I imagined it had before Karo syrup hijacked it nearly 80 years ago. When I was researching the history of pecan pies, I'd repeatedly run across a close cousin to transparent pies: sirop (syrup) pies. They were made in almost the same way, but usually added cream to the filling. How could that be bad? For the heck of it, I added in ½ cup cream with the sugars for my pie. Tasters loved the creamy, custardy transformation it wrought. Unfortunately, the cream made the filling looser. The maple syrup, I learned, was also partly to blame; it has a higher water content than corn syrup. To better bind the filling and get a sliceable pie, I replaced the three whole eggs with six yolks, which have less water than whites, and thus bind more firmly.

All that was left was the nuts. Bringing out their flavor was as simple as toasting them before they went into the pie. Five to 10 minutes in a 350-degree oven gave them enough crunch and flavor to hold their own in the filling.

Most recipes suggest simply pouring the filling into an unbaked pie shell. But when I did so, the bottom crust came out soggy and undercooked. As soon as the pie went into the oven, the uncooked bottom crust soaked up the uncooked liquid filling. Some recipes solve the problem by prebaking the crust, but could I avoid the extra step? Up to this point I'd been baking the pie at a steady 350 degrees on the middle rack of the oven. What if I started it at a high temperature (450 degrees), then immediately turned down the dial to a gentle 325 degrees? I hoped the initial high heat would give the bottom crust a head start, and the subsequent low temperature (it took 15 minutes for the temperature inside the oven to come down to 325 degrees) would prevent the eggs from curdling. At the same time, I lowered the oven rack. The intense heat from below would help set the crust. The result was just as I'd hoped: a crisp, golden bottom crust.

To the dismay of my tasters, pecan pie needs to completely cool before you can eat it. Otherwise, as I learned through gluttony and error, the filling won't firm to the proper consistency, so the pie won't slice nicely. Cooling took about four hours, at which point the filling was silky yet firm; the flavor a mild caramel with hints of molasses; and the nuts a toasty, crunchy counterpoint. The other thing that happened after four hours? My tasters threatened to kill me if I didn't let them have a piece.

—DIANE UNGER, *Cook's Country*

Old-Fashioned Pecan Pie

SERVES 8 TO 10

Regular or mild molasses tastes best in this pie. Serve with Bourbon Whipped Cream (recipe follows) if desired.

1 cup maple syrup

1 cup packed (7 ounces) light brown sugar

½ cup heavy cream

1 tablespoon molasses

4 tablespoons (½ stick) unsalted butter, cut into ½-inch pieces

½ teaspoon salt

6 large egg yolks, lightly beaten

1½ cups pecans, toasted and chopped

1 recipe Single-Crust Pie Dough, fitted into a 9-inch pie plate and chilled (recipe follows)

1. Adjust an oven rack to the lowest position and heat the oven to 450 degrees. Heat the syrup, sugar, cream, and molasses in a saucepan over medium heat, stirring occasionally, until the sugar dissolves, about 3 minutes. Remove from the heat and let cool, about 5 minutes. Whisk the butter and salt into the syrup mixture until combined. Whisk in the egg yolks until they are incorporated.

2. Scatter the pecans evenly in the pie shell. Carefully pour the filling over the pecans. Place the pie in the oven and immediately reduce the oven temperature to 325 degrees. Bake until the filling is set and the center jiggles slightly when the pie is gently shaken, 45 to 60 minutes. Transfer the pie to a wire rack and cool for 1 hour, then refrigerate until set, about 3 hours and up to 1 day. Bring the pie to room temperature and serve.

Bourbon Whipped Cream
MAKES ABOUT 2 CUPS

Although any style of whiskey will work here, we like the smokiness of bourbon, and since it's Southern, it fits right in.

1 cup heavy cream

2 tablespoons bourbon

4½ teaspoons light brown sugar

½ teaspoon vanilla extract

With an electric mixer on medium speed, beat the cream, bourbon, sugar, and vanilla until stiff peaks form, about 2 minutes. (The whipped cream can be refrigerated for up to 4 hours before serving.)

Single-Crust Pie Dough
MAKES ENOUGH FOR ONE 9-INCH SINGLE-CRUST PIE

1¼ cups (6¼ ounces) unbleached all-purpose flour

1 tablespoon sugar

½ teaspoon salt

3 tablespoons vegetable shortening, cut into ½-inch pieces and chilled

4 tablespoons (½ stick) unsalted butter, cut into ¼-inch pieces and chilled

4–6 tablespoons cold water

1. Process the flour, sugar, and salt together in a food processor until combined. Scatter the shortening over the top and pulse until the mixture resembles coarse cornmeal, about 10 pulses. Scatter the butter pieces over the top and pulse the mixture until it resembles coarse crumbs, about 10 pulses. Transfer the mixture to a bowl.

2. Sprinkle 4 tablespoons of the cold water over the mixture. Stir and press the dough together, using a stiff rubber spatula, until the dough sticks together. If the dough does not come together, stir in the remaining water, 1 tablespoon at a time, until it does.

3. Turn the dough onto a sheet of plastic wrap and flatten into a 4-inch disk. Wrap the dough tightly in the plastic wrap and refrigerate for at least 1 hour.

4. Let the chilled dough soften slightly at room temperature. Roll the dough out on a lightly floured counter to a 12-inch circle, about ⅛ inch thick. Roll the dough loosely around the rolling pin and unroll into a 9-inch pie plate, leaving at least a 1-inch overhang. Ease the dough into the plate by gently lifting the edge of the dough with one hand while pressing into the plate bottom with the other hand. Leave any dough that overhangs the plate in place.

5. Trim the overhang to ½ inch beyond the lip of the pie plate. Fold the overhang under itself; the folded edge should be flush with the edge of the pie plate. Using your thumb and forefinger, flute the edge of the dough. Cover with plastic wrap and freeze until firm, about 30 minutes, before filling or baking. (The dough can be refrigerated, wrapped tightly in plastic wrap, for up to 2 days, or frozen for up to 1 month. Let the frozen dough thaw on the countertop until malleable before rolling out).

LEMON CHESS PIE

UNLESS YOU LIVE IN THE SOUTH, YOU MAY NOT know about chess pie. You should. Dating back to the 1800s, this pie is a cousin to custard and translucent pies. Rich and intense, it's made from everyday ingredients most cooks had in their pantry, namely lots of eggs (an 1870 recipe I found included 16), lots of sugar (that same recipe called for a pound), lots of butter, sometimes milk or cream, and, to thicken, either flour or cornmeal. The cornmeal floats to the top, helping create a delicate, crackly crust that adds to the pie's appeal. One common variation is Lemon Chess Pie. The lemon flavor balances a homespun, very sweet, but by no means ordinary pie.

I tested recipes old and new. None was perfect. They ranged from sour to over-the-top sweet. Some were like meringue, others thick and jellied, none creamy and custardy as befits chess pie. Although butter is a key ingredient, too much made the filling greasy. An ideal recipe would get the proportions right. Also, I wanted to give this old-fashioned pie an update, making a good thing better for the 21st century. Based on my initial tests, I combined 1¾ cups sugar (considerably less than the norm), 4 tablespoons butter, four eggs, 1 tablespoon each flour and cornmeal, and 2 teaspoons lemon juice.

With four eggs, my pie wasn't firm enough. I went up by one (good), then tried adding extra yolks for extra richness (bad, eggy overload). Recipes called for as little as 4 tablespoons butter or as many as 16. With the latter, the butter oozed out and puddled on the plate. At 8 tablespoons, it made its mark pleasantly and added richness I'd previously hoped to get with the egg yolk.

Did I need both flour and cornmeal in the filling? Nope, tests showed. Nor did I need cornstarch, as some recipes suggested. I replaced the flour (which tasted raw) with an extra tablespoon of cornmeal. I was briefly stumped when tasters complained the pie was now gritty. The problem neatly solved itself when, waiting for the pie shell to chill, I prepared the filling. As the combined filling ingredients sat, the cornmeal softened.

After testing various amounts of lemon juice and zest, I landed on 3 tablespoons juice and 1 tablespoon zest for a delicately tart flavor. Milk or cream is sometimes added to make chess pie creamier. My tasters found they muted the lemon. I also tried orange zest, lemon and vanilla extracts, nutmeg, even black pepper. Some things are better left alone.

To mix the filling, I started with the food processor, for ease. Any grandmother could have told me that old ways may be as good—or better: The processor aerated the mixture, making the baked filling foamy. In the end, simply mixing in a bowl, whisking in the melted butter last, proved easiest and best.

I poured the filling into a pie crust that I'd partially baked to ensure it would stay crisp (see "Docking the Crust," page 239) and baked it for 30 minutes. As it emerged from the oven, I decided to accentuate the slightly crunchy crust that forms on top by sprinkling the pie with sugar. It took several hours for the pie to set up, and when I tasted it at last, I understood why chess pie has stood the test of time.

—DIANE UNGER, *Cook's Country*

Lemon Chess Pie

SERVES 8

Regular yellow cornmeal (not stone ground) works best here. Make the filling before baking the shell so the cornmeal has time to soften. Adding the filling when the pie shell is still warm reduces the pie's cooking time slightly.

- 5 **large eggs**
- 1¾ **cups (12¼ ounces) plus 1 teaspoon sugar**
- 1 **tablespoon grated lemon zest plus 3 tablespoons fresh lemon juice**
- 2 **tablespoons cornmeal (see note)**
- ¼ **teaspoon salt**
- 8 **tablespoons (1 stick) unsalted butter, melted and cooled slightly**
- 1 **recipe Single-Crust Pie Dough, fitted into a 9-inch pie plate and chilled (page 236)**

1. Whisk the eggs in a large bowl until smooth. Slowly whisk in 1¾ cups of the sugar, the lemon zest and juice, cornmeal, and salt until combined. Whisk in the butter.

2. Following the photos on page 239, poke the pie shell all over with a fork. Refrigerate for 40 minutes, then

LEMON CHESS PIE

freeze for 20 minutes. Adjust an oven rack to the upper-middle position and heat the oven to 450 degrees. Bake the shell until small bubbles appear and the surface begins to look dry, about 8 minutes. Remove the shell from the oven and reduce the oven temperature to 325 degrees.

3. Whisk the filling briefly to recombine. Scrape the filling into the prepared pie shell and bake until the filling's surface is light brown and the center jiggles slightly when shaken, 35 to 40 minutes. Sprinkle with the remaining 1 teaspoon sugar. Cool the pie completely on a wire rack, about 4 hours. Serve. (The pie can be refrigerated, covered with plastic wrap, for up to 2 days.)

NOTES FROM THE TEST KITCHEN

DOCKING THE CRUST

Custard pies have the unique problem in that their loose filling can make a tender pie crust soggy, so many custard pie recipes, including those for chess pie, typically require you to blind bake the crust, or bake the empty pie shell filled with pie weights until it's set. We found a quicker way to parbake that avoids the need for pie weights and still keeps our crust crisp.

1. Use a fork to poke holes all over the pie shell. The holes will allow steam to escape when the pie crust is baking, in turn helping the shell hold its shape.

2. Refrigerate the crust for 40 minutes, then freeze it for 20 so the gluten in the flour can relax, and the fat in the crust can firm up and hold its shape in the oven.

3. Parbake the shell at high heat, removing it from the oven once it starts to bubble (after about 8 minutes); the shell will look dry, and the holes will fill.

APPLE UPSIDE-DOWN CAKE

PINEAPPLE AND UPSIDE-DOWN CAKE ARE NEARLY synonymous. But long before the introduction of canned pineapple in the early 1900s sparked a craze for pineapple in baked goods, upside-down cakes were made with seasonal fruit such as apples. The technique was straightforward: Pour melted butter and brown sugar into a pan or skillet, add sliced apples, spread cake batter over them, and bake. The apples caramelize on the bottom of the pan, revealing a layer of burnished amber fruit when the cake is upturned.

After testing a few recipes, however, I understood why sweet, juicy pineapple had overshadowed the humble apple. Rather than a luscious topping full of deeply fruity, caramelized flavor, the apple slices tasted bland and watery and seemed more garnish than topping. To restore apple-pie order to this upside-down cake, I would need to start from the top down—or, rather, from the bottom up.

I started by trying several good baking varieties of apples: sweeter Golden Delicious and Braeburns as well as more tart Cortlands and Granny Smiths. Cortlands in particular boasted that fresh-from-the-orchard flavor and complexity, but their flesh broke down and turned mushy. Braeburns were too sweet after being caramelized in sugar. Golden Delicious worked reasonably well, but the notably crisp texture and sharper acidity of Granny Smiths worked best.

I then turned my attention to the rest of the topping. The ingredients and method were roughly the same in most recipes: Melt about 4 tablespoons of butter and ⅔ cup light brown sugar in a saucepan, pour the mixture into a 9-inch round cake pan, fan two sliced apples across the top, spread cake batter over them, and slide the pan into the oven. But when I inverted the cake onto a plate and cut a slice, I found that the two apples had cooked down to a shriveled layer, with patches of cake peeking through.

The obvious solution? Add more apples. When three apples didn't provide enough apple heft, I sliced up a fourth. I expected a substantial topping steeped with fruit flavor but instead got a cake jammed with unevenly cooked apples—some slices made contact with the pan and caramelized; the rest just steamed and their surplus moisture left the cake gummy.

MAKING APPLE UPSIDE-DOWN CAKE

1. Precook half of the apples in butter to deepen their flavor and reduce their volume, which in turn allows more to be added.

2. Add the raw apples, brown sugar, and lemon juice to the pan and cook briefly to preserve the fresh flavor.

3. Transfer the apple topping to a cake pan and gently press it into an even layer.

4. Spread the batter over the apple topping and bake.

5. Let the cake cool in the pan for 20 minutes to help set the apple topping, then invert the cake onto a wire rack to keep the bottom dry.

Then I recalled that we'd faced a similar dilemma with our Deep-Dish Apple Pie a few years back: how to cram in lots of apples without flooding the dessert with juice. In that case, our solution was to precook the apples to draw out excess moisture before baking. Following suit, I sautéed four sliced apples in a few tablespoons of butter until they just softened slightly and developed a deep golden color, then added the brown sugar, waited for the crystals to dissolve, and poured the topping into the cake pan, followed by the batter. Voilà! Not only did precooking the fruit release excess moisture, it allowed me to fit all four apples into the pan if I pressed them down gently. What's more, all of the fruit was infused with caramelized flavor, even if it didn't touch the pan.

There was just one problem: Precooking sacrificed fresh apple flavor. Hoping to strike a compromise, I tried cooking half of the apples, then folding in the remainder before turning the topping into the pan. This was an improvement. A few more tests revealed that slicing the uncooked apples thinner (¼ inch) let them bake evenly with the apples that had been sliced ½ inch thick and sautéed. All this full-flavored topping needed was a squirt of fresh lemon juice to add brightness and balance.

There was still the cake to contend with. I had been using the standard butter cake called for in the typical pineapple version. While its tender texture worked fine for pineapple upside-down cake, which needed less fruit, it was buckling under the weight of the 2 pounds of apples. The creaming method for this cake—wherein you beat the butter with the sugar, beat in the eggs, and then alternately fold in the dry and liquid ingredients (in this case, just milk)—was to blame. Creaming creates lots of air bubbles that produce lightness, volume, and delicate texture. For a coarser crumb, I would need to use the so-called quick-bread method, in which the butter is melted and the liquid and dry ingredients are mixed separately before being combined together. The melted butter introduces less air into the batter than creamed butter, for a sturdier crumb. Sure enough, the cake made with this approach was moist with a more substantial crumb that held up under the topping.

That said, compared to the intense apple topping, the cake tasted a little lackluster. Trading the milk for either yogurt or buttermilk improved matters, but sour cream was a standout. Its subtle tang balanced the sweetness of the cake and complemented the caramelized apple. I also swapped ¼ cup of white sugar for light brown sugar, which offered a hint of molasses. Sprinkling a tablespoon of cornmeal into the dry ingredients added earthy flavor and a pleasantly coarse texture.

This apple cake was perfect—until the upside-down part came in. Most recipes call for a stay of 5 or 10 minutes in the pan before inverting the cake onto a serving plate, but this caused the bottom of the cake to steam, resulting in a gummy base. In addition, the apples slid off, while the piping-hot caramel dripped down the sides of the cake like sauce over ice cream. Letting the cake rest in the pan for a good 20 minutes allowed the apple topping to set. Afterward, turning the cake out onto a rack rather than a plate to finish cooling let the bottom of the cake breathe, avoiding sogginess. How 'bout them apples?

—YVONNE RUPERTI, *Cook's Illustrated*

Apple Upside-Down Cake

SERVES 8

You will need a 9-inch nonstick cake pan with sides that are at least 2 inches high for this cake. Alternatively, use a 10-inch oven-safe stainless steel skillet (don't use cast iron) to both cook the apples and bake the cake, with the following modifications: Cook the apples in the skillet and set them aside while mixing the batter (it's OK if the skillet is still warm when the batter is added) and increase the baking time by 7 to 9 minutes. If you don't have either a 2-inch high cake pan or an oven-safe skillet, use an 8-inch square pan.

TOPPING

- 4 **Granny Smith or Golden Delicious apples (about 2 pounds), peeled and cored**
- 4 **tablespoons (½ stick) unsalted butter, cut into 4 pieces**
- ⅔ **cup packed (4⅔ ounces) light brown sugar**
- 2 **teaspoons fresh lemon juice**

CAKE

- 1 **cup (5 ounces) unbleached all-purpose flour**
- 1 **tablespoon cornmeal (optional)**
- 1 **teaspoon baking powder**
- ½ **teaspoon salt**
- ¾ **cup (5¼ ounces) granulated sugar**
- ¼ **cup packed (1¾ ounces) light brown sugar**
- 2 **large eggs**
- 6 **tablespoons (¾ stick) unsalted butter, melted and cooled slightly**
- ½ **cup sour cream**
- 1 **teaspoon vanilla extract**

1. FOR THE TOPPING: Butter the bottom and sides of a 9-inch round, 2-inch-deep nonstick cake pan and set aside. Adjust an oven rack to the lowest position and heat the oven to 350 degrees.

2. Halve the apples from pole to pole. Cut 2 of the apples into ¼-inch-thick slices and set aside. Cut the remaining 2 apples into ½-inch-thick slices. Heat the butter in a 12-inch skillet over medium-high heat. When the foaming subsides, add the ½-inch-thick apple slices and cook, stirring 2 or 3 times, until the apples begin to caramelize, 4 to 6 minutes. (Do not fully cook the apples.) Add the ¼-inch-thick apple slices, brown sugar, and lemon juice and continue to cook, stirring constantly, until the sugar dissolves and the apples are coated, about 1 minute longer. Following the photo on page 240, transfer the apple mixture to the prepared pan and lightly press into an even layer. Set aside while preparing the cake.

3. FOR THE CAKE: Whisk the flour, cornmeal (if using), baking powder, and salt together in a medium bowl and set aside. Whisk the granulated sugar, brown sugar, and eggs together in a large bowl until thick and homogeneous, about 45 seconds. Slowly whisk in the butter until combined. Add the sour cream and vanilla and whisk until combined. Add the flour mixture and whisk until just combined. Pour the batter into the pan and spread evenly over the fruit. Bake until the cake is golden brown and a toothpick inserted into the center comes out clean, 35 to 40 minutes.

4. Cool the pan on a wire rack for 20 minutes. Run a paring knife around the sides of the cake to loosen. Place a wire rack over the cake pan. Holding the rack tightly, invert the cake pan and wire rack together, then lift off the cake pan. Place the wire rack over a baking sheet or large plate to catch any drips. If any fruit sticks to the pan bottom, remove and position it on top of the cake. Let the cake cool for 20 minutes (or longer to cool it completely), then transfer to a platter, cut into pieces, and serve.

VARIATIONS

Apple Upside-Down Cake with Almonds
Follow the recipe for Apple Upside-Down Cake, combining ⅓ cup finely ground toasted almonds with the flour and adding 1 teaspoon almond extract with the sour cream and vanilla in step 3.

Apple Upside-Down Cake with Lemon and Thyme
Follow the recipe for Apple Upside-Down Cake, adding 1 teaspoon finely grated lemon zest and 1 teaspoon finely chopped fresh thyme leaves with the sour cream and vanilla in step 3.

STRAWBERRY STACK CAKE

UNABLE TO SPARE EGGS AND BUTTER NEEDED FOR tender layer cakes, Depression-era Appalachian cooks combined Spartan resources and patience into something just as good: stack cake. Thin spiced molasses rounds were sandwiched together with stewed dried apples and left to "ripen." After a couple of days, the filling moistened the sturdy layers, yielding a soft, fruity, robustly flavored cake. Stack cakes were often served for special occasions; they were both impressive and convenient, since they were prepared days in advance. Traditional recipes call for sorghum and lard. Could I update the recipe and use strawberries to adapt the cake for summer?

After gathering several stack cake recipes, I noticed they divided into two schools. In one, cookie dough is rolled out, cut into rounds, and baked in a cast-iron skillet, one round at a time; the other style yields a pourable cake-style batter that is baked in cake pans in the oven. I narrowed the recipes to five, representing both styles, and baked off more than 30 layers, which I then assembled into cakes, sandwiching them with strawberry jam (I'd work on the filling later). Tasters vetoed the cakes made with pourable batter. After two

days in the refrigerator, they were soggy, simply too delicate to hold up to the filling. The cakes made with cookie-like layers were better. In the best of the lot, the sturdy cookie layers had softened to a tender Fig Newton–like texture. But there was plenty of work to do. The molasses and warm spices in the cake (from a traditional recipe) made sense with apples but not with strawberries. And with 3 cups of commercial jam needed to fill all those layers, the cake was too sweet.

I thought a basic sugar cookie would suit strawberries better, so I followed the most successful recipe from my first round of testing, beating the shortening with granulated sugar instead of molasses. When the mix was fluffy, I beat in eggs, vanilla extract, and buttermilk, which lent a slightly cakey personality. Finally, I added flour and leaveners. Tasters loved the just-tender texture of this shortening-based "cake," but now that the molasses was gone, we could actually taste the shortening.

Replacing the shortening with butter yielded layers that were too crumbly. A combination of half butter and half shortening was better, but with such a short ingredient list (and so many layers) we could still taste the artificial shortening. That's when my thoughts turned to cream cheese. Like shortening, cream cheese is high in fat and low in moisture. Keeping the butter in my working recipe for its rich flavor, I ditched the shortening for cream cheese. Two days later the cake was ready for tasting. The cream cheese worked perfectly, with an unexpected benefit: Its gentle tang was a nice foil to the sweet berry filling.

Next goal: Simplify. Rather than baking the layers one at a time in a cast-iron skillet, I tried rolling out the dough, cutting it into rounds, and baking the rounds on baking sheets. But rolling and trimming the dough was as tedious as the original method. A few recipes suggested pressing the dough into the bottom of round cake pans and then baking. This press-in-the-pan method was a breeze, but since few home cooks have more than two cake pans, they'd still be tied to the oven for three rounds of baking. Then it occurred to me: Why not combine the methods by first pressing the dough into a pan and then moving the rounds to a baking sheet? After some trial and error, I found I could easily transfer the rounds from the cake pan to the baking sheet by lining the pan with an oversize parchment round and using the parchment as a sling to lift out the dough. Also, decreasing the layer size to 8 inches allowed two rounds to fit snugly on each baking sheet.

STRAWBERRY STACK CAKE

MAKING STRAWBERRY STACK CAKE

Instead of laboriously rolling out half a dozen layers, we divide the dough into 6 equal pieces and use an easy pat-in-the-pan method.

1. Position a 9-inch parchment round over an 8-inch pan, pressing the paper snugly into the pan edges.

2. Using lightly floured hands to prevent sticking, press a dough disk evenly over the bottom of the cake pan.

3. Lift the parchment to transfer the rounds to a baking sheet. Two rounds should fit on a large baking sheet.

THE BEST VANILLA ICE CREAM

Vanilla ice cream makes a great match for our Strawberry Stack Cake. We asked manufacturers of the eight top-selling brands of vanilla ice cream which of their styles was most popular, then we put them before our tasters to find the best. While texture varied from the softness of Marshmallow Fluff to dense as snowballs and color from almost yellow to grayish, what mattered most to tasters was vanilla taste. Tasters strongly preferred brands containing real vanilla extract over those containing synthetic vanilla. Though a small amount of stabilizers wasn't a bad thing (as seen in our winner), ice creams with an excess of them came across as gummy and pasty, and additives used in lieu of egg yolks didn't pass muster either. Finally, the less air incorporated into the ice cream (known as overrun), the better, as our top two ice creams also had the lowest overrun. Our winner, **Ben & Jerry's Vanilla**, was praised for its "indulgent" vanilla flavor that "built in intensity." (See page 298 for more information about our testing results.)

I still couldn't bake all six layers at once, but two oven trips was a huge improvement.

I was ready to tackle the filling. Tasters insisted I use fresh berries. My first impulse was to process the strawberries (I used 2½ pounds) with sugar (½ cup), but as I'd feared, the juicy puree made the cake soggy. The dried apples used in the original filling inspired me to add dried fruit, hoping it would absorb some of the moisture. Since dried strawberries aren't readily available, I pureed dried apples with the berries. Yet even at ½ cup, the addition didn't improve things much. It was time for Plan B: maceration, a common technique to draw out the juices of fresh fruit. I tossed the strawberries with sugar, let the mixture sit for 30 minutes, and then discarded the juices and processed the berries. The cake was less saturated, but it was also less flavorful. And no wonder; I'd just tossed out much of the flavor with the juices.

With every no-cook trick exhausted, I decided to simmer the strawberries on the stovetop to concentrate and reduce their juices. I cooked the berries and sugar until thick and jammy. A couple of tablespoons of lemon juice gave the berries a bright, balanced flavor. Once the berry mixture cooled, I assembled the layers and tucked the cake away. Though some recipes claim that "two days are required to consummate the marriage of fruit filling and cake," my patience had been pushed to the limit. After the stack cake had rested for just eight hours, I cut myself a sliver. It was ready to go. The cooked strawberry mixture had softened and moistened the cake layers, but they were by no means soggy. And with only a small amount of added sugar, the berry flavor was front and center. To be sure the stack cake would stand the test of time, we sampled it daily, and although we'd polished it off by day three, I'm pretty sure an even riper slice wouldn't have been turned down.

—CALI RICH, *Cook's Country*

Strawberry Stack Cake

SERVES 12

You can substitute frozen berries for the fresh. Our favorite rimmed baking sheet, the Lincoln Foodservice Half-Size Heavy Duty Sheet Pan, is 17¾ by 12⅞ inches, which allows you to bake 2 cake layers at a time. If using a smaller baking sheet, you'll need to bake 1 layer per sheet. Let the sheet cool completely between baking the layers.

FILLING

2½ pounds fresh strawberries, hulled and halved

½ cup (3½ ounces) granulated sugar

2 tablespoons fresh lemon juice

Pinch salt

CAKE

5 cups (25 ounces) unbleached all-purpose flour

1 teaspoon baking powder

1 teaspoon baking soda

½ teaspoon salt

¼ cup buttermilk (see page 103)

2 teaspoons vanilla extract

8 tablespoons (1 stick) unsalted butter, softened

4 ounces cream cheese, softened

2½ cups (17½ ounces) granulated sugar

2 large eggs

2 tablespoons confectioners' sugar

1. FOR THE FILLING: Bring the strawberries, sugar, lemon juice, and salt to a simmer in a large saucepan over medium heat. Mash the strawberries with a potato masher and cook until thick and jam-like, about 30 minutes (the mixture should measure 2¾ cups). Transfer to a shallow dish and refrigerate until cool, about 30 minutes.

2. FOR THE CAKE: Adjust the oven racks to the upper-middle and lower-middle positions and heat the oven to 350 degrees. Whisk the flour, baking powder, baking soda, and salt together in a bowl. Combine the buttermilk and vanilla in a measuring cup. With the electric mixer on medium-high speed, beat the butter, cream cheese, and granulated sugar until light and fluffy, about 2 minutes. Beat in the eggs, 1 at a time, until combined, then the buttermilk mixture. Reduce the speed to low and add the flour mixture gradually until combined.

3. Divide the dough into 6 equal pieces. Pat each piece into a 5-inch disk, wrap it in plastic wrap, and refrigerate until firm, about 30 minutes. Meanwhile, cut six 9-inch parchment rounds. Following the photos on page 244, line an 8-inch round cake pan with a parchment round and press the chilled dough disk into the bottom of the lined pan. Transfer the round to a rimmed baking sheet. Repeat, placing the second round ½ inch apart from the first round. Repeat with 2 additional disks on a second rimmed baking sheet. Bake until just golden around the edges, 16 to 20 minutes, switching and rotating the sheets halfway through. Cool for 10 minutes on the sheets, then transfer to the counter to cool completely. Repeat with the remaining dough.

4. TO ASSEMBLE: Place 1 cooled cake round on a serving platter. Spread ½ cup of the cooled berry mixture over the cake, leaving a ½-inch border uncovered, then top with another cake round. Repeat with the remaining berry mixture and cake rounds, finishing with cake. Cover with plastic wrap and refrigerate until the cake has softened, at least 8 hours or up to 3 days. Dust with confectioners' sugar and serve. (Both the berry mixture and cake rounds can be frozen for up to 1 month. Freeze the cooked and cooled berry mixture in an airtight container. Wrap the individual cake rounds in plastic wrap and foil. Bring all the components to room temperature before assembling.)

ANGEL FOOD CAKE

ANGEL FOOD CAKE HAS A VERY SHORT INGREDIENT list—mostly egg whites, sugar, and flour. As with so many simple recipes, the devil is in the details. To name a few, if you don't sift the flour, separate the egg whites with tremendous care, and fold with a gentle touch, the majestic, snowy-white cake turns out depressingly dense, squat, and wet. Over seven weeks in the kitchen, we baked more than 100 angel food cakes to discover, once and for all, what matters, what doesn't, and how to achieve perfection.

Unlike most other cakes, angel food cake uses no butter or oil—you don't even grease the cake pan. It doesn't call for baking soda or baking powder, either, relying solely on beaten egg whites for its dramatic height. It's cooled in the pan it is baked in, upside down and suspended in the air. To make angel food cake, you whip egg whites with sugar and cream of tartar until white peaks form, fold in flour and flavorings, and bake.

Given the brevity of the recipe and the constancy of ingredients and basic method, it's puzzling how widely the outcomes can vary. Several experienced test cooks recently baked angel food cakes from nearly identical recipes on the same day in the same kitchen with the same equipment. Some of the cakes were tender and

MAKING ANGEL FOOD CAKE

1. Process the sugar in a food processor until fine and powdery to ensure a light and fluffy cake. Measure out half of the sugar and reserve. Add the flour mixture to the remaining sugar and process to aerate.

2. Separate each egg over a small bowl, so that one sloppily cracked egg won't ruin the whole batch (the whites will not whip properly if they contain specks of yolk). Cold eggs are easier to separate than warm eggs.

3. Start whipping on medium-low speed until foamy, which will allow more air to be trapped within the egg whites. Add cream of tartar (which is acidic) to help the whites to get a nice loft when whipping.

4. Increase the mixer speed to medium-high and whip the whites to soft, billowy mounds. Gradually whip in the reserved, processed sugar 1 tablespoon at a time, which helps make the whipped whites sturdier.

5. Sift the flour mixture into the whipped egg whites in three additions—for easier incorporation. Folding the ingredients together helps preserve the fluffy, airy texture of the whipped whites.

6. If your cake pan does not have feet, invert the baked cake over the neck of a heavy-bottomed bottle or a large funnel. Let the cake cool completely upside down to ensure the crumb has the fluffiest texture.

statuesque with a delicate crumb, others misshapen and heavy. Why?

Even I, an experienced baker, grew intimidated by the dire warnings I read while researching recipes. But through testing I discovered several steps that made no difference or could be streamlined. To begin with, cold egg whites will whip to the same volume as room-temperature eggs (they'll just take a few minutes longer). And don't panic if you slightly under- or overbeat them. We tried both, several times, and our cakes turned out respectably regardless. Next, you do indeed need to sift the flour—but not nearly as much as you think. And if you jump up and down in front of the oven or open the door to take a peek, several times, your cake won't fall.

Some steps do matter. The real key to angel food cake lies in voluminous, stable egg whites. The merest speck of yolk precludes whipping them to peaks; even just ½ teaspoon of yolk in 12 whites prevented peaks from forming. Adding cream of tartar to foamy whites is a step I found in many recipes, and one worth keeping since it offered insurance against deflated whites. It is acidic, which helps stabilize egg whites, as would lemon juice or vinegar, but you would be able to taste those.

As for the flour, some recipes call for sifting it up to eight times. I tried making a cake with flour at the opposite extreme, skipping sifting entirely, but the resulting cake was squat. After a multitude of tests, I came up with a creative solution that maximized the results. I put the flour in the food processor to aerate it quickly and then sifted it just once. I also found that cake flour was far superior to all-purpose. Whereas the latter produced cakes that tasters said had a texture resembling Wonder Bread, cake flour, which is finer than all-purpose, produced a delicate, tender crumb and was easier to incorporate into the whites. The exact amount of flour used was also critical. No matter what I tried, the cake was slightly wet and spongy when I used 1 cup of flour. In despair I added just 2 tablespoons additional flour and my cake had a flawlessly tender texture time after time.

For the sugar, I tested cakes made with both plain granulated sugar and confectioners' sugar, and both were acceptable, but somewhat heavy. Simply putting the granulated sugar in the food processor was a happy medium: fine, light, and clump-free sugar that wouldn't deflate the egg whites.

After almost two months of baking as many as six cakes a day, I finally had what I thought was the perfect recipe. But would it produce consistently good results for everyone? I gave it to several inexperienced bakers. Each produced identical tall, sweet stunners. I couldn't rest until I found out if they'd run into any problems. Their answer was better than angels singing: "Piece of cake!"

—LYNN CLARK, *Cook's Country*

Angel Food Cake

SERVES 10 TO 12

Do not use all-purpose flour. Our tasters unflatteringly compared a cake made with it to Wonder Bread. If your angel food cake pan does not have a removable bottom, line the bottom of the pan with parchment paper. In either case, do not grease the pan (or the paper).

1 cup plus 2 tablespoons (4½ ounces) cake flour (see note)
¼ teaspoon salt
1¾ cups (12¼ ounces) sugar
12 large egg whites
1½ teaspoons cream of tartar
1 teaspoon vanilla extract

1. Adjust an oven rack to the lower-middle position and heat the oven to 325 degrees. Whisk the flour and salt in a bowl. Process the sugar in a food processor until fine and powdery, about 1 minute. Reserve half of the sugar in a small bowl. Add the flour mixture to the food processor with the remaining sugar and process until aerated, about 1 minute.

2. With an electric mixer on medium-low speed, beat the egg whites and cream of tartar until frothy, about 1 minute. Increase the speed to medium-high. With the motor running, slowly add the reserved sugar and beat until soft peaks form, about 6 minutes. Add the vanilla and mix until incorporated.

3. Sift the flour mixture over the egg whites in 3 additions, folding gently with a rubber spatula after each addition until incorporated. Scrape the mixture into a 12-cup ungreased tube pan.

4. Bake until a toothpick inserted into the center comes out clean and cracks in the cake appear dry, 40 to 45 minutes. Cool, inverted, to room temperature, about 3 hours. To unmold, run a knife along the interior of the pan and turn the cake out onto a platter. Serve.

VARIATIONS

Lemon–Poppy Seed Angel Food Cake

Follow the recipe for Angel Food Cake, adding 2 tablespoons grated lemon zest and 2 tablespoons fresh lemon juice from 2 to 3 lemons along with the vanilla extract in step 2. Fold 1 tablespoon poppy seeds into the batter along with the flour in step 3.

Chocolate-Almond Angel Food Cake

Follow the recipe for Angel Food Cake, replacing ½ teaspoon of the vanilla extract with ½ teaspoon almond extract in step 2. Fold 2 ounces finely grated bittersweet chocolate into the batter along with the flour in step 3.

Café au Lait Angel Food Cake

Follow the recipe for Angel Food Cake, adding 1 tablespoon instant coffee or espresso powder to the food processor along with the flour in step 1. Replace ½ teaspoon of the vanilla with 1 tablespoon coffee liqueur in step 2.

INDIVIDUAL FALLEN CHOCOLATE CAKES FOR TWO

FALLEN CHOCOLATE CAKE IS AN INTENSE, RICH chocolate cake that ranges in texture from a dense, brownie-like consistency to something altogether more ethereal. It's essentially undercooked chocolate cake. And while it's a restaurant staple, those recipes aren't always translated well for the home kitchen. Nevertheless, I thought this cake would make the perfect dessert for two—only a handful of ingredients are required, and the finished cakes look so posh, they have the ability to transform any supper into a special-occasion dinner.

To begin, I had to decide on the basic method. Melting chocolate and butter together is the standard protocol found in most recipes, but from there I had two choices: I could either whip the egg yolks and whites separately and then fold them together, or I could whip whole eggs and sugar to create a thick foam. Tasters agreed that the latter method proved superior, as it delivered the rich, moist texture I was after, and it kept the recipe simple and streamlined. That left me with a recipe that consisted of melting

INDIVIDUAL FALLEN CHOCOLATE CAKES

chocolate and butter; whipping whole eggs, sugar, and flavorings into a foam; and then folding the two together. Pretty simple.

My next step was to determine how much of each ingredient I would need for two cakes. After considerable testing, I decided that 2 tablespoons of melted butter and 2 ounces of bittersweet chocolate made the dessert just moist enough and delivered a good jolt of chocolate without being overbearing. The egg quantity, however, was perhaps the most crucial element, affecting texture, richness, and moisture. I tested cakes made with two whole eggs (these had a light and spongy texture), one whole egg plus one yolk (these were moist and dark), and one whole egg (rich but light, moist, intense, and dark). The single whole egg gave me the best cakes overall, with both the flavor and texture I was after. And although some recipes use very little or no flour, I found that a modest amount (a mere tablespoon for the pair) gave the cakes some structure and lift—making them less fudge-like and more cake-like.

To bake the cakes, I greased two 6-ounce ramekins, and for an extra boost of chocolate dusted them with cocoa powder. With the dishes ready and the batter portioned, I turned my attention to oven temperatures, baking the cakes at 350, 400, and 450 degrees. At the highest temperature, the tops of the cakes were slightly burned yet the centers were a bit too runny. At 350 degrees, the dessert took on a more cake-like quality, but not in a good way—tasters noted the cakes were too dry. Choosing the middle ground, I found that 400 degrees for 10 minutes worked best, yielding a light, cake-like perimeter around a moist well of intense, gooey chocolate.

When it came to unmolding the cakes, I found it best to start by running a small knife around the edges; then I could gently invert each ramekin onto its own plate. Lifting the ramekins too soon resulted in cracked cakes, so I let the ramekins rest on the plates for a minute until the cakes completely separated from the baking dishes.

Tasters agreed, with a dusting of confectioners' sugar and a few berries sprinkled on top, these ultra-chocolaty, molten-in-the-middle cakes would turn any dining room into a four-star restaurant.

—DAN ZUCCARELLO, *America's Test Kitchen Books*

Individual Fallen Chocolate Cakes for Two

SERVES 2

These elegant cakes are slightly underbaked so that their centers remain a little saucy. Greasing the ramekins with butter and dusting with cocoa powder help to ensure that the cakes release from the ramekins cleanly. The cakes are best served warm with a dollop of whipped cream and fresh berries. You will need two 6-ounce ramekins for this recipe.

    Cocoa powder, for the ramekins
2   tablespoons unsalted butter, softened
2   ounces bittersweet or semisweet chocolate, chopped
¼   teaspoon vanilla extract
1   large egg
2   tablespoons granulated sugar
    Pinch salt
1   tablespoon unbleached all-purpose flour
    Confectioners' sugar, for dusting (optional)

1. Adjust an oven rack to the middle position and heat the oven to 400 degrees. Butter two 6-ounce ramekins and dust with cocoa powder.

NOTES FROM THE TEST KITCHEN

THE BEST CHOCOLATE ICE CREAM

Our Fallen Chocolate Cake recipe is unbeatably rich, and we expect the same intensity from our chocolate ice cream. But with so many options, which should you buy? We gathered the eight best-selling chocolate ice creams for a blind tasting. Since every product in the lineup uses Dutch-processed cocoa powder as its sole source of chocolate flavor, we learned it couldn't be the type of chocolate that distinguishes premium ice creams. It's richness, which comes from egg yolks (mass market brands replace egg yolks with emulsifiers) and lower overrun (the amount of air churned into the ice cream). But in the end, our rankings revealed the biggest factor for tasters was deep chocolate flavor. Our winner, **Ben & Jerry's Chocolate Ice Cream**, had the deepest chocolate flavor as well as being rich and creamy. Still, two mass-market brands, both boasting big chocolate flavor, came in close behind. (See page 299 for more information about our testing results.)

2. Combine the butter and chocolate in a medium microwave-safe bowl and microwave on high until melted, 1 to 3 minutes, stirring often. Stir in the vanilla.

3. In a large bowl, whip the egg with an electric mixer on medium-low speed until foamy, about 1 minute. Increase the speed to medium-high and whip the egg to soft, billowy mounds, about 1 minute. Gradually whip in the granulated sugar and salt; continue to whip the egg until very thick and pale yellow, 5 to 10 minutes longer.

4. Scrape the whipped egg mixture on top of the chocolate mixture, then sift the flour over the top. Gently fold the mixtures together with a large rubber spatula until just incorporated and no streaks remain.

5. Divide the batter between the prepared ramekins, smooth the tops, and wipe any drops of batter off the sides. Place the ramekins on a rimmed baking sheet and bake the cakes until they have puffed about ½ inch above the rims of the ramekins and jiggle slightly in the center when shaken very gently, 10 to 13 minutes.

6. Run a small knife around the edges of the cakes. Gently invert each ramekin onto an individual serving plate and let sit until the cakes release themselves from the ramekins, about 1 minute. Remove the ramekins, dust the cakes with confectioners' sugar (if using), and serve immediately.

VARIATION

Individual Fallen Chocolate-Orange Cakes for Two
Follow the recipe for Individual Fallen Chocolate Cakes, stirring ½ teaspoon grated orange zest and 1 teaspoon orange-flavored liqueur into the melted chocolate with the vanilla in step 2.

REDUCED-FAT GERMAN CHOCOLATE CAKE

GERMAN CHOCOLATE CAKE (WHICH IS IN FACT, ALL-American, named after the man who developed the variety of chocolate—German's Sweet Chocolate—used in the cake) cuts an impressive swath: Three layers of chocolate cake sandwiched with a gooey caramel frosting that brims with coconut and pecans. If you don't find its towering stature intimidating, surely all the calories (almost 750) and the fat (45 grams) in just a single slice will make you think twice. But how do you shave calories from a cake that's defined by its cloying sweetness and lavish use of butter, egg yolks, and nuts?

Full-fat German chocolate cakes are mild and moist, and hew closely to the recipe on the back of the German's Sweet Chocolate box, made from a mix of flour, butter, German's chocolate, eggs, buttermilk or sour cream, and plenty of sugar. The frosting is made by heating sweetened condensed or evaporated whole milk with butter, egg yolks, coconut, and pecans.

Cutting portion size to cut calorie count isn't our normal approach, but typical slices of this cake are gargantuan. After several tests I determined that slimming the recipe from three layers to two still yielded ample slices. Now I could work on minimizing the fat.

Switching from full-fat to low-fat sour cream and trimming the butter from 8 to 3 tablespoons slashed about 50 calories and almost 6 grams of fat per slice. For the chocolate, I wanted to retain the old-fashioned, mild flavor that distinguishes this cake, yet generate enough chocolate impact to hold its own against the caramel-coconut-pecan frosting. I rejected German's chocolate, which tastes of sugar, not chocolate. After many rounds of testing, I found a combination of chopped milk chocolate and Dutch-processed cocoa worked best.

The cake was now lower in calories yet flavorful, so I had a bit of wiggle room to adjust the frosting. A base of fat-free evaporated milk instead of whole saved 10 calories and almost 2 grams of fat per slice. For deeply caramelized flavor, I used all brown sugar. Then I reduced the amount of butter from 6 tablespoons to 2, which saved about 30 calories and almost 4 grams of fat per portion.

Fatty egg yolks usually thicken the frosting. Substituting egg whites improved my numbers but made the frosting grainy. Cooking down the evaporated milk on the stovetop failed to thicken the icing. But 3 tablespoons of cornstarch did the trick. To finish the frosting, I added a moderate amount of chopped pecans and sweetened coconut (though you'd think unsweetened would be the lighter choice, a little research revealed that ounce for ounce, sweetened coconut has fewer calories and less fat than unsweetened. Sweetened coconut contains more water, and more water means fewer calories per cup of coconut.) With no loss in deliciousness, my cake now had just 340 calories and 13 grams of fat per slice. Not bad at all.

—KRIS WIDICAN, *Cook's Country*

Reduced-Fat German Chocolate Cake

SERVES 12

For an accurate measurement of boiling water, bring a full kettle of water to a boil, then measure out the desired amount. Avoid fat-free sour cream, which will make the cake gummy. Toast the coconut and nuts in a 325-degree oven, shaking the pan often, for about 15 minutes.

CAKE

- 3 ounces milk chocolate, chopped
- 3 tablespoons Dutch-processed cocoa powder
- ⅓ cup boiling water
- 1⅓ cups unbleached all-purpose flour
- ½ teaspoon baking soda
- 3 tablespoons unsalted butter, softened
- ½ cup (3½ ounces) packed brown sugar
- ⅓ cup (2⅓ ounces) granulated sugar
- ½ teaspoon salt
- 3 large eggs, at room temperature
- 1 teaspoon vanilla extract
- ½ cup low-fat sour cream, at room temperature

FROSTING

- 1 cup fat-free evaporated milk
- 3 tablespoons cornstarch
- 2 tablespoons unsalted butter
- ⅔ cup (4⅔ ounces) packed brown sugar
- ¼ teaspoon salt
- 1 tablespoon vanilla extract
- ⅓ cup pecans, toasted (see note) and chopped fine
- ½ cup sweetened shredded coconut, toasted (see note)

1. FOR THE CAKE: Adjust an oven rack to the lower-middle position and heat the oven to 350 degrees. Grease and flour two 9-inch cake pans. Whisk the chocolate, cocoa, and boiling water in a bowl until smooth and let cool. Combine the flour and baking soda in a separate bowl. With an electric mixer on medium-low speed, beat the butter, sugars, and salt until combined. Increase the speed to medium and beat until the mixture lightens in color and sticks to the sides of the bowl, about 1 minute. Scrape down the bowl, then add the eggs, 1 at a time, and mix until well combined, about 45 seconds. Reduce the speed to low and add the chocolate mixture and vanilla until incorporated. Add the flour mixture in 3 additions, alternating with 2 additions of sour cream, and mix until just combined.

2. Divide the batter into the prepared pans and bake until a toothpick inserted in the center comes out clean, 10 to 15 minutes. Cool the cakes in the pans for 10 minutes, then turn them out onto a wire rack and cool completely, at least 1 hour.

3. FOR THE FROSTING: Whisk the evaporated milk, cornstarch, butter, brown sugar, and salt in a medium saucepan over medium-high heat until bubbling, about 3 minutes. Continue to cook until the mixture is thickened, about 1 minute. Off the heat, stir in the vanilla and all but 1 tablespoon each of the pecans and coconut. Cool to room temperature.

4. Place 1 cake round on a platter. Spread with half of the frosting, then top with the second cake. Spread the remaining frosting over the top of the cake. Sprinkle with the remaining pecans and coconut and serve. (Once the cakes are cooled in step 2, they can be wrapped in plastic wrap and stored at room temperature for up to 2 days.)

ULTIMATE CHOCOLATE CUPCAKES

IF CUPCAKE APPEAL IS ALL ABOUT GETTING THE BEST attributes of cake in a portable package, the irony is that most of today's highly specialized cupcake bakeries either can't deliver the goods—a moist, tender crumb capped with just enough creamy, not-too-sweet frosting—or they deviate from the classic model. To keep us interested, bakers tend to doll up the standbys with gimmicky alternatives like "Cinnamon Chai Pecan Sticky," "Mojito," and "Caramel Apple." And the core elements—cake and frosting—are barely palatable.

Call me old-fashioned, but I prefer a simple, decadent chocolate cupcake any day. To get a sense of what's on the market, I held two tastings: one for chocolate cupcakes I'd gathered from half a dozen famous bakeries around the country and another for a handful of published recipes I baked myself. The results were grim. The bakery and homemade confections alike were fraught with a cupcake Catch-22: If the cakes packed decent chocolate flavor, their structure was too crumbly. Conversely, if the cakes balanced moisture and tenderness without crumbling, the chocolate turned wimpy. I was beginning to understand what I was up against.

INNER SECRET FOR SUPER-CHOCOLATY CUPCAKES

CHOCOLATE, INSIDE AND OUT

After packing lots of chocolate into the batter, we raised the bar one notch higher by filling the cupcake with a dollop of truffle-like ganache.

MAKING MERINGUE-STYLE BUTTERCREAM

Whereas uncooked frostings tend to be greasy and grainy, our Swiss meringue buttercream gets its satiny-smooth texture from whisking the egg whites and sugar in a double boiler, then whipping the mixture with softened butter.

1. Whisk the egg white mixture until it is foamy and registers 150 degrees on an instant-read thermometer.

2. Beat the mixture in a standing mixer until slightly cooled, then add the softened butter, 1 tablespoon at a time.

3. Add the vanilla and any additional ingredients (such as melted, cooled, chocolate) specific to the type of icing you choose to make, then whip until light and fluffy.

DECORATING CHOCOLATE CUPCAKES

While developing the recipe for Ultimate Chocolate Cupcakes with Ganache Filling, we experimented with countless decorating techniques. Here are two of our favorites:

FLAT TOP WITH COATED SIDES

1. Place 2 to 3 tablespoons of frosting on each cupcake, forming a thick layer. Using a small offset spatula, spread to create a flat top.

2. Using the spatula, smooth the edges of the frosting so they are flush with the sides of the cupcake. Reflatten the top as necessary.

3. Place a topping such as chopped nuts on a plate. Holding the cupcake at its base, gently roll the outer edges of the frosting in the topping.

PIPED

1. Place the frosting in a pastry bag fitted with a ½-inch plain or star tip. Starting at the outside edge and working inward, pipe the frosting into a spiral.

2. Sprinkle lightly with a topping, if desired.

There was one recipe I hadn't tried: my favorite chocolate cake. It features a double whammy of cocoa powder (½ cup) and melted bittersweet chocolate (3 ounces), plus the chocolate-enhancing flavor of brewed coffee (½ cup). These elements, when combined with tangy buttermilk (an appropriately less sweet alternative to regular milk), make for moist cake with unabashed chocolate intensity. Figuring a cupcake is just a pint-size version of a cake, I mixed up the batter, portioned it into a muffin pan, and popped it into the oven. About 18 minutes later, we dug in—and the swooning began. Here, my tasters declared, was a chocolate cupcake that really tasted like chocolate. The only problem? Piles of ultra-tender crumbs littering the countertop. As fork food, this rich, tender cake was ideal, but eaten without utensils, it was more of a cleanup project.

I quickly fingered the cocoa and melted chocolate as culprits in the too-tender crumb. Specifically, the texture suffered from too little gluten development and too much fat. Gluten forms when proteins in flour bind together with liquid and become pliable; the more the proteins are worked into the liquid (the cake batter), the more gluten develops, and the stronger the crumb. Fat (like chocolate), meanwhile, acts as a tenderizer to create a delicate crumb.

Because all that cocoa powder contains no gluten-forming proteins, it dilutes the flour, while the extra fat from the chocolate made this cake too tender for cupcakes. To strengthen the batter I had to cut back on both chocolate components. Fifty percent less cocoa and two-thirds less bittersweet chocolate later, I had perfectly portable (if slightly dry) cupcakes—and predictably feeble chocolate flavor.

I needed to work in more chocolate without disrupting the batter's structure. On a whim, I tossed a handful of chocolate chips into the batter; unfortunately, this produced warm bits of gooey chocolate that cooled into hard, distracting lumps. Stymied, I figured my only alternative was to make do with what little chocolate I had and try to ramp up its flavor.

Thus began my experiments in eccentric chocolate flavor enhancement, gleaned from self-professed chocoholics' claims on the Internet, such as combining chocolate (which derives most of its complex taste through the Maillard reaction when the cacao beans are roasted) with other sources of Maillard-produced flavor compounds such as liquid smoke, full-bodied beers, even flour that I smoked on the grill for an hour. These ideas led to dead ends, as did stirring in glutamate-rich flavor enhancers like miso paste or soy sauce. Not only were these confections no more chocolaty, their flavor ranged from fermented to salty, sour, ashy, or bitter.

Getting back to more conventional tactics, if I had to work with less chocolate, the least I could do was take advantage of the one chocolate-enhancing ingredient I was already using: coffee. Mixing the cocoa with hot coffee eked out more chocolate flavor. Then I wondered if I could exchange the other liquid component—buttermilk—for even more. The effect might benefit me twofold, since the taste of rich dairy products typically obscures other flavors. So I swapped out the buttermilk and increased the amount of coffee to ¾ cup. Bingo. The chocolate flavor was noticeably more pronounced. (To activate the baking soda without the buttermilk's acid, I added 2 teaspoons of white vinegar.) I still had another dairy ingredient to consider: butter. I had my doubts, but trying more neutral-flavored vegetable oil in place of melted butter seemed worth a shot. The result? Not a dramatic leap, but definitely a good move. In a side-by-side tasting, even the skeptics picked the oil-only cupcakes, citing fuller, unadulterated chocolate flavor. Even better, this batch was extra moist.

I'd done all I could think of to boost the existing chocolate flavor when a colleague suggested I toughen up the structure of the cupcake that I had. That way, I could add back the extra chocolate without tenderizing it too much. I tried adding an extra egg or two, but this made the texture rubbery. Next, I overmixed the batter to stimulate gluten development (as if I were kneading bread dough), but all that bought me was a weary arm. However, thinking about bread baking gave me a hint: bread flour. Specifically engineered for gluten development, bread flour contains more protein than all-purpose flour and turned out a cupcake that was markedly less crumble-prone, but not tough.

With newfound room for more fat, I began to add back some of the chocolate. Tablespoon by tablespoon, I traded flour for cocoa powder until the latter maxed out at ⅓ cup, and worked the bar chocolate back up to 3 ounces for the most unapologetically chocolaty (and still sturdy) cake yet.

Still, the chocoholic in me was holding out for more. Thinking back to my attempt with chocolate chips, I missed those pockets of molten chocolate when the cake was still warm and wondered if there was another means to that end. Perhaps a mixture that would stay almost fluid even after it cooled—such as a chocolate ganache? I melted a standard ganache mixture of 2 ounces bittersweet chocolate and 2 tablespoons heavy cream (plus 1 tablespoon of confectioners' sugar for a hint of sweetness), let the mixture cool until slightly firm, and then spooned a teaspoon of it onto each cupcake before baking. As the cupcakes baked, the ganache sank into the batter, but a little bit too far—a problem solved by thinning the ganache with 2 more tablespoons of cream. I'd hit chocolate nirvana.

Now, about that frosting. Too many of the bakery cupcakes we sampled paraded swirly tufts of gritty, sickly-sweet icing that cracked and disintegrated like cotton candy. I was after something more refined. A second dose of chocolate ganache took the chocolate intensity too far, but tasters thought a fluffy seven-minute meringue frosting felt insubstantial. Buttercream seemed like a reasonable compromise, but tasters vetoed the graininess of quick versions calling for simply beating butter together with confectioners' sugar.

That left me with cooked buttercreams, and I opted for the Swiss meringue variety, where egg whites and granulated sugar are heated over a double boiler, then whipped with knobs of softened butter. The result is silky and decadent, without the weight and greasiness of other rich frostings. Velvety with just enough sweetness, this buttercream crowned the cake perfectly and even lent itself to a number of easy flavor variations. After more than two months and 800 cupcakes baked, I finally had the perfect, ultimate version.

—YVONNE RUPERTI, *Cook's Illustrated*

Ultimate Chocolate Cupcakes with Ganache Filling

MAKES 12 CUPCAKES

Use a high-quality bittersweet or semisweet chocolate for this recipe, such as one of the test kitchen's favorite baking chocolates, Callebaut Intense Dark Chocolate L-60–40NV or Ghirardelli Bittersweet Chocolate Baking Bar. Though we highly recommend the ganache filling, you can omit it for a more traditional cupcake. For simple decorating techniques, see page 252.

GANACHE FILLING

2 ounces bittersweet chocolate, chopped fine (see note)

¼ cup heavy cream

1 tablespoon confectioners' sugar

CHOCOLATE CUPCAKES

3 ounces bittersweet chocolate, chopped fine (see note)

⅓ cup (1 ounce) Dutch-processed cocoa powder

¾ cup hot coffee

¾ cup (4⅛ ounces) bread flour

¾ cup (5¼ ounces) granulated sugar

½ teaspoon salt

½ teaspoon baking soda

6 tablespoons vegetable oil

2 large eggs

2 teaspoons white vinegar

1 teaspoon vanilla extract

1 recipe frosting (recipes follow)

1. FOR THE GANACHE FILLING: Place the chocolate, cream, and confectioners' sugar in a medium microwave-safe bowl. Microwave until the mixture is warm to the touch, 20 to 30 seconds. Whisk the mixture until smooth, then refrigerate until just chilled, no longer than 30 minutes.

2. FOR THE CUPCAKES: Adjust an oven rack to the middle position and heat the oven to 350 degrees. Line a standard-size muffin pan (cups have ½-cup capacity) with baking-cup liners. Place the chocolate and cocoa powder in a medium bowl. Pour the hot coffee over the mixture and whisk until smooth. Refrigerate until completely cool, about 20 minutes. Whisk the flour, sugar, salt, and baking soda together in a medium bowl and set aside.

3. Whisk the oil, eggs, vinegar, and vanilla into the cooled chocolate-cocoa mixture until smooth. Add the flour mixture and whisk until smooth.

4. Divide the batter evenly among the muffin pan cups. Place one slightly rounded teaspoon of the ganache filling on top of each cupcake. Bake until the cupcakes are set and just firm to the touch, 17 to 19 minutes. Cool the cupcakes in the muffin pan on a wire rack until cool enough to handle, about 10 minutes. Carefully lift each cupcake from the muffin pan and set on a wire rack. Cool to room temperature before frosting, about 1 hour.

5. TO FROST: Mound 2 to 3 tablespoons of the frosting on the center of each cupcake. Following the photos on page 252, use a small icing spatula or butter knife to ice each cupcake. (The cupcakes can be made up to 24 hours in advance and stored unfrosted in an airtight container.)

Creamy Chocolate Frosting

MAKES ABOUT 2¼ CUPS

Cool the chocolate to between 85 and 100 degrees before adding it to the frosting. If the frosting seems too soft after adding the chocolate, chill it briefly in the refrigerator and then rewhip it until creamy.

- ⅓ cup (2⅓ ounces) sugar
- 2 large egg whites
- Pinch salt
- 12 tablespoons (1½ sticks) unsalted butter, softened and cut into 12 pieces
- 6 ounces bittersweet chocolate, melted and cooled (see note)
- ½ teaspoon vanilla extract

1. Combine the sugar, egg whites, and salt in the bowl of a standing mixer, then place the bowl over a pan of simmering water. Following the photos on page 252, heat the mixture, whisking gently but constantly, until slightly thickened and foamy and it registers 150 degrees on an instant-read thermometer, 2 to 3 minutes.

2. Using the whisk attachment, beat the mixture on medium speed in a standing mixer until it reaches the consistency of shaving cream and is slightly cooled, 1 to 2 minutes. Add the butter, 1 piece at a time, until smooth and creamy. (The frosting may look curdled after half of the butter has been added; it will smooth with additional butter.) Once all the butter is added, add the cooled melted chocolate and the vanilla and mix until combined. Increase the speed to medium-high and beat until light, fluffy, and thoroughly combined, about 30 seconds, scraping the beater and sides of the bowl with a rubber spatula as necessary. (The frosting can be made up to 24 hours in advance and refrigerated in an airtight container. When ready to frost, place the frosting in a microwave-safe container and microwave briefly until just slightly softened, 5 to 10 seconds. Once warmed, stir until creamy.)

VARIATIONS

Creamy Malted Milk Chocolate Frosting

Follow the recipe for Creamy Chocolate Frosting, reducing the sugar to ¼ cup, substituting 6 ounces milk chocolate for the bittersweet chocolate, and adding ¼ cup malted milk powder to the frosting with the vanilla extract in step 2.

Creamy Vanilla Frosting

Follow the recipe for Creamy Chocolate Frosting, omitting the bittersweet chocolate and increasing the sugar to ½ cup. (If the final frosting seems too thick, warm the mixer bowl briefly over a pan of simmering water. Then place the bowl back on the mixer and beat on medium-high speed until creamy.)

Creamy Peanut Butter Frosting

For an extra hit of peanut flavor, we like to garnish these cupcakes with ½ cup chopped peanuts.

Follow the recipe for Creamy Chocolate Frosting, omitting the bittersweet chocolate, increasing the sugar to ½ cup, and increasing the salt to ⅛ teaspoon. Add ⅔ cup creamy peanut butter to the frosting with the vanilla extract in step 2.

Creamy Butterscotch Frosting

Follow the recipe for Creamy Vanilla Frosting, substituting ⅓ cup packed dark brown sugar for the granulated sugar and increasing the salt to ½ teaspoon.

CHEWY BROWNIES

YES, IT WAS A DICEY ADMISSION TO MAKE TO MY colleagues as we discussed brownies we crave most. Some praised fudgy specimens, while others talked up moist, fluffy cakey confections. But then it slipped out: my nostalgia for the satisfying chewiness of the just-add-eggs-and-oil brownies I grew up eating at family picnics and bake sales. Nobody said anything. Then one ally voiced her support, and another followed. Pretty soon, any previous high-minded idea of what makes a brownie irresistible had been eclipsed by the memory of versions from a cardboard box.

Of course, everyone agreed that box-mix brownies are all about texture, as even the best suffer from a

MAKING A FOIL SLING

1. Fold an 18-inch length of foil lengthwise to an 8-inch width. Fit the foil into the length of a 13 by 9-inch baking dish, pushing it into the corners and up the sides of the pan; allow the excess to overhang the pan edges.

2. Fit a 14-inch length of foil into the width of the pan, perpendicular to the first sheet (if using extra-wide foil, fold the second sheet lengthwise to a 12-inch width). Spray with nonstick cooking spray.

CHEWY BROWNIES: IT'S ABOUT THE FAT

The secret to a box-mix brownie's chewy texture boils down to the ratio of saturated to unsaturated fat.

BOX FORMULA
28% saturated fat
72% unsaturated fat

Besides containing the optimal ratio of fat types, box brownies make use of highly processed powdered shortening to achieve a chewy texture.

CLASSIC FORMULA
64% saturated fat
36% unsaturated fat

Classic brownies are made with all butter for a high proportion of solid, saturated fat that leads to a tender, not chewy, texture.

OUR FORMULA
29% saturated fat
71% unsaturated fat

Our brownies contain a low-tech combo of butter and vegetable oil that creates a similar chew—and imparts a richer taste than shortening.

markedly artificial, even waxy chemical sweetness. My goal was clear: a homemade brownie with chewiness (and a shiny, crackly top) to rival the box-mix standard—but flush with a rich, all-natural chocolate flavor.

I rounded up as many recipes as I could find with "chewy" in the title. It became clear why the box brownie has retained its foothold: Not one could actually lay claim to such a quality. All brownie recipes are composed of the same basic ingredients: fat (usually butter), eggs, salt, sugar, vanilla, flour (typically all-purpose), and of course chocolate (most often from an unsweetened bar). For fudgy brownies, use less flour and more chocolate; for cakey, do the reverse. None of the so-called chewy brownie recipes I consulted did anything different—their ratios of fat and chocolate tended to produce brownies somewhere between fudgy and cakey for a texture that was merely soft, not chewy. Their mixing techniques were also the same.

I then tried recipes with unusual techniques or ingredients, from substituting condensed milk and biscuit mix for the flour to baking brownies on a pizza stone to underbaking the brownies and then chilling them in an ice bath. All failures.

Clearly, I was on my own. I tried to think of other chewy baked goods. Brown sugar cookies came to mind. Because brown sugar and corn syrup both attract and retain water, cookie dough containing high levels of these ingredients bakes up moister and chewier than the exact same dough made with drier white sugar. Thinking a similar concept might work for my brownies, I took one of the chewier recipes I found calling for 4 ounces unsweetened chocolate, 8 ounces butter, 5 ounces flour, 2 eggs, and 14 ounces sugar and replaced the white sugar with a combination of brown sugar and corn syrup. Not only did it do nothing for texture, but it also managed to lose the shiny, crackly crust. Regular sugar would have to stay.

It was time to call for reinforcements. I consulted with our science editor to see if he knew of any tricks boxed brownies use to achieve their chewiness. He responded with a phrase that completely changed the direction of my research: high-tech shortening system.

When I saw the "partially hydrogenated soybean and cottonseed oils" on the brownie-mix box, I had dismissed them as fats. But it turns out the key to the texture of a box brownie resides in the specific types and amounts of fat it includes. Fat can be divided into two broad types—saturated and unsaturated. Both types consist of carbon atoms strung together in long chains. In predominantly saturated fats such as shortening (a.k.a. partially hydrogenated vegetable oil), each of these carbon atoms has the maximum number of hydrogen atoms attached to it. The hydrogen acts as a buttress to keep the carbon chains rigid, so they pack together, forming a fat that is solid even at room temperature. Unsaturated fats, such as vegetable oils, have fewer hydrogen atoms, resulting in a fat that is liquid at room temperature. The right combination of rigid and flexible chains—the shortening system—is what gives box brownies their unique texture.

Box brownie mixes come with the saturated-fat component. When a cook then adds unsaturated vegetable oil to this mix, the liquid fat and powdered solid fat in the mix combine in a ratio designed to deliver maximum chew. So I would have to discover the perfect proportion of liquid to solid fat—without the aid of high-tech fats used by brownie mix manufacturers.

I'd keep the butter as my saturated fat—a far more flavorful choice than vegetable shortening, which manufacturers resort to for shelf stability. To simplify my calculations, I eliminated the melted chocolate and used cocoa powder, which contains very little fat by comparison. Once I figured out the ideal fat ratios, I could put the bar chocolate back in. For an unsaturated fat, I stuck to the box-mix choice: vegetable oil.

Next I devised a series of recipes that all had roughly the same amount of total fat, but with varying ratios of butter to vegetable oil. Brownies containing mostly saturated fat baked up tender and not at all chewy, while brownies made with mostly unsaturated fat were the chewier ones. Eventually, I hit on the magic formula: 29 percent saturated fat to 71 percent unsaturated—or about a 1–3 ratio. To see how these figures compared to my gold standard Ghirardelli Chocolate Supreme box-mix brownies, I crunched the numbers on the back of the mix. Bingo! They virtually mirrored my results, with 28 percent saturated fat to 72 percent unsaturated.

But even with the 1–3 ratio, problems persisted: My brownies left a slick of grease on the plate, and with cocoa powder the sole source of chocolate, their flavor was lackluster. I attacked the greasiness first. Careful to stay close to the 1–3 ratio, I decreased the fat content overall, but this gave me dry brownies. Emulsifiers can help prevent fats from separating and leaking out during baking. While recently developing a recipe for vinaigrette, we found that mayonnaise—an emulsion itself—was able to keep the dressing from separating. Though it seemed an odd move, I tried replacing some of the oil in my recipe with mayo. It worked surprisingly well, but tasters were seriously taken aback when the "secret ingredient" was revealed. Delving deeper, I identified the active emulsifier in the mayonnaise as lecithin, a phospholipid that occurs naturally in egg yolks. The simple addition of two extra yolks to my recipe in exchange for a little oil made greasiness (and the mayonnaise) a thing of the past.

Now I could finally deal with the chocolate flavor. I first tried tweaks that wouldn't affect the fats. Espresso powder deepens chocolate flavor, and stirring 1½ teaspoons into the boiling water along with the cocoa helped, but I knew I could do better. A little research revealed that although the total fat in unsweetened chocolate is lower per ounce than in an equivalent amount of butter, it contains a similar ratio of saturated to unsaturated fat. This fact suggested that I could replace 2 tablespoons of butter (1 ounce) with 2 ounces of unsweetened chocolate and still stay very close to the ideal fat ratio. And with the unsweetened chocolate providing more pure chocolate flavor, I cut the cocoa powder back to ⅓ cup.

I had just about homed in on the perfect chewy chocolaty brownie when one last thought occurred to me: Only chocolate that is melted and incorporated into the batter actually affects the ratio of fats in the mix. Theoretically, I should be able to incorporate as many chocolate chunks into the mixed batter as I wanted, and as long as they didn't melt until the batter started baking, it should have no effect on texture. I whipped up another batch, folding in a full 6 ounces of bittersweet chocolate chunks just before baking. The results were as close as any cook could come without the benefits of industrial processing on her side: chewy, fudgy bars with gooey pockets of melted chocolate that evoked images of bake sales past, but with complex flavor and just enough adult flourish to lift them out of the realm of child's fare.

—ANDREA GEARY, *Cook's Illustrated*

Chewy Brownies

MAKES 2 DOZEN 2-INCH BROWNIES

For an accurate measurement of boiling water, bring a full kettle of water to a boil, then measure out the desired amount. For the chewiest texture, it is important to let the brownies cool thoroughly before cutting. If your baking dish is glass, cool the brownies for 10 minutes, then remove them promptly from the pan (otherwise, the superior heat retention of glass can lead to overbaking). While any high-quality chocolate can be used, our preferred brands of bittersweet chocolate are Callebaut Intense Dark Chocolate L-60–40NV and Ghirardelli Bittersweet Chocolate Baking Bar. Our preferred brand of unsweetened chocolate is Scharffen Berger.

- ⅓ cup (1 ounce) Dutch-processed cocoa powder
- 1½ teaspoons instant espresso (optional)
- ½ cup plus 2 tablespoons boiling water (see note)
- 2 ounces unsweetened chocolate, chopped fine
- 4 tablespoons (½ stick) unsalted butter, melted
- ½ cup plus 2 tablespoons vegetable oil
- 2 large eggs
- 2 large egg yolks
- 2 teaspoons vanilla extract
- 2½ cups (17½ ounces) sugar
- 1¾ cups (8¾ ounces) unbleached all-purpose flour
- ¾ teaspoon salt
- 6 ounces bittersweet chocolate, cut into ½-inch pieces

1. Adjust an oven rack to the lowest position and heat the oven to 350 degrees. Following the photos on page 256, line a 13 by 9-inch baking dish with a foil sling, lightly coat with vegetable oil spray, and set aside.

2. Whisk the cocoa powder, espresso powder (if using), and boiling water together in a large bowl until smooth. Add the unsweetened chocolate and whisk until the chocolate is melted. Whisk in the melted butter and oil. (The mixture may look curdled.) Add the eggs, yolks, and vanilla and continue to whisk until smooth and homogeneous. Whisk in the sugar until fully incorporated. Add the flour and salt and mix with a rubber spatula until combined. Fold in the bittersweet chocolate pieces.

3. Scrape the batter into the prepared pan and bake until a toothpick inserted halfway between the edge and center comes out with just a few moist crumbs attached, 30 to 35 minutes. Transfer the pan to a wire rack and cool for 1½ hours.

4. Using the foil overhang, lift the brownies from the pan. Return the brownies to the wire rack and let cool completely, about 1 hour. Cut into 2-inch squares and serve. (The brownies can be stored in an airtight container at room temperature for up to 4 days.)

SHORTBREAD

IF YOUR EXPERIENCE WITH SHORTBREAD IS LIMITED to bland, chalky specimens from a tin, you might wonder how this bar came to be one of the British Isles' most famous teacakes. But when shortbread is made well, it's easy to understand why it earned a reputation as a favorite of high-ranking palates from Mary, Queen of Scots to Elizabeth II. The best are tawny brown and crumble in the mouth with a pure, buttery richness.

And yet, its history left few clues to reproducing a good version. The basics have changed little: Combine flour, sugar, butter, and salt, pat the dough into a round, and bake. But recipes I unearthed varied in their proportions. Some called for equal parts butter and flour, and some for only half this ratio; several included ingredients like rice flour or cornstarch. Results were all over the map. While some cookies crumbled in my hand before I could take a bite, others were sturdy to a fault, and still others turned out either greasy or overly airy and cakelike. Moreover, nearly every version suffered from some degree of uneven cooking and overbrowning.

I decided to first limit my ingredients to the basic four. For proportions, I settled on a moderate 4-5 ratio, with 8 ounces butter, 10 ounces flour, ⅔ cup sugar, and ¼ teaspoon salt. For the mixing method, I tested the most traditional approach, which is like making pie crust: Cut the butter and dry ingredients together until they form wet crumbs, then pack the crumbs together into a dough. I also made one batch in which I creamed the butter and sugar before adding the flour. For a third batch, I employed reverse creaming, mixing the flour and sugar before adding the butter.

Shortbread traditionally takes one of three shapes: one large circle with a hole cut in the center (this ensures

SHORTBREAD

even cooking) and scored into wedges; individual round cookies; or rectangular "fingers." Settling on the wedge shape, I pressed the dough into a 9-inch disk, made a hole in the center using a biscuit cutter, and placed the short-bread in a 450-degree oven for a few minutes. Following the high-low baking protocol, I then reduced the oven temperature to 300 degrees and continued to bake the cookies for an hour before scoring and cooling them.

The traditional, packed-crumb method produced cookies that were crumbly in some spots and brittle in others. Regular creaming incorporated too much air. Reverse creaming, which creates less aeration, yielded the best results and was the way to go. I reduced the butter from 16 to 14 tablespoons for a pliable dough with plenty of buttery flavor that wasn't too greasy. I swapped the white sugar for confectioners' sugar to smooth out the texture. I had made progress, but these cookies were somewhat tough and not as crisp as I wanted.

Intuition told me a higher oven temperature would drive more moisture from the cookies. I baked a batch entirely at 450 degrees, but the edges started over-browning after 10 minutes, while the inner portion remained wet. I then realized that baking shortbread is analogous to cooking a roast: The higher the oven temperature, the less even the cooking, and the more prone to overcooking the edges will be. I tried again, baking a second batch at 450 degrees for five minutes (to set the dough) and then lowering the temperature to 250 degrees. Better, but still not perfect.

Early shortbread was made by leaving the dough in a warm oven heated by dying embers. What if I briefly baked the shortbread, shut off the oven, and left it inside until it was completely dry? With just 15 minutes or so of "real" baking and an hour with the oven turned off the results were striking: This batch was dry through and through, with an even, golden brown exterior.

Next I focused on toughness. I needed to limit gluten development. Gluten, the protein matrix that lends baked goods structure and chew, forms naturally when liquid (here from the butter) and all-purpose flour are combined, even without kneading. Various 21st-century recipes have tried to solve this problem by substituting low-protein, gluten-free rice flour for some of the all-purpose flour. I gave it a try, and its crumbly texture looked promising. But when I took a bite, I found these cookies were woefully bland. Cornstarch (another gluten-free ingredient used in some modern recipes) yielded equally insipid results.

I needed to curb gluten development without compromising flavor. Scanning the pantry shelves, I spotted a possible solution: old-fashioned oats. Oats have a nutty flavor and contain few of the proteins necessary for gluten development; on top of that, they're traditional to early shortbread recipes. I ground some oats to a powder in a spice grinder and substituted ¾ cup of this home-milled oat flour for some of the all-purpose flour, keeping my fingers crossed. The resulting cookies had a promising crisp and crumbly texture, but the oats muted the buttery flavor. Still, I knew I was on the right track. For my next batch, I used less oat flour and supplemented it with a modest amount of cornstarch. This worked handsomely. The cookies were now perfectly crisp and flavorful, with an appealing hint of oat flavor.

I had one last problem to solve: spreading. As buttery shortbread bakes, it expands, losing its shape. I tried baking the dough in a traditional shortbread mold with ½-inch-high sides, but it still widened into an amorphous mass. The dough needed a substantial barrier. My solution? A springform pan collar. I set the closed collar on a parchment-lined baking sheet, patted the dough into it, and then opened the collar to give the cookie about half an inch to spread out.

History had repeated itself, and I now had the finest shortbread of its time.

—J. KENJI LOPEZ-ALT, *Cook's Illustrated*

Shortbread

MAKES 16 WEDGES

Use the collar of a springform pan to form the short-bread into an even round. Mold the shortbread with the collar in the closed position, then open the collar, but leave it in place. This allows the shortbread to expand slightly but keeps it from spreading too far. See page 292 for information on our favorite rolled oats for baking.

½ cup old-fashioned rolled oats
1½ cups (7½ ounces) unbleached all-purpose flour
⅔ cup (2⅔ ounces) confectioners' sugar
¼ cup cornstarch
½ teaspoon salt
14 tablespoons (1¾ sticks) unsalted butter, cold, cut into ⅛-inch-thick slices

1. Adjust an oven rack to the middle position and heat the oven to 450 degrees. Pulse the oats in a spice grinder or blender until reduced to a fine powder, about 10 pulses (you should have ¼ to ⅓ cup oat flour). Using a standing mixer fitted with paddle attachment, mix the oat flour, all-purpose flour, sugar, cornstarch, and salt on low speed until combined, about 5 seconds. Add the butter to the dry ingredients and continue to mix on low speed until a dough just forms and pulls away from the sides of the bowl, 5 to 10 minutes.

2. Place the collar of a 9 or 9½-inch springform pan on a parchment-lined rimmed baking sheet (do not use the springform pan bottom). Following the photos, press the dough into the collar in an even ½-inch-thick layer, smoothing the top of the dough with the back of a spoon. Place a 2-inch biscuit cutter in the center of the dough and cut out the center. Place the extracted round alongside the springform collar on the baking sheet and replace the cutter in the center of the dough. Open the springform collar, but leave it in place.

3. Bake the shortbread for 5 minutes, then reduce the oven temperature to 250 degrees. Continue to bake until the edges turn pale golden, 10 to 15 minutes longer. Remove the baking sheet from the oven and turn off the oven. Remove the springform pan collar. Use a chef's knife to score the surface of the shortbread into 16 even wedges, cutting halfway through the shortbread. Using a wooden skewer, poke 8 to 10 holes in each wedge. Return the shortbread to the oven and prop the door open with the handle of a wooden spoon, leaving a 1-inch gap at the top. Allow the shortbread to dry in the turned-off oven until pale golden in the center (the shortbread should be firm but giving to the touch), about 1 hour.

4. Transfer the baking sheet to a wire rack; cool the shortbread to room temperature, at least 2 hours. Cut the shortbread at the scored marks to separate and serve. (Wrapped well and stored at room temperature, the shortbread will keep for up to 7 days.)

VARIATION

Chocolate-Dipped Pistachio Shortbread
Follow the recipe for Shortbread, adding ½ cup finely chopped toasted pistachios to the dry ingredients in step 1. Bake and cool the shortbread as directed. Once the shortbread is cool, melt 8 ounces finely chopped bittersweet chocolate in a small heatproof bowl set over a pan of almost-simmering water, stirring once or twice, until smooth. Remove from the heat, then stir in 2 ounces more finely chopped bittersweet chocolate until smooth. Carefully dip the base of each wedge in the chocolate, allowing the chocolate to come halfway up the cookie. Scrape off the excess with your finger and place the wedges on a parchment-lined rimmed baking sheet. Refrigerate until the chocolate sets, about 15 minutes.

NOTES FROM THE TEST KITCHEN

MAKING SHORTBREAD

1. Press the dough into a closed springform pan collar set on a parchment-lined rimmed baking sheet, then smooth it over with the back of a spoon.

2. Cut a hole in the center of the dough with a 2-inch biscuit cutter, then replace the cutter in the empty hole.

3. Open the collar and bake the shortbread for 5 minutes at 450 degrees, then lower the oven temperature to 250 degrees and bake the shortbread another 10 to 15 minutes.

4. Score the partially baked shortbread into wedges, then poke 8 to 10 holes in each wedge.

5. Return the shortbread to the turned-off oven to dry, propping open the door with a wooden spoon or stick.

LEMON YOGURT MOUSSE

THOUGH MOST EVERYONE LOVES A COOL SCOOP OF ice cream—myself included—every now and then I want something a little lighter. Lemon mousse, with its sunny flavor and creamy yet light and fluffy texture, has recently become a standby in my home kitchen. But while its texture is light, like any traditional mousse, its egg yolk–enriched base combined with whipped cream, egg whites, and sugar is actually heavy on the fat (one ½-cup serving can contain up to 12 grams of fat). Could I cut some of the fat from the traditional mousse yet maintain the same appealing creamy, smooth texture and bright flavor? Just as frozen yogurt serves as the lighter cousin to ice cream, I wondered if I couldn't come up with a lemon yogurt mousse that was just as refreshing as its full-fat counterpart.

I started by rounding up a few existing recipes, all of which substituted yogurt for the heavy cream. Some also cut out the yolks entirely, and others involved whipping the egg whites with sugar over the heat (similar to making a seven-minute icing). While the icing technique for the egg whites showed good promise (it offered more structure than standard whipped egg whites), in general the results revealed a host of problems. Some were stiff

NOTES FROM THE TEST KITCHEN

MAKING LEMON YOGURT MOUSSE WITH BLUEBERRY SAUCE

1. Pour the blueberry sauce into the bottom of six 4-ounce ramekins and let them chill in the refrigerator until needed.

2. Spoon the mousse into the chilled ramekins on top of the sauce. Loosely cover with plastic wrap and refrigerate the mousse until chilled and set, 6 to 8 hours.

and springy like a creamy Jell-O; Others were foamy; and almost all were watery and separated. And then there were the issues with lemon flavor. Some recipes I made were lip-puckeringly sour while others barely registered any lemon flavor at all. Clearly, I needed to set out on my own. I wanted a smooth, creamy mousse and bright lemon flavor.

I made two decisions upfront. First, I would proceed without egg yolks. While the yolks contribute richness and a silky texture to the standard mousse, I didn't want the added fat and would find a way to create similar satisfying results without them. Besides, they made for a heavier mousse and I was after lightness. Second, I would rely on Greek yogurt for the yogurt component. It has a dense, creamy texture that the test kitchen has found works well in a number of lighter creamy desserts (as well as dips).

With those two decisions made, I was ready to experiment. I began with the texture and structure. There are two main components of a standard mousse: whipped cream and whipped egg whites. When folded together, they provide a suspension of fat and protein that gives mousse its distinctly creamy yet airy texture. Obviously I would need to find a way to achieve similar results with yogurt in lieu of the heavy cream. I already knew from early tests that a simple swap of one for the other wouldn't work. Unlike with heavy cream, whipping yogurt will not do much in terms of lightening and aerating. As a result, the whipped egg whites can't incorporate with the heavier yogurt to create the proper suspension. You end up with a dense, separated lemon pudding with the lemon juice pooling at the bottom of the ramekins. Whipping the egg whites with the sugar, icing-style, offered more structure, but not enough. I would need to create more suspension and lift.

First I tried adding more egg whites to the standard three in most recipes. I tested incorporating four and five whipped egg whites (sweetened with sugar) into a basic mousse base made with Greek yogurt and a few tablespoons of lemon juice. But each added egg white only made things worse, resulting in mousse that tasters pronounced "too eggy," with an unappealing texture. I went back to three egg whites—and to the drawing board.

In the test kitchen we often use gelatin to give structure to custard-based desserts like panna cotta and chilled soufflés. It seemed worth a try here. I started by soaking a packet of gelatin (2½ teaspoons) in warm water until dissolved, then I added it to the cooked egg whites. The results told me I was heading in the right direction; this mousse held together and the wateriness was gone. But this mousse was too stiff. Working backward from the 2½ teaspoons, I tested lesser amounts in ½-teaspoon intervals. I found the perfect structure came from ¾ teaspoon of gelatin, giving me a creamy, smooth mousse.

Up to this point I had been using full-fat Greek yogurt. I wondered if the texture would suffer if I used 2 percent or fat-free Greek yogurt instead, so that I could cut a few more calories and fat. It did. Tasters unanimously agreed that the full-fat yogurt was essential to the creaminess. The lower-fat versions lacked flavor and created a spongy texture.

But even with full-fat yogurt, tasters felt my recipe was missing some of the richness that they expected in a mousse. Crunching the numbers, I found I had a little wiggle room to add back some fat, so I whisked ¼ cup of heavy cream (full-fat recipes call for 1 cup or more) into the yogurt. This gave the mousse just the richness my tasters craved.

Finally, I could focus on flavor. I wanted a bright lemon zing that would complement the tanginess of the yogurt; however, I knew I had to be careful. Lemon juice whisked in with the yogurt added great lemon flavor, but too much liquid created a watery mousse. A few tests proved 3 tablespoons was the limit. Still, I wanted more lemon flavor. Lemon zest packs a powerful lemony punch, and 1½ teaspoons added the right amount without making the mousse bitter.

Tasters all liked the mousse as it was, but I thought it might be nice to dress it up a bit so I developed three simple berry sauces. I simply cooked blueberries, raspberries, and strawberries with a little sugar, pureed them, and strained them through a fine-mesh strainer. But spooning these sauces over the mousse didn't look as attractive as I hoped; it looked more like an afterthought. Then a fellow test cook mentioned fruit-on-the-bottom yogurt. What if I put the sauce in the ramekins before adding the mousse and letting them set? It was easy enough to do, and my tasters loved swirling the sauce into their mousse at the table. Of course, they also loved that each serving had half the fat of full-fat lemon mousse—just 6 grams. This dessert was the perfect treat for a hot summer day.

—KELLY PRICE, *America's Test Kitchen Books*

Lemon Yogurt Mousse with Blueberry Sauce
SERVES 6

You can substitute 1 cup frozen blueberries for the fresh berries.

BLUEBERRY SAUCE
- ¾ cup fresh blueberries (about 4 ounces)
- 2 tablespoons sugar
- 2 tablespoons water
- Pinch salt

MOUSSE
- 3 tablespoons water
- ¾ teaspoon unflavored gelatin
- ½ cup whole milk Greek yogurt
- ¼ cup heavy cream
- 1½ teaspoons grated lemon zest plus 3 tablespoons fresh lemon juice
- 1 teaspoon vanilla extract
- ⅛ teaspoon salt
- 3 large egg whites
- 6 tablespoons (2¾ ounces) sugar
- ¼ teaspoon cream of tartar

1. FOR THE BLUEBERRY SAUCE: Bring the blueberries, sugar, water, and salt to a simmer in a medium saucepan over medium heat, stirring occasionally. Cook until the sugar is dissolved and the fruit is heated through, 2 to 4 minutes.

2. Transfer the mixture to a blender and puree until smooth, about 20 seconds. Strain the puree through a fine-mesh strainer, pressing on the solids to extract as much puree as possible (you should have about ½ cup). Spoon the sauce evenly into six 4-ounce ramekins and refrigerate until chilled, about 20 minutes.

3. FOR THE MOUSSE: Meanwhile, pour the water into a small bowl, sprinkle the gelatin evenly over the top, and set aside to let the gelatin hydrate for 10 minutes. In a separate bowl, whisk the yogurt, heavy cream, lemon zest, lemon juice, vanilla, and salt together until smooth.

4. Whisk the egg whites, sugar, and cream of tartar together in a large bowl (or the bowl of a standing mixer). Set the bowl over a large saucepan of barely simmering water, making sure the water does not touch the bottom of the bowl. Heat the mixture, whisking constantly, until it has tripled in size and registers about 160 degrees on an instant-read thermometer, 5 to 10 minutes.

5. Off the heat, quickly whisk in the hydrated gelatin until melted. Whip the warm mixture with an electric mixer on medium-high speed until it forms stiff, shiny peaks, 4 to 6 minutes. Add the yogurt mixture and continue to whip until just combined, 30 to 60 seconds.

6. Divide the mousse evenly among the chilled ramekins with the blueberry sauce, cover tightly with plastic wrap, and refrigerate until chilled and set, 6 to 8 hours. Serve chilled. (The strained sauce can be refrigerated in an airtight container for up to 2 days. The finished mousse can be refrigerated for up to 24 hours before serving.)

VARIATIONS

Lemon Yogurt Mousse with Raspberry Sauce
For the sauce, substitute 1 cup raspberries for the blueberries.

Lemon Yogurt Mousse with Strawberry Sauce
For the sauce, substitute 1 cup halved strawberries for the blueberries and reduce the amount of water to 2 teaspoons.

FRESH BERRY GRATINS

FRESH BERRIES ARE GOOD ENOUGH TO EAT PLAIN or with a dollop of whipped cream. But when the occasion demands a more dressed-up dessert, my thoughts turn to berry gratin. This dessert is made by spreading fruit in a shallow vessel, covering it with a topping, and baking until the fruit releases its juices and the topping turns crisp and browned. Possibilities range from pastry cream to croissant crumbs to ground almonds to—my favorite—the ethereally light and foamy Italian custard called *zabaglione*.

Zabaglione is a custard that is whisked together from just three ingredients: egg yolks, sugar, and alcohol. It sounds simple, but the whisking is done over heat, so you have to be careful not to overcook the mixture and to whisk for just long enough to transform the egg yolks to the ideal thick, creamy, foamy texture.

Heat would also prove tricky for the berries—too much and they turn soupy and lose freshness; too little and they barely warm through. I wanted juicy, firm berries covered in frothy zabaglione and topped with a lightly browned crust.

Starting with a traditional zabaglione of three egg yolks, 2 tablespoons of sugar, and 3 tablespoons of sweet Marsala, I set out to first finesse the general gratin assembly and baking steps. I wanted individual gratins and a variety of fruit (raspberries, strawberries, blueberries, and blackberries). I divided 3 cups of berries among four small dishes, spooned the zabaglione over, and baked the gratins in a 400-degree oven until the custard developed a golden-brown crust. Unfortunately, beneath the beautiful custard lurked overcooked berries.

Thinking that increasing the heat might help the zabaglione brown faster and avoid overcooked berries, I ran tests increasing the temperature in 25-degree increments. But even at 500 degrees, the berries were still turning mushy by the time the topping browned. Only when I used the broiler was I able to produce a lightly browned crust and gently warmed berries. But now the berries weren't sufficiently juicy.

I tried tossing the berries with sugar to draw out their juices, sprinkling 2 teaspoons of granulated sugar (and a pinch of salt) over the berries and letting the mixture sit for 30 minutes. Then I topped the juicy berries with the custard and broiled the gratins. Success: The custard was golden brown, and the berries were warmed, with just the right texture.

I could now concentrate on the zabaglione. Up to this point, I had been whisking the yolks, sugar, and Marsala in a makeshift double boiler. I combined the ingredients in a large bowl, placed the bowl over a pot of simmering water, and whisked constantly. The custard proved finicky: Sometimes it cooked too quickly and bits of congealed yolk ruined it. At other times, it seemed underdone: Traditional recipes call for whisking just until soft peaks form, but this was insufficient and the zabaglione ended up thin and frothy.

I made three tweaks. First, I turned the heat down, keeping the water to barely a simmer. Second, I compared zabagliones made in metal and glass bowls: The metal bowl conducted heat more quickly, making the custard likely to overcook. I chose a thick glass bowl for even, gentle cooking. Finally, to get the right texture, I didn't stop whisking when soft peaks formed; instead, I waited until the custard became slightly thicker, the texture of hollandaise sauce.

Next up was flavor. Tasters said the zabaglione made with Marsala was a bit sweet. I experimented with

Grand Marnier (too orangey), Muscat (too intense), and Sauternes (exceedingly sweet). Then I changed course, trying a crisp, dry Sauvignon Blanc. Its clean flavor allowed the berries to shine, but now, no matter how long I whisked, my zabaglione was so frothy, it verged on runny. A close examination of the labels revealed that the key difference was sugar: Marsala, Grand Marnier,

and dessert wines like Sauternes all have much more dissolved sugar than Sauvignon Blanc and are therefore more viscous. My choices were to add sugar to the white wine or to find another way of supporting those bubbles.

Taking the sugar up to ¼ cup helped to keep my zabaglione stable, but now it was achingly sweet. Even 3 tablespoons was too much. Next, I tried swapping out the sugar for equal amounts of viscous corn syrup and honey, but the results were still runny.

It was time for a thickener. Cornstarch increased the viscosity of the custard, but it also made it taste starchy and chalky. I tried gelatin, but it made the mixture somewhat jellylike. What about whipped cream? I was concerned that it would mute the wine's clear flavor, but I gave it a shot. I carefully folded a few tablespoons of whipped cream into my cooked, slightly cooled zabaglione and then spooned it over the berries. Finally, I had a light, smooth, and creamy concoction cut with a touch of dry wine. The only missing element? A slight crunch. Sprinkling the custard with a mixture of brown and white sugar before broiling created a crackly, caramelized crust. I had finally achieved my goal.

—YVONNE RUPERTI, *Cook's Illustrated*

NOTES FROM THE TEST KITCHEN

STAGES OF ZABAGLIONE

As it cooks, zabaglione gradually transforms from liquid and thin to creamy and thick. Here's what to expect.

1. The mixture starts out fluid and loose. Whisking develops foamy air bubbles, which lighten the mixture as it heats.

2. With further whisking and cooking, the mixture expands, thickens, and begins to turn creamy.

3. The zabaglione is ready when it is glossy and creamy, with a consistency resembling hollandaise sauce.

GRATIN DISHES

For our Individual Fresh Berry Gratins, we wanted broiler-safe mini gratin dishes that were shallow enough to ensure maximum surface area for a lightly browned, nicely crisp crust. We tested four dishes; one was flimsy, and a few were ridiculously pricey. Our favorite, the **Le Creuset Petite Au Gratin Dish**, $9.95, heated evenly and offered a generous surface for good browning.

Individual Fresh Berry Gratins

SERVES 4

When making the zabaglione, make sure to cook the egg mixture in a glass bowl over water that is barely simmering. Glass conducts heat more evenly and gently than metal. If the heat is too high, the yolks around the edges of the bowl will start to scramble. Constant whisking is required. Although we prefer to make this recipe with a mixture of raspberries, blackberries, blueberries, and strawberries, you can use 3 cups of just one type of berry. Do not use frozen berries. A broiler-safe pie plate or gratin dish can be used in place of the individual gratin dishes. To prevent scorching, pay close attention to the gratins when broiling.

BERRY MIXTURE

- 3 cups fresh mixed berries (raspberries, blueberries, blackberries, and strawberries; strawberries stemmed and halved lengthwise if small, quartered if large), at room temperature
- 2 teaspoons granulated sugar
  Pinch salt

ZABAGLIONE

- **3 large egg yolks**
- **3 tablespoons granulated sugar**
- **3 tablespoons dry white wine**
- **2 teaspoons light brown sugar**
- **3 tablespoons heavy cream, chilled**

1. FOR THE BERRY MIXTURE: Toss the berries, sugar, and salt together in a medium nonreactive bowl, then divide the mixture evenly among 4 shallow 6-ounce gratin dishes set on a rimmed baking sheet. Set aside.

2. FOR THE ZABAGLIONE: Whisk the egg yolks, 2 tablespoons plus 1 teaspoon of the granulated sugar, and the wine in a medium glass bowl until the sugar is dissolved, about 1 minute. Set the bowl over a saucepan of barely simmering water (the water should not touch the bottom of the bowl) and cook, whisking constantly, until the mixture is frothy. Following the photos on page 265, continue to cook the mixture, whisking constantly, until it is slightly thickened, creamy, and glossy, 5 to 10 minutes (the mixture will resemble hollandaise and form loose mounds when dripped from the whisk). Remove the bowl from the saucepan and whisk constantly for 30 seconds to cool slightly. Transfer the bowl to the refrigerator and chill until the egg mixture is completely cool, about 10 minutes.

3. Meanwhile, adjust an oven rack 6 to 7 inches from the broiler element and heat the broiler. Combine the brown sugar and remaining 2 teaspoons granulated sugar in a small bowl.

4. In a large bowl, whisk the heavy cream to soft peaks, 30 to 90 seconds. Using a rubber spatula, gently fold the whipped cream into the cooled egg mixture. Spoon the zabaglione over the berries and sprinkle the sugar mixture evenly over the zabaglione. Let stand at room temperature for 10 minutes, until the sugar dissolves into the zabaglione.

5. Broil until the sugar is bubbly and caramelized, 1 to 4 minutes. Serve immediately.

VARIATION

Individual Fresh Berry Gratins with Lemon Zabaglione

Follow the recipe for Individual Fresh Berry Gratins, replacing 1 tablespoon of the wine with 1 tablespoon fresh lemon juice and adding 1 teaspoon grated lemon zest to the yolk mixture in step 2.

Individual Fresh Berry Gratins with Honey-Lavender Zabaglione

Heat 2 teaspoons dried lavender and ¼ cup dry white wine in a small saucepan over medium heat until barely simmering; remove from the heat and let stand for 10 minutes. Strain the wine through a fine-mesh strainer and discard the lavender (you should have 3 tablespoons wine). Follow the recipe for Individual Fresh Berry Gratins, replacing the white wine with the lavender-infused wine and replacing 1 teaspoon granulated sugar with 2 teaspoons honey in step 2.

BAKED APPLE DUMPLINGS

APPLE DUMPLINGS ARE A HOMESPUN COMBINATION of warm pastry, concentrated apple flavor, raisins, butter, and cinnamon. In the 19th century, every homemaker could toss off a biscuit or pie dough and deftly wrap it 'round the stuffed apples. They tied up the dumplings in cheesecloth, boiled or steamed them, and served them with sauce; latter-day cooks prefer to bake them. The dumplings were so loved that in the animated 1937 classic film, Snow White's ability to make them persuaded the Seven Dwarfs to let her stay. Somehow they've fallen off our collective radar screen, but we say if a Disney cartoon character could make apple dumplings, surely the modern American cook can.

But it turns out, successfully sealing an apple in dough isn't easy. And baking produced crunchy apples inside overcooked crusts, apples that turned to mush, and gummy dough at folds and crimps. Finally, because most dumplings are baked in sauce, their bottoms get soggy.

I made some dumplings using store-bought pie dough, a shortcut many recipes take. While acceptable in a pie, where the filling stars, it was a letdown in dumplings. No question I'd be making my own dough. I also knew I'd bake my dumplings. Boiling and steaming couldn't produce crust worthy of the word. My first real decision, then, was pie versus biscuit dough. Raw pie dough tore, and baking ruptured it at the seams and sent it sliding down the shoulder of the fruit like an unzipped dress. Meanwhile, steam from the baking apple had turned the dough gluey.

Moving on to biscuit dough, I gradually increased the fat in a favorite test kitchen recipe from 8 tablespoons

BAKED APPLE DUMPLINGS

butter (for flavor) and 4 tablespoons shortening (for tenderness) to 10 and 5 tablespoons, respectively. Mixed with 2½ cups flour, 2 teaspoons baking powder, and ¾ cup buttermilk, they yielded a sturdy, tender dough. This dough formed tender, fluffy biscuits that absorbed the apple juices everywhere, except where the dumplings had been sitting in sauce. Why bake them in syrup, anyway? I'd just serve the sauce on the side.

I baked the dough-wrapped apples in a 425-degree oven—our favored temperature for biscuits. Now, the bottom crusts were crisp, but so were the apples. I'd been using Granny Smiths, a test kitchen favorite for baking, but were they to blame? Regardless, tasters

complained they were too tart. After a series of tests, tasters picked sweeter Golden Delicious, which were better in terms of flavor, but they were still too crisp.

An old recipe suggested using three-quarters of each apple if the apples were big. I adapted the idea, cutting the apples in half, then I seeded and cored them and filled the hollows with cinnamon sugar, raisins, and butter. I wrapped each half, cut a hole in the tops to let steam escape, brushed the dumplings with beaten egg white, and sprinkled them with cinnamon sugar.

Twenty-five minutes later, after the apple juices had started to bubble and the kitchen smelled fantastic, I pulled the dumplings from the oven. The apples were

NOTES FROM THE TEST KITCHEN

MAKING APPLE DUMPLINGS

1. Scoop out the core and seeds, taking care not to pierce the bottom of the apple halves.

2. Divide the butter mixture among the apple halves, filling the hollows.

3. Fold the corners of the dough up to enclose the apple, overlapping and crimping to seal.

4. Arrange the dumplings on a baking sheet, brush with egg white, and sprinkle with cinnamon sugar.

TWO ROTTEN APPLES

HEATSTROKE
Some apples, such as McIntosh, can't take the heat. They turn into applesauce before the pastry is baked.

EXTRA CRUNCHY
Whole apples are barely cooked when the pastry is done. To avoid that, we use halved Golden Delicious.

THE BEST CINNAMON

These days, cinnamon is anything but a standardized commodity. Labels advertise various origins and make claims such as "extra fancy" or "gourmet." But does all the pageantry really amount to anything? We gathered 10 supermarket and mail-order brands and tested them in applesauce, cinnamon buns, and rice pudding. In the end, we found that while our tasters had their favorites, most brands of cinnamon rated reasonably well as long as they were used before their expiration date. Our favorite was a mail-order cinnamon, **Penzeys Extra Fancy Vietnamese Cassia Cinnamon** (left), which exhibited "warm clove" and "fruity" notes. But if you don't want to spend the money ($5.45 for 1.7 ounces) or wait for it to show up in the mail, our supermarket best buy, **Durkee Ground Cinnamon** (right), scored almost as well with tasters, who praised its unique complex and woodsy flavor, but cost about $2 less. (See page 293 for more information about our testing results.)

perfect, the biscuits tender and buttery, and tasters could even finish a serving.

On the stovetop I boiled a syrup of sugar and water, alongside several variations. The winning sauce used equal parts apple cider and water, to which I added sugar, cinnamon, butter, and lemon. I drizzled the dumplings with sauce and sighed in contentment. I was remembering something I'd read in an 1888 *Good Housekeeping* article on apple dumplings: "This time-honored dish does not appear on our tables as often as its excellent qualities would warrant." My recipe could have changed that.

—DIANE UNGER, *Cook's Country*

Baked Apple Dumplings

SERVES 8

Use a melon baller or a metal teaspoon measure to core the apples. We like to serve the dumplings warm with vanilla ice cream and Cider Sauce (recipe follows). Other sweet, moderately firm apples, such as Braeburns or Galas, can be used in this recipe.

DOUGH

- 2½ cups (12½ ounces) unbleached all-purpose flour
- 3 tablespoons sugar
- 2 teaspoons baking powder
- ¾ teaspoon salt
- 10 tablespoons (1¼ sticks) unsalted butter, cut into ½-inch pieces and chilled
- 5 tablespoons vegetable shortening, cut into ½-inch pieces and chilled
- ¾ cup cold buttermilk

APPLES

- 6 tablespoons sugar
- 1 teaspoon ground cinnamon
- 3 tablespoons unsalted butter, softened
- 3 tablespoons golden raisins, chopped
- 4 Golden Delicious apples
- 2 egg whites, lightly beaten

1. FOR THE DOUGH: Process the flour, sugar, baking powder, and salt together in a food processor until combined. Scatter the butter and shortening over the flour mixture and pulse until the mixture resembles wet sand. Transfer the mixture to a bowl. Stir in the buttermilk until a dough forms. Turn the dough out onto a lightly floured counter and knead briefly until the dough is cohesive. Press the dough into an 8 by 4-inch rectangle. Cut in half crosswise, wrap each half tightly in plastic wrap, and refrigerate until firm, about 1 hour.

2. FOR THE APPLES: Adjust an oven rack to the middle position and heat the oven to 425 degrees. Combine the sugar and cinnamon in a small bowl. In a second bowl, combine the butter, raisins, and 3 tablespoons of the cinnamon sugar mixture. Peel the apples and halve them through the equator. Following the photos on page 268, remove the core and pack the butter mixture into each apple half.

3. On a lightly floured counter, roll each dough half into a 12-inch square. Cut each 12-inch square into four 6-inch squares. Working 1 at a time, lightly brush the edges of each dough square with the egg white and place an apple half, cut side up, in the center of each square. Gather the dough 1 corner at a time on top of the apple, crimping the edges to seal. Using a paring knife, cut a vent hole in the top of each dumpling.

4. Line a rimmed baking sheet with parchment paper. Arrange the dumplings on the prepared baking sheet, brush the tops with egg white, and sprinkle with the remaining cinnamon sugar. Bake until the dough is golden brown and the juices are bubbling, 20 to 25 minutes. Cool the dumplings on the baking sheet for 10 minutes. Serve.

Cider Sauce

MAKES ABOUT 1½ CUPS

To make this sauce up to 2 days in advance, reduce the cider mixture until it measures 1½ cups, then refrigerate. When ready to serve, return the mixture to a simmer and whisk in the butter and lemon juice off the heat.

- 1 cup apple cider
- 1 cup water
- 1 cup sugar
- ½ teaspoon ground cinnamon
- 2 tablespoons unsalted butter
- 1 tablespoon fresh lemon juice

Bring the cider, water, sugar, and cinnamon to a simmer in a saucepan and cook over medium-high heat until thickened and reduced to 1½ cups, about 15 minutes. Off the heat, whisk in the butter and lemon juice. Drizzle the sauce over the dumplings and serve.

TEST KITCHEN RESOURCES

* Every product tested may not be listed in these pages. Please visit www.cooksillustrated.com to find complete listings and information on all products tested and reviewed.

BEST KITCHEN QUICK TIPS

PACKET O' SPICE

Spices and herbs are a must in soups and stews, but some (like bay leaves, whole peppercorns, and cloves) have to be fished out before serving. To make removal easy, Jenny Hattori of Salinas, Calif., creates individualized spice packets.

1. Fill a tea filter bag made for loose tea with spices, tightly tie the packet closed with kitchen twine, and add it to the pot.

2. When your dish is ready, simply remove the packet.

GOOD TO THE LAST DROP

The last few drops of mustard in a nearly empty jar can be difficult to scrape out. Rachel Mazor of Brooklyn, N.Y., uses up every last bit by making a quick mustard vinaigrette like the following:

Add 3 parts extra-virgin olive oil and 1 part vinegar to the jar, along with salt and pepper to taste. Add garlic, herbs, or other seasonings, if desired. Place the lid on the jar and shake well to blend the dressing, then serve.

PARCHMENT PAPER SUBSTITUTE

Leaya Chang of New York, N.Y., was about to bake a cake when she realized that she didn't have any parchment paper to line the bottom of the pan. After a quick look around her kitchen, she decided to try using a large (8- to 10-cup) basket-style paper coffee filter. She greased an 8-inch cake pan, placed the flattened filter in the bottom of the pan, sprayed it with nonstick cooking spray, and poured in the cake batter. It worked perfectly, without any special trimming to make the coffee filter fit inside the pan.

IMPROMPTU STRAINER

After using her rasp-style grater to zest lemons, Isabell Berger of Williamsville, N.Y., found that if she turned the grater over, she could also use it to strain the pits and pulp from the juice.

RECYCLING LEFTOVER PICKLE JUICE

Instead of tossing out a jar of pickle juice after finishing the last pickle, Diane Talts of Goodyear, Ariz., uses the tangy liquid to make a new condiment. She adds thinly sliced onions to the juice and lets them marinate in the refrigerator for a few days. The drained pickled onions can be used as a topping for hot dogs or hamburgers or in salads. This method also works well with the spicy packing juice from vinegar peppers.

KOSHER SALT SHAKER

When sprinkling kosher salt on foods such as steak, it can be hard to get an even coating using your hands. But the holes on a salt shaker are too small to allow the large grains to pass through. Beth Jones of North Augusta, S.C., has found a solution. She stores her kosher salt in a clean spice jar with a shaker top. The holes are the perfect size to dispense the large grains.

EASIER FAT-SKIMMING

Skimming fat from a simmering pot of soup or stock often means chasing it around a bubbling surface. To make this task easier, Tom Dube of Somerville, Mass., moves the pot to one side of the burner so that only half has contact with the heat. The simmering bubbles on the heated side push the fat to the cooler side, making it easier to skim.

PREVENTING ICE CRYSTALS ON ICE CREAM

When exposed to air, ice cream quickly develops unappealing ice crystals and freezer burn. To cut down on air exposure and keep ice cream as fresh as possible, Carrie Kellogg of Warren, Mich., uses the following method (which also frees up freezer space).

1. As the ice cream is eaten, cut off the empty part of the container with scissors or a knife.

2. Replace the lid and return the container to the freezer.

VINEGAR FLY TRAP

Since so-called fruit flies are actually vinegar flies attracted to the odor of fermenting fruits and vegetables, Laura Carrigan of New York, N.Y., devised a simple solution to rid her kitchen of these annoying pests.

Place a few drops of dish soap in a small bowl of vinegar on the counter and stir to combine. The vinegar lures the flies into the liquid, and the soap breaks the surface tension, preventing them from escaping.

STICKY SPOONS

When measuring small amounts of sticky liquid like honey or corn syrup, Kristina Katori of Oakland, Maine, runs the measuring spoons under hot water before using them. A heated spoon keeps the sticky liquid runnier, which helps it release more easily.

VINEGAR DISHWASHER RINSE AGENT

Lucy Trifiro of Madbury, N.H., has found a cheaper, environmentally friendly alternative to the rinse agent used in dishwashers. She fills the compartment with plain white vinegar, which works just as well to keep spots from forming and costs mere pennies per load.

RESCUING A BROKEN SAUCE

Sometimes a finicky sauce, such as beurre blanc, can separate and break if it gets too hot. Trudy Barkas of Davenport, N.Y., says that all is not lost. Simply remove the pan from the heat and whisk an ice cube into the sauce until it comes back together.

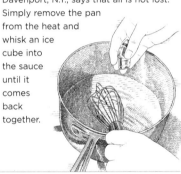

STEAMED CORN FOR A CROWD

Kelly McKinney of Broken Arrow, Okla., wanted to steam a large amount of corn but didn't have a big enough pot. Here's the solution she devised.

1. Cut 2 onions into 1-inch-thick slices, separate them into rings, and arrange them on the bottom of a roasting pan. Fill the pan with 1 inch of water and place ears of shucked corn on the onions. Cover the pan with foil and seal tightly.

2. Set the pan over two burners and steam over high heat until tender, about 10 minutes.

TAMING RED PEPPER FLAKES

Erv Slaski of Simpsonville, S.C., finds that large flakes of red pepper give off overly intense bursts of heat in food. To get a more even distribution of spiciness, he now uses a pepper mill to produce a finer grind.

Fill a pepper mill with red pepper flakes. Grind the amount you want over the food. (Grinding the flakes releases more flavor, allowing you to use less.)

BEST KITCHEN QUICK TIPS

LEVEL MEASURING

To measure dry ingredients accurately, teaspoons and tablespoons should be leveled off with a straight edge. Tanya Farrow of Philadelphia, Pa., finds the flat spout of a baking powder canister ideal for accomplishing this task, eliminating the need to drag out a leveling tool such as a butter knife.

1. Store a frequently used ingredient, such as salt, in a clean baking powder canister.

2. When measuring, scrape the spoon against the level edge of the opening.

ANOTHER WAY TO PEEL BEETS

Kassandra Calderon of Peach City, Ga., loves eating beets but hates the stains they leave behind. To keep her hands stain-free, she grasps the cooked (and slightly cooled) beets with a plastic bag, such as one used for produce. Then, working from the outside of the bag, she rubs the skins right off.

IN-A-PINCH PIE PLATE

During the holidays, pie baking is in full swing at the home of Vilma Walker of Anaheim, Calif. In need of an extra pie plate, she scoured her cabinets and found the perfect alternative: a seasoned cast-iron skillet. (Make sure the skillet is 9 or 10 inches in diameter to keep the volume and baking times consistent with the recipe.)

REVIVING OLD CARROTS

When Tricia Walton of Elmira, N.Y., finds that her carrots have gone limp, she brings them back to life by peeling them and soaking them in water in the refrigerator overnight. The carrots absorb the water, which crisps them back up.

DIY DECORATING TOOL

Professional bakers use tools such as an icing comb to decorate the sides of frosted cakes. Kirk Davis of Orlando, Fla., discovered that he could easily make his own.

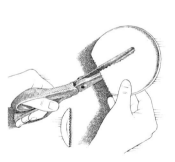

1. Using pinking shears, cut out a wedge from a plastic lid (such as the top of a cottage cheese container).

2. Drag the wedge along the sides of a frosted cake to create an attractive raised design.

SHARPENING VEGETABLE PEELERS

Elizabeth Kutchner of Sheboygan, Wis., finds her vegetable peeler dulls quickly, no surprise given its daily workout in her kitchen. To bring back its edge, she runs the back of a paring knife along the blade at a 45-degree angle. The metal spine of the paring knife acts as a hone, aligning the tiny metal "teeth" of the blade.

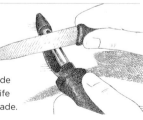

HANDS-FREE SEASONING

Josh Haselmann of St. Paul, Minn., came up with this clever trick to keep his hands clean when seasoning chops, steaks, or cutlets.

1. Sprinkle a plate or other flat surface liberally with salt and pepper (or other seasonings), then lay the meat on the plate.

2. Season the top side of the meat. Use tongs to transfer the meat to the stovetop or grill.

SWEETER ONIONS

Diane Farrell of Mount Carroll, Ill., enjoys onions in her salads but finds their flavor harsh when raw. She tempers them with the following method.

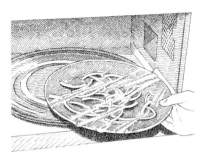

1. Place the onion slices on a microwave-safe plate, cover with plastic wrap, and microwave on high power for 15 to 30 seconds.

2. Once they're cool, toss the mellowed onions into your salad.

UNDILUTED FRUIT PUNCH

Chilling fruit punch or sangria with ice cubes can water it down. Gloria Saenz of Seguin, Texas, has a clever alternative. She freezes assorted chunks of fruit, such as apple, orange, pineapple, pear, peach, and grapes, on a baking sheet for 1 to 2 hours (depending on the size of the fruit). She then adds the frozen fruit to the drink. Not only does the fruit help keep the drink cold, it can be eaten at the end.

EASY OLIVE SLICING

If you're making nachos or another dish that requires lots of sliced olives, individually cutting each olive can be tedious. James C. Eakes of Ketchikan, Alaska, found that his egg slicer speeds up the process.

Depending on the size of the olives, set two or three in the egg slicer and push down to slice. If a coarse chop is desired, turn the olives 90 degrees and slice again.

ENSURING PERFECTLY ROUND COOKIES

To avoid giving her icebox cookies a flat side, Nidia Medina of Brooklyn, N.Y., rests the cylinders of cookie dough on a bed of rice when chilling them in the fridge. Once sliced, her cookies are perfect circles.

AN EXTRA UTENSIL RACK

Looking for extra space to hang ladles and whisks, Michelle Whalen of Poughkeepsie, N.Y., fastened a cooling rack to the wall. Attaching S-hooks to the rack allows utensils (and cookware) of any size to hang easily.

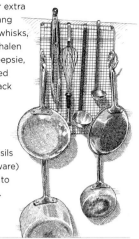

CHEAPER KNIFE PROTECTORS

Adam Staley of Austin, Texas, uses sheets of inexpensive magnetic paper, easily found at an office goods store, to make covers for his individual knives.

Fold the paper in half lengthwise. Using the blade as a guide, trim the paper to fit the knife.

RESCUING HARD-TO-PEEL EGGS

It's easy to peel freshly boiled eggs, but after they sit in the refrigerator for a day or two, the task becomes more difficult. Cheryl Kremkow of New York, N.Y., uses this method to make the shell release more easily.

1. Submerge the hard-cooked eggs in hot water for 1 minute.

2. Transfer the eggs to ice water and submerge for 1 minute more. The shell will now peel off more easily.

ESSENTIAL KITCHEN EQUIPMENT

Sixteen years of developing recipes and testing pots, pans, knives, tools, and gadgets have taught us not only which items are essential to any well-equipped kitchen, but also the most durable, high-quality brands to choose. Here are the 38 must-haves in our kitchen that we recommend for yours.

COOKWARE

1. ALL-CLAD Stainless 12-Inch Fry Pan $110

This roomy skillet can cook a family-sized meal. The traditional finish allows food to stick, developing the crusty brown bits of fond that contribute flavor.

2. ALL-CLAD Stainless 4-Quart Saucepan (with lid) $194.99

BEST BUY **CUISINART Multiclad Unlimited 4-Quart Saucepan** $69.99

3. CALPHALON Contemporary Nonstick 2½-Quart Shallow Saucepan $29.95

For even cooking, we prefer saucepans made of stainless steel sandwiching an aluminum core in a style of construction known as "tri-ply." A 4-quart saucepan is just the right size for making rice or blanching vegetables; a 2-quart saucepan is good for smaller jobs like heating milk or melting butter. For a cheaper alternative, consider nonstick.

4. T-FAL Professional Total Non-Stick Fry Pan, 12.5 Inches $34.99

Nonstick is great for delicate, quick-cooking foods like fish or eggs—but don't spend big bucks since the coating wears off within a few years.

5. LODGE LOGIC 12-Inch Cast-Iron Skillet $32.95

Nothing tops cast iron when it comes to creating a flavorful, deeply browned crust on steaks and other foods.

6. LE CREUSET 7¼-Quart Round French Oven (with lid) $269

This incredibly versatile Dutch oven made of enameled cast iron is ideal for soups, stews, stocks, braises—even frying and baking.

BEST BUY **TRAMONTINA 6½-Quart Cast-Iron Dutch Oven** $54.95

7. CUISINART Chef's Classic Stainless 12-Quart Stockpot (with lid) $69.95

Lighter than a Dutch oven, a 12-quart stockpot is used mainly for boiling water for pasta, corn, and lobster. This brand's inexpensive price tag is just right for a pot with limited use.

8. CALPHALON Contemporary Stainless Roasting Pan with Rack $129.99

Don't buy nonstick; the dark finish camouflages the crusty brown bits you need to make gravy for roasted meats. This pan's gently flared shape makes stirring and deglazing easy.

KNIVES

9. VICTORINOX Fibrox (formerly Victorinox Forschner) 8-Inch Chef's Knife $24.95

Our inexpensive, lightweight favorite has a high-carbon stainless steel blade that stays sharper longer and a nonslip handle.

10. VICTORINOX Fibrox 4-Inch Paring Knife $12.95

This knife's sharp, agile blade and firm, comfortable grip can handle close work like paring fruit and slivering garlic.

11. WÜSTHOF 10-Inch Classic Bread Knife $89.95

The long, slightly flexible blade and serrations on this knife are good for cutting bread, tomatoes, and cake.

BEST BUY **VICTORINOX Fibrox 10¼-Inch Curved Blade Bread Knife** $24.95

12. CHEF'S CHOICE Model 130 Professional Sharpening Station $149.95

A sharpener is different than a sharpening steel, which merely repositions a knife's cutting edge, rather than actually sharpening it. Electric is a must for restoring nicked, damaged, or very dull blades.

13. ACCUSHARP Knife and Tool Sharpener $10.99

For knives that aren't severely dulled or damaged, our favorite manual sharpener is an affordable, handy option.

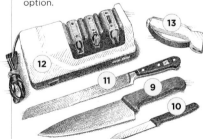

BAKEWARE

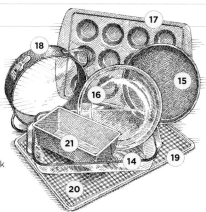

14. PYREX Bakeware 13 x 9-Inch Baking Dish $8.95

A multitasker for cakes, lasagna, and casseroles. Oven-safe glass browns nicely and can handle metal utensils.

15. CHICAGO METALLIC Professional Lifetime 9-Inch Nonstick Round Cake Pan $15.95

High, straight sides and a dark nonstick finish deliver better browning; you'll need two for most recipes.

16. PYREX Bakeware 9-Inch Pie Plate $2.99

Tempered glass, rather than metal, makes it easier to track browning results; plus, glass won't react with acidic fruit to give fillings a tinny flavor.

17. WILTON Avanti Everglide Metal-Safe Nonstick Muffin Pan $13.99

Choose a sturdy, medium-weight, dark-colored muffin tin like this one for better heat absorption and deeper browning.

18. FRIELING'S Handle-It Glass Bottom 9-Inch Springform Pan $42.95

Removable sides make a springform essential for cakes like cheesecake and ice cream cake that would be impossible to unmold from a standard cake pan.

19. LINCOLN FOODSERVICE Half-Size Heavy Duty Sheet Pan $15.99

20. CIA BAKEWARE 17 x 12-Inch Cooling Rack $15.95

BEST BUY **LIBERTYWARE Cross Wire Cooling Rack Half-Sheet Pan Size** $5.25

A multitasking duo with duties beyond baking—keep two of each on hand. We use our rimmed baking sheet for cookies, oven fries, and veggies. And we place the cooling rack within it to roast meat.

21. WILLIAMS-SONOMA Nonstick Goldtouch 8½ x 4½-Inch Loaf Pan $21

The gold-colored nonstick coating on our favorite loaf pan yields baked goods with an even, lightly browned crust.

MEASURING TOOLS

22. AMCO Basic Ingredient 4-Piece Measuring Cup Set $11.50

These durable stainless steel cups boast rims flush with the long handles, making leveling off dry ingredients easy.

23. CUISIPRO 4-Cup Deluxe Liquid Measuring Cup $14.95

A pour spout and handle are musts in liquid measuring cups. Read from above, the plastic Cuisipro measures more accurately than a glass Pyrex cup.

24. CUISIPRO Stainless Steel Oval Measuring Spoons $13.95

We like that these sturdy, elongated spoons are slim enough to dip into narrow spice jars.

25. COOPER-ATKINS Oven Thermometer $6.12

The best insurance against varying oven temperatures. This model sports a hook, base stand, and clearly marked numbers.

26. OXO Food Scale $49.99

For close to 100 percent accuracy when baking, weigh your ingredients on a scale; digital models with large readout displays like this one are the easiest to read.

27. POLDER 3-in-1 Clock, Timer, and Stopwatch $15.12

This test kitchen favorite has a lengthy time range (1 second to at least 10 hours) and can count up after the alarm goes off.

28. THERMOWORKS Splashproof Super-Fast Thermapen $96

Forgo guesswork and pinpoint exactly when food is done. We call the Thermapen the Ferrari of thermometers for its fast, accurate readings and long probe.

BEST BUY **CDN ProAccurate Quick-Read Thermometer** $16.95

UTENSILS

29. BEST MANUFACTURERS 12-Inch Standard French Whisk $10.50

Our favorite all-purpose French whisk is long and agile, with tines that don't bend and twist with prolonged use.

30. FANTE'S French Rolling Pin with Tapered Ends (model #1528) $6.99

This long, thin, tapered rolling pin is gentler on delicate dough than standard rolling pins.

31. RUBBERMAID Professional 13½-Inch High Heat Scraper $18.99

Not your grandmother's spatula. Besides scraping bowls and icing cakes, this heatproof spatula made of silicone can also stir sauces on the stove.

32. OXO Good Grips Box Grater $17.95

Razor-sharp grates and a collecting cup make this model a standout.

33. OXO Good Grips 12-Inch Locking Tongs $12.95

The scalloped edges on these tongs get a better grip on food.

34. KUHN RIKON Easy-Squeeze Garlic Press $20

This press boasts easy-to-squeeze plastic handles and an efficient plunger.

35. MESSERMEISTER Pro-Touch Swivel Peeler $6.95

The blade on this peeler is extremely sharp and maneuverable enough to glide across the curves of potatoes, apples, and carrots.

36. MESSERMEISTER Take-Apart Shears $19.95

The "take-apart" feature on these shears allows for thorough cleaning.

37. ARCHITEC The Gripper Nonslip Cutting Board $14.99

We like this dishwasher-safe board for its durable surface and skid-free bottom.

38. RSVP INTERNATIONAL Endurance Precision Pierced 5-Quart Colander $32.95

Hundreds of tiny holes allow water to drain quickly without losing so much as a pea.

PERFECT COFFEE 101

You can spend $20 a pound for premium coffee, but unless it's fresh and you're using proper brewing techniques, it's a waste of money. Here's what you need to know to make the perfect cup.

BUYING AND STORING TIPS

THE BASICS

- **DO** buy loose beans in small quantities no more than a few days from the roasting date (ask before you buy); our testing has shown that roasted beans are ready for the compost pile after just 10 to 12 days. Buy from a local roaster or a store that sells a high volume, upping your chances of buying beans from a recently roasted batch.

- **DO** buy prebagged coffee in a heat-sealed, aluminized Mylar bag with a one-way degassing valve. This valve (sometimes no more than a bump) releases carbon dioxide to stop the bag from inflating while keeping out oxygen, which turns coffee stale. Unopened, these bags keep beans as fresh as the day they were roasted for up to 90 days (the outer limit for beans in such packaging cited by roasters including George Howell Terroir Coffee Company, in Acton, Mass., and national retailer Peet's Coffee & Tea). Of course, as soon as you open the bag, the clock starts ticking on freshness.

- **DON'T** rely on expiration dates. We've found some supermarket brands of coffee with expiration dates as far as two years out from the roasting date.

- **DON'T** buy preground coffee. Grinding speeds oxidation and the deterioration of flavor. When we compared coffee brewed from just-ground beans with coffee brewed from beans ground 24 hours earlier, tasters overwhelmingly preferred the coffee brewed from freshly ground beans. Grinding the night before is also not optimal: Studies show the exposed coffee cells begin to break down within the hour.

FLAVOR COUNTDOWN

To determine how long coffee maintains ideal flavor after roasting, we bought 30 bags of beans from the same batch, packaged within hours of roasting in one-way valve bags. Over two weeks, we prepared two pots of coffee daily: one made with beans from a just-opened bag, the other using beans stored on the counter in a sealed zipper-lock bag with the air pressed out. A few very discriminating tasters noticed a change in taste after just a few days of storage; many tasters noticed a deterioration after 10 days; most tasters agreed the coffee tasted markedly less fresh after 12 days. Bottom line: Opened beans stored in an airtight container should be used within 10 to 12 days.

WHERE TO STORE BEANS: COUNTER, FRIDGE, OR FREEZER?

If you finish a bag of beans in less than 10 to 12 days, store them either in the original bag or in a zipper-lock bag away from heat and light. If you plan to keep beans longer than this time frame, store them in the freezer to limit contact with air and moisture. (Never store coffee in the fridge; it will pick up off-flavors.) It is best to portion beans (whether storing on the counter or in the freezer) in small zipper-lock bags in one-day allotments to keep air and moisture exposure to a minimum.

BEST BREWING PRACTICES

1. USE FILTERED WATER: A cup of coffee is about 98 percent water, so if your tap water tastes bad, your coffee will too. But don't bother with bottled water; just use a filtration pitcher.

2. HEAT TO PROPER TEMPERATURE: The most desirable flavor compounds in coffee are released in water between 195 and 205 degrees. Our tasters judged coffee brewed at 200 degrees as having the fullest, roundest flavor. Once water has boiled (212 degrees), let it rest for 10 to 15 seconds.

3. USE THE RIGHT GRIND, BREW FOR THE RIGHT TIME: Brewing time will dictate how you grind the coffee. In general, the longer the brewing time, the coarser the grounds should be. Don't try to adjust strength by changing the grind; grounds that are too fine for your brewing method will result in overextraction, while grounds that are too coarse will be underextracted.

4. ADD THE RIGHT AMOUNT: The norm is 2 tablespoons ground beans per 6 ounces water. If you prefer stronger or weaker coffee, adjust the amount of grounds; changing the amount of water can lead to over- or underextraction, since the less water you use, the shorter the brewing time and vice versa.

5. KEEP THE POT CLEAN: Coffee beans contain oils; every time you brew a pot, some is left behind. Over time, that oil will make your coffee taste rancid. Rinse your pot with hot water after each use and scrub apparatus with hot soapy water at least once a week.

RECOMMENDED BREWING METHODS

While we can't dispute the convenience of an automatic drip coffee maker, we've learned that most models brew crummy coffee—they don't heat the water to the ideal temperature, and the brewing times are too long or too short. Unless you're willing to splurge on the one coffee maker we really like, the Technivorm Moccamaster Coffee Maker, $265, we recommend a French press (the Bodum Chambord 8-Cup French Press, $39.95, is our favorite) or manual drip.

FRENCH PRESS

HOW IT WORKS: A French press (or plunger pot) directly infuses ground coffee in just-boiled water. Once properly extracted, the grounds are pressed to the bottom of the carafe.

WHY WE LIKE IT: Because the coffee's oils are not filtered out, this method yields coffee nearly as full-bodied as espresso. It also allows you to control water temperature and brew time.

DOWNSIDE: Cleaning requires taking apart the pieces.

THE RIGHT GRIND: Medium-coarse (a little coarser than couscous).

1. Add 2 tablespoons coffee for every 6 ounces water (preheat pot first with hot tap water).

2. Add just-boiled water steadily, saturating all the grounds.

3. Using long spoon or chopstick, stir coffee to aid extraction.

4. Add lid and steep coffee for about five minutes (four minutes for smaller pots).

5. With even pressure, steadily press down filter.

MANUAL DRIP

HOW IT WORKS: Place ground coffee in a wedge-shaped filter holder and pour water over it into a container below.

WHY WE LIKE IT: The manual drip allows the natural acidity of coffee to shine through, yielding bright, flavorful coffee. As with the French press, you control water temperature and brew time.

DOWNSIDE: Since you have to add water in batches, you can't leave the kitchen during brewing.

THE RIGHT GRIND: Medium (like coarse cornmeal) for paper filters; medium-fine (like fine cornmeal) for metal filters.

1. Add 2 tablespoons coffee for every 6 ounces water to filter (warm thermos with hot tap water).

2. Pour ½ cup just-boiled water over grounds, saturating thoroughly; let stand for 30 seconds.

3. Pour remaining hot water over grounds, in batches if necessary, stirring gently after each addition.

FRESHNESS TEST

To check if your beans are fresh, scoop ½ cup into a zipper-lock bag and press out all the air, then seal the bag and leave it overnight. If the beans are within 7 to 10 days of roasting, they will make the bag puff up from the carbon dioxide that they release. If the bag remains flat, then the beans are not producing gas—a sign they've passed the point of peak freshness.

PUFFED = STILL FRESH

FLAT = PAST THEIR PRIME

THE BEST SMALL APPLIANCES

Small appliances promise convenience—but the wrong ones can wind up as clutter. Here's our guide to top-quality workhorses and test kitchen champs. After nearly two decades testing small appliances, we know how to identify keepers—the most useful, durable, and high-quality equipment and brands. (Don't look for an electric wok on this list.) While a few items are not inexpensive, they're worth the investment for better cooking and baking.

FOOD PROCESSOR

KITCHENAID 12-Cup KFP750 Food Processor $199.95

This peak performer aced all our vegetable prep tests, chopping and slicing as evenly and cleanly as an expertly wielded knife—but a lot faster. It went on to win perfect scores pureeing steamed broccoli into soup and cutting fats into flour for pastry. The 12-cup bowl is spacious enough for an extra-large batch of pizza dough, but you can also attach a 4-cup mini bowl and blade for smaller chores like chopping a handful of parsley.

BEST BUY
CUISINART Pro Custom 11 $169

For $30 less, the Cuisinart is also a stellar performer. Its only downside? It's less of a chopping champ than the KitchenAid.

BLENDER

KITCHENAID 5-Speed KSB580 Blender $149.99

When frozen cocktails beckon, only a blender offers impeccable ice-crushing power. Because food processors can leak, a blender is also a better bet for swirling smoothies, soups, and purees. Our favorite boasts a tapered, V-shaped jar and four blades (each positioned at a different angle, the better to catch and pulverize foods) that left nary a lump or trace of pulp in smoothies made with rock-hard frozen berries and fibrous mango.

BEST BUY
KALORIK BL Blender $47.95

If you're fine with a slower pace, look to the far-cheaper Kalorik, which excelled at core tasks, despite taking a longer time to get the job done.

IMMERSION BLENDER

KALORIK Sunny Morning Stick Mixer $25

If you already own a blender or food processor (or both), why bother with a smaller appliance with the same blending function? Because with this tool, there's no need to blend in batches, and it's easy to rinse off and toss back into the drawer. Our top choice aced our tests and has a detachable plastic shaft and wide blade cage that makes for easy cleanup.

HANDHELD MIXER

CUISINART Power Advantage 7-Speed Hand Mixer $49.95

Not big on baking? A handheld mixer isn't as powerful as a stand mixer, but a good model still does a decent job whipping, creaming, and mixing. Even with thick cookie dough, the metal beaters on our winner offer smooth, steady, controlled mixing action.

ELECTRIC KNIFE SHARPENER

CHEF'S CHOICE Model 130 Professional Sharpening Station $149.95

An electric sharpener has the edge over manual options because it doesn't just sharpen, it also removes nicks and notches. Our favorite includes spring-loaded blade guides that hold the blade against the sharpening wheels at the proper angle, ensuring a fine, polished edge.

STAND MIXERS

KITCHENAID Professional 600 Series 6-Quart Stand Mixer $399.99
CUISINART 5.5-Quart Stand Mixer $299

These two stand mixers ranked neck and neck in our testing. Both are pricey—but they're powerhouse performers, masters at whipping egg whites, creaming butter and sugar, kneading basic bread dough, and mixing even the stiffest cookie dough. The Cuisinart 5.5-Quart Stand Mixer includes not only an efficient dough hook but modern updates such as a digital timer with automatic shut-off and a splashguard attachment.

BEST BUY ### KITCHENAID Classic Plus Stand Mixer, 4.5-Quart $199.99

This stand mixer (reviewed in a separate testing of inexpensive stand mixers) has a smaller capacity and less brute force than our winners, but still performed remarkably well in our tests.

TOASTER

HAMILTON BEACH Michael Graves Design 4-Slice Toaster, $37.99

A toaster shouldn't break the bank, but it should produce toast that's evenly browned on both sides. Our top choice has a similar number of heating elements on each side of the toasting slots; browning overall was more consistent from batch to batch than in other models we tested. Extra-wide slots accommodate bagels.

SLOW COOKER

CROCK-POT Touchscreen Slow Cooker $129.99

A slow cooker (or crockpot) cooks pot roasts, beans, and stews with slow, steady heat. Turn it on, leave the house, and return hours later to a finished dish. Our winner cooked pot roast, meaty tomato sauce, and French onion soup perfectly. It has a control panel that is simple to set and clearly indicates that the cooker was programmed.

ELECTRIC KETTLE

CAPRESSO H20 Plus Glass Kettle $59.95

This sleek appliance shaves minutes off the wait for boiling water, sits on a separate base to conserve stovetop space, and includes automatic shut-off/boil-dry safeguards. The 6-cup glass carafe is easy to pour and clean—plus we like the view of rising bubbles as water boils.

DON'T GET BURNED: TOASTER OVENS

Toaster ovens have been known for making lousy toast, plus their small size and typically inconsistent heating elements make them inadequate ovens. We found these problems persist, even in a new generation of models tricked out with convection capability, digital displays, and custom cookware. Our one recommended model, the **Krups 6-Slice Digital Convection Toaster Oven FBC2**, $249.99, cooked food more evenly than the other models we tested, offering reliable cooking, user-friendly controls, solid construction, and even decent toast. But since it is expensive, we only recommend it if you want to invest in a higher-end toaster oven for small cooking projects. You can do equally well with an ordinary toaster and your full-size oven.

ICE CREAM MAKER

WHYNTER SNÖ Professional Ice Cream Maker $219.99

Home ice cream machines fall into two types: pricey self-refrigerating models that let you make batch after batch, or cheaper models with a removable canister that must be refrozen each time. Our favorite self-refrigerating model makes incredibly creamy, dense, smooth ice cream that's firm enough to eat right away.

BEST BUY **CUISINART Automatic Frozen Yogurt, Ice Cream, and Sorbet Maker** $49.95

COFFEE GRINDER/ SPICE GRINDER

CAPRESSO Cool Grind 501 $19.95

Like many blade grinders, this one can struggle to grind evenly. But it has two features we value highly: a large capacity and a deep cup that contains grinds without spilling. It also works well as a spice grinder— buy two, one for coffee and another for spices (unless you don't mind coffee with a hint of spice, or vice versa).

WAFFLE MAKER

CHEF'S CHOICE WafflePro Express $69.95

Waffle irons have a specific job, yet the marketplace is still rife with machines turning out pallid, soggy results. Our favorite model stood out for speedily cooking a perfect waffle in the promised shade, and emitting a loud beep to let us know when breakfast was ready.

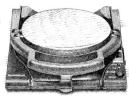

ELECTRIC GRIDDLE

BROILKING Professional Griddle $99.99

Our winner is roomy enough for eight pieces of French toast, and it's made of heavy-duty cast aluminum, which evenly distributes heat for perfectly browned pancakes and crisp bacon. The removable backsplash stops grease from splattering.

BEST BUY **WEST BEND Cool-Touch Nonstick Electric Griddle** $51.95

This has a smaller surface area but cooks equally well.

AUTOMATIC DRIP COFFEE MAKER

TECHNIVORM Moccamaster Coffee Maker KBT-741 $265

The only automatic coffee maker we like achieves perfect temperatures for brewing and keeps the coffee hot in a thermal carafe (instead of turning acrid in a glass carafe on a hot plate). It's easy to use and brews exceptionally smooth, balanced coffee. Sure, it's expensive—but not compared to a year's worth of Starbucks. (Still have sticker shock? Try a manual drip filter or French press.)

KEEPING A CLEANER, SAFER KITCHEN

Some of the most effective ways to cut down on harmful bacteria in the kitchen aren't what you'd think. Here's what you need to know to keep things as clean—and safe—as possible.

CLEANING BASICS

Depending on factors such as moisture, temperature, surface porosity, and the particular strain of bacteria, microbes can live as long as 60 hours on your sink or cutting board. But you don't need anything special to clean a kitchen—for the most part, we rely on old-fashioned soap and hot water or a bleach solution.

ALL HANDS UNDER WATER

Washing your hands is one of the best ways to stop the spread of food-borne pathogens. Wash before and during cooking, especially after touching raw meat and poultry. The U.S. Food and Drug Administration (FDA) recommends at least 20 seconds in hot, soapy water. How long is that? Try singing "Happy Birthday."

SANITIZE YOUR SINK

Studies have found that the kitchen sink is crawling with even more bacteria than the garbage bin (the drain alone typically harbors 18,000 bacteria per square inch). The faucet handle, which can reintroduce bacteria to your hands after you've washed them, is a close second. Though we've found that hot soapy water is amazingly effective at eliminating bacteria, for added insurance, clean these areas frequently with a solution of 1 tablespoon bleach per quart of water (the bleach will also kill off some of those microbes in the drain).

CLEANING SPONGES

The wet environment of a sponge is the next worst offender after the kitchen sink; whenever possible, use a paper towel or a clean dishcloth instead to wipe up. If you do use a sponge, disinfect it. To find the best method, we tried microwaving, freezing, bleaching, and boiling sponges that had seen a hard month of use in the test kitchen, as well as running them through the dishwasher and simply washing them in soap and water. Lab results showed that microwaving and boiling were most effective, reducing bacteria counts from the millions to an untroubling 1,000 CFUs. Since sponges can burn in a high-powered microwave, we recommend boiling them for 5 minutes.

CUTTING-BOARD CLEANUP

If you can't use a dishwasher (which won't work for some boards), is bleaching the next best method for eliminating bacteria from your board? We sent boards to a lab, where they were colonized with salmonella, then washed with hot soapy water, a bleach solution, or undiluted vinegar. All methods were equally effective at reducing bacteria.

WASHING PRODUCE

Forget buying expensive fruit and vegetable washes. A spray bottle filled with 3 parts water and 1 part white vinegar works just as well to clean smooth-surfaced produce such as apples and pears. Just spray, then rinse under tap water. In our tests, this method removed 98 percent of surface bacteria. It's also good practice to wash produce that has inedible rinds and peels, such as melons, because cutting into a contaminated peel can drag pathogens inside. Delicate fruit, like berries, can be washed in a bowl filled with three parts water and one part white vinegar: Drain, rinse with tap water, and then spin dry in a salad spinner lined with paper towels.

PREVENTING CROSS-CONTAMINATION

One of the most important rules of food safety is to keep raw and cooked foods separate. Never place cooked food on a plate or cutting board that has come into contact with raw food, or vice versa, and wash any utensil (including a thermometer) that comes in contact with raw food before reusing it. These additional steps will help you avoid cross-contamination.

DON'T RECYCLE USED MARINADE

Used marinade is contaminated with raw meat juice and is therefore unsafe to consume. If you want a sauce to serve with cooked meat, make a little extra marinade and set it aside before adding the rest to the raw meat.

PUT UP A BARRIER

Items that come in contact with both raw and cooked food, like scales and platters, should be covered with plastic wrap or aluminum foil to create a protective barrier. Once the item has been used, the wrap—and any bacteria—can be discarded. Similarly, wrapping your cutting board with plastic wrap before pounding meat and poultry will limit the spread of bacteria.

SAFER SEASONING

Though bacteria can't live for more than a few minutes in direct contact with salt (which quickly dehydrates bacteria, leading to cell death), it can live on the edges of a box or shaker. To avoid contamination, we grind pepper into a small bowl and then mix it with salt. This way, we can reach into the bowl for seasoning without having to wash our hands every time we touch raw meat or fish. Afterward, the bowl goes right into the dishwasher.

DON'T RINSE YOUR MEAT

Avoid rinsing raw meat and poultry. Rinsing is more likely to spread contaminants around the sink than send them down the drain. Since brined meats need to be rinsed before cooking, make sure to thoroughly clean the sink and surrounding areas after rinsing.

USING A THERMOMETER

TAKE YOUR FOOD'S TEMPERATURE

A reliable instant-read thermometer (see page 277 for our favorite models) will gauge whether cooked food has been brought up to a safe temperature.

TAKE YOUR FRIDGE'S TEMPERATURE

A good refrigerator thermometer (we like the Maverick Cold-Chek Digital Refrigerator/Freezer Thermometer, $19.99) will tell you if your fridge and freezer are cooling properly. Check regularly to ensure that your refrigerator is between 35 and 40 degrees; your freezer should be 0 degrees or below. Different foods are safest at different temperatures; see the chart below for our recommendations. Keep in mind that the back of a refrigerator is the coldest. Make sure that raw meat is stored well-wrapped and never on shelves that are above other food.

FOOD	IDEAL TEMPERATURE
Fish and Shellfish	30 to 34 degrees
Meat and Poultry	32 to 36 degrees
Dairy Products	36 to 40 degrees
Eggs	38 to 40 degrees
Produce	40 to 45 degrees

AVOIDING THE TEMPERATURE DANGER ZONE

Most bacteria thrive between 40 and 140 degrees Fahrenheit. Within this "danger zone," bacteria double about every 20 minutes, quickly reaching harmful levels. As a general rule, food shouldn't stay in this zone for more than two hours (one hour if the room temperature is over 90 degrees).

DEFROST IN FRIDGE

Defrosting should always be done in the refrigerator, not on the counter at room temperature, where bacteria can multiply readily. Always place food on a plate or in a bowl while defrosting to prevent any liquid it releases from coming in contact with other foods. Most food will take 24 hours to thaw fully. (Larger items, like whole turkeys, can take far longer. Count on about 5 hours per pound.)

COUNTER-INTUITIVE COOLING

Though it may go against your instincts, don't put hot foods in the fridge immediately after cooking. This will cause the temperature of the refrigerator to rise, potentially making it hospitable to the spread of bacteria. The FDA recommends cooling foods to 70 degrees within the first two hours after cooking and 40 degrees within four hours after that. We stay within these guidelines by cooling food on the countertop for about an hour, until it reaches 80 to 90 degrees (food should be just warm to the touch), then transferring it to the fridge.

REHEAT RAPIDLY

When food is reheated, it should be brought through the danger zone as quickly as possible—don't let it come slowly to a simmer. Bring leftover sauces, soups, and gravies to a boil and make sure casseroles reach at least 165 degrees, using an instant-read thermometer to determine whether they're at the proper temperature.

THE ESSENTIAL PANTRY

Besides proper techniques, the best recipes depend on the best ingredients. Here are our favorite brands of important staples to keep in your pantry. Ingredients within categories are listed in order of preference. Asterisks indicate available through mail order.

BEANS
CHICKPEAS
Pastene
WHITE
Westbrae Organic Great
Northern
Progresso Cannellini

BREAD
WHITE SANDWICH
Arnold Country Classics
Pepperidge Farm Farmhouse
Hearty
WHOLE WHEAT
Pepperidge Farm 100%
Natural

BREAD CRUMBS
Ian's Panko

BROTH
BEEF
Rachael Ray Stock-in-a-Box
All-Natural Beef Flavored
Stock
CHICKEN
Swanson Certified Organic
Free Range
Better Than Bouillon
VEGETABLE
Swanson Vegetarian

CAPERS
Reese Non Pareil
Roland Nonpareille

CHILI POWDER
Spice Islands
Pendery's Top Hat Chile
Blend*

CHOCOLATE
DARK (BITTERSWEET)
Callebaut Intense,
L-60–40NV
Ghirardelli Bittersweet
Baking Bar
MILK
Dove
Scharffen Berger
MILK CHIPS
Hershey's
SEMISWEET CHIPS
Ghirardelli 60% Cacao
BITTERSWEET
Hershey's Special Dark
Mildly Sweet
UNSWEETENED
Scharffen Berger
Callebaut
Ghirardelli
WHITE CHIPS
Guittard Choc-Au-Lait

CINNAMON
Penzeys Extra Fancy
Vietnamese Cassia*
Durkee

CLAM JUICE
Bar Harbor

COCOA POWDER
Callebaut*
Droste

COCONUT MILK
FULL-FAT
Chaokoh
LIGHT
A Taste of Thai Lite

CORNMEAL
WHOLE GRAIN
Arrowhead Mills

FLOUR
UNBLEACHED ALL-PURPOSE
King Arthur
Pillsbury

HOT SAUCE
Frank's RedHot Original

KETCHUP
Hunt's
Heinz Organic

MAPLE SYRUP
Maple Grove Farms Pure
Maple Syrup
Highland Sugarworks

MAYONNAISE
Hellmann's Real (known as
Best Foods on West Coast)
Hellmann's Light

MIRIN
Mitoku Organic Mikawa
Eden

MOLASSES
Grandma's Mild or Robust
Brer Rabbit Mild or Full Flavor

MUSTARD
DIJON
Grey Poupon
Maille
WHOLE GRAIN
Grey Poupon Harvest
Grey Poupon Country Dijon

OATS
FOR BAKING
Quaker Old-Fashioned Rolled
FOR COOKING
Bob's Red Mill Organic
Steel-Cut

OIL
EXTRA-VIRGIN OLIVE
CALIFORNIA
California Olive Ranch
Arbequina*
Sciabica's Sevillano Variety
Fall 2008 Harvest*
EXTRA-VIRGIN OLIVE
SUPERMARKET
Columela
Lucini Italia Premium Select*
Colavita
PURE OLIVE SUPERMARKET
DaVinci
Colavita
VEGETABLE
Crisco Natural Blend
Mazola Canola

PAPRIKA
The Spice House Hungarian
Sweet*
Penzeys Hungarian Sweet*

PASTA
EGG NOODLES
Light 'n Fluffy Wide
ELBOW MACARONI
Barilla
FARFALLE
Mueller's
FRESH
Buitoni
LASAGNA NOODLES
(NO-BOIL)
Barilla
PENNE
Mueller's
SPAGHETTI
Ronzoni
SPAGHETTI, WHOLE WHEAT
Bionaturae

PEPPERCORNS
BLACK
Kalustyan's Indian Tellicherry*
Morton & Bassett Organic

PEPPERS
ROASTED RED
Dunbars Sweet

PRESERVES
RASPBERRY
Smucker's
STRAWBERRY
Welch's

RICE
ARBORIO
RiceSelect
BASMATI
Tilda Pure

RICE (continued)
LONG-GRAIN WHITE
Lundberg

SALT
Maldon Sea Salt
Fleur de Sel de Camargue
Morton Coarse Kosher

SOY SAUCE
FOR COOKING
Lee Kum Kee Tabletop
FOR DIPPING
Ohsawa Nama Shoyu Organic

TOMATOES
CRUSHED
Tuttorosso
Muir Glen Organic
DICED
Hunt's
PASTE
Amore
PUREED
Hunt's
Progresso
WHOLE
Progresso Italian-Style
Redpack

TUNA
IN WATER
Chicken of the Sea Solid
White Albacore
Starkist Solid White Albacore
IN OLIVE OIL
Ortiz Bonito del Norte

VANILLA EXTRACT
McCormick Pure
CF Sauer Co. Gold Medal
Imitation

VINEGAR
APPLE CIDER MAILLE
Spectrum Naturals Organic
BALSAMIC
Lucini Gran Riserva
Monari Federzoni
RED WINE
Spectrum Naturals Organic
Pompeian
WHITE WINE, FOR
COOKING
Colavita Aged
WHITE WINE, FOR
VINAIGRETTE
Spectrum Naturals Organic
Cascadian Farm 100%
Organic

COOKING WITH PANTRY INGREDIENTS

RICE RULES

For drier, fluffier long-grain or basmati rice, follow these suggestions.

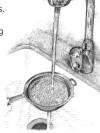

RINSE IT: Rinsing raw grains removes surface starch that will otherwise absorb water during cooking, causing grains to stick.

GRAB A TOWEL: Once the rice is cooked, cover the pan with a clean kitchen towel, replace the lid, and allow the rice to sit off heat for 10 minutes. The towel will soak up steam and prevent stickiness.

COOKING WITH WINE

The best all-purpose cooking wines are medium-bodied, non-oaked varieties that aren't too sweet.

REDS Go with blended (nonvarietal) American and Australian wines, or a French Côtes du Rhône.

WHITES We prefer clean, crisp, dry Sauvignon Blancs to sweet Rieslings or heavily oaked Chardonnays, which can dominate subtle flavors.

SHOPPING TIP

Since wine has a brief shelf life—only a few days after a bottle is opened—we recommend boxed wines, which store the liquid in an airtight, bladderlike plastic sack that collapses as the wine is removed. Dry vermouth, with a shelf life of several months, makes a good substitute for white wine.

SUBSTITUTION

Broth can work just fine as a nonalcoholic replacement for wine in soups and stews. For every ½ cup broth used, stir in ½ teaspoon red or white wine vinegar or lemon juice before serving.

PASTA DOS AND DON'TS

- **DO** remember to salt the pasta water for a properly seasoned dish: 1 tablespoon table salt to 4 quarts water.

- **DON'T** add oil to the water; it will make the pasta slick and prevent the sauce from sticking.

- **DO** let a little water cling to the cooked pasta to help the sauce adhere.

- **DON'T** rinse the cooked pasta; it washes away starch and makes the pasta taste watery.

CANNED BEANS: OBSERVE THE 30-MINUTE RULE

When adding canned beans to soups and stews, simmer them for a full 30 minutes to give them time to take on the flavor of other ingredients. Always drain and rinse first; the salty, starchy packing liquid can throw off recipes.

DRIED BEANS: BRINE 'EM

Forget conventional wisdom warning against salting beans before they're cooked. Our testing revealed that adding salt to the overnight soaking liquid (2 teaspoons per quart of water)—in effect "brining" the beans— yields better-seasoned and more evenly cooked results.

DRIED HERBS

While in most cases dried herbs can't compete with fresh, our tests found some important exceptions: Bay leaf, thyme, oregano, rosemary, marjoram, and sage will work fine in moist preparations cooked for at least 20 minutes (like chili or poultry stuffings). These herbs are able to maintain their flavor even through the drying process.

EMERGENCY SUBSTITUTIONS

CANNED BEANS FOR DRIED

For every pound of dried beans called for, you'll need 58 ounces of canned beans (3 to 4 cans, depending on size).

TURNING WHITE SUGAR INTO BROWN

White sugar combined with molasses is an excellent substitute for brown sugar. Pulse the two in a food processor or simply add the proper amount of molasses along with the other wet ingredients.

1 cup granulated sugar + 1 tablespoon molasses = 1 cup light brown sugar

1 cup granulated sugar + 2 tablespoons molasses = 1 cup dark brown sugar

MAKING CAKE FLOUR

With just 6 to 8 percent protein, cake flour imparts a more tender, delicate texture to baked goods than all-purpose. Here's how to make an approximation.

2 tablespoons cornstarch + ⅞ cup all-purpose flour = 1 cup cake flour

USING DRIED HERBS FOR FRESH

Dried herbs are more potent than fresh; if you have to substitute dry for fresh, use half of the amount called for in the recipe.

4 tablespoons fresh oregano = 2 tablespoons dried oregano

GARLIC 101

From pungent and fiery to sweet and nutty, garlic is capable of delivering a range of flavors—depending on how you prep and cook it. Here are our proven methods for getting the right results.

BUYING

Choose loose garlic heads, not those sold in cellophane-wrapped boxes, so you can examine them closely. Pick heads without spots, mold, or sprouting. Squeeze them to make sure they're not rubbery and that there aren't any soft spots or missing cloves. The garlic shouldn't have much of a scent; if it does, you're risking spoilage.

SOFTNECK

Of the two main garlic varieties, your best bet at the supermarket is softneck, since it stores well and is heat tolerant. This variety features a circle of large cloves surrounding a small cluster at the center.

HARDNECK

Distinguished by a stiff center staff surrounded by large, uniform cloves, hardneck garlic has a more intense, complex flavor. But since it's easily damaged and doesn't store as well, wait to buy it at the farmers' market.

ELEPHANT GARLIC

The huge individual cloves of so-called elephant garlic—which is actually a member of the leek family—are often sold alongside regular garlic. We find it far milder than regular garlic and don't recommend it for recipes.

STORING

With proper storage, whole heads of garlic should last at least a few weeks.

- **DO** store heads in a cool, dark place with plenty of air circulation to prevent spoiling and sprouting.

- **DON'T** store cut garlic in oil for more than 24 hours. This may seem like an easy way to preserve leftovers, but since the bacteria that cause botulism grow in exactly this kind of oxygen-free environment, it's actually a health hazard.

PREPPING

How garlic is handled can have a dramatic impact on flavor.

- **DO** remove any green shoots from cloves before chopping. They contain bitter-tasting compounds that persist even after cooking.

- **DO** pay attention to how fine you chop garlic. The finer the mince, the stronger the flavor (see "Manipulating Garlic's Flavor," page 287).

- **DON'T** chop garlic in advance. In tests, we've found that since garlic flavor comes from the compound allicin—which is released and starts to build only when the cloves are ruptured—the longer cut garlic sits, the harsher its flavor.

THREE WAYS TO SKIN A CLOVE

Crushing the clove is the easiest way to remove the skin from garlic you plan to mince. When a whole clove is called for, try the other two tips.

CRUSH: Press against the garlic firmly with the flat side of a chef's knife to loosen the skin.

ROLL: The E-Z-Rol Garlic Peeler, $8.95, relies on hand friction to quickly and efficiently remove the skin from cloves placed inside it.

MICROWAVE: Place the garlic on a microwave-safe plate and cook on high power 10 to 20 seconds; cool and peel.

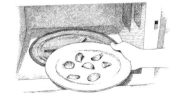

TWO WAYS TO MAKE GARLIC PASTE

In dishes such as aïoli and pesto, a paste adds the most robust garlic flavor and keeps the garlic's texture unobtrusive.

SALT AND DRAG: Sprinkle a mound of minced garlic with a coarse salt such as kosher. Repeatedly drag the side of a chef's knife over the mixture until it turns into a smooth puree.

GRATE: Rub cloves against the sharp, fine holes of a rasp-style grater to reduce garlic to a paste.

WHAT'S THE YIELD?

Because of garlic's intense flavor, the size of the cloves can really make a difference in your cooking. Besides specifying the quantity and size of the cloves, our recipes offer teaspoon or tablespoon measurements for minced garlic (our most common preparation) so there's no doubt that you're using the right amount. Illustrations are true to size.

EXTRA-LARGE CLOVE
1 tablespoon minced

LARGE CLOVE
2 teaspoons minced

MEDIUM CLOVE
1 teaspoon minced

SMALL CLOVE
½ teaspoon minced

COOKING

- **DO** wait to add garlic to the pan until other aromatics or ingredients have softened (push these to the perimeter) to avoid browning and the creation of bitter compounds.

- **DON'T** cook garlic over high heat for much longer than 30 seconds; you want to cook it only until it turns fragrant. And make sure to stir constantly.

- **DO** add garlic to a cold pan when it is the only flavoring and cook it over low to medium heat to give it time to release its flavors and keep it from burning.

MANIPULATING GARLIC'S FLAVOR

Garlic's pungency emerges only after its cell walls are ruptured, triggering the creation of a compound called allicin. The more a clove is broken down, the more allicin—and the more flavor (and aroma)—are produced. Thus you can control the amount of bite garlic contributes to a recipe by how fine (or coarse) you cut it. Cooking also affects flavor intensity. Garlic is sharpest when raw. When it's heated above 150 degrees, its enzymes are destroyed and no new flavor is produced; only flavor created up to the inactivation temperature remains. This is why toasted or roasted garlic has a mellow, slightly sweet flavor. Alternatively, garlic browned (or overbrowned) at very high temperatures (300 to 350 degrees) results in a bitter flavor. (Garlic chips are the exception, since they are mellowed first, then crisped, which creates a sweet flavor with only hints of bitterness.)

TYPE OF GARLIC	RESULTING FLAVOR
Roasted whole head	Very mild, sweet, caramel-like
Toasted whole clove	Mellow and nutty
Slivered and sautéed	Mellow
Minced and sautéed	Full and rounded
Pressed and sautéed	Very robust, harsh
Raw paste	Sharp and fiery

GARLIC SUBSTITUTES

Though we almost always prefer a fresh clove to processed garlic, there are times when substitutes can come in handy.

POWDER: Since garlic powder (made from pulverized dehydrated minced garlic) will not burn in the oven, we sometimes prefer it to fresh garlic in spice rubs, breading, and dishes such as roasted potatoes. Substitute ¼ teaspoon garlic powder for each clove of fresh garlic.

PREPEELED: Even if kept unopened in its original packaging, prepeeled garlic lasts only about two weeks before turning yellowish and developing an overly pungent aroma. Still, in tests we found its flavor comparable to that of fresh cloves, if used before yellowing. Make sure to buy prepeeled cloves that look firm and white.

DEHYDRATED MINCED: Because this product takes a long time to rehydrate and packs none of the punch of fresh garlic, we avoid it altogether.

PRESS CREDENTIALS

In our experience, a good garlic press can break down cloves more finely and evenly—and quickly—than the average cook wielding a knife. (Note: The fine mince can lead to stronger garlic taste.) Plus, with a good garlic press, you don't even have to stop and peel the cloves. We squeezed hundreds of cloves with 13 different models to find the best tool for the job: the Kuhn Rikon Easy-Squeeze Garlic Press, $19.95.

ALL-PURPOSE VEGETABLE OILS

With the range of vegetable oil varieties available and profusion of names like "Vegetable Plus!" and "Natural Blend," it's hard to know which one to pick—or whether it even matters. We tested 10 vegetable oils, all produced by the three companies dominant in the industry (we excluded the harder-to-find, more expensive peanut oil and olive oil) in two applications: mayonnaise and french fries. We rated them on greasiness (for fries), texture (in mayonnaise), presence of off-flavors (if any), and overall appeal. While tasters noticed significant differences among the oils in these tests, when we tested the top- and bottom-ranked oils again, in white cake and vinaigrette (where oil played a subordinate role) tasters could hardly differentiate between the two. Our top-ranking oil, though not by much, performed well in every application. It has the unusual addition of sunflower oil, which we found provides checks and balances on flavor and freshness, even under high heat. Oils are listed in order of preference.

RECOMMENDED

CRISCO Natural Blend Oil (canola, sunflower, and soybean)
PRICE: $5.75 for 48 oz.
MAYONNAISE: ★★★
FRYING: ★★★
BAKING: ★★★
VINAIGRETTE: ★★★
COMMENTS: In mayonnaise, the "very clean" taste of this blend outperformed the rest. Despite containing canola and soybean oils (which can contribute off-flavors), it was utterly "neutral and balanced" in fries. Still, in cake and vinaigrette, it performed no better than our bottom-ranked oil.

MAZOLA Canola Oil
PRICE: $5.53 for 48 oz.
MAYONNAISE: ★★★
FRYING: ★★★
COMMENTS: The "clean flavor" of this oil gave mayonnaise a "nice, light" taste. In fries, while a few sensitive tasters noticed some fishiness, the majority gave it the thumbs-up for a neutral taste that let potato flavor "shine through."

CRISCO Pure Vegetable Oil (soybean)
PRICE: $3.99 for 48 oz.
MAYONNAISE: ★★★
FRYING: ★★★
COMMENTS: Though criticized by some for being "slightly greasy" in both the mayonnaise and the fries, overall its taste was "neutral" in both applications—just how we like our vegetable oil to be.

CRISCO Corn Oil
PRICE: $5.95 for 48 oz.
MAYONNAISE: ★★
FRYING: ★★★
COMMENTS: While tasters disliked most corn oils in mayonnaise, this brand was the exception, earning low but acceptable scores, with only a few tasters detecting a "cardboard" aftertaste. In fries, it shone: "Great. No negatives."

CRISCO Canola Oil
PRICE: $5.75 for 48 oz.
MAYONNAISE: ★★★
FRYING: ★★
COMMENTS: This oil contributed to a "pleasant-tasting" mayonnaise with a "creamy" texture. Fries, however, didn't have that "clean burst of fresh fry flavor," and some tasters detected an aftertaste "like spent oil."

RECOMMENDED (continued)

WESSON Vegetable Oil (soybean)
PRICE: $3.99 for 48 oz.
MAYONNAISE: ★★
FRYING: ★★
COMMENTS: Most tasters deemed this oil "inoffensive" in mayonnaise, but some noted a slight "greasy" consistency. In fries, tasters were divided: Half found it an agreeably silent partner to the potatoes; others complained of "weird," "metallic" off-flavors.

RECOMMENDED WITH RESERVATIONS

WESSON Canola Oil
PRICE: $5.99 for 48 oz.
MAYONNAISE: ★★★
FRYING: ★
COMMENTS: This oil drew accolades for producing a mayonnaise that was "mellow" and "silky." But it finished last in the fries test; taster complaints ranged from "sour" to "disgusting fish flavor."

MAZOLA Corn Oil
PRICE: $5.49 for 48 oz.
MAYONNAISE: ★
FRYING: ★★★
COMMENTS: Like the two bottom-ranked corn oils, this product tanked in the mayo tests, producing a sauce with "rancid," "turpentine-like" flavors. Fries were a different story altogether: "These are great; no off-flavors."

MAZOLA Corn Plus! Oil (corn and canola)
PRICE: $4.49 for 48 oz.
MAYONNAISE: ★
FRYING: ★★★
COMMENTS: In mayonnaise, this corn-canola blend exhibited an aftertaste so "pungent," one taster likened it to "blue cheese." But like other corn oils, in fries it was a marvel, producing fries with "nutty," "buttery" flavor.

WESSON Corn Oil
PRICE: $5.44 for 48 oz.
MAYONNAISE: ★
FRYING: ★★★
BAKING: ★★★
VINAIGRETTE: ★★★
COMMENTS: Although "like licking metal—funky" in mayo, french fries made in this oil tasted "good, unadulterated." Most tasters found it indistinguishable from our top brand in cake and vinaigrette.

CALIFORNIA EXTRA-VIRGIN OLIVE OILS

While olives are not new to California, olives here have mostly been harvested for eating—until recently. Today California produces a small fraction of the olive oil consumed in the United States each year, but since the key to good extra-virgin olive oil is freshness, the potential benefits of buying domestic are built in. We wondered if California already sells olive oils as good as our favorite imports, so we purchased 10 bottles from the state's largest and most established producers, and compared them in a tasting that also included our favorite import, Columela. The favorite California variety in the tasting notably came in just behind first-place Columela by a mere half a point on a scale of 0-10, winning big for its fresh olive flavor. So while Columela may remain our favorite overall, several of the California oils we tasted were in the same class. The California growers have clearly struck something promising. The oils are listed in order of preference. Prices for mail-order oils do not include shipping (though two producers offer free shipping).

RECOMMENDED

CALIFORNIA OLIVE RANCH Arbequina
PRICE: $13.97 per half liter
OLIVE: Arbequina, unfiltered
COMMENTS: This oil by North America's largest olive oil producer came in just a fraction of a point behind our imported favorite (Columela), winning out over other California oils with a similar profile: full, fruity olive flavor and little bitterness or pungency. "Lovely, nutty, and fruity," with notes of "lemon," "vanilla," and "honey." "Quite buttery and round and almost sweet," tasters raved. "The aftertaste is fresh, pure olive."

SCIABICA'S Sevillano Variety Fall 2008 Harvest
PRICE: $26.60 per half liter
OLIVE: Sevillano, unfiltered
COMMENTS: "Green, pungent, and moderately bitter," agreed tasters. "Tastes like it's fresh," with a "spicy, peppery aroma and a buttery aftertaste" and notes of "fennel/licorice," "green apple," and "green grass"; flavors are "harmonious" and "balanced," "surprisingly sweet," "like fresh peas." "Smells like sun-warmed hay, very clean and soft." One taster simply wrote: "Olive-y goodness."

PACIFIC SUN Tehama County Blend
PRICE: $12 per half liter
OLIVES: Mission and Ascolano, unfiltered
COMMENTS: A blend of mild, late-harvest Mission olives with peppery, early-harvest Ascolano olives, this oil impressed tasters as "buttery, not bitter at all," "not pungent" but "mild," "smooth," "floral," like "roses," with a "fruity aroma" and notes of "passion fruit, pineapple," and "melon" with a "nutty" finish, "like walnuts." "Nice flavor, more complex than most."

LUCERO Ascolano
PRICE: $28 per half liter, free shipping for orders $50 and up
OLIVE: Ascolano, unfiltered
COMMENTS: "Unusually fruity," this olive oil "tastes like olives in a fruity, rounded way." Tasters found it "apple-y and fresh, with a peppery kick" and "strong," with "cut-grass," "clover," or "grapefruit" notes. "Tastes like it smells." One summed it up as "slightly too bitter, but perfectly balanced potency."

RECOMMENDED WITH RESERVATIONS

DaVERO Dry Creek Estate
PRICE: $37.33 per half liter
OLIVES: Field blend of Leccino, Frantoio, Maurino, and Pendolino, planted at a ratio of 50%, 25%, 15%, and 10%, unfiltered
COMMENTS: "Wow, it sure does taste like fresh olive oil. Reminiscent of green herbs and artichokes," wrote one taster. "Complex and almost zesty," agreed another. Others found this blend too "harsh" in a way that "overpowered the fruitiness," though one taster noted, "Bitter at first, but mellows nicely."

MCEVOY RANCH Traditional Blend
PRICE: $28 per half liter
OLIVES: Frantoio, Leccino, Pendolino, Maurino, Coratina, and Leccio del Corno, organic and unfiltered
COMMENTS: "Quite pungent, very bitter flavor, like olive leaves and pits," "like swallowing an M-80 of cayenne," "horseradish strong!" "like fresh ground peppercorns," or "rosemary grass." "Tastes quite young," wrote one taster; "like a peppered apple," and "almost too potent," said others.

STELLA CADENTE L'Autunno Blend
PRICE: $25 per half liter
OLIVES: Leccino, Frantoio, Pendolino, Coratina, and Mission, unfiltered
COMMENTS: "Light and fruity," this oil started out tasting "subtle" and "buttery." "Really tame," said one taster, while others remarked on "citrusy" or "lemony" notes. Several were turned off by a "viscous," "greasy" texture and a slightly "musty" smell, as well as a "harsh," almost "sour" aftertaste that was "sharp" and "stays with you." One taster concluded, "Everything in balance but meek and mild."

APOLLO Mistral Blend
PRICE: $26.60 per half liter
OLIVES: Picholine, French Columella, Groussane, and Ascolano, organic and filtered
COMMENTS: "Extreme peppery kick with a lot of bitterness," "super-green," "very pungent." This "complex" oil had "big fruit and spice," with tasters describing "unripe flavors." Some picked up off-notes, including "copper penny" or "gasoline." "Astringent" and (to some) "overwhelming," it was also "vaguely nutty," "like cashews."

WHOLE WHEAT PASTA

We recently bought 18 nationally distributed brands of whole wheat and multigrain spaghettis and put them to the test, eating them with olive oil and with sauces. Three brands earned the "recommended" status, but two were whole grain imposters, with refined wheat as their first ingredient. Most 100 percent whole wheat and 100 percent whole grain pastas fell to the bottom. However, Bionaturae Organic 100% Whole Wheat Spaghetti boasted a good chewy and firm texture, making it our top pick. The manufacturer's secret? Custom milling (which ensures good flavor), extrusion through a bronze, not Teflon, die (which helps build gluten in the dough), and a slower drying process at low temperatures (which yields sturdier pasta). Pastas appear in order of preference; protein and fiber are per 2-ounce serving.

RECOMMENDED

BIONATURAE Organic 100% Whole Wheat Spaghetti
PRICE: $3.49 for 16 oz.
PERCENTAGE OF WHOLE GRAINS: 100
PROTEIN: 7g FIBER: 6g
INGREDIENTS: Organic whole durum flour
COMMENTS: Tasters lauded this spaghetti for its "earthy," "wheaty," "nutty," "full" flavor, which was "heartier than white pasta, without being too wheaty." It also boasted a "pleasantly chewy," "firm" texture. Its "good blend of whole wheat flavor and regular-pasta texture" worked well with our sauces.

HEARTLAND Perfect Balance Spaghetti
PRICE: $1.19 for 14.5 oz.
PERCENTAGE OF WHOLE GRAINS: 21
PROTEIN: 7g FIBER: 3g
INGREDIENTS: Enriched durum semolina, whole wheat durum flour
COMMENTS: This spaghetti earned accolades for its "buttery," "smooth," "springy," "firm" texture. Only 21 percent whole grain, it tasted "the most like white pasta" of any in the lineup, serving as a "neutral" background for marinara and pesto.

BARILLA Plus Multigrain Spaghetti
PRICE: $2.50 for 14.5 oz.
PERCENTAGE OF WHOLE GRAINS: 0
PROTEIN: 10g FIBER: 4g
INGREDIENTS: Semolina, grain and legume flour blend (lentils, chickpeas, egg whites, spelt, barley, flaxseed, oat fiber, oats), durum flour, niacin, iron, thiamine mononitrate, riboflavin, folic acid
COMMENTS: It's no surprise that this spaghetti "doesn't taste like whole wheat pasta," as it contains no whole grains. Tasters enjoyed the "mildly nutty, wheaty" taste along with its "firm, chewy" texture (though a few found the texture "stiff").

RECOMMENDED WITH RESERVATIONS

HEARTLAND Plus Spaghetti
PRICE: $1.29 for 14.5 oz.
PERCENTAGE OF WHOLE GRAINS: 0
PROTEIN: 9g FIBER: 4g
INGREDIENTS: Enriched semolina, grain and legume flour blend (lentils, egg whites, oat fiber, flaxseed, whole grain barley flour, whole oat flour)
COMMENTS: "I think I like this because it doesn't taste like it's whole grain." Others liked the "mild nutty flavor," which had a "neutral" flavor when paired with marinara and pesto. Its high protein content made it a "workout for your chompers."

GIA RUSSA 100% Whole Wheat Spaghetti
PRICE: $2.99 for 16 oz.
PERCENTAGE OF WHOLE GRAINS: 100
PROTEIN: 8g FIBER: 5g
INGREDIENTS: Whole wheat durum flour
COMMENTS: Tossed with pesto, this spaghetti was "nutty and robust"; but plain, it was likened to eating "wheat germ" and tasted "a little sour." With marinara, the overpowering wheat flavor seemed "milder." Though it had "good chew," many felt it was "gritty," "like cardboard."

DAVINCI 100% Whole Wheat Spaghetti
PRICE: $3.99 for 12 oz.
PERCENTAGE OF WHOLE GRAINS: 100
PROTEIN: 7g FIBER: 5g
INGREDIENTS: Whole durum wheat semolina
COMMENTS: This spaghetti had "good flavor," but "not much whole wheat flavor." When paired with marinara and pesto, it had a "neutral," "subtle wheat taste," but tasters couldn't get past the "gummy," "doughy" texture.

BARILLA Whole Grain Spaghetti
PRICE: $1.39 for 13.25 oz.
PERCENTAGE OF WHOLE GRAINS: 51
PROTEIN: 7g FIBER: 6g
INGREDIENTS: Whole durum wheat flour, semolina, durum wheat flour, oat fiber
COMMENTS: Its heavy "bran" flavors were "not terrible," but made this "hippie-food" spaghetti taste "more like oats than wheat." The "skinny" strands cooked up "mealy" and "mushy." Tasters said the texture was like "sandpaper," "gritty," and "stale."

RONZONI Healthy Harvest Whole Wheat Blend
PRICE: $2 for 13.25 oz.
PERCENTAGE OF WHOLE GRAINS: 63
PROTEIN: 7g FIBER: 5g
INGREDIENTS: Durum whole wheat flour and semolina blend, whole flaxseed meal, wheat fiber, thiamine mononitrate, niacin, riboflavin, iron, folic acid
COMMENTS: Though this spaghetti's "healthy, earthy" flavor appealed to a few, it overwhelmed most. Some detected a "mildly fishy" flavor as well as the taste of "stale vitamins." The "chewy, gummy noodles stick to my teeth," complained one taster.

REDUCED-FAT POTATO CHIPS

We held a blind tasting of eight national brands of low-fat potato chips to find out if any could be an acceptable stand-in for the classic, full-fat (10 grams of fat per ounce) favorite. Not surprisingly, we liked best the ones that reduced the fat the least. Manufacturers reduce the fat in one of three ways: One method bakes, oils, and salts potato slices; they contain 3 grams of fat per serving. Another takes sliced potatoes, quickly fries them, then removes some of the oil picked up by steaming and baking. This second style results in 6 to 7 grams of fat per serving. Finally, some reduced-fat chips are made by combining sugar, binders, and leaveners with dehydrated potatoes to form a dough, which is cut into "chips" and baked. These have between 1½ and 3 grams of fat per serving. The chips made using the hybrid fry-then-bake method were the big winners. Chips are listed in order of preference; total fat and sodium is per 1-ounce serving.

HIGHLY RECOMMENDED

RUFFLES Reduced Fat
PRICE: $3.99 for 9 oz.
TOTAL FAT: 7g
SODIUM: 180mg
COMMENTS: "Hey, now, that's good," said one surprised taster about these "rich, salty, and crisp" chips with "nice potato flavor." These chips, which contain only potatoes, oil, and salt, "don't taste low-fat." They're "greasy and fatty-tasting—in a good way." Surely it didn't hurt that they are heavily salted.

LAY'S Kettle Cooked Reduced Fat Extra Crunchy Potato Chips
PRICE: $3.29 for 8.5 oz.
TOTAL FAT: 6g
SODIUM: 160mg
COMMENTS: These chips actually scored the highest for flavor ("clean," "great potato flavor") and finished only a hair behind the Ruffles overall. The prevailing opinion? "Look real, taste real." Most—but not all—tasters appreciated the "super-crunchy," "almost hard" texture. "I'm trying to figure out how these are healthy," said one satisfied taster.

RECOMMENDED

CAPE COD 40% Reduced Fat Potato Chips
PRICE: $3.49 for 8 oz.
TOTAL FAT: 6g
SODIUM: 110mg
COMMENTS: "Tastes like a regular potato chip" with "robust potato flavor" and "superb crunch." However, a few tasters noticed an "odd, fishy flavor"; we know that canola oil sometimes imparts such a flavor. Also, these chips have the least sodium of any in our lineup. A few tasters missed the salt.

RECOMMENDED WITH RESERVATIONS

BAKED! RUFFLES Original Potato Crisps
PRICE: $3.79 for 9 oz.
TOTAL FAT: 3g
SODIUM: 200mg
COMMENTS: "Very hard, very sweet, very bad," one taster said. Others disliked their "way too salty" flavor. They are, however, the highest-rated chips of the baked-only variety. "I'm almost convinced this was once a potato," said one taster.

NOT RECOMMENDED

BAKED! LAY'S Original Potato Crisps
PRICE: $3.79 for 9 oz.
TOTAL FAT: 2g
SODIUM: 180mg
COMMENTS: These "artificial-looking and -tasting" chips scored last for flavor. Tasters compared them to "salty paper" and "packing peanuts." They were also judged "too sweet" with "zero potato flavor."

KETTLE BRAND Lightly Salted Baked Potato Chips
PRICE: $3.69 for 4 oz.
TOTAL FAT: 3g
SODIUM: 135mg
COMMENTS: These chips are made from oil, salt, and thick slices of skin-on potatoes baked until quite brown, a trait that divided tasters into two camps: "nutty" and "earthy" versus "burnt" and "ashtray aftertaste." "I like the roasted flavor," said one taster, "but it's odd for a chip." Said another, "Tastes the way a burning hair dryer smells."

UTZ Baked Original Potato Crisps
PRICE: $3.49 for 8.5 oz.
TOTAL FAT: 1.5g
SODIUM: 150mg
COMMENTS: Tasters compared the flavor to instant mashed potatoes and the texture to "dried potato puree" or "something that's been run over by a steamroller." No wonder this brand tanked in our ratings. As one taster concluded, "Not sure what these taste like, but it definitely isn't good."

HERR'S Original Baked Potato Crisps
PRICE: 99¢ for 1.85 oz.
TOTAL FAT: 2g
SODIUM: 180mg
COMMENTS: With "zero potato flavor" and notes of "powdered milk," "fake butter," and "greasy doughnuts," these "sugary" chips won few fans. In the words of one grimacing colleague, "most unpleasant" of all.

OATS

Though instant oatmeal has remained popular since its inception by Quaker in 1922, interest has swung back lately toward slower-cooking traditional oats, with stores offering Irish-style steel-cut, Scottish-style stone-ground, and organic varieties in addition to instant, quick, and five-minute "old-fashioned" rolled oats. And while Quaker used to be virtually the only brand, the number has lately proliferated. Is one style better as a hot cereal or for baking? Do any of the newcomers offer a better oatmeal than Quaker? We recently held several tastings to get the answers. In the end, steel-cut oats, with their firm chewy texture and full oat flavor, won the day for breakfast, while rolled oats proved best for baking (the stone-ground Scottish oats in our tasting did not fare well). If you want to buy one type of oatmeal for baking and breakfast, we recommend our second-ranked brand in the rolled oat category, Quaker, which cooks quickly and aced our baking tests. Scores were averaged, and the oats appear, grouped by style, in order of preference.

Steel-Cut Oats

RECOMMENDED

BOB'S RED MILL Organic Steel-Cut Oats
PRICE: $3.45 for 24 oz. (14¢ per oz.)
COMMENTS: Tasters praised these steel-cut oats for "buttery goodness," and "great oat flavor," that is "earthy" and "nutty," "whole grain-y in a good way," "rich and complex."

ARROWHEAD MILLS Organic Steel-Cut Oats Hot Cereal
PRICE: $2.99 for 24 oz. (12¢ per oz.)
COMMENTS: Its texture appealed to many tasters, and its "toasty," "nutty," "brown-rice" or "barley" flavor was "complex" and "hearty." "Like a warm granola bar," one taster raved.

COUNTRY CHOICE Organic Steel-Cut Oats
PRICE: $4.79 for 30 oz. (16¢ per oz.)
COMMENTS: "Good oat flavor, slightly sweet." "A very nice balance of creaminess and crunch," "toasty and substantial," and "earthy." However, a few tasters found it "a bit horsey."

HODGSON'S MILL Premium Steel-Cut Oats
PRICE: $1.95 for 18 oz. (11¢ per oz.)
COMMENTS: "Good all-around earthy, sweet oat flavor," said tasters, who praised its "natural-tasting," "full-flavored, hearty" and "strong" oat flavor. Several tasters found it slightly "slimy" or "mucilaginous."

RECOMMENDED WITH RESERVATIONS

QUAKER Steel-Cut Oats
PRICE: $4.69 for 24 oz. (20¢ per oz.)
COMMENTS: Tasters were split on this oatmeal, with some calling it "mild," with "very plain oat flavor, a good canvas." Others called it "bland," "middle-of-the-road," and "a bit mushy" and "gooey."

MCCANN'S Steel-Cut Irish Oatmeal
PRICE: $7.49 for 28 oz. (27¢ per oz.)
COMMENTS: Though some tasters thought this pricey imported oatmeal had "a good chew" and "very earthy flavor," others said it was "too mild, almost timid," "like cardboard or paper pulp," with an "odd aftertaste," that was slightly "bitter" and "vegetal," like "raw seeds" or "grass."

Rolled Oats

RECOMMENDED

BOB'S RED MILL Organic Extra Thick Rolled Oats
PRICE: $2.40 for 16 oz. (15¢ per oz.)
COMMENTS: "Nice, rich," "good oat flavor—seems real," like "sweet semolina," with "nutty, barley" "browned" overtones and a "good texture" that is "nice and plump," with a "decent chew," while being "creamy and cohesive."

QUAKER Old-Fashioned Rolled Oats
PRICE: $4.99 for 42 oz. (12¢ per oz.)
COMMENTS: Offering a "slight chew," and "subtle sweetness," Quaker's most well known style of oatmeal "felt and tasted very natural," with a texture that tasters deemed "good—plump and crunchy," "hearty," and "with a tiny bit of snap." Its flavor had "good oat-y, toasty notes."

NOT RECOMMENDED

ARROWHEAD MILLS Organic Old-Fashioned Oatmeal Hot Cereal
PRICE: $3.99 for 16 oz. (25¢ per oz.)
COMMENTS: Tasters decried this oatmeal as "gooey," "like textured thick water." "Awful. I was afraid to swallow." Its flavor was mild to the point of "no flavor at all." In sum: "Starchy, cardboard-y, and one-dimensional."

BOB'S RED MILL Old-Fashioned Rolled Oats
PRICE: $4.49 for 32 oz. (14¢ per oz.)
COMMENTS: While tasters really liked this company's "Extra Thick" rolled oats, they disliked these thinner oat flakes, which became "too mushy," "gluey," and "sticky" and lacked the thicker flakes' appeal. Tasters called them "bland" with "no flavor."

COUNTRY CHOICE Organic Old-Fashioned Oats
PRICE: $3.39 for 18 oz. (19¢ per oz.)
COMMENTS: "Very mushy and no flavor," "earthy flavor but bad texture, like slurry," "mushy and viscous and raggedy—take it away!" complained tasters, who found "nothing good here. Bland, like cardboard." "Tastes like grass, with a slight chemical aftertaste."

CINNAMON

In recent years this spice has become anything but a standardized commodity, with labels touting various origins and making claims such as "extra fancy" or "gourmet." We gathered 10 supermarket and mail-order brands and tested them in applesauce, cinnamon buns, and rice pudding. We stuck to the more vibrant and complex-tasting, familiar variety known as Cassia cinnamon (what you find in most U.S. supermarkets) rather than the mild-mannered Ceylon variety (which is what most other countries prefer). In every application, tasters declared that heat, complexity of flavor, and texture were what mattered most. Our top-ranked cinnamons had a spicy heat that built gradually, with complex yet balanced flavors and aromas, and a fine texture that couldn't be detected when mixed into food. Nevertheless, most brands rated reasonably well as long as they were used before their expiration date. The cinnamons appear below in order of preference.

RECOMMENDED

PENZEYS Extra Fancy Vietnamese Cassia Cinnamon
PRICE: $5.45 for 1.7 oz. ($3.21 per oz.)
ORIGIN: Vietnam
COMMENTS: "Slightly smoky" and filled with complex "warm clove" and "fruity" flavors, its spiciness was "strong, yet not overpowering"; it "started mellow, then built to a spicy finish." When it was baked into cookies and cinnamon buns, tasters could detect "toasty" flavors and "clove and floral" aromas.

DURKEE Ground Cinnamon
PRICE: $3.50 for 1.75 oz. ($2 per oz.)
ORIGIN: Indonesia
COMMENTS: Nearly tied with the winner, this grocery store cinnamon was "unique," "complex," "woodsy," and "floral." Tasters perceived a "finely ground texture" that "incorporated wonderfully" into food. It reminded tasters of "cloves," "allspice," and "nutmeg." Its "fruity, floral" flavors were evident in the cookies and cinnamon buns.

SMITH AND TRUSLOW Freshly Ground Organic Cinnamon
PRICE: $26 for four 0.8-oz. jars ($8.13 per oz.)
ORIGIN: Vietnam
COMMENTS: Freshly ground to order, this mail-order brand is the most expensive cinnamon in our lineup. Described as "woodsy," "citrusy," and "floral," it was a favorite for a "remarkably sweet" flavor that "gradually gets hotter."

ADAMS Ground Cinnamon
PRICE: $3.99 for 2.33 oz. ($1.71 per oz.)
ORIGIN: Indonesia and China
COMMENTS: The "sweet," "complex" flavor of this cinnamon from a Texas spice company tasted of "cardamom" and "cloves." Described as "rather fruity," this cinnamon was a little too "floral-tasting" for some. Others sensed a faint flavor of "Red Hots candy."

MORTON & BASSETT Ground Cinnamon
PRICE: $5.19 for 2.2 oz. ($2.36 per oz.)
ORIGIN: Indonesia
COMMENTS: This "warm" cinnamon had "fruity" and "honey" flavors that made it "easy on the palate." But the "mild cinnamon taste" seemed to "wash out at the end," leaving tasters wanting more spiciness.

RECOMMENDED WITH RESERVATIONS

SAUER'S Ground Cinnamon
PRICE: $3.50 for 2.25 oz. ($1.56 per oz.)
ORIGIN: Indonesia
COMMENTS: This cinnamon possessed a "peppery," "fragrant" profile, but was "somewhat weak" with "very little heat" and tasted "more floral than spicy." "Reminds me of my grandma's potpourri," commented one taster. Another asked, "Is this true cinnamon?" In sum: "Underwhelming."

SPICE ISLANDS Ground Saigon Cinnamon
PRICE: $4.75 for 1.9 oz. ($2.50 per oz.)
ORIGIN: Vietnam
COMMENTS: This "sweet and warm" cinnamon with "clove" notes was "pleasant" and "slightly smoky" with "moderate heat" and a "pronounced Red Hots candy flavor" that started strong but "faded quickly." Some noticed a "rather gritty" texture. Others complained about a "medicinal flavor" and "artificial" aftertaste.

MCCORMICK Gourmet Collection Saigon Cinnamon
PRICE: $4.69 for 1.87 oz. ($2.51 per oz.)
ORIGIN: Vietnam
COMMENTS: This cinnamon was called "quite strong" and "earthy" by some, but many found it "flat," "one-dimensional," "ho-hum" and "generic," like "Hot Tamales candy" that "doesn't blow my head off." Other tasters felt it was "harsh and bitter," evoking "soap" or even "furniture polish."

TONE'S Ground Cinnamon
PRICE: $6 for 8 oz. (75¢ per oz.)
ORIGIN: Indonesia
COMMENTS: This "average" cinnamon was described as "muted," "meek," and "dull"—"simply not hot." It initially tasted like "Big Red chewing gum" but then "really mellowed out at the finish." Some tasters noticed a "dusty" quality. Overall, it was "run-of-the-mill" with "very little depth."

MCCORMICK Ground Cinnamon
PRICE: $2.99 for 2.37 oz. ($1.26 per oz.)
ORIGIN: Indonesia
COMMENTS: This cinnamon had a "peppery finish" and possessed a "very assertive," "Red Hots candy" taste, but its flavor had "little complexity" that faded when baked in cookies and cinnamon buns. Some tasters detected a "gritty, dusty" texture; others found it "musty" and "stale" with a "chemical flavor and metallic finish."

CREAMY ITALIAN DRESSINGS

Here in the test kitchen, we always make our own salad dressing, but we know on occasion convenient bottled dressing gets called into action in numerous home kitchens. In the hopes of finding an acceptable supermarket creamy Italian dressing to fill the role, we rounded up six top-selling brands, readied our salad spinner, and called in a panel of cooks and editors to taste each dressing plain and with iceberg lettuce. The results? We still prefer homemade, and we can't recommend any store-bought bottles more strongly than "with reservations." Two, Marzetti and Marie's, are acceptable. They have the least sodium per serving, aren't too sweet, and have no off-flavors. And not only do they have the most fat of those we tasted, but it's also the type of fat that matters. Each dressing has vegetable oil as its primary fat source, but the fats listed next in the Marzetti dressing are egg yolk and buttermilk; in Marie's, sour cream, whole egg, and egg yolk. These ingredients give our winners creamy flavor and texture. With the exception of Marie's and Newman's Own, the dressings contain chemical additives and preservatives, a fact that didn't correlate to our preferences. Top-ranked Marzetti, for example, contains high-fructose corn syrup, preservatives, and artificial color. Newman's Own, which finished second to last, has none of those additives. While our top dressings are passable in a pinch, we still suggest you make your own. Dressings are listed in order of preference; total fat and sodium are per 2-tablespoon serving.

RECOMMENDED WITH RESERVATIONS

MARZETTI Creamy Italian Dressing with Cracked Peppercorns
PRICE: $2.79 for 16 oz.
TOTAL FAT: 14g
PRIMARY SOURCES OF FAT: Soybean oil, egg yolk, buttermilk
SODIUM: 220mg
COMMENTS: Tasters thought the "spicy," "peppery" flavors lent a "nice bite" of "freshness." "Archetypical creamy Italian," said one taster about the "nice combo of spices and herbs." Some tasters were put off by a "tangy," "astringent," "vinegar-heavy" taste. But on the whole, we found Marzetti "very flavorful" and "decent all around."

MARIE'S Creamy Italian Garlic
PRICE: $3.99 for 16 oz.
TOTAL FAT: 19g
PRIMARY SOURCES OF FAT: Soybean oil, sour cream, whole egg, egg yolk
SODIUM: 135mg
COMMENTS: This refrigerated "homemade-tasting" dressing contains sour cream, making it much thicker than other samples. Some tasters liked that, others didn't. The sour cream made it either winningly "thick, rich, and buttery" or "too thick—almost like paste" and "better suited to a dip." One taster wished it had more herb flavor.

WISH-BONE Creamy Italian
PRICE: $1.49 for 8 oz.
TOTAL FAT: 10g
PRIMARY SOURCE OF FAT: Soybean oil
SODIUM: 240mg
COMMENTS: Our panel was split on the "chunky bits," with some calling them "odd chewy bits" and others appreciating the "good crunch of veggies." "Like school cafeteria dressing, in a good way," said one, adding "I like it." Several tasters mentioned the "balanced" flavors, but others found it "sour" and didn't think much of the "slimy" texture, either.

RECOMMENDED WITH RESERVATIONS *(continued)*

KEN'S STEAK HOUSE Creamy Italian
PRICE: $2.50 for 16 oz.
TOTAL FAT: 13g
PRIMARY SOURCES OF FAT: Vegetable oil (soybean and/or canola), sour cream solids (milk)
SODIUM: 300mg
COMMENTS: Tasters struggled to identify the distinctive seasoning (listed only as "spice" on the label), guessing nutmeg, caraway, oregano, allspice, dried basil, and "stale potpourri." "Not bad, but not creamy Italian," observed one. "Sweet, but with good balanced acidity," said another. Naysayers compared it to "corn syrup mixed with mayo and oregano."

NOT RECOMMENDED

NEWMAN'S OWN Creamy Italian
PRICE: $3.49 for 16 oz.
TOTAL FAT: 14g
PRIMARY SOURCES OF FAT: Vegetable oil (soybean and/or canola), egg yolk, buttermilk powder, Romano cheese, Parmesan cheese
SODIUM: 270mg
COMMENTS: The fresh-looking ingredient list gave us high hopes—which were soon dashed. The "very cheese-heavy" flavor tasted "like the green can," one taster said. "Smells like funky cheese, tastes like unwashed socks," said another. The cheese was "gritty and dry," the dressing "one-dimensional" and "too salty."

KRAFT Creamy Italian
PRICE: $3.29 for 16 oz.
TOTAL FAT: 11g
PRIMARY SOURCE OF FAT: Soybean oil
SODIUM: 250mg
COMMENTS: Our tasters had almost nothing nice to say about this "inedibly sweet," "slimy" dressing, which finished dead last for flavor, texture, and perceived freshness. First impression: "Smells like Elmer's glue." Lasting impression: "Overly sweet fake flavor." Other comments included "wet dog-y," "plasticky," and "I wouldn't let this touch my lettuce."

BOTTLED BARBECUE SAUCES

Sometimes home cooks just don't have the time or ingredients to whip together homemade barbecue sauce, and chances are you have a bottle of the store-bought stuff in your refrigerator. But is it the best-tasting option? We gathered eight top-selling national brands and asked tasters to sample each one cooked (broiled on chicken thighs) and raw (on its own and as a dip for chicken nuggets). We'd argue the all-American supermarket style of barbecue sauce should be on the sweet side and balance tang, smoke, and tomato flavor. In fact, total sugars proved the determining factor in our tasting, as sauces with higher total sugars performed better (though one proved it's possible to have too much). And not all sugars are created equal. Our top two are the only sauces in our lineup that list molasses as their third ingredient; other brands contain it, but in lower relative concentrations. Our winner, Bull's-Eye, also contains no high-fructose corn syrup (HFCS); white sugar is its primary sweetener. Because sugar caramelizes more slowly than HFCS, it was easy to get a thick, glossy glaze from Bull's-Eye when broiling without it burning. (Admittedly, the only other HFCS-free variety in our tasting finished last, though it reached a personal best in the broiled chicken test.) If you must buy your sauce, our advice is to avoid those with HFCS and look for molasses. Sauces are listed in order of preference; total sugars is per 2-tablespoon serving.

RECOMMENDED

BULL'S-EYE Original Barbecue Sauce
PRICE: $2.39 for 18 oz.
TOTAL SUGARS: 11g
COMMENTS: This "robust," "spicy" sauce won points for its "great, sticky crust" in the broiled chicken tasting. It also finished first as a dip for chicken nuggets. Tasters praised it as "fresh-tasting, smoky, and tomatoey," "tangy," and with a "good balance of smoky and sweet." "Almost perfect," one noted.

RECOMMENDED WITH RESERVATIONS

KC MASTERPIECE Original Barbecue Sauce
PRICE: $3.69 for 28 oz.
TOTAL SUGARS: 12g
COMMENTS: This "potent" sauce has "a pleasant kick" that one taster described as "very sweet and tangy with a smoky hook." A second taster "could eat this one right out of the bottle," but several others detected distasteful hints of "raisins" and "prunes." Everybody, however, liked its "velvety" texture.

SWEET BABY RAY'S Award Winning Barbecue Sauce
PRICE: $1.67 for 18 oz.
TOTAL SUGARS: 16g
COMMENTS: Tasters said the burn and spice were nice, but the sugar content ("way too sweet") was not. This sauce has the most total sugars and lists high-fructose corn syrup first.

HUNT'S Original Barbecue Sauce
PRICE: $1.25 for 21.6 oz.
TOTAL SUGARS: 11g
COMMENTS: Tasters thought this "thin," middle-of-the-road sample tasted like "sweet and sour sauce," "melted fruit roll-ups," and "barbecue Jolly Ranchers." "Middling potency and sweetness, not a standout but fine" and "solid if uninspiring."

RECOMMENDED WITH RESERVATIONS *(continued)*

KRAFT Original Barbecue Sauce
PRICE: $1.89 for 18 oz.
TOTAL SUGARS: 10g
COMMENTS: Tasters were divided. Some appreciated the fact that this sauce "packs a punch" and liked its deep smoky flavor. Others judged that same smoke flavor as "overwhelming" and "harsh."

NOT RECOMMENDED

JACK DANIEL'S Original No. 7 Recipe Barbecue Sauce
PRICE: $2.99 for 19 oz.
TOTAL SUGARS: 8g
COMMENTS: We heard a chorus of complaints. "Robitussin," "juniper," "nail polish remover," "rancid beer," and "sweat socks" were among the unpleasant flavors tasters detected. Tasters also found it "way too smoky." "Tastes so awful I spit it out."

STUBB'S Original Bar-B-Q Sauce
PRICE: $4.49 for 18 oz.
TOTAL SUGARS: 4g
COMMENTS: "I wouldn't call this barbecue sauce," one taster observed about this "peppery," "sour," and "acidic" sauce. The "tomato and vinegar flavors are not balanced or united," said another. Several thought it resembled "spicy ketchup or marinara sauce," not barbecue sauce.

TEXAS BEST Barbecue Sauce
PRICE: $4.99 for 17.5 oz.
TOTAL SUGARS: 3g
COMMENTS: With drastically less total sugars than our winner, it's no surprise tasters found this Texas-style sauce "an apple among oranges." We liked it in a previous tasting, but the formula has since changed twice. This was the only brand with no molasses, which our tasters missed. They complained about this "very acidic," "tomato-heavy" sauce.

CANNED BLACK BEANS

With typically just three main ingredients—beans, water, and salt—you would think all canned black beans would be about the same. But our blind tasting of six national brands—three of them organic—proved from brand to brand, they can taste plenty different. We tasted each plain (drained and rinsed) and in a test kitchen recipe for black bean soup. The results neatly separated into three brands we like and three we don't. Predictably, our tasters had a strong preference for well-seasoned beans. The three brands that scored the highest—Bush's Best, Goya, and Progresso—all have more than 400 milligrams of sodium per half-cup serving; the three low-scoring brands, all of them organic, contain much less (simply adding more salt didn't help). Texture was important, too, as tasters disliked mushy beans (the three organic brands again). The difference between firm and mushy beans hinges on a balance between chemistry (in the form of salt and other additives) and process (how hot and how long the beans are cooked during canning). Salt accelerates the softening of beans by breaking down the pectin in the cell walls. So you need salt for good flavor, but too much can make the beans mushy. This is why two of our salty, highly ranked brands, Goya and Progresso, add calcium chloride, which counteracts the softening power of sodium by strengthening the pectin in the cell walls of the beans. So how does Bush's achieve firm beans with lots of salt and no calcium chloride? That's proprietary manufacturing information, we're told, but odds are that to preserve more of their firm texture, Bush's quickly processes their beans with less heat than the other brands (the three organic brands are dramatically overcooked). Beans are listed in order of preference; sodium is per ½-cup serving.

RECOMMENDED

BUSH'S BEST Black Beans
PRICE: $1.49 for 15 oz.
INGREDIENTS: Prepared black beans, water, salt
SODIUM: 480mg
COMMENTS: Tasters appreciated the "clean," "mild," and "slightly earthy" flavor of these beans, and several specifically called out the "good salt level." We liked the beans' "firm," "almost al dente" texture when we tasted them plain. In the soup, the beans were especially "creamy."

GOYA Black Beans/Frijoles Negros
PRICE: 89¢ for 15.5 oz.
INGREDIENTS: Black beans, water, salt, calcium chloride
SODIUM: 460mg
COMMENTS: This brand finished a close second to Bush's. These beans, which have almost as much sodium as the winner, won praise for "nutty," "balanced," "briny" flavor and "good firm texture," both plain and in the soup.

PROGRESSO Black Beans
PRICE: $1.59 for 19 oz.
INGREDIENTS: Soaked black beans, water, salt, calcium chloride
SODIUM: 400mg
COMMENTS: Tasters rated these beans slightly softer than Bush's and Goya but still acceptable, somewhat "firm" and "creamy." Their flavor was good but unremarkable tasted plain, approaching "mellow" or even "bland," tasters said. Likewise, in the soup, we found them "creamy but not overly flavorful." A solid if uninspiring choice.

NOT RECOMMENDED

EDEN Organic Black Beans
PRICE: $1.39 for 15 oz.
INGREDIENTS: Organic black turtle beans, water, kombu seaweed
SODIUM: 15mg
COMMENTS: With the least sodium per serving in our lineup by far, it's no wonder our tasters found them "flat," "bland," and "tasteless." They did score slightly better in the soup, where other flavors masked some of their deficiencies. Kombu seaweed is very rich in flavor-enhancing MSG (in fact, a Japanese scientist first discovered MSG in kombu), but the overall sodium was too low to make a difference. Tasters couldn't place the flavor as seaweed, but the kombu, we guess, added something: We detected hints of "tar," "bleach," and "soap."

WALNUT ACRES Organic Whole Black Beans
PRICE: $1.77 for 15 oz.
INGREDIENTS: Organic prepared black beans, water, sea salt
SODIUM: 85mg
COMMENTS: Tasters were impressed by the appearance of these "plump" beans, but not their "pasty," "blown-out" texture or "weak, muddy" flavor. When cooked in the soup, these mushy beans almost disintegrated.

WESTBRAE NATURAL Organic Vegetarian Black Beans
PRICE: $1.71 for 15 oz.
INGREDIENTS: Water, organic black beans, sea salt
SODIUM: 140mg
COMMENTS: "Total mush." "No salt discerned." "Watery." Tasters also detected off-flavors from "dirt" to "cardboard" to "coffee"—nothing we want in our black beans. "On the plus side, you could puree them with a dirty look."

CANNED CHICKEN NOODLE SOUP

Even "gourmet" canned chicken noodle soups can't match the long-cooked goodness of what Grandma could make. But when the need for soup hits quickly, today's busy cooks often reach for the canned version. We wanted to determine which, if any, were worth buying, so we heated eight nationally available canned soups and called in our tasters. The keys, we learned, are no off-flavors or odd textures and plenty of salt—our top four soups had the most sodium (notably, when we added enough salt to a low-sodium entry to match the level of the winner, tasters still disliked it). The soups we rated highest fell into two camps: meaty soups with good flavor and texture and brothy, inexpensive condensed soups, whose scores seemed to be inflated by nostalgia. Our top four also contain MSG, or monosodium glutamate, which enhances meaty, savory flavor. Our top soup did contain the highest percentage of chicken, but more chicken alone couldn't save an otherwise bad soup. The amounts of vegetables and noodles were less important than their texture. Only one brand is recommended, and none received our top rating ("highly recommended"). Soups are listed in order of preference; sodium is per 1-cup serving.

RECOMMENDED

PROGRESSO Traditional Chicken Noodle
PRICE: $2.50 for 19 oz.
SODIUM: 950mg
MSG: Yes
PERCENTAGE OF CHICKEN (out of total soup—broth and solids—weight, 3 cans averaged): 9.6%
COMMENTS: This "salty, but in a really good way" and "robust" soup with "meaty-tasting broth" received the highest scores for both flavor and texture. The noodles "still have some bite," and it contained the highest percentage of chicken that "actually seemed real."

RECOMMENDED WITH RESERVATIONS

PROGRESSO Traditional Hearty Chicken & Rotini
PRICE: $2.50 for 19 oz.
SODIUM: 960mg
MSG: Yes
PERCENTAGE OF CHICKEN: 7.2%
COMMENTS: While some tasters questioned the "weird noodle choice," most praised the "good chicken-y flavor" and "rich, savory broth." A few tasters, however, found the broth "gummy" and "viscous."

CAMPBELL'S Condensed Homestyle Chicken Noodle
PRICE: $1.89 for 10.75 oz.
(makes 21.72 oz. when reconstituted)
SODIUM: 940mg
MSG: Yes
PERCENTAGE OF CHICKEN: 1.6%
COMMENTS: "I know this is ghetto, but I love it," one taster said about this "kid-friendly" soup. The minuscule amount of chicken was deemed "mushy." "Nice and salty and not complex."

CAMPBELL'S Condensed Chicken Noodle Soup
PRICE: $1.49 for 10.75 oz.
(makes 21.72 oz. when reconstituted)
SODIUM: 890mg
MSG: Yes
PERCENTAGE OF CHICKEN: 1.3%
COMMENTS: Even with its "squishy" chicken and "bloated" noodles (and no vegetables), most tasters thought this familiar soup had a "nicely balanced" if "somewhat bland" broth.

NOT RECOMMENDED

MUIR GLEN Organic Chef Inspirations Chicken Noodle Soup
PRICE: $3.29 for 18.8 oz.
SODIUM: 880mg
MSG: No
PERCENTAGE OF CHICKEN: 5.1%
COMMENTS: Tasters were not excited about the "overly vegetal," "very herby" flavor. The "tough and chewy," "hard and dry" meat didn't help matters, nor did the "wobbly," "mushy" noodles.

CAMPBELL'S Select Harvest Healthy Request Chicken with Egg Noodles
PRICE: $3.19 for 18.6 oz.
SODIUM: 480mg
MSG: No
PERCENTAGE OF CHICKEN: 4.5%
COMMENTS: According to the label, the soup is "98% fat-free" and "lower sodium." Tasters didn't need the label to notice the reduced salt, which made for a "flat" and "flavorless" soup. Tasters also identified an unappetizing "metallic," "aluminum" flavor.

HEALTHY CHOICE Old Fashioned Chicken Noodle Soup
PRICE: $2.50 for 15 oz.
SODIUM: 480mg
MSG: No
PERCENTAGE OF CHICKEN: 7.9%
COMMENTS: While tasters liked the texture ("full-bodied broth, firm noodles"), they disliked the "sour, oniony, vegetal" taste, and they really missed the salt. "No flavor, no seasoning." "Tastes flat."

WOLFGANG PUCK Organic Chicken with Egg Noodles Organic Soup
PRICE: $2.59 for 14.5 oz.
SODIUM: 760mg
MSG: No
PERCENTAGE OF CHICKEN: 4.6%
COMMENTS: This "murky," "funky," "scary-looking" brew scored last for both flavor and texture. Tasters were especially put off by the "nasty" bits of dark chicken meat. "Tastes exactly as it looks: like mud."

VANILLA ICE CREAM

To find the best vanilla ice cream, we put the most popular styles of the best-selling brands before our tasting panel. In the end, they strongly preferred brands containing real vanilla extract over those containing synthetic vanilla. But there were other secondary factors. For years manufacturers have used additives to keep ice cream viscous and creamy as it is inevitably subjected to thawing and refreezing, and while a small amount of stabilizers wasn't a bad thing, ice creams with an excess came across as gummy. And additives used to mimic the complex, fatty flavor traditionally provided by egg yolks couldn't hold a candle to those with the real thing. Finally, the less air incorporated into the ice cream (known as overrun), the better. Our top two ice creams also had the lowest overrun. Ice creams are listed in order of preference; sugar and total fat are per ½-cup serving.

HIGHLY RECOMMENDED

BEN & JERRY'S Vanilla
PRICE: $4.39 per pint
SUGAR: 19g TOTAL FAT: 14g OVERRUN: 24%
INGREDIENTS: Cream, skim milk, liquid sugar, water, egg yolks, fair-trade certified vanilla extract with vanilla bean seeds, guar gum, carrageenan
COMMENTS: Tasters praised the "indulgent" vanilla flavor that "built in intensity" and the "deep, creamy, hazelnut aftertaste."

RECOMMENDED

HÄAGEN-DAZS Vanilla
PRICE: $3.50 per 14-oz. container ($4 per pint)
SUGAR: 21g TOTAL FAT: 17g OVERRUN: 26%
INGREDIENTS: Cream, skim milk, sugar, egg yolks, vanilla extract
COMMENTS: This brand had a "creamy, dense, and smooth" texture. While some called it "jam-packed with vanilla punch," others found the flavoring "raw and too strong."

WELLS BLUE BUNNY All Natural Vanilla
PRICE: $3.10 per 1.75-quart container (89¢ per pint)
SUGAR: 16g TOTAL FAT: 9g OVERRUN: 78%
INGREDIENTS: Milk, cream, sugar, skim milk, grade A nonfat dry milk, egg yolks, natural vanilla extract, vanilla beans
COMMENTS: Tasters loved the "lingering" vanilla flavor, but a few complained this ice cream tasted more like milk than vanilla. Its "light and fluffy" texture was "foamy." "This reminds me of soft-serve."

BREYERS Natural Vanilla
PRICE: $5.49 per 1.5-quart container ($1.83 per pint)
SUGAR: 14g TOTAL FAT: 7g OVERRUN: 94%
INGREDIENTS: Milk, cream, sugar, natural vanilla flavor, natural tara gum
COMMENTS: While several tasters praised this ice cream's vanilla flavor as "very intense" and "clean," others pointed out that it "quickly dissipates." It lost points for having an "icy, crumbly" texture.

RECOMMENDED WITH RESERVATIONS

FRIENDLY'S Vanilla
PRICE: $5.49 per 1.5-quart container ($1.83 per pint)
SUGAR: 11g TOTAL FAT: 8g OVERRUN: 94%
INGREDIENTS: Milk, cream, corn syrup, skim milk, sugar, whey protein concentrate, whey, buttermilk, vanilla extract, guar gum, mono- and diglycerides, xanthan gum, carrageenan, annatto extract and turmeric (for color)
COMMENTS: Some enjoyed the "custardy" texture; others found it "Play-Doh-like." But the "muted, weak" vanilla flavor was what really knocked it down in the rankings.

BLUE BELL Homemade Vanilla
PRICE: $6.65 per 2-quart container ($1.66 per pint)
SUGAR: 21g TOTAL FAT: 8g OVERRUN: 46%
INGREDIENTS: Milk, cream, sugar, skim milk, high-fructose corn syrup, corn syrup, natural and artificial vanilla flavor, cellulose gum, vegetable gums (guar, carrageenan, carob bean), salt, annatto color
COMMENTS: Tasters disliked this ice cream's "over the top" vanilla flavor that tasted "artificial," concluding, "This is not adult ice cream." Most also panned its insubstantial texture.

TURKEY HILL Vanilla Bean
PRICE: $5.29 per 1.5-quart container ($1.77 per pint)
SUGAR: 12g TOTAL FAT: 7g OVERRUN: 94%
INGREDIENTS: Milk, cream, sugar, corn syrup, whey, nonfat milk, mono- and diglycerides, vanilla, guar gum, vanilla bean, carrageenan
COMMENTS: "Fake," "medicinal" vanilla flavor helped demote this previous winner. While some found its "cotton candy–like" texture appealing, the majority did not.

NOT RECOMMENDED

EDY'S GRAND Vanilla
PRICE: $5.59 per 1.5-quart container ($1.86 per pint)
SUGAR: 14g TOTAL FAT: 8g OVERRUN: 97%
INGREDIENTS: Skim milk, cream, sugar, corn syrup, cellulose gum, mono- and diglycerides, guar gum, carrageenan, annatto color, dextrose, natural flavor
COMMENTS: Downgraded for its "unremarkable, fading vanilla flavor" (notice vanilla is not in its ingredient list), this brand's "fluffy, marshmallow-y" texture put it at the bottom.

CHOCOLATE ICE CREAM

We thought premium brands would blow mass-market options out of the water for our tasting of the eight best-selling chocolate ice creams. However, while premium ice creams distinguish themselves by their richness and creamy texture (which comes from the presence of egg yolks and lower overrun, an industry term that refers to the amount of air churned into ice cream), our results proved our tasters care most about deep chocolate flavor. Mass-market brands may be light, fluffy, and sweet, but two in our lineup definitely taste like chocolate, earning them spots just behind our winner, a premium brand. Ice creams are listed in order of preference; total fat is per ½-cup serving.

RECOMMENDED

BEN & JERRY'S Chocolate
PRICE: $3.99 for 1 pint
INGREDIENTS: Cream, liquid sugar, water, skim milk, fair-trade certified cocoa processed with alkali, guar gum, carrageenan, egg yolks
TOTAL FAT: 14g OVERRUN: 22%
COMMENTS: This "very chocolaty," "pleasantly creamy" ice cream had "darker" and "more concentrated" flavor than the others. Most equated it with "perfection"; a few compared it with "burnt coffee."

FRIENDLY'S Rich & Creamy Classic Chocolate
PRICE: $2.99 for 1.5 quarts
INGREDIENTS: Milk, cream, skim milk, sugar, corn syrup, cocoa processed with alkali, whey protein concentrate, whey, buttermilk, guar gum, mono- and diglycerides, xanthan gum, carrageenan
TOTAL FAT: 8g OVERRUN: 94%
COMMENTS: This ice cream won points for its "smooth," "light" texture and "ultra-creamy mouthfeel." The flavor reminded a few of "frozen hot cocoa."

EDY'S Grand Rich & Creamy Chocolate
PRICE: $3.09 for 1.5 quarts
INGREDIENTS: Milk, cream, skim milk, sugar, cocoa processed with alkali, cellulose gum, mono- and diglycerides, guar gum, carrageenan, dextrose
TOTAL FAT: 8g OVERRUN: 97%
COMMENTS: This brand was "super chocolaty" and full of "very dark flavor." It rated second only to Ben & Jerry's for chocolate flavor. But it lost points for its texture: "Like a frozen pudding, not especially creamy."

WELLS BLUE BUNNY Chocolate Champion
PRICE: $3.19 for 1.75 quarts
INGREDIENTS: Milk, cream, buttermilk, sugar, whey, corn syrup, cocoa processed with alkali, guar gum, mono- and diglycerides, sodium phosphate, cellulose gum, sodium citrate, carageenan, polysorbate 80, yellow 6 lake, blue 2 lake, red 40, yellow 5, blue 1, red 40 lake
TOTAL FAT: 6g OVERRUN: 97%
COMMENTS: This brand had a "creamy finish" that tasted "whipped." Flavor was less impressive: "More sweet than chocolate." A few said it was "excellent on all counts."

RECOMMENDED WITH RESERVATIONS

HÄAGEN-DAZS Chocolate
PRICE: $3.50 for 14 ounces
INGREDIENTS: Cream, skim milk, sugar, egg yolks, cocoa processed with alkali
TOTAL FAT: 17g OVERRUN: 25%
COMMENTS: We expected better results, given the low overrun. But tasters found it "kind of blah," although its "smooth," "firm" texture gave it a respectable standing. One happy taster called this sample "chocolaty without seeming too 'mature.'"

BLUE BELL Dutch Chocolate
Price: $6.65 for 2 quarts
INGREDIENTS: Milk, cream, sugar, skim milk, high-fructose corn syrup, cocoa processed with alkali, cellulose gum, vegetable gums (guar, carrageenan, carob bean), salt, flour, soy flour
TOTAL FAT: 9g OVERRUN: 45%
COMMENTS: A few tasters praised its "good bittersweet balance"; most described it as "nothing special." It was "a bit chalky" and "lacking thick and creamy consistency." As one taster put it, it felt "like cool nothing in my mouth—chocolate cloud vapor."

NOT RECOMMENDED

TURKEY HILL Dutch Chocolate Original Recipe Premium
PRICE: $4.99 for 1.5 quarts
INGREDIENTS: Milk, cream, sugar, corn syrup, cocoa processed with alkali, whey, nonfat milk, mono- and diglycerides, guar gum, carrageenan
TOTAL FAT: 7g OVERRUN: 94%
COMMENTS: "Tastes like cheap chocolate chips" one taster said about this brand, which had the least chocolate flavor, according to our panel. They found the texture "too airy and frothy."

BREYER'S All Natural Chocolate
Price: $5.49 for 1.5 quarts
INGREDIENTS: Milk, cream, sugar, cocoa processed with alkali, whey, natural tara gum, natural flavor
TOTAL FAT: 7g OVERRUN: 94%
COMMENTS: "Grainy," "icy," and "not substantial enough." Tasters noted a "processed taste" and lack of "bold chocolate flavor." Several tasted "alcohol," "sour milk," and "Robitussin."

LARGE SAUCEPANS

Now that even low-cost manufacturers are offering fully clad cookware—a construction that features alternating layers of materials extending from the cooking surface up the sides, ensuring more even cooking—we wondered if we still needed to shell out $200 for our former favorite in this category, the All-Clad Stainless 4-Quart Saucepan. In our testing, we found that the real differences came down to design and maneuverability. Pans that were particularly heavy or had poorly designed handles did not rate well, nor did those with sharp corner angles that prevented a whisk from getting into the corners. Happily, we found that a good-quality, fully clad, easy-to-maneuver pan could be had for just $69.99, but in the end our old favorite still reigned supreme. Saucepans are listed in order of preference.

RECOMMENDED	PERFORMANCE	TESTERS' COMMENTS
ALL-CLAD Stainless 4-Quart Saucepan with Lid and Loop MODEL: 5204LP WEIGHT: 3.3 lb. PRICE: $194.99 MATERIAL: 18/10 stainless steel interior, aluminum core, magnetized stainless steel exterior	COOKING: ★★★ DESIGN: ★★½	Our champ held on to its title for heating slowly and evenly enough to prevent the onions from scorching and the pastry cream and rice from overcooking. Our only quibbles: It lacks a rounded pouring lip, and some testers complained that the handle's angle felt awkward and that its sharp upper edge dug into their fingers.
CUISINART MultiClad Unlimited 4-Quart Saucepan `BEST BUY` MODEL: MCU194-20 WEIGHT: 2.4 lb. PRICE: $69.99 MATERIAL: 18/10 stainless steel interior, hard anodized aluminum exterior	COOKING: ★★½ DESIGN: ★★½	This lightweight pan performed virtually identically to our winner (the biggest difference is that it cooks a little faster), and its handle garnered compliments like "well-balanced" and "comfortable." The rolled lip helped to ensure a spill-free pour. Its biggest flaw: the interior scratched easily.
J.A. HENCKELS Classic Clad 4-Quart Saucepan with Lid MODEL: 40316-200 WEIGHT: 3.25 lb. PRICE: $85.99 MATERIAL: Stainless steel interior, aluminum core, stainless steel exterior	COOKING: ★★★ DESIGN: ★★	A good performer overall, this pan cooks beautifully. But when it came to design, testers were split: Some appreciated the thick, arched handle, while others dubbed it "bulky" and struggled when pouring. As one tester put it, this pan would be perfect "if it never had to leave the stove."

RECOMMENDED WITH RESERVATIONS	PERFORMANCE	TESTERS' COMMENTS
TRAMONTINA Gourmet 4-Quart Tri-Ply-Clad Stainless Steel Saucepan MODEL: 80116/514 WEIGHT: 3.35 lb. PRICE: $49.97 MATERIAL: 18/10 stainless steel interior, aluminum alloy core, magnetic stainless steel exterior	COOKING: ★★½ DESIGN: ★★½	Nearly identical to All-Clad in looks, this pan cooked a tiny bit faster. But most testers complained about it feeling "top-heavy" and "unbalanced," with a handle too thin to accommodate its weight, which made the helper handle more of a necessity than a bonus feature.
CUISINOX Elite 3.6-Liter (3.8-Quart) Covered Saucepan MODEL: POT320 WEIGHT: 3.2 lb. PRICE: $159.90 MATERIAL: 18/10 stainless steel interior, aluminum core, magnetic stainless steel exterior	COOKING: ★★½ DESIGN: ★★	This saucepan heated slightly faster than our top pans, resulting in a few onions that overbrowned. Though it is one of the lightest pans, its shape and handle angle did little to help distribute the weight, making it nearly impossible to pour 1½ quarts of water without using the helper handle.

NOT RECOMMENDED	PERFORMANCE	TESTERS' COMMENTS
VIKING Professional Cookware 3-Quart Saucepan MODEL: DW1607 WEIGHT: 3.5 lb. PRICE: $199.95 MATERIAL: 18/10 stainless steel interior, aluminum core, 18/10 magnetized stainless steel exterior	COOKING: ★★★ DESIGN: ★½	Despite seven layers of three different types of metal, this pan performed only marginally better than pots costing a fraction of its price. What's more, its frame was "unwieldy," with a poorly placed handle that was also "hard to grip."
DEMEYERE Atlantis 3.2-Quart Saucepan with Lid MODEL: 41420+41520 WEIGHT: 3.5 lb. PRICE: $274.95 MATERIAL: 18/10 stainless steel interior, copper core, stainless steel exterior	COOKING: ★★½ DESIGN: ★	This model produced perfectly browned onions and fluffy pilaf, but pastry cream stuck then curdled in this pan's sharp corners. Testers complained about bottom-heaviness and angle of the handle made pouring liquid "terribly uncomfortable."

"HYBRID" CHEF'S KNIVES

The familiar all-purpose chef's knife has a thick, wedge-shaped blade that can push through tough foods and a curved edge that allows the blade to rhythmically rock when chopping. It won't chip or break easily and it's simple to resharpen. By contrast, in Japan there isn't one all-purpose knife, but instead various specialized knives; all are extremely thin, with a razor-sharp cutting edge honed on just one side that allows for incredibly precise cutting. These Japanese knives have a straighter edge than a chef's knife and are typically made of very hard steel to support the thinness of the blade. Only recently have knife makers merged the two styles. Called the *gyutou* (ghee-YOU-toe) in Japan, this hybrid knife fuses Japanese knife making with Western knife design. The result is a feather-light, lethally sharp, and wonderfully precise knife. We tested eight hybrid knives and our winning traditional chef's knife. Interestingly, our traditional knife beat out all but two of the hybrids, the Masamoto VG-10 and the Misono UX-10, and the sheer pleasure of using these knives' sleek, well-designed blades makes them a worthy addition to any cook's knife block. Knives are listed in order of preference.

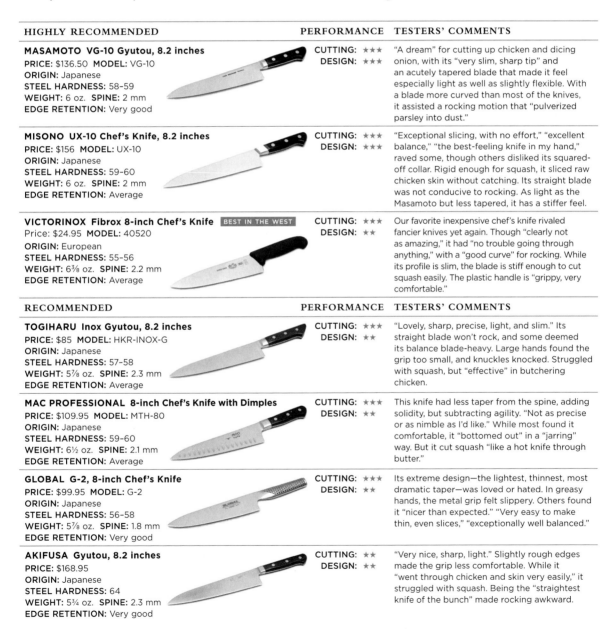

HIGHLY RECOMMENDED	PERFORMANCE	TESTERS' COMMENTS
MASAMOTO VG-10 Gyutou, 8.2 inches PRICE: $136.50 MODEL: VG-10 ORIGIN: Japanese STEEL HARDNESS: 58–59 WEIGHT: 6 oz. SPINE: 2 mm EDGE RETENTION: Very good	CUTTING: ★★★ DESIGN: ★★★	"A dream" for cutting up chicken and dicing onion, with its "very slim, sharp tip" and an acutely tapered blade that made it feel especially light as well as slightly flexible. With a blade more curved than most of the knives, it assisted a rocking motion that "pulverized parsley into dust."
MISONO UX-10 Chef's Knife, 8.2 inches PRICE: $156 MODEL: UX-10 ORIGIN: Japanese STEEL HARDNESS: 59–60 WEIGHT: 6 oz. SPINE: 2 mm EDGE RETENTION: Average	CUTTING: ★★★ DESIGN: ★★★	"Exceptional slicing, with no effort," "excellent balance," "the best-feeling knife in my hand," raved some, though others disliked its squared-off collar. Rigid enough for squash, it sliced raw chicken skin without catching. Its straight blade was not conducive to rocking. As light as the Masamoto but less tapered, it has a stiffer feel.
VICTORINOX Fibrox 8-inch Chef's Knife BEST IN THE WEST Price: $24.95 MODEL: 40520 ORIGIN: European STEEL HARDNESS: 55–56 WEIGHT: 6⅜ oz. SPINE: 2.2 mm EDGE RETENTION: Average	CUTTING: ★★★ DESIGN: ★★	Our favorite inexpensive chef's knife rivaled fancier knives yet again. Though "clearly not as amazing," it had "no trouble going through anything," with a "good curve" for rocking. While its profile is slim, the blade is stiff enough to cut squash easily. The plastic handle is "grippy, very comfortable."

RECOMMENDED	PERFORMANCE	TESTERS' COMMENTS
TOGIHARU Inox Gyutou, 8.2 inches PRICE: $85 MODEL: HKR-INOX-G ORIGIN: Japanese STEEL HARDNESS: 57–58 WEIGHT: 5⅞ oz. SPINE: 2.3 mm EDGE RETENTION: Average	CUTTING: ★★★ DESIGN: ★★	"Lovely, sharp, precise, light, and slim." Its straight blade won't rock, and some deemed its balance blade-heavy. Large hands found the grip too small, and knuckles knocked. Struggled with squash, but "effective" in butchering chicken.
MAC PROFESSIONAL 8-inch Chef's Knife with Dimples PRICE: $109.95 MODEL: MTH-80 ORIGIN: Japanese STEEL HARDNESS: 59–60 WEIGHT: 6½ oz. SPINE: 2.1 mm EDGE RETENTION: Average	CUTTING: ★★★ DESIGN: ★★	This knife had less taper from the spine, adding solidity, but subtracting agility. "Not as precise or as nimble as I'd like." While most found it comfortable, it "bottomed out" in a "jarring" way. But it cut squash "like a hot knife through butter."
GLOBAL G-2, 8-inch Chef's Knife PRICE: $99.95 MODEL: G-2 ORIGIN: Japanese STEEL HARDNESS: 56–58 WEIGHT: 5⅞ oz. SPINE: 1.8 mm EDGE RETENTION: Very good	CUTTING: ★★★ DESIGN: ★★	Its extreme design—the lightest, thinnest, most dramatic taper—was loved or hated. In greasy hands, the metal grip felt slippery. Others found it "nicer than expected." "Very easy to make thin, even slices," "exceptionally well balanced."
AKIFUSA Gyutou, 8.2 inches PRICE: $168.95 ORIGIN: Japanese STEEL HARDNESS: 64 WEIGHT: 5¾ oz. SPINE: 2.3 mm EDGE RETENTION: Very good	CUTTING: ★★ DESIGN: ★★	"Very nice, sharp, light." Slightly rough edges made the grip less comfortable. While it "went through chicken and skin very easily," it struggled with squash. Being the "straightest knife of the bunch" made rocking awkward.

"GREEN" SKILLETS

Traditional nonstick coatings use two controversial chemicals (PFOA and PTFE), so it's no surprise that the nonstick skillet is getting its turn to "go green." In our testing of 12-inch "green" skillets, not a single one was without flaw in terms of cooking performance, and none were ideally designed or as durable as our traditional pan. And while two of the new coatings are entirely free of the chemicals, a third merely eliminates one of them. And because of their newer technology, these skillets require more resources to manufacture than the traditional, two factors that make whether they are really green debatable. Until technology improves, we're sticking with the traditional nonstick or a well-seasoned cast iron. Skillets are listed in order of preference.

RECOMMENDED WITH RESERVATIONS

	PERFORMANCE	TESTERS' COMMENTS
SCANPAN Professional 12.25-inch Fry Pan MODEL: 60003200 PRICE: $129.95 COATING: Contains PTFE, no PFOA BASE MATERIAL: Compressed aluminum with ceramic titanium COOKING SURFACE: 10.75 in. WEIGHT: 3.3 lb.	NONSTICK PERFORMANCE: ★★★ DESIGN: ★★ DURABILITY/ SCRATCHING: ★★	Steaks seared well and browned evenly on the generous surface area, and fish and scrambled eggs cooked without sticking. Metal utensils left slight scratches, but overall this pan had the most durable surface of the models and performed closest to traditional nonstick. Still, it was unbalanced, heavy, and a standard 12-inch lid will not fit it.
EARTH PAN 12-inch Hard Anodized Skillet MODEL: 19495EPR PRICE: $39.95 COATING: Silicone copolymer BASE MATERIAL: Hard anodized aluminum COOKING SURFACE: 9.62 in. WEIGHT: 2.18 lb.	NONSTICK PERFORMANCE: ★★ DESIGN: ★★ DURABILITY/ SCRATCHING: ★★	At first this pan easily released food, but after days of testing, we noticed deterioration of the nonstick surface, fond that began to build up when we cooked, and light but visible scratches. However, the skillet felt comfortable, and sautéing was quick and easy, though a few testers felt the handle was a little low and awkward.
DEMEYERE-RESTO 12.6-inch Ecoglide Frying Pan without Lid MODEL: 85632 PRICE: $139.99 COATING: Contains PTFE, no PFOA BASE MATERIAL: Stainless steel COOKING SURFACE: 10.75 in. WEIGHT: 3.9 lb.	NONSTICK PERFORMANCE: ★★★ DESIGN: ★ DURABILITY/ SCRATCHING: ★	Far too heavy and cumbersome, but the nonstick quality was excellent. It took noticeably longer to heat than other skillets, but once the pan was at temperature, food browned evenly. Scrambled eggs turned out light and fluffy, though the coating became severely scratched when we used metal utensils.

NOT RECOMMENDED

	PERFORMANCE	TESTERS' COMMENTS
GREENPAN 12.5-INCH Frypan MODEL: 355051 PRICE: $84.95 COATING: Ceramic BASE MATERIAL: Hard anodized aluminum COOKING SURFACE: 9 in. WEIGHT: 2.55 lb.	NONSTICK PERFORMANCE: ★★ DESIGN: ★★ DURABILITY/ SCRATCHING: ★	This ceramic-coated aluminum pan performed well at first but slipped as testing went on. Eggs and fish released easily, but we struggled to cook steak evenly. The higher vertical sides and small cooking surface cramped food; it discolored and scratched severely. The comfortable, heat-resistant handle was a bright spot.
CUISINART GreenGourmet 12-inch Skillet with Helper Handle MODEL: GG22-30H PRICE: $69.95 COATING: Ceramic BASE MATERIAL: Hard anodized aluminum COOKING SURFACE: 9 in. WEIGHT: 3.4 lb.	NONSTICK PERFORMANCE: ★ DESIGN: ★ DURABILITY/ SCRATCHING: ★★	The extra handle came in handy on this heavy pan, but it couldn't outweigh its generally subpar performance. Scrambled eggs stuck to the sides and rivets. The vertical sides and smaller cooking surface crowded steaks, which burned on the outside before they cooked through. Stir-fry results were good and wear and tear was minimal.
STARFRIT Alternative Eco Pan 11-inch Fry Pan MODEL: 30432-003-0000 PRICE: $33.60 COATING: Ceramic BASE MATERIAL: Cast aluminum COOKING SURFACE: 9.62 in. WEIGHT: 2.25 lb.	NONSTICK PERFORMANCE: ★ DESIGN: ★ DURABILITY/ SCRATCHING: ★	The handle on this flimsy pan started to loosen after the first few tests, and because it is not heat-resistant, the pan couldn't go in the oven. Temperature was hard to control; eggs stuck. Steaks were crowded and steamed. Fish stuck and ripped when we tried to remove it from the skillet. The pan sustained deep scratches.

HAND-HELD MIXERS

Even if you own a standing mixer, there are some jobs, like whipping cream or beating eggs, where it's just easier to grab a hand-held model. Over the years, however, we've been disappointed; they can be little more than glorified whisks. We headed into the kitchen with seven leading models of hand-held mixers to see if we could separate the wimps from the workhorses. Many had their shortcomings, including lack of power and excessive splattering. But our winner can handle just about everything but kneading bread dough as well as a standing mixer—at a fraction of the price. Mixers are listed in order of preference.

HIGHLY RECOMMENDED		PERFORMANCE	TESTERS' COMMENTS

CUISINART Power Advantage 7-Speed Hand Mixer
MODEL: HM-70
PRICE: $49.95
WEIGHT: 2 lb. 8 oz.

RANGE OF SPEEDS: ★★★
DESIGN: ★★★
LIGHT WHIPPING: ★★★
HEAVY MIXING: ★★★
MASHED POTATOES: ★★

Powerful enough to whip and beat almost as quickly as a stand mixer, its extra-low speed also let us incorporate light ingredients with no mess. The motor was quiet, and the simple digital controls, separate beater-release lever, and contoured handle made the mixer a pleasure to use. A swiveling cord helps left-handed users.

KITCHENAID Professional 9-Speed Hand Mixer
MODEL: KHM9P
PRICE: $79.99
WEIGHT: 2 lb. 5⅜ oz.

RANGE OF SPEEDS: ★★★
DESIGN: ★★★
LIGHT WHIPPING: ★★★
HEAVY MIXING: ★★★
MASHED POTATOES: ★★

This model has the low speeds needed for mess-free mixing. Its lightweight body, quiet motor, digital speed controls, and separate button for beater release contributed to its high score. But it cost $30 more than the Cuisinart, dropping it to second place.

RECOMMENDED WITH RESERVATIONS		PERFORMANCE	TESTERS' COMMENTS

BLACK & DECKER Power Pro 250-Watt Hand Mixer
MODEL: MX300
PRICE: $20.95
WEIGHT: 2 lb. 4⅝ oz.

RANGE OF SPEEDS: ★
DESIGN: ★
LIGHT WHIPPING: ★★★
HEAVY MIXING: ★
MASHED POTATOES: ★

This turbo-charged mixer whipped and creamed at breakneck speed. But its lowest speed was way too fast—spraying flour, cream, and batter everywhere. Its motor was deafening, and its useless spatula attachment trapped batter before popping off.

SUNBEAM Heritage Hand Mixer
MODEL: 3156
PRICE: $39.99
WEIGHT: 2 lb. 7⅛ oz.

RANGE OF SPEEDS: ★
DESIGN: ★
LIGHT WHIPPING: ★★★
HEAVY MIXING: ★
MASHED POTATOES: ★

Although it whipped and mixed quickly, there was little difference between low and high speeds. Even set to "low," it sprayed batter and flour. Large, circular vents provided retro style—but had nooks that trapped food.

OSTER 6-Speed 250-Watt Hand Mixer
MODEL: 2577
PRICE: $34.15
WEIGHT: 3 lb.

RANGE OF SPEEDS: ★
DESIGN: ★
LIGHT WHIPPING: ★★★
HEAVY MIXING: ★
MASHED POTATOES: ★

We liked the retractable cord, but even on "low," this souped-up mixer left more food outside than in the bowl. Its weight made our arms ache, and it should come with earplugs.

NOT RECOMMENDED		PERFORMANCE	TESTERS' COMMENTS

HAMILTON BEACH 6-Speed Hand Mixer
MODEL: 62695V
PRICE: $29.99
WEIGHT: 2 lb. 8⅜ oz.

RANGE OF SPEEDS: ★
DESIGN: ★
LIGHT WHIPPING: ★★
HEAVY MIXING: ★
MASHED POTATOES: ★

Adequate for whipping, creaming, and mixing, but its fast "low" speed splattered ingredients. The cheap speed dial didn't match actual speeds. And a burning smell during the mashed potatoes test made us wonder how long this mixer would last.

PROCTOR SILEX Plus Hand Mixer
MODEL: 62545
PRICE: $15.99
WEIGHT: 1 lb. 14 oz.

RANGE OF SPEEDS: ★
DESIGN: ★
LIGHT WHIPPING: ★★
HEAVY MIXING: ★
MASHED POTATOES: ★

This lightweight, inexpensive mixer with a handy snap-on storage case did a decent job of whipping, beating, and creaming. But it struggled with thick cookie dough. The strong burning smell as we mashed potatoes indicated a weak motor.

IMMERSION BLENDERS

Immersion blenders are simpler to use and clean than ordinary blenders and food processors, but can they produce comparable results? We tested several models making smoothies and pesto to find out. We quickly learned why most immersion blenders come with "mixing cups." For a number of jobs, the tapered cup keeps food close to the blades so the blender works more effectively. Meanwhile, the protective cage around the blades must allow blended food to exit without being sucked back into the vortex. Blenders need strong motors to generate circulation, especially for large pots of soup, and while multiple speeds sound great, we only used high and low. We preferred models with big buttons that were easy to hold down. Weight factored in, too; just try holding a too-heavy blender with one hand while drizzling oil into egg yolks to make mayonnaise. Immersion blenders should be easy to clean, and models with dishwasher-safe, detachable shafts were best. Those with cramped cages that trapped food lost points. In the end, we found that the cheapest in our lineup was also our favorite. Immersion blenders are listed in order of preference.

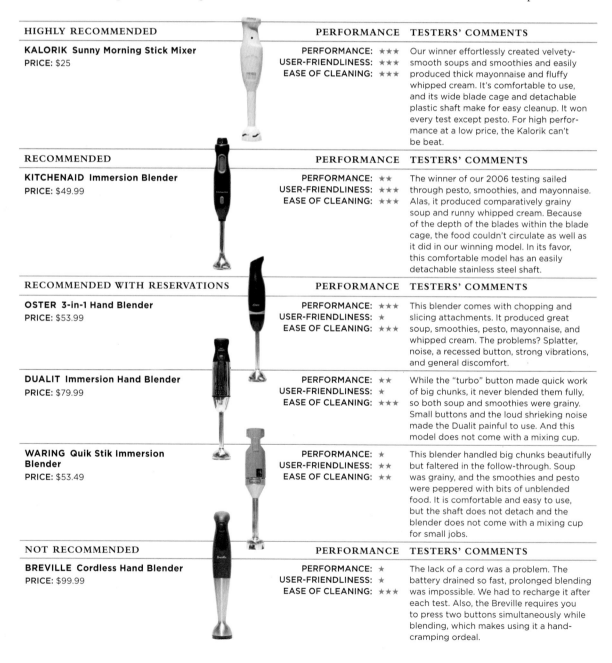

HIGHLY RECOMMENDED	PERFORMANCE	TESTERS' COMMENTS
KALORIK Sunny Morning Stick Mixer PRICE: $25	PERFORMANCE: ★★★ USER-FRIENDLINESS: ★★★ EASE OF CLEANING: ★★★	Our winner effortlessly created velvety-smooth soups and smoothies and easily produced thick mayonnaise and fluffy whipped cream. It's comfortable to use, and its wide blade cage and detachable plastic shaft make for easy cleanup. It won every test except pesto. For high performance at a low price, the Kalorik can't be beat.

RECOMMENDED	PERFORMANCE	TESTERS' COMMENTS
KITCHENAID Immersion Blender PRICE: $49.99	PERFORMANCE: ★★ USER-FRIENDLINESS: ★★★ EASE OF CLEANING: ★★★	The winner of our 2006 testing sailed through pesto, smoothies, and mayonnaise. Alas, it produced comparatively grainy soup and runny whipped cream. Because of the depth of the blades within the blade cage, the food couldn't circulate as well as it did in our winning model. In its favor, this comfortable model has an easily detachable stainless steel shaft.

RECOMMENDED WITH RESERVATIONS	PERFORMANCE	TESTERS' COMMENTS
OSTER 3-in-1 Hand Blender PRICE: $53.99	PERFORMANCE: ★★★ USER-FRIENDLINESS: ★ EASE OF CLEANING: ★★★	This blender comes with chopping and slicing attachments. It produced great soup, smoothies, pesto, mayonnaise, and whipped cream. The problems? Splatter, noise, a recessed button, strong vibrations, and general discomfort.
DUALIT Immersion Hand Blender PRICE: $79.99	PERFORMANCE: ★★ USER-FRIENDLINESS: ★ EASE OF CLEANING: ★★★	While the "turbo" button made quick work of big chunks, it never blended them fully, so both soup and smoothies were grainy. Small buttons and the loud shrieking noise made the Dualit painful to use. And this model does not come with a mixing cup.
WARING Quik Stik Immersion Blender PRICE: $53.49	PERFORMANCE: ★ USER-FRIENDLINESS: ★★ EASE OF CLEANING: ★★	This blender handled big chunks beautifully but faltered in the follow-through. Soup was grainy, and the smoothies and pesto were peppered with bits of unblended food. It is comfortable and easy to use, but the shaft does not detach and the blender does not come with a mixing cup for small jobs.

NOT RECOMMENDED	PERFORMANCE	TESTERS' COMMENTS
BREVILLE Cordless Hand Blender PRICE: $99.99	PERFORMANCE: ★ USER-FRIENDLINESS: ★ EASE OF CLEANING: ★★★	The lack of a cord was a problem. The battery drained so fast, prolonged blending was impossible. We had to recharge it after each test. Also, the Breville requires you to press two buttons simultaneously while blending, which makes using it a hand-cramping ordeal.

PASTRY BRUSHES

Manufacturers have released many new models since our previous testing of pastry brushes, when the OXO Good Grips Silicone Pastry Brush won top honors. We tested eight other models painting egg wash on dumplings, basting grilled chicken, oiling a hot pan, and more. Our old winner remained on top. Brushes are listed in order of preference.

HIGHLY RECOMMENDED	PERFORMANCE	TESTERS' COMMENTS
OXO Good Grips Silicone Pastry Brush MODEL: 1071062 PRICE: $6.99 MATERIAL: Silicone	EGG WASH: ★★★ BARBECUE SAUCE: ★★★ CRUMBS: ★★★ SMELL TEST: ★★★ DESIGN: ★★★	This lightweight brush features perforated flaps in the bristles that hold liquid, even watery egg wash. It was delicate enough to paint pastry and brushed barbecue sauce evenly and thickly. The angled head helped reach tight spots and kept sauce off the counter when we set it down.

RECOMMENDED	PERFORMANCE	TESTERS' COMMENTS
KAISERFLEX Large Basting Brush/ Pastry Brush MODEL: 682044 PRICE: $10 MATERIAL: Silicone	EGG WASH: ★★★ BARBECUE SAUCE: ★★ CRUMBS: ★★★ SMELL TEST: ★★★ DESIGN: ★★	Thin, flexible bristles delicately painted egg wash, spread softened butter evenly on baguettes, and painted hot oil on pans. But heavy barbecue sauce dripped off slightly too much, and the metal handle was somewhat awkward to grasp.

RECOMMENDED WITH RESERVATIONS	PERFORMANCE	TESTERS' COMMENTS
MARIO BATALI Italian Kitchen Silicone Pastry Brush MODEL: 0-49120 PRICE: $7.99 MATERIAL: Silicone	EGG WASH: ★ BARBECUE SAUCE: ★★★ CRUMBS: ★★ SMELL TEST: ★★ DESIGN: ★★★	This brush's big bristles spread barbecue sauce like a champ but struggled to paint egg wash evenly on pastry and tore crumbs from delicate cake. The handle felt comfortable and sturdy in our hands. Great for barbecue sauce.
OXO Good Grips Pastry Brush MODEL: 73881 PRICE: $6.99 MATERIAL: Natural Boar's Bristle	EGG WASH: ★★★ BARBECUE SAUCE: ★ CRUMBS: ★★★ SMELL TEST: ★★ DESIGN: ★★★	Modeled like our winner, it's no surprise this brush got top marks in design and comfort. But its natural boar bristles curled and burned in the heat, held smells, and clumped with barbecue sauce.

NOT RECOMMENDED	PERFORMANCE	TESTERS' COMMENTS
ATECO Flat Pastry Brush MODEL: 60215 PRICE: $4.10 MATERIAL: Natural Boar's Bristle	EGG WASH: ★★★ BARBECUE SAUCE: ★ CRUMBS: ★★★ SMELL TEST: ★ DESIGN: ★★	This natural bristle brush is a true pastry brush, gently brushing away crumbs. Its silicone collar held bristles tightly. But keep it away from heat and heavier basting jobs.
CUISINART Silicone Basting Brush MODEL: 89456 PRICE: $7.99 MATERIAL: Silicone	EGG WASH: ★★ BARBECUE SAUCE: ★ CRUMBS: ★★★ SMELL TEST: ★★★ DESIGN: ★	The flat, wide plastic handle was awkward and slippery, but this brush maneuvered adequately around pastry folds, and wiped away cake crumbs like a gentle breeze. We had trouble applying barbecue sauce on chicken—its bristles couldn't convey enough sauce.
ORIGINAL KAISER Backform Wooden Pastry Brushes, Set of 2 MODEL: 660516 PRICE: $8 ($4 per brush) MATERIAL: Natural Boar's Bristle	EGG WASH: ★★ BARBECUE SAUCE: ★★ CRUMBS: ★★★ SMELL TEST: ★ DESIGN: ★	These bristles are built like cheap paintbrushes. They spread oil and egg wash fairly easily, but barely picked up liquid and lacked the bulk to spread barbecue sauce. Their strong point, due to the featherweight design, was in brushing cake crumbs.
DKB HOUSEHOLD USA/ZYLISS Silicone Basting Brush MODEL: 50540 PRICE: $10 MATERIAL: Silicone	EGG WASH: ★ BARBECUE SAUCE: ★ CRUMBS: ★★ SMELL TEST: ★ DESIGN: ★	This brush has a perforated flap inside the bristles, but its one stiff flap (versus the OXO's three) struggled to hold egg wash and oil yet wouldn't let go of barbecue sauce. Consequently, pastry became dripping wet, while chicken was barely coated.
ALL-CLAD Pastry Brush MODEL: T-132 PRICE: $21.95 MATERIAL: Natural Boar's Bristle	EGG WASH: ★ BARBECUE SAUCE: ★ CRUMBS: ★ SMELL TEST: ★ DESIGN: ★	At this price, we expected top-notch performance, but this brush failed every test. The bulky bristles began shedding after the first use. They picked up barbecue sauce and softened butter but refused to release them, and they curled and browned to a crisp in the heat.

GRILL COOKWARE

Grill grates are designed to contain and cook smaller, more fragile foods without special preparation for fear of losing them to the fire below, and without sacrificing good flavor and charring or browning. We rounded up models in all styles and a range of materials for testing. Grill woks failed us, causing food to steam, and pans with a nonstick coating emitted fumes, giving food a chemical smell and taste. Pans are listed in order of preference.

HIGHLY RECOMMENDED	PERFORMANCE	TESTERS' COMMENTS
WEBER Professional-Grade Grill Pan MODEL: 6435 PRICE: $19.99 SIZE: 14 x 11 in. MATERIAL: Stainless steel	COOKING: ★★★ DESIGN: ★★★ USER-FRIENDLINESS: ★★★ CLEANUP: ★★★	This sturdy pan was well designed, with ⅛-inch slits rather than holes, so that even chopped onion pieces didn't fall through. Its four raised sides kept food on the pan when we stirred; raised handles helped us lift it off the grill easily with heavy mitts. Good heat retention meant good browning.
WILLIAMS-SONOMA Mesh Grill-Top Fry Pan MODEL: 9684432 PRICE: $29.95 DIAMETER: 9 in. MATERIAL: Stainless steel mesh	COOKING: ★★★ DESIGN: ★★★ USER-FRIENDLINESS: ★★★ CLEANUP: ★★★	Lightweight and maneuverable, this model caramelized and gave excellent grill flavor to food. Though it blackened, the mesh did not trap food or become difficult to clean. The cooking surface is larger than it appears because of flared sides. We wish the metal handle were removable, so we couldn't accidentally touch it with bare hands.

RECOMMENDED	PERFORMANCE	TESTERS' COMMENTS
BARBECUE GENIUS Stainless Steel Gourmet Grill Topper MODEL: 19401 PRICE: $25 SIZE: 13¾ x 10½ in. MATERIAL: Stainless steel	COOKING: ★★★ DESIGN: ★★ USER-FRIENDLINESS: ★★ CLEANUP: ★★★	We liked this pan's heat-retaining stainless steel and moderately raised handles. The holes were small enough to keep food from falling out. However, a wide strip of unperforated metal around each edge allowed food to steam, and the rim only extended to three sides. The pan also warped slightly.
CHARCOAL COMPANION Large Porcelain-Coated Griddle MODEL: CC 3080 PRICE: $16.99 SIZE: 16 x 10½ in. MATERIAL: Porcelain-coated steel	COOKING: ★★ DESIGN: ★★★ USER-FRIENDLINESS: ★★★ CLEANUP: ★★	A solid performer, thanks to four raised sides, easy-to-grip handles, a generous cooking surface, and square ¼-inch holes. On the other hand, it warped slightly when cooking fish, and over time the porcelain coating acquired a gunky film that was hard to scrub away.

RECOMMENDED WITH RESERVATIONS	PERFORMANCE	TESTERS' COMMENTS
CHARCOAL COMPANION Enamel Cast-Iron Griddle MODEL: CC 3515 PRICE: $49.99 SIZE: 15½ x 12 in. MATERIAL: Enameled cast iron	COOKING: ★★ DESIGN: ★★ USER-FRIENDLINESS: ★★ CLEANUP: ★★	This heavy pan had large oval and medium-sized round holes that let smaller onions and potatoes drop into the fire. But it excelled at caramelizing any vegetables that stayed in the pan as well as grilling delicate fish; plus, it retained heat beautifully on cold days. Winter grillers, take note.

NOT RECOMMENDED	PERFORMANCE	TESTERS' COMMENTS
GRILL PRO Porcelain-Coated Grill Topper MODEL: 97121 PRICE: $19 SIZE: 13¾ x 10½ in. MATERIAL: Porcelain-coated steel	COOKING: ★★ DESIGN: ★★ USER-FRIENDLINESS: ★★ CLEANUP: ★★	Completely covered with ⅜-inch round holes and featuring three raised sides, this porcelain-coated topper provided good grill exposure. Yet it warped badly, and the porcelain coating became gunky after repeated use.
MR. BAR B Q Deluxe Stainless Steel Skillet MODEL: 06058P PRICE: $20.50 DIAMETER: 9⅞ in. MATERIAL: Stainless steel with wood handle	COOKING: ★★ DESIGN: ★ USER-FRIENDLINESS: ★ CLEANUP: ★★	The folding (but not removable) wood handle was for storage rather than cooking: It snapped down into our food when we attempted to position it vertically to close the charcoal grill lid, and its metal trim got red-hot.

GRILL TONGS

Small design nuances have a huge impact on how well tongs handle asparagus or corn, flip a whole chicken, or turn a floppy rack of ribs. Grill tongs must keep hands a comfortable distance from the fire, but we had to work to lever heavy foods when they were too long. The best models had shallow, scalloped pincers that slid under food and held on yet didn't gouge. Though bulky tongs proved to have strong teeth for moving hefty foods, the added weight made jobs more difficult. The best pairs hit the spot between lightweight and sturdy. A little springy tension and the ability to easily open and close proved important. Tongs must open wide to handle everything from corn to whole chickens. We liked the easy-to-use lock of our winner from OXO; others had overactive locks that haphazardly stuck. Tongs are listed in order of preference.

HIGHLY RECOMMENDED	PERFORMANCE	TESTERS' COMMENTS
OXO Good Grips 16-inch Locking Tongs PRICE: $14.99 MATERIAL: Stainless steel, rubber handle WEIGHT: 8 oz. LENGTH: 17½ in.	PINCERS: ★★★ TENSION: ★★★ STURDINESS: ★★★	Comfortable, lightweight, and sturdy, these passed every test with top marks. The pincers picked up spears of asparagus in one swoop, cupped corn firmly, and did not damage tender rib meat. One tester said, "I could perform heart surgery with these."

RECOMMENDED	PERFORMANCE	TESTERS' COMMENTS
WEBER STYLE Tongs PRICE: $10.99 MATERIAL: Stainless steel, rubber handle WEIGHT: 8 oz. LENGTH: 19 in.	PINCERS: ★★★ TENSION: ★★★ STURDINESS: ★★	Almost identical to our top tongs, these felt easy and natural in our hands. Shorter than advertised—a usable length of 16 inches instead of 19, with a 3-inch lock—they gripped ribs, hot coals, and multiple asparagus spears. The pincers angled inward a little sharply, cutting into rib meat.

RECOMMENDED WITH RESERVATIONS	PERFORMANCE	TESTERS' COMMENTS
KINGSFORD Texas Turner Tongs PRICE: $12 MATERIAL: Stainless steel, hardwood handle WEIGHT: 9.6 oz. LENGTH: 17½ in.	PINCERS: ★★ TENSION: ★★ STURDINESS: ★★★	Strong, solid arms made maneuvering heavy items easy; however, several testers objected to their stiff tension and oversize handles. They also locked erratically as we used them, and the sharp lock was uncomfortable to push.

NOT RECOMMENDED	PERFORMANCE	TESTERS' COMMENTS
OUTSET Rosewood Extra-Long Locking Tongs PRICE: $14.95 MATERIAL: Stainless steel, rosewood handle WEIGHT: 15.2 oz. LENGTH: 22¼ in.	PINCERS: ★★ TENSION: ★ STURDINESS: ★★	We liked this pair's smooth, ridged wood grip as well as its dexterity at picking up ears of corn. But they were too heavy and long to work comfortably or control smaller items like asparagus, and too big for cooks with smaller hands.
LODGE Camp Dutch Oven Tongs PRICE: $10.95 MATERIAL: Stainless steel WEIGHT: 6.4 oz. LENGTH: 15¾ in.	PINCERS: ★★ TENSION: ★ STURDINESS: ★★	The flimsiest, lightest, and shortest in our lineup, these tongs had a locking bar that constantly slid down. Pincer tips did not align, so picking up asparagus was a challenge, although they gripped ribs and hot coals marginally well. We also knocked off points for stiff tension and a choppy open-and-close motion.
STEVEN RAICHLEN 19.5-inch Locking Tongs PRICE: $17.99 MATERIAL: Stainless steel, plastic handle WEIGHT: 14.4 oz. LENGTH: 19½ in.	PINCERS: ★★ TENSION: ★ STURDINESS: ★★	Extra-large pincers were great for holding large slabs of ribs but not so great at picking up thin asparagus. At nearly 1 pound, they were uncomfortably heavy, with unnecessarily large grips and too-tight tension. One tester noted that they felt like exercise equipment.
CUISINART Professional Grill Tongs PRICE: $19.99 MATERIAL: Stainless steel, rubber handle WEIGHT: 15.2 oz. LENGTH: 18 in.	PINCERS: ★★ TENSION: ★ STURDINESS: ★	These unusual tongs had pronounced teeth that cut into meat and made getting under ribs and around corn and chicken difficult. They managed a decent, if shaky, grip on asparagus and coals but opened too narrowly for foods larger than corn. As far as we could tell, the scooper arm was useless.

VACUUM SEALERS

If you find yourself with an extra bounty of food, you likely freeze your stockpile, but just one month later you inevitably have food encrusted with freezer burn. We tested eight vacuum sealers to find out if they can really keep food fresher in the freezer. We tested freezing coffee, strawberries, steak and chicken breasts, even a Thanksgiving dinner. Countertop models proved more reliable than handheld models at making a good seal, and our favorites all had sensors to detect overflowing liquids. After one month, our top four models continued to hold up well, but only the Pragotrade was frost-free. After another month, it was still working well. However, this model requires a lot of counterspace and a large budget. For most people, the FoodSaver V2240 is a better choice. It was the easiest to use and kept a respectable seal after a month. Sealers are listed in order of preference.

HIGHLY RECOMMENDED	PERFORMANCE	TESTERS' COMMENTS
PRAGOTRADE Vacuum Sealer Pro 2300 PRICE: $469.95 ROLL (PER FOOT): 38¢ QUART BAG: 26¢	FROST-FREE: ★★★ EASY TO USE: ★★	This was the only model with bags strong enough to keep frozen food perfectly sealed and frost-free after two months. But it was expensive, large, and heavy, and you must press on the lid during vacuuming. Only for the devoted freezer-owner.

RECOMMENDED	PERFORMANCE	TESTERS' COMMENTS
FOODSAVER V2240 Vacuum Sealer Kit `BEST BUY` PRICE: $99.99 ROLL (PER FOOT): 56¢ QUART BAG: 55¢	FROST-FREE: ★★ EASY TO USE: ★★★	Easy to use, this model was much smaller and lighter than our winner, sealing food tightly and quickly. After a month, tiny air pockets formed around food, but packages stayed sealed with minimal frost. At two months: early signs of freezer burn.
RIVAL Seal-A-Meal VS107 Food Saver with Hold Release PRICE: $63.02 ROLL (PER FOOT): 50¢ QUART BAG: 45¢	FROST-FREE: ★★ EASY TO USE: ★★	This relatively lightweight model was harder to use than the FoodSaver V2240, but it sealed as tightly. After a month, we saw tiny air pockets and frost, but packages stayed sealed. At two months: early signs of freezer burn.

RECOMMENDED WITH RESERVATIONS	PERFORMANCE	TESTERS' COMMENTS
FOODSAVER V3840 Vacuum Sealer Kit PRICE: $173.97 ROLL (PER FOOT): 50¢ QUART BAG: 45¢	FROST-FREE: ★★ EASY TO USE: ★	This model sealed as tightly as the other FoodSaver, but it isn't worth the extra $73. Sitting vertically to save space, it's still wider than other models. The sealing slot is too narrow, and we found no difference between "dry" and "moist" food functions.

NOT RECOMMENDED	PERFORMANCE	TESTERS' COMMENTS
REYNOLDS Handi-Vac Vacuum Sealer PRICE: $18.35 QUART BAG: 35¢	FROST-FREE: ★ EASY TO USE: ★★★	As long as food didn't get caught in the zipper, this handheld device made a tight seal at first. But after one month, bags of coffee that had been brick-hard were loose, and other foods were covered in frost.
ZIP VAC Portable Food Storage System PRICE: $29.99 QUART BAG: 67¢	FROST-FREE: ★ EASY TO USE: ★★★	This handheld model sealed tightly, but broke after just six uses. (A backup unit had similar problems.) If food got near the zipper, it wouldn't seal. After a month in the freezer, bags lost their seal. And while the device is cheap, its bags are not.
OLISO Frisper Vacuum Sealer PRICE: $59.99 QUART BAG: 60¢	FROST-FREE: ★ EASY TO USE: ★★	This model works by puncturing a hole in a reusable bag to draw out air, then heat-sealing around the hole. But its vacuum was too weak for a tight seal, especially around curvy strawberries, and was so loud we wanted earplugs.
DENI Freshlock Turbo II Vacuum Sealer PRICE: $97.99 ROLL (PER FOOT): 62¢ QUART BAG: 75¢	FROST-FREE: ★ EASY TO USE: ★	This model is a hassle (you have to press on different corners and seal three sides of a roll to make a bag). Bags felt cheap, the thin melting wire almost broke after three uses, and its vacuum was weak.

FIRE EXTINGUISHERS

According to the National Fire Protection Association, cooking mishaps are the number-one cause of home fires and home fire injuries, so it pays to have an extinguisher you can use effectively. We tested nine fire extinguishers on burning vegetable oil and cotton dish towels. Six were traditional ABC extinguishers designed to fight the three most common types of home fires: combustible material (A), flammable liquid (B), and electrical (C). We also tested two in small aerosol cans and another "designer" canister. The ABC, or "multipurpose," devices are filled with monoammonium phosphate, which forms a barrier between the fuel and oxygen, but it also scars appliance surfaces. The BC extinguishers contain nondamaging sodium bicarbonate, a pressurized spray of baking soda, which coats the fuel to similarly cut off its supply of oxygen. The nontraditional models used proprietary water-based formulas. All in the latter category failed to impress us. Our top two models (both traditional) finished neck-and-neck, but because one was a nondamaging BC-type, that made it our top pick. Extinguishers are listed in order of preference. Products with a UL rating have been tested by Underwriters Laboratories, an independent product safety and compliance certification firm. The number indicates the approximate square feet of coverage and the letters represent the types of fires it is designed to put out.

HIGHLY RECOMMENDED	PERFORMANCE	TESTERS' COMMENTS
KIDDE Kitchen Fire Extinguisher MODEL: 21005753/FX10K PRICE: $18.97 UL RATING: 10-B:C EXTINGUISHING AGENT: Dry chemical (sodium bicarbonate) POTENTIAL TO DAMAGE KITCHEN SURFACES: No	FIREFIGHTING ABILITY: ★★★ EASE OF USE: ★★★ LACK OF SIDE EFFECTS: ★★	Extremely fast, powerful, well-directed spray that quickly extinguished grease fire and burning dish towels, leaving a comfortable sense that plenty more spray was left in canister. Created noxious fumes and messy residue
KIDDE ABC Dry Chemical Fire Extinguisher MODEL: 466142 (also known as FA110) PRICE: $19.99 UL RATING: 1-A:10-B:C EXTINGUISHING AGENT: Dry chemical (monoammonium phosphate) POTENTIAL TO DAMAGE KITCHEN SURFACES: Yes	FIREFIGHTING ABILITY: ★★★ EASE OF USE: ★★★ LACK OF SIDE EFFECTS: ★★	Big, focused spray with spot-on aim that took only a few seconds to put out grease and towel fires. Forceful spray extinguished dish towel, then blew it off heat source. Created noxious fumes and left messy residue.

RECOMMENDED	PERFORMANCE	TESTERS' COMMENTS
FIRST ALERT Kitchen Fire Extinguisher MODEL: KFE2S5 PRICE: $22.34 UL RATING: 5-B:C EXTINGUISHING AGENT: Dry chemical (sodium bicarbonate) POTENTIAL TO DAMAGE KITCHEN SURFACES: No	FIREFIGHTING ABILITY: ★★★ EASE OF USE: ★★ LACK OF SIDE EFFECTS: ★★	Pulling off this model's odd plastic cap seemed an unnecessary extra step that cost valuable seconds. Effective once in use, with concentrated coverage offering good control and aim. Created noxious fumes and messy residue.
FIRST ALERT Multipurpose Fire Extinguisher MODEL: FE1A10GO PRICE: $21.99 UL RATING: 1-A:10-B:C EXTINGUISHING AGENT: Dry chemical (monoammonium phosphate) POTENTIAL TO DAMAGE KITCHEN SURFACES: Yes	FIREFIGHTING ABILITY: ★★★ EASE OF USE: ★★ LACK OF SIDE EFFECTS: ★★	The pin was so hard to pull out we had to put canister down and use both hands. Effective at putting out grease fire; powerful spray extinguished dish towel and blew it off burner. Created noxious fumes and messy residue.

RECOMMENDED WITH RESERVATIONS	PERFORMANCE	TESTERS' COMMENTS
FIRST ALERT Tundra Fire Extinguishing Spray MODEL: AF-400 PRICE: $14.97 UL RATING: None EXTINGUISHING AGENT: Liquid (proprietary formula) POTENTIAL TO DAMAGE KITCHEN SURFACES: No	FIREFIGHTING ABILITY: ★★ EASE OF USE: ★★★ LACK OF SIDE EFFECTS: ★★★	This can was as easy to use as Reddi-wip. Contents were drippy but mostly went where directed. Extinguished grease fire but left dish towel slightly smoldering. Also, one of the four cans tested clogged and stopped working.
BUCKEYE Multipurpose Dry Chemical Fire Extinguisher MODEL: 2.5 SA ABC PRICE: $29.90 UL RATING: 1-A:10-B:C EXTINGUISHING AGENT: Dry chemical (monoammonium phosphate) POTENTIAL TO DAMAGE KITCHEN SURFACES: Yes	FIREFIGHTING ABILITY: ★★★ EASE OF USE: ★★ LACK OF SIDE EFFECTS: ★	Very direct, narrow spray easily extinguished both types of fires. But quality was inconsistent: Pin slid out too easily on one model and got stuck on another. Fumes burned eyes and constricted throats.

PLASTIC FOOD STORAGE CONTAINERS

Finding a good food storage container shouldn't take as much thought or effort as it often does. We selected eight BPA-free plastic food storage containers (research links BPA to various health issues), choosing square or rectangular as close as possible to 8-cup capacity, and tested each for leaking, durability, odor-retention, and design. We put them in the microwave, the freezer, and the refrigerator. We ran them through dozens of dishwasher cycles, submerged them in water, and dropped them to see how they held up. Containers are listed in order of preference.

HIGHLY RECOMMENDED	PERFORMANCE	TESTERS' COMMENTS
SNAPWARE MODS SIZE: Large rectangle, 8 cups PRICE: $6.99 MODEL: 98213 72915 MATERIAL: Polypropylene with silicone gasket DISHWASHER PLACEMENT: Lid on top rack only	LEAKS: ★★½ ODORS: ★★★ MICROWAVE: ★★★ DURABILITY: ★★★ DESIGN: ★★★	Simple snap-down lid sealed easily throughout testing. Though it allowed a few drops of water in during first submersion test, after dishwashing, seal was perfect. Flat, rectangular shape encourages quick cooling or heating and stacks easily, with lid attaching to bottom.

RECOMMENDED	PERFORMANCE	TESTERS' COMMENTS
LOCK & LOCK Classic Food Storage Container SIZE: Rectangle, 8 cups PRICE: $7.49 MODEL: HPL818 MATERIAL: Polypropylene with silicone gasket DISHWASHER PLACEMENT: Top rack only	LEAKS: ★★½ ODORS: ★★★ MICROWAVE: ★★ DURABILITY: ★★★ DESIGN: ★★	Sturdy, with secure seal. Performed dependably overall but leaked a few drops during first submersion test—though seal improved after dishwashing 50 times. Stained slightly more than others after microwaving chili, and has taller, deeper shape that we find less practical.
OXO Good Grips Top Container SIZE: Medium rectangle, 9.3 cups PRICE: $7.99 MODEL: 1172700 MATERIAL: Polypropylene with silicone gasket DISHWASHER PLACEMENT: Top rack only	LEAKS: ★★½ ODORS: ★★★ MICROWAVE: ★★ DURABILITY: ★★½ DESIGN: ★★	When new, this container leaked when submerged, but after dishwashing 50 times, seal improved (though lid bowed, making it stiffer to seal). Stained slightly more than others and has taller, deeper shape than preferred.
FRESHVAC PRE Vacuum Food Storage SIZE: Square, 9.3 cups PRICE: $5.99 MODEL: 1-2200S MATERIAL: Polypropylene DISHWASHER PLACEMENT: Lid on top rack only	LEAKS: ★★★ ODORS: ★★★ MICROWAVE: ★★ DURABILITY: ★ DESIGN: ★	We struggled to achieve perfect airtight seal after dishwasher test—unless lid was aligned right, "vacuum" tab wouldn't operate. Shape is low but too rounded and bulbous for efficient storage. Minuscule "date dial" popped off during drop test.

RECOMMENDED WITH RESERVATIONS	PERFORMANCE	TESTERS' COMMENTS
GLADWARE Deep Dish SIZE: Rectangle, 8 cups PRICE: $5.97 for set of 3 MODEL: 12587 70045 MATERIAL: Polypropylene DISHWASHER PLACEMENT: Top and bottom racks	LEAKS: ★★ ODORS: ★ MICROWAVE: ★ DURABILITY: ★ DESIGN: ★★	Performed acceptably new but became alarmingly soft in microwave. After 50 dishwasher cycles, it degraded: Seal leaked profusely, chili stained, and fishy odor hung on. Best for a potluck—it's cheap and you won't care if you don't get it back.

NOT RECOMMENDED	PERFORMANCE	TESTERS' COMMENTS
STERILITE Ultra-Seal SIZE: Rectangle, 8.3 cups PRICE: $6.49 MODEL: 0322 MATERIAL: Polypropylene with silicone gasket DISHWASHER PLACEMENT: Top rack only	LEAKS: ★ ODORS: ★★★ MICROWAVE: ★★ DURABILITY: ★ DESIGN: ★	We had high hopes for this container, but seal was uneven; because lid lacked rigidity, corners leaked badly even when new. (Second new model had same flaws.) Flap popped open during drop test. Chili stained more than in other containers.
ZIPLOC Snap 'N Seal SIZE: Large rectangle, 9.5 cups PRICE: $4.55 for set of 2 MODEL: 10885 MATERIAL: Polypropylene DISHWASHER PLACEMENT: Top rack	LEAKS: ★ ODORS: ★★★ MICROWAVE: ★ DURABILITY: ★ DESIGN: ★	Despite being roomy, felt cheap and flimsy. Extremely leaky, both before and after 50 dishwasher cycles. Not on a par with better containers in lineup, or even with fellow "disposable" container by Glad. Its only virtue: rock-bottom price.
RUBBERMAID Lock-its SIZE: Square, 9 cups PRICE: $12.99 MODEL: 7K95 MATERIAL: Polypropylene DISHWASHER PLACEMENT: Top and bottom racks	LEAKS: ★½ ODORS: ★★★ MICROWAVE: ★ DURABILITY: ★ DESIGN: ½	Usually dependable brand flopped—poorly made flap seals distorted in microwave, popping back up when pressed down. (Second model shared these flaws.) Top flew off in drop test. We like "Easy Find" lid, which sticks to bottom of container, but that was its only asset.

DISH TOWELS

We recently tested eight towels in search of one that would soak up liquid, dry dishes without streaks or destruction, and look good as new after washing. Testing proved that while innovative materials promise better absorption, they often failed to deliver. In the end, we preferred the feel and absorbency of cotton, but terry cloth was too bulky, and flimsy herringbone and flour sack towels couldn't stand up to demanding kitchen work. Only the NOW Designs Ripple Towel passed all our tests with near perfect scores. Towels are listed in order of preference.

RECOMMENDED	PERFORMANCE	TESTERS' COMMENTS
NOW DESIGNS Ripple Towel PRICE: $7.95 MATERIAL: 100% ribbed cotton ORIGINAL SIZE: 30 x 20½ in. SHRINKAGE: 17%	ABSORPTION: ★★ STAIN RESISTANCE: ★★★ DRYING DELICACY: ★★★ DURABILITY: ★★★	A champion at soaking up spills, this well-proportioned towel left glassware streak-free and easily slipped into the smallest champagne flute. It shrank slightly but its shape didn't distort. Just one trip through the washer and dryer got the stains out.
CALPHALON Kitchen Towel Ensembles PRICE: $6.99 MATERIAL: 100% combed cotton terrycloth ORIGINAL SIZE: 29¼ x 16 in. SHRINKAGE: 18%	ABSORPTION: ★★ STAIN RESISTANCE: ★★★ DRYING DELICACY: ★ DURABILITY: ★★★	Extremely sturdy, this towel remained almost stain-free and new-looking, even after multiple washes. However, the thick material made drying champagne flutes and wine glasses treacherous.

RECOMMENDED WITH RESERVATIONS	PERFORMANCE	TESTERS' COMMENTS
MU Microfiber Dish Towel PRICE: $8.99 MATERIAL: microfiber; 80% polyester, 20% polyamide ORIGINAL SIZE: 24 x 16 in. SHRINKAGE: 9%	ABSORPTION: ★★ STAIN RESISTANCE: ★★ DRYING DELICACY: ★★ DURABILITY: ★★	Testers hated the feel of this towel. It soaked up 1 cup of water, more than any other towel tested, in the dangling towel test, but didn't do as well with an actual spill. Mustard stains remained visible.
BAMBOO Kitchen Towel, Set of 3 PRICE: $25.99 ($8.66 per towel) MATERIAL: 100% bamboo ORIGINAL SIZE: 31 x 20 in. SHRINKAGE: 35%	ABSORPTION: ★★ STAIN RESISTANCE: ★ DRYING DELICACY: ★★ DURABILITY: ★★	Stains left their mark and its large size was cumbersome, but this towel absorbed ⅔ cup of water. Soft as a baby blanket, it was an odd choice for a kitchen towel but proved gentle enough to dry delicate items.

NOT RECOMMENDED	PERFORMANCE	TESTERS' COMMENTS
A.R.E. NATURALS Bamboo Kitchen Towel, Set of 3 PRICE: $24.99 ($8.33 per towel) MATERIAL: 60% bamboo, 40% cotton ORIGINAL SIZE: 29 x 17½ in. SHRINKAGE: 53%	ABSORPTION: ★★ STAIN RESISTANCE: ★ DRYING DELICACY: ★★ DURABILITY: ★	While it absorbed fairly well, this towel shrank by more than 50 percent. By the end of testing, it was extremely distorted and was discolored by stains—more of a rag than a dish towel.
MOPPINE Oven Mitts by Rachael Ray, Set of 3 PRICE: $22.95 (Item # 647453), ($7.65 per towel) MATERIAL: 100% cotton ORIGINAL SIZE: 27 x 17½ in. SHRINKAGE: 27%	ABSORPTION: ★★ STAIN RESISTANCE: ★ DRYING DELICACY: ★ DURABILITY: ★	This towel-oven mitt combo sounded like a great idea, but it performed poorly. Though quite absorbent, it stained and quickly became frayed. As a mitt, it was unstable and slippery. If the towel gets wet, you can't use it as an oven mitt because heat transfers through.
NOW DESIGNS Floursack Teatowel Collection, Set of 3 PRICE: $14.99 ($4.99 per towel) MATERIAL: 100% cotton ORIGINAL SIZE: 35 x 23½ in. SHRINKAGE: 18%	ABSORPTION: ★ STAIN RESISTANCE: ★ DRYING DELICACY: ★★ DURABILITY: ★	Towel or tablecloth? Giant and awkward, this towel got in the way during every test. The thin material struggled to absorb, with the towel simply floating on top of liquid. By the end of testing, the material was stained and thinning.
SHAMWOW! Set of 4 large and 4 small PRICE: $19.99 ($2.50 per towel) MATERIAL: rayon ORIGINAL SIZE: 24 x 19½ in. SHRINKAGE: 13%	ABSORPTION: ★★ STAIN RESISTANCE: ★ DRYING DELICACY: ★ DURABILITY: ★	Not only did this gimmicky towel not soak up "12 times its weight in liquid" as promised, but it practically disintegrated by the end of testing. We avoided the dryer, but the shoddy material still pilled and shredded after one wash.

CONVERSIONS & EQUIVALENCIES

SOME SAY COOKING IS A SCIENCE AND AN ART. We would say that geography has a hand in it, too. Flour milled in the United Kingdom and elsewhere will feel and taste different from flour milled in the United States. So, while we cannot promise that the loaf of bread you bake in Canada or England will taste the same as a loaf baked in the States, we can offer guidelines for converting weights and measures. We also recommend that you rely on your instincts when making our recipes. Refer to the visual cues provided. If the bread dough hasn't "come together in a ball," as described, you may need to add more flour—even if the recipe doesn't tell you so. You be the judge.

The recipes in this book were developed using standard U.S. measures following U.S. government guidelines. The charts below offer equivalents for U.S., metric, and Imperial (U.K.) measures. All conversions are approximate and have been rounded up or down to the nearest whole number. For example:

1 teaspoon = 4.929 milliliters, rounded up to 5 milliliters
1 ounce = 28.349 grams, rounded down to 28 grams

VOLUME CONVERSIONS

U.S.	METRIC
1 teaspoon	5 milliliters
2 teaspoons	10 milliliters
1 tablespoon	15 milliliters
2 tablespoons	30 milliliters
¼ cup	59 milliliters
⅓ cup	79 milliliters
½ cup	118 milliliters
¾ cup	177 milliliters
1 cup	237 milliliters
1¼ cups	296 milliliters
1½ cups	355 milliliters
2 cups	473 milliliters
2½ cups	592 milliliters
3 cups	710 milliliters
4 cups (1 quart)	0.946 liter
1.06 quarts	1 liter
4 quarts (1 gallon)	3.8 liters

WEIGHT CONVERSIONS

OUNCES	GRAMS
½	14
¾	21
1	28
1½	43
2	57
2½	71
3	85
3½	99
4	113
4½	128
5	142
6	170
7	198
8	227
9	255
10	283
12	340
16 (1 pound)	454

CONVERSIONS FOR INGREDIENTS COMMONLY USED IN BAKING

Baking is an exacting science. Because measuring by weight is far more accurate than measuring by volume, and thus more likely to achieve reliable results, in our recipes we provide ounce measures in addition to cup measures for many ingredients. Refer to the chart below to convert these measures into grams.

INGREDIENT	OUNCES	GRAMS
Flour		
1 cup all-purpose flour*	5	142
1 cup cake flour	4	113
1 cup whole wheat flour	5½	156
Sugar		
1 cup granulated (white) sugar	7	198
1 cup packed brown sugar (light or dark)	7	198
1 cup confectioners' sugar	4	113
Cocoa Powder		
1 cup cocoa powder	3	85
Butter†		
4 tablespoons (½ stick, or ¼ cup)	2	57
8 tablespoons (1 stick, or ½ cup)	4	113
16 tablespoons (2 sticks, or 1 cup)	8	227

* U.S. all-purpose flour, the most frequently used flour in this book, does not contain leaveners, as some European flours do. These leavened flours are called self-rising or self-raising. If you are using self-rising flour, take this into consideration before adding leavening to a recipe.
† In the United States, butter is sold both salted and unsalted. We generally recommend unsalted butter. If you are using salted butter, take this into consideration before adding salt to a recipe.

OVEN TEMPERATURES

FAHRENHEIT	CELSIUS	GAS MARK (imperial)
225	105	¼
250	120	½
275	130	1
300	150	2
325	165	3
350	180	4
375	190	5
400	200	6
425	220	7
450	230	8
475	245	9

CONVERTING TEMPERATURES FROM AN INSTANT-READ THERMOMETER

We include doneness temperatures in many of our recipes, such as those for poultry, meat, and bread. We recommend an instant-read thermometer for the job. Refer to the table above to convert Fahrenheit degrees to Celsius. Or, for temperatures not represented in the chart, use this simple formula:

Subtract 32 degrees from the Fahrenheit reading, then divide the result by 1.8 to find the Celsius reading.

EXAMPLE:

"Roast until the thickest part of a chicken thigh registers 175 degrees on an instant-read thermometer." To convert:

175° F − 32 = 143°
143° ÷ 1.8 = 79.44°C, rounded down to 79°C

INDEX

A

B

I

Ice cream
    chocolate, taste tests on, 249, 299
    preventing ice crystals on, 273
    vanilla, taste tests on, 244, 298
Ice cream makers, ratings of, 281
Immersion blenders, ratings of,
    31, 280, 304
Individual Fallen Chocolate Cakes for Two,
    247–50, *248*
Individual Fallen Chocolate-Orange Cakes
    for Two, 250
Individual Fresh Berry Gratins, 264–66
    with Honey-Lavender Zabaglione, 266
    with Lemon Zabaglione, 266
Indoor Pulled Pork with Sweet and Tangy
    Barbecue Sauce, 158–61
Ingredients, pantry
    cooking with, 285
    cooking with wine, 285
    emergency substitutions, 285
    essential food items, 284
Ingredients, tastings of
    andouille sausage, 158
    barbecue sauce, 295
    black beans, canned, 227, 296
    black peppercorns, 106
    California olive oil, 14, 288
    chicken noodle soup, 297
    cinnamon, 268, 293
    coffee, decaffeinated, 90
    creamy Italian dressing, 294
    hot sauce, 11
    ice cream, chocolate, 249, 299
    ice cream, vanilla, 244, 298
    kosher dill pickles, 154
    liquid smoke, 124
    oats, 292
    pasta, whole wheat, 110, 290
    potato chips, reduced-fat, 149, 291
    rice, long-grain white, 158
    saffron, 36
    sandwich bread, 229
    seven-grain cereal, 126
    vegetable oil, 103, 288
Insulated carriers, ratings of, 121

J

Joe Booker Stew, 43–44, *45*

K

Ketchup, favorite brands, 284
Kettles, electric, ratings of, 281
Kitchen cleaning basics
    cleaning sponges, 282
    sanitizing sink, 282
    washing cutting boards, 282
    washing hands, 282
    washing produce, 282
Kitchen food safety
    cooling food on countertop, 283
    defrosting food in refrigerator, 283
    preventing bacterial spread, 283
    preventing cross-contamination, 283
    refrigerator food storage, 283
    reheating food, 283
    rinsing meat and poultry, 283
    safe handling of marinades, 283
    seasoning foods, 283
    using thermometers, 283
Kitchen quick tips
    cast-iron skillet "pie plates," 274
    DIY cake decorating tool, 274
    easy olive slicing, 275
    ensuring round icebox cookies, 275
    hands-free meat seasoning, 274
    hard-to-peel boiled eggs, 275
    homemade spice packets, 272
    impromptu lemon juice strainer, 272
    inexpensive knife protector, 275
    keeping ice cream fresh, 273
    kosher salt shaker, 272
    makeshift utensil rack, 275
    making fruit "ice cubes," 275
    measuring dry ingredients, 274
    measuring sticky liquids, 273
    mellowing harsh flavor of onions, 275
    parchment paper substitute, 272
    peeling beets, 274
    quick mustard vinaigrette, 272
    recycling pickle juice, 272
    rescuing a broken sauce, 273
    reviving limp carrots, 274
    sharpening vegetable peelers, 274
    skimming fat from liquids, 272
    steaming corn for a crowd, 273
    taming red pepper flakes, 273
    trapping fruit flies, 273
    vinegar dishwasher rinse agent, 273
Kitchen scales, ratings of, 277
Kitchen timers, ratings of, 277